THE ENCYCLOPEDIA OF
JEWISH LIFE
Before and During the Holocaust

Editor in Chief **Shmuel Spector**

Consulting Editor **Geoffrey Wigoder**

Foreword by **Elie Wiesel**

Volume III
Seredina-Buda – Z

YAD VASHEM
Jerusalem

NEW YORK UNIVERSITY PRESS

Washington Square, New York

These three volumes are an abridgment of the multi-volume Encyclopedia of Jewish Communities published in Hebrew by Yad Vashem.

The publication was supported by a grant of the Memorial Foundation for Jewish Culture.

Foreword by Elie Wiesel translated from the French by Fred Skolnik

First pubished in the U.S.A. in 2001 by
NEW YORK UNIVERSITY PRESS
Washington Square
New York, NY 10003
www.nyupress.nyu.edu

Library of Congress Cataloging-in-Publication Data
The Encyclopedia of Jewish life before and during the Holocaust / edited by Shmuel Spector,
consulting editor: Geoffrey Wigoder; foreword by Elie Wiesel
p.cm.
Three-volume set: ISBN 0-8147-9356-8 (cloth)
Volume I: ISBN 0-8147-9376-2 (cloth)
Volume II: ISBN 0-8147-9377-0 (cloth)
Volume III: ISBN 0-8147-9378-9 (cloth)
1. Jews—Europe—History—Encyclopedias. 2. Jews—Africa, North—Encyclopedias.
3. Holocaust, Jewish (1939-1945)—Encyclopedias. 4. Europe—History, Local.
5. Africa, North—History, Local. I. Spector, Shmuel. II. Wigoder, Geoffrey, 1922-1999
DS135.E8 E45 2001
940'.04924—dc21 2001030071

Prepared, edited and produced by The Jerusalem Publishing House,
39 Tchernichovski Street, Jerusalem, Israel.

Printed in China

SEREDINA-BUDA   Sumy dist., Ukraine. Jews settled in the early 19th cent. and numbered a few hundred at the end of the cent. Russian soldiers killed 25 on 19 March 1918. The J. pop. was 1,176 in 1926 and 463 (total 7,134) in 1939. The Germans captured the town on 1 Oct. 1941. In Dec. 1941, they murdered over 100 of the remaining Jews.

SEREDNE   (Hung. Szerednye) Carpatho-Russia, Czechoslovakia, today Ukraine. Jews probably settled in the first half of the 18th cent. Three families were living there in 1746. The J. pop. then rose to 256 in 1830 and 389 (total 1,107) in 1880. After WWI, the community maintained an elementary school for 100 pupils. The J. pop. increased to 599 in 1921 and 619 in 1941. Sixteen Jews were artisans and 13 tradesmen. There were three J. butchers, a few farmers, and several professionals. With the arrival of the Hungarians in March 1939, the Jews were pushed out of work. In 1940–41, dozens were drafted into labor battalions, some being sent to forced labor camps and others to the eastern front, where most perished. In late July 1941, a number of J. families without Hungarian citizenship were expelled to the Ukraine and murdered.

About 500 Jews were deported to Auschwitz on 17 May 1944. Some Jews were able to join the Czechoslovakian army and fought against the Nazis on the eastern front. A few dozen survivors returned after the war but most soon abandoned the town.

SEREDZIUS   (Yid. Srednik) Kaunas dist., Lithuania. Jews first settled in the 18th cent. In the 19th cent. there were two synagogues and a hasidic *shtibl*. The J. pop. in 1897 was 1,174 (71% of the total). Prior to WWI, many emigrated to the U.S. and South Africa. After WWI, half of those exiled to Russia returned. Between the World Wars, the J. pop. continued to fall due to a Lithuanian boycott of J. merchants. The community maintained a Hebrew school, a synagogue, and social welfare organizations. The Zionist movement won widespread support. In 1940, the J. pop. was about 500 (42%). After the German conquest of 1941, the men were shot at Vilkija on 28 Aug. 1941 while the women and children were murdered at the nearby village of Skrebenai.

SEREGELYES   Fejer dist., Hungary. Jews arrived in 1860 and numbered 127 in 1880 and 93 in 1930. The

Group of rabbis, Seredne, Czechoslovakia

congregation was Neologist. On 5 June 1944, the Jews were deported to Auschwitz via Szekesfehervar.

SERES (Serres, Serrai, Siroz, Siris) Macedonia, Greece. Jews were present in S. in the 12th cent. In 1453 the Ottomans transferred most of the Jews to Istanbul, where they formed their own congregation. A Romaniot community continued to exist but dwindled from the early 16th cent., when an influx of Spanish and Portuguese Jews predominated. The J. pop. in 1520–35 was 325 (total 5,465). By the end of the cent., the Romaniot community no longer existed and a well-knit Sephardi community was organized. During this period, S. became a center of Torah study and Kabbalah. By the early 17th cent., however, it lost its scholarly prominence, although Kabbalism was popular until the mid-19th cent. At the end of the 18th cent., the community's only synagogue was destroyed and replaced with a new, magnificent synagogue that seated 2,000. In the 19th cent., most Jews engaged in banking and traded in cotton, wheat, opium, anise, and industrial goods. Toward the end of the cent. S. experienced a financial setback and many Jews left for Salonika, Kavala, Ksanthi, and Drama. J. children received only religious education until the mid-19th cent., when a modern J. school was opened. By the early 20th cent., when the J. pop. peaked at 2,000 (1904), there were a number of social welfare organizations, a library, and a club. Prior to the Balkan wars (1912–13) there were some 1,300 Jews in S., but by Oct. 1912 the J. pop. had dropped to 988. Before the Bulgarian invaders left S. in July 1913, they set it on fire; 115 (out of 140) J. homes were burned down and the Great Synagogue was destroyed. Many then left S. and only a few families remained. After WWI, the occupying Bulgarians ordered the 90 J. families in S. to leave. The Greeks soon reentered S. (Oct. 1918) and some J. families returned with them. The Sephardi community was slowly rehabilitated, although anti-J. sentiments developed amongst the Greeks at that time. Most Jews worked in the tobacco industry, which also attracted J. families from Kavala, Drama, and Ksanthi. In the 1920s, a new synagogue and a new school building were erected. An economic crisis in the early 1930s left many families unemployed; two charity organizations operated at that time. Prior to WWII there were about 600 Jews in S. The Bulgarians occupied S. and in Feb. 1942 imposed restrictions on J. movement. Soon afterwards, youths were drafted into forced labor and many Jews began to flee S. In March 1943, J. possessions were confiscated and then on 4 March, 471 Jews were arrested. After being held for three days in a tobacco factory they were transferred – along with the Jews of Drama and Kavala – to transit camps in Bulgaria, where sanitary conditions were extremely poor. On 18–19 March they were boarded on ships and conveyed into German hands. During the voyage, a number of Jews were offloaded onto tugboats, several of which were sunk in the Danube River. From there the Jews were transferred to the Treblinka death camp. Only three Jews survived the death camp. A few others, who joined the underground movements, survived the war in hiding. The community was not revived after the war; only one Jew lived in S. in 1983.

SERGO (until 1937 and in 1940–78, Kadiyevka; in 1978–91, Stakhanov; from 1991, Kadiyevka) Voroshilovgrad dist., Ukraine. The Jews settled in this coal mining town in the early 20th cent., their number increasing under the Soviets to 922 (total 67,974) in 1939. The Germans captured the city on 12 July 1942 and murdered the few Jews who had neither escaped nor been evacuated.

SERNIKI Volhynia dist., Poland, today Ukraine. Despite a rural residence ban, Jews numbered 932 in 1897 (total 2,549). They were mainly engaged in the lumber industry. Under the Germans, 150 J. men were murdered on 8 Aug. 1941. Another 550 were executed near Solomir on 9 Sept. 1942. Of the 500 who fled, 279 reached the forests, some to fight as partisans.

SEROCK Warsaw dist., Poland. Jews traded there in the 17th cent. An organized community was established in the early 19th cent. and numbered 2,054 (52.5% of the total) in 1897. As a result of WWI, the Red Army's brief occupation (1920), and Polish antisemitism, J. economic life declined. Most earned a bare subsistence, and during the 1920s, with help provided by the Joint Distribution Committee, a workers' cooperative and a people's bank were set up to relieve the distress. Agudat Israel and its allies won the communal elections of 1931, and J. representatives later made up a third of the city council. After the German occupation (9 Sept. 1939), 300 townsmen – mostly Jews – were arrested and maltreated. Some died. Of those aged 18–45, 150 were deported to the Soviet border. On 5 Dec. 1939, all the other Jews were marched to Nasielsk, where they were beaten, robbed, and then sent in two trains on a roundabout three-day journey. One train reached Biala Podlaska and the other the Lublin dist. in Poland. The deportees shared the fate of local Jews. Of S.'s 3,000 Jews in 1939, fewer than 300 survived WWII, mainly in the USSR.

SEROKOMLA Lublin dist., Poland. Jews settled in the early 19th cent. and numbered 140 (total 977) in 1921. On 22 Sept. 1942, the Jews of S., together with Jews from nearby villages, about 200 in all, were executed in the course of 11 hours outside the village. Some fled to the forest and joined a J. partisan group led by David Weinstein.

SETA (Yid. Shat) Kedainiai dist., Lithuania. Jews first settled in the 17th cent. A Karaite community existed from 1664 to 1709. In the second half of the 19th cent., the J. community suffered from fires and famine. In 1897 the J. pop. was 1,135 (68% of the total). Until 1898 children studied in a *heder,* after which a J. school was established. Zionist and Bundist organizations were active. Many emigrated to South Africa and the U.S. in the mid-1930s as a consequence of the deteriorating economy and anti-J. boycott. The community maintained two synagogues and a Hebrew school. In 1940 the J. pop. was 350 (24%). After the Germans captured the city in June 1941, the Jews were taken to Kedainiai, where they were murdered together with the local Jews on 28 Aug.

SEVASTOPOL Crimea, Russia, today Ukraine. Jews first settled in the old period when the city was called Khersones. The modern community was founded in the late 18th cent. and in 1784 included a few families from Galicia. J. residence was banned in 1829 and the Jews were expelled in 1834. In the Crimean War (1854–55), Jews participated in the defense of the city. As a reward, certain groups were allowed to return. In 1897, the J. pop. rose to 3,910 (total 53,595). There were about 70 Krimchak families there and 830 Karaites. Despite restrictions, numerous J. religious and cultural institutions operated, including a *talmud torah,* two private schools, a library, and a synagogue. In 1939, under the Soviets, the J. pop. was 5,988 (total 109,104). The Germans captured the city on 3 July 1942. On 12 July, they murdered about 4,200 Jews from S. and its environs in gas vans and ditches near the villages of Starye Shuly and Boltechekrak.

SEVERINOVKA (until 1917, Potockoe) Odessa dist., Ukraine. The J. pop. was 234 (total 1,190) in 1897 and 164 in 1926. Jews were attacked in a pogrom in 1905. The Germans captured the town in mid-Aug. 1941 and soon afterwards murdered the few Jews who had neither fled nor been evacuated.

SEVLUS (Hung. Nagyszollos; Yid. Szhelish) Carpatho-Russia, Czechoslovakia, today Ukraine. Jews probably settled in the first half of the 18th cent. Two J. families were living there in 1768. Their number increased to 150 in 1830 and 880 (total 4,381) in 1880. A yeshiva with dozens of students was opened in the mid-19th cent. and a Great Synagogue (apparently built of stone) was erected in the early 20th cent. Many J. refugees arrived from Galicia during WWI, including Hasidim with their leaders. The J. pop. grew significantly after the war, reaching 2,913 in 1921 and 4,262 (total 13,331) in 1941. The community maintained numerous welfare and charity organizations. It also supported a yeshiva run by R. Yitzhak Eizik Weiss, head of the hasidic Spinka dynasty. A Hebrew school with an enrollment of 150 children was also active. Most of the city's trade was in J. hands. Jews also owned two banks, three flour mills, two distilleries, a canning factory, a brickyard, and a number of farms employing Jews. Jews were also represented in the professional class with four doctors, two veterinarians, six lawyers, and three engineers. A few were administrative officials. In the period of the Czechoslovakian Republic, the Zionists were very active and the J. National Party exerted much influence, winning 11 of the 36 seats in the municipal council in 1921 and furnishing a deputy mayor. Agudat Israel was also popular and founded a Beth Jacob school for girls. The Maccabi sports club had a branch in the city. The Hungarians occupied S. in March 1939 and in 1940 drafted hundreds of Jews into forced labor battalions, sending many to the eastern front, where some died. In late July or early Aug., dozens of J. families without Hungarian citizenship were expelled to the Ukraine. Some were murdered there while others were able to return home after being held in a transit camp. In early 1944, a number of Jews were executed for alleged membership in an underground organization. After the German occupation of Hungary in March 1944, a *Judenrat* was appointed and thousands of Jews from the area were brought to the city. Between 27 May and 4 June 1944, the 12,000 Jews in S. were deported to Auschwitz in three transports.

SEVSK Oriol dist., Russia. Jews probably settled in the late 19th cent., numbering 279 (total 8,553) in 1926 and 113 in 1939. The few who remained after the German occupation of 1 Oct. 1941 were murdered.

SEYTLER (from 1944, Nizhnegorskyi) Crimea, Russia, today Ukraine. A few J. families were present before the publication of the May Laws of 1882 banning J. residence in Russian villages. Within a framework of various restrictions, a number of J. grain merchants were permitted to live near the local railway station in 1895 in order to carry on their trade. Many Jews arrived in the 1920s during the period of J. agricultural settlement in the Crimea. In addition to colonies like Bet Lekhem and Kherut near the urban center of Itchki, there were a number of J. kolhhozes in the area such as Bluchendorf with 663 Jews in 1926 and Rabotnik with 60 J. families in 1932. In 1939, there were only 82 Jews (total 3,152) in the town. The Germans occupied S. in late Oct. or early Nov. 1941. Sixty-four Jews were murdered in the first half of Dec., 53 in the town and 11 in one of the nearby J. kolkhozes.

SFANTUL GHEORGHE (Hung. Sepsiszentgyorgy) N. Transylvania dist., Rumania. A J. community was established in 1787, and in 1867 was officially recognized as the central community of the district. In 1897, S. joined the Hungarian Neologist community organization, and a synagogue seating 300 was built in 1903. The J. pop. in 1930 was 378 (3% of the total). A number of Jews owned large factories. The Jews participated in cultural life and some served on the municipal council. In the Holocaust the community shared the fate of the rest of Transylvanian Jewry. A ghetto was created in May 1944 holding, in addition to the local community, Jews from the Trei Scaune, Ciuc, and Odorhei districts. On 4 June, all 3,000 ghetto inhabitants were deported to Auschwitz. After the war a few dozen survivors gathered in S. but soon left.

SFAX Sfax dist., Tunisia. The medieval J. community is known from the 11th cent., importing textile products from Egypt and Syria and exporting mainly olive oil. The Almohads destroyed the community in

the mid-12th cent. According to local tradition, the modern community was founded in the 18th cent. when wealthy Moslems invited J. jewelers from Djerba to settle. By the mid-19th cent., it numbered about 150 families and included a large number of Leghornian Jews maintaining commercial ties with Malta and Italy. Many fled to Tripoli during the 1864 rebellion, returning to find their homes and stores in ruins. Resistance to the French occupation in 1881 was also spirited, causing Jews and Christians in S. to seek refuge on European warships anchored opposite the city. The J. pop. rose to 2,722 in 1909 and 3,466 (total 43,333) in 1936, with S. the second largest city in Tunisia after Tunis. From 1905, the community, as elsewhere in Tunisia, was managed by a J. Relief Fund (Caisse de Secours et de Bienfaisance). It maintained 11 synagogues, most of them in the J. quarter outside the city walls. J. children studied in French public schools, in two Alliance schools set up for boys and girls in 1905, and in the *talmud torah* system. The first Zionist society, Ohavei Zion, was founded in 1913 and had 130 members. A second group, Herzliyya, was set up by Felix Allouche. In 1924, Allouche founded the weekly *Reveil Juif*, the most influential Zionist newspaper in North Africa. It was published in S. until 1931 and then moved to Tunis. Allouche's activities made S. one of the most important centers of Zionism in Tunisia. He also played a leading role along with other local Jews in the founding of the Revisionist movement in Tunisia in 1926. Betar began operating in S. in 1931 and under local auspices spread to Mahdia. As part of its Zionist program, it started a Hebrew theater group and choir in S. while the Revisionists dominated elections to the Zionist Congresses. In 1926, the J. scout movement (UUJJ) also set up a local branch. Occasional outbursts of violence marked relations with the Arabs. In the riots of Aug. 1917, 50 Moslem soldiers in the French army went on a rampage, killing one Jew and injuring others as they looted J. stores. Others were injured in three days of rioting in July 1932, with jewelry stores a particular target of looters. In the latter instance, Arab nationalism fanned the flames of economic discontent, with Zionist activity in S. and events in Palestine adding a further dimension to Arab-J. friction. Of the 870 J. breadwinners in S. in 1936, 250 were in trade, 279 in industry and crafts, and 210 were day laborers. Jews owned five of the city's six business establishments dealing in oil and seven of

Jewish-owned store in Sfax, Tunisia, c. 1900 (Beth Hatefutsoth Photo Archive, Tel Aviv/photo courtesy of Yad Vashem, The Holocaust Martyrs' and Heroes' Remembrance Authority, Jerusalem)

11 dealing in grain. In protest against Nazi policy the Jews of S. boycotted German products in the 1930s. The period of Vichy rule had little affect on the Jews but with the arrival of the Germans in Nov. 1942, a regime of forced labor and extortion was introduced. The community was ordered to supply 100 workers, mostly to unload German trucks and build shelters, and to pay heavy fines. Cars, radios, and other property were confiscated. The Jews also suffered from indiscriminate Allied bombardments. Many fled to nearby Arab villages to seek shelter. The city was liberated on 10 April 1943, leaving the Jews in straitened economic circumstances and with a feeling of deep disappointment in the behavior of France. Zionist activity was renewed and by March 1944 the movement had 650 members, at first maintaining a measure of ideological neutrality and resisting the attempts of Tze'irei Tziyyon and the religious Zionist groups in Tunis to win its support. Subsequently, most of the Zionist groups set up branches in S. and after the establishment of Israel emissaries

from the state began to arrive. A Hebrew teacher arrived from Israel in 1954 and set up classes for 200 students. In the same year, a roof organization was established for all the pioneer movements, including Gordonia, Deror, Bnei Akiva, Ha-No'ar ha-Tziyyoni, and a much weakened Betar. Jews left in illegal *ha'pala* operations. The continuing economic plight of the city's Jews further stimulated emigration. Between 1946 and 1956, the J. pop. dropped from 4,223 to 3,168 and in June 1956 alone, 885 Jews left for Israel. In 1976, 205 Jews remained in S.

SHAKHTY Rostov dist., Russia. Jews settled in the 1920s and numbered 303 (total 114,134) in 1939. The Germans occupied S. on 21 July 1942, murdering about 100 Jews in Aug.

SHALOM ALEYHEM Nikolaiev. S. was a J. colony with 341 J. inhabitants in the late 1920s. In the early 1930s, 90% of the farm workers in the settlement were Jews. The few Jews who had neither fled nor been evacuated were murdered within a month of the German occupation of Aug. 1941.

SHAMKI Minsk dist., Belorussia. S. was founded as a J. agricultural colony in the late 19th cent. In 1898, it numbered 255 Jews and in 1924–25 the entire J. pop. of 310 Jews was apparently still engaged in farming. However, in the early 1930s, the number of J. farming families dropped to five. The Germans arrived in early July 1941 and in Sept. murdered about 700 Jews from S. and its environs together with the Jews of the Kholopenitsi area.

SHAMOVO Mogilev dist., Belorussia. An organized community was in existence by 1759. In 1897 the J. pop. was 759 (total 915). In 1924–25, under the Soviets, 44 families (246 Jews) earned their livelihoods in agriculture and in 1926 the J. pop. was 607, with most engaged in crafts. A kolkhoz with 26 J. families was founded nearby in 1930. The community was served by a rabbi and operated a clandestine *heder*. The Germans occupied S. in July 1941. The remaining 500 Jews were murdered at the J. cemetery in a major *Aktion* on 2 Feb. 1942. A few succeeded in escaping to the forest where they joined the partisans.

SHARGOROD Vinnitsa dist., Ukraine. J. settlement probably commenced in the late 16th cent., with a synagogue constructed in the Moorish style. As a border town, S. with its Jews was subjected to attacks by Tartars, Cossacks, and Haidamaks. The J. pop. was 2,219 in 1765 and 3,989 (total 5,529) in 1897. In the late 19th cent. most Jews were artisans (around 300) or tradesmen (operating most of the town's 125 stores). In the early 20th cent., a state J. school for girls was opened and at the start of the next decade, two private J. schools were in operation (one for boys, the other co-educational). In the Soviet period, a J. council (soviet) and elementary school were active. Most Jews were employed in a number of cooperatives and kolkhozes.

The folk orchestra of the Jewish high school in Shargorod, Ukraine, 1937

In 1939, the J. pop. was 1,664. The Germans captured the town on 22 July 1941. In Sept., it was annexed to Transnistria and a ghetto and J. police force were established. In Oct.–Nov., the Rumanians expelled about 5,000 Jews to the ghetto, mainly from Bukovina and also from Bessarabia. This brought the ghetto pop. up to nearly 7,000 with the 1,800 Jews of S. and the surrounding area. By June 1942, 1,449 had died of typhus, mostly among the refugees. Another 1,000 were transferred to ten local villages on 30 June. In May 1943, 175 Jews were mobilized for forced labor at the village of Trichati near Nikolaev. On 1 Sept. 1943, 2,731 Jews from Bukovina and 240 from Bessarabia were still residing in the ghetto.

SHAROVKA Kamenets-Podolski dist., Ukraine. Jews settled in the 16th cent. Their pop. was 114 in 1765, 581 in 1897, and 647 (total 2,455) in 1926. The Germans captured the town on 8 July 1941. In Oct. 1942, the Jews were brought to Yarmolintsy, where they perished.

SHATAVA Kamenets-Podolski dist., Ukraine. J. settlement commenced in the 16th cent. The J. pop. was 164 in 1765 and 1,135 (total 2,670) in 1897, dropping to 434 in 1926 under the Soviets. The Germans arrived on 10 July 1941, executing 300 Jews from the area in the fall.

SHATILKI Polesie dist., Belorussia. J. settlement began in the late 18th cent. with five Jews present in 1789. Probably about 500 Jews lived there in the Soviet period, with a J. elementary school (four grades) and a J. council (soviet) active. Two kolkhozes supporting 42 J. families were set up near the town in 1930. The Germans arrived in early July 1941. In Feb.–March 1942, they murdered the remaining 351 Jews.

SHATILOVO Vitebsk dist., Belorussia. In 1930, 28 J. families were employed at the Lekert kolkhoz founded in 1928. After their arrival in mid-July 1941, the Germans murdered the few Jews who had neither fled nor been evacuated.

SHATSK Minsk dist., Belorussia. Jews probably settled at the turn of the 18th cent., numbering 20 in 1811 and 810 (total 967) in 1897. Their pop. dropped to 780 in 1923. In the mid-1920s, under the Soviets, about 11

families farmed while most of the others were members of three artisan cooperatives. A three-year J. school was opened in 1924. The Germans occupied the town in early July 1941 and, toward the end of Sept., murdered 635 people, 450 of them Jews from S.

SHCHEDRIN Polesie dist., Belorussia. S. was founded in 1842 as a J. farm settlement and had a J. pop. of 4,022 (total 4,234) in 1897. Thirty J. families were still farming in the late 19th cent. while a large number of Jews engaged in the lumber trade. In 1926, the J. pop. was 1,759. A J. council was established in 1924. In 1929, 264 Jews did not have the right to vote. A multinational kolkhoz, set up nearby in 1929, provided employment for 187 J. families. A J. elementary school was started in 1920 and attended by 190 children in 1930. A separate J. school served kolkhoz families. In the late 1930s, there were about 420 J. families in the settlement, half employed in agriculture and 30% earning their livelihoods from crafts. The J. school and J. council were shut down in the late 1930s. The Germans arrived in July 1941 and in March 1942 murdered the 1,500 Jews there at the J. cemetery.

SHCHORS (until 1935, Snovsk) Chernigov dist., Ukraine. The town developed from a farm after a train station was built there in 1874. In 1897, Jews numbered 985 (total 2,379) and in 1939, 1,402. The Germans captured S. on 3 Sept. 1941 and on 24 Nov., they murdered 50 J. men. In Jan 1942, a few dozen J. children were shot and a few days later about 80 more men were executed. The women and remaining children were murdered at a later date. On 20 Sept. 1942, a few dozen Jews from the surrounding villages were brought to S. for execution.

SHCHORSK Dnepropetrovsk dist., Ukraine. The J. pop. was 83 in 1939 (total 2,667). After their arrival in mid-Aug. 1941, the Germans murdered the few Jews who had neither fled nor been evacuated.

SHENDEROVKA Kiev dist., Ukraine. The J. pop. was 761 (total 3,966) in 1897. The mainstay of the J. economy was the town's weekly market day, particularly the twice-monthly grain and cattle markets. Most were Hasidim. In 1926, under the Soviets, the J. pop. was 409. The Jews were murdered after the arrival of the Germans in WWII.

SHEPETOVKA Kamenets-Podolski dist., Ukraine. Jews probably settled in the 17th cent. and numbered 317 in 1765. In the late 18th and early 19th cents., S. was a hasidic center, particularly in the time of R. Pinhas Shapira of Koretz (1726–91). In 1897, the J. pop. was 3,880 (48.3% of the total). Under the Soviets, a J. elementary school founded in 1927 had an enrollment of 300 in 1933. In 1939, the J. pop. was 4,844. The Germans captured the town on 5 July 1941, murdering over 4,000 Jews from S. and its environs in July–Aug. A ghetto was established in early 1942. In fall 1942, it was liquidated when several thousand of its J. inhabitants were murdered.

SHEVCHENKOVO (until the mid-1820s and from 1944, Dolinskaya) Kirovograd dist., Ukraine. J. settlement probably commenced in the late 19th cent. The J. pop. was 57 in 1897 and 245 (total 10,015) in 1926 under the Soviets. The Germans captured S. on 8 Aug. 1941 and on 7 Nov. murdered 63 Jews.

SHIRIAEVO Odessa dist., Ukraine. A stone synagogue was built in the first half of the 19th cent. The J. pop. was 567 (total 1,889) in 1897 and 293 in 1939. A. J. elementary school was still operating in the early 1930s. The Germans captured S. on 6 Aug. 1941. On 24 Sept., 108 Jews were murdered, including 21 from neighboring settlements. The Germans murdered 114 people (including 28 children) in the area, nearly all of them Jews.

SHIROKOYE Dnepropetrovsk dist., Ukraine. Jews settled in the late 19th cent. and numbered 325 (total 9,017) in 1939. The Germans captured the town in mid-Aug. 1941 and murdered hundreds of Jews from the area in Sept., including the Jews of P.

SHKLOV Mogilev dist., Belorussia. Jews settled in the early 17th cent. and reached a pop. of 1,367 in 1766. They engaged in petty trade and, as wholesalers, dealt in cloth, silk, and cattle. J. merchants were guild members while most of the petty traders were unregistered. A J. printing press published religious books. An organized community was in existence from the late

Heder *children during recess, Shepetovka, Ukraine (The Russian Ethnographic Museum, Petersburg/photo courtesy of Yad Vashem, The Holocaust Martyrs' and Heroes' Remembrance Authority, Jerusalem)*

18th cent. In the 19th cent., the community maintained a Great Synagogue, 13 prayer houses, and an orphanage for 50 children. In 1897, the J. pop. was 5,422 (78% of the total). S. was the birthplace of Yehoshua Zeitlin (1742–1822), scholar and *shtadlan*. In the Soviet period, 17 prayer houses were filled to capacity on the Sabbath and in particular on J. holidays. A J. theater and J. elementary school were also active. By 1926, the J. pop. had dropped to 3,119, decreasing even further in 1939 to 2,132 (26% of the total). Three nearby kolkhozes supported 50 J. families in the 1930s, among them a J. kolkhoz with 30 families. The Germans arrived in July 1941, establishing a ghetto for 3,200 Jews from S. and its environs. A second ghetto with 2,700 J. inhabitants was set up in the neighboring village of Ryzhkovichi. Groups of young Jews were regularly executed in both ghettoes. Some escaped to the forests. In early Oct., the Ryzhkovichi ghetto was liquidated when the Jews were executed near the village of Zareche. The Jews in the town ghetto were also murdered there and at the local linen-processing factory at around the same time.

SHLISSELBURG (in 1944–92, Petrokrepost; today Shlisselburg) Leningrad dist., Russia. Jews probably settled after the Oct. 1917 Revolution. Their pop. was 57 in 1926 and 47 (total 9,715) in 1939. The Germans occupied S. on 8 Sept. 1941 and murdered the small number of Jews still there: a few at Chudovo on 17 Sept. and six in March 1942.

SHOLOKHOVO Dnepropetrovsk dist., Ukraine. Jews first settled in the Soviet period, probably in the late 1920s or early 1930s. The Germans occupied S. in mid-Aug. 1941. On 18 Oct. they murdered at least 191 Jews who had survived the previous *Aktion* carried out in Sept. by an *Einsatzkommando 6* unit.

SHOSTKA Sumy dist., Ukraine. Jews probably settled in the late 18th cent. and numbered 1,842 (total 7,000) in 1897. In 1939, 370 remained. The Germans captured S. on 27 Aug. 1941. Those Jews who had neither fled nor been evacuated were murdered in the *Aktions* of winter 1942 and on 19 July 1942.

Marketplace of Shklov, Belorussia (Raphael Abramovitch/photo courtesy of Yad Vashem, The Holocaust Martyrs' and Heroes' Remembrance Authority, Jerusalem)

Jewish self-defense, Shpola, Ukraine, 1919 (The Central Archive for the History of the Jewish People, Jerusalem/photo courtesy of Yad Vashem, The Holocaust Martyrs' and Heroes' Remembrance Authority, Jerusalem)

SHPIKOV Vinnitsa dist., Ukraine. Jews numbered 21 in 1765 and 1,875 (total 4,901) in 1897. In the Soviet period, a J. elementary school (four grades) was in operation. A nearby J kolkhoz provided employment for a few dozen J. families (46 farmers in 1932). A J. council (soviet) was active in the mid-1920s. In 1939, the J. pop. was 895. The Germans captured S. on 22 July 1941, annexing it to Transnistria. On 18 Dec. 1941, the Rumanians expelled the Jews of the region to the Rogozna camp and from there, on 19 Aug. 1943, to Pechera, where 539 were tortured and murdered.

SHPOLA Kiev dist., Ukraine. The J. pop. was 251 in the late 18th cent. and 5,388 in 1897. On 18–19 Feb. 1897, Ukrainian townsmen and peasants from the nearby villages extensively looted and destroyed J. property. In 1919, General Denikin's White Army troops attacked the Jews. In the Soviet period, 95 local J. families founded a kolkhoz nearby. A J. council (soviet) was active in S., repairing houses, paving roads, installing street lighting on the road to the kol-khoz, and even organizing help in the sowing season. About 150 Jews worked in a furniture factory opened in 1934. Most children studied at the J. school started in 1923. In 1939, the J. pop. was 2,397. The Germans occupied S. on 30 July 1941. On 9 Sept., the Jews were ordered to list the names of professional personnel in S. These, numbering 160, were executed. In late Sept., a ghetto was established, where 10–12 died every day. On 15 April 1942, Jews were sent to the Dariev and other camps. On 15 May, 760 J. women, children, and elderly people were murdered. A total of 225 able-bodied men were sent to the Brodetsk camp where they were executed in Dec. 1942. Another 105 were executed at the Shostkiv camp. The last Jews of S. were murdered in early 1943.

SHTERNDORF Nikolaiev dist., Ukraine. S. was a J. colony with a J. rural council and elementary school (125 students in 1931) in the Soviet period. The Germans arrived in Aug. 1941 and in Sept. murdered about 340 Jews from S. and its environs.

SHTEYNGARDSKI (county) Krasnodar territory, Russia. The Germans occupied the area in Aug. 1942 and murdered 57 Jews (local residents and refugees) in mid-Oct.

SHULIATINO Vitebsk dist., Belorussia. S. was founded in 1852 as a J. agricultural colony on state land and had a J. pop. of 99 in 1898. The Germans captured S. in July 1941 and presumably murdered the Jews there.

SHUMIACHI Smolensk dist., Russia. Jews probably settled at the turn of the 17th cent. An organized community existed by the mid-18th cent. The J. pop. was 1,190 in 1847 and 2,523 (total 3,991) in 1897. In the Soviet period, the J. pop. dropped to 1,394 in 1926 and 744 in 1939. A J. kolkhoz employed dozens of J. families in the 1920s and a J. school and club were functioning. The Germans captured S. on 1 Aug. 1941, confining the Jews in a ghetto in early Oct. and murdering about 400 on 18 Nov. A few others were subsequently flushed out of hiding and also murdered.

SHUMILINO Vitebsk dist., Belorussia. Jews were only permitted to settle in the late 19th cent. In 1926, under the Soviets, their pop. was 483 (total 1,042), dropping to 376 in 1939. A four-year J. elementary school was opened in 1925. The Germans occupied S. on 8 July 1941. A closed ghetto holding about 400 Jews was established in Aug. On 19 Nov. they were murdered outside the town.

SHYROKI LUH (Hung. Szeleslonka) Carpatho-Russia, Czechoslovakia, today Ukraine. Jews probably settled in the 18th cent. and after abandoning the town returned in the early 19th cent. Nine Jews were present in 1830, the J. pop. then growing to 62 (total 972) in 1880, 131 in 1921, and 190 in 1941. A pogrom occurred after WWI. The Hungarians occupied the town in March 1939. In Aug. 1941, they expelled a number of J. families without Hungarian citizenship to Kamenets-Podolski, where they were murdered. The rest of the Jews were deported to Auschwitz in late May 1944.

SIANKI Lwow dist., Poland, today Ukraine. The J. pop. in 1921 was 119. The Jews were possibly deported to the Belzec death camp in the second half of 1942, directly or via Turka.

SIAUDINE (Yid. Sha'udine) Sakiai dist., Lithuania. The J. pop. in 1923 stood at 130 (30% of the total), dropping to 70 in 1940. After the German conquest of 1941, the Jews were taken to Sakiai on 5 July and shot nearby.

SIAULENAI (Yid. Shavlan) Siauliai dist., Lithuania. Jews first settled in the 17th cent., building a beautiful synagogue at mid-cent. In the late 1800s, many emigrated to the U.S. and South. Africa. In 1861, the community became famous throughout Russia for a blood libel in which a Jew accused his own father of murdering a Christian boy. The J. pop. in 1897 was 547 (53% of the total). Between the World Wars, emigration to Lithuania's big cities and abroad was so great that not enough Jews remained to finance a J. school. The Zionist movement enjoyed widespread support. The J. pop. in 1940 numbered 20 families. After the German invasion in June 1941, Lithuanian nationalists sent all the Jews to Zagare, where they were murdered on 2 Oct. 1941.

SIAULIAI (Yid. Shavl) Siauliai dist., Lithuania. Jews first settled in the 17th cent. In 1731, the community received permission to establish itself formally. A magnificent synagogue was built in 1749. In 1775, the J. community was granted the right to appoint judges to adjudicate intracommunal disputes. The J. pop. in 1797 was 2,757 (88% of the total). During the Polish rebellions against Russian rule in 1831 and 1863, Jews suffered at the hands of both sides. In 1839, the Russians granted Jews the right to vote in municipal elections. In the mid-19th cent. many Jews left the city because of the community's inability to pay debts and taxes owed to the government. Government expulsions of Jews from neighboring villages in 1840 and from the western border communities in 1850 brought many Jews to S., thus increasing the poverty among local Jews. When Czar Alexander II came to power in 1855, the J. community's debts were canceled and the expulsions repealed, allowing Jews to return to their villages. These steps, together with the development of transportation facilities, ushered in a period of prosperity in the second half of the 19th cent., in which the Jews played an important role building factories for processing hides and tobacco and for producing soap, beer, and iron moldings. Among the most prominent was the tannery of Hayyim Frenkl, one of the largest in Russia and employing thousands of

Lag ba-Omer in Siauliai, Lithuania, 1933 (Beth Hatefutsoth Photo Archive, Tel Aviv/courtesy of Ya'akov Machat, Israel)

workers. A series of epidemics caused by polluted wells, fires, a blood libel in the 1860s, and the fear that anti-J. riots in Russia would spill over into Lithuania led many Jews to emigrate, primarily to South Africa. In 1897 the J. pop. was 6,990 (43%). During WWI, the Jews were expelled from S. and in 1915 the retreating Russian army burned down the center of the town, where Jews lived. With aid from relatives in South Africa and the U.S., and from the Joint Distribution Committee, the returnees built modern homes. Trade and industry flourished. A J. community council ran community affairs from 1919 to 1926, when the Ezra society took its place. Several Jews were elected to the municipal council. One Jew served as deputy mayor for 20 years. The community maintained, in addition to the original 18th cent. synagogue, several smaller ones, a number of hasidic *minyanim*, several prayer groups organized according to occupation, and a yeshiva established in 1909. Community social welfare institutions included a hospital established in 1891. After WWI, an orphanage, old age home, and dental and eye clinics for children were established. S. had Zionist sympathizers from the beginning of the Hovevei Zion

period. Both the Zionists and Bund were well represented in S. and a number of pioneers made their way to Palestine prior to WWI and played key roles in the settlement of Rehovot, Kefar Saba, and Petah Tikva. Until the mid-19th cent. J. children attended a *heder*. Among the more progressive schools subsequently established was a state J. school for girls, by the poet Yehuda Leib Gordon, who lived in S. in 1860–65. Following WWI, the community supported several Hebrew elementary schools; a Hebrew kindergarten; two Hebrew high schools, secular and religious; two libraries, one Zionist and one Yiddishist; and two ORT vocational schools. There were also a Yiddish elementary school and kindergarten. From 1924, a Yiddish newspaper, *Die Zayt* appeared. By the mid-1930s antisemitism took the form of physical attacks on Jews, a boycott of J. businesses, a campaign against signs in Hebrew letters, heavy taxes, a blood libel, and the removal of the marketplace from the J. neighborhood.

On the outbreak of WWII, the J. pop. of S. was 6,600. The annexation of Lithuania by the Soviet Union and the subsequent nationalization of factories

The Frenkl shoe factory, employing Jewish workers in Siauliai, Lithuania (Beth Hatefutsoth Photo Archive, Tel Aviv)

and stores severely undermined the economic position of the J. pop. In the first two weeks following the German invasion on 26 June 1941, Lithuanian nationalists and intellectuals murdered over 1,000 Jews prior to the establishment of two separate ghettoes into which all Jews were ordered on 15 Aug. A committee, referred to as "the delegation" and consisting of Jews who volunteered to serve, acted as a liaison to the Lithuanians and Germans. Its secretary was Eliezer Yerushalmi, who kept a "Ghetto Diary," an account of events in the ghetto. The diary was later presented by the Soviets in the International Military Tribunal in Nuremberg and published in Israel. As the two ghettoes were not large enough, about 1,000 Jews were taken to Zagare and Bubliai and executed. Until the end of Sept., about 300 were murdered in several *Aktions*. Up to end of Sept., a forced labor regime was instituted and Jews were sent to work at Frenkl's factory, to a nearby airfield under construction, and to dig peat. Ghetto workshops provided enough income to establish a hospital within the ghetto. From 15 Aug. 1942, J. women were forbidden to give birth on pain of death. To prevent pregnant women and their families from being killed,

J. doctors performed abortions and put newborn babies to death. In Sept. 1943, the German SS took over the ghettoes and converted them into a concentration camp. In Jan. 1943, the ghetto pop. numbered 4,836. From the end of Sept. through Oct. 1943 many were transferred to six labor camps. All those at the camps were returned to the ghetto in July 1944, as the front moved toward Lithuania. On 5 Nov. 1943, the "Children's *Aktion*" took place in which the Germans rounded up the elderly and J. children when parents were away at work. Soviet air force bombers mistakenly hit the ghetto, killing inmates. Between 17 and 19 July, trains emptied the ghetto, bringing the remaining 3,000 Jews to the Stutthof concentration camp. From there many were sent to other concentration camps, mostly around Dachau. About 500 survived the war in addition to the few who had escaped previously.

SIBIU   (Hung. Nagyszeben; Ger. Hermannstadt) S. Transylvania dist., Rumania. In 1878, the J. community organized, establishing a synagogue and other communal institutions. In 1881, the Jews were subjected to a blood libel, but after five days, the tensions eased without any harm befalling community members. One of the first Zionist organizations in Hungary was founded in S. in 1898. In 1918, an Orthodox Sephardi congretation was established. Zionist youth movements were active between the World Wars. In 1923, a group of ultra-Orthodox Jews set up a separate congregation, building a synagogue and a yeshiva. The J. pop., which stood at approximately 586 in 1880, rose to 1,441 in 1930 (3% of the total). Antisemitic manifestations were rife between the World Wars. At the outbreak of WWII, S. became the district center for Jews mobilized for forced labor. After 23 Aug. 1944, S. was the center for J. refugees from the frontier areas. After the war the community expanded to about 2,000, but in 1947–48 the majority left, many for western countries, some to Israel.

SIC (Hung. Szek) N. Transylvania dist., Rumania. Jews settled in the mid-19th cent. The J. pop. in 1930 was 50 (2% of the total). On 3 May 1944 the community was transferred to the Gherla ghetto and later to the Cluj ghetto. On 26 May the Jews were deported to Auschwitz.

SICKENHOFEN Hesse, Germany. Established around 1600, the J. community numbered 79 (15% of the total) in 1880, but declined rapidly. Eight Jews remained in 1933 and two years later the community disbanded.

SID Croatia, Yugoslavia, today Republic of Croatia. A community existed between the World Wars. In 1931 the J. pop. was 63 (total 5,926). All perished in the Holocaust.

SIDI BOU-ZID Gafsa dist., Tunisia. A small community of about 70 Jews originating in Gabes existed from the early 20th cent. Jews were tailors and cloth merchants and traded in the *alafa* plant. During WWII and the German occupation, they took refuge with the Bedouins. Their fate after WWII is unknown.

SIDRA Bialystok dist., Poland. J. settlement began in the late 17th cent. Most Jews depended on the weekly market day to earn their livelihoods. The J. pop. reached 742 (total 1,165) in 1897, declining sharply in 1921 to 455 (total 897) through emigration. Including refugees, 520 Jews were present when the Germans arrived in June 1941. In Sept. they were expelled to the Suchowola ghetto, joining 2,500 from other towns. On 2 Nov. 1942 all were sent to the Kelbasin transit camp near Grodno and from there to Auschwitz.

SIECIECHOW Kielce dist., Poland. A few J. families were present in the 19th cent. and 118 Jews (total 998) in 1921. There is a lack of information about the fate of the Jews of S., but it is believed that in summer 1942 all the Jews were deported by the Germans to the Treblinka death camp via Kozienice.

SIEDLCE Lublin dist., Poland. Jews were present by 1577. The community was presumably destroyed in the Chmielnicki massacres of 1648–49. In the 18th cent., Jews were living in S. in relative prosperity and in the 1790s the town's proprietress sold the Jews a few dozen stores there. However, the situation of the Jews worsened in the late 19th cent. when they failed to enter modern fields of industry and commerce and many of the distilleries that had been a traditional J. source of income closed down. The J. pop. grew from 2,908 in 1827 to 11,440 in 1897 and 16,820 (total 30,742) in 1910, and then declined to 14,685 in 1921 (total 31, 687). In 1931 the J. pop was 14,793 (total 38,876). A new synagogue was erected in 1856, with religious life marked by the conflict between Hasidim and *Mitnaggedim*. The former (mainly followers of Gur, Aleksandrow, Amshinov) maintained their own *shtiblekh* while various artisan groups also had *minyanim*. In 1926, R. Avraham Pinhas Morgenstern began to lead a congregation of Lomazy and Radzyn Hasidim. A small group of *maskilim* was active from the 1820s and Hovevei Zion organized a group after the Kattowitz Conference in 1884, the community having had a long history of ties to Eretz Israel. A J. hospital was founded in 1890 and an orphanage and old age home in the first decade of the 20th cent. In 1904, the community's first Hebrew school was founded. Large numbers of Jews arrived prior to WWI as a new period of prosperity set in, marked by a building boom caused partly by the city's frequent fires which sometimes destroyed entire quarters. Shoemaking was also a major J. trade, with 135 artisans employing 190 salaried workers and apprentices, and the 38 bootmakers employing an additional 90. The industry also employed numerous merchants and was supported by two J. banks. Needleworkers and hatmakers were also prominent among the Jews. The Bund, which became active in 1900, organized the city's first strikes. In 1903, small Po'alei Zion and Zionist Socialist groups also began to operate. The revolutionary activity of 1905–06, including the assassination of the local police chief, led to a pogrom, carried out on 8 Sept. 1906 by the Russian cavalry. Indiscriminate shooting killed 31 Jews and wounded 150. Hundreds more were arrested while 1,025 J. homes were damaged and 59 stores looted. Under the German occupation in WWI, Jews were seized for forced labor and many suffered from hunger and disease. The community also cared for 2,000 J. refugees. Nonetheless, public life flourished, and in 1917 the publication of the Balfour Declaration inspired the Zionists. A number of reformed *hadarim* teaching Hebrew and modern subjects were also opened. Antisemitic outbreaks continued after WWI, with 1,000 Jews arrested by the authorities in 1920 for alleged collaboration with the Soviets in the Polish fight for independence. Twenty were executed. The immediate postwar period found 8,000 Jews in need of relief. During the 1920s, Jews became active in the burgeoning textile industry but in the 1930s they suffered from discriminatory government measures and the competition of newly organized Polish cooperatives. Community life continued unabated. A Tarbut Hebrew school was opened in 1926, enrolling 216 children in 1930 and becoming a focus of cultural activity. J. libraries throughout the city housed 23,000 volumes and a number of J. periodicals were published, including the *Shedletser Vokhnblat* from 1922 to 1939. R. Shaul Ze'ev Bergenstein, one of the founders of the Beth Jacob school system, was head of a large yeshiva until leaving for Palestine in 1932.

About 2,000 people, including many of the city's 15,000 or so Jews, were killed in the German bombardments of Sept. 1939. During the first occupation of the Germans, Jews were robbed and persecuted and many Jews fled with the retreating Red Army, When the Germans returned permanently on 10 Oct. a regime of forced labor and extortion was instituted under a *Judenrat*. On 24 Dec. 1939, the synagogue was burned

Jewish merchants in Siedlce market square at the beginning of the German occupation, Poland

down. Many Jews were sent to labor camps in the Lublin area. About 1,200 J. refugees from Kalisz and other cities in western Poland arrived in March 1940. Six Jews were murdered in March 1941 in retaliation for an alleged attempt on a German soldier's life. In spring 1941, two ghettoes were set up, one accommodating about 10,000 Jews, the other 2,000. On 21 Aug. 1942, 400 Ukrainians, joined by Polish police and SS troops, surrounded the larger ghetto and the next day 10,000 Jews were deported to the Treblinka death camp and 2,000 were executed in the J. cemetery. The J. medical staff and 100 patients were murdered in the J. hospital and 200 Jews found hiding were also shot on the spot. Most of the 2,000 Jews in the small ghetto were dispersed among 20 local labor camps. Those who remained behind were crowded 30 to a room. On 25 Nov. 1942, 2,000 of the surviving Jews were marched to the Gonshie-Barki ghetto, joined by 1,000 Jews from surrounding towns. On 30 Nov., they were ordered back to S. Hundreds were murdered on the way by their Ukrainian guards. The rest were loaded onto a waiting train and deported to Treblinka. Five hundred Jews still employed in the local labor camps were killed off in the early months of 1943. About 2,000 Jews survived the war, 1,200 of them in the Soviet Union.

SIEGBURG Rhineland, Germany. The first J. family settled in 1287. The medieval community maintained a cemetery, prayer house, and *mikve*. The Jews were expelled in 1440–48, returning only in the early 17th cent. Their pop. was 82 in 1816 and reached a peak of 376 in 1905. The community continued to use the medieval cemetery but erected a synagogue in 1841 and started a J. elementary school in 1892. The Jews were active in local life and from 1846 were represented as a rule on the municipal council. In 1919, a Jew served as chairman of the local branch of the DDP (German Democratic Party). In 1933, the J. pop. was 219. In 1934, Agudat Israel initiated a pioneer training program preparatory to *aliya* to Palestine. It attracted youngsters from all over Germany, especially those of Polish origin, and some worked on local farms. About 200 passed through the program until it was closed down in 1937. Program graduates were among the founders of Kibbutz Hafetz Hayyim. On *Kristallnacht* (9–10 Nov. 1938), six J. stores were looted and the synagogue was set on fire. Most J. men were sent to the Dachau concentration camp.

Those who did not manage to emigrate to safety were deported in 1941–42. About 100 perished in the Holocaust.

SIEGELSBACH Baden, Germany. Jews settled in the early 18th cent. and reached a pop. of 104 in 1848. The pop. dropped to nine in 1933. Of these, six emigrated to the U.S. and three died of natural causes.

SIEGEN Westphalia, Germany. A. J. couple first settled in 1815. Numbering only 17 individuals in 1853, the community began to grow in 1870, reaching a peak pop. of 130 in 1925. The private J. school opened in 1871 became a public institute in 1901. A synagogue was consecrated in 1904. The community was moderately liberal, introducing a harmonium into the synagogue. The cemetery (established in 1871) was vandalized in 1905 with 16 tombstones seriously damaged. It was closed in 1912 because of difficulty of access and the community received a piece of land in the new municipal cemetery for J. burial. In June 1933, the J. pop. was 115. By Nov. 1938 all J. businesses had been "Aryanized" and 56 Jews had left, 19 to other German cities and the rest to other countries. On *Kristallnacht* (9–10 Nov. 1938), local SS troops set the synagogue on fire. Windows of J. homes were smashed and 11 J. men were sent to concentration camps. In May 1939, 41 Jews remained. Four Jews committed suicide shortly before the rest were deported to the death camps in 1942–43. Seven J. women married to non-Jews remained in Sept. 1944. They were deported to the east and subjected to forced labor until the end of the war.

SIELEC (I) Polesie dist., Poland, today Belarus. An organized J. settlement is known from 1623. After WWI, the J. pop. dropped from an 1897 high of 866 (total 2,684) to 250. In May 1942, the Jews were brought to Bereza Kartuska and from there sent to Brona Gora on 15 July for liquidation.

SIELEC (II) Lwow dist., Poland, today Ukraine. The J. pop. in 1921 was 175. Those Jews not fleeing to Soviet territory in Sept.–Oct. 1939 were possibly deported to the Belzec death camp via Sokal in fall 1942.

SIELEC (III) Lublin dist., Poland. A community of 15 Jews is known from the late 17th cent. Between the

World Wars, 40–50 J. families lived there. With the addition of 80 refugees from Cracow, the J. pop. rose to 450 under the German occupation in WWII. In 1942, the Jews were deported to the Sobibor death camp via Wlodawa.

SIEMIANOWICE SLASKIE Silesia dist., Poland. Jews numbered 367 in 1870 (total 9,052) and 200 in 1913. After WWI the German J. pop. was replaced by Polish Jews. These fled the German occupation in Sept. 1939, leaving behind just 30 German Jews, who were expelled to Jaworzno in late 1940 and shared the fate of the local Jews.

SIEMIATYCZE Bialystok dist., Poland, today Belarus. Jews arriving from Lithuania are mentioned in 1582 and formed a prosperous community. They enjoyed extensive privileges but at the same time many economic restrictions were imposed, such as a ban on manufacturing alcoholic beverages. Up to the 18th cent. the Jews of S. were under the jurisdiction of the Tykocin community, leading to much friction between them. By the 17th cent. they constituted an organized community, building a synagogue in 1670 and replacing it with a new one in 1799. From 1750, under the rule of Prince Jablonski, the town's new proprietor, the community was subjected to tight control in many spheres. J. autonomy was further limited under the Prussians (1795–1807). Jews nonetheless made S. one of Polesie's commercial centers, with a small number of Jews leasing estates and conducting foreign trade. Jews also traded extensively in metals and manufactured copperware. The community suffered from a massive fire in 1824 and a cholera epidemic in 1830. During the Polish rebellion of 1863, Cossack troops pillaged and abused the Jews. Two more fires and another cholera epidemic struck in the latter part of the 19th cent. By 1878, the J. pop. was 3,600 (total 4,634). From the late 19th cent. until the outbreak of WWI, economic conditions deteriorated, leaving most Jews impoverished and leading to emigration to the U.S. and Eretz Israel. The Bund and the Zionists became active in the early 20th cent. Economic hardship continued after WWI, with the Joint Distribution Committee aiding the community. In 1919 a Kadima Hebrew school was founded, soon joining the Tarbut network. The J. pop. in 1921 was 3,716 (total 5,694). The Hehalutz organization began to operate in the same year. During the Soviet occupation of 1939–41, many

Jews were drafted into the Red Army and others joined the retreat as the Germans approached in June 1941. SS troops murdered seven Jews as alleged collaborators with the Soviets and gave the Polish police a free hand to abuse the J. pop. A *Judenrat* was soon appointed, charged with providing "contributions" and forced labor, which included 10–12-year-old children. A ghetto was sealed off on 1 Aug. 1942. On 9 Sept. 1942, the town's 6,500 Jews, along with 1,500 brought earlier to the ghetto from Drohiczyn, Mlinik, and Grodsk, were deported to the Treblinka death camp; 150 were shot trying to escape and about 80 found refuge in the forest.

SIENA Tuscany, Italy. A J. settlement existed in S. in 1229, mainly comprised of moneylenders. In 1348, the Jews were accused of bringing the plague to the town. In the 15th cent., two Franciscan friars attacked the local Jews in their sermons. In 1437, the Jews were forced to wear the J. badge. Between 1543 and the end of the 16th cent., at least 11 Jews graduated as physicians from the University of S. In 1571, Duke Cosimo I confined the Jews to a ghetto. In 1786 a new synagogue was built. When French troops entered S. in March 1799, local Jews were given full emancipation, but they were soon attacked by rebels against French domination and on 28 June 1799, 19 Jews were killed and the synagogue looted. In memory of that event, the community holds a special fast day on the 25th of Sivan. Following the violence, some Jews left the town. The community numbered 300 members in 1814 and 290 in 1853. Among the spiritual leaders of the community in the 19th cent. were R. Menahem Azariah Hayyim Castelnuovo and Shemuel Nissim. The Jews gained full civil rights in 1859. In 1873, the community numbered 275 members dropping to 160 in 1925. According to the 1930 law reforming the J. communities, S. was included in the district of Florence. In 1935, part of the old ghetto was destroyed. By 1936, there were 20 Jews left in S. During WWII, 14 local Jews were deported to extermination camps. By 1948, the community numbered 100 members; in 1970, 70.

SIENIAWA Lwow dist., Poland, today Ukraine. Jews were the first to settle in S. in the late 17th cent. and constituted a majority of the pop. until WWII. In the 18th cent. the community was one of the most important in the region. In 1856, R. Yehezkel Shraga Halberstam established his dynastic court there, making S. the center of Zanz Hasidism and attracting thousands of visitors, to the benefit of local tradesmen. In this period and up to WWI, the J. pop. averaged 2,000–2,500, set back somewhat by a big fire in 1889. In WWI the Jews suffered from arson, looting, and violence, leaving the J. pop. at 1,071 in 1921. Between the World Wars the Zionists increased their activity, formerly suppressed by the Hasidim. From Sept. 1939 to June 1941, the town was under Soviet rule, which shut down J. commerce and community life. The Germans entered the town on 22 June 1941 and instituted a regime of forced labor and sporadic killing. After a winter marked by near starvation, refugees swelled the J. pop. to 1,800 in June 1942. On 20 July, most were sent to the Pelkinia transit camp for selection, most being deported to the the Belzec death camp. A final 600 or so were murdered at the J. cemetery in May 1943.

SIENKIEWICZOWKA Volhynia dist., Poland, today Ukraine. Jews numbered around 120 (total pop. 500) after WWI. The Germans captured S. on 26 June 1941. Many Jews hid with Czech families as the others were brought to the Horochow ghetto at the end of Oct., where they were shot on 8 Sept. 1942.

SIENNICA Warsaw dist., Poland. An organized community existed from the 1820s, growing to 560 (total pop. 988) in 1921. All the Jews were deported by the Germans to the Treblinka death camp on 18 Oct. 1942.

SIENNO Kielce dist., Poland. Jews settled in the 16th cent. In the 19th cent., Avraham Yehoshua Heschel served as rabbi, later gaining fame as a religious philosopher in the US. The J. pop. was 735 (total 1,686) in 1921. Under the German occupation in WWII, its number rose to 2,000 with the arrival of 1,000 refugees. All were deported to the Treblinka death camp in Oct. 1942.

SIERADZ Lodz dist., Poland. Jews first settled here in 1436 but the community grew only in the mid-18th cent. In 1822 the Jews were confined to a ghetto but the measure was rescinded in 1862. The J. pop. in 1897 was 2,357 (34.5% of the total) and in 1921 grew to 2,835 (total 9,284). Zionist groups began to function after WWI, and Agudat Israel dominated the community council. Antisemitic manifestations were

widespread during the 1930s. When the Germans entered the city on 3 Sept. 1939, some Jews were sent to internment camps in Germany and others murdered in German army camps. In Dec. 1939, Jews were expelled to Sandomierz and in 1940 or 1941 another 1,000 were sent to Zdunska Wola. In 1942, there were 1,100–1,400 Jews in the ghetto and on 24-27 Aug. 1942 the majority were deported to Chelmno and about 190 to the Lodz ghetto.

SIERPC (Yid. Sheps) Warsaw dist., Poland. Jews are first mentioned in the mid-18th cent., living in a separate quarter and engaging in petty trade A few exported grain or leased estates and by the late 19th cent. 40% of breadwinners were artisans. A synagogue was built in 1895 and Gur, Aleksandrow, and Plotsk Hasidim maintained *shtiblekh* and were embroiled in disputes with a minority of *Mitnaggedim*, who formed a separate congregation in 1859. The community was reunited in the 1890s by R. Yehiel Mikhal Goldshlak (d. 1918), a Gur Hasid and proponent of religious Zionism who officiated in the community for 53 years. The J. pop. rose from 1,185 in 1827 to 2,935 in 1897 and declined to 2,861 in 1921 (total 6,722). Before WWI immigration to the west was stepped up among the young. The shortlived Bolshevik occupation of 1920 was accompanied by confiscations of J. property and the execution of a number of wealthy Jews. After the war, the community was supported by the Joint Distribution Committee and overseas relatives. Almost all the J. political parties were active in the community. Agudat Israel was involved in community institutions while Zionist influence continued to grow. A Tarbut Hebrew school founded in 1932 enrolled 200 children. The economic boycott of the 1930s severely undermined J. livelihoods. The Germans captured the city on 8 Sept. 1939, pillaging J. stores with active local participation and introducing a regime of forced labor and persecution. The synagogue was burned down on 29 Sept. On 8 Nov., 3,000 Jews, mostly women, children, and the old, were expelled in the direction of Nowy Dwor, most reaching Warsaw. The remaining 400 workers were confined to a ghetto, joined by another 100 Jews filtering back to the city. On 6 Jan. 1942, all were transported to Strzegowo, dying of starvation or disease in the ghetto or being sent on to the death camps.

SIESIKIAI (Yid. Sesik, Sheshik) Ukmerge dist.,

Beth Jacob school, Sierpc, Poland, 1936

Lithuania. According to the 1926 census, there were 125 Jews in S. Most were engaged in the grain trade. They maintained a small synagogue. The Zionist movement won widespread support. Most of the youth emigrated to South Africa. In 1940, the J. pop. stood at 70. The Lithuanians murdered all the Jews after the German occupation of June 1941.

SIEU   (Hung. Sajo) N. Transylvania dist., Rumania. A J. community was founded in the early 19th cent. In 1930, the J. pop. was 324 (18% of the total). In April 1944, the J. pop. was transferred to the Drago-miresti ghetto and then deported to Auschwitz.

SIEU MAGHERUS   (Hung. Sajomagyaros) N. Transylvania dist., Rumania. Jews first settled in the early 19th cent. In 1930 the J. pop. was 63 (6% of the total). In May 1944, the Jews were transferred to Bistrita and in June deported to Auschwitz.

SIEWIERZ   Kielce dist., Poland. Jews were banned from residence until 1862. In 1939, they numbered 229. All were expelled by the Germans to Zawiercie in summer or fall 1942 and from there deported to Auschwitz.

SIGHET   (Sighetul Marmatiei; Hung. Maramarossziget) N. Transylvania, Rumania. Jews first settled in the 17th cent., engaged in distilling spirits and in money-lending. They traded in furs, textiles, and steel with the Jews of Poland and Galicia. Members of the community joined the Shabbatean and even the Frankist movements. The first synagogue was built in 1770. The Great Synagogue was consecrated in 1836 and remained standing until the Holocaust. The J. pop. increased from 431 in 1830 to 4,960 in 1890 (30% of the total). Feuds between the various hasidic sects over the appointment of rabbis and ritual slaughter broke out from the early 19th cent. In 1887 the community split over the decision to join the national association of Orthodox congregations. The breakaway faction called itself the "Sephardi Community." R. Yekutiel Teitelbaum (1808–83) founded the S. hasidic dynasty and established a yeshiva. Among the erudite rabbinical scholars who lived in S. were R. Yehuda Modern and R. Shelomo Leib Tabak. A press established in 1874 printed over 200 works in Hebrew up to 1944. It printed the Hebrew weekly *Ha-Tor* as well as other periodicals in Yiddish and Hebrew. In the years prior to WWI, two Yiddish-Hungarian weeklies were published. Due to its proximity to the border, the Jews of S. suffered greatly during WWI at the hands of the Russian invaders. In 1919, returning soldiers from various armies attacked and robbed Jews, and self-defense units were organized. Between the World Wars the economic situation of the Jews was difficult and the Joint Distribution Committee provided assistance, funding an orphanage and weaving workshops. Jews engaged in the lumber trade, dominated the export of fruit, particularly apples, and constituted the majority of the town's doctors. The J. pop. in 1930 was 11,075 (40% of the total). In 1931, a group of Orthodox working youth joined the Agudat Israel youth section and established a training farm. During this pe-

riod, leaders of hasidic sects established courts, e.g., R. Pinhas Hagar of Borsa, R. Eliezer Ze'ev Rosenbaum of Craciunesti, R. Moshe Hagar of Kosov and R. Yaacov Yissakhar Dov Rosenbaum of Slatina. In the mid-1920s, the Orthodox community opened an elementary school attended by hundreds of pupils. In the 1930s, there were 150 students studying at the yeshiva. Zionism struck roots in S. in 1906 and it became one of the strongest movements in Transylvania. Dr. Eliyahu Blanck, chairman of the Zionist organization, translated Herzl's *Der Judenstaat* into Hungarian and established the first Hebrew school in S. Mizrachi was the dominant Zionist movement with its national headquarters situated in S. for some time. In 1935, a group of 400 Jews from S. and the surrounding area immigrated to Palestine and settled in Rehovot. The Zionist organizations published a number of periodicals in Hebrew, Yiddish, and Hungarian. Nobel Prize laureate Elie Wiesel, born in S. in 1926, has commemorated the J. community in his books.

Soon after the entry of Hungarian troops in Sept. 1940, J. business licenses were canceled and the economic situation of the Jews declined. The J. pop. in 1941 was 10,144 (39% of the total). Several hundred Jews who did not possess Hungarian citizenship were

Weaving class at the Torah im Derekh Eretz Yeshiva, Sighet, Rumania, 1930s (Beth Hatefutsoth Photo Archive, Tel Aviv/photo courtesy of Yad Vashem, The Holocaust Martyrs' and Heroes' Remembrance Authority, Jerusalem)

expelled in July 1941 and most were murdered in Kamenets-Podolski. Others were transferred to ghettoes and deported to Auschwitz. In 1942 hundreds of young Jews were drafted into labor battalions in the Ukraine, where they died of starvation or were murdered. During 1943–44, S. was inundated with J. refugees from Poland who later moved on to Budapest. The J. pop. of 15,000 (including Jews from the surrounding villages) was ghettoized on 20 April 1944. The behavior of the Germans and gendarmes was particularly cruel. At the end of April SS officers Adolf Eichmann and Dieter Wisliceny visited the ghetto. The J. pop. was deported to Auschwitz from 16 to 21 May 1944. After the war, Jews returned to S. and by 1947 the community numbered over 2,000. In the 1950s the majority left mainly for Israel.

SIGHISOARA   (Hung. Szgesvar; Ger. Schassburg) S. Transylvania dist., Rumania. A J. community was founded in the 1860s and maintained a synagogue and a yeshiva with 30–40 pupils. In 1930 the J. pop. was 173 (1% of the total). On 27 Nov. 1940, economic sanctions were imposed on the Jews and they were forced to forfeit their property. Despite the war, a J. school was opened in 1942. The language of instruction was Yiddish. The J. community, provided aid to

some 2,000 refugees. After the war, J. community life returned to normal.

SIGULDA   (Ger. Segewald) Livonia dist., Latvia. In 1935 the J. pop. was 15 (total 1,618). The Jews were murdered by the Germans with Latvian assistance shortly after their arrival in July 1941.

SIKLOS   Baranya dist., Hungary. Jews were present in the Roman period. The modern community dates from the early 19th cent. Jews played an important role in the economic life of the area, establishing local banks, an electricity plant, and other enterprises. A J. school was opened in 1848 and a large synagogue was constructed in 1864, with the congregation becoming Neologist and exercising jurisdiction over many smaller settlements. The J. pop. was 438 in 1880 and 453 in 1930. On 14 May 1944, the Jews were brought to Barcs for deportation to Auschwitz.

SILALE   (Yid. Shilel) Taurage dist., Lithuania. Jews first settled in the 18th cent. Three synagogues were in operation and the Hovevei Zion movement attracted a folowing. At the end of the 19th cent., many emigrated to the U.S., South Africa, and some to Palestine. The J. pop. in 1897 was 786 (56% of the total). Communal

Burial of damaged Torah scrolls and prayer books, Silale, Lithuania, 1924

life centered around Zionist activities. Fires devastated the community in 1930 and 1939. The J. pop. in 1939 was 350 (27%). After the German invasion in June 1941, on 7-8 July, all the J. men were killed. The women and children were murdered that fall in a nearby forest.

SILENE Zemgale (Courland) dist., Latvia. The J. community was founded in the 19th cent. and numbered 285 in 1897, with many trading in forest products. In WWI most reached Vitebsk after expulsion by the Russians. The J. pop in 1935 was 189 (total 1,022). The Jews were presumably murdered by the Germans in the second half of 1941.

SILIANA Ouled Aoun dist., Tunisia. The J. community, which sprang up in the beginning of the 20th cent., numbered 104 in 1936 and 120 (7% of the total) in 1946. Few details are known about community life. In WWII, the Germans did not occupy S.

SILUTE (Yid. Haidekrug) Silute dist., Lithuania. Jews lived here from the late 18th cent. and numbered 100-150 under Lithuanian rule (1923-39). Persecution of Jews began in 1938. When Germany annexed the area in March 1939, all the Jews fled to Lithuania proper, perishing in the Holocaust. The Germans constructed labor camps in S. and its surroundings to which more than 500 Jews were brought from other towns; few survived.

SILUVA (Yid. Shidleve) Raseiniai dist., Lithuania. Jews first settled in the 18th cent. A synagogue was built in the 19th cent. The J. pop. in 1897 was 506 (42% of the total). In the 1922 elections for the Lithuanian Sejm (parliament), the Jews voted overwhelmingly for the Zionists. In the late 1920s and 1930s, antisemitic incidents and an anti-J. boycott led many to emigrate to South Africa. The J. pop. in 1938 numbered about 80 families. After the German conquest of 1941, the Germans transferred all the Jews to Ribukai, where they were put to forced labor until 21 Aug., when all were killed.

SIMEIZ Crimea, Russia. Jews were accorded formal residence rights in 1903 but a few were apparently present before that time. In 1939, their pop. was 180 (total 4,497). The Germans occupied S. on 8 Nov. 1941, murdering the few Jews who remained in Dec.

SIMFEROPOL Crimea, Russia, today Ukraine. J. settlement commenced with the founding of the city in the late 19th cent. The J. pop. was 471 in 1803, rising to 8,951 Ashkenazi Jews (total pop. 49,078) in 1897, with another 500 Krimchaks and 1,000 Karaites. About 22% of the Jews were engaged in petty trade and crafts. Many Jews were employed in the city's tobacco factories and printing houses, J.-owned in many cases. Two *talmudei torah*, two J. schools (for boys and girls), a vocational school for girls, and a public library operated in the early 20th cent. The community also maintained a J. hospital (founded in 1853) and various welfare organizations. The Zionists and the Bund were active at the turn of the 19th cent. The newspaper *Molot* appeared in 1906 and *Yevreyskaya Obschina* in 1918. In Oct. 1905, 42 Jews were killed in a pogrom. After the Feb. 1917 Revolution, many Jews were elected to the local council (soviet) and a special J. self-defense unit was formed to defend the Jews against rioters. After the Bolsheviks seized power in the city in Jan. 1918, the unit was disbanded and Zionist members of the local council were dismissed. Leftist Zionist organizations like Hashomer Hatzair and the left-wing faction of Po'alei Zion continued to operate openly in the early 1920s and then clandestinely until 1927. S. was one of the centers for the dispersion of J. farm settlers coming into the Crimea. In 1932, there were nine J. agricultural settlements in the county, attached to two J. rural councils and including 324 families. The number of J. farmers dropped to 900 in 1933. The construction of a J. vocational school was begun in 1928 with the support of the Joint Distribution Committee. A J. high school was still open in 1937 and presumably a number of J. elementary schools were operating in the 1920s. In 1939, the J. pop. of S. was 22,771 (total 142,634). The Germans captured the city on 1 Nov. 1941. According to their count, there were 12,000-14,000 Jews present at the time. *Sonderkommando 11b* forces commenced executing Jews on 9 (or 11) Dec. and by 13 Dec. had murdered over 10,000 along with 2,250-2,500 Krimchaks. According to another source, 17,600 Jews from S. and its environs were murdered in 1941 and another 3,000 in 1942.

SIMKAICIAI (Yid. Shimkaytz) Raseiniai dist. Lithuania. The J. pop. in 1940 was 30 (7.5% of the total). Following the German conquest of 1941, Lithuanian nationalists took all the able-bodied Jews to the village of Zuveliskiai and shot them. The remaining Jews were killed together with the Jews of Raseiniai on 29 Aug. 1941.

SIMLEUL SILVANIEI (Hung. Szilagysomlyo) N. Transylvania dist., Rumania. Jews founded a community in the 1830s and engaged in the wine and spirit industry. A synagogue was built in 1839 and a J. school in 1891. The last rabbi, R. Shelomo Zalman Ehrenreich (1899–1944), was one of the most erudite scholars in Transylvania and Hungary. The yeshiva he headed had up to 80 students. A Hebrew press was founded in 1904 by Shelomo Halevi Heimlich, printing J. scholarly works and continuing to function up to the Holocaust. Zionist activity began in 1924 but declined in the 1930s. The J. pop. in 1941 was 1,496 (16% of the total). In May 1944, the J. pop. of S. and 8,000 Jews from the surrounding areas were ghettoized in the village of Ceheiu under the worst conditions in N. Transylvania. There were attempts to escape from the ghetto. The Jews were deported to Auschwitz in transports on 29 May, 3 June, and 6 June. A J. community was reestablished after the war but the majority left mainly for Israel.

SIMMERN Rhineland, Germany. Jews probably arrived in the late 14th cent. Five J. families were present in 1722 and the community reached a peak pop. of 143 in 1832. A J. school operated since 1824 and a synagogue was consecrated in 1911. In 1933, the J. pop. was 81 (total 3,528). About 20 Jews remained in the late 1930s, with at least a dozen emigrating to Palestine and another dozen to the U.S. Four Jews were deported on 12 April 1940, seven on 30 April, and the last two on 25 June. At least 12, and probably more, perished in the Holocaust.

SIMNAS (Yid. Simne) Alytus dist., Lithuania. A J. community is first mentioned in the 18th cent. The J. pop. was 736 in 1856, dropping to 493 in 1897 (34%). During WWI, the Russian army expelled the Jews to Russia, some of whom returned later. Between the World Wars several *hadarim* and a Hebrew school operated. The community also had a large library of Hebrew and Yiddish works. The Zionist movement won widespread support. In 1930 there were 150 J. families in S. After Germany's invasion in June 1941, Lithuanian nationalists ordered all Jews who

Jewish elementary school, Simnas, Lithuania

had fled to return, on pain of death. Men were seized for forced labor and a 100 young men were murdered at the end of Aug. On 12 Sept. 1941, the remaining 400 Jews were brutally murdered in the Kalsninkai forest. Among those who escaped the slaughter was Dr. Abba Gefen (Weinstein), who subsequently served as Israel's ambassador to Rumania.

SIMONTORNYA   Tolna dist., Hungary. The J. settlement developed from the mid-18th cent. Most Jews worked at a J. hide-processing plant. The Jews formed a Neologist congregation in 1869. A school was opened in 1896. During the White Terror attacks (1919–21), several Jews were killed. In 1944 the J. pop. was 80. All the Jews were deported to Auschwitz on 5 July 1944 via Bonyhad and Pecs.

SIMONYS   (Yid. Shimantz) Panevezys dist., Lithuania. The J. pop. in 1886 was approximately 34 (30% of the total), rising to 79 in 1923. After the German conquest of 1941, the Jews were killed together with other Jews from the area in fall 1941.

SINELNIKOVO   Dnepropetrovsk dist., Ukraine. Jews settled in the late 19th cent. and numbered 259 in 1897. In 1919, they were attacked in a pogrom by General Denikin's White Army soldiers. In the Soviet period, the J. pop. was 1,309 (total 12,581) in 1926 and 740 in 1939. The Germans captured S. on 2 Oct. 1941, murdering about 200 Jews on 13 May 1942.

SINGEN   Baden, Germany. Jews first settled in 1900. The J. pop. in 1933 was 44 (affiliated to Konstanz). All left by May 1939.

SINGHOFEN   Hesse–Nassau, Germany. Jews from S. and neighboring villages established a community in the early 19th cent., numbering 70 in 1843. By 1925 the community had dwindled to 22 and, after it disbanded in 1938, the Nazis destroyed the synagogue.

SINIAWKA   Nowogrodek dist., Poland, today Belarus. In the late 19th cent. the Jews of S. engaged in farming and leasing and some traded in lumber. In 1921 they numbered 379 (total 514) after enduring a reign of terror unleashed by Polish soldiers in the aftermath of WWI. Hehalutz became active in the early 1920s and later a Tarbut Hebrew school was opened. German *Wehrmacht* units entered S. in late June

1941. In Aug. an *Einsatzgruppe* unit arrived and murdered the entire J. pop. outside the town.

SINSHEIM   (in J. sources, Zonsheim) Baden, Germany. A J. settlement existed in the second half of the 13th cent. During the Black Death persecutions of 1348-49, Jews from Worms and Speyer were given refuge there, but most were massacred. Few Jews were present until the modern community began to develop in the 18th cent. In 1827, S. became the seat of the district rabbinate with jurisdiction over 20 communities until it was attached to the Heidelberg rabbinate in 1875. In 1836 a synagogue was erected and the J. pop. reached 135 in 1871, thereafter declining steadily to 71 in 1933. In the Nazi era, the Jews were isolated socially and economically. Fifty-one emigrated, some after first leaving for other German cities. Fifteen were deported to the camps, two surviving. Another four were victims of euthanasia killings.

SINTEREAG   (Hung. Somkerek) N. Transylvania dist., Rumania. Jews first settled in early 18th cent. and engaged in the export of farm produce and fruit. The J. pop. in 1930 was 131 (12% of the total). The economic situation of the Jews deteriorated prior to the Holocaust. On 5 May 1944, the J. pop. was transferred to Beclean and then to the Dej ghetto, from where it were deported to Auschwitz.

SIOFOK   Veszprem dist., Hungary. Jews settled in the early 19th cent. The J. pop. grew to 578 in 1886 as S. became a commercial center and vacation site largely owing to J. initiative. A synagogue was erected in 1869. After WWI, 300 Jews from the region were murdered at S., which had become a center of White Terror activity. In 1930, 287 Jews remained. In May 1944, they were brought to Veszprem and on 29 May deported to Auschwitz. Some 100 survivors reestablished the community, but it gradually dispersed.

SIRET   (Ger. Seret), Bukovina, Rumania. A J. community existed in the mid-16th cent. In 1912-18, the mayor was a Jew and Jews were members of the municipal council. Most of the Jews engaged in commerce. Zionist activity began at the turn of the century. During WWI, Jews fled from the conquering Russians. Those who returned found their property destroyed. The Rumanian authorities persecuted the Jews, licenses of J. members of the free professions were revoked, and J. officials were removed from their positions. The J. pop. in 1930 was 2,121 (14% of the total). In 1936, R. Barukh Hager of the Vizhnitz dynasty was appointed community rabbi and opened a yeshiva. Zionist youth movements were active between the World Wars. On 20 June 1941, the J. pop. was marched to Dornesti, then moved to Craiova and Calafat, and finally deported to Transnistria. In 1944, Soviet troops liberated 460 S. Jews in Dzurin, 400 of whom immigrated to Palestine.

SIROKE Slovakia, Czechoslovakia, today Republic of Slovakia. Jews settled in the late 18th cent. Their pop. was 64 (total 1,060) in 1880 and 40 in 1940. Under Slovakian rule, they were deported via Presov to Demblin in the Lublin dist. of Poland on 12 May 1942.

SIROTINO Vitebsk dist., Belorussia. The J. pop. was 269 in 1847 and 1,766 (89% of the total) in 1897. In the early 20th cent., Jews were employed in

the linen-processing industry as well as in trade and crafts. In 1926, under the Soviets, their pop. dropped to 660. A four-year J. elementary school was opened in the same year. The Germans occupied S. in early July 1941. A ghetto for the 170 remaining Jews was set up in Aug. The Germans first murdered all J. men and later, on 24 Sept., women, children, and the old.

SIRVINTOS Ukmerge dist., Lithuania. Jews first settled in the 18th cent. In the late 19th cent., many Jews were Zionists and Haskala adherents. The J. pop. in 1897 was 1,413 (76% of the total), dropping to about 700 in 1940. During WWI the Jews were expelled to Russia; two-thirds returned after the war. In the 1930s, many emigrated to South Africa, the U.S., Cuba, Mexico, and Palestine. After the German invasion in June 1941, German soldiers burned the three synagogues and Jews suspected of connections with the Soviet regime were sent to Ukmerge and killed. In Aug. the Jews were forced to live in a ghetto. On 18 Sept. all were killed in the Pivonija forest.

Teachers with students at Jewish school, Sirvintos, Lithuania

SISAK Croatia, Yugoslavia, today Republic of Croatia. Jews first settled there in the 1860s and numbered 230 in 1931 (total pop. 10,915). The community was destroyed in the Holocaust by the Ustase. A children's camp was established where over 7,000 children (Serb and J.) were treated with extreme cruelty. In Sept. 1942, 2,000 were killed with typhus germs.

SITKOVCY Vinnitsa dist., Ukraine. Jews settled in the mid-18th cent. Ten were present in 1765. In the Soviet period, many worked in a sugar refinery. In 1939, the J. pop. was 217. The Germans occupied S. on 23 July 1941 and in Aug. 1942 murdered 106 Jews from S. and its environs at Raygorod.

SITNIA Polesie dist., Belorussia. S. was a J. colony founded in 1835 on leased land. In 1898, the pop. was 219. In the mid-1920s, about 200 Jews were engaged in agriculture. A Yiddish school was in operation in the Soviet period. The Germans arrived in late Aug. 1941, soon murdering the few Jews who had not fled or been evacuated.

SITTARD Limburg dist., Holland. Jews lived in S. between 1300 and 1350. J. traders settled in the early 16th cent. but at the end of the cent. the Jews were expelled. Settlement began again in the 17th cent., particularly from the 1650s, and a community was formed in the 18th cent. It grew significantly in the 19th cent.; a synagogue was inaugurated in 1853 and a number of social welfare organizations were established. A J. school was founded in 1851. Many Jews were involved in the town's cultural life. The J. pop. in 1891 was 181 (total 5,608). A large number of refugees reached S. in the 1930s and by 1941 they numbered 90. The J. pop. was 136 in 1941 and 52 in nearby Geleen. Some 120 Jews were deported from summer 1942 until April 1943, 113 of whom perished in Auschwitz and Sobibor. Only one returned from the camps. Sixteen survived in hiding.

SIVAC Vojvodina dist., Yugoslavia. A J. community was organized in the 19th cent. The J. pop. was 47 in 1940 (total pop. over 9,000); all were sent to Auschwitz and only one survived.

SIVERSKYI Leningrad dist., Russia. Jews probably first settled after the Oct. 1917 Revolution. They numbered 14 in 1926 and 172 (total 9,090) in 1939. The Germans occupied the town in late Aug. 1941 and in Jan. 1942 murdered 93 Jews and gypsies (apparently the last to be found in S.).

SKADOVSK Nikolaiev dist., Ukraine. Jews settled in the early 20th cent. and in the Soviet period numbered 172 in 1926 and 201 (total 6,628) in 1939. The Germans arrived on 13 Aug. 1941 and on 11 Oct. murdered about 250 Jews from S. and its environs.

SKAISTA Latgale dist., Latvia. The J. pop. in 1930 was 16. Those not escaping to the Soviet Union were murdered by local Latvians after the German occupation around the end of June 1941.

SKAITSKALNE (Yid. Shimberg) Zemgale (Courland) dist., Latvia. An organized J. community was present in the 1840s, growing to 429 in 1897 (total 562). In the 1880s Lithuanian Jews without residence rights filtered into the town. S. served as a Torah center for the region, with Courland and Lithuanian rabbis meeting there each year. Habad Hasidism was also influential. The Jews were expelled in WWI, with only half returning (202 Jews in 1920) and the J. pop. dropping further to 135 in 1935. The Jews were murdered shortly after the arrival of the Germans around the end of June 1941.

SKALA (I) Tarnopol dist., Poland, today Ukraine. Jews are mentioned from 1570 but the community was apparently wiped out in the Chmielnicki massacres of 1648-49 and the subsequent Swedish and Hungarian invasions. Recovering late in the 17th cent., it reached a peak pop. of 3,449 (total 6,154) in 1880, declining thereafter through steady emigration. Jews were active as distillers and brewers as well as dealing in agricultural produce. Chortkov and Vizhnitz Hasidim maintained rival courts and Haskala and Zionism made modest inroads in the late 19th cent. In WWI, the J. pop. was twice expelled by the Russians and decimated by starvation and a cholera epidemic as well as subsequently being hounded by the Petlyura gangs, Polish soldiers, and the Bolsheviks. By 1921, the J. pop. was 1,555. With the Soviet border closed between the World Wars, J. trade suffered considerably, with heavy taxes, competition from the cooperatives, and anti-J. propaganda adding further hardship. The Zionists offered supplementary Hebrew education and maintained a 5,000-volume library. The Soviet regime

Street leading to synagogue in Skaitskalne, Latvia, 1930

The Kolatacz family of Skala celebrating a wedding, Poland

of 17 Sept. 1939 brought an end to J. commercial and community life. The Hungarian army entered S. on 14 July 1941. The community aided thousands of J. refugees from Carpathia passing through the town in July on their way to mass extermination even though it was itself subjected to forced labor and extortion Persecution was stepped up when the Germans arrived in early Aug. 1941. Through the *Judenrat*, up to 150 Jews a day were demanded for work on farms or at German headquarters. Later others were sent to labor camps. Refugees from the surrounding villages exacerbated the housing problem and swelled the rolls of the impoverished. The Gestapo arrived on 25 Sept. 1942 and immediately organized an *Aktion*, rounding up around 700 Jews and sending the able-bodied to the Janowska Road camp while deporting the others to the the Belzec death camp The remainder were ordered to the Borszczow ghetto, with the exception of a few dozen doing farm work or menial tasks for the Germans. They too were expelled over the next year. Of the hundreds who had escaped the net, almost all were hunted down and murdered by Germans and Ukrainians. Some of the young Jews joined the partisans.

SKALA (II)   Kielce dist., Poland. Jews settled in the late 18th cent. In the 19th cent., most were employed as peddlers and tailors, with some maintaining shops and stalls. In the late 19th cent., a few manufactured such food products as jam and groats. The J. pop. rose to 604 in 1921 (total 3,543). The Zionists and Agudat Israel were active between the World Wars. The Germans arrived in Sept. 1939, establishing a *Judenrat* and sending the able-bodied to labor camps. On 27 Aug. 1942, the rest were brought to the Slomniki transit camp and on 6–7 Sept. deported to the Belzec death camp. On 10 Nov., the remaining Jews were rounded up and shot.

SKALAT   Tarnopol dist., Poland, today Ukraine. Jews are first mentioned in 1613 and maintained an organized community from the late 17th cent. Despite extensive emigration, stepped up after a devastating fire in 1895, the J. pop. held to a level of around 3,000 (45–55% of the total) from the 1880s on (In 1921 the J. pop. was 2,919 out of total 5,937.) The arrival of refugees in WWI contributed to the continuing trend of economic decline. Some relief was provided by the business generated yearly by the numerous hasidic visitors between Lag ba-Omer and Shavuot, when

the Husyatin rabbi stayed there. Zionist activity intensified between the World Wars, but was curtailed with the Soviet annexation in Sept. 1939 as was all commercial life. Jews, however, held important administrative posts under the Communists and around 200 fled with the Red Army with the arrival of the Germans on 7 July 1941 A Ukrainian pogrom claimed 560 J. lives, most of the victims being forced to leap to their deaths from the towers of the municipal building. Forced labor and extortion followed, with Jews confined to a special quarter and the first consignment of 600 of the infirm deported to the Belzec death camp around the end of Aug. 1942. In the fall, Jews from the neighboring settlements were expelled to the town. On 21 Oct., a mass *Aktion* resulted in the deportation of a further 3,000, and 153 dead. Another 1,100 were sent to the Belzec death camp on 9 Nov. The remaining Jews were now sealed into a ghetto with 300 confined to a labor camp within the town. Around 700 of the ghetto dwellers were rounded up and murdered beside open pits on 7 April 1943 and another 600 on 9 June. Two hundred of the labor camp inmates were executed on 30 June. Of the hundreds hiding out in the forests, many were hunted down. About 30 young Jews joined the partisans and 190 Jews were still alive to greet the Soviet liberators on 22 March 1944.

SKALBMIERZ   Kielce dist., Poland. Jews only settled here in 1880, forming an organized community with a synagogue and cemetery in the early 20th cent. and numbering 609 (total 1,715) in 1921. About 400 remained when the Germans arrived in Sept. 1939. A *Judenrat* was established in Sept. 1940 under a regime of forced labor and 1,000 J. refugees arrived from Cracow. On 29 Aug. 1942, all were brought to the Slomniki transit camp. The able-bodied were sent to the Pokrowice labor camp, the sick and old were murdered, and the rest deported to the Belzec death camp.

SKALICA   (Hung. Szakolca) Slovakia, Czechoslovakia, today Republic of Slovakia. The J. presence was nearly continuous from the Middle Ages to WWII, making the community one of the oldest in Slovakia. A cemetery was consecrated in 1750 and beside it a synagogue in 1760. J. property was seriously damaged in peasant riots in 1848. After the split of 1869, the community established a Neologist congregation and in 1876 built a new synagogue. The J. pop.

reached a peak of about 300 (total 5,000) in the 1880s and then declined as the young left for the big cities, dropping to 135 in 1921. Jews were active in public life between the World Wars and served on the municipal council. The Zionists were also active. In 1940, 86 Jews remained, included in the German defense zone (*Schutzzone*) and consequently subjected to the abuse of Nazi soldiers. In 1940-41, the authorities closed down 23 J. businesses. In late March 1942, young Jews were deported and on 20 April, 131 Jews from S. and the neighboring settlements were sent to Auschwitz via Zilina. Smaller transports followed in July.

SKAPISKIS (Yid. Skopishok, Skopishkis) Rokiskis dist., Lithuania. By 1870, the Jews in S. had established a synagogue. In 1897, the J. pop. was 1,010 (85% of the total). The Jews engaged in peddling and trade. When economic conditions worsened, partly because of antisemitism among Lithuanian merchants, many young Jews emigrated, mainly to South Africa. There were two *batei midrash*, one belonging to the Kapost Hasidim, the other to the *Mitnaggedim*. Following the German occupation of 1941, S.'s 40 J. families were transferred to Rokiskis and then murdered together with the Jews of that town.

SKARYSZEW Kielce dist., Poland. Jews are first mentioned in the late 18th cent., when they were granted the right to found a community by King Stanislaw Augustus Poniatowski. Their first rabbi, Eliezer Teitelbaum, served from 1908 until his death at 94 in 1941. The J. pop. was 820 (total 2,072) in 1921. After the German occupation of Sept. 1939, the Jews enjoyed relative quiet until confined to a ghetto in May 1942. On 18 Aug. 1942, its 1,800 residents, including refugees, were transferred to Szydlowiec and from there deported to the Treblinka death camp.

SKARZYSKO-KAMIENNA Kielce dist., Poland. Jews settled in the late 19th cent. During the 20th cent., Gur, Aleksandrow, and Amshinov Hasidim maintained 15 *shtiblekh*. In 1918, Jews were victimized in a pogrom. Their pop. grew to 1,590 (total 8,163) in 1921. Some were employed in the metalworking industry and organized into a trade union in 1925 by the Bund, which became the largest J. political party in the city. The Zionists were active from 1916 and Agudat Israel opened its doors in 1924. The Germans captured S. on 6 Sept. 1939, instituting a reign of terror

with the murder of five Jews and exacting an exorbitant "contribution" from the community. The pop. of the ghetto established in March 1941 increased from 2,000 to 5,000 with the arrival of refugees from Plock and Lodz in early 1942. At the same time, Hassag, the German munitions factory operating in S. with Polish forced labor, was converted into a labor camp where 23,000 Jews were ultimately brought, 17,000 perishing there. The ghetto was liquidated on 28 Sept 1942, when 3,500 Jews were deported to the Treblinka death camp and 500 of the able-bodied sent to the labor camp. The labor camp was liquidated in Aug. 1944, when 700 Jews were shot and 6,000 transferred to other labor camps or deported to the Buchenwald concentration camp. Five survivors were murdered in Feb. 1946 by Polish nationalists.

SKAUDVILE Taurage dist., Lithuania. Jews first settled in the 18th cent., establishing a synagogue and yeshiva in the 19th cent. The J. pop. of 1,012 in 1897 (72% of the total) remained stable down through the years. Unlike most places in Lithuania, the Jews were not expelled during WWI. The Zionists enjoyed considerable support in S. J. children studied in a Tarbut Hebrew school and *talmud torah*. When the Lithuanian merchants association persuaded town officials to move the market away from the center of town, Jews were adversely affected and many emigrated. After the German invasion in June 1941, J. men were taken to the Puzai forest outside the town and murdered. The remaining Jews were executed on 15 Sept. 1941 in the Griblaukis forest.

SKAUNE Latgale dist., Latvia. J. farmers were present for a few generations before WWI, numbering

Jewish house in Skaudvile, Lithuania

144 (a quarter of the pop.) in 1910. Many left after the war but the Jews still managed to maintain community institutions and for the most part identified as Zionists. Most fled to the Soviet Union on the approach of the Germans in June 1941. About a dozen, mostly elderly couples, were murdered in the town by the Germans and Latvians.

SKAWINA   Cracow dist., Poland. Jews did not settle until the residence ban was lifted in 1860 under Austrian rule. They numbered 100 in 1890 and 280 in 1921 (total 2,444). J. property was looted in the riots of Nov. 1918. The Germans expelled 150 to Miendzyrzec Podlaski in April 1941. A stream of refugees brought the pop. up to 2,000 by the time the community was liquidated on 29–30 Aug. 1942, when 180 were murdered (children and the sick and old), the able-bodied sent to the Plaszow concentration camp, and the rest to the Belzec death camp.

SKEPE   Warsaw dist., Poland. In 1852, Jews established a community which numbered 350 in 1921. During the Holocaust, they were probably expelled to other cities.

SKIDEL   Bialystok dist., Poland. Jews arrived in the late 17th cent. A devastating fire in 1880 left many homeless. The J. pop. doubled from 1,062 in 1878 to 2,222 (total 2,790) in 1897 after an influx of Jews from the villages in the wake of Czar Alexander III's 1882 May Laws. Many worked in the tanning industry developed by the Tartars in the town. Haskala made inroads in the late 19th cent. During the German occupation of WWI (1915–18), Jews suffered from food shortages and forced labor. The J. pop. in 1921 was 1,936 (total 2,907). After WWI, J. tradesmen resumed their commercial activities with the aid of J. credit facilities but heavy taxes again undermined their livelihoods. A Bund-sponsored CYSHO school enrolled 200–250 children as Bund influence grew among young Jews in the years of economic crisis. Others attended a Tarbut school under Zionist influence. Under Soviet rule in 1939–41, most Jews worked in nationalized factories. The Germans entered the town in June 1941 after a heavy bombardment destroyed many J. homes. The Jews were put to forced labor and in Aug. 1942 confined to a ghetto under a *Judenrat*. On 2 Nov. 1942 they were marched to the notorious Kelbasin transit camp near Grodno, becoming the first Jews

to arrive there. A few days later they were deported to Auschwitz.

SKIEMONYS   (Yid. Shkumian) Utena dist., Lithuania. The J. pop. was 160 in 1886 and 128 in 1923 (22% of the total). After the German occupation of 1941, the Jews were probably transferred to Anyksciai, where they were murdered together with the local Jews on 29 Aug. 1941.

SKIERBIESZOW   Lublin dist., Poland. Dating back to the 15th cent., the J. community in S. numbered 106 in 1921. The Germans murdered 82 Jews in Nov. 1941 and the last 14 in May 1942.

SKIERNIEWICE   Lodz dist., Poland. Although J. residence was restricted, the community increased threefold between 1827 and 1857 and in 1897 numbered 4,333 (28% of the total). This was due mainly to the jobs and trade generated by the building of the czar's residence in S., the laying of the Warsaw–Vienna railway line running through the town, and the establishment of S. as the district administrative center. Jews also provided supplies to the Russian forces garrisoned there and met the needs of J. soldiers serving with them. The hasidic courts in S. also attracted thousands of followers. Zionist groups were established in the early 20th cent. At the beginning of WWI, Jews were expelled by the Russians on the pretext that they supported the Germans, but returned with the German conquest of 1915. Tiferet Zion, a leading Zionist organization, attracted several hundred members. The situation of the Jews worsened between the World Wars and many Jews moved to other cities or emigrated overseas. During the 1930s, there were manifestations of antisemitism and boycotts of J. enterprises. Agudat Israel was founded in S. in 1918 and its members regularly served as chairmen of the community council. In 1921, the J. pop. was 4,371 (total 20,064). In 1939, the 4,300 J. residents were persecuted by the Nazis, who allowed the Poles to pillage J. shops and duly filmed the proceedings. The synagogue was burned down. A *Judenrat* was set up which was required to supply men for forced labor and provide for the 2,400 refugees who arrived in the town by early 1941. Seven thousand Jews were ghettoized in 1940 in the most squalid quarter of the town. Permission was granted on 24 Jan. 1941 for Jews to leave the town and there was a mass evacuation to surrounding towns and to Warsaw until by 1 March 1941 no Jews remained. In fall 1945, 43 survivors returned, but left in 1946.

SKIRSNEMUNE (Yid. Skirsnemune, Skirstimman) Raseiniai dist., Lithuania. The J. pop. was 171 in 1897 (12% of the total), dropping to about about 100 (14%) in 1923. All the Jews were murdered in fall 1941 after the German occupation.

SKOCZOW Silesia dist., Poland. The small number of Jews who settled (266, or less than 10% of the total in 1890) were mostly well-to-do. They opened factories and in their liberal, assimilationist milieu regarded themselves in many instances as "Germans of the J. persuasion." Only with the arrival of Galician Jews between the World Wars did Zionism gain a foothold. Antisemitism intensified in the 1930s. Persecution and physical abuse accompanied the German occupation of 1 Sept. 1939. Sixty J. males aged 14–60 were expelled to the area under Soviet annexa-

tion on 27 Oct.; the remaining 140 were confined to a single building in Nov. and in May 1940 expelled to Myszhkow and Lazy to share the fate of the local Jews.

SKOKI Poznan dist., Poland. A J. community of 338 existed in 1770, dwindling to 182 in 1895 (total 1,319) and fewer than 50 in Sept. 1939. All were expelled by the Germans to General Gouvernement territory shortly after the occupation.

SKOLE Stanislawow dist., Poland, today Ukraine. Jews are found from the early 18th cent., the J. pop. growing steadily to 3,099 (total 6,425) in 1910. From the 1840s, many were employed in the lumber industry, including around 100 in the largest match factory in Galicia. Toward the end of the cent., Jews found work in the burgeoning tourist trade. Early in the 20th cent. the Zionists gained political control of the community, with their ramified activity continuing between the World Wars. Agudat Israel was influential in

Cast of "Der Yeshiva Bocher," Skole, Poland, 1933

Entire Book of Proverbs and first chapter of Book of Psalms written on back of postcard in 15 hours and 20 minutes by Moshe Fuchs of Tucholka and Skole, Poland

traditional circles. In 1938, the J. pop. was 2,670 (of a total 8,000). Antisemitism intensified in the 1930s and the Soviet annexation of Sept. 1939 brought commercial and community life to an end. The Hungarian army arrived early in July 1941. The Germans took over the town a month later and set up a *Judenrat* as a vehicle of extortion and demanded that all J. males between 14 and 60 report for forced labor. In Dec., 20 J. sawmill workers deemed unfit were murdered in the forest. On 2–4 Sept. 1942 about 100 of the infirm were killed in the town during an *Aktion* that sent the "unproductive" to Stryj for deportation to the Belzec death camp. Most of the remaining 900 Jews were confined to two labor camps which, thinned out by selections and flight, were finally liquidated by execution in June and Aug. 1943. The Germans and Ukrainians continued to hunt down the dozens of Jews who had fled to the forests.

SKOLOSZOW Lwow dist., Poland. The J. pop. in 1921 was 188 (total 2,650). The Jews probably shared the fate of Radymno's Jews in the Holocaust.

SKOPIN Riazan dist., Russia. The J. pop. was 104 in 1923. Those Jews who had neither fled nor been evacuated were murdered on 25–28 Feb. 1942 during the German occupation.

SKOPJE (Serb./Turk. Uskub) Macedonia, Yugoslavia. Jews probably lived in S. from the early Roman period until its destruction by an earthquake in 518. Jews are mentioned again in 1337 and a 17th cent. synagogue plaque mentions the existence of a J. community and synagogue from 1366. In the 13th–15th cents., Jews arrived from Western Europe and later from the Slavic countries. At the end of the 15th cent. and early in the 16th cent., Iberian J. refugees joined the community, which adopted their Sephardi traditions. Documents from the 16th and 17th cents. record the trade between the Jews of S. and Jews of other com-

Business school students on an outing, Skopje, Yugoslavia, 1926 (Itzhak Adizis/photo courtesy of Yad Vashem, The Holocaust Martyrs' and Heroes' Remembrance Authority, Jerusalem)

munities. In the 17th cent. the walled J. quarter was located in the center of S. The messianic doctrines of Shabbetai Zvi from the mid-17th cent. had a powerful effect on the Jews of S. and spread from there to surrounding localities. With the war between Austria and Turkey (S. had been in Turkish hands from 1392) in 1688-89, most of the Jews left S. The victorious Austrians counted 3,000 Jews amongst its 60,000 inhabitants. They burned down the city for fear of a plague and out of strategic considerations. Some Jews died and some escaped. The remnant was taken into captivity and held under inhuman conditions. Some were killed. A ransom was demanded of other European communities for their release and J. emissaries were sent for this purpose. In 1690 the Turks regained control of S. Some surviving Jews then returned and found their quarter burned and plundered. The J. community slowly revived and by 1765 numbered 1,063. In 1879 the J. quarter was destroyed in a fire and in 1892 the J. pop. numbered only 700. From the early 20th cent. the

community's schools were supervised by the Alliance Israelite. During the Balkan war of 1913, many Jews from neighboring towns came to S. After WWI, Zionism and welfare agencies proliferated and religious activity dwindled. Despite equal rights, J. trade was impeded in the aftermath of the war and poverty spread. In the 1930s many of the community's members, especially the rich, left the J. quarter for a new neighborhood, where a third synagogue was founded. In 1931 there were 2,641 Jews in S. (total 68,334). On 5 Oct. 1940, Yugoslavian laws were introduced restricting J. commercial activity. On 6 April 1941 the Germans attacked Yugoslavia and entered S. the following day. The Jews suffered a wave of pillaging and then S. was handed over to the Bulgarians. The Jews were fired from their jobs and property was confiscated. Zionist activity was banned and some Jews were even deported to Bulgaria. In fall 1941, over 300 Jews escaping persecution in Belgrade reached S. Early in 1943 rumors of deportation spread and some fled to find a haven in Italian Albania. On 11 March 1943 all the Jews of S. were concentrated in a factory with no sanitary facilities or food. Between 22 and 29 March they were taken to the Treblinka death camp; none lived. Among those who survived the Holocaust were Jews with Spanish or Italian citizenship and a number of partisan fighters, as well as doctors and pharmacists who were necessary to the Bulgarians to fight epidemics. After the Holocaust some 300 returned to their homes.

SKORODNOYE Polesie dist., Belorussia, today Belarus. The J. pop. was 422 (total 674) in 1897. In the Soviet period, a J. elementary school (four grades) was in operation, with an enrollment of 58 in 1928. Most Jews earned their livelihoods as artisans; some farmed small plots of land. The Germans occupied the town in July 1941 and murdered about 300 Jews.

SKRUDALIENE Courland dist., Latvia. The J. pop. was 19 in 1935 (total 236). The remaining Jews were murdered shortly after the German occupation of June 1941.

SKRUNDA Kurzeme (Courland) dist., Latvia. The J. community included fewer than a dozen families between the World Wars (1–3% of the total pop.), mainly trading in agricultural produce. At the beginning of the German occupation around the end of June 1941, all the Jews were murdered outside the town.

SKRYGALOVO Polesie dist., Belorussia. Jews numbered 37 in 1811 and 417 (total 784) in 1897. Seventeen Jews from S. and its environs were murdered and nearly all J. homes looted in a pogrom staged by the Balakhovich brigade in 1920. In 1923, the J. pop. was 866. A J. elementary school (four grades) was active in the 1920s. The Germans occupied S. in late Aug. 1941. Some Jews succeeded in fleeing. The rest were presumably murdered.

SKRYHICZYN Lublin dist., Poland. Jews lived on the estate attached to the village in the 19th cent. It was purchased by Etta Raizl Rotenberg, who, with her two sons, set up a sawmill, dairy, and horse-breeding farm. The family became the community's benefactors. In 1921, the J. pop. was 188 (total 267), mostly followers of Gur Hasidism. The Rotenberg estate was broken up in the 1920s, with a number of Jews pur-

Playing chess on the banks of the Bug River, Skryhiczyn, Poland, 1920s

chasing parcels of land. Many members of the family left for South America and the U.S. Some came to Palestine, joining family members who had come earlier in the cent. to help found the village of Kinneret. When the Germans arrived in Sept. 1939, peasants staged a pogrom in which six members of one family were murdered. The Jews were expelled on 22 Nov. 1941, apparently to the Hrubieszow ghetto, and from there deported to the Sobibor death camp in June 1942.

SKRZYNNO Lodz dist., Poland. Jews lived there from the 19th cent. and in 1897 numbered 191 (35% of the total). During WWII the Jews were forced by the Germans to work in the nearby quarries. In Oct. 1942, the 200 Jews (including refugees) were sent to Opoczno and then deported to the Treblinka death camp.

SKULSK Lodz dist., Poland. The independent community dates from the mid-19th cent. and numbered 185 in 1897 (25% of the total). In July 1940 some of the Jews were dispersed by the Germans to the Zagorow, Grodziec, and Rzgow ghettoes and murdered in Oct. 1941 in the Kazimierz Biskupi forest.

SKUODAS   Kretinga dist., Lithuania. Jews first settled in the 17th cent. A magnificent synagogue, one of the oldest in Lithuania, was built in the early 18th cent. There were another three synagogues. Until 1879 children studied in a *heder* and *talmud torah*. That year H. Soloveitchik, a Haskala adherent, founded a school. In 1884 a a modernized *heder* was established, to be followed by two Hebrew schools and a Hebrew kindergarten prior to WWI. The J. pop. in 1897 stood at 2,292 (60% of the total). For many years all commerce in S. was dominated by Jews but in 1929 a network of non-J. businesses began to develop, with the purpose of undercutting the Jews. Many Jews emigrated subsequently to the U.S. and South Africa. The Zionist movement won widespread support, especially among the youth. In 1940 the J. pop. was 2,200 (50%). In the Soviet period (1940–41), Zionist and Hebrew activities were prohibited and businesses nationalized. With the German invasion of June 1941, many Jews tried to escape but found the roads blocked. Some younger people, however, made their way to Russian-controlled territory. Jews suspected of having connections with the Soviet regime were shot. Lithuanian nationalists then took all the Jews from their homes and executed the men. A week later most of the women and children were murdered and the remaining few in Aug. or Sept. 1941.

SKVIRA   Kiev dist., Ukraine. Jews probably settled in the late 17th cent. and numbered 262 in 1765 and 2,184 (total 17,958) in 1897. The weekly market day and 16 yearly fairs were an important source of income for the Jews, most of whom were Hasidim. Yitzhak Twersky served as rabbi. The community maintained social welfare agencies and provided monetary grants to Jews inducted into the czar's army. In the late 19th cent., a private boys' school and two general schools for girls were founded. S. was the birthplace of Ahad Ha-Am (Asher Hirsch Ginsberg; 1856–1927), founder of spiritual (cultural) Zionism. On 23 Oct. 1917, six Jews were seriously injured and J. stores and homes looted in local rioting and in Feb. 1919 Ukrainian gangs staged a further pogrom. In 1939, under

the Soviets, the J. pop. was 2,243, with a J. council (soviet) and Yiddish-language elementary school in operation. The Germans captured S. on 14 July 1941 and on 20 Sept. executed the Jews at one of the cemeteries.

SLADKOVODNOYE   Zaprozhe dist., Ukraine. Jews from Rowne (Volhynia) and the Tchernigov region founded S. as a J. colony in 1853. By 1858, it had a pop. of 561 (mostly Jews). In 1881, J. and German residents organized to defend themselves drove off Ukrainian rioters. The J. pop. was 430 in 1897 and 345 in 1926. In 1929, S. was included in the Novo-Zlatopol J. Autonomous Region. A J. elementary school was still open in S. in the late 1930s. The Germans captured S. in the first half of Oct. 1941. On 12–13 Dec., 107 Jews were murdered. The rest were expelled to Novo-Zlatopol, where 92 were executed.

SLANY   Bohemia, Czechoslovakia. Jews settled in the late 19th cent. after a long-standing residence ban. A synagogue and J. school were opened in 1865 and in 1930 the J. pop. was 85 (total 9,739). In Feb. 1942, the Jews were deported to the Theresienstadt ghetto via Kladno. Half of them were soon sent east (to Lublin, the Treblinka death camp, Izbica, and Trawniki) and the others were dispatched to Auschwitz in 1943–44. Few survived.

SLATINA   Walachia dist., Rumania. The J. community was founded in 1880. The Hovevei Zion movement functioned from 1898. In 1899 the J. pop. was 212. In Sept. 1940, the Iron Guard instituted a reign of terror and forced J. merchants to hand over their shops to its members. J. males were drafted into forced labor battalions in Jan. 1941 and some were sent to Transylvania. In 1939, the community assisted J. refugees from Poland and in June 1941 from towns and villages in Moldavia. Most of the exiles returned after the war and in 1947, 107 Jews were living there.

SLAVGOROD   Dnepropetrovsk dist., Ukraine. Jews settled in the late 19th cent. and numbered 189 (total 1,299) in 1897. In the Soviet period, the J. pop. declined to 123 in 1926 and 13 in 1939. After their arrival on 2 Oct. 1941, the Germans murdered the few Jews still there. The Germans murdered 118 people in S. and its environs, most of them probably Jews.

SLAVIANOSERBSK   Voroshilovgrad dist., Uk-

Jewish street in Slatina, Rumania (Beth Hatefutsoth Photo Archive, Tel Aviv/courtesy of Jiri Fiedler, Prague)

raine. Jews probably settled in the 19th cent. In 1847, the town's 55 Jews founded an organized community and built a prayer house. In 1897, the J. pop. was 143. The Germans occupied S. on 12 July 1942 and murdered the few Jews who had neither escaped nor been evacuated.

SLAVKOV U BRNA (Ger. Austerlitz) Moravia, Czechoslovakia. Jews are known from the late 13th cent. Many arrived from Brno after the expulsion of 1454. Jews owned fields, orchards, and vineyards and dominated the salt trade until losing the monopoly in 1660. The J. quarter burned down in 1762 and 40 died in a cholera epidemic in 1836 and others in 1866. The J. pop. was 544 in 1857, dropping to 66 (total 4,554) in 1930. The Jews were apparently deported to the Theresienstadt ghetto together with the Jews of Brno in late 1941–early 1942 and from there sent to the death camps of Poland, few surviving.

SLAVNOE Vitebsk dist., Belorussia. The J. pop. before WWII was about 200. Most Jews were artisans and an agricultural cooperative was active in the town. A synagogue remained open until 1933 and a J. elementary school until 1937. The Germans occupied S. on 6 July 1941. A ghetto was established on 9 July. On 15 March 1942, all 143 Jews there were executed near the village of Gliniki.

SLAVONSKA POZEGA Croatia, Yugoslavia, today Republic of Croatia. Jews first settled there after the mid-19th cent. Violent antisemitism broke out after WWI. The community numbered 468 in 1931 (total 7,125) and 123 in 1940. It was destroyed in the Holocaust.

SLAVONSKI BROD Croatia, Yugoslavia, today Republic of Croatia. In the 1870s there were 16 J. families in S. Zionism was introduced in the first years of the 20th cent. In 1931 there were 462 Jews there (total 13,776). In WWII over 40 Jews participated in the partisan fighting against the Fascists. The Jews of S. were murdered in death camps and only a dozen survived the Holocaust.

SLAVUTA Kamenets-Podolski dist., Ukraine. There were 246 J. poll tax payers in 1765. A J. printing press operated in S. in 1792–1836. In the early 19th cent., Jews contributed to the development of local industry, establishing factories for producing cloth, paper, soap, and candles and a sawmill, foundry, and flour mill. In 1897, their pop. was 4,891 (total 8,454). In the Soviet period, most Jews worked in artisan cooperatives, factories, and the government bureaucracy. J. clubs and schools operated in the city. In 1934, an ancient four-story synagogue designed by an Italian architect was torn down. In 1939, the J. pop. was 5,102. The Germans captured S. on 7 July 1942. On 18 Aug., they executed 322 Jews and on 30 June another 911. A ghetto was established. Most of the Jews were murdered on 26 June 1942: 800 at the foot of a hill called Bald Mt.; 2,000 in the forest near the S.–Tashki road; and 10,000 near the water tower at the army barracks. Another 300 Jews were buried alive near the Pioneer camp. The Germans murdered a total of 13,000 Jews in S., including Jews from the provinces of S. and Berezdov. The notorious Eastern Front Hospital with its many prisoners of war was located in S. and here J. prisoners of war were murdered.

SLAVYANSK (until 1784, Solyanoy, Tor) Stalino dist., Ukraine. Jews probably settled in the early 19th cent. after the city became a center of the salt, porcelain, and iron-smelting industries. In 1897, the Jews numbered 469 (total 15,792), some engaging in salt exports. J. laborers began arriving during the Soviet period. In 1939, the J. pop. was 2,050 (total 77,842). The Germans captured the city on 26 Sept. 1941. On 2–5 Dec., 420 J. families were murdered at the local quarries.

SLAWATYCZE Lublin dist., Poland. Jews settled in the late 18th cent. Numbering about 150 families in the 19th cent., they engaged in the wool and grain trade and contributed to the industrialization of S. by establishing a glass factory and home textile industry. Their pop. was 902 (total 1,868) in 1921. After WWI, the Zionists expanded their activities, surpassing the Hasidim in influence. In 1939, the J. pop. was 1,542. Many escaped to Soviet-held territory on the approach of the Germans in Sept. 1939. The Germans set up a *Judenrat* and ghetto. In Feb. 1940, they murdered 32 Jews. On 13 June 1942, most of the Jews were brought to Lomazy and murdered there in Aug. The remnant was deported to the Treblinka death camp on 27 Oct. via Miendzyrzec Podlaski.

SLAWKOW Kielce dist., Poland. A few Jews settled in S. before a residence ban was lifted in 1862, en-

abling the J. pop. to rise to 610 (total 3,750) in 1921. In 1838, a Jew established a factory for manufacturing steel nails, screws, and wire After WWI, it employed 1,200 workers, a quarter of them Jews. The Joint Distribution Committee helped many recover from the ravages of WWI. Between the World Wars, the Zionists were active, opening new branches and a training kibbutz. As a result of a devastating fire and the economic situation, many young people left S. for South America in the 1930s. On their occupation in Sept. 1939, the Germans murdered 98 Jews from S. and its environs who were trying to return home after failing to reach Soviet-occupied territory in eastern Poland. In Nov. The Germans established a *Judenrat* and instituted a regime of forced labor. Towards the end of 1941, a ghetto was set up. On 10 June 1942, the Germans dragged the Jews out of their homes for a selection that sent many to the labor camps and workshops in Bendzin and Sosnowiec. On June 12, the rest were loaded on railway cars, probably bound for Auschwitz.

SLESIN Lodz dist., Poland. Jews lived there from the early 19th cent. and in 1884 numbered 270 (22% of the total). On 15 May 1940 the Jews were expelled to Zagorow and Grodziec and shared the fate of the Jews there.

SLIEDRECHT Zuid-Holland dist., Holland. The community was established in the 19th cent. and numbered 52 in 1901. A J. school operated there. In 1941 the J. pop. was 16 (total 14,284). All but three Jews were deported and perished in the Holocaust.

SLOBODA Vitebsk dist., Belorussia. S. was founded as a J. farm settlement on private land in 1831. In 1898 the J. pop. was 185. In the mid-1920s, under the Soviets, 33 J. families earned their livelihoods from agriculture. A J. kolkhoz founded in 1930 supported 26 J. families. The Germans occupied S. in July 1941. Jews continued working at the kolkhoz for a short while after the arrival of the Germans. In the fall they were murdered in the forest near the kolkhoz.

SLOBODKA (I) Vilna dist., Poland, today Belarus. Jews probably arrived with the founding of the settlement in the latter half of the 19th cent. and numbered around 40 families (total 200) in 1925. J. tradesmen traveled each week to Drujsk in the absence of a local market. A large Polish army base in the area was another important source of income. On their arrival in June 1941 the Germans instituted a regime of forced labor. In winter 1942 all the Jews were expelled to the Widze ghetto and from there dispersed among various labor camps, where 149 perished.

SLOBODKA (II) Odessa dist., Ukraine. Under the Soviets, the J. reading room, which had served as a clubroom, was closed down in the 1920s though the J. school was still operating in the early 1930s. In 1939, the J. pop. was 117 (total 2,584). After occupying the town on 27 July 1941, the Germans murdered the few Jews who had neither fled nor been evacuated.

SLOBODZEYA (Slobozia) Moldavia, today Republic of Moldova. The 19th cent. J. settlement received community services from neighboring Jadova. It numbered 605 (total 28,706) in 1807 and 107 in 1939. During the peasant revolt of 1907, the Jews fled their homes. After the German-Rumanian occupation of early Aug. 1941, five Jews were seized for forced labor and of the 72 residents murdered by the Germans, most were Jews.

SLOKA (Yid. Schlok) Vidzeme (Livonia) dist., Latvia. In 1811, 429 Jews were registered as citizens of S. to enable them to trade in nearby Riga, where J. residence was severely restricted. When many were permitted to settle in Riga the number of J. residents in S. dropped, to 204 in 1897 (total 2,190). The town was demolished in WWI, after which only 23 Jews lived there (ten in 1935). In WWII a labor camp for Riga Jews working in the peat bogs was set up in S.

SLOMNIKI Kielce dist., Poland. Jews settled in the early 19th cent. and numbered 904 in 1897 and 1,460 (total 4,797) in 1921. Most of the Jews were tradesmen, the larger merchants dealing in lumber and grain and a few owning large textile, shoe, and food supply stores. In 1926, a fire destroyed the *beit midrash*, which was rebuilt in 1930 and operated alongside hasidic *shtiblekh* (Aleksandrow and others). Although the Orthodox dominated the community, a number of Zionist groups were active, comprising 200 members in 1931 and sending 12 on *aliya* by 1939. In 1927, Polish landlords demanded exorbitant rents, forcing those unable to pay out on the streets. S. was captured by the Germans on 6 Sept. 1939 and included in General Gouvernement territory. A *Judenrat* was appointed

and most Jews continued working in their previous occupations under various restrictions and the threat of abuse by visiting German officers and policemen. Some were subjected to forced labor. A ghetto was never established in S. In 1940–1941, 1,000 refugees increased the J. pop. to 2,250. The first *Aktion* was carried out on 4–8 June 1942, when a large group was deported to the Belzec death camp after the disabled were murdered and 36 of the young selected for labor in the Plaszow concentration camp. The 1,000 remaining Jews were among the 6,000–8,000 surviving Jews of Miechow prov. herded into a nearby transit camp to await deportation. About 1,000 were sent to work, probably in Plaszow. Hundreds of the sick and old along with infants were executed beside freshly dug ditches before the rest were sent to the Belzec death camp on 6 or 7 Sept. 1942. Another 200 were rounded up in Nov. and executed in the Chodow forest. Four survivors were murdered after the war, causing many to leave S.

SLONIM Nowogrodek dist., Poland, today Belarus. Jews are first mentioned in the late 15th cent. and formed an independent community from around 1626. A great stone synagogue was erected in 1642. In 1660 the community suffered from the depredations of Stefan Czarniecki's irregular Polish troops in the war against the Swedes. From the outset of settlement, J. merchants maintained commercial ties with Lublin and Poznan and in the late 17th cent. trade expanded to include the port of Koenigsberg, where grain and lumber were shipped. In the 18th and 19th cents. Jews also traded in hides, furs, and steel and in the late 19th cent. in farm machinery and matches. In 1826 the town's first textile factory was founded by a Jew, employing 20 Jews among its 35 workers, and later in the cent. other J. textile factories were established as well as a distillery, steampower station, and yeast, soap, metalworking, and cigarette paper factories. The presence of a Russian garrison stimulated J. commerce, as did the construction of new army barracks in 1901. At the turn of the 19th cent., a third of J. breadwinners were artisans (800 in number, comprising a majority in the city) and Jews owned about 150 stores in the market. The J. pop. rose from 1,340 in 1817 to 5,476 in 1862, reaching a peak of 18,381 (total 22,350) in 1889. Thereafter economic and political circumstances (the pogroms and anti-J. measures of the 1880s) sparked a process of accelerated emigra-

Market next to synagogue in Slonim, Poland

tion, mainly to the U.S., reducing the J. pop. to 11,515 in 1897. The famous S. yeshiva, founded in 1815 by R. Shelomo Zalman Kahana, enrolled 800 students in the late 19th cent. It was later headed by Avraham ben Yitzhak Weinberg, who founded the hasidic S. dynasty in the 1850s. Many of its followers established themselves in Tiberias. After the death of R. Avraham's successor, R. Shemuel Weinberg, in 1916, a new branch was established in Baranowicze. In the late 19th cent. there were 24 synagogues and prayer houses and numerous hasidic *shtiblekh* in S. Most were destroyed in a devastating 1881 fire that gutted 900 homes and almost all of the city's stores and warehouses. The Bund and Zionist groups became active in the early 20th cent. Another great fire destroyed 600 homes in 1918 and under wartime conditions an estimated 1,500 Jews died of starvation. In 1921, when the J. pop. was 6,917, at least a third of J. families were on relief. The economic crisis of the 1930s led to further

deterioration. Community welfare services were extensive, including an orphanage, maternity ward, and old age home, while the TOZ organization sent 500 children to summer camps. In addition to the Mizrachi and Agudat Israel religious schools, 160–200 children studied at a Tarbut school. The Zionist youth movements all had their own culture clubs. In 1931 the J. pop. was 8,605. Under the Soviet occupation of 1939–41, flight from western Poland brought the J. pop. up to around 20,000. About 1,000 Jews, mostly refugees, were exiled to the interior of the Soviet Union. The Germans captured the city in late June 1941, instituting a *Judenrat* and a regime of severe persecution. On 17 July, about 1,200 Jews were executed near the village of Pietralewicze. Forced labor and fines followed. A ghetto was established in late Aug. On 14 Nov. 1941, another 9,000 Jews were murdered at Czepielow, including all residents of the orphanage and old age home. The final *Aktion* took place on 29 June 1942

Heder in Slonim, Poland, 1938

when as many as 10,000 Jews were again brought to Pietralewicze for execution. The 800 Jews left in the ghetto were murdered a few months later. About 400 Jews escaped to the forests, many joining partisan units, mainly the Shchors 51 Company.

SLOVECHNO Zhitomir dist., Ukraine. Jews arrived in small numbers in the mid-18th cent. In 1897, their pop. was 885 (total 1,570). The Soviet-J. writer Itzik Kipnis (1896–1974) was born in S. On 16–19 July 1919, the Petlyura gangs initiated a pogrom and killed 60 Jews, including children. In 1939, the J. pop. was 879. The Germans captured S. on 18 Aug. 1941. Local Jews were brought to Korosten for execution while Jews from the surrounding villages were executed in S. itself.

SLOVENI Vitebsk dist., Belorussia. The J. pop. was 446 (total 751) in 1897. A J. kolkhoz with six families was founded in 1929. The Germans arrived in July 1941. All of the 120 remaining Jews were concentrated in one street until executed on 16 March 1942.

SLOVENSKY MEDER (Hung. Totmegyer) Slovakia, Czechoslovakia, today Republic of Slovakia. The J. pop. was over 100 in 1921 with a synagogue and

cemetery in use. In mid-June 1944, the Jews were deported to Auschwitz.

SLUPCA Lodz dist., Poland. The community was founded in the 1870s and numbered 751 in 1897 (20% of the total). In Feb. 1940, several hundred Jews were expelled by the Germans to Tarnow and Bochnia. On 17–18 July 1941, the remainder were transferred to Rzgow and in Oct. murdered in the Kazimierz Biskupi forest.

SLUPIA NOWA Kielce dist., Poland. Jews settled in the early 19th cent. The development of quarries drew many Jews to S. and in 1921 the J. pop. numbered 956 (total 2,160). In 1929, 300 were left homeless after a fire. Rioting Poles pillaged and beat Jews as the Germans prepared to enter the town in Sept. 1939. Most of the town's 800 Jews were deported to the Treblinka death camp in Sept.–Oct. 1942 via Bodzentyn or Suchedniow. A local labor camp with up to 4,000 inmates operated in 1941–43.

SLUTSK Minsk dist., Belorussia. Jews are first mentioned in 1583. In the early 17th cent., the community came under the jurisdiction of Brest-Litovsk and in the late 17th cent. it was one of the five leading communities in the Lithuanian Council. In 1765, the J. pop. was 1,577. R. Yisrael Yehuda Leibl, one of the leading *Mitnaggedim*, was born and lived in S. in the 18th cent. The J. pop. rose to 5,897 in 1847 and 10,264 (total 14,349) in 1897. In the late 19th cent., the Szkolishche quarter, one of the three in the city, was inhabited entirely by Jews. Jews earned their livelihoods mainly in petty trade and crafts, their commercial life centering around three weekly market days and four yearly fairs. A few were farmers. In the early 1880s, the community built a hospital. S. was the birthplace of the writer Yitzhak Dov Berkowitz (1885–1967) and the poet Yaakov Cahan (1881–1960). The J. pop. reached a peak of 11,887 on the eve of WWI. During their withdrawal from the city, commencing on 8 July 1920, Polish soldiers pillaged and burned J. homes, and murdered a number of Jews. The S. yeshiva (a branch of the famous Slovodka yeshiva founded in the late 19th cent.) moved to Kletsk in Poland after the Polish retreat. In the Soviet period, the J. pop. dropped to 8,358 in 1926 and 7,392 in 1939. In 1939, most Jews were employed in artisan cooperatives (as tailors, shoemakers, printers) or worked in kolkhozes (over

100 J. families in two mixed kolkhozes in the early 1930s). In the mid-1930s, a J. elementary school (founded in 1924 with 700 students) and a J. secondary school were still open. A kindergarten and children's home were operating in the late 1920s. In 1928, R. Yehezkel Abramsky published two issues of *Yagdil Torah*, the only Orthodox periodical to be published in the Soviet Union (first published in 1908). In 1925, R. Sanomirski and a number of his students were brought to trial for operating a clandestine yeshiva. The last rabbi of S., Yitzhak Hachmark, was active in the community (also clandestinely) until 1930. The Germans captured the city on 26 June 1941. By late Oct. they murdered, with the aid of their Lithuanian collaborators, about 2,800 Jews (other sources have 1,000) near the village of Makrita. The remaining Jews and apparently a large number of Polish refugees were concentrated in two ghettoes (in Nov. 1941 or Jan. 1942). One was located in an open field just outside the city and intended for the old, children, and those unfit for work; the other was situated in the center of the city, where 5,000 Jews were held in 40 buildings. Thousands of Jews from nearby settlements were also brought to the ghetto. In May or July 1942, hundreds of Jews (including 700 children) were murdered near Makrita and on 8 Nov. 1942, about 5,000 from the city ghetto were executed. In the last *Aktion*, on 8 Feb. 1943, the Germans and their Latvian helpers murdered 1,600 Jews at the village of Zhurino (or Zhurovo). Dozens of Jews who escaped to the forests joined partisan groups. In all, the Germans murdered 14,000–18,000 Jews in the two ghettoes.

SLUTZK (until 1918 and from 1944, Pavlovsk) Leningrad dist., Russia. Jews probably settled in the early 20th cent. The J. pop. was 281 in 1926 and 2,013 (total 30,798) in 1939. The Germans entered S. on 16 Sept. 1941, murdering the Jews who had not fled or been evacuated.

SLUZEWO Warsaw dist., Poland. Jews settled there in the 18th cent. Economic pressures reduced their number from 560 in 1857 to 252 (17.5% of the pop.) in 1921. The Nazis subjected them to forced labor and established a ghetto, which was liquidated in May 1942.

SMEDEREVO (among Jews, Simindra) Serbia, Yugoslavia. Jews lived in S. from the early 19th cent. De-

spite anti-J. measures, the community grew to 139 in 1896 (total 6,875). In 1940, the J. pop was 83. All but three perished in the Holocaust.

SMIDOVICH Crimea, Russia, today Ukraine. Five families from Roslavl in the Smolensk dist. founded S. in 1926 as a J. agricultural settlement. In 1932, the J. pop. was 320. The Germans occupied S. in late Oct. 1941 and murdered 31 Jews in April 1942. Twenty J. families returned after the liberation but most apparently left some time afterwards.

SMIELA Kiev dist., Ukraine. The J. pop. of S. and the surrounding settlements was 927 in 1765. In 1897, the J. pop. of S. was 7,475 (total 15,000). Most of the city's 176 shopkeepers and 256 artisans were Jews. A pogrom on 3 May 1881, left seven Jews dead, dozens injured, and J. homes and stores looted. In April 1882, following a fire and further riots, 300 Jews were left homeless, 100 stores were looted, and 50 Jews injured. The synagogue and prayer house were destroyed. On 20 Aug. 1919 General Denikin's White Army soldiers murdered 30 Jews and destroyed J. homes and stores. In 1939, under the Soviets, 3,428 Jews remained. Some worked in a sugar refinery and a barrel factory and others were members of artisan cooperatives. The Germans captured S. on 5 Aug. 1941 and within a short time murdered 3,000 residents of the city, most of them Jews. A large number of Jews were also murdered in an *Aktion* in early 1943.

SMILDE Drenthe dist., Holland. Jews settled towards the end of the 18th cent. and their numbers increased significantly from the early 19th cent. The community numbered 67 in 1850 but dwindled thereafter. The J. pop. in 1941 was 13 (total 6,384). In the Holocaust 12 were deported and perished; one survived in hiding.

SMILOVICHI Minsk dist., Belorussia. The J. pop. was 462 in 1765 and 2,094 (total 3,133) in 1897. On 7 or 8 July 1920, retreating Polish soldiers beat and robbed Jews in S. In 1926, under the Soviets, the J. pop. dropped to 1,748. Many Jews worked at a multinational kolkhoz (with over 240 Jews and Tartars) and in four J. kolkhozes founded within the town or nearby. Another 400 Jews were members of six artisan cooperatives. A J. elementary school (founded in 1922) was still open in the early 1930s and a J. rural council was active in the mid-1920s. The Germans occupied the town in late June 1941. On 14 Oct., they murdered 1,388 Jews and other local residents.

SMILTENE Vidzeme (Livonia) dist., Latvia. The J. community was formed in the 1880s, attracting Lithuanian Jews at the turn of the cent. and growing to 278 (total 2,357) in 1920. About 20 young Jews joined the Latvian army in 1919 and participated in the struggle for independence. The J. elementary school founded in 1920 was the first in Livonia and a Zionist youth movement also began to operate in that year. The arrival of the Soviets in 1940 brought nationalization of J. businesses and an end to communal life. The Germans took the town in early July 1941. On 8 Aug. the Latvian police executed S.'s 200 Jews.

SMOLENSK Smolensk dist., Russia. Jews were probably living in S. in the late 13th cent. In 1611, after the town was captured from the Russians, King Sigismund III of Poland banned J. residence. Nonetheless, 80 Jews were present in 1616. Following the Russian reconquest in 1654 and the truce of Andruszow in 1667, the Jews were required to convert. Many preferred captivity or even death. Some who converted attained high positions in the Russian Empire, such as Peter Shafirov, an intimate advisor to Czar Peter I. The J. pop. grew despite the residence ban. The 11 Oct. 1881 census gave a figure of 2,933 Jews in S. (total 33,890). They mainly engaged in trade (lumber, grain, and flax) and crafts. In the late 19th cent., a *talmud torah* was opened which soon became a J. school. During WWI, thousands of refugees arrived in S. from western Russia. The J. pop. continued to grow after the Oct. 1917 Revolution and reached 12,887 (total 78,520) in 1926 and 14,812 in 1939. All J. religious and welfare institutions were closed down by the late 1920s. S. was the birthplace of the well-known aeronautical engineer and fighter plane designer Semyon Lavochkin. The Germans captured S. on 16 July 1941. In late July they ordered the city's Jews into a ghetto. Hundreds died from starvation and the cold in the winter. About 2,000 Jews were murdered in mid-July 1941, either by gassing or by firing squads near the village of Magalenschina.

SMOLEVICHI Minsk dist., Belorussia. Jews are first mentioned in 1699. In 1897 their pop. reached 1,927 (total 3,037). Under the Soviets, a J. elementary school was founded in 1920 and attended by 250 children in 1926. It was still operating in the early 1930s. A J. council (soviet) was also active in the mid-1920s. Some of the Jews worked at two J. kolkhozes. In 1939, the J. pop. was 1,385. After their arrival in 1941, the Germans concentrated 2,000 Jews from S. and the surrounding area in a ghetto. Apparently they shot 118 people soon after their arrival, most of them Jews, for alleged connections with the partisans. On 24 or 28 Aug., together with two Lithuanian companies, they executed 1,400–1,540 Jews in the Gorodishche forest. Another 400 Jews were murdered around 13 Sept.

SMOLIANY Vitebsk dist., Belorussia. Jews are first mentioned in the late 16th cent. and numbered 530 in 1765 and 1,704 (79% of the total) in 1897. By 1926, under the Soviets, the J. pop. dropped to 950. Fifty-eight J. breadwinners were artisans and 18 families earned their livelihoods in agriculture. The Germans captured S. on 9 July 1941. A ghetto for 700 Jews, including refugees from Minsk, Borisov, Orsha, and Dubrovno, was established on 9 March 1942. Many died of hunger and disease. All were murdered on 5 April.

SMOLNIK Slovakia, Czechoslovakia, today Republic of Slovakia. Permanent J. settlement commenced in the late 19th cent. The J. pop. reached a peak of 95 (total 2,385) in 1919 and then dropped to 42 in 1940. Most of the young joined Hashomer Hatzair between the World Wars. Antisemitic outbursts occurred throughout the 1930s and were stepped up after the Munich Agreement of Oct. 1938 with Jews forced to wear the yellow badge long before its institution in Slovakia as a whole. In 1941, J. businesses were closed down and on 19 May 1942 most of the Jews were deported to Izbica in Poland via Spisska Nova Ves.

SMORGONIE (Smorgon) Vilna dist., Poland, today Belarus. Jews first arrived in the 17th cent. and by 1651 formed an independent organized community. In 1765 the Jews numbered 649. About 40 J. farming families lived in an adjacent settlement, working the land until WWI. In the 19th cent. a flourishing hide-processing industry developed in the city, including 54 factories and 30 workshops, with the majority of workers Jews. The J. pop. grew to 6,743 (total 8,908) in 1897. There were seven prayer houses, including *shtiblekh* for Habad and Koidanov Hasidim, as well as three small *yeshivot*, a *talmud torah*, an old age home, and a small hospital. Among the community's rabbis was Yehuda Leib Gordin (1903–1910), author of *Teshuvat Yehuda* and a supporter of the Zionists. Two of his sons opened a secular Hebrew school in 1908 in the face of spirited Orthodox opposition. The Bund became active among J. factory workers, agitating for better working conditions, and participated in the revolutionary events of 1905. In 1915, rampaging Cossacks attacked the community in a night of murder, rape, and looting as 40 J. soldiers endeavored to protect the victims. During WWI the town was virtually destroyed. Jews received assistance from relief organizations as their pop. dropped to 2,500 (total 5,000) between the World Wars. Jews owned 140 of the town's 150 stores and about 50 shoemakers stood out among the artisans but competition, heavy taxes, and boycotts undermined their livelihoods. A Tarbut Hebrew school enrolled 200 children in 1936 and the Hehalutz organization and Zionist youth movements were active. Among prominent natives of S. were David Raziel (1910–41), commander of the Irgun Tzeva'i Le'ummi, and the writers A. Kabak (1880–1944) and Moshe Kulbak (1896–1940). After two years of Soviet rule (1939–1941) the Germans took S. on 26 June 1941, establishing two separate ghettoes in Sept. In Oct. 1942, 1,600 Jews were sent to the Oszmiana ghetto to share the fate of local Jews. Others perished after being sent to Lithuanian or Estonian labor camps or the Kovno ghetto

Main street of Smorgonie, Poland

while some were executed directly in the Ponary woods near Vilna on 26 April 1943.

SMORZE MIASTECZKO Stanislawow dist., Poland, today Ukraine. The J. pop. was 129 in 1921. The Jews were expelled to Stryj for liquidation in Sept. 1942.

SMOTRYCH Kamenets-Podolski dist., Ukraine. An organized community existed by 1712. In 1765 the J. pop. was 275 and in 1897, 1,725 (total 3,900). A Hovevei Zion group became active towards the end of the 19th cent. Later additional organizations began operating: Po'alei Zion, Tze'irei Tziyyon, Mizrachi, the Orthodox Mahaneh Yisrael, and the Bund. A Hehalutz group was started in 1921, most of its members subsequently emigrating to Palestine. In the Soviet period, Jews founded a kolkhoz with 62 families. In 1939, the J. pop. was 1,075. The Germans arrived on 8 July 1941, murdering 40 Jews in the first days of the occupation. In the fall, they murdered 670, expelling the rest to the Dunayevtsy ghetto, where they were executed on 18 Oct. 1942.

SNEEK (Snits) Friesland dist., Holland. Individual J. families lived in S. throughout the 18th cent. Their number increased from 1809. A community was organized in 1817 and a synagogue was built in 1836. The J. pop. in 1892 was 141. A branch of the Alliance Israelite and a Zionist organization were opened in the early 20th cent. The J. pop. in 1941 was 43 (total 17,390). In the Holocaust 25 Jews were hidden by local residents and saved. The rest were deported and perished.

SNEGORKA Kiev dist., Ukraine. The J. pop. in 1939 was 147 (total 3,043). The Germans occupied S. in July 1941 and apparently murdered the local Jews together with the Jews of Titiev prov.

SNEGUROVKA Nikolaiev dist., Ukraine. In 1931 a J. kolkhoz (called Royter Putilovets) was founded next to S., becoming binational with 26 Ukrainian and 18 J. families in 1932. The J. pop. of S. was 224 (total 5,065) in 1939. The Germans captured S. on 18 Aug. 1941 and on 15 Sept. murdered about 160 Jews. The few remaining Jews in the area were murdered in Sept. 1942.

SNEZHNOYE (until 1864, Vasilievka), Stalino

Doors of Ark of the Law, Smotrych, Ukraine, 1746

dist., Ukraine. Jews arrived in the early 20th cent. after the discovery of anthracite deposits in the area. In 1939, they numbered 114 (total 16,156). The Germans captured S. on 31 Oct. 1941. Three Jews from S. and nine from Novo-Donbas (in Russia's Rostov dist.) are known to have been murdered in the city.

SNIADOWO Bialystok dist., Poland. The J. settlement dates from the second half of the 16th cent. The J. pop. reached 1,081 (total 1,203) in 1857 and 1,300 at the end of the 19th cent. but after the community was expelled in WWI by the Russian army, just 386 returned by 1921, most of the others settling in Lomzha or emigrating overseas. Those remaining suffered from anti-J. riots and economic boycotts in the 1930s. The Germans executed over 50 Jews after

their arrival in June 1941. The rest were expelled to the Lomzha ghetto on 2 Nov. 1941 and deported to Auschwitz in Jan. 1943.

SNIATYN Stanislawow dist., Poland, today Ukraine. J. settlers are mentioned in 1563 and were accorded wide-ranging rights, the J. pop. growing to 4,206 in 1900 (total 11,500). The Zionists were active from 1894 and a Baron Hirsch school, eventually enrolling 187 students, was set up in 1900. A fire in 1906 left 200 J. families homeless and the establishment of a Ukrainian cooperative in 1911 cut into J. business. After the tribulations of WWI, 3,248 Jews remained. An anti-J. boycott led to a further deterioration of economic conditions, with Po'alei Zion and the Bund now competing for support among J. workers.

After the Soviet withdrawal in June 1941, Rumanian forces entered S., pillaging and murdering Jews with the active participation of the Ukrainian populace. The arrival of the Hungarians introduced a measure of restraint but the latter instituted a regime of forced labor that was stepped up when the Germans took over the town in Sept. Sporadic killing through the fall claimed 500 J. lives. About 5,000 Jews, including refugees from the surrounding settlements, were packed into the local sports arena in mid-April 1942 (Passover) and after a week of intense suffering and random killing deported to the Belzec death camp. A final 1,500 were sent to Belzec on 7 Sept.

SNINA (Hung. Szinna) Slovakia, Czechoslovakia, today Republic of Slovakia. Jews are mentioned in the census of 1725, with Galician families arriving from the early 19th cent. and giving the community a hasidic cast. A synagogue was built in 1842 and a new one in 1893. A J. elementary school was opened in the early 1860s. The J. pop. grew from 118 in 1828 to 209 (total 2,749) in 1900 and 399 in 1921. The Zionists and Agudat Israel became active after WWI. Most Jews engaged in trade. The Slovakian authorities forced them out of business in 1941. After the expulsion of J. children from the public schools in 1940, a regional J. school was opened in S. On 22 March 1942, 50 young J. women from S. and its environs were dispatched to Poprad en route to Auschwitz. A few dozen young men were then sent to the Majdanek concentration camp and most of the others were deported to the Chelm ghetto in the Lublin dist. of Poland on 11 May. In May 1944, the remaining members of the community were deported to western Slovakia. Some managed to hide and others captured by the Germans were sent to the concentration camps.

SNITKOVKA Kamenets-Podolski dist., Ukraine. Jews numbered 98 in 1847 and 231 (total 1,436) in 1897. The Nazis captured the town in the latter half of July 1941. The Jews of S. were murdered in 1942 with the Jews of the Letichev region.

SNOW Nowogrodek dist., Poland, today Belarus. Jews probably arrived in the 16th cent. In 1897 they numbered 526 (total 707) but their number declined from the early 20th cent. and stood at 401 in 1921. Most of the Jews were murdered by the Germans on 17 June 1942; 88 who escaped were lured back by false promises of a reprieve and murdered three days later.

SNOWIDOWICZE Volhynia dist., Poland, today Ukraine. The J. pop. was 78 in 1921 (total 1,289). In the Holocaust, the Jews were probably brought to the Rokitno ghetto for liquidation.

SNYTHKOV Vinnitsa dist., Ukraine. In 1765, 281 Jews were living in S. and the neighboring villages. Their pop. increased to 1,126 (total 2,886) in 1897. A wooden synagogue dated to the 18th cent. Most of the town's 40 stores belonged to Jews. In 1927, under the Soviets, the J. pop. was 1,181. From the late 1920s, a few dozen J. families earned their livelihoods in a J. kolkhoz. A J. elementary school was open until the 1930s. The Germans occupied S. on 23 July 1941, looting the J. kolkhoz and murdering several Jews. A ghetto was established for the Jews of the area and dozens of J. families from across the Dniester River. On 19 Aug. 1942, the Jews in the ghetto were expelled to Murovanye Kurilovtsy, where most were murdered within two days.

SOBEDRUHY Bohemia (Sudetenland), Czechoslovakia. A community with a synagogue probably existed in the late 15th cent. The Jews left c. 1500 after a devastating fire left them homeless. They returned in the late 16th cent. The community flourished again in the 18th cent., the J. pop. numbering about 300 in 1733. Until the mid-19th cent., few non-Jews lived in S. Jews owned many factories and maintained an elementary school from 1820. In 1893, their pop. was 393 but many left from the late 19th cent, reducing the J. pop. to 51 (total 2,189) in 1930. The Jews left for other places in Bohemia after the annexation of the Sudetenland to the German Reich in Sept. 1938.

SOBERNHEIM Rhineland, Germany. Jews are first mentioned in 1336 and were victims of the Black Death persecutions of 1348–49. Settlement was soon renewed, with Jews earning their livelihoods as moneylenders, wine and textile merchants, and livestock traders. In 1808 a local Jew was chosen as a deputy to the Assembly of J. Notables in Paris. A synagogue was consecrated in 1859 but the community remained under the jurisdiction of the Bad Kreuznach regional congregation, only becoming independent in 1926. A J. elementary school was in operation by 1840. During the 19th cent., Jews began opening stores and business establishments, mainly dealing in textiles. One store became the largest department store in the town and a small, domestic sock-knitting business, started by Sarah Marom, a widow with nine children, became a huge family enterprise employing 800 workers. The J. pop. was 131 in 1843 and 109 (total 3,479) in 1905. In 1888, a Jew was first elected to the municipal council. Afterwards, Jews also served as deputy mayors (mostly members of the wealthy Marom family). The Zionists were active between the World Wars but the majority of the community did not identify with the movement. In religion, most were Liberal (15% being considered Orthodox). Harmonious relations generally prevailed with the German pop. These, however, eroded somewhat during the Weimar period. In the March 1933 Reichstag elections, 42% of the local vote went to the Nazi Party. In 1933, the 34 J. families in S. owned 19 businesses. All were subjected to boycott pressures and most closed in 1935–36, the last of them in 1938 (including the Marom factory, sold at the end of the year) along with homes and land still in J. hands. Social ostracization accompanied the boycott as Jews were insulted, spat upon, and beaten in the streets. Only a small minority continued to help the Jews. On *Kristallnacht* (9–10 Nov. 1938), the synagogue and J. homes were seriously damaged and the J. cemetery was desecrated. The last 13 Jews were moved to five houses and in spring and summer 1942 deported to the east where they died. Of the 150 Jews present in S. in the Nazi period, 76 emigrated (46 to the U.S.) while 23 left for other German cities. At least 31 perished in the Holocaust.

SOBESLAV Bohemia, Czechoslovakia. The J. community was established in the late 19th cent. though Jews were possibly present before then. In 1930, the J. pop. was 78 (total 4,200). In Nov. 1942, the Jews were deported to the Theresienstadt ghetto via Tabor and in Sept. and Oct. 1943 most were sent from there to Auschwitz.

SOBIENIE JEZIORY (Yid. Sabin) Lublin dist., Poland. Jews settled in the late 19th cent. and numbered 1,439 (total 1,888) in 1921. Following the war, Zionist activity developed and a library opened. The Germans established a *Judenrat* and a ghetto whose pop., swelled by refugees, rose to 6,000 in Sept. 1941. As a regional concentration point en route to the death camps, S. contained 8,000 Jews on 2 Oct. 1942, when an *Aktion* sent all to the Treblinka death camp.

SOBKOW Kielce dist., Poland. Jews settled in the late 18th cent., founding a school and synagogue by the beginning of the 19th cent. They numbered 646 (total 1,117) in 1897. After WWI, the economic crisis and heavy taxes reduced many to penury. During WWII, refugees increased the J. pop. from 565 to 800, confined to the ghetto established by the occupying Germans. On 28 Aug. 1942, they were expelled to Jendrzejow and a month later, after a selection for the labor camps, deported to the Treblinka death camp.

SOBOLEVKA Vinnitsa dist., Ukraine. Twelve Jews were present in 1765. The J. pop. reached 1,121 (total 5,745) in 1897. In the Soviet period, most Jews were employed in artisan cooperatives and a sugar refinery. Others (75 families in 1930) worked on a J. kolkhoz that was dismantled in 1934. A J. council (soviet) and J. elementary school (four grades) were in operation. In 1939, the J. pop. was 434. The Germans occupied S. on 28 July 1941. On 27 May 1942, 382 Jews were murdered in a forest near Dobzhuk. The few skilled workers left alive were murdered later, making a total of 405 killed.

SOBOLEW-PLACE Lublin dist., Poland. Jews probably settled in the early 19th cent. and maintained a prayer house serving the neighboring villages. In 1921, their pop. was 561 (total 976). Between the World Wars, Zionist activity was extensive. The Germans captured the town on 17 Sept. 1939 and set up a *Judenrat* in late 1939 and a ghetto in fall 1940. Refugees from Garwolin, Maciejowice, and other places doubled the ghetto pop. to 1,710 in July 1941. In Oct. 1942, all were deported to the Treblinka death camp. A new ghetto established in Dec. held 1,400 Jews from the area, enticed from their hiding places by false promises that they would not be harmed. In Jan. 1943 they were also sent to the Treblinka death camp. Several survivors returned to S. after the war but when three were killed, the remainder left.

SOBOTA Lodz dist., Poland. Jews first settled here in the early 16th cent. and by 1897 numbered 325 (49% of the total). At the outbreak of WWII, Jews fled to other towns and the remainder were expelled to Glowno in 1940.

SOBOTISTE Slovakia, Czechoslovakia, today Republic of Slovakia. Jews may have been present in the Middle Ages. In 1738 a community of 18 families was formed under the protection of Count Nyary. A synagogue was erected in 1763 and the J. pop. rose to 387 in 1787 but the community suffered under the Count's successor. In 1848–49, J. property was damaged in peasant riots. In 1869, the J. pop. reached a peak of 619 (total 2,762) but then dropped to 361 in 1880 as the young left for the big cities. R. Yaakov Koppel Reich served the community in 1860–72, afterwards becoming chief rabbi of Budapest. He was followed by R. Yehuda Gruenwald (1881–91), later head of the Satmar yeshiva. In the 1930s, the J. pop. was 70–75. Under Slovakian rule, J. businesses were "Aryanized" in 1941 and most of the Jews were deported to the death camps in spring 1942.

SOBRANCE Slovakia, Czechoslovakia, today Republic of Slovakia. Jews are believed to have settled in the late 17th cent. Their pop. grew from 106 in 1828 to 349 (total 1,074) in 1880 with S. becoming the seat of a regional rabbinate with 34 settlements under its jurisdiction. R. Moshe Simha Friedman served the community from 1891 to 1940 and ran a yeshiva attended by a few dozen students. A synagogue and J. elementary school were also opened in the late 19th cent. After WWI, Mizrachi was the largest Zionist movement. Jews owned 28 business establishments, 11 workshops, and a big flour mill. Among the large neighboring settlements were Nemecka Poruba (nearly 150 Jews in 1919) and Vysna Rybnica (162 Jews in 1930). There were 395 Jews in S. in 1941. Dozens were seized for forced labor in 1940–41 after the Hungarian occupation, some perishing on the eastern front. In July 1941, J. non-Hungarian nationals were deported to the occupied Ukraine, where they were murdered. Most of the other Jews were deported to Auschwitz on 17 May 1944. Of the postwar community of 182, many emigrated to Israel in 1949.

SOCHACZEW Warsaw dist., Poland. The first record of Jews living here is a royal document from 1426. In the succeeding centuries, the community suffered from continuing antisemitism, including economic strictures and blood libels resulting in the execution of Jews. S. was an important J. community in Greater Poland and its delegates served as *shtadlanim* in the Great Sejm (1788–92). In the late 19th cent., S. became a hasidic center. R. Avraham Bornstein, known as Reb Avremele Sochaczewer, was regarded as a leading halakhic authority and was the head of the Alexsandrow Hasidim with many followers. In 1897, most of the J. pop. of 3,776 were Hasidim. During WWI, most of the Jews left S., a site of bitter battles, mainly for Warsaw. The Russian garrison, which controlled the area, was hostile to those who remained. After the Germans captured the city, about half the Jews returned, sheltering in cellars and storerooms. When the Poles took control, their soldiers severely abused the Jews. In order to establish order in S., a militia was set up in Nov. 1918, in which both Jews and Poles participated. In 1925, half the members of the town council were Jews (but only three in 1939). Most of the time the Zionists led the community. The 1930s saw increased incitement against the Jews, whose 1931 pop. was 3,011 (28% of the total). A blood libel in 1933 alleging that Jews had kidnapped a Christian woman for ritual purposes sparked violent attacks. At the trial, the woman testified that the story was fabricated. With the outbreak of WWII, many Jews fled. When German soldiers entered S. on. 9 Sept. 1939, they dragged elderly and infirm Jews out of their houses and murdered them in cold blood. Several hundred Jews per day were sent to forced labor. In Jan. 1940, the Jews were ordered to establish a *Judenrat* responsible for the enforcement of Nazi orders and the administration of J. affairs. A year later, 900 Jews were deported to Zhyrardow and a ghetto was established. However, ghetto residents were soon deported, on 15 Feb. 1941, to the Warsaw ghetto. The fate of the Jews of S. was that of the others in the Warsaw ghetto: most died under ghetto conditions or in the death camps to which they were deported in 1942.

SOCHOCIN Warsaw dist., Poland. A permanent J. settlement began to develop in the late 18th cent. In the 19th cent. most Jews were artisans; they also gained control of trade, particularly in grain and wool. Jews owned a distillery and beer brewery and many were employed in the burgeoning oyster-shell button industry. In 1897 the J. pop. reached a peak of 449. Prominent among the community's rabbis was Tuvia Yehuda Tavyomi, who served from 1909 to 1936. In WWI the Jews suffered from Russian and Polish depredations and in its aftermath saw their livelihoods undermined by economic boycotts. Zionist activity commenced in 1916. The Germans arrived in

Sept. 1939 and annexed S. to East Prussia (Ciechanow county), The town's *Volksdeutsche* immediately looted J. homes. The Germans destroyed the synagogue and instituted a regime of forced labor and fines. The 90 J. families (including 18 refugee families) were confined to a ghetto. In Oct. 1941, all 300–350 Jews were expelled to Pomiechowek and then to the Dzialdowo transit camp, from which they were dispersed, ultimately to perish.

SODEN, BAD   see BAD SODEN.

SOEGEL   Hanover, Germany. Jews were living there in 1771 and established a community that numbered 49 by 1842. Despite Catholic objections, they built a synagogue after their original prayer house was destroyed in a fire in 1840. They acquired a burial ground in 1850 and maintained a close association with the Jews of Lathen, who formed a semi-independent community. Children from Lathen and neighboring Werlte attended the J. elementary school in S., where Moses Speier taught for over 40 years (1896–1939). From a J. pop. of 68 in 1895, the community grew to 92 (over 6% of the pop.) in 1913. It remained Orthodox and a branch of the Agudat Israel movement was established after WWI. Members, including Lathen and Werlte Jews, founded a women's league, a youth club, and a branch of the Central Union (C.V.) When the Nazis came to power in 1933, there were 80 Jews in S. and 51 in Werlte. Over the next five years they were robbed of their farms and property, expelled from the cattle trade, and systematically impoverished. On *Kristallnacht* (9–10 Nov. 1938), SA troops burned local synagogues and sent J. men to the Dachau or Sachsenhausen concentration camp. Of the remaining Jews, 35 were deported to the Riga ghetto in 1941 and at least 27 to the Theresienstadt ghetto in 1942; 67 perished in the Holocaust. From Werlte, 14 Jews emigrated and 12 were deported to Riga. Three survived.

SOEST   Westphalia, Germany. Jews settled by the mid-13th cent. at the latest. The community, which opened a cemetery, included nine taxpayers in 1330–35. The Jews were expelled in the Black Death persecutions of 1348–49. In the mid-15th cent. the community numbered 50 and was considered large for the time. No further information is available until the early 19th cent. A synagogue with a classroom was consecrated in 1822 and a new cemetery was opened in 1832. The community reached a peak pop. of 296 in 1885. Jews were well integrated in the life of the city, joining local societies from 1841 and also serving on the municipal council. In 1929, the synagogue was renovated and enlarged. It was also equipped with an organ. In 1932, the J. pop. was 192. Jews owned 44 business establishments, including two department stores. On *Kristallnacht* (9–10 Nov. 1938), SA and SS troops broke into the synagogue, destroying the furnishings and religious books and setting the building on fire along with the J. school building next door. J. stores were vandalized and some looted while J. men were taken into "protective" custody and dispatched to concentration camps. On the eve of the outbreak of war in 1939, 42 Jews remained, the others having emigrated or moved to other localities in Germany. At least 50 perished in the Holocaust.

SOETERN   Oldenburg, Germany. The J. community in S., which existed prior to the Thirty Years War (1618–48), numbered only 44 in 1791. In 1846, the J. pop. was 233 but dropped to 107 in 1900. The community maintained a synagogue from 1838, a school (1831–1909), and a cemetery dating back to 1650. In 1933, there were 90 Jews living in S. A Jew was arrested in March 1933 for "Communist agitation," and, as a Polish citizen, deported to Poland. On *Kristallnacht* (9–10 Nov. 1938), the Nazis smashed the synagogue windows, then assembled the Jews of S. and forced them to wreck the synagogue. The cemetery was desecrated and both J. businesses and homes were looted and wrecked. Some Jews were maltreated and at least one was taken to the Dachau concentration camp, where he probably perished. By 1939, 36 Jews from S. had moved elsewhere in Germany. Although 27 managed to emigrate, some fell into Nazi hands in the locatlities were they had hoped to find shelter. The remaining Jews, at least 12, were deported in April and July 1942.

SOFIEVKA   Dnepropetrovsk dist., Ukraine. Jews settled in the late 19th cent., numbering 390 (total 9,327) in 1897 and 425 in 1926. In 1939, 67 remained. These were murdered by the Germans after they captured the city in mid-Aug. 1941, probably in May 1942.

SOHREN   Rhineland, Germany. Twenty-two Jews were living in S. in the early 19th cent. The J. pop.

rose to 83 in 1843 and then fell to 65 (total 858) in 1885 and 26–28 in 1932–33. Eighteen Jews emigrated before *Kristallnacht* (9–10 Nov. 1938), and two to France afterwards. Five Jews were deported to the camps in July 1942. Ten Jews perished in the Holocaust. The synagogue opened in 1858 was sold to the village in Dec. 1938 and transferred to the Koblenz J. community in 1954. The J. cemetery, dating back to the first half of the 19th cent., was desecrated in 1978.

SOKAL (Yid. Sikal) Lwow dist., Poland, today Ukraine. Jews are recorded from the early 16th cent. and constituted an urban class trading mainly in farm produce. Those settling in the early 17th cent. apparently arrived from neighboring Belz, whose hasidic court set the tone of J. life in S. from the early 19th cent. The community grew steadily, reaching a pop. of 2,408 in 1880 (total 6,725) and 5,220 in 1931. Five of the town's six brickyards were owned by Jews in the early 20th cent. as well as plywood, soap, and candle factories, sawmills, and printing presses. Antisemitic propaganda was stepped up in the 1930s. The Soviet annexation of Sept. 1939 brought J. commercial life to a virtual end and imposed administrative restrictions on Zionist and Bund activists. With the German occupation of 23 June 1941, Ukrainian police rounded up 400 Jews and after a selection murdered most of them near the brickyard outside the town. Forced labor and extortion followed with starvation claiming many lives in the winter of 1941–42. In a mass *Aktion* on 17 Sept. 1942, 2,000 Jews were deported to the Belzec death camp and on 15 Oct. a ghetto was set up for the refugee-swelled J. pop. of over 5,000. A typhoid epidemic claimed an average of over 20 lives a day. A second *Aktion* commenced on 28 Oct. with another 2,500 sent to the Belzec death camp. Many attempted to escape but were hunted down by the Germans with the aid of a hostile local pop., including roaming gangs of Ukrainian nationalists who killed on sight. Sporadic killing continued through the winter and spring of 1943. In the final *Aktion* of 27 May 1943, the remaining Jews were executed outside the town.

SOKOLETS Kamenets-Podolski dist., Ukraine. Jews numbered 356 in 1765 and 747 (27% of the total) in 1897. In the Soviet period, a J. rural council (soviet) was active and in 1923 the J. pop. was 505. The Germans occupied the town in early July 1941 and on 31 Aug. murdered 1,224 Jews in S. and at Zhvanchik.

SOKOLIKI GORSKIE Lwow dist., Poland, today Ukraine. The J. pop. was 292 in 1921. The Jews were deported to the Belzec death camp in the second half of 1942, directly or via Turka.

SOKOLKA Bialystok dist., Poland. Jews possibly settled in the latter half of the 16th cent. In 1698 they received a wide-ranging charter of privileges from King Augustus II, granting them freedom of worship and the right to hold property and engage in commerce. In 1765 the J. pop. stood at 522. Under Prussian rule (1795–1807) economic conditions worsened under the burden of heavy taxes and trade restrictions. Though restrictions remained in force under subsequent Russian rule, J. tradesmen benefited from the proximity of a Russian army camp and in the late 19th cent., tanneries established as an offshoot of the rapid industrial development of Bialystok employed hundreds of Jews. Thirteen factories were owned by Jews. The Jews operated a wide variety of community institutions, including a synagogue, four *battei midrash*, two hasidic *shtiblekh* (Karlin and Kotsk-Gur), and numerous social welfare organizations. The J. pop. rose from 1,457 in 1857 to 2,848 (total 8,000) in 1897. During the German occupation in WWI, economic life came to a standstill, with food shortages and forced labor the lot of the Jews. However, J. political life continued and Zionist groups, active since the late 19th cent., proliferated. In the first elections to the community council in 1919 the Zionists won the majority of the votes and a Zionist was selected as chairman. In the aftermath of the war, economic recovery was slow because of the loss of the Russian market and discriminatory government measures. Many Jews left for Palestine and the the U.S. as the economic crisis left the majority of Jews on the threshold of penury. In 1921 the J. pop was 2,821 (total 6,086). Their situation improved somewhat in the 1927–35 period but again deteriorated in the years preceding WWII, leading to a renewed wave of emigration. The majority of the community's children attended Tarbut and Yavne Hebrew schools. Under Soviet rule in 1939–41, the Jews were integrated into the new cooperative and bureaucratic system. The Germans entered the city on 24 June 1941, establishing a *Judenrat* and a sealed ghetto where the Jews were packed 16 to a room and denied food from outside its walls. Twenty-five young Jews were taken out of their homes and murdered at a nearby village. On 5 Nov. 1942, after a selection, the Jews were transported to the notorious Kelbasin transit camp near Grodno and after six weeks of torture and starvation deported to the Treblinka death camp. The 200 Jews left in the ghetto with another 200 brought in from neighboring towns to work at a boot factory were sent to Auschwitz on 23 Feb. 1943.

SOKOLOV (I)   Zhitomir dist., Ukraine. J. settlement began in the mid-18th cent. and reached a pop. of 239 (total 770) in 1897 and nearly 500 in the 1920s. Many Jews were artisans. The Jews were murdered in the initial period of the German occupation (commencing 10 July 1941).

SOKOLOV (II)   (previously, Falknov nad Ohri) Bohemia (Sudetenland), Czechoslovakia. Jews were present in the first half of the 15th cent. New families arrived after 1848 and, in all, in the 1840-96 period, 259 births were registered along with 62 marriages and 120 deaths. A synagogue was erected in 1897 and the community grew to 208 in 1921. In 1930, 170 Jews remained (total 11,381). Most of the Jews left the Sudetenland on the signing of the Munich Agreement in Sept. 1938. The rest were deported to the Theresienstadt ghetto and the death camps of Poland in 1942. The Nazis destroyed the synagogue and the J. cemetery. The postwar community numbered 231 in 1948.

SOKOLOW (I)   Stanislawow dist., Poland, today Ukraine. Jews apparently settled in the 16th cent. and continued to live in S. despite residence restrictions. In the late 19th cent. the J. pop. was 229 (somewhat less than half the total pop.). In Aug. 1942 the Jews were expelled by the Germans to Bolechow, where they shared the fate of the local Jews.

Jewish soldiers in the Polish army, Sokolka, Poland, 1930 (Beth Hatefutsoth Photo Archive, Tel Aviv/courtesy of Shimon Kruglak, Israel)

SOKOLOW (II)   Lwow dist., Poland. Jews settled in the late 17th cent., reaching a pop. of 2,155 (45% of the total) in 1890. A devasting fire in 1904 destroyed almost all J. homes (600), causing hundreds to move elsewhere. In 1905 peasants rioting at a village fair beat and looted J. peddlers. At the end of WWI the community, numbering 1,351, received support from the Joint Distribution Committee. Zionist activity, which had commenced in 1893, intensified from 1917. Under the German occupation, a ghetto was set up in 1941 and filled with refugees. In June 1942 the Jews were expelled to Rzeszow after a selection marked out 35 for immediate execution; most were deported from there to the Belzec death camp a month later.

SOKOLOW (III)   Lublin dist., Poland. Jews probably settled in the early 17th cent. as petty traders, tanners, shoemakers, and furriers, enjoying equal rights with Christian artisans under a royal privilege of 1665. The J. pop. grew from 1,186 in 1827 to 5,329 (total 9,738) in 1893. In 1931 the J. pop was 5,027 (total 9,918). In the late 19th cent., Kotsk-Gur, Aleksandrow, Kalushin, and Ruzhin Hasidim maintained *shtiblekh*. The Bund became active in 1900 and Po'alei Zion in 1905, with many of those participating in the strikes and demonstrations of the period emigrating afterwards due to persecution as a result of their revolutionary activities. In 1910, a fire destroyed most J. homes and the *beit midrash*, which was replaced by a big synagogue. During WWI, R. Yitzhak Zelig Morgenstern founded a hasidic court and a yeshiva serving the entire region. It had a postwar enrollment of 150. During the war, six out of nine city council members were Jews. The war led to increased emigration and economic hardship. Following the war, Polish soldiers killed six Jews accused of helping the Russian Army. Despite the traditional Orthodox orientation of the community, Zionist influence increased, with many religious families sending their children to Mizrachi's Yavne school. Agudat Israel ran a Beth Jacob school

Jewish family in Sokolow, 1916–17 (Beth Hatefutsoth Photo Archive, Tel Aviv/courtesy of Polska Academia Nauk, Warsaw)

for girls. Anti-J. riots instigated by the Endecja (National Democrat) Party erupted in 1937 and 1938. With the outbreak of WWII, many young Jews fled with the retreating Red Army in Sept. 1939. The occupying Germans established a *Judenrat* in late 1939 and sent 1,000 Jews to the Korczow labor camp. A ghetto was also established where 2,000 J. refugees from Kalisz and the Lodz area were sent and many died of starvation and disease. Periodically groups of Jews were sent to unknown destinations. On 10 Oct. 1942, all were deported to the Treblinka death camp. The Korczow labor camp was liquidated on 26 Nov. 1942. A few managed to escape and join the partisans.

SOKOLOWKA Tarnopol dist., Poland, today Ukraine. Jews are mentioned from 1629, the growing community receiving equal rights from the town's proprietor in the first half of the 18th cent. In 1880 the pop. stood at 983 (almost half the total) but by 1921 had declined to 460 as a result of emigration and WWI. The arrival of the Germans in early July 1941 inaugurated a regime of persecution with the Jews expelled to the Zloczow or Brody ghetto in Nov. 1942.

SOKOLY Bialystok dist., Poland. Jews probably first settled in the 18th cent. Their pop. grew to 1,377 in 1857 (total 1,509). Most were poor, selling goods and services at the weekly market and monthly fair or in the surrounding villages. A synagogue, *beit midrash*, and cemetery were opened in the late 19th cent. The J. pop. leveled off at around 1,500 after WWI. Economic conditions were difficult and the Zionists, Bund, and Agudat Israel were all active. After the Soviet occupation of Sept. 1939–June 1941, the Germans entered the town on 24 June 1941 and subjected the Jews to a reign of terror with their Polish collaborators. A *Judenrat* was appointed to supply forced labor and meet extortionate demands. The J. pop. was 1,500 in 1941, including refugees. Many of the young fled, a group of 100 reaching the forests in fall 1942. On 2 Nov. 1942, 500 Jews were deported to the Treblinka death camp. Most of those escaping were hunted down and murdered by Polish gangs.

SOKUL Volhynia dist., Poland, today Ukraine. A hundred Jews were living here in the late 18th cent. In the Holocaust, the Jews were probably taken to the Rozyszcze ghetto for liquidation.

SOLDIN (Pol. Mysliborz) Brandenburg, Germany, today Poland. Evidence of a J. presence can be found from the first half of the 14th cent., the middle of the 15th cent., and 1690. A settlement developed at the end of the 18th cent. There were 117 Jews in 1840 and the community maintained a synagogue and a cemetery. When the Nazis came to power in 1933, there were 36 Jews. The last J. business was sold in Nov. 1938. In Nov. 1944, there was one Jew in S., married to a non-J. partner. No further information about the fate of the Jews of S. is available, but it may be assumed that those who did not manage to emigrate were deported to the east.

SOLEC NAD WISLA Kielce dist., Poland. A small J. community existed in the 17th cent. In 1921, the Jews numbered 843 (total 2,513). The Germans entered S. on 9 Sept. 1939 and in Dec. 1941 set up a ghetto whose 800 residents were transferred to Tarlow in Nov. 1942 for deportation to the Treblinka death camp. In Feb. 1943, a family of Poles was executed for helping Jews.

SOLECZNIKI WIELKIE Vilna dist., Poland, today Belarus. Jews may have arrived in the 18th cent. Most were shopkeepers and peddlers doing the bulk of their business on the weekly market day. The J. pop. numbered 134 in 1866 and 570 (total 1,200) in 1922. Economic conditions remained difficult after WWI despite aid from the relief organizations and relatives abroad, with increasing antisemitism in the 1930s. Zionist influence was widespread between the World Wars, especially among the young. The Germans arrived in late June 1941, appointing a *Judenrat* and instituting a regime of forced labor. In Oct. 1941 all the Jews were expelled to the Dziewieniszki ghetto and from there to the Woronowo ghetto. On 11 May 1942, all but a few dozen workers were murdered in the nearby Bilorowski forest. The rest were sent to Lida. After organizing an escape to the forest they joined the partisans.

SOLENYE Kalinin dist., Russia. On 19 Oct. 1941 the Germans murdered 38 local Jews.

SOLIMAN Grombalia dist., Tunisia. J. settlement probably dates from the 17th cent., when Spanish exiles arrived mainly from Algiers and Oran with others from Leghorn bearing Italian citizenship. In the early

19th cent. a drought brought an end to the community, which was only reestablished in the early 20th cent. by seven of the original founding families. A few owned big farms with olive orchards, vineyards, groves, and livestock. Jews also owned seven of the town's 14 olive oil presses and enjoyed general prosperity. The J. pop. was 212 in 1909 and 182 (total 4,127) in 1936. The wealthy Levi family managed community affairs and built a synagogue which also housed the *talmud torah*. Most children attended the French public school. In Dec. 1942 and again in March 1943, Jews were mobilized for forced labor under the German occupation. Most evaded recruitment in S., preferring registration in distant Nabeul rather than Tunis on the correct assumption that conditions would be more amenable there. The last Allied bombardment of S. on 9 May 1943, a day before S. was liberated, killed seven Jews in a death toll of 730 and destroyed most of the town including the synagogue. After the war, many young Jews joined the Neo-Dustur movement to preserve good relations with the Arabs. Most Jews left for Tunis preparatory to emigration to Israel or France.

SOLINGEN Rhineland, Germany. Continuous J. settlement started in the 18th cent. A cemetery was opened in 1718 and a prayer house in 1787. Numbering only 32 individuals in 1804, the J. pop. rose to 182 in 1871 and a peak of 328 in 1905. A synagogue was consecrated in 1872. Jews owned four factories, including two large ones manufacturing metal products, and one J. factory owner was active in municipal affairs. In 1932, the J. pop. was 280. Many emigrated in the first months of Nazi rule, leaving 217 in June 1933. On *Kristallnacht* (9–10 Nov. 1938), SA and SS troops burned the synagogue and vandalized most J. homes and stores. One Jew was shot to death in his home and 32 were arrested, some being sent to the Dachau concentration camp. In May 1939, 78 Jews remained, including several in mixed marriages. In all, about 140 Jews emigrated, most of them to safe havens, and about 50 moved to other localities in Germany. In Oct. 1941 and July 1942, 24 were deported from S. to the death camps. Jews in mixed marriages were sent to the Theresienstadt ghetto in 1944, and survived the war.

SOLIVAR Slovakia, Czechoslovakia, today Republic of Slovakia. The J. pop. was 103 in 1830 and about 50 in 1940. Most were deported to the Lublin dist. of Poland in May 1942.

SOLNECHNOGORSK Moscow dist., Russia. There were 324 Jews in the area in 1939, most in S., the majority apparently arriving after the Oct. 1917 Revolution. The Germans during their short period of occupation (from 23 Nov. to 12 Dec. 1941) murdered the few Jews who had not fled or been evacuated, as well as those in the villages of Parfenovo and Glazovo.

SOLOBKOVTSY Kamenets-Podolski dist., Ukraine. The J. pop. was 411 in 1765 and 1,307 (39% of the total) in 1897. A J. printing press was founded in 1802. Pogroms were staged against the Jews on 23 Nov. 1917 and 20 Aug. 1919. In the Soviet period, a J. council and kolkhoz were active. The J. pop. was 940 in 1939. The Germans arrived on 9 July 1941, executing 194 J. families in Aug.–Dec. Another 26 families were executed at the Dunayevtsy railroad station. In all, 787 Jews were murdered in 1941.

SOLOTWINA Stanislawow dist., Poland, today Ukraine. The 17th cent. community grew to nearly 2,000 in the late 19th cent. (around 50% of the total), with a Baron Hirsch school for over a hundred children as well as a Hebrew school. The Russians burned almost all J. homes in WWI and the J. pop. dropped to 610 by 1921. In Sept. 1942 the Jews were expelled by the Germans to Stanislawow, where they were killed or sent to the Belzec death camp.

SOLT Pest–Pilis–Solt–Kiskun dist., Hungary. Jews settled in the early 19th cent. and numbered 159 in 1880. Many left in the wake of the post-WWI White Terror attacks (1919–21). In 1930, 53 remained. The young men were taken to forced labor in 1941, with most perishing. On 17 June 1944, the Jews were deported to Auschwitz via Kalocsa.

SOLTSY Leningrad dist., Russia. Jews probably settled in the early 20th cent. In 1939 they numbered 156 (total 8,972). The Germans arrived on 22 July 1941 and within a few days murdered about 150 Jews from S. and its environs.

SOLTVADKERT Pest–Pilis–Solt–Kiskun dist., Hungary. Jews settled in the late 18th cent, marketing wines and farm produce. The community maintained a J. school, *heder, talmud torah*, and yeshiva. A synagogue was consecrated in 1889. During the White Terror attacks (1919–21), J. stores were burned and robbed. In 1930, the Jews numbered 384. After the German occupation of March 1944, 28 were deported to Austria; the rest were sent on 29 June to Auschwitz via Kecskemet.

SOLY Vilna dist., Poland, today Belarus. A community of 245 was present in 1847, increasing to 530 in 1897 (total 981). In WWI, 28 J. homes were destroyed. In 1930 there were about 130 families (about half the total). The community was rehabilitated with the aid of the YEKOPO relief organization, but Polish competition undermined J. livelihoods between the World Wars. After the arrival of the Germans in late June 1941 a *Judenrat* and ghetto were established under a regime of forced labor. Later S. became one of the four ghettoes where the smaller J. communities of the Vilna area were sent. However, in spring 1943 all the Jews were evacuated and instead of being resettled in Vilna and Kovno as promised were routed to Ponary, where they were killed.

SOMBOR Vojvodina dist., Yugoslavia. Jews first settled in S. towards the end of the 18th cent. and a community was established in the 1820s. Zionist youth activity began in 1912 and by the 1930s the community was largely Zionist. The economic hardship of the 1930s was felt by the Jews and welfare organizations were set up. In 1940 the Jews numbered 1,620 (total 32,000). In April 1941 the Hungarians arrived and many Jews were arrested. In July some were seized for forced labor; only a few survived. The community continued to function until 5 April 1944, when the German invaders sent all the Jews to Backa Topola and from there to Auschwitz. Only a few were taken to Bergen-Belsen and survived. More than two-thirds of the community perished in the Holocaust. It was reestablished after the war.

SOMBORN (now part of Freigericht) Hesse–Nassau, Germany. Although Jews lived there from 1707, an independent community was not established until 1905. It numbered 47 in 1905 and 1933. Most Jews left by 1938, 11 emigrating to the U.S.

SOMCUTA MARE (Hung. Nagysomkut) N. Transylvania dist., Rumania. A J. community was founded in the 1820s and served as a center for 34 communities in the area. The first rabbi, Azriel Yitzhak Klar, was one of the leading rabbis of Transylvania. Zionist activity began in 1926 and increased greatly during the 1930s. The J. pop. in 1941 was 897 (28% of the total). In May 1944, the J. pop. was transferred to the Baia Mare ghetto and then deported to Auschwitz. After the war about 200 survivors returned, but the majority soon left, mainly for Israel.

SOMERSETA Latgale dist., Latvia. The J. settlement was founded in the 19th cent. and numbered around 100 families on the eve of WWI. Flight to the Crimea in WWI and emigration to Palestine reduced the J. pop. to 57 (total 282) in 1935. Most were murdered in a nearby forest shortly after the German occupation of July 1941.

SOMMERHAUSEN Lower Franconia, Germany. A J. community is known from the mid-18th cent., with a synagogue and school in the 19th. The Jews numbered 105 in 1816 and 21 in 1933 (total 1,109). Ten emigrated and nine left for other German cities in 1936–1941. J. homes were wrecked on *Kristallnacht* (9–10 Nov. 1938), and the last two Jews were deported to the Theresienstadt ghetto and Auschwitz, respectively, in 1942–43.

SOMOGYSZIL Somogy dist., Hungary. Jews settled in the late 18th cent. They organized in 1810, founding a synagogue in 1835 and a J. school in 1860. In 1869, when the congregation became Neologist, the Jews numbered 394. By 1941, the J. pop. had dropped to 40. The Jews were deported to Auschwitz via Kaposvar on 1–2 July 1944.

SOMOTOR Slovakia, Czechoslovakia, today Republic of Slovakia. Jews probably settled in the early 18th cent. A synagogue was erected in 1890. The J. pop. rose from 79 in 1880 to a peak of 179 (total 640) in 1910 and then dropped to 127 in 1941, when the Hungarians seized dozens for forced labor. Most perished on the eastern front. On 17 April 1944, the remaining Jews were sent to the Satoraljaujhely ghetto and from there deported on 21 May to Auschwitz.

SOMPOLNO Lodz dist., Poland. Jews lived there from the late 18th cent. and between 1823 and 1862 only by special permission. The J. pop. in 1897 was

641 (22.5% of the total) and in 1939 about 1,200. In 1940 the Jews were ghettoized and on 2 Feb. 1942 they were deported to Chelmno.

SONDERSHAUSEN Thuringia, Germany. Jews lived there in the early 14th cent. and in the first half of the 15th cent., suffering persecution during the Black Death disturbances of 1348–49. In the late 17th cent., a J. community with a prayer hall is mentioned. In the 18th cent., the community acquired a cemetery. In 1826, a new synagogue was dedicated. The J. pop. numbered 40 J. families in 1835 and 130 Jews in 1884. Most of the 67 Jews who lived in S. in 1933 left the town before the outbreak of war, emigrating to the the U.S., Australia, New Zealand, England, and Palestine. On *Kristallnacht* (9–10 Nov. 1938), the synagogue was destroyed. Those Jews who remained (19 in 1939) were deported to the Riga and Theresienstadt ghettoes.

SONNEBERG Thuringia, Germany. In the 1860s a few J. traders settled in S. Around 1900, 40 Jews from S. established a J. community together with 25 Jews from neighboring settlements. They maintained a J. cemetery which was part of the Christian cemetery. The J. pop. was 46 in 1925 and 36 in 1933. On *Kristallnacht* (9–10 Nov. 1938), all J. men in the town were arrested and forced to march through the streets holding antisemitic signs. Anti-J. slogans were painted on the walls of J. homes. In 1939, 13 Jews remained. No further information is available about their fate.

SONTHEIM Wuerttemberg, Germany. The early J. settlement was attacked in the Rindfleisch massacres of 1298 and again in 1304. The permanent settlement dates from the second half of the 15th cent., when seven families expelled from Heilbronn lived there. The Jews prospered in the 18th cent. as cattle and horse traders though still under the yoke of the Teutonic Order with its heavy taxation. Under Wuerttemberg rule from 1805, the Jews expanded their economic base, setting up a spinning mill and shoe factory. The J. pop. reached a peak of 103 in 1807 (10% of the total) with accelerated emigration setting in in the second half of the 19th cent. The 60 Jews of neighboring Horkheim were also part of the community from 1832 (dwindling to 17 in 1910). A. J. school was founded in the 1830s and in 1907 the Wilhelmsruhe Old Age Home opened. When the Nazis came to power in 1933, 31 Jews remained in S., immediately subjected to severe persecution. The old age home became a refuge for pensioners throughout southwest Germany, sometimes housing as many as 150. It was seriously vandalized by the SA on *Kristallnacht* (9–10 Nov. 1938), and in Nov. 1940 its residents were expelled, most perishing in the camps. Of the town's Jews, 22 emigrated by 1940; the other nine were sent to the Riga and Theresienstadt ghettoes and perished.

SONTRA Hesse-Nassau, Germany. Jews first lived there in 1367, but a permanent community was not established until about 1710. Its members, small traders and peddlers, were religiously observant and their high birthrate expanded the community to 114 (6% of the pop.) in 1885. Affiliated with Kassel's rabbinate, they maintained an elementary school and a synagogue, but their number declined to 72 in 1933. On 8 Nov. 1938 Jews were attacked and by 1939 most had left, 40 emigrating (25 to the U.S.). At least 17 perished in Nazi camps.

SOPOCKINIE (Yid. Sopotkin), Bialystok dist., Poland. An organized community was established in the second half of the 18th cent. with the consecration of a synagogue and cemetery. Many fled in WWI as Jews suffered abuse and persecution under the German occupation. The J. pop. dropped from 1,674 in 1897 to 888 (total 1,774) in 1921. With the closing of the borders after the war and the curtailment of the transit trade with Lithuania, the J. economic position deteriorated. Most Jews were reduced to peddling and petty trade. Their situation was exacerbated by anti-J. boycotts and the general economic crisis, leading many, particularly the young, to leave S. Nonetheless J. cultural and political life flourished. The Zionists controlled the community council and Hehalutz was the most active organization. Under the Soviet occupation of Sept. 1939–June 1941, J. stores were nationalized and J. artisans organized in cooperatives. The Germans captured the town on 22 June 1941. All the Jews were imprisoned at the nearby Teulin monastery. In June 1942 all the men except skilled workers were sent to Starosielce for forced labor; the rest of the pop. was ghettoized in S. In Nov. 1942 the Jews of S. became the first of 25,000–30,000 Jews in the Grodno and Bialystok areas to be transferred to the Kelbasin transit camp, held there under subhuman conditions until deported to the Treblinka and Auschwitz death camps around the end of the year.

SOPRON   Sopron dist., Hungary. The J. settlement dates from the Middle Ages. Mostly employed as moneylenders, the Jews were continually persecuted. After the expulsion of 1526, Jews only returned to trade in the 18th cent. under the protection of the House of Esterhazy. The modern community developed in the 19th cent. By 1881, Jews numbered 1,152, increasing to 2,483 in 1920. Jews traded in grain, cattle, and wine and founded two weaving mills that were among the most important in the country. The ancient synagogue was possibly built in 1350. Neologist and Orthodox synagogues were erected in 1876 and 1891, respectively. A J. school was built in 1852. The J. pop. dropped after WWI when the Austrian annexation of western Burgenland curtailed economic development. In 1941, the J. pop. was 1,861. On 22 April 1944, the Jews were confined in a ghetto. On 5 July, 3,000 Jews, including inhabitants of neighboring towns, were deported to Auschwitz. Forty-two Jews were

Ark of the Law in the old synagogue of Sopron, Hungary. Believed to have been built in 1350

transported to Budapest as part of the Kasztner group. Some 8,000 Jews, members of the labor battalions stationed in S., are believed to have died there in the course of 1945. A postwar community of 300 gradually dwindled.

SORAU   (Pol. Zary) Brandenburg, Germany, today Poland. Jews lived occasionally in S. probably in the 14th and the 16th cents. A permanent J. settlement developed only in the 18th cent. In the first half of the 19th cent., the Jews of S. (50 in 1849) were attached to the Guben community. They later formed their own community, and maintained a synagogue and a cemetery. In 1880, there were 154 Jews in S. When the Nazis came to power in 1933, there were 90 Jews still living in S. In May 1939 there were 72 Jews and 19 persons of partial J. origin (*Mischlinge*). It may be assumed that those who did not emigrate were deported to the east. In Nov. 1944, there were seven Jews, probably protected by marriage to non-Jews, still living in S.

SOROCA   Bessarabia, Rumania, today Republic of Moldova. Jews first settled in the 17th cent. after receiving permission from the princes of Moldavia to live, trade, and work there. They engaged in the sale of agricultural produce. A committee elected every three years represented them before the authorities and governed the community. During his term as rabbi (1800-09), R. David Shelomo Ivshitz established a yeshiva that attracted students from throughout Rumania. The first synagogue was built in 1775. After 1812, Jews were granted permission to trade throughout the Russian empire but were forbidden to purchase land in built-up areas. Jews from Podolia, the Ukraine, and Galicia, as well as Lithuania and Latvia, were attracted to settle in the Bessarabian steppes by offers of land, agricultural machinery, and exemption from army service. The J. pop. in 1864 was 4,135 (76% of the total). Jews were the main growers and sellers of tobacco and grapes. They also owned transports on the Dniester River. The Jews' economic situation declined from the 1880s as a result of falling grain prices and recurrent droughts. Hundreds of Jews who were not registered as citizens were expelled from outlying villages and arrived in S. destitute. A burden on the hard-pressed J. community, they increased the J. pop. to 9,200 in 1880–81. Although more and more Jews returned to working the land and growing fruit, vegetables, and tobacco, the majority worked as artisans. Throughout the 1890s, hundreds of Jews emigrated to the U.S. and to the Baron Hirsch colonies in Argentina. The agronomist Akiva Ettinger (1872–1945) came to S. in 1898 on behalf of the ICA and set up an agricultural college for 200 J. youth, He taught J. farmers to improve their crops by modern methods, established a cannery, and founded loan funds and schools in neighboring J. communities. A Great Synagogue was built and 12 prayer houses functioned mainly for the artisan organizations. A J. hospital with an outpatient wing and pharmacy was opened in 1886. At least one or two Jews were appointed to the municipal council by the regional authorities and Hasidim of various sects were prominent in the community. In 1861 a government-sponsored J. school was opened with a secular curriculum as well as J. studies; a vocational training department was added in 1885. A branch of Hovevei Zion was founded in 1890 with 200 members who were instrumental in introducing the study of modern Hebrew into J. educational institutions. In the 1906 elections to the first Duma, 11 of the 18 representatives were Jews. In 1919, a branch of the the U.S. Committee for Aid to Bessarabian Jews and Ukrainian Refugees was established to aid the thousands of Jews who came to S. during WWI and the Russian Revolution of 1917. The Zionist Ha-Tehiyya organization was founded in 1919 and in 1921 a group of about 120 pioneers trained at the ICA plant nursery established by Ettinger. In 1919–20 a Tarbut high school was opened with 105 pupils in 1931–32. A Tarbut elementary school had 158 pupils. The J. pop. in 1930 was 5,452 (36% of the total). Attempts to organize a democratically elected community council after the 1917 Revolution caused friction and elections were held only in June 1934. The murder by border police of six young Jews attempting to cross the Dniester River in Jan. 1932 and the accusation that they were Communists elicited reactions from the press and questions in the Rumanian parliament. Antisemitic manifestations increased and in 1936 land near the city walls belonging to Jews was expropriated, including prayer houses. In June 1941 the Soviet authorities transferred several hundred Jews to Floresti and then exiled them

Members of Keren Hayesod committee, Soroca, Rumania, 1921 (Beth Hatefutsoth Photo Archive, Tel Aviv/courtesy of Zalman Keynan, Israel)

to Siberia. After the Rumanian army entered S. at the beginning of July, 200 Jews were murdered by the local gendarmes and more by the army. The J. pop. was deported to Transnistria and was among the 10,000 Jews murdered in the Cosauti forest.

SOROKSAR Pest–Pilis–Solt–Kiskun dist., Hungary. Jews settled in the second half of the 19th cent. Most worked in nearby Budapest. The community organized in 1885, establishing a school in 1872. The J. pop. was 357 in 1910 (3% of the total) and 243 in 1941. The Jews were deported via Budapest and Bekesmegyer to Auschwitz on 30 June 1944. Survivors reestablished the community but it soon dispersed.

SOSNICA Lwow dist., Poland. The J. pop. was 100 in 1921. Some Jews were expelled to Soviet-held territory in 1939 and met their end there after the German conquest of 1941; others were deported to the Belzec death camp in 1942.

SOSNITSA Chernigov dist., Ukraine. Jews settled in the late 18th cent. and numbered 1,842 (total 7,000) in 1897. Most trade and crafts were in their hands. A J. kolkhoz was active in the 1920s. The J. pop. dropped between the World Wars, reaching 370 in 1939. The Germans arrived on 6 Sept. 1941 after some of the Jews fled. Seventy-eight were murdered on 10 and 16 Nov.

SOSNOWICA Lublin dist., Poland. A J. community of 514 was present in 1897, dropping to around 300 between the World Wars (about half the total pop.). The Germans arrived in early Oct. 1939, immediately killing 30 Jews and instituting a regime of forced labor. In 1941, refugees arrived from Mlawa and Lublin. In April 1942 Gestapo and SS officers forcibly removed all J. children to an unknown destination and all traces of them disappeared. In Nov., the rest of the Jews were taken to the Wlodawa ghetto for deportation to the Sobibor and Treblinka death camps. Many young people managed to escape to the forests.

SOSNOWIEC Kielce dist., Poland. The first Jew, Avraham Blumenthal of Modzejow, settled in 1859, authorized by the Russians to act as the city's customs agent. Others followed, including Hasidim (Radomsko, Aleksandrow, Sochaczew, Kotsk), with the community attached to Bendzin until 1898. A cemetery was dedicated in 1893, a synagogue in 1906, and a J. hospital in 1912 as the J. pop. grew from 2,291 in 1897 to 13,646 (total 97,086) in 1921. The Zionists organized their first group in 1897–98, with the young poet Hayyim Nahman Bialik among its leading activists and one of the city's first Hebrew teachers (1897–1900). A J. labor movement also developed in the late 19th cent. with the Bund and Po'alei Zion operating clandestine cells in 1906–08. At the outset of WWI, the Joint Distribution Committee helped Jews cope with severe food shortages, compounded by the arrival of thousands of J. refugees. After WWI, J. merchants and craftsmen organized themselves into influential associations, capable of providing credit to members. In 1921, Jews operated 368 workshops and business establishments, over half in the garment industry. The residence of R. Shelomo Hanokh ha-Kohen Rabinowich of Radomsko, who founded and supported 36 *yeshivot* throughout Poland, attracted thousands of hasidic followers. By 1931 the J. pop. reached 30,805. Zionist activity also expanded and 3,000 attended a lecture by Bialik when he returned to the city in 1931. The Betar group founded after Vladimir Jabotinsky's visit in 1927 had 200 members prior to WWII and the Maccabi sports club founded in 1916 had 600 members in 1926 and sent a large contingent to the Maccabiah Games in Palestine in 1932. J. elementary and secondary schools were in operation along with a J. business school, ORT classes, and a Beth Jacob school for 300 girls. The J. hospital was expanded to include 90 beds and an old age home completed in 1933 accommodated 40 residents. In the 1930s antisemitism intensified with occasional outbreaks of violence. Some 9,000 Jews fled east on the approach of the Germans, who entered S. on 4 Sept. 1939 and in the first days of the occupation murdered 30 Jews and introduced a regime of severe persecution. Subsequently Jews were evicted from choice apartments, a large "contribution" was exacted from the community, and all males under the age of 55 were subjected to forced labor. J. businesses were taken over and given to German "trustees." A *Judenrat* was established with Moshe Merin at its head. In Dec. 1939, he was made chairman of the Central *Judenrat* for Eastern Upper Silesia and began a controversial career guided by the view that some Jews would have to be sacrificed to the Germans in order to save others. The Central Office was abetted by 200 J. policemen and wielded considerable authority over local *Judenrat* councils. By late 1940, 2,880

Jews were working in labor camps. Another 3,000, including 2,000 tailors, were employed in "shops" producing clothing and other articles for the German army and regarded as a way of avoiding forced labor. In March 1941, 3,000 J. refugees from Oswiencim were brought to S. and Bendzin, increasing the J. pop. of S. to 24,249. On 11 May 1942, when J. police failed to round up 1,500 Jews, Merin threatened to report them to the Germans and the 1,500 Jews were subsequently deported to Auschwitz. In June, another 2,000 were sent there, including hospital patients, orphans, and residents of the old age home. On 12 Aug., 22,000 Jews gathered in the city's sports field for selection despite the urging of Zionist youth movement members not to comply. About 4,000 were sent to Auschwitz, beginning on 15 Aug. In summer 1942, Merin opened two labor camps for refugees as a hedge against deportation and the local sewing shop increased its workforce to 4,000. In fall 1942

the Germans set up a ghetto for 14,000 Jews in the Srodula suburb and another for 6,000 in the Old City. Under Merin's orderly supervision, the move was completed in March 1943. In June 1943, the Germans decided to liquidate all the Jews of Upper Silesia with Merin himself dispatched to Auschwitz on 19 Aug. On 23–24 June, only 1,200 Jews were found in the city for deportation since many were in hiding. On 1 Aug., nearly 800 German soldiers and police arrived for the final *Aktion* and within eight days, 30,000 Jews from S. and from Bendzin were deported to Auschwitz and another 400 shot while resisting. The last 1,200 Jews in the labor camps were sent to Auschwitz in Dec. 1943 and Jan. 1944. After meeting with Mordekhai Anielewicz, commander of the J. Fighting Organization (ZOB), in May 1942, the Zionist youth groups decided to form an underground organization. Its activities led to clashes with the *Judenrat*, which turned in several underground members, including

Jewish kindergarten in Sosnowiec, Poland, 1929 (Beth Hatefutsoth Photo Archive, Tel Aviv)

the leader of the Hashomer Hatzair group, 21-year-old Tzevi Dunski, who was hanged by the Germans in Auschwitz. A few dozen were able to escape to Slovakia and Hungary. Others were apprehended by the Germans, and a few were killed in armed clashes. After the war, some 2,440 Jews returned to S. from the Soviet Union but by late 1946 most had left Poland in the face of the country's violent antisemitism.

SOUK EL-ARBA (also Jendouba) Souk el-Arba dist., Tunisia. J. tradesmen from Tunis settled in the newly created town in the late 19th cent, later joined by Jews from Nabeul, Sousse, Beja, and even Algeria. Among the pop. were many Jews who had been nomads a short time before. The J. pop. was 184 in 1909 and 230 (total 4,011) in 1936. Jews were active in the oil industry and dominated local trade. The organized community was recognized in 1901 and managed by a committee, the J. Relief Fund (Caisse de Secours et de Bienfaisance), as elsewhere in Tunisia. A synagogue was established at the end of the 19th cent. Community life revolved around the synagogue in its traditional dress. In WWII, the community was spared the German occupation and barely felt the racial laws of the Vichy regime. After the war, the Joint Distribution Committee helped the community recover and Torah ve-Avodah, initiated by the local rabbi, became active on behalf of the Zionists. Most Jews left for Israel after Tunisia attained its independence in 1956, with a minority emigrating to France.

SOUK EL-KHEMIS Souk el-Khemis dist., Tunisia. Jews settled in S. in the early days of the French Protectorate (1881). They numbered 50 in 1909, 78 (6% of the total) in 1936, and 111 (4.5%) in 1946. There was no J. quarter or synagogue. Services took place in a private home. There was a *shohet* but no rabbi or *mohel*. The French acted to prevent anti-J. Arab riots. In WWII, the Germans did not occupy S., but the town suffered from German bombings and the passage of Allied armies to the front. The Joint Distribution Committee helped the community reestablish itself after the war. Following Tunisian independence in 1956 S.'s Jews left, first for Tunis, then Israel.

SOULTZ-SOUS-FORETS Bas-Rhin dist., France. A J. community was established in the 18th cent., numbering 164 members in 1783. The community numbered 415 members in 1865. The local synagogue

was inaugurated in 1897. In 1936 there were 116 Jews in S. During WWII, all were expelled to the south of France, with the rest of the Jews from Alsace-Lorraine. Bombing destroyed the synagogue during the war. In 1965, there were 18 Jews in S.

SOUSSE Sousse dist., Tunisia. The J. settlement possibly dates from the Punic period and was destroyed in the Vandal and Byzantine invasions of the 5th–6th cents. A well-established community existed in the Zeirid period (10th–11th cents.), when Jews were active in the flourishing textile industry. S. also became an important religious center after the destruction of Kairouan in 1057. S. was destroyed by the Almohads c. 1159. Though Jews probably returned under the Hafsids in the 15th–16th cents, the community was not heard from again until the 18th cent. The new community was founded under the Husseini dynasty at the turn of the 18th cent. by Leghornian merchants, known as Gorni or Grana, who made S. their second largest settlement in Tunisia after Tunis. Their European connections gave them commercial advantages over local Jews and Moslems and brought economic prosperity to the city. In 1824, the J. pop. was estimated at 1,000 and in 1853 at 1,600 with 150 of the 400 J. families of Leghornian origin and the rest native (Touansa) Jews. The two segments of the pop. formed separate communities, each with its own president (*qa'id*) but with a shared (sectioned) cemetery and common synagogues, *dayyanim*, teachers, and butchers. In 1864, violent anti-J. rioting broke out against the background of the bey's constitutional reforms of 1857 and 1861 granting the Jews equal rights. A cholera epidemic in 1867 claimed many J. lives. With the institution of French rule in 1881, many Jews arrived from the coastal area seeking work and the economic position of the Leghornian Jews improved still further as they were quick to adopt modern technological innovations in industry. Eugenio Lumbroso founded the first mechanical oil press in Tunisia in S., exporting the product to Marseille for the manufacture of soap there. He also built a soap factory between S. and Mahdia. Jews also exported wool and the *alafa* plant to France and England. Between the World Wars, the J. pop. was 3,500–3,700 (20–25% of the total). In 1936, although the number of J. wholesalers and retailers was declining, they still comprised 30% of the city's total, while manufacturers and artisans comprised 25% of the total and a professional class was rapidly emerging. In the late 1930s, economic conditions took a turn for the worse, partly due to the drought, partly due to the moratorium on debts declared by the bey in response to Arab nationalist pressure. Another decree by the bey, dating back to 19 Aug. 1900, established a single community council for the Leghornian and Touansa Jews, called the J. Relief Fund (Caisse de Secours et de Bienfaisance) and charged with maintaining the needy and the community's religious institutions. R. Yosef Ghez (1860–1934) officiated in 1906–28, afterwards becoming chief rabbi of Tunisia. He was also president of the rabbinical seminary in S. and a staunch supporter of the Zionists. He was succeeded by R. Shalom Fallah and R. David Bochobza. The community maintained six synagogues from the early 20th cent., the largest and oldest holding 300 worshipers. A seventh synagogue was erected between the World Wars and one was destroyed in WWII. The custom of making a pilgrimage to the grave of R. Pinhas Uzan in Moknine also became popular between the World Wars, under the influence of the many Jews from there who settled in S. in the 1920s, including jewelers and gold and silver merchants. J. children

attended French public schools and an Alliance school founded in 1883 as well as *talmudei torah* attached to the synagogues for afternoon study and a number of *yeshivot*. The Alliance school reached an enrollment of 221 in 1912 but subsequently declined. The French cultural influence was paramount in S.; however, there was also a rich Judeo-Arabic culture whose flagbearer was the weekly journal *al-Najma*, founded by Mahluf Najar and published from 1920 to 1961. It included political and cultural essays and serialized fiction. Najar also founded a local J. theater company. French influence expressed itself in the predominance of French among the European languages spoken by the Jews, replacing the Italian of the Leghornians, particularly after the rise of the Fascists in Italy in 1922. A Tunisie Francaise society, publishing a daily newspaper of the same name, was in the forefront of the J. struggle for equal rights and French citizenship. Zionist interest could be traced to the correspondence between R. Avraham Uzan of S. and Theodor Herzl in 1901. A Tirahem Zion society was founded in 1916, raising funds for Palestine and promoting the study of Hebrew. The Maccabi sports club operated in 1920–32; the UUJJ

The Gaba bookstore, Sousse, Tunisia, 1950s (Beth Hatefutsoth Photo Archive, Tel Aviv/courtesy of Bernard Allali, Paris)

scout movement from 1927; and Hashomer Hatzair and the Revisionists from 1931. Relations with the Arabs were generally good, although Moslem soldiers occasionally rioted, as in 1898 and 1900. In Aug. 1917, local mobs joined Arab soldiers from the French garrison in a 12-day spree of looting. In WWII, Jews came under the racial laws of the Vichy regime, with many dismissed from the civil service and J. children expelled from the city's French secondary school and from the youth brigade enlisted in the Vichy war effort. In Nov. 1942, Tunisia was occupied by the Germans. Most Jews fled after the heavy Allied bombardment of 13 Dec. 1942, seeking refuge in places like Moknine and bartering their belongings in order to live. The Jews of S. were registered for forced labor in Moknine and put to work repairing roads and unloading ships even during air raids. In March 1943 the Jews were forced to pay a collective fine of FF15 million. Personal possessions (typewriters, bedding, watches, jewelry etc.) were also confiscated. Within the nearly deserted city, J. homes were looted by German soldiers and local Arabs. S. was liberated on 12 April 1943. The Jews returned over a period of six months, finding it difficult to recover from the depredations of the war. The professional and educated class began leaving for Tunis while traditional community life revived around the synagogues. The Zionist youth movements intensified their activity and groups of 20–30 youngsters began leaving illegally for Israel via Tunis and France. One group of 17 among 27 on a flight to Oslo for tuberculosis treatment was killed when the plane crashed. The publicity exposed clandestine *aliya* activities and caused the French to tighten controls. By 1956 most Jews had left for Israel with a minority emigrating to France.

SOVATA   (Hung. Szovata) N. Transylvania dist., Rumania. An organized J. community existed from the 1890s. The J. pop. in 1930 was 90 (3% of the total). In May 1944 the Jews were transferred to the Targu-Mures ghetto and in June deported to Auschwitz.

SOWLINY   Cracow dist., Poland. The J. pop. in 1921 was 120 (total 1,920). The Jews were probably expelled to Limanowa for extermination in summer 1941.

SPANDAU   Brandenburg, Germany. There was a J. community from the 13th cent. A cemetery is men-

tioned in 1324 and a synagogue in 1342. The community probably suffered during the Black Death persecutions of 1348–49. It came to an end in 1510 as a result of the Host desecration trial in Berlin in which two Jews from S. were among those executed and which led to the expulsion of all Jews from Brandenburg. There is evidence of another settlement emerging in 1692. The J. pop. was 43 in 1801 and 78 in 1858. In 1855, S. Jews became part of the Nauen district synagogue community, but in 1894 they established their own community. A synagogue was dedicated in 1895, a cemetery having been opened already in 1865. Many Jews attained a high standard of living, and some were elected to the city council. In 1910, the J. pop. was 316. After WWI, immigrants from Eastern Europe swelled the pop., so that in 1929 the community numbered 680 officially (and possibly more). In 1930, the synagogue was attacked and antisemitic slogans appeared throughout the town. In June 1933, the J. pop. of S. was 725, dropping to 381 in 1937. On *Kristallnacht* (9–10 Nov. 1938), the synagogue was set on fire, J. businesses were wrecked, and J. men were arrested and taken to the Sachsenhausen concentration camp. Soon afterwards, the S. community, with 205 members in May 1939, was incorporated into the Berlin community. The cemetery was closed in 1940 and remains were reinterred at the J. cemetery in Berlin-Weissensee. Those who did not manage to emigrate were deported together with Berlin's Jews, except those married to non-Jews.

SPANGENBERG   Hesse–Nassau, Germany. Jews lived there from the mid-17th cent., opening a new synagogue in 1846 and numbering 133 (8% of the total) in 1871. After WWI, a branch of the J. Youth League Association was active. The J. school's closure in 1925 limited J. teaching to religious instruction. Affiliated with Kassel's rabbinate, the community still numbered 109 (5%) in 1933. By Nov. 1938, however, Nazi violence had forced the Jews to dispose of their synagogue; most left, 24 emigrating.

SPAS   Stanislawow dist., Poland, today Ukraine. The J. pop. in 1921 was 113. The Jews were probably expelled to Dolina for liquidation in spring–summer 1942.

SPAS-DEMENSK   Smolensk dist., Russia. Jews probably settled at the turn of the 19th cent. Their pop. was 161 in 1926 and 84 in 1939. The few who remained after the German occupation in early fall 1941 were murdered.

SPERMEZEU (Hung. Ispanmezo) N. Transylvania dist. Rumania. A small J. community existed from the early 19th cent. A J. school was opened in the early 20th cent. The J. pop. in 1930 was 154 (9% of the total). On 5 May 1944 the Jews were transferred to the Dej ghetto; 161 of the 210 Jews living in S. in 1944 died in extermination camps.

SPEYER Palatinate, Germany. Members of the illustrious Italian Kalonymus family from Mainz arrived in the 1070s, joined by others fleeing the Mainz riots of 1084. They were invited to live in Altspeyer under the protection of Bishop Ruediger Hutzman, who claimed he wished "to magnify the dignity of the place." They were allowed to build a wall around their settlement in the village, given land for a cemetery, and accorded the privilege of unrestricted trade and moneylending activities. Emperor Henry IV confirmed and expanded their rights in 1090. They were also accorded civil rights (*Buergerrecht*) in the city as permanent residents with the right to acquire land. The Jews lived both in the walled village settlement and in the city center near the market and cathedral where most of their community institutions were located, including a synagogue in existence from before 1096 and what was perhaps the oldest *mikve* in Central Europe, dating from before 1128. A synagogue was also consecrated in Altspeyer in 1104 to enable the Jews there to pray near their homes following the massacre of ten Jews in S. by Crusaders on the Sabbath in 1096 during the First Crusade. Yehuda ben Kalonymus headed a *beit midrash*. The community was one of the leading religious centers of Germany, ranking with Worms and Mainz and with them constituting the supreme rabbinical court in Germany. Among its outstanding scholars were R. Yitzhak ben Asher ha-Levi and R. Kalonymus ben Yitzhak (d. 1128–29), known respectively as founders of the tosafist and mystic schools of S. The mystical doctrines of Kalonymus were passed down to his son Shemuel he-Hasid, founder of Hasidei Ashkenaz, by his student Elazar Hazan ben Meshullam. Other well-known rabbis and halakhists were Yekutiel ben Moshe and his son Moshe, David ben Shemuel ben David ha-Levi, and Eliakim ben Meshullam ha-Levi. The energetic response of

the bishop in the wake of the Crusader depredations of 1096 saved the community from the fate of the Worms and Mainz communities, but in 1195 ten more Jews were murdered and all J. homes burned in the wake of a blood libel. From the early 13th cent., authority over the Jews passed gradually from the bishop to the municipality. A 12-member council (*Judenrat*) governed the community but despite its stability it began to lose its status as a spiritual center. In 1286, a number of Jews joined a large group that emigrated to Eretz Israel under the influence of Meir of Rothenburg. Jews were active as wine merchants and also dealt in dyes and medicinal drugs. From the mid-12th cent, their moneylending activities gained increasing importance, as in all the Rhineland. The community ended in 1349 in the Black Death massacres with a few fleeing and a few converting to save themselves. Jews were formally readmitted to the city in 1352, again under the protection of the municipality, mainly because of their importance as moneylenders. But restrictions imposed on the profession in 1387 and the city's defeat in 1389 at the hands of the Palatinate led to economic decline, exacerbated by a series of expulsions in the 15th and 16th cents. After the 1534 expulsion, Jews were not present again until 1621. In 1622, 47 were living under the protection of the municipality. However, new restrictions followed and in 1688 they were again expelled. J. settlement was only renewed under the French after the institution of equal rights. In 1808, Jews numbered 80. Their pop. grew steadily throughout the cent., reaching 539 (total 15,589) in 1880. In 1848, 61% of Jews were merchants and 25% practiced trades (including butchers). Later Jews opened shoe, cigarette, and woodworking factories. In trade, livestock dealers were prominent. Between 1863 and 1907, Jews were regularly elected to the municipal council and the jurist Karl Adler, a native of S., became one of the first two Jews to be elected to the Bavarian Landtag in 1869. Jews were also active in local organizations like the Red Cross and glee club. A J. elementary school was started in 1831 with 42 pupils and a new synagogue was consecrated in 1837, also housing the school and a *mikve*. Ludwig Schloss taught in the school 52 years, also becoming chairman of the community and one of its leading figures. Because of its Liberal tendencies, manifested in the introduction of an organ into the synagogue in 1850 and confirmation exercises in the Protestant style for both boys and girls, the community was in constant conflict with the

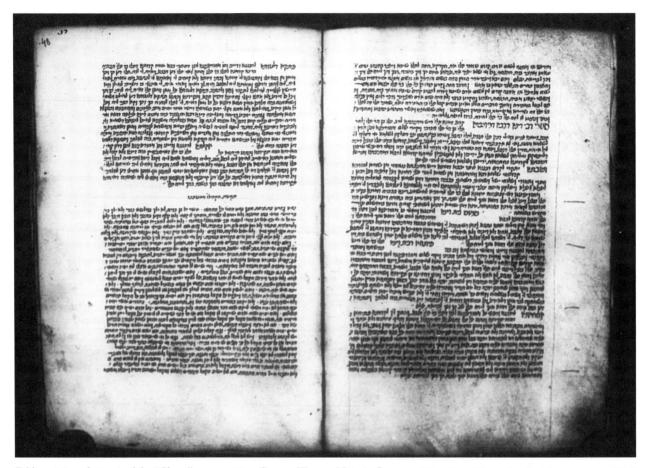

Takkanot *(regulations) of the "Shum" communities (Speyer, Worms, Mainz), Germany (Montefiore Library, London/photo courtesy of Beth Hatefutsoth, Tel Aviv)*

regional rabbinate, particularly from 1865 when the Orthodox Dr. Adolf Salvendi was at its helm. The J. pop. dropped to 403 in 1910 and the downward trend continued in the Weimar period owing to a declining birthrate and emigration to bigger cities like Mannheim and Frankfurt. Jews continued to be involved in local life.

In 1933, the J. pop. was 269. With the rise to power of the Nazi regime, J. stores were burned and the economic and social isolation of the Jews commenced. The situation worsened in late 1934 and by Sept. 1936, ten J. businesses had been closed or sold. Only 50 J. wage earners now remained in the city. In the 1933–36 period, 84 Jews left S.; another 30 left in 1937. Of these, 33 moved to other German cities and 81 emigrated, including 45 to the U.S. Fifteen more left by Oct. 1938. J. youth and sports clubs remained active and Hebrew and English courses were offered in the community. The Zionists also became more active. On *Kristallnacht* (9–10 Nov. 1938), the synagogue

was burned, J. homes and stores were vandalized, and the J. cemetery was desecrated. J. men were sent to the Dachau concentration camp and detained for weeks and months. Another 60 Jews left by May 1939. Sixty remained in Oct. 1940. On 21–22 Oct., 51 were deported to the Gurs concentration camp in southern France in the general expulsion of Jews from the Palatinate and Baden. Of these, ten managed to emigrate. Of the others, 12 perished in France and 24 were murdered in Auschwitz; five survived. In all, at least 42 Jews perished in the Holocaust.

SPEZIA Genoa dist., Italy. In 1910, there were 60 Jews residing in S. In 1918, local Jews established an association to provide J. education and to meet the community's charitable and religious needs. According to the 1930 law reorganizing the J. communities, S. was included in the dist. of Genoa. By 1936, the number of Jews in S. was 100. In 1937, small J. communities were established in S. and San Remo. In 1948, the community numbered 108 persons.

SPISSKA BELA (Hung. Szepesbela) Slovakia, Czechoslovakia, today Republic of Slovakia. Jews settled after 1840, founding a Status Quo congregation in 1870 and only opening a cemetery in the early 20th cent. as the community grew slowly to a pop. of 111 in 1880 and a peak of 185 (total 3,041) in 1919. A synagogue was erected in 1922 and the Zionists and WIZO became active. The Kleinberger family owned a distillery and a sawmill employing about 100 workers. In 1940, 52 Jews remained. In the Slovakian state, they were severely persecuted by local Germans, who vandalized their homes and stores. In early April 1942, a number of families were deported to Auschwitz. Most of the others were sent to the Lublin dist. ghettoes on 16 May.

SPISSKA NOVA VES (Hung. Iglo) Slovakia, Czechoslovakia, today Republic of Slovakia. Jews settled in the mid-19th cent. The community formed a Status Quo congregation after 1869, consecrating a splendid synagogue in 1899. A J. elementary school was opened in 1872 with an enrollment of 50–60 children. The J. pop. grew from 156 in 1869 to 620 (total 9,301) in 1900 and 733 in 1930. The Zionists became active in the early 20th cent. and after WWI, most of the young were attracted to their youth movements, with some young people emigrating to Palestine. The J. National Party was also influential and in the 1920s, five Jews sat on the municipal council. Jews also held other public positions. In the 1930s, about 20 families split off and founded an Orthodox congregation with its own *beit midrash* for prayer services. A blood libel in 1935 aroused much anti-J. agitation among the German pop. Jews dominated trade and owned 62 business establishments along with 23 workshops and a number of factories, including a sawmill and wood-processing plant employing 250 workers. After the establishment of the Slovakian state in March 1939, the German pop. frequently attacked Jews. Jews were also compelled to give up their businesses and were seized for forced labor by the authorities. The arrival of 285 refugees from Bratislava in 1941 pushed the J. pop. up to over 1,000. In late March 1942 about 150 of the young were deported to the Majdanek concentration camp and Auschwitz, respectively. A few dozen families were deported to Auschwitz, on 17 April. On 29 May, over

250 were sent to the Lublin dist. of Poland with the able-bodied men being sent to Majdanek and the rest to Izbica. Altogether 80% of the Jews were deported in 1942. Most of the others fled the city before the Germans arrived in Sept. 1944, many fighting with the partisans and the Czechoslovakian army. The postwar community of 200 rapidly dwindled through emigration.

SPISSKA SOBOTA Slovakia, Czechoslovakia, today Republic of Slovakia. The J. pop. was 104 in 1940. The community was under the jurisdiction of the Poprad rabbinate and maintained a synagogue and cemetery.

SPISSKA STARA VES (Hung. Ofalu) Slovakia, Czechoslovakia, today Republic of Slovakia. J. refugees from Galicia settled in the late 18th cent., forming an organized community by the 1820s and maintaining a synagogue, *heder*, and *talmud torah*. Their pop. rose to a peak of 303 (total 1,244) in 1910 and then dropped to 217 in 1940. In the Czechoslovakian Republic, Jews were active in public life. They owned 11 business establishments, three taverns, and two butcher shops. The Zionists became active in the 1920s, mainly through Mizrachi, WIZO, and the youth movements. Agudat Israel supported Orthodox education. A regional J. elementary school was opened in 1939–40. In the Slovakian state, Jews were forced out of their businesses and mobilized for forced labor. On 25 March 1942, dozens of young J. girls were deported to Auschwitz. Young men were sent to the Majdanek concentration camp in early April and families were transported to Izbica in the Lublin dist. (Poland) on 29 May. In all, 80% of the Jews of S. and its environs were sent to the death camps in 1942.

SPISSKA VLACHY (Hung. Szepesolaszi) Slovakia, Czechoslovakia, today Republic of Slovakia. Jews probably settled in 1848. A synagogue, cemetery, and J. school were opened around the turn of the 19th cent. and the J. pop. rose to a peak of 161 (total 2,442) in 1919. The Zionists and Agudat Israel were active after WWI. In 1940, local Germans were constantly attacking the 146 Jews in the community, vandalizing their synagogue and businesses. In 1941, the Slovakian authorities closed down or "Aryanized" J. businesses. In late March and early April 1942, 54 young Jews were deported, the men to the Majdanek concentration camp and the women to Auschwitz. On 29 May, about 70 Jews were deported to Izbica in the Lublin dist. (Poland); others were sent to Auschwitz in the summer.

SPISSKE PODHRADIE (Hung. Szepesvaralja) Slovakia, Czechoslovakia, today Republic of Slovakia. Jews first settled in 1840. A synagogue was built in 1871 but soon burned down; a new one was constructed in 1905. A *talmud torah* for 40 children was opened in the 1870s and a J. elementary school for 60 in the 1880s as the J. pop. rose above 250. After WWI, the community reached a pop. of above 400 (14% of the total). The Zionists became active in the 1920s, particularly WIZO. Agudat Israel was active in Orthodox education. With the outbreak of war, local Germans and inhabitants of nearby settlements attacked Jews. J. children were expelled from public schools in 1940. J. businesses were "Aryanized" in 1941 and men seized for forced labor. In March 1942, dozens of young J. women were deported to Auschwitz, followed by dozens of young men sent to the Majdanek concentration camp. Over 200 Jews were deported to the Lublin dist. on 29 May 1942, the men to the Majdanek concentration camp, the others to Izbica. A few dozen more were deported to Auschwitz in the summer. Additional families were deported in Sept. 1944. In all, 416 Jews perished in the Holocaust.

SPITHENCY Vinnitsa dist., Ukraine. The J. pop. was 937 (total 2,607) in 1897 and 774 in 1926. A pogrom was staged in 1918. The Germans arrived on 21 July 1941. They murdered the Jews in two stages: some in Oct., together with the Jews of Pliskov; the remaining 290 in April 1942.

SPLIT (Ital. Spalato) Croatia, Yugoslavia, today Republic of Croatia. Jews lived in the region from the second cent., when they participated in the thriving trade of the period. Signs of J. community life in the Middle Ages have been discovered, but more detailed information on the Jews and a J. community in S. dates to the 16th cent. In 1592 a Jew by the name of Daniel Rodriguez founded a new and efficient land trade route based in S. In return for his contribution to the great expansion of commerce, Rodriguez requested and received from the Venetian government equal rights and privileges for the Jews of the Venetian Republic,

including S. The Jews helped defend S. during the wars against the Turks, especially in 1645-69. In the 18th cent. they dealt mostly in trade and loans, both of which were crucial to the economy of S. The J. community was well organized from the early 17th cent. and included welfare organizations. From 1777 attitudes to the Jews worsened and the Venetian government restricted J. trade and movement in S. In 1778 the Jews were restricted to the confines of a ghetto. They numbered 279 that year in a total pop. of 3,000-5,000. In 1807, however, the ghetto was opened by the new French rulers. Throughout the 19th cent., the Jews contributed to the economy and culture of S. After WWI they continued in trade and some entered the professional class. Social and cultural activities took place within the community. Zionist activity also took root during this period. In 1940 the J. pop. peaked at 400 (total 40,000). In 1941 the Italians invaded Dalmatia and the Jews then assisted some 3,000 refugees from Poland, Austria, and Czechoslovakia who passed through S. until the end of 1942. The assistance included education, material essentials, and health care. Most of the Jews joined S.'s underground movement. The youth gathered weapons in the synagogue basement and participated in the war of liberation in 1942-43. On 12 June 1942, Fascist fundamentalists destroyed the synagogue, plundered its contents, and burned its archives and library. Worshipers were beaten as they left the synagogue, and J. shops were wrecked the next day. On 17 Sept. 1943, the Italians capitulated to the Germans and terrible persecutions began. Those who had not been able to escape (mostly the elderly and children) were arrested by the Germans and were taken to forced labor and then to the death camps. Of S.'s remaining 284 Jews, 114 joined the fighting against the Fascists. A total of 150 Jews from S. died in the Holocaust, including 29 partisan fighters in armed clashes. The community was reconstituted after the war.

SPRENDLINGEN (I) Mainz-Bingen dist., Hesse, Germany. Jews lived there in the 17th cent. and founded one of the largest village communities in the region, numbering 177 (9% of the total) in 1861. Only 39 Jews were left, however, to mark their synagogue's 100th anniversary in 1925. On *Kristallnacht* (9–10 Nov. 1938), the synagogue was vandalized and J. men were beaten and then sent to a concentration camp. Fifteen Jews still remained in 1939.

SPRENDLINGEN (II)   Offenbach dist. (now part of Dreieich), Hesse, Germany. Jews living there from 1765, established a community in 1831, and numbered 112 (4% of the total) in 1871. The Nazi boycott forced two-thirds of the 107 Jews to leave before *Kristallnacht* (9–10 Nov. 1938), when their synagogue was destroyed. A total of 57 Jews emigrated and 20 moved elsewhere; the last 16 were deported in 1942.

SPROTTAU   (Pol. Szprotawa) Lower Silesia, Germany, today Poland. There was a Street of the Jews in 1380 but after being expelled no Jews were present until the early 19th cent. In 1825, the J. pop. was 27, rising to 90 in 1852. The community maintained a prayer house, a J. school operating out of a private home in 1838–39, and a cemetery in 1881. The J. pop. dropped in the late 19th cent. and stood at 44 in 1925 and 37 in 1933. On *Kristallnacht* (9–10 Nov. 1938), the prayer house was burned and J. stores were destroyed. Thirteen Jews remained in May 1939 and two married to non-Jews in Nov. 1942. No further information is available on the fate of the Jews under the Nazis. Presumably those who did not emigrate perished following deportation.

SREM   Poznan dist., Poland. Jews first settled in the 16th cent. in a quarter especially constructed for them. By 1816 the J. pop. stood at 1,566 (total 2,696), with 223 of the 473 J. breadwinners engaged in peddling, 89 in trade and brokerage, and 142 in farming. A new synagogue was erected in 1851 and a J. elementary school was in operation. Wide-ranging cultural activity was initiated in the late 19th cent. Emigration to big German cities like Berlin and Breslau increased in the late 19th cent., reducing the J. pop. to 607 in 1895 and 103 in 1921. The 26 Jews remaining on the eve of WWII were expelled by the Germans to General Gouvernement territory on 7 Nov. 1939.

SREMSKA MITROVICA   Serbia, Yugoslavia. A J. community was established in the 19th cent. The J. pop. in 1931 was 132 (total 13,839). In the Holocaust the Jews were deported to death camps, including 500 German Jews who had arrived in the hope of emigrating.

SROCKO   Lodz dist., Poland. In the 19th cent. Jews leased land in the village (known as "J. Srocko") but by the beginning of the 20th cent. Jews no longer worked these plots. In Oct. 1942, all 600 Jews (most of them refugees) were expelled to Piotrkow and then deported to the Treblinka death camp.

SRODA   Poznan dist., Poland. Jews settled after the Prussian annexation in 1793, some operating farms in the surrounding countryside. An organized community with a synagogue and elementary school was soon formed, reaching a pop. of 338 (total 2,183) in the town itself in 1843. The Zionists became active in 1906. Fifty Jews remained when the Germans arrived in Sept. 1939. A few were executed and the rest expelled to General Gouvernement territory.

STACHOW   Polesie dist., Poland, today Belarus. The J. pop. in 1921 was 140 (total 1,849). The Jews were presumably brought to the Stolin ghetto for liquidation on 11 Sept. 1942

STADEN   Hesse, Germany. Established around 1700, the J. community numbered 87 (about 22% of the total) in 1828 but dwindled to 22 by 1933. Its synagogue was vandalized on *Kristallnacht* (9–10 Nov. 1938), and all the remaining Jews left before WWII.

STADSKANAAL   Groningen dist., Holland. A community developed in the 1840s and numbered 260 in 1911, when 50 children were studying in the J. school. The J. pop. in 1941 was 186 (total 19,791). During the Holocaust 160 were deported to the east, 44 survived in hiding, and two returned from the camps. J. life was renewed after the war.

STADTHAGEN   Schaumburg-Lippe, Germany. Although some Jews lived in medieval S. (Grevenalveshagen), no community existed until about 1635, when daily services were held in a private home. The small community (which numbered 57 Jews in 1907) had a synagogue, built in 1858, but religious services only took place on major festivals. During the Weimar Republic, Jews were active in the Masonic lodge and the glee club. In June 1933, there were 62 Jews registered in S. Anti-J. violence alarmed the townspeople to such an extent that the burgomaster had three SS men arrested and punished for hooliganism — a decision upheld by the public prosecutor (1935). On *Kristallnacht*, Nazis destroyed the synagogue. Eleven Jews moved to other German cities and 23 emigrated (about 18 to safe havens) before WWII. At least 21 Jews were deported to the ghettoes of Riga, Warsaw, and Theresienstadt in 1941–42; only one survived.

STADTLENGSFELD Thuringia, Germany. Jews settled in S. around 1359 and probably established a cemetery at that time. They were then persecuted and/or expelled, but the exact date is unknown. A J. settlement developed at the beginning of the 17th cent. In 1825, the J. pop. was 566 (25% of the total). A synagogue was erected around this time and the community employed a rabbi. Around 1900, there were 100 Jews in S.; in 1925, 35; and in 1932, 32. A few days after *Kristallnacht* (9–10 Nov. 1938), the synagogue as well as J. businesses and houses were vandalized. No further information is available about the fate of the Jews of S.

STADTOLDENDORF Braunschweig, Germany. Jews settled c. 1810 after residing in the area since the 18th cent. The industrialist Avraham Yosef Rothschild arrived in the city in 1815, contributing greatly to its economic development, mainly by establishing a large knitting mill. A synagogue and cemetery were consecrated around the 1850s. In 1871, the J. pop. was 53, rising to 83 in 1895 and then declining to a level of about 50 in the 1910–25 period. In 1933, the J. pop. was 47. In Aug. 1937, the owners of the Rothschild knitting mill were arrested for alleged currency violations, forced to pay a heavy fine, and deprived of ownership of the mill. Two died serving their sentences in the Sachsenhausen concentration camp. On *Kristallnacht* (9–10 Nov. 1938), the synagogue was burned and the only J. store still open in the city was looted. About ten J. men were sent to the Buchenwald concentration camp for over a month. In May 1939, 42 Jews remained, but 16 managed to leave by the end of the year. Of those who stayed behind, 16 were deported to the east in March and July 1942. The last two, J. women married to non-Jews, were deported in Feb. 1945.

STAKLISKES (Yid. Stoklishok) Alytus dist., Lithuania. Jews first settled at the beginning of the 18th cent. In the 1880s many emigrated to the U.S.. The J. pop. in 1897 was 808 (37% of the total). Between the World Wars Jews emigrated to the U.S. and South Africa, with some young people going to Palestine. Many participated in Zionist activities. The J. pop.

in 1940 was about 70 families. Under the Soviets (1940–41) businesses were nationalized and Zionist activity banned. After the German invasion in June 1941, Lithuanian nationalists killed several J. activists accused of supporting the Soviet regime. Those still alive were murdered in various places by Aug. 1941.

STALINDORF (until 1931, Chemerisk; in 1944–61, Stalinskoye; from 1961, Zhovtnevoye) Dnepropetrovsk dist., Ukraine. S. was founded in the 1920s as a J. farm settlement by Jews from Vinnitsa, Vitebsk, Zhitomir, Proskurov, and Kamenets-Podolski. In 1931, the seat of the J. Autonomous Region was transferred to S. from Izluchistoye, remaining there until the Nazi occupation in 1941. The J. pop. grew from 555 in 1930 to about 1,200 in 1935 and then dropped to 748 (total 1,569) in 1939. The number of Jews in the entire region fell from a peak of 13,207 in 1935 to 7,312 (total 32,967) in 1939. Most Jews in the region were farmers belonging to the 40 J. kolkhozes founded there in the early and mid-1920s. The S. rural council (soviet) had jurisdiction over about 4,000 Jews and an overall pop. of more than 7,520 in 1932. From 1931, S. housed a rural theater group (belonging to the J. kolkhozes), a theater house with 400 seats, a J. school, and a teachers' college. A J. newspaper, *Der Stalindorfer Emes*, appeared from 1933. In the mid-1930s, Yiddish was used extensively in local government offices, the law courts, etc., but in the late 1930s the situation took a turn for the worse. Yiddish declined as an official language, the J. schools became Russian and Ukrainian, and the J. newspaper was closed down. The Germans captured S. in mid-Aug. 1941. Executions commenced in Sept., with most of the Jews murdered in May 1942: 450 on 2 May and in late May another few hundred. The Nazis murdered over 3,900 Jews in the former J. Autonomous Region.

STALINGRAD (until 1925, Carycyn; from 1961, Volgograd) Stalingrad dist., Russia. Jews settled in the late 19th cent. and reached a pop. of 893 (total 55,000) in 1897. The community maintained a prayer house at this time. In the Soviet period, the J. pop. rose to 1,985 in 1926 and 4,325 (total 356,507) in 1939. After the Germans entered the city, the Gestapo murdered the Jews. The Germans also murdered in the S. area many Jews who had been evacuated from the western parts of the Soviet Union. On 25 Sept. 1942, 12 Jews were murdered at the German Stalindorf kol-

Street show in town square of Stakliskes, Lithuania

Jewish kolkhoz theater group putting on performance of Perez Markish's play Nit Gedaygt *("Don't Worry"), Stalindorf, Ukraine*

khoz. In the Voroshilovski area, another 45 were murdered in the same month at the village of Peregruznoye in addition to 43 at Vodino and 68 at Aksayi in Aug. and 164 at Kamenka in early Oct. 1942.

STALINO (until 1924, Yuzovka; from 1961, Donetsk) Stalino dist., Ukraine. Jews settled in the late 19th cent. following the opening of coal mines and a British-built steel mill in 1869. Most were artisans, with a number of wealthy merchants. A handsome synagogue was built 1887 and the community maintained various charitable institutions including a *talmud torah* for 20 needy children. The J. pop. was 3,168 (total 28,076) in 1897. Many were killed and injured in a three-day pogrom that broke out on 17 Oct. 1905. In 1926, about 500 J. breadwinners were artisans; 300 worked at the steel mill (including 60 skilled workers); 250 worked in construction; and 100 were employed in a leather goods factory. About 110 children attended a J. elementary school. Only the elderly frequented the synagogue. In 1928, Jews represented a third of the 4,000 seasonal workers at the steel mill. In the two textile and leather goods factories, 70–90% of the workers were Jews and in 1932, over 3,000 construction workers were Jews. The J. pop. rose after S. became a dist. center in 1932 but the community's relative weight in the overall pop. declined as its pop. reached 24,991 (total 466,268) in 1939. The Germans captured the city on 20 Oct. 1941. A ghetto for all the Jews was set up in the center of the city near the Lenin Culture Palace. They were subjected to 15–17 hours of forced labor a day without food or medical attention. Hundreds died every day. A few hundred Jews were murdered in an *Aktion* carried out in Dec. 1941. The Maria mine in the eastern suburbs of the city became the mass burial ground of Nazi victims, most being hurled into the shafts alive. Between 50,000 and 75,000 residents of S. and the surrounding area were murdered in this way, including an estimated 15,000 Jews.

STALLUPOENEN (Rus. Nesterov), East Prussia, Germany, today Russia. The J. pop. numbered 57 in 1843; 132 in 1880; and 60 in 1925. The community maintained a synagogue and a cemetery. In 1933, there were 48 Jews still living in S. On *Kristallnacht*

Synagogue in Stalino, Ukraine, 1931

(9–10 Nov. 1938), the synagogue was destroyed. No information is available about the fate of the community under Nazi rule.

STANESTII DE JOS Bukovina, Rumania, today Ukraine. Jews from Galicia and Russia settled in the late 19th cent. The J. pop. in 1890 was 909 (30% of the total). Jews had a monopoly on trade in alcohol and tobacco. They were persecuted by the invading Russians in 1914 and fled when the Russians reconquered S. in 1916. The J. pop. in 1930 was 622. On 28 June 1941, Ukrainians murdered 54 Jews, and on 28 July the J. pop. was transferred to Vascauti. On 1 Aug. it were moved to Edineti, large numbers dying on the way. The remaining 272 were deported to Transnistria.

STANIN Lublin dist., Poland. The J. pop. stood at 131 in 1921 (total 643). The Jews were probably deported to the Treblinka death camp by the Germans in Sept.–Oct. 1942.

STANISIC Vojvodina dist., Yugoslavia. There was a J. community existing from the mid-18th cent. The J. pop. in 1931 was 80 (total 7,596). It was destroyed in WWII.

STANISLAVCHIK Vinnitsa dist., Ukraine. Jews numbered 22 in 1765 and 1,207 (total 5,142) in 1897. A *talmud torah* was open in the early 20th cent. Under the Soviets, a separate J. council (soviet) and J. school (four grades) were active for a short while. In 1939, the J. pop. was 301. The Germans arrived on 16 July 1941. After S. was annexed to Transnistria in early Sept., hundreds of Jews from Bukovina and Bessarabia were expelled there. Many died under the harsh ghetto conditions. Of those expelled, 81 were still in the ghetto in early Sept. 1943.

STANISLAWCZYK Tarnopol dist., Poland, today Ukraine. The J. community grew to 795 or half the pop. in 1880 but declined steadily through emigration to 165 in 1921. The Germans entered S. on 25 June 1941 after two years of Soviet rule and the Ukrainians immediately took to robbing and beating Jews. Many fled in Oct. 1942 on the eve of an *Aktion* deporting Jews to the Belzec death camp but most were subsequently hunted down and murdered by the Germans and Ukrainians.

STANISLAWOW (I) (Stanislav) Stanislawow dist., Poland, today Ukraine. Jews arrived with the founding of the town in 1654 by Count Jendrzej Potocki. They received extensive trade and residence privileges and in the 18th cent. replaced the Armenians as the leading merchants there. J. artisans also gained a dominant position, increasing from 69 to 645 in the 19th cent. and comprising twice the number of non-J. artisans, with a third engaged in tailoring. In the second half of the 19th cent. Jews became active in industry. Of the 50 factories existing in 1875, 35 were J.-owned, employing 278 Jews. Of nearly 3,000 breadwinners at the turn of the cent., half were tradesmen and a third salaried workers. Two families dominated the community. The Horowitz family supplied the community with rabbis from 1784 until the Holocaust while the wealthy Halperns endowed its institutions. Yoel Halpern held the Galician salt monopoly and founded a J. hospital in 1837. Avraham Halpern headed the community for many years and was elected to the Austrian parliament in 1848. Jews were well represented on the municipal council and a Jew served as mayor from 1897 to 1919. The J. pop. rose from 2,237 in 1792 to 10,028 in 1880 and 15,253 (total 33,280) in 1910. A synagogue that remained standing until WWII was consecrated in 1777. In the second half of the 19th cent. the Haskala movement began to spread. A Reform synagogue was opened in the 1860s and after it closed a new one was completed in 1899 with Markus (Mordekhai Ze'ev) Braude (1869–1949) as preacher. A Baron Hirsch school operated in 1899–1907. Orthodox children were educated under the *heder* system. A Safah Berurah school for Hebrew study was founded in 1903 and enrolled 200 students in 1911. About 350 J. students studied at the municipal high school in 1903 and 100 young men from all over Galicia, in addition to local Jews, studied at the Or Hayyim yeshiva founded in 1906. The leading J. political party in the late 19th cent. was the assimilationist Shomer Israel. The Zionists became active in the 1880s, with Dr. Braude one of their most influential adherents and for awhile leader of the Zionist Organization in Galicia. Numerous J. periodicals also appeared during the period. During WWI, the Jews experienced a relatively mild Russian occupation and public life was resumed on the return of the Austrians in 1915. In 1920, roaming Petlyura gangs attacked Jews until the arrival of the Polish army; many Jews fell victim to hunger and disease. By 1921, 730 J. factories and workshops were in operation, employing

Synagogue in Stanislawow, Poland, 1931

over 1,000 Jews, a third of them in a big hide-processing plant. Clothing production was the predominant light industry and 726 of the city's 800 stores were J.-owned. The community also numbered 130 J. lawyers. The community continued to operate extensive welfare services, supporting about 500 orphans and organizing summer camps and hot meals for the needy. A J. secondary school was founded in 1924 and reached an enrollment of 487 in 1932. Another 370 studied at the J. elementary school, 260 at J. vocational schools, and 400 in the *talmud torah* operated by Agudat Israel. The dominant force in the community was the Zionist movement with its youth organizations. In the 1930s, antisemitism intensified and Jews suffered from the economic boycott organized by the Polish and Ukrainian cooperatives. In 1931 the J. pop. was 24,825 (total 72,350).

On the outbreak of WWII thousands of J. refugees flooded the city. The Soviets arrived in Sept. 1939, closing down J. community institutions and nationalizing J. businesses while exiling a number of prominent

J. figures. Artisans were organized into cooperatives. In 1940 many of the refugees as well were exiled to the interior of the Soviet Union. On the withdrawal of the Red Army in June 1941, local Ukrainians commenced a reign of terror, cut short only by the arrival of the Hungarian army on 2 July. A few thousand starving and exhausted refugees from Carpathia were housed at the Rodolf Flour Mill as the J. pop. of S. swelled to over 40,000. The Germans took over the city on 26 July, joining local Poles and Ukrainians in attacking Jews. A *Judenrat* was immediately appointed. In early Aug., 500–1,000 members of the J. intelligentsia were massacred in the Pawlacze forest. Jews were ordered to turn in their valuables and were arbitrarily tormented and murdered. On 12 Oct. 1941 Jews living in the center of the city were ordered to the local market. Over 10,000 were led to the J. cemetery and murdered systematically beside a freshly dug mass grave after being stripped naked. *Judenrat* members and their families were murdered after being forced to watch the massacre. At nightfall the few thousand who remained alive were sent home. In Dec. the remaining 30,000 Jews were transferred to a closed ghetto, where thousands were left without homes and had to be accommodated in warehouses, garages, and prayer halls. On 31 March 1942, the public shelters, orphanage, old age home, and Rodolf Mill were emptied of their J. inhabitants and 5,000 were deported to the Belzec death camp. Jews were now officially classified according to employment status and those less useful were rounded up in the thousands. They were sent to the Rodolf Mill, which now served as a concentration camp for those earmarked for extermination and contained Jews from the surrounding area as well. Most were sent on to Belzec while others were murdered in the J. cemetery or at the Mill. In a new *Aktion* on 12 Sept. 1942, 5,000 Jews were seized from their homes and deported to Belzec while hundreds more, including patients in the two ghetto hospitals, were murdered on the spot. The number of Jews locally employed was cut down, with many sent to the Janowska Road labor camp in Lwow. Those still working locally for the Germans were housed in separate camps. In Jan. 1943 the liquidation of the ghetto commenced as Jews were removed and shot street by street in a process lasting two months. A number of young Jews escaping into the forests during the 1942 *Aktion*s organized themselves into partisan groups with other Jews. One was led by Anda Luft, a young chemical engineer, who died fighting when her group was surrounded by the Germans. Around 1,500 of S.'s Jews survived the war, most in the Soviet Union.

STANISLAWOW (II) Warsaw dist., Poland. Jews first settled in the late 17th cent., reaching a pop. of 601 (total 2,082) in 1897. The town's 400 Jews were confined to a ghetto by the Germans after their arrival in Sept. 1939. All the Jews were deported to the Treblinka death camp on 25 Sept. 1942.

STARA BYSTRICA (Hung. Obeszterce) Slovakia, Czechoslovakia, today Republic of Slovakia. An independent community was founded in the mid-18th cent., reaching a pop. of 140 in the early 20th cent. In 1930, 64 Jews remained. Those still there in 1942 were deported to the death camps.

STARA DALA (Hung. Ogyalla) Slovakia, Czechoslovakia, today Republic of Slovakia. Jews apparently settled in the first half of the 18th cent, most earning their livelihoods as shopkeepers and peddlers. Synagogues were erected in the early 19th cent. and in 1880, when the J. pop. reached a peak of 272 (total

2,523). A J. elementary school was also opened in 1880. After WWI, the J. pop. dropped to 118 with another 100 or so in neighboring Pribeta. Most local businesses were in J. hands. The Zionists were active. In 1941, 87 Jews remained. Under Hungarian rule, many were seized for forced labor, some dying on the eastern front. On 23 June 1944, those who remained behind were deported to Auschwitz via Komarno.

STARA KANJIZA Vojvodina dist., Yugoslavia. Jews first settled there in the early 19th cent and numbered 223 by 1931 (total 19,108). None survived the Holocaust.

STARA LUBOVNA (Hung. Olublo) Slovakia, Czechoslovakia, today Republic of Slovakia. Jews apparently settled in the 1820s and founded an organized community at mid-cent. A synagogue was probably erected in the 1880s as the J. pop. rose to about 200. After WWI, Jews were active in public life. Their pop. rose to 273 in 1921 (total 1,937) and 334 in 1940. Jews owned 37 business establishments, 14 workshops, a sawmill, flour mill, and soap factory.

Yeshiva students, Stara Kanjiza, Yugoslavia

The Zionists became active in the 1920s with Hashomer Hatzair, Bnei Akiva, and Betar representing the youth movements. Agudat Israel also operated a large local branch. A regional J. school was opened in 1940 in the hostile environment of the Slovakian state. In 1941, the German minority looted J. homes and stores while the authorities forced Jews out of their businesses and seized them for forced labor. In 1942, dozens of young Jews were deported: the women to Auschwitz on 22 March and the men to the Majdanek concentration camp on 1 April. Others were transported from May through the summer to death camps in the Lublin dist. of Poland and to Auschwitz. Of the remaining 58 Jews, the Germans murdered 21 on 16 Oct. 1944. Others escaped and a few fought against the Nazis.

STARA MORAVICA (Hung. Kossulhfalva or Omoravicza) Vojvodina dist., Yugoslavia. Jews first lived there in the 19th cent. and numbered 78 in 1931 (total 8,034). Community members were murdered by the Hungarians while some died in the labor battalions in the Ukraine, or in Auschwitz.

STARA SOL Lwow dist., Poland, today Ukraine. Jews were present from the early 17th cent., living largely off the salt trade until the government monopoly between the World Wars cut into their livelihoods. Emigration reduced the J. pop. from its 1880 peak of 416 (total 1,347) to 211 in 1921. After Soviet annexation (1939–41) the Germans entered S. on 2 July 1941. In March and Aug. 1942 the Jews were deported to Sambor, where they shared the fate of the local Jews.

STARA TURA (Hung. Otura) Slovakia, Czechoslovakia, today Republic of Slovakia. Two J. families from Moravia were present in the 1720s. A synagogue and *beit midrash* were opened in the early 19th cent. while the J. pop. rose to 80 in 1828 and 134 (total 5,819) in 1880. J. homes and stores were looted and vandalized in peasant riots in 1848. The J. pop. dropped to 57 in 1921 and 42 in 1940. The Slovakian authorities closed down J. businesses in 1941. After the young were deported to Auschwitz and the Majdanek concentration camp in late March 1942, the rest of the Jews were transported to the Opole ghetto in the Lublin dist. of Poland.

STARAYA SINYAVA Kamenets-Podolski dist., Ukraine. Jews are first mentioned in 1570, when there were nine J. houses in the town. The community was apparently wiped out in the Chmielnicki massacres of 1648–49. J. life gradually revived and in 1765 the J. pop. was already 834. In 1897, it was 2,279 (49% of the total). A pogrom was staged against the Jews in June 1919. In the Soviet period, a J. council (soviet) was active. In 1939, the J. pop. was 1,237. The Germans occupied S. on 14 July 1941, and on 19 Aug. they murdered 300 Jews. The rest were concentrated in a ghetto. Most were murdered on 23 June 1942 after expulsion to Staro-Konstantinov. Another 80 were shot in S. in summer 1943. The killing site in S. was a big ditch north of the local sugar refinery.

STARAYA USHITSA (until 1826, Ushitsa) Kamenets-Podolski dist., Ukraine. Jews numbered 202 in 1765 and 1,583 (14% of the total) in 1897, with 38% of breadwinners engaged in trade, especially in farm produce. Seventy-one families (242 Jews) earned their livelihoods sewing clothes. Two J. private schools were operating in 1910. In the late 1920s, 70% of the Jews were "classless." To provide them with work, two cooperatives were organized, for shoemakers and tailors. A J. kolkhoz was also founded. A J. council and J. school (named after Shalom Aleichem in 1926) were active. In 1939, the J. pop. was 753. The Germans captured the town on 7 July 1941, executing 820 Jews on 22 July. Jews from Studenitsa were also executed there. Skilled workers were brought to Kamenets-Podolski, where they perished. In all, the Germans murdered 3,109 Jews from S. and the surrounding area.

STARAYIA RUSSA Leningrad dist., Russia. Jews probably settled in the mid-19th cent. and numbered 624 (total 15,000) in 1897. In the Soviet period, the J. pop. first rose to 1,301 in 1926 but then dropped to 828 in 1939. The Germans captured the town on 9 Aug. 1941 and murdered about 2,000 Jews from S. and the surrounding settlements.

STARGARD (Pol. Stargard Szczecinski) Pomerania, Germany, today Poland. Jews were allowed to live and trade in S. after 1665, despite initial resistance from the local authorities. Toward the end of the 17th cent., a J. community developed and a cemetery was established. By 1765, 35 families were living in the town, and 77 in 1812. S. was one of the largest J. communities in Pomerania. By 1900, the J. pop. was 620. The community was Liberal, having introduced an organ for its religious services. A synagogue was built in 1913. Several Jews served on the city council from the 1850s. In 1921, in the context of the debate about the massive immigration into Germany of East European Jews (*Ostjuden*), a concentration camp was set up in S., in which undesirable members of the group were incarcerated and often abused. When the Nazis came to power in 1933, the S. community had shrunk to 310 members. In Aug. 1935 a series of anti-J. demonstrations was held and boycott measures were intensified with many businesses refusing to serve Jews. The Polish Jews were deported across the Polish border in Oct. 1938. On *Kristallnacht* (9–10 Nov. 1938), the synagogue was destroyed. By May 1939, only 81 Jews and 33 persons of partial J. origin (*Mischlinge*) remained in S. Those who failed to emigrate were deported on 12–13 Feb. 1940 to the Lublin dist. (Poland) together with the Jews of Stettin. Polish-J. prisoners of war were incarcerated in S.

STAROBELSK Voroshilovgrad dist., Ukraine. Jews settled in the 19th cent. and numbered 196 (total 14,419) under the Soviets in 1939. The Germans arrived on 13 July 1942, murdering 200 people, among them Jews, alongside the road to Svatovo in July–Aug.

STAROBIN Minsk dist., Belorussia. J. settlement probably dates from the turn of the 18th cent. The J. pop. rose from 85 in 1811 to 1,494 (total 2,315) in 1897. During the civil war (1918–21), Jews were attacked by soldiers from the Balakhovich brigade as well as by Polish soldiers in summer 1920. In the early 1920s, under the Soviets, about 40 J. families were employed in draining a few hundred acres of land earmarked for J. farms. In the late 1920s and early 1930s about 60 J. families earned their livelihoods in a mixed kolkhoz with a J. majority. A J. school founded in 1922 had an enrollment of 180 in 1926 while in the early 1920s nearly all J. boys studied in "illegal" *hadarim*. In 1939, the J. pop. was 1,210. The Germans entered the town in late June 1941. On 22 or 27 Aug., they murdered 200 J. men. The remaining Jews were expelled to the Slutzk ghetto, sharing the fate of the Jews there. A few escaped to the forests and joined the partisans.

STARODUB Oriol dist., Russia. J. settlement apparently commenced in the 17th cent. Chmielnicki's Cos-

sack troops massacred many Jews in 1648 and in 1708 local residents murdered about 50. The J. pop. rose from 319 in 1801 to 2,558 in 1847 and 5,109 (total 12,000) in 1897. The community maintained four synagogues. The children attended a state J. school. Almost all petty trade was in J. hands and Jews were also prominent as artisans. In 1905, several Jews were killed in a pogrom while J. property was extensively damaged and a synagogue burned down. In 1910, J. children also attended a *talmud torah* and a private school for girls. In the Soviet period, the J. pop. dropped to 3,317 in 1926 and 1,629 in 1939. The Germans occupied S. on 18 Aug. 1941. In late Sept. over 1,400 Jews were transferred to a ghetto. A few hundred men were murdered for resisting the move. On 1 March 1942, another 800 were executed.

STAROGARD Pomerania dist., Poland. Jews only settled permanently after the Prussian annexation in 1772. The merchant Avraham Peter Kaufmann founded a family there that was influential throughout Pomerania. In 1851 family members set up a shoe factory. The Goldfarb family ran a tobacco factory and like the Kaufmanns were philanthropists, founding three old age homes. In 1849 a new synagogue and an elementary school were opened. The J. pop. reached a peak of 529 (total 6,634) in 1885. Untypically, many subsequently moved to villages or estates rather than the big cities. The last 40 Jews were murdered by the Germans in the months after their occupation in Sept. 1939.

STARO-KONSTANTINOV Kamenets-Podolski dist., Ukraine. Jews settled in the mid-16th cent. They were attacked by the Cossacks in 1648, 1651, and 1702. The J. pop. grew to 9,212 (total 16,527) in 1897 with the opening of several J.-owned factories in the 19th cent. In the early 20th cent., a *talmud torah* and J. elementary school were active in the community. In 1939, under the Soviets, the J. pop. was 6,743. A J. school with ten grades was founded in 1939. Two J. elementary schools were also operating. A J. kolkhoz was founded in 1926 and functioned until WWII. The Germans captured S. on 8 July 1941, setting up a ghetto and *Judenrat* in Aug. During July-Aug., 4,000 Jews were executed outside the city in a number of *Aktions*. Another 3,000 were murdered in June 1942.

STAROMINSKAYA Krasnodar territory, Russia.

After their arrival on 5 Aug. 1942, the Germans executed 63 Jews outside the village.

STAROSELYE Mogilev dist., Belorussia. The J. pop. was 106 in 1880 and 867 in 1897, dropping to 512 (total 1,203) in 1923 under the Soviets. In 1924–25, 34 Jews were farmers but most earned their livelihoods as artisans. The authorities opened a J. school in 1921 but it soon closed because the community refused to recognize it. A Yiddish literary circle was active in the town. The Germans occupied S. in early Aug. 1941. In Sept. they executed over 200 Jews beside a pit in the Brinkovo forest. A few escaped and joined the partisans.

STARO-ZAKREVSKI MAYDAN (from 1944, Stari Maydan) Kamenets-Podolski dist., Ukraine. S. was founded on state land in 1846 as a J. colony with 62 families (303 Jews) working 1,600 acres of land. In 1897, the J. pop. was 519 (total 595). A pogrom was staged in July 1919. In the Soviet period, a J. rural council (soviet) and 120 J. farm units (in 1928) were active. The Germans occupied the village in mid-July 1941. The Jews who failed to escape were executed in Sept. 1942 with the rest of the Jews in the Volkovinets region.

STARUNIA Stanislawow dist., Poland, today Ukraine. The J. pop. in 1921 was 168. The Jews were possibly expelled to the Rodolf Mill camp in Stanislawow for liquidation in Sept. 1942.

STARYE DOROGI Minsk dist., Belorussia. Jews probably settled in the late 19th cent., numbering 55 (total 515) in 1897. However, only in 1903 were they accorded the legal right to reside in the town. During the Soviet period, some Jews were employed in nearby kolkhozes. A J. council (soviet) was established in 1925 and a J. elementary school was still open in 1931 and a synagogue in the mid-1930s. In 1939, the J. pop. was 1,085 (total 4,241). The Germans arrived in late June 1941 and in Sept. probably murdered 363 J. families from S. and the surrounding area

STARYI KRYM Crimea, Russia, today Ukraine. A Khazar J. community existed in the ninth cent. when the town was called Fullakh. At the turn of the 19th cent. a limited number of Jews from the western parts of Russia were allowed to settle. In 1939, the J. pop. was 104 (total 5,143). Shortly after the arrival of the Germans on 2 Nov. 1941, 105 Jews from S. and its environs were murdered.

STARYI OSKOL Kursk dist., Russia. J. settlement probably dates to the early 20th cent. In 1926, the J. pop. was 106 (total 11,000). The few Jews who had neither fled nor been evacuated were murdered after the arrival of the Germans on 2 July 1942.

STARY SAMBOR (Yid. Alt Stat) Lwow dist., Poland, today Ukraine. Jews are first mentioned in 1544. In 1890 the J. pop was 1,613 (total 3,482). Steady emigration in the face of economic hardship reduced it to 1,534 in 1921. During and after WWI the Jews suffered rapine and persecution at the hands of the Cossacks and Ukrainians. In 1923 a fire left 384 J. families homeless. The Germans gave the Ukrainians a free hand for one day on their occupation of the town on 3 July 1941 with the result that 22 Jews were murdered at the J. cemetery before a gathering of Ukrainian citizens. Many Jews were expelled to the neighboring Sambor ghetto in March 1942, as were most of the rest on 5-6 Aug., for ultimate deportation to the Belzec death camp.

STARY SONCZ Cracow dist., Poland. Jews are first mentioned in 1469 but only formed an organized community under Austrian rule with the end of residence restrictions in 1860. The J. pop. stood at 666 (total 5,156) in 1910. All J. stores were looted in 1898 and declining economic conditions and the rigors of WWI led to emigration, the J. pop. standing at 553 in 1921. The Halberstam hasidic dynasty of Zanz provided the community with rabbis. Under the German occupation, a *Judenrat* was set up at the end of 1939 and a ghetto crowding together 1,000 Jews including refugees was established in spring 1942. On 17 Aug., after the sick and old were murdered, all were expelled to Nowy Soncz for deportation to the Belzec death camp.

STASSFURT Saxony, Germany. Clear evidence of Jews in S. during the Middle Ages dates back to 1434 and the end of the 15th cent. In 1842, a new J. settlement was established. The Jews rented a room for prayer and in 1872 set up a cemetery. In 1892, an officially recognized synagogue community was established, which reached a peak of 68 members in 1901,

Teachers and students celebrating Lag ba-Omer, Staszow, Poland, 1938 (Beth Hatefutsoth Photo Archive, Tel Aviv/courtesy of M. Karmi, Israel)

shrinking to 25 in 1925. When the Nazis came to power in 1933, there were 21 Jews in S. Prayer services were moved to a private apartment, but probably stopped by 1935. On *Kristallnacht* (9–10 Nov. 1938), several Jews were arrested and J. businesses were looted. One family and several young people managed to escape abroad; two families were deported to the east.

STASZOW Kielce dist., Poland. Jews settled in 1526 when the town received municipal status. In 1610, they were expelled and a number executed after a blood libel. Some apparently remained and, although there was another blood libel in 1688, the residence ban was lifted in 1690. Jews were allowed to consecrate a synagogue and cemetery in 1718 and granted a charter of rights in 1722 permitting them to engage in unlimited trade and practice crafts. In the 18th cent., the J. pop. grew along with J. prominence in the local economy. Under Austrian rule after the Third Partition of Poland in 1795, the Jews were subjected to heavy taxes and in the Grand Duchy of Warsaw (1807–15) they were further restricted in an effort to bring about their assimila-

tion. In 1809, Jews were required to reside in a J. quarter. Conditions improved in the late 19th cent. as the J. pop. rose to 4,885 (total 7,893) in 1897 and Jews dominated the retail trade and claimed a large share of the wholesale trade in grain, lumber, and alcoholic beverages. The presence of the Russian army until 1906 also stimulated business. However, on its departure, economic conditions declined and many Jews required relief. The Bund became active among J. workers and artisans in 1906. In WWI, rampaging Cossacks pillaged J. property. Between the World Wars, Mizrachi became the first and one of the biggest Zionist parties. The Zionists were strongly opposed by Agudat Israel, which founded a Beth Jacob school for girls, a Beit Yosef yeshiva, and an important bank. Violent antisemitism characterized the 1930s, but a J. group of 120 sports club members provided defense against attacks. In 1931 the J. pop was 4,805 (total 9,147). The Germans arrived on 7–8 Sept. 1939, appointing a *Judenrat* in Nov. and instituting a regime of forced labor as refugees arrived from Kalisz and Lodz. On 15 June 1942 a ghetto was sealed off and in June and Oct., large groups of Jews were executed. On 8 Nov. 1942, 6,000 Jews

Jewish resident of Staszow, Poland (Beth Hatefutsoth Photo Archive, Tel Aviv/courtesy of M. Karmi, Israel)

were deported to the Belzec and Treblinka death camps; another 189 caught hiding were murdered. The last few hundred Jews were dispatched to Treblinka on 10 Jan. 1943.

STAUDERNHEIM Rhineland, Germany. The J. pop. was 45 in 1808; 71 (total 1,000) in 1858; and 24 in 1932. Twelve Jews remained in May 1939 and the last three were deported to the camps in July 1942. The synagogue (consecrated in 1896) was vandalized on *Kristallnacht* (9–10 Nov. 1938).

STAVISHCHE Kiev dist., Ukraine. The J. pop. was 699 in 1765 and 3,917 (total 8,161) in 1897. Most Jews were Hasidim. In the late 19th cent., a *talmud torah* and a private boys' school combining religious and general studies were opened. Four Jews were murdered in riots on 15 June 1919. In 1939, under the Soviets, the J. pop. was 319. The Germans occupied S. in July 1941 and two weeks later murdered all J. males up to the age of 60. The women and children were murdered in Oct.

STAWISKI Bialystok dist., Poland. An organized community was formed in the mid-17th cent., encouraged by the nobility for its economic activity and permitted to build houses near the castle. A splendid synagogue was consecrated in 1813 with fortresslike walls and towering arches. The J. pop. reached 2,234 (total 2,570) in 1857. Most Jews earned their livings in petty trade and crafts. The best known of the community's rabbis was Hayyim Leib Rothenberg-Mishowski (1878–98). R. Reuven Katz, who served after WWI and helped set up small *yeshivot* in the region's towns, became vice president of the American Rabbinical Council in 1931 and later chief rabbi of Petah Tikva for 32 years. The trend of emigration that set in late in the 19th cent. continued through WWI, reducing the J. pop. to 1,920 in 1921. During WWI the Jews were subjected to forced labor and suffered from food shortages under the German occupation but were able to maintain public life. In its aftermath they were subjected to the depredations of General Haller's irregular Polish troops. With the return to normalcy, Zionist activity was renewed, with Hehalutz sending a group of pioneers to Palestine in 1924. Most Jews remained, with a small middle class comprised of storekeepers and a few of the artisans. Under the month-long German occupation of Sept. 1939, J. men were sent to an East Prussian transit camp and the remaining Jews subjected to a reign of terror with active Polish participation. The Germans returned on 27 June 1941 after two years of Soviet rule and unleashed a brutal pogrom in early July in which Polish mobs wielding iron bars slaughtered 300 Jews. On 15 Aug. the Gestapo arrived, murdering the able-bodied beside antitank ditches near the village of Matwica and 500 of the old and young in the Kyszlinecki forest. The 60 surviving Jews, skilled workers and their families, were confined to a ghetto. On 2 Nov. 1942 they were transferred to the Bogusze concentration camp and shortly thereafter deported to the Treblinka and Auschwitz death camps. Few of the town's 2,000 Jews survived the Holocaust.

STAWISZYN Kalisz dist., Poland. An independent community existed from the mid-19th cent. The J. pop. in 1884 was 656 (31% of the total) and in 1939 about 800. In Jan. 1940 some of the Jews were transferred to Kalisz and on 12 Feb. the remainder were expelled to Kozminek, where they suffered the same fate as the local Jews.

R. Freidman on a Sabbath stroll, Stefanesti, Rumania

STEBLEV Kiev dist., Ukraine. Eight Jews were present in 1775 and a few dozen in the 19th cent. In 1887, the J. pop. was 1,472 (total 5,746). Some Jews worked at a sugar refinery and others at a spinning and weaving mill. Most were Hasidim. In Aug. 1919, a gang of 400 rioters attacked the Jews but J. self-defense units succeeded in driving off the attackers before they could do any damage. In 1923, under the Soviets, the J. pop. was 700. A Yiddish-language school was opened in the town and a J. kolkhoz was founded nearby. After their arrival in Aug. 1941, the Germans murdered the Jews.

STEBNIK Lwow dist., Poland, today Ukraine. Jews lived there from the late 19th cent. The J. pop. in 1921 was 134 (total 2,341). In the face of Ukrainian violence after the German occupation in July 1941, most fled to neighboring towns before final deportation to the Belzec death camp.

STECOWA Stanislawow dist., Poland, today Ukraine. The J. pop. in 1921 was 118. The Jews were probably murdered or fled in Sept.–Dec. 1941 with the remnant expelled to Sniatyn for extermination in July 1942.

STEDUM EN LOPPERSUM Groningen dist., Holland. This united community was formed in 1877 and included Middelstum. The J. pop. in 1889 was 83. No Jews remained in S. by the early 20th cent.; there were six in Loppersum and 11 in Middelstum in 1941. All but one were deported and perished in the Holocaust.

STEENWIJK Overijssel dist., Holland. J. settlement began in the late 17th cent. and increased from the mid-18th cent. The community grew rapidly and was financially stable throughout the 19th cent. A J. school was built in 1849. The J. pop. in 1890 was 225 (total 5,360). A number of social welfare and religious organizations were established. The J. pop. in 1941 was 93. In the Holocaust 47 Jews perished in the Sobibor concentration camp, Auschwitz, and other camps. With assistance from local inhabitants, 42 survived in hiding. J. life was renewed immediately after the Holocaust. The neighboring J. communities in Blokzijl and Vollenhove were disbanded before WWII. They dated from the 18th cent.: Blokzijl had a peak pop. of 108 in 1860 while there were 77 Jews in Vollenhove in 1813.

STEFANESTI   Moldavia dist., Rumania, today Republic of Moldova. S. was founded around several inns which Jews established here in the early 17th cent. In 1886, the 2,886 Jews constituted 77% of the pop. and maintained three synagogues. The majority traded in wheat imported from Bessarabia or in lime which they prepared themselves. The court of the Ruzhin hasidic dynasty was located there. J. houses and the synagogue were destroyed in a fire in 1873. Between the World Wars, Jews sent eight representatives to the municipal council. The J. pop. in 1930 stood at 2,361 (27% of the total). In summer 1940, retreating Rumanian soldiers attacked Jews and many fled to Bessarabia. After the outbreak of the Soviet-Rumanian war in June 1941, the J. pop was forced to march to Sulita. When they returned two weeks later, they found their property destroyed by Soviet bombing and pillaged by their neighbors. The J. pop. was drafted into labor battalions and many died. Some were charged as Communists and sent to the Taru-Jiu concentration camp and from there to Transnistria.

STEINACH AN DER SAALE   Lower Franconia, Germany. Jews were among the victims of the Armleder massacres of 1336. The modern community was founded no later than the second half of the 17th cent. Thirty-six Jews emigrated to North America in 1830–54. The J. pop. reached a peak of 144 (total 801) in 1880, with a synagogue built in mid-cent. and a J. public school operating until 1924. The J. pop. declined to 39 in 1933. Thirty-one left in 1934–41. On 11 Nov. 1938, the night after *Kristallnacht*, the synagogue and J. homes were vandalized. Of the six Jews remaining in 1942, four were deported to Izbica in the Lublin dist. (Poland) via Wuerzburg on 25 Apr. and two to the Theresienstadt ghetto on 23 Sept. 1942.

STEIN AM KOCHER   Baden, Germany. The first Jews settled during the Thirty Years War (1618–48). The community grew to a peak of 93 in 1825 (total 954) and then declined steadily to nine in 1933. Most emigrated and a few perished in the camps.

STEINAU AN DER ODER   (Pol. Scinawa Mala) Lower Silesia, Germany, today Poland. The J. community maintained a synagogue from 1861 and a cemetery. It numbered 105 in 1884. Seven families (about 40 Jews) remained in 1931. Their fate in the Nazi era is unknown. Presumably those who did not emigrate were deported and perished.

STEINBACH A. DONNERSBERG   Palatinate, Germany. The J. pop. was 60 in 1804; 91 in 1848; and 75 (total 693) in 1875. The community maintained a synagogue and cemetery (the latter established in 1850). In 1932, 22 Jews remained, dwindling to six in 1939. They were deported to the Gurs concentration camp in Oct. 1940. At least five Jews perished in the Holocaust.

STEINBACH A. GLAN   Palatinate, Germany. There was a J. community in the 18th cent., growing to 217 (a third of the total) in 1848 and then declining to 119 in 1900 and 32 in 1932. A J. elementary school operated about 80 years before closing in 1916. The synagogue erected in 1725 was wrecked on *Kristallnacht* (9–10 Nov. 1938) and the 13 Jews remaining in S. were ejected from the village during the riots and their homes looted. Another 13 Jews emigrated in the Nazi period. The last four Jews were deported to the Gurs concentration camp in Oct. 1940 and then sent to Auschwitz in Aug. 1942. The cemetery, which dates back to 1755, was desecrated by the Nazis and again in 1979 and 1986.

STEINHART   Middle Franconia, Germany. The Jews were expelled in 1560 and maintained a presence through the 17th and 18th cents., numbering 149 (total 362) in 1810. The community ended in 1883 when the few remaining Jews joined the Oettingen community.

STEINHEIM   Westphalia, Germany. Although Jews are first mentioned in 1602 and numbered 40 a hundred years later, a synagogue was only consecrated in 1884. The community reached a peak pop. of 160 in 1885, dropping to 59 by 1933. The synagogue, which had ceased to be used for prayer in 1936, was a target of thieves and vandals even before *Kristallnacht*. On *Kristallnacht* (9–10 Nov. 1938), SA troops destroyed its contents, the work of destruction being completed by the German army in Dec. 1938. Seven Jews were sent to the Buchenwald concentration camp. In 1942,

18 Jews were deported to the death camps. Altogether 32 Jews perished in the Holocaust.

STENDAL Saxony, Germany. By the 1260s, there was already a community. It suffered during the Black Death persecutions of 1348–49 and in 1446. The Jews were expelled together with those from Brandenburg following a Host desecration trial in Berlin in 1510 in which two local Jews were burned at the stake. Jews only began to resettle towards the end of the 18th cent. In 1857, the local Jews were affiliated to the Tangermuende community. In 1861, the community hired its own teacher and in 1865 established a cemetery. A synagogue was consecrated in 1887. In 1905, the J. pop. was 93. When the Nazis came to power in 1933, there were 61 Jews in S. On *Kristallnacht* (9–10 Nov. 1938), the synagogue was gutted by fire. In 1939, there were only 23 Jews in the city. It may be assumed that those who did not manage to escape were deported, with the exception of three Jews still living in S. in Oct. 1942, probably protected by marriage to non-Jews.

STENZHYCA Lublin dist., Poland. J. residence was officially allowed only after the Third Partition of Poland in 1795. J. economic distress persisted between the World Wars. The J. pop. was 125 (total 1,530) in 1921. Thirty J. families remained in WWII. The Germans set up a *Judenrat* in late 1939 and forced the Jews to work on the roads and in the hospitals and to supply services to the army. In summer 1941, Jews were sent to the Demblin labor camp. On 6 May 1942, the rest were sent to Demblin and most were deported to the Sobibor death camp.

STEPAN Volhynia dist., Poland, today Ukraine. Jews are first mentioned in 1569; few remained after the Cossack wars of the mid-17th cent. but recovery was rapid. Jews numbered 1,854 in 1897 (total 5,137) and 1,337 in 1921 (total 4,064). Many engaged in the grain trade. S. was famous for its Hasidism, with links to the Berezne, Neskhizh, and Turzysk dynasties. Zionist activity expanded after WWI. The Germans took the town on 17 July 1941, established a *Judenrat*, and instituted a regime of persecution and forced labor, sending groups of the young to the Kostopol labor camp. A ghetto crowding together 3,000 Jews including refugees was set up on 5 Oct. 1941. On 24 Aug. 1942 they were brought to freshly dug pits near Kostopol and murdered; of the 500 fleeing before the *Aktion*, 300 were immediately caught by Ukrainian peasants and returned while dozens of others later died or were killed.

STEPANTSY Kiev dist., Ukraine. Twelve Jews were present in 1765. Their pop. reached 3,171 in 1866 but all were expelled in 1882. In 1903, they were allowed to return and numbered 3,389 (total 7,436) in the same year. J. livelihoods revolved around the town's weekly market day and yearly fair. Most Jews were Hasidim. R. Nahman he-Hasid, author of a number of Torah studies, served as the community's rabbi. On 14 Feb 1919, the Petlyura gangs murdered 99 Jews and injured about 300. In 1923, under the Soviets, the J. pop. was 668. The Germans occupied S. in July 1941 and murdered all the Jews.

STERBFRITZ (now part of Sinntal) Hesse–Nassau, Germany. The community, numbering 169 (16% of the total) in 1885, was affiliated with the rabbinate of Hanau. After WWI it had members in Oberzell, but only five pupils attended its community school. More than half of the 92 Jews who remained in 1933 left before *Kristallnacht* (9–10 Nov. 1938), when the synagogue's interior was destroyed; 28 emigrated and at least 15 perished in the Holocaust.

STERDYN Lublin dist., Poland. Jews are first mentioned in the early 19th cent. The J. pop. was 278 in 1865, rising to 710 (total 802) in 1921. Under the German occupation a *Judenrat* was appointed in late 1939 and refugees increased the J. pop. to 900. All were deported to the Treblinka death camp on 10 Oct. 1942.

STERKRADE Rhineland, Germany. Jews first arrived in 1830 and formed a single community with Holten. Their pop. rose from 25 in 1865 to 58 (total 21,205) in 1905 and 130 in 1925. The community was composed of both Liberal and Orthodox Jews, with public prayer only on the Sabbath and holidays. At the end of the Weimar period, most Jews engaged in trade, their businesses including the large Mayer and Klestadt clothing outlet. Ninety Jews remained in 1933. J. stores were subjected to an ongoing boycott campaign by local Nazis; "Jews Not Welcome Here" signs were put up in the parks; and J. children were expelled from the public schools. Five Polish Jews were expelled from the city in Oct. 1938 and J. homes and stores were destroyed on *Kristallnacht* (9–10 Nov. 1938). At least 36 Jews emigrated in the Nazi period, 12 to Palestine. In late Oct. 1941, 11 were deported to the Lodz ghetto. Six others were also subsequently deported. All perished.

STERNBERK Moravia (Sudetenland), Czechoslovakia. The medieval J. community ended in expulsion in 1577. The J. pop. was 128 in 1880 and 62 in 1930 (less than 0.5% of the total). Jews founded most of the city's textile factories. The Jews left S. when the Sudetenland was annexed to the German Reich in fall 1938. Some emigrated, others were deported to the death camps of Poland in 1942, and a few survived the Holocaust in the Theresienstadt ghetto.

STETTIN (Pol. Czczecin) Pomerania, Germany, today Poland. Although Jews are first mentioned in 1261, they had probably been living in the town for some time. The community appears to have suffered major decimation in the wake of the Black Death persecutions of 1348–49. There was no J. cemetery, and the dead were probably buried in Greifswald. In 1492–93, the Jews of S., along with all the Jews in Pomerania, were expelled on charges of desecration of the Host. In the 17th cent. Jews were again found in S., but they were banned from permanent residence until the 18th cent. In 1753 there were two Jews employed at the Prussian mint in S., one engaged in supplying silver. A modern community developed in 1812, numbering 18 Jews (probably family heads plus dependents) in 1818. By 1843, there were 519 Jews in S. In the 1820s, the community established a cemetery, bath house, and religious school. The first synagogue was built in 1834–35 and a decade later there is evidence of the first rabbi. In the mid-19th cent., Jews from Posen and West Prussia settled in S., increasing the pop. to 1,823. As a result of this immigration, an Orthodox prayer room existed from 1867 in addition to the community synagogue. A new synagogue was built in 1875 and the presence of an organ demonstrated the Liberal orientation of the community. The antisemitic riots which broke out in Pomerania when the Neustettin synagogue was burned down in 1881 led to three days of clashes in S. but there was no damage to J. property. In 1905, the J. pop. of S. was 3,001 (2% of the total). In 1930, the J. pop. was 2,703. The community maintained a wide variety of social, cultural, and welfare associations and institutions, including local branches of the Central Union (C.V.) and the German Zionist Organization; various youth associations; an orphanage (1874); an old age home (1893); a day nursery and day care center; a children's holiday camp; a community newsletter with a circulation of 1,200 (1916); and a lending library (1919). Orthodoxy was strengthened in 1928, when a *talmud torah* and a *mikve* were set up. In 1933, there were 2,365 Jews living in S. As early as 1933, many community members were taken into "protective" custody by the Nazis and maltreated. In 1934, there were numerous anti-J. demonstrations and religious services were disrupted. In 1937, three adolescents murdered a J. businessman: two of the perpetrators were sentenced to lengthy jail sentences and one to death. The community managed to establish a J. elementary school in 1934, which enrolled 78 students in 1935. It was probably closed in 1936 or shortly afterwards. By 1937, the community numbered 1,903. In Oct. 1938, some 70 J. families without German citizenship were deported to Poland. On *Kristallnacht* (9–10 Nov. 1938), the synagogue and J. clubhouses were set on fire and businesses and homes were wrecked and looted. J. men were arrested and taken to the Sachsenhausen concentration camp. Until 1939, the Palestine Office operated in S., organizing the emigration of Jews from the city and its environs. By May 1939, the community numbered 1,117. At least 800 Jews from S. were deported to the Lublin dist. (Poland) on 11–12 Feb. 1940 in a transport which included Jews from the whole of Pomerania. The 30 or so children of the orphanage were taken to Berlin and Hamburg, and later deported from there. In 1941–42, the last of the city's Jews, mainly elderly people, who had lived in the community's old age home, were deported also. In Oct. 1942, there were just 79 Jews living in the city, probably protected by marriage to non-Jews. Of the deportees, only a few survived. After 1945, Polish Jews settled in the city and established a new community, but in 1946 some were murdered in the pogroms occurring at the time throughout Poland. In 1959, the community had 1,050 members, but most Jews left the city in the mid-1960s, moving to other Polish cities or emigrating.

STEYR Upper Austria, Austria. Jews first settled in the beginning of the 14th cent., operating primarily as moneylenders. They were expelled in a wave of blood libels in 1420. The Jews returned during the late 18th cent., but anti-J. feeling kept the settlement from developing until after the 1848 revolution. In 1870, the community was recognized as an independent body, but under the auspices of Linz. In 1874, the community established a J. cemetery and a J. elementary school. In 1892, the community became completely independent of Linz. In 1894, a synagogue was inaugurated. Jews mainly engaged in the textile trade and were represented in the professional class as pharmacists, doctors, and lawyers. By 1891, the J. pop. stood at 174, declining to 82 in 1934. In 1931, with the emergence of Nazi youth movements, antisemitism became more virulent and from time to time J. shops were damaged. By the end of 1938, 47 Jews succeeded in emigrating. Their property was confiscated. On *Kristallnacht* (9–10 Nov. 1938), the synagogue was burned down and J. men arrested. They were beaten and then released shortly after. By the end of 1939, the 11 remaining Jews in S. had been sent to Vienna and from there to the death camps in the east. After the war, J. refugees from Hungary and Poland reestablished a small community.

STIP Macedonia, Yugoslavia. Jews lived in S. from the 15th cent. In 1890 there were 350 Jews and by 1910 they numbered 750 (total 25,000). The Jews suffered during the Balkan wars (1912–13) and in Oct. 1912 the Bulgarians expelled the Jews, who found shelter in Salonika. The Jews eventually returned to revive the community and rebuild their quarter in the now Serbian town. In the 1930s, there were two Zionist youth organizations. In 1941, S. came under Bulgarian control and the Jews were forced to wear a yellow badge. On 11 March 1943 they were taken by train to Skopje, where they were held with the local Jews and then deported with them to the Treblinka death camp. Only four out of some 600 Jews from S. survived the Holocaust.

STITNIK (Hung. Csetnek) Slovakia, Czechoslovakia, today Republic of Slovakia. Jews settled in the 1850s, forming a Status Quo congregation with a synagogue and cemetery and maintaining a pop. of about 70 (5% of the total) until 1940, when it dropped to 43. In 1941, the Jews were forced out of their businesses and in June 1942 they were deported to Auschwitz and to the Lublin dist. of Poland.

STKACIN Slovakia, Czechoslovakia, today Republic of Slovakia. The community numbered 137 in 1930, maintaining a synagogue and cemetery. All the Jews were sent to the death camps in 1942. In the nearby village of Kolbasov, Ukrainian nationalists arriving from Poland murdered 11 Holocaust survivors on 6 Dec. 1945, apparently with local collaboration.

STOBYCHWA Volhynia dist., Poland. The J. pop. of over 100 apparently abandoned the settlement permanently during WWI.

STOCKERAU Lower Austria, Austria. Jews were present at the end of the 17th cent., engaged in moneylending. In 1854, religious services were held in a private home and in 1903 a synagogue was inaugurated. A J. cemetery was consecrated in 1874. In 1905, the community gained the status of a religious association (*Kultusverein*). Jews were engaged in trade. In 1934, the J. pop. stood at 130, thereafter declining sharply. After the *Anschluss* (13 March 1938), shops and private property was confiscated. After *Kristallnacht* (9–10 Nov. 1938), the Protestant Church took over the synagogue. Shortly after, there were no Jews living in S.

STOCKSTADT AM RHEIN Hesse, Germany. Numbering 67 (about 6% of the total) in 1871, the J. community declined to 15 by 1880. Of the last ten Jews in 1933, six emigrated in 1937.

STOCZEK (I) Bialystok dist., Poland. The J. pop. in 1921 was 112 (total 1,064). The Jews were expelled by the Germans to Bialowiezha in Aug. 1941 and then to Pruzhany before final deportation to Auschwitz on 28 Jan. 1943.

STOCZEK (II) (Yid. Stok) Lublin dist., Poland. Despite a longstanding residence ban, 228 Jews were present by 1856, their number increasing, with the arrival of many Hasidim to 1,221 (total 1,636) in 1921. After WWI, Jews formed mutual aid societies to foster economic recovery. Despite the traditional orientation of the community, many of the young joined the Zionists. Antisemitic rioting left 42 injured on 23 Aug. 1937. After the German occupation of Sept. 1939, 200 young Jews were sent to labor camps and a *Judenrat* and ghetto were set up. On 22 Sept. 1942, all were deported to the Treblinka death camp after 100 of the sick and old were murdered.

STOCZEK LUKOWSKI Lublin dist., Poland. After a longstanding residence ban, the J. settlement grew rapidly in the late 19th cent., numbering 1,962 (total 2,951) in 1921. Between the World Wars, the Zionists were active. In the 1930s, antisemitism intensified, with attacks on J. schoolchildren and shopkeepers. The German occupation of Sept. 1939 was accompanied by severe persecution. A *Judenrat* and ghetto were set up, with a typhoid epidemic claiming many victims in summer 1941. At the end of Aug., all but 200 of the able-bodied were deported to Parysow. On 27 Sept. 1942, the Jews of S. were sent together with those of Parysow to the Treblinka death camp. One hundred were murdered on the way.

STOD Bohemia, Czechoslovakia. Jews are known from the 17th cent. In the late 19th cent., the Salz family founded the first malt factory in Bohemia. In 1930, the J. pop. was 57 (2% of the total). In 1942, the Jews were deported to the Theresienstadt ghetto together with the Jews of Prague and from there sent to the death camps of the east.

STODOLISCHE Smolensk dist., Russia. J. settlement probably commenced in the late 19th cent. The J. pop. was 329 (total 535) in 1926 and 232 in 1939. After their arrival in S. in the first half of Aug. 1941, the Germans murdered the few Jews who had not fled or been evacuated.

STOICISZKI Vilna dist., Poland, today Belarus. Jews settled in 1865 on estate land confiscated by the Russians from the Polish nobility and established a farm settlement where the pop. grew to 262 in 1898. They cultivated livestock, cereal crops, vegetables, and fruit trees, and sold their produce in the neighboring towns. After the arrival of the Germans in June 1941, their property was divided among local Poles and Lithuanians and on 20 Sept. 1941 all 310 were expelled via Haiduciszki to the Poligon camp, where they were murdered on 7–9 Oct. 1941 with the 8,000 Jews of Swienciany province.

STOJANOW Tarnopol dist., Poland, today Ukraine. Jews first arrived in 1629, gaining control of trade and a number of crafts, including the construction of wooden houses. The J. pop. reached a peak of 726 (a quarter of the total) in 1900. Most identified with Belz Hasidism. The Zionists only became active between the World Wars, when all children attended Polish public schools. Antisemitism increased in the 1930s and with the arrival of the Germans on 24 June 1941 the Ukrainians began pillaging J. homes. A regime of forced labor and terror soon prevailed. In an *Aktion* on 12 Sept. 1942 (Rosh Hashanah) all but a handful were rounded up and deported to the Belzec death camp after the old and infirm were murdered in the town.

STOK Lublin dist., Poland. The J. pop. was 167 in 1921 (total 705). Most Jews left for nearby settlements on the outbreak of WWII. The remaining Jews were deported to the Treblinka death camp via Lukow in Oct. 1942.

STOLBERG Rhineland, Germany. The local J. community grew only from the middle of the 19th cent., numbering 54 individuals in 1890 and a peak of 86 in 1900. It dropped again to 49 (total 17,000) in 1925–32 and 40 in June 1933. The community maintained a prayer room in a private house and a cemetery was established in 1860. About half the Jews moved to nearby Aachen in the Nazi period. The rest emigrated to Holland, China, Bolivia, and South Africa. On *Kristallnacht* (9–10 Nov. 1938), the two J. stores were damaged. The last two Jews were brought to Eschweiler in July 1941 and from there deported to the Theresienstadt ghetto in March 1942. In all, at least 18 Jews perished in the Holocaust.

STOLIN Polesie dist., Poland, today Belarus. Jews began to settle around the mid-17th cent. In 1794, R. Asher Perlov, son of "Aharon the Great," founder of Karlin Hasidism, established his court in S., which was maintained until WWII, with a yeshiva founded in 1922. A Hovevei Zion group was formed in 1898 and the Bund became active in the early 20th cent., agitating among workers and organizing J. self-defense. The J. pop. reached 2,966 in 1921 (total 4,763). After the Feb. 1917 Revolution, J. public life revived, with a Tarbut school the center of Zionist activity. The Germans appeared on 22 Aug. 1941, instituting a regime of forced labor and establishing a *Judenrat*. About 1,500 women and children arrived from Dawidgrodek in late Aug. and with other refugees brought the pop. of the ghetto, established in May 1942, up to 7,000, racked by hunger and disease. On 11 Sept. 1942 (Rosh Hashanah eve), all were brought to pits near the local airfield and shot.

The rabbi of Stolin leading procession to his son's wedding, Poland

STOLOWICZE Nowogrodek dist., Poland, today Belarus. Jews probably settled under the auspices of the Radziwills in the late 16th cent. In 1897 they numbered 515 (total 929). Many engaged in agriculture between the World Wars, with emigration under straitened economic circumstances reducing the J. pop. to about 350 at the time of the German occupation of 27 June 1941. A *Judenrat* was appointed on 1 Sept. 1941 and a ghetto was established in Jan. 1942. Most of the Jews were executed outside the town on 12 May 1942.

STOLP (Pol. Slupsk) Pomerania, Germany, today Poland. There is mention of a Jew in S. in 1705. In 1812, there were 63 Jews; in 1852, 599; and in 1880, 958. S. was the second largest community in Pomerania after Stettin. A cemetery was consecrated in 1815 and a synagogue in 1840. There was a rabbi in 1841 and a school was opened. The community became Liberal, establishing a mixed choir and introducing an organ in the big new synagogue consecrated in 1902. At this time, the community also maintained a community center and an old age home which provided for both J. and non-J. residents. The antisemitic riots which broke out in Pomerania when the Neustettin synagogue was burned down in 1881 spread to S. J. property was destroyed and businesses looted. Similar riots occurred in 1900. When the Nazis came to power in 1933, the J. pop. was 470. By Sept. 1935, J. businessmen were facing financial ruin due to Nazi boycott measures. On *Kristallnacht* (9–10 Nov. 1938), the synagogue was set on fire and most J. men were arrested and deported to the Sachsenhausen concentration camp. By May 1939, about half the community had emigrated. There were still 215 Jews and 46 persons of partial

J. origin (*Mischlinge*) living in S. From 1940 onwards, the Jews were obligated to perform forced labor and compelled to move to the community's old age home. Most of the remaining Jews were deported in two transports: on 9–10 July 1942 to Auschwitz and in Aug. 1942 to the Theresienstadt ghetto. By April 1944, only 42 Jews married to non-Jews remained in S. They were compelled to leave the city together with the German pop. when the town became part of Poland at the end of the war.

STOLPCE Nowogrodek dist., Poland, today Belarus. Jews probably settled in the latter 16th cent. under the auspices of the Radziwill family. In 1622 the Lithuanian Council discussed a blood libel that had occurred in S. A synagogue was erected in the early 17th cent. The Jews were prominent in the Neiman River grain trade and at the turn of the 19th cent. owned most of the town's 16 stores. In 1897 their number was 2,409 (total 3,754). Zionist activity commenced in the early 20th cent. After WWI, J. life revived somewhat as the ruined city became a provincial capital. The prewar J. public school joined the Tarbut network and Zionist activity expanded. The Germans arrived on 27 June 1941, murdering about 200 of the town's 3,000 Jews on 29 June. A *Judenrat* and ghetto were soon established, and 87 more Jews were murdered on 25 July. Hundreds were shipped to labor camps. An armed resistance group of 11 escaped to the forest but most of the other Jews were executed on 22 Sept. 1942; those left behind as workers were murdered toward the end of the year.

STOLZENAU AN DER WESER Hanover, Germany. Dating from 1700, the community numbered around 15 families in 1778, when Yehiel Hildesheimer and Shemuel Levi headed the town's yeshiva. The prospering community built a synagogue in 1834 and maintained an elementary school in 1892–1925. Good relations prevailed with the non-J. pop. Between 1855 and 1900, the J. pop. grew to over 100 (6–7% of the total). Members were strictly Orthodox and held daily prayer services until WWI. The communities of S. (45–50 Jews) and neighboring Leese (55) amalgamated in 1922. On *Kristallnacht* (9–10 Nov. 1938), the Nazis blew up the synagogue and burned Torah scrolls in the marketplace. While J. cemeteries remained intact, the last Jews were deported in 1942. At least 13 from S. and three from Leese perished.

STOMPORKOW Lodz dist., Poland. In 1906 only three J. families lived here and in 1939 there were 30 families. After the German occupation, the influx of refugees increased the community to 490 and in spring 1942 all were transferred to Radoszyce and then to the Treblinka death camp.

STOPNICA (Yid. Stavnich) Kielce dist., Poland. Jews are first mentioned in the mid-17th cent., living under a collective privilege. The J. pop. grew from 1,014 in 1827 to 3,692 (total 5,569) in 1908. In 1921 the J. pop. was 3,328 (total 4,902). In WWI, the Jews suffered from the depredations of Russian troops and were attacked by Polish antisemites in 1919. The Orthodox controlled the community and its institutions, but many joined the Zionists between the World Wars. The Bund and Agudat Israel were also active, the latter founding a Beth Jacob school for 150 girls. The Germans captured the town on 8 Sept. 1939, setting fire to a J. neighborhood and killing four. In early 1940, a *Judenrat* was established. In April, 12 Jews were seized from the Passover table and murdered. In 1941 a ghetto was set up, crowding together 5,300 Jews, mainly deportees from Lodz, Cracow, and Radon. By June, 400 had died of hunger and disease. On 5 Sept. 1942, 400 of the disabled were executed, 1,500 of the young sent to the Skarzysko-Kamienna labor camp, and 3,000 deported to the Treblinka death camp. A small group of 70 left behind to sort and classify J. property was subsequently dispersed to labor camps.

STORNDORF Hesse, Germany. The J. community, established in 1750, numbered 200 (about 21% of the total) in 1871, dwindling to 25 in 1933. On *Kristallnacht* (9–10 Nov. 1938), Nazis destroyed the synagogue's interior and in Sept. 1939, when all the Jews had left, S. was declared "free of Jews" (*judenfrei*).

STOROJINETI Bukovina, Rumania, today Ukraine. A J. community was founded in the second half of the 19th cent. and numbered 1,601 in 1880 (a third of the total pop.) A yeshiva was opened, and in 1904 a high school was founded which closed in 1934. During WWI, Russian soldiers and local Ukrainians plundered J. property and many Jews fled to Austria. In 1930 the J. pop. was 2,480. In 1937 the Goga-Cuza regime boycotted J. stores and the Iron

Guard attacked Jews. Zionist activity began at the end of the 19th cent., and Zionist youth groups functioned after WWI. In 1940, J. property was confiscated by the Soviets, and in spring 1941, hundreds of families were exiled. In June, when Rumanian and German forces attacked the Jews and plundered their property, 300 Jews fled to Cernauti. The remaining Jews were ghettoized and groups were deported daily to Transnistria, the last on 13 Oct. 1941. Only a tenth of them survived.

STRAKONICE Bohemia, Czechoslovakia. Jews are first mentioned in 1499. In 1509 (or 1511) two were apparently burned at the stake following a blood libel. Throughout the 19th cent., Jews specialized in the manufacture of fez-type hats for export to Turkey. A new synagogue was built in 1860. The J. pop. was 326 (total 7,112) in 1890 and then dropped steadily to 169 in 1930 and 82 in 1942. Most of the Jews were deported to the Theresienstadt ghetto via Klatovy on 26 Nov. 1942 and from there to Auschwitz in Jan. and Sept. 1943. At least 71 perished.

STRALSUND Pomerania, Germany. Evidence of Jews in S. dates from 1282. The medieval community was expelled or murdered in the Black Death persecutions of 1348–49. In the 17th cent., several Jews were granted temporary permission to live and trade in the town. After the opening of the local mint in 1758 several so-called "mint Jews" (*Muenzjuden*) received permission to settle in S. and a J. community began to develop, numbering 172 in 1797. A cemetery was established in 1765 and a synagogue in 1787. The J. pop. of 67 in 1852 began to rise when the port of S. was connected to the railroad network in 1863. In 1900, the J. pop. numbered more than 100 individuals. Leopold Tietz (c. 1880) and Adolf Wertheim (c. 1900) opened department stores which were of considerable economic importance for S. and formed the basis of the department store chains the two men initiated. When the Nazis came to power in 1933, there were 140–160 Jews in S. In Oct. 1938, 22 Polish Jews were deported across the Polish border. On *Kristallnacht* (9–10 Nov. 1938), the synagogue was burned, J. businesses were wrecked, and about 30 men were arrested and deported to the Sachsenhausen concentration camp. In May 1939, 69 Jews and 53 persons of partial J. origins (*Mischlinge*) were still living in S. About 40 Jews were deported to the Lublin dist. (Poland) together with the Jews of Stettin on 12 Feb. 1940. Altogether,

at least 53 Jews from S. were deported, either directly from the town or from places where they had hoped to find shelter. All perished. Only six Jews married to non-Jews were living in S. at the end of the war.

STRAMTURA (Hung. Szurdok; Yid. Strimtere) N. Transylvania dist., Rumania. An organized J. community existed from the early 19th cent. The J. pop. in 1930 was 369 (11% of the total). In April 1944 the Jews were transferred to the Viseul de Sus ghetto and later deported to Auschwitz.

STRANANY Slovakia, Czechoslovakia, today Republic of Slovakia. The J. pop. in 1940 was 150. The Jews were deported to the Lublin dist. of Poland on 8 May 1942 together with the Jews of Michalovce.

STRASBOURG (Ger. Strassburg) Bas-Rhin dist., France. The earliest evidence of a J. presence dates back to the 12th cent. when Benjamin of Tudela visited the community. The Jews fled the town during the anti-J. persecutions associated with the Third Crusade in the 13th cent. During the Black Death persecutions of 1348–49, 2,000 Jews who refused to accept baptism were burned to death on 13 Feb. 1349. In spite of the town's decision to prohibit the settlement of Jews for a period of 100 years, a number of Jews were admitted into the town from 1396 on. At least 25 families resided in S. when all were officially expelled at the end of 1388. Until the French Revolution, no permanent residence was permitted, but Jews could enter the city during the day for business purposes. When S. came under French sovereignty in 1681, anti-J. measures were eased so that in time of war, neighboring Jews could take temporary refuge in the town. In 1770, Herz Cerfberr, army purveyor, obtained for his family and 68 other Jews the right to reside in S. This was the beginning of the modern community. In 1806, seven delegates represented the 1,500 Jews of S. at the Assembly of J. Notables. Immediately after the constitution of the consistories, Yosef David Sinzheim, until then the chief rabbi of S., became the chief rabbi of the central consistory. The community numbered about 1,500 members in 1834 and 2,820 in 1861. The first official synagogue was established in 1805, followed by others in 1834 and 1892 and by the very impressive Quai Kleber synagogue in 1898. Charitable and educational institutions in S. were first established in 1835, with a society encouraging

Cigale Singer, a 5-year-old Jewish girl, wearing an Alsacian dress at a school event, Strasbourg, France, 1929

work among the poor; the Ecole de Travail Israelite followed in 1842; and then the Societe de Secours Mutuel des Israelites de Strasbourg in 1849. In 1853, Hospice Elisa was established for the old and in 1878 the Hadassa J. hospital. A rabbinical seminary existed for a short while in 1885. From 1871, S. came under German rule. The community consisted of 3,088 Jews (total pop. 85,000). By 1905, the community numbered 5,111. In 1907, a museum dedicated to the Jews of Alsace was inaugurated. After WWI, Alsace became a haven for J. immigrants from Eastern Europe (40% of the Jews in 1920s were not originally from S.). In 1919, the Mizrachi organization established a branch. Beside the *talmud torah* and the J. school the Ecole Israelite des Arts et Metiers was active in the 1920s. University graduates founded an Institut de Science Juive, where J. studies were taught. In 1926, the cornerstone of a home for 65 young girls

was laid. In 1930, the chief rabbi of Bas-Rhin, Isaie Schwartz, established the Ligue pour le Repos Sabbatique (L.R.S), numbering 568 members. In 1931, there were nearly 8,500 Jews in S., with over 60% born in France. From 1927, the *Souvenir et Science* journal published articles about the heritage of local J. communities. In Sept. 1939, when WWII broke out, the entire pop. of S., including 10,000 Jews, was evacuated to the southwest of France. The S. Jews were dispersed in more than 50 localities. Members of the community were active in the resistance movement. Its rabbis, Rene Hirschler, Robert Brunschvig, and Elie Cyper, and youth leader Leo Cohn, were arrested and deported to death camps. Samy Klein and Aron Wolf, also rabbis, were killed in the course of their resistance work. It is estimated that during the war over 1,000 Jews were killed either through deportation or in combat. After liberation, 8,000 returned and together with J. settlers from North Africa there were 14,000 Jews in S. in 1964.

STRATYN Stanislawow dist., Poland, today Ukraine. Jews, mainly from Rohatyn, settled in the second half of the 17th cent. The community grew with the establishment of a hasidic dynasty there but declined from a peak pop. of 593 (75% of the total) in 1880 to 155 in 1921. Those not murdered by rampaging Ukrainians after the Soviet withdrawal in late June 1941 were probably liquidated by the Germans in 1942.

STRAUBING Lower Bavaria, Germany. Jews traded in the town in the 13th cent. and inhabited a J. quarter in the early 14th. The Jews were all murdered in Sept. 1338 in the wake of the massacre of the Jews in nearby Deggendorf and the renewed community was again destroyed in the Black Death persecutions of 1348–49. In 1442, a third community was expelled within the framework of the general expulsion from Munich. The modern community was founded in the late 19th cent. and numbered 141 in 1910 (total 22,021). In the Nazi era the Jews suffered from a strict economic boycott, with J. property "Aryanized" on 24 Nov. 1938, two weeks after *Kristallnacht* (9–10 Nov. 1938), when the synagogue was vandalized. In the 1933–42 period, ten Jews left Germany and another 19 took up residence in other German cities. Of the remaining 30, most were expelled to Piaski in the Lublin dist. (Poland) and to the Theresienstadt ghetto on 2 April and 23 Sept. 1942. The community established after the war by concentration camp survivors numbered 119 in 1970.

STRAUSBERG Brandenburg, Germany. Jews were living in S. in the 13th and 14th cents. A settlement comprising two families in 1720 developed at the beginning of the 18th cent. The J. community numbered 62 in 1812 and 55 in 1880. It established a synagogue in 1817 and maintained a cemetery. In June 1933, about four months after the Nazis came to power, there were 69 Jews in S. On *Kristallnacht* (9–10 Nov. 1938), the synagogue and the cemetery were laid waste and J. stores were wrecked. By May 1939, there were 38 Jews and 21 persons of partial J. origin (*Mischlinge*) in S. Those Jews who did not manage to emigrate were deported. The last eight, mainly elderly, were deported on 13 April, 1942. Only one Jew, probably protected by marriage to a non-Jew, was still registered as living in S. in Oct. 1942.

STRAZ Bohemia (Sudetenland), Czechoslovakia. Jews are mentioned in 1331 and numbered 47 families in the first half of the 19th cent. A new synagogue was built in 1882 after a devastating fire in 1867. Thirty-one Jews remained in 1930. Most left after annexation to the Third Reich; those who remained behind were probably deported to death camps via the Theresienstadt ghetto. The Nazis burned the synagogue in Nov. 1938.

STRAZNICE Moravia, Czechoslovakia. Jews are mentioned in 1490. Their pop. grew to 569 in 1848 but afterwards declined steadily as many Jews left for the big cities, especially Vienna. A synagogue was erected in 1804 and a J. elementary school and library were opened in 1862. Most Jews were merchants trading their goods in Hungary. In 1848, the community was granted political autonomy. In 1930, the J. pop. was 194 (total 5,225). The Jews were apparently deported to the Theresienstadt ghetto together with the Jews of Brno in early 1942. From there they were sent to the death camps of Poland.

STREDA NAD BODROGOM Slovakia, Czechoslovakia, today Republic of Slovakia. The J. pop. was 127 in 1930 and 115 in 1941. Most were deported to Auschwitz in May 1944.

STREDNI APSA (Hung. Kozepapsa; Yid. Mitl Apsa) Carpatho-Russia, Czechoslovakia, today Ukraine. Jews apparently arrived in the early 18th cent. with two families present in 1728. In 1880, their pop. was 258 (total 2,287). A few dozen students attended a small yeshiva. Many families earned their livelihoods in agriculture. Nineteen engaged in trade and eight in crafts. There was also a J.-owned flour mill and farm. The J. pop. rose to 431 in 1921 and then dropped to 412 in 1941. Most of the young were members of Zionist youth movements (Hashomer Hatzair, Betar) or Tze'irei Agudat Israel. The Hungarians occupied S. in March 1939, forcing the Jews out of work. In 1941, they drafted dozens of young Jews into forced labor battalions, sending some to the eastern front, where most died. In late July, they expelled a number of families (30 Jews) to Kamenets-Podolski, where they were murdered. In late May 1944, the rest were deported to Auschwitz. A few survivors returned after the war but most soon left for Czechoslovakia.

STREHLEN (Pol. Strzelin) Lower Silesia, Germany, today Poland. Jews were present by the end of the 14th cent. A synagogue is mentioned in 1439 and a Street of the Jews in 1441. Nothing more is heard about the Jews until the reestablishment of the community in the 19th cent. In 1845, the community numbered 86, rising to 163 in 1880. It maintained a synagogue and cemetery. Paul Ehrlich, future Nobel Prize laureate in medicine, was born in S. in 1854. The J. pop. began to decline in the late 19th cent. and stood at 36 in 1932. On *Kristallnacht* (9–10 Nov. 1938), J. stores were destroyed. Fourteen Jews remained in May 1939. No further information is available about the fate of the Jews under the Nazis. Those who failed to emigrate were presumably deported and perished.

STRELNA Leningrad dist., Russia. The J. pop. was 41 in 1926 and 319 (total 16,455) in 1939. The few Jews who had not fled or been evacuated were murdered after the German occupation of mid-Jan. 1942.

STRENCI (Ger. Stackeln) Livonia dist., Latvia. Jews arrived between the World Wars and numbered a few dozen (less than 2% of the total). Those not fleeing to the Soviet Union were murdered by the Germans with Latvian assistance after their arrival in July 1941.

STRESHIN Gomel dist., Belorussia. The J. pop. was 113 in 1789 and 1,179 in 1897. In the 1920s, under the Soviets, 42% of the Jews were artisans and blue-collar workers. Of the three agricultural cooperatives that were set up near the town in 1919, one was J. with 12 J. families; the other two employed 17 J. families. A J. kolkhoz founded in 1919 had 46 families in 1930. In 1925, there were 70 children at a J. school. A J. council (soviet) was established in the same year. In 1939, the J. pop. was 531 (33% of the total). The Germans occupied S. in Aug. 1941 after many of the Jews had been evacuated. Those remaining were robbed of their belongings and herded into a ghetto under conditions of starvation and overcrowding. In early April 1942, the 242 Jews there were expelled to the Zhlobin ghetto and were among the 480 Jews executed on 14 April.

STRIBRO   Bohemia (Sudetenland), Czechoslovakia. Jews were present in the Middle Ages. The modern community was established after 1850 with a synagogue erected in 1879. The J. pop. grew to 171 (total 4,600) in 1910 and was 127 in 1930. Jews were active as merchants, dealing primarily in clothing, grain, and livestock. They also operated a distillery, glass factory, and wood-processing plant. After the annexation of the Sudetenland to the Third Reich in Sept. 1938, the Jews left the city.

STRIEGAU   (Pol. Strzegom) Lower Silesia, Germany, today Poland. Jews lived in S. before 1350. In 1410, local rioters beat 73 Jews to death. In 1454, all the Jews were expelled and the Great Synagogue was converted into a church. J. settlement was renewed in the 19th cent. A cemetery was opened in 1815 and a prayer house was consecrated in 1846. In 1849, the J. pop. was 120, increasing to 150 in 1880 but subsequently declining. In 1927, the J. pop. was 94 and on the eve of the Nazi era it was 74. The Central Union (C.V.) was active in this period. With the J. pop. dropping further, the community was formally dissolved in 1936 and in 1937 numbered only 17. On *Kristallnacht* (9–10 Nov. 1938), J. business establishments were destroyed. In 1939 six Jews remained and by Nov. 1942 four Jews married to non-Jews. No further information is available about the fate of the community under Nazi rule. Presumably those Jews unable to emigrate perished after deportation.

STRIJEN   Zuid-Holland dist., Holland. A community was formed in the 19th cent. and numbered 52 in 1901. The J. pop. in 1941 was 16 (total 4,819). Fifteen were deported and perished in the Holocaust.

STROMIEC-ZAGAJNIK   Kielce dist., Poland. Jews are first mentioned in the late 19th cent. and numbered 189 (total 293) in 1921. The Germans deported the Jews to the Treblinka death camp via the Bialobrzegi ghetto in Oct. 1942.

STROPKOV   Slovakia, Czechoslovakia, today Republic of Slovakia. According to tradition, Jews were present in the late 17th cent. and expelled in 1700. A few J. families from Poland settled in the early 18th cent. and in the 1770s, Hasidim from Galicia began to arrive, soon dominating the community. More arrived in the 19th cent. as the J. pop. grew to 1,189 (total 2,531), maintaining nearly that level until WWII. Under the influence of its rabbis, Hasidism spread to other communities in eastern Slovakia, with Zanz Hasidism predominating. R. Yekutiel Yehuda Teitelbaum of Drohobycz led the hasidic congregation from 1833, R. Yehezkel Shraga Halberstam from 1870, and R. Avraham Shalom Halberstam in 1898–1933. A new synagogue was consecrated in 1894 with the old one becoming a hasidic *shtibl*. The local yeshiva had 50 students in 1928. The Zionists became active in the 1920s with Mizrachi the leading movement and Hashomer Hatzair, Bnei Akiva, and Betar attracting the youth. Agudat Israel with its own youth movement and Beth Jacob school for girls was influential in Orthodox circles. Jews served on the municipal council and owned 73 of the town's 94 business establishments along with 25 workshops and a number of factories. In 1939–40, the community opened a school for 200 children. The Slovakian authorities closed down J. businesses in 1941 and seized Jews for forced labor. Young J. men were deported to the Majdanek concentration camp and the women to Auschwitz in March–April 1942. On 24 May, families were deported, including 650 Jews to Rejowiec in the Lublin dist. (Poland), where most perished. The few dozen Jews with certificates of protection were dispersed in western Slovakia in May 1944. Twenty-six joined the partisans. Most of the 110 Jews in the postwar community left for Israel in 1949.

STRUEMPFELBRUNN   Baden, Germany. Jews are first mentioned in 1757. The community reached a peak pop. of 73 in 1860. At the end of the cent.

most were cattle traders. In 1933, 19 Jews remained (total pop. 612). On *Kristallnacht* (9–10 Nov. 1938), the synagogue and J. homes were heavily damaged and the J. guest house was destroyed while J. men were sent to the Dachau concentration camp. J. emigration began in 1938. The eight Jews remaining in Oct. 1940 were deported to the Gurs concentration camp and another three were deported after leaving S. Nine perished in the camps.

STRUNA   Vitebsk dist., Belorussia. S. was founded as a farm settlement and in 1930, 88 J. families were employed at a nearby kolkhoz started in 1929. The Germans arrived in July 1941, murdering the remaining Jews.

STRUSOW   Tarnopol dist., Poland. Jews are first mentioned in 1624, with the J. pop. growing to 735 (a quarter of the total) in 1900. The community was liquidated by the Germans toward the end of 1942, when most were sent to the Belzec death camp.

STRYJ   (Yid. Stry) Stanislawow dist., Poland, today Ukraine. Jews are first mentioned in 1563 and a J. quarter outside the city walls was established in 1575. In 1689 a synagogue was built within the city as townsmen became reconciled to the J. presence. Jews engaged in moneylending and tax farming, operated distilleries, flour mills, and salt mines, and traded in horses. In the 16th and 17th cents. the community came under the auspices of Przemsyl but in the 18th cent. it became independent with eight smaller communities attached to it. By the early 19th cent. most of S.'s more substantial merchants were Jews, dealing in grain and farm produce, cattle and wine J. artisans included tailors, furriers, carpenters, and blacksmiths. Three of Galicia's ten cloth printers were local Jews. Nonetheless, at mid-cent. two-thirds of the community, which had grown to 650 families, lived in straitened economic circumstances. The coming of the railroad in the second half of the 19th cent. contributed to the city's commercial and industrial development, with the J. pop. growing to 6,572 in 1890 and 10,718 (total 30,942) in 1910. Petty trade still prevailed among the Jews but accelerated building activity gave work to J. contractors, engineers, and carters. In

Jewish funeral in Stryj, Poland, 1905

1886, a devasting fire destroyed most of the town, leaving 7,000 homeless, most of them Jews. The Austrian J. philanthropist Baron Hirsch contributed liberally to the rehabilitation of the city and brick dwellings replaced the wooden ones. Among the community's illustrious rabbis were Aryeh Leib ben Yosef ha-Kohen Heller (1788-1815), author of *Ketzot ha-Hoshen*, and Yaakob Lorbeerbaum (1830-32), one of the great scholars of the age. Dr. Philip Fruchtman represented Jews and Poles in the Sejm from 1873 to 1909 and also served as S.'s mayor for a number of years. The leading social force in the community until WWI was the assimilationist Shomer Israel. A J. hospital was built and a J. boarding school opened. The Zionists became active in the 1880s and, with most children in public schools, initiated in 1903 the establishment of a school for supplementary Hebrew language instruction. A period of economic stagnation set in after WWI. The Polish Butchers' Law lowered the number of J. butchers from 60 to ten in 1937 and many shopkeepers were reduced to operating market stalls while others left the city. The Zionists now became the leading social and political force in the community. The J. pop. in 1932 was 10,869. In the late 1930s, antisemitism intensified and only the arrival of the Soviets in Sept. 1939 prevented a pogrom by local Ukrainians and peasants under the shortlived German occupation. The Soviets closed down J. institutions and nationalized J. businesses while craftsmen were organized into cooperatives. Hundreds of J. refugees were exiled to the Soviet Union along with a number of community leaders. Hundreds more joined the Red Army or left with the Soviets as the Germans reentered the city on 2 July 1941. A number of Jews were immediately murdered in retaliation for Soviet executions of Ukrainian nationalists. A *Judenrat* was appointed to regulate the provision of forced labor and Jews were evicted from coveted apartments by the Germans. In Sept. 1941 a mass *Aktion* was carried out in which over 1,000 Jews were murdered in the Holobotow forest outside the city. At the end of the year Jews were concentrated in the quarter later to be sealed off as a ghetto. In May 1942, some were sent to the Belzec death camp and others were murdered in the streets in a new *Aktion*. On 3 Sept., in another mass *Aktion* carried out by German and Ukrainian police with the assistance of Ukrainian nationalist youth, 5,000 Jews were rounded up for deportation to Belzec and 500 murdered in the ghetto. Another 2,000 were deported on 17-18 Oct. Sporadic

killing continued through the winter of 1942-1943 while others fell victim to starvation and disease. Around the end of Feb. 1943, 1,000 Jews were murdered inside the city and on 22 May another 1,000 were executed at the local cemetery. Final liquidation of the ghetto took place on 3 June when houses in the ghetto were systematically burned down to flush out Jews in hiding. The last *Judenrat* members and J. police were also murdered. Over the next two months, the Jews in local labor camps were also executed. Groups of Jews who escaped from the ghetto during the *Aktions* wandered through the nearby forests, many being murdered by Ukrainian nationalists. Only a few lived to see the liberation in Aug. 1944.

STRYKOW Lodz dist., Poland. J. wool traders settled in the late 17th cent. The S. hasidic dynasty founded here by R. Efrayyim Fishel (d. 1824) and his followers spread throughout Poland. The J. pop. was 1,799 in 1897 (59% of the total) and about 2,000 in 1939. Between the World Wars home workshops were set up by Jews, serving factories in Lodz and other towns. In Dec. 1939 S. was annexed to the Reich and the 1,600 Jews were expelled to Glowno, where they shared the fate of the local Jews. In April or May 1942 the remaining Jews were transferred to Brzezany and then to the Lodz ghetto.

STRYZHAVKA Vinnitsa dist., Ukraine. Jews numbered 272 in 1765 and 795 (total 2,200) in 1897. Entire families were wiped out in a pogrom in summer 1918. In 1926, under the Soviets, the J. pop. was 413. The Germans captured S. on 19 July 1941 and murdered 227 Jews, apparently all who remained, on 10 Jan. 1942.

STRZEGOWO Warsaw dist., Poland. Jews settled in the late 19th cent., dominating trade and growing to a pop. of 591 (total 1,853) in 1921. Between the World Wars J. merchants dealt in grain and livestock but many Jews were also peddlers and shopkeepers. Most of the J. political parties in Poland were represented. A Tarbut school was founded in the 1930s and Agudat Israel ran a Beth Jacob school for girls. With the advance of the Germans in Sept. 1939, the *Volksdeutsche* took over the town, targeting the Jews for persecution and abuse. A *Judenrat* was set up in summer 1940 under a regime of forced labor. A ghetto was established in Oct. 1941, with the J. pop. swelling to around 2,000 after 1,000 refugees arrived from Sierpc and Biezun on 6 Jan. 1942 and another 200 in flight from *Aktion*s in various other ghettoes. About a tenth of the ghetto pop. died under the difficult conditions that prevailed. Others were murdered by German police and *Volksdeutsche*. On 2 Sept. 1942, 20 men were publicly hanged on petty charges. On 2 Nov. the elderly were transferred to the Mlawa ghetto and from there deported to the Treblinka death camp. On 24 Nov. the rest of the J. pop. was brought to Mlawa and immediately sent to the gas chambers of Auschwitz with the local Jews.

STRZELISKA NOWE   Lwow dist., Poland, today Ukraine. Jews apparently arrived in the second half of the 17th cent. and from the mid-19th cent. the community was dominated by Belz Hasidism. A fire in 1913 and the tribulations of WWI contributed to reducing the J. pop. from 1,597 (total 2,672) in 1900 to 771 in 1921. The community was expelled to Bobrka by the Germans in the second half of 1942.

STRZELNO   Poznan dist., Poland. Jews first settled after the annexation to Prussia in 1772, with a community organized in the early 19th cent. as the J. pop. grew and prospered. Jews numbered 432 (total 4,000) in 1885, after which a process of emigration set in, reducing the J. pop. to 141 in 1910 and 61 in 1939. Nobel Prize-winning physicist Albert Michelson (1852–1931) was born in S. The few Jews remaining after the German invasion of Sept. 1939 were expelled by the Germans to General Gouvernement territory shortly after the occupation.

STRZELSK   Volhynia dist., Poland, today Ukraine. During the Holocaust the community of about 30 families was expelled by the Germans to Sarny for liquidation.

STRZEMIESZYCE WIELKIE   Kielce dist., Poland. Jews first settled in the late 19th cent. and numbered 1,304 (total 10,328) in 1921, with many working for the railroad or as agents in local chemical factories. A synagogue was established in 1908. The Zionists were active from the early 20th cent. After the German occupation of 6 Sept. 1939, a *Judenrat* and ghetto were established. Four hundred refugees arriving in April 1940 increased the J. pop. to 1,800. Jews were sent to labor camps in Silesia. Two ghetto shops established

by the *Judenrat* specialized in tailoring and recycling scrap iron. In early 1942, 500 Jews were sent to work in Bendzin; in May, 400 were deported to Auschwitz; and on 15 June, 1,000 were transported directly to the gas chambers there.

STRZYLKI   Lwow dist., Poland, today Ukraine. The J. pop. in 1921 was 242 (total 1,430). In Aug. 1942 the Jews were expelled by the Germans to Sambor en route to the Belzec death camp.

STRZYZOW   Lwow dist., Poland. Jews were present from the late 15th cent., constituting a majority of the pop. in the 18th cent. as well as one of the largest communities in the area, with a unique baroque-style synagogue that remained standing until WWII. J. traders were active in cattle trading in neighboring Frysztak, and some Jews worked as carters and porters. As artisans, the Jews were tailors, watchmakers, and locksmiths. The wealthy held leases connected with the estates of the local aristocracy. In the 19th cent., natural disasters set the community back: a cholera epidemic in 1860 and a fire in 1895 leaving 100 families homeless. The J. pop. stood at 859 in 1880 and 1,104 in 1921. R. Naftali Tzevi Ropshitser and R. Tzevi Elimelekh Shapira of Dynow served as local rabbis. The rivalry between their hasidic dynasties subsequently divided the community. Zionist activity commenced in 1907. Antisemitism made itself felt in a blood libel in 1882 and riots in 1898. Further violent disturbances occurred in 1918 and 1919. Between the World Wars, heavy taxation, boycotts, the competition of the Polish cooperatives, and the transfer of the provincial seat from the town eroded the economic position of the Jews. The Zionists expanded their activities, operating a training farm for 100 young pioneers in the 1933–37 period. The German *Wehrmacht* arrived on 10 Sept. 1939 and immediately inaugurated a reign of terror. A *Judenrat* was appointed. However, through 1940–41, the Jews were able to pursue their livelihoods to a certain extent and confinement in labor camps was rare, though conditions among the town's 300 refugees were severe. Another 1,000 were brought in from the Warsaw ghetto in April or May 1941 and temporarily camped in the area, benefiting from what little support the community could provide. All the 1,300 Jews in S. were expelled to the Rzeszow ghetto on 26–28 June 1942 after the sick and weak were murdered. Most were deported to the Belzec death camp in July.

STUBNIANSKE TEPLICE (Hung. Stubnyafurdo) Slovakia, Czechoslovakia, today Republic of Slovakia. Jews settled in the late 19th cent., organizing a Neologist community with a synagogue and cemetery in the early 20th cent. The J. pop. rose to a peak of 120 (total 372) in 1919 with most basing their livelihoods on the local mineral springs and operating hotels and restaurants. The Zionists and the J. National Party had wide support. After the establishment of the Slovakian state in March 1939, Jews were harassed by local Germans and pushed out of their businesses by the authorities. They were deported to the Lublin dist. (Poland) on 8 June 1942.

STUDENETS Mogilev dist., Belorussia. Jews numbered 179 (11% of the total) in 1880. A *beit midrash* was erected in the late 19th cent. In 1923, under the Soviets, the J. pop. was 85. The Germans occupied S. in Aug. 1941, murdering the few Jews still there.

STUDENITSA Kamenets-Podolski dist., Ukraine. Jews probably settled in the 17th cent. In 1703, Cossacks attacked them. Their pop. was 274 in 1765 and 556 (total 1,911) in 1897. In 1926, under the Soviets, it was 363. The Germans occupied S. in early July 1941. The Jews were executed at Staraya Ushitsa on 22 July 1942. Skilled workers were transferred with their families to the Kamenets-Podolski ghetto, where they perished.

STUHM (Pol. Sztum) East Prussia, Germany, today Poland. A J. cemetery in S. indicates the presence of Jews there in the 18th cent. A synagogue was dedicated in 1862. The J. pop. numbered 97 members in 1880; 106 in 1895; and 70 in 1925. When the Nazis took power in 1933, there were 46 Jews in S. By May 1939 there were only 13. No information about the fate of the Jews of S. under Nazi rule is available.

STULPICANI Bukovina, Rumania. The Jews numbered 609 in 1910 but only 151 in 1930. In June 1941, the J. pop. was transferred to Gura-Humorului and in Oct. deported to Transnistria. Few survived.

STUPAVA (Hung. Stomfa) Slovakia, Czechoslovakia, today Republic of Slovakia. Jews are mentioned in 1600 but were probably present in the late Middle Ages, perhaps as temporary residents. From 1722, the Jews lived under a special privilege from Count Palffy

that accorded them commercial and religious rights and served as a model for other communities in Slovakia. An influx of Moravian J. families increased the J. pop. to 128 in 1736. A synagogue was erected in 1803 and a J. elementary school was opened c. 1860. The J. pop. reached a peak of 819 (total 3,374) in 1828 but began to decline at mid-cent. as families left for the big cities, mainly Bratislava. In the early 20th cent., about half the Jews were shopkeepers and peddlers with a J. pop. of about 300. The Zionists became active before WWI. Mizrachi became the largest movement and Agudat Israel was also active after WWI. In 1940, the J. pop. was 191. In the Slovakian state, J. children were expelled from the public school and J. businesses were shut down while men were mobilized for forced labor. About 20 J. girls were deported to Auschwitz via Patronka on 25 March 1942. Young men were sent to the Majdanek concentration camp via Sered in early April and families were deported to Auschwitz and the death camps in the Lublin dist. (Poland) later in the spring. Most of the small number that remained behind were sent to the death camps in late summer 1944.

STUTTGART Wuerttemberg, Germany. A small J. community was in existence in the early 13th cent., living in a special quarter with a synagogue, cemetery, and other public facilities. Most of the Jews were burned to death in the Black Death massacres of 1348–49 and the survivors expelled. Jews were again present in small numbers in the late 14th cent., engaging in moneylending and trade until expelled about a hundred years later. Permanent J. settlement was not renewed until the early 19th cent., but individuals lived there previously, including Court Jews such as Joseph Suess Oppenheimer (1699–1738), Duke Alexander's financial advisor, Nathaniel Seidel, master of the Wuerttemberg mint in 1747, and the Seligmann brothers, who were granted the salt-mine concession for Wuerttemberg in 1759. In 1802 the Kaulla family founded the royal bank of Wuerttemberg, which became the most important financial institution in southern Germany. In 1807, 92 Jews were present. The community rose to a pop. of 3,015 in 1880 and 4,291 in 1910 (total 286,218). Unlike most other J. communities in Germany, the Jews of S. had a relatively high birthrate. Intermarriage was high, reaching a pre-WWI peak of 24% in 1907. The community engaged mainly in banking and large-scale commerce and operated facto-

Synagogue in Stuttgart, Germany, built in 1832

ries for producing textiles, shoes, furniture, and cigarettes and the first distilleries in the city. In 1873 an outburst of violence caused much damage to J. homes and stores until stopped by the army. With official recognition of the community in 1834, Joseph Maier (1797–1874) became Wuerttemberg dist. rabbi, instituting a new German-language prayer service. The Reform trend was continued by his successor, Moses Wassermann (1811–92), who successfully defended the J. faith in a defamation trial in Ulm (the Rohling Trial). Orthodox circles countered by forming the Adass Jeshurun congregation in 1878. A synagogue was consecrated in 1861 and a new cemetery was opened in 1876. Children studied at municipal schools and received their supplementary J. education in the community's religious school, where 592 students were enrolled in 1910–11. At that time, 20 J. charitable organizations were operating in the city, managing 378 separate welfare funds. S. was also the seat of Wuerttemberg Jewry's state-wide organizations. During WWI, in the wake of Cossack depredations, East European Jews settled in the city (the first having arrived from Czarist Russia in 1890 in flight from the pogroms). The J. pop. reached a peak of 4,548 (total 341,967) in 1925. There was a measure of antisemitic agitation in the Weimar period. J. communal life remained rich and active, with widespread youth organizations, though in the face of assimilation the Zionists made small impact, an exception being among the Orthodox youth of the Adass Jeshurun congregation. Assimilation and increasing intermarriage led to the founding of a *beit midrash (Lehrhaus)* in 1925 offering a variety of courses in Judaism and with such guests as Martin Buber engaging in dialogues with Christian theologians and university professors.

At the commencement of Nazi rule in 1933, the Jews maintained their strong economic position, owning 166 large wholesale and retail establishments and 106 factories. J. civil servants were fired from their jobs and the economic boycott was variously enforced against J. businesses. In Feb.–March 1936, Jews were severely beaten in the basement of Gestapo headquarters. By the end of 1937, 1,342 Jews had emigrated, including 180 children to Palestine within the framework of Youth Aliya. The community made great efforts to sustain its social and cultural life, with the Zionists now becoming more active and a J. elementary school opened in 1934 and enrolling 213 children in 1936–37. Vocational training and foreign-language courses were also opened. Karl Adler founded the J. Arts Council, which provided employment for J. artists. On *Kristallnacht* (9–10 Nov. 1938), the synagogue was set on fire, communal property was impounded, and J. stores were heavily damaged. Around 800 J. men were detained, some of them being sent to the Welzheim and Dachau concentration camps, and community institutions were shut down. In 1939, 2,093 Jews were evicted from their homes on the basis of a new regulation requiring Jews to vacate apartments rented from non-Jews. In 1940, Jews were subjected to forced labor in German munitions factories and in 1941 public prayer was banned. In 1940–41, 600–800 of the aged were transferred by the Germans to improvised old age homes throughout the country from which they were ultimately deported to the east. Mass deportations commenced on 1 Dec. 1941, when 1,000 Wuerttemberg Jews, including 318 from S. and its last 50 schoolchildren, were sent to the Riga ghetto as part of the SS plan to deport 50,000 German and Czech Jews to the east. Another 93 were part of a group of 350 Jews deported to Izbica in the Lublin dist. (Poland) on 26 April 1942, which included the last children in Wuerttemberg and the last doctors and nurses at J. hospitals. A third group of 49 of the sick and aged, with 13 from S., was dispatched directly to the gas chambers of Auschwitz on 13 July. On 22 Aug., 53 S. Jews were part of a consignment of 1,072 transported to the Theresienstadt ghetto and between 1 March 1943 and 14 Feb. 1945 a further 400–500 Wuerttemberg Jews were deported to Theresienstadt and Auschwitz. In all, 1,175 of the Jews of S.

were deported. At least 1,000 perished. After the war a new community was formed, numbering 1,176 in 1946, with most subsequently emigrating. About 350 Jews were living there in 1990.

STUTTGART-BAD CANSTATT Wuerttemberg, Germany. The J. settlement commenced in 1826, becoming a suburb of Stuttgart in 1905 but forming an independent community from 1871 to 1936. In 1876 a synagogue was completed where a Reform service was instituted with an organ and mixed choir, while the Orthodox minority worshiped with the Adass Jeshurun congregation in Stutttgart proper. Jews were active as manufacturers of textiles and corsets and as dealers in down. The Zionist writer and industrialist Leopold Marx (b. 1889) was an outstanding public figure in Wuerttemberg, founding the Stuttgart *Lehrhaus* with Otto Hirsch. The J. pop. grew to 484 in 1900 (total 26,497). In 1933, the J. pop. was 261. On *Kristallnacht* (9–10 Nov. 1938), the synagogue was burned down and J. men were detained at Dachau and other concentration camps. Most of the city's Jews managed to emigrate, leaving 18 at the outbreak of war. These were expelled to the east in 1941–44.

SUBACIUS (Yid. Subotch) Panevezys dist., Lithuania. Jews lived in S. in the 19th cent. and built a magnificent *beit midrash*. In 1897 the J. pop. was 376 (45% of the total). At the turn of the cent. many emigrated to South Africa and between the World Wars to the west, with a few to Palestine. In 1940 the J. pop. was 50 (7% of the total). After the German occupation of 1941, the Jews were persecuted by Lithuanian nationalists and all were killed at the nearby Ilciunai forest.

SUBATA (Yid. Shubitz, Subitz) Zemgale (Courland) dist., Latvia. A J. community existed in the early 19th cent., divided between Lithuanian Orthodoxy and Habad Hasidism. The J. pop. rose to a peak of 978 in 1897 (total 2,047), thereafter declining steadily. Jews were especially active in the flax trade. The Jews were expelled by the Russians in 1915 and with postwar emigration their number declined to 387 in 1935. A J. public school was opened after WWI with Yiddish and Hebrew as the languages of instruction and in 1930 a Russian-language J. school existed. The Germans captured the town in June 1941. In summer or fall 1941 all the Jews were murdered in a nearby forest together with a number of J. refugees from Lithuania, first the children before their parents' eyes, then the others.

SUBOTICA (Hung. Szabadka) Vojvodina dist., Yugoslavia. The first records of a J. presence date back to 1743. In 1775, permanent residence rights were granted to the Jews and a community took root. A synagogue was built in 1802 and functioned until it was replaced by a magnificent new synagogue in 1903. In the mid-19th cent. the Jews suffered economic repression and the community established welfare organizations for the needy. In 1867 the Jews received equal rights. This increased the prosperity and power of the community. In 1868 the community was represented at a national conference of Hungarian communities and joined the new movement of Reform Judaism. At the end of the 19th cent., the Orthodox Jews, who held separate services, constituted 10% of the community. It was the Orthodox community of S. that initiated the nationwide Association of Orthodox Communities in 1921. In 1900 the Jews numbered 3,026 in a total pop. of 83,593. From its establishment and until the Holocaust, the J. community's prominence in various sectors, such as trade, banking, and the free professions, exceeded its proportion in the general pop. (3%–6% on the average). During WWI, the community extended its welfare activities, volunteering in the hospitals, sending packages to soldiers, caring for widows and orphans, and feeding the needy. After WWI the community quickly improved its relations with the new Yugoslavian government. The government for its part curbed nascent antisemitism as Hungarian nationalists accused the Jews of betrayal and Yugoslavian and Serbian nationalists charged them with being pro-Hungarian. During these years and in the 1930s the J. economy improved and the Jews continued to play their part in trade, industry, and the professions. A high proportion of J. youth went on to higher education. J. cultural life also improved with organized activity in music, literature, popular entertainment, and sports. A J. hospital was opened in Aug. 1923, earning a nationwide reputation for the high level of its treatment and services. Prior to WWII J. aliens were expelled to Hungary, while refugees from Nazi Germany, Austria, Czechoslovakia, Poland, and Hungary swarmed to S. and received assistance from the community. Zionism developed prior to WWI and the local branch of the Zionist Organization was opened in 1921. In the 1930s about a dozen pioneers

emigrated to Palestine. Prior to the Holocaust, S. was the fourth largest J. community in Yugoslavia with 6,500 Jews in 1931 (total 100,058). In April 1941 the Hungarians entered S. The Jews were dismissed from public and most private positions and stores were seized. Many were taken for forced labor and others were tortured and forced to sell their property for a fraction of its value. From July 1941 the Hungarians struck at their opponents, including many J. partisans and underground activists who were operating in S. Most of the Jews arrested in these groups were executed or died in prisons and camps. In Feb. 1943 survivors of the forced labor battalions were taken into captivity by the Soviets as hostages and then freed to join a Yugoslavian brigade. On 20 March 1944, the German army entered S. and in April the remaining Jews were gathered into ghettoes. In June, the 3,200 remaining members of the community were deported to the death camps. Only a few managed to escape and join the partisans; several children were saved. About 320 Jews survived the death camps. On 10 Oct., S. was liberated and survivors of the death camps, partisan fighters, and released hostages began to return. Some 75% of the community's 6,000 Jews perished in the Holocaust. The Reform and Orthodox congregations were reestablished after the war and the community was speedily rehabilitated. In 1948, some 800 out of the 1,200 Jews there left for Israel.

SUCANY Slovakia, Czechoslovakia, today Republic of Slovakia. Jews were apparently present in the early 18th cent. The community began to grow significantly in the early 19th cent., establishing a synagogue and the first J. elementary school in the dist. After rising to 133 in 1828 and 266 (total 1,914) in 1880, the J. pop. commenced to decline steadily through emigration to the big cities. A new synagogue was built after a fire destroyed the old one in 1842 and the community formed a Neologist congregation later in the cent. Jews prospered economically, operating a number of factories before and after WWI. The Zionists became active between the World Wars with the young joining Hashomer Hatzair. In 1940, 106 Jews remained. The young were sent to Auschwitz and the Majdanek concentration camp at the end of March 1942; another 42 Jews were deported to the death camps of the Lublin dist. of Poland in early June.

SUCEAVA (Yid. Shutz) Bukovina, Rumania. Jews

first settled in the 15th cent. A permanent community existed in the early 18th cent. Prince Mihai Sturza granted the Jews some 140 acres of his land in perpetuity and it remained J. property even between the World Wars. In 1890 the J. pop. was 3,751 (36% of the total). During the last 20 years of the 19th cent. Jews were prominent in building, banking, landholding, and the professions. Jews also held senior positions on the municipal council. The first synagogue was built in the mid-18th cent. and up to the outbreak of WWII, 12 prayer houses served the community. Zionist activity began in the early 20th cent. and the first convention of all Zionist organizations in Bukovina was held in S. in 1902. The opening of the border between Bukovina and Rumania after WWI greatly improved the economic situation of the Jews. The J. political party and the Bund had branches in S. and in 1922 it was the seat of the Union of J. Communities in Bukovina. A J. high school was opened between the World Wars. From 1928 the Zionist parties controlled the community council and in 1929 they received 38% of the votes in the municipal council. In 1940, antisemitic persecution and killings began when S. became the center of government and army headquarters. The J. pop. in 1941, was 3,253. In July 1941, thousands of Jews expelled from the surrounding towns and villages found refuge in S. In June 1941, 150 Jews were taken as hostages and imprisoned in the synagogue. Acts of terror were stepped up in Aug.–Sept. 1941 and on 10 Oct., the Jews of S. were deported via Atachi to Transnistria. Some 800 Jews succeeded in getting to Shargorod and thus survived.

SUCHA Cracow dist., Poland. The community began to consolidate after 1860 with the end of residence restrictions in Galicia and the establishment of the town as a railroad junction. Hasidism (Bobow, Belz, and Czchow) dominated the community and together with traditional circles suppressed Zionist activity. In 1890 the J. pop. stood at 188 (less than 5% of the total) and in 1921 at 332. Many fled in WWI, though the Russians never took the town. In Nov. 1918, J. property was looted in local rioting and in the 1930s anti-J. agitation and the competition of the Polish cooperative seriously hurt the J. economy. Under the German occupation from 4 Sept. 1939, refugees nearly doubled the J. pop. to 600 in 1941. In June 1942 around 220 were deported to Auschwitz after a selection. Of the others, 300 were employed at the waterworks in Biel-

sko, mostly engaged in rechanneling the Skawa River. Seemingly, living conditions were ideal but the illusion was shattered in May 1943 when mothers and children were deported to Auschwitz together with the weak and old (120 in number); the others were dispersed to various labor camps.

SUCHA BRONKA (Hung. Szuhabaranka) Carpatho-Russia, Czechoslovakia, today Ukraine. J. settlement began in the early 19th cent. with the J. pop. standing at 14 in 1830 and 50 (total 803) in 1880. It rose to 113 in 1921 under the Czechoslovakians and then dropped to 107 in 1941. The Hungarians arrived in March 1939, drafting a number of Jews into labor battalions and sending them to forced labor camps. In late July 1941, a few families without Hungarian citizenship were expelled to Kamenets-Podolski and murdered. The rest were deported to Auschwitz on 19 May 1944.

SUCHEDNIOW Kielce dist., Poland. Jews settled in the late 19th cent., numbering 912 (total 4,105) in 1921. The Orthodox dominated the community, but between the World Wars the Zionists were also active. The Germans captured S. on 7 Sept. 1939, setting up a *Judenrat* under a regime of forced labor and exacting an exorbitant "contribution" from the community. In Feb. 1941, 2,000 refugees from Plock arrived and in June a ghetto was established. By Aug. 1942, new refugees increased the J. pop. to over 4,000. After a selection for the Skarzysko-Kamienna labor camp on 22 Sept. 1943, 3,000 Jews were deported to the Treblinka death camp. Poles helped about 30 remaining Jews hide from the Germans. In Sept. 1944, Poles from S. also helped hide members of the J. Fighting Organization (Z.O.B.) after the Warsaw uprising.

SUCHOSTAW Tarnopol dist., Poland, today Ukraine. The community grew to 614 (total 2,282) in 1880 but fell to 378 after the tribulations of WWI. Husyatin-Ruzhin Hasidism prevailed, with the Zionists active between the World Wars. The Jews were expelled by the Germans to neighboring Chorostkow in 1942 and were eventually killed.

SUCHOWOLA Bialystok dist., Poland. Jews first arrived in the 17th cent. and in 1698 were accorded the right to set up stalls in the market and build houses by King Augustus the Saxon. J. trade developed further

15th cent. synagogue Suchostaw, Poland

upon annexation to Prussia following the Third Partition of Poland in 1795, with Jews dominating the marketplace and the prosperous among them building a new quarter called "The Hill." Throughout the 19th cent. the J. grain trade with Germany and Russia expanded and Jews set up a steam-operated flour mill. In 1897 the J. pop. reached 1,944 (total 3,203). In 1921 the J. pop was 1,262 (total 2,457). Haskala made inroads at the end of the cent., producing a reformed *heder* and a drama circle. During the German occupation of WWI the Jews were subjected to forced labor and in 1920 were robbed and persecuted by General Haller's Polish troops. In the aftermath of the war, economic conditions deteriorated and most Jews were reduced to petty trade with the peasant pop. and required assistance from the Joint Distribution Committee. A number of the young emigrated to Palestine through the Hehalutz organization. Most children attended a Tarbut Hebrew school. With the arrival of refugees after the outbreak of WWII, the J. pop. rose from 1,500 in 1937 to 5,100 in 1942. After the arrival of the Germans in late June 1941, the Jews were terrorized by Polish mobs until confined to a ghetto. On 2 Nov.

1942, the Jews were transferred to the Kelbasin transit camp near Grodno and on 16 Feb. 1943 they were deported to Auschwitz.

SUDAK Crimea, Russia, today Ukraine. A J. community existed in the tenth cent. The modern community was probably founded in the late 19th cent. In 1939, the J. pop. of S. was 58 (total 3,246). In all the area there were only 79 Jews. A few Jews were murdered after the arrival of the Germans on 2 Nov. 1941. Another 25 were murdered in Feb. 1942 and the last group of 75 in 1944, shortly before the Red Army liberated S.

SUDARGAS (Yid. Sudarg) Sakiai dist., Lithuania. Jews first settled here at the turn of the 19th cent. and numbered 627 in 1856. Between the World Wars most of the J. youth moved to Kovno. The J. pop. in 1940 was about 30 families. All the Jews were killed after the German occupation of 1941.

SUDILKOV Kamenets-Podolski dist., Ukraine. Jews settled in the 17th cent. In 1705–06 they were victimized in Cossack attacks. Their pop. was 397 in 1765 and 2,713 (total 5,551) in 1897. Pogroms were staged against the Jews in 1917 and 1919. In 1939, under the Soviets, the J. pop. was 1,311. The Germans captured S. in early July 1941. On 20 Aug., they murdered 471 Jews. The rest were expelled to the Shepetovka ghetto, where most perished.

SUDZHA Kursk dist., Russia. Jews probably settled in the early 20th cent. and numbered 53 in 1926. The few remaining Jews were murdered by the Germans after their arrival on 18 Oct. 1941.

SUECHTELN Rhineland, Germany. A protected J. family was present in 1663, increasing to two families in the early 18th cent. and six in the late 18th cent. In the first half of the 19th cent., the J. pop. was about 25. It grew to 51 (total 9,371) in 1905 and then fell to 22 in June 1933. The community maintained a cemetery from 1845. Most Jews left in the Nazi period. In Dec. 1941 and July 1942, the six remaining Jews were deported to the east.

SUFLION (Soufli) Thrace, Greece. A small number of Jews lived in S. in the early 20th cent. The J. pop. in 1940 was 40. In May 1943, 32 Jews were deported to Auschwitz via Salonika on 9 May.

SUGENHEIM Middle Franconia, Germany. Jews are known from the early 17th cent. and a synagogue was built in 1756. At the time, the Jews inhabited a special quarter (*Judengasse*). In 1837 the J. pop. stood at 160 (total 760), dropping to 42 in 1933 and 15 by 1938. On *Kristallnacht* (9–10 Nov. 1938), the synagogue and J. school were vandalized. The remaining Jews left by 11 Jan. 1939. The five Jews of the attached community of Ullstadt (a community of 40–50 in the first half of the 19th cent. whose cemetery served 11 other communities) left in 1934.

SUHL Saxony, Germany. Evidence of Jews in S. dates from 1315. In spite of several expulsions, J. settlement was continuously renewed. At the beginning of the 18th cent., Jews were restricted to a settlement outside the town gates. The first J. resident was allowed to acquire a house within the city only in 1848. In 1856, the ten J. families from S. set up a community together with the Jews of Heinrich. In 1880, the community numbered 91, establishing a cemetery in 1905 and a synagogue in 1906. By the time the Nazis assumed

Market day in Sudilkov, Ukraine

power in 1933, the community numbered 120 (about 40 households). The general boycott of 1 April 1933 led to the first emigrations. By April 1938, there were only 24 J. households in S. On *Kristallnacht* (9–10 Nov. 1938), the synagogue was burned down, and in 1939 only 20–30 Jews still lived in S. Those who did not manage to escape had to move to "J. houses." All were deported in 1942, with the exception of two Jews who were probably protected by marriage to non-Jews.

SUKHARI Mogilev dist., Belorussia. An organized community with a *beit midrash* existed in the 19th cent. In 1897, the J. pop. was 446 (86% of the total). A kolkhoz supporting 24 J. families was founded in 1930. The Germans arrived in July 1941, probably murdering the Jews in the fall.

SUKHINICHI Smolensk dist., Russia. Jews probably settled in the late 19th cent., numbering 66 in 1926 and 98 (total 10,620) in 1939. After their arrival on 7 Oct. 1941, the Germans murdered the Jews, with 23 families from S. and its environs executed in a last *Aktion* on 25 Dec.

SULEJOW (Yid. Silow) Lodz dist., Poland. Jews were not permitted to live in S. until the early 19th cent. They were subjected to blood libels and pogroms but eked out a living from the limestone quarries nearby. In 1897 the J. pop. was 1,881 (40% of the total). Between the World Wars the Jews provided services to vacationers in the surrounding villages. Eighty of the 93 houses belonging to Jews, and the synagogue, were destroyed in German bombardments at the beginning of WWII with numerous casualties; many fled to nearby villages. The influx of refugees increased the J. community to 1,577 by July 1942. All were expelled to Piotrkow in Oct. 1942 and on 14–21 Oct. deported to the Treblinka death camp.

SULINGEN Hanover, Germany. The community numbered 18 in 1814 and grew to 78 (5% of the total) in 1871. It maintained a synagogue and an elementary school. Jews living in Kirchdorf, Scholen, Varrel, and three other townships belonged to the community, which dominated the meat trade. Of the 31 Jews registered in 1933, 22 emigrated, mostly to Argentina, South Africa, and Palestine. In June 1938, S. was declared "free of Jews" (*judenrein*). The six re-

maining Jews eventually perished in the Riga and Lublin ghettoes.

SULITA (I) Bukovina, Rumania. In 1941, the J. community, numbering some 30 families, was transferred to Campulung and then to Transnistria. Few survived.

SULITA (II) Moldavia dist., Rumania, today Republic of Moldova. A J. community existed here in 1820. In 1866, 80% of the Jews were artisans and the rest merchants. The J. pop. in 1899 numbered 1,830 (63% of the total). On 19 March 1907, 3,000 peasants entered the city and destroyed J. property. The Iron Guard exiled the community leadership to Targu-Jiu in fall 1940. In June 1941, the J. pop. of 1,096 was deported to Harlau and Botosani. About a third of the community returned after the war.

SULMIERZYCE (Yid. Silmarzitz) Lodz dist., Poland. Thirteen J. families lived here in 1842. In 1921 the J. pop. was 157 (total 1,133). At the outbreak of WWII the 30 J. families fled.

SULZBACH Saar, Germany. The J. pop. was 31 in 1895 and 45 (total 0.5%) in 1927. In 1935, 106 Jews trying to reach France sought temporary refuge in the area. Two Jews remained in 1939. Five died in the Holocaust.

SULZBACH-ROSENBERG Upper Palatinate, Germany. Jews possibly arrived when the town was founded in the mid-13th cent. The community was destroyed in the Black Death persecutions of 1348–49 and only reestablished in the mid-17th cent. In the 1670s Jews expelled from Vienna began settling and in 1685 the 12 J. families in S. were granted a charter of privileges. In 1687 a synagogue was dedicated. A local printing press began publishing Hebrew books in 1669 and achieved great fame in the J. world under the management of R. Moshe Bloch (1684–1694) and the Frankel-Arnstein family (1694–1851). Its edition of the *Zohar* and its prayer books enjoyed wide circulation. In the 18th cent. a number of Court Jews were active in the town, including Jacob Josef, who served as *parnas* in 1722–70, and Nathan Schwabacher, who replaced him. In 1822 a devastating fire destroyed the synagogue and left 40 J. families homeless. A new synagogue was built in 1827 and a J. public school was opened in 1837. The J. pop. stood at 164 in 1871 (down from a peak of 336 in 1810) and dropped steadily to a total of nine Jews in 1933 (total pop. 6,800). The synagogue was impounded in 1934 and turned into a museum. Its religious articles were sent to Amberg and destroyed on *Kristallnacht* (9–10 Nov. 1938). Five Jews emigrated in 1934–36. The last Jew was sent to the Theresienstadt ghetto on 21 Jan. 1943.

SULZBUERG Upper Palatinate, Germany. The first settlers were refugees from the Rindfleisch massacres of 1298 (from Neumarkt, Berching, and Freystadt). They engaged in moneylending and the cattle trade under the tolerant rule of the ducal house of Wolfstein (until annexation to Bavaria in 1740). The community was virtually destroyed in the Thirty Years War (1618–48) and numbered 12 families in 1705. In 1756 legal residence was limited to 30 families. In the second half of the 18th cent. the Jews suffered from numerous economic restrictions, forcing them to engage mainly in petty trade and the cattle business. A new synagogue was dedicated in 1799 and a J. public school was opened in 1835. In 1867 the J. pop. was 180 (total 759) and thereafter declined steadily to 16 in 1933. Five emigrated by *Kristallnacht* (9–10 Nov. 1938), when the synagogue was vandalized. Seven were expelled to Piaski in the Lublin dist. (Poland) on 2 April 1942 and three to the Theresienstadt ghetto on 23 Sept. 1942.

SULZBURG Baden, Germany. Jews arrived in the early 16th cent. and were expelled in 1615 with the rest of the Jews of the region. The J. settlement was renewed in 1716 by four families expelled from Switzerland and Alsace. From 1727 to 1827, S. was the seat of the chief rabbinate of Upper Baden. Throughout the 18th and 19th cents. the Cahan and Weil families stood at the head of the community. Gustav Weil (1798–1889), the noted Orientalist, was the first J. lecturer to receive tenure at Heidelberg University without converting. In 1823 a synagogue was consecrated and at the J. elementary school English was taught to prepare the young for emigration to the U.S. Anti-J. rioting occurred during the revolutionary disturbances of 1848 and on the eve of J. emancipation in 1862. The J. pop. grew steadily to a peak of 416 in 1864 (total 1,296) but then declined sharply, numbering 84 in 1933. Under the Nazis the economic boycott was sys-

tematically enforced, with the licences of J. cattle traders revoked and Jews forced to liquidate their businesses. On *Kristallnacht* (9–10 Nov. 1938), the synagogue and cemetery were vandalized and Jews were sent to the Dachau concentration camp. In all, 47 Jews emigrated and ten moved to other German cities. The last 27 Jews were deported to the Gurs concentration camp on 22 Oct. 1940. Eight others were sent to concentration camps after leaving S. In all, 24 perished.

SUMEG Zala dist., Hungary. Jews are mentioned in 1699. A J. school was opened in 1850 and a synagogue was erected in 1866. The J. pop. was 302 in 1880 and 296 in 1930. In mid-May 1944, the Jews were brought to the Zalaegerszeg ghetto and on 4 July deported to Auschwitz. The community was reestablished after the war, but most left by 1958.

SUMPERK Moravia, Czechoslovakia. Jews were probably present in the first half of the 15th cent. They were expelled in 1585 following an outbreak of the plague. The J. pop. was 162 in 1900 and 199 (total 15,718) in 1930. In Sept. 1942, the Jews were deported to the Theresienstadt ghetto via Ostrava. Nearly all were then sent on to Maly Trostinec (Belorussia). Only one survived.

SUMY Sumy dist., Ukraine. Jews were allowed to trade at the town's fairs under various restrictions from 1835 and began settling in 1858. In 1897, they numbered 797 (total 27,564) and in 1926, 2,418. In 1917, a Hebrew elementary school with an enrollment of 150 children was founded. In the same year, three Jews were elected to the municipal council. The J. pop. dropped to 1,851 in 1939. The Germans captured S. on 10 Oct. 1941. On 5 Dec. 1941, the Jews were registered, made to wear the yellow badge, and ordered to report for forced labor. On 6–7 Feb. 1942, 1,000 Jews were murdered near a brickyard outside the city. Another 102 held in the local jail were murdered in May–June 1942. In March 1943, the Hungarian army brought a J.-Hungarian company of over 250 workers to the city. All were executed within a few days. In 1959, 1,300 Jews were living in S.

SUPRASL Bialystok dist., Poland. The first Jews settled in the late 17th cent. From the mid-19th cent. Jews worked in the textile industry developed by German entrepreneurs. A new brick synagogue with stained glass windows was built in the 1860s. The J. pop. grew to 538 (total 3,091) in 1878. A weaving mill purchased in the early 20th cent. by the Citron family became the largest factory in the region, employing 700–1,300 workers. Other J.-owned textile plants began to develop. On the eve of WWI, Jews expanded into the lumber industry, setting up two sawmills. After WWI, most of the J. political parties were active, as were the Zionist youth movements. A Tarbut Hebrew school was the center of the community's cultural life. The revival of the textile industry and increasing tourism assured full employment for the Jews despite the general economic crisis in Poland. In 1921 the J. pop. was 390 (total 2,322). The Germans arrived on 28 June 1941, murdering 13 Jews within a month and instituting a regime of forced labor. On 2 Nov. 1942, apprised of an immanent *Aktion*, 270 of the town's 400 Jews fled to the forest. The rest were transferred to the old Polish cavalry barracks near Bialystok and soon deported to the Treblinka death camp. The Jews in the forest formed the Kadima partisan group under the command of Sasha Suchaczewski of Warsaw. Others died fighting in the Bialystok ghetto uprising.

SUPURUL DE JOS (Hung. Alsoszouor) N. Transylvania dist., Rumania. Jews settled in the late 19th cent. The J. pop. in 1930 was 118 (7% of the total). A J. community also existed in the neighboring village of Supurul de Sus (Hung. Felsoszopor) which in 1920 numbered 82. In May 1944, both communities were transferred to the Simleul Silvaniei ghetto and then deported to Auschwitz.

SURANY Slovakia, Czechoslovakia, today Republic of Slovakia. Jews were apparently present in the 17th cent. Their numbers grew significantly in the late 18th cent., reaching 211 in 1787 and 409 in 1840. R. Feivl Plaut served the community in 1850–93, making S. a national center of religious life with a famous yeshiva. A Great Synagogue was built in the 1820s and a J. elementary school for 70–80 students was opened in the 1850s. R. Yehuda Gruenwald, one of Hungary's greatest rabbis, succeeded R. Plaut. The community's last rabbi was Meir Yehuda Frei (1903–44). During his ministry, 31 settlements came under the auspices of the local rabbinate and enrollment at the yeshiva increased to 300, with many coming from various coun-

tries. From 1900 through WWII, the J. pop. was 700–800 (10–15% of the total). Owing to R. Frei's opposition, the Zionist movement was limited in influence, although Bnei Akiva operated from the 1920s and the Maccabi sports club was active. An Agudat Israel branch was opened in 1919. Jews were prominent in trade, particularly in farm produce, lumber, building materials, and clothing, and owned most of the town's business establishments. The Hungarians annexed the town in Nov. 1938, undermining J. livelihoods and mobilizing men for forced labor. This reduced the J. pop. to 570 in 1941. On the arrival of the Germans in March 1944, 524 Jews remained. In late May, 400 Hungarian gendarmes rounded them up and confined them in an improvised ghetto near the Great Synagogue. On 10 June, 1,115 Jews from S. and its environs were transferred to the central ghetto in Nove Zamky. From there, on 14 June, they were deported to Auschwitz.

SURAZH (I) Bialystok dist., Poland. Jews first appeared in the 16th cent., remaining until the town secured a *de non tolerandis Judaeis* privilege in the 17th cent. Only a handful were present in 1800, forming an organized community in the course of the 19th cent. and reaching a peak pop. of 368 (total 1,599) in 1897. Thereafter the J. pop. dropped sharply through emigration, mainly to the U.S. and Argentina, leaving 120 in 1921 and 40 when the Germans arrived in June 1941. In spring 1942, the 330 surviving Jews from the area were concentrated in the J.-owned hide-processing plant in the town and from there taken out for execution.

SURAZH (II) Oriol dist., Russia. Jews probably settled in the late 18th cent. Their pop. rose from 229 in 1802 to 1,652 in 1847 and 2,398 (total 4,000) in 1897. Two synagogues were in use in 1870. Most Jews engaged in petty trade and crafts. Jews were beaten and robbed in a pogrom staged in Oct. 1905 and again victimized in 1918 at the hands of Red Army soldiers. A J. boys' school was in operation in 1910. In 1939, under the Soviets, the J. pop was 2,052. The Germans occupied S. on 17 Aug. 1941. The Jews were confined in a ghetto and in March 1942 about 700 were executed at the village of Kislovka. After the war, the bodies were disinterred and reburied in a common grave in the J. cemetery.

SURAZHI Vitebsk dist., Belorussia. J. settlement

commenced in the late 18th cent. The J. pop. grew from 848 in 1863 to 1,246 (total 2,731) in 1897. In 1905, Jews were attacked in a pogrom. A state J. school emphasizing vocational training was in operation in the early 20th cent. Red Army soldiers staged another pogrom in 1918, during the Russian civil war. In the mid-1920s, under the Soviets, 31 J. breadwinners earned their livelihoods in crafts and 20 in agriculture. A J. elementary school was attended by 100 children. In 1939, the J. pop. was 461. The Germans occupied S. on 12 July 1941. On 2 Aug., 700 Jews, including refugees from Vitebsk and Yanovichi, were led to pit filled with explosives and blown up.

SURDUC N. Transylvania dist., Rumania. Jews settled in the late 18th cent. In 1930 the J. pop. was 125 (10% of the total). In May 1944 the community was transferred to the Simleul Silvaniei ghetto and in June deported to Auschwitz.

SURTY Slovakia, Czechoslovakia, today Republic of Slovakia. Jews probably settled in the first half of the 18th cent. Their pop. grew steadily after the arrival of Galician refugees in the first half of the 19th cent., reaching 171 (total 1,037) in 1919. In 1944, after the German occupation, 100 Jews remained. They were deported to Auschwitz in May.

SUSICE Bohemia, Czechoslovakia. Jews are mentioned in 1562 but a J. community was only established in the mid-17th cent. In 1692, the Jews were forced to live in a special quarter and wear distinctive clothing. A synagogue was erected in 1659–60 (burning down in 1707). A new synagogue was built in 1859. After the 1866 riots in Bohemia and in S., anti-J. incidents proliferated. In the early 20th cent., Jews helped develop the town's well-known match industry. Their pop. rose to 300 in 1860 but then declined steadily to 112 (total 6,856) in 1930. The synagogue was closed down in Oct. 1941 and the remaining Jews were deported to the Theresienstadt ghetto via Klatovy in Nov. 1942. Most were sent to Auschwitz in Sept. 1943.

SUVAINISKIS (Yid. Suvainishok) Rokiskis dist., Lithuania. Jews lived here from the late 18th cent. In 1897 the J. pop. was 684 (80% of the total). A Hebrew school operated between the World Wars. For economic reasons, many emigrated to the U.S., South Africa, and Palestine. In 1930 the J. pop. was 200. All the Jews were killed after the German occupation of 1941.

SUWALKI Bialystok dist., Poland. The J. community originated in the beginning of the 19th cent. and by 1897 totaled 5,747. It was one of the most important communites in the region and distinguished rabbis officiated there, including the proto-Zionist R. Shemuel Mohilewer. In 1859, a J. hospital was established. Jews from S. participated in the Polish uprising of

Market square in Suvainiskis, Lithuania

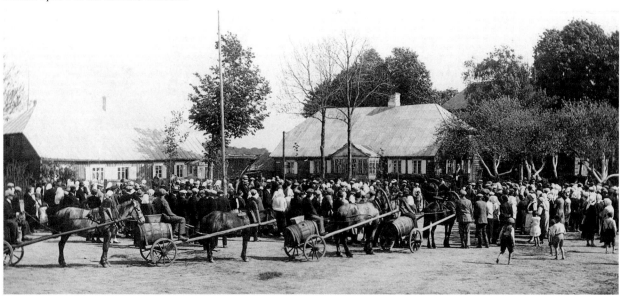

1863. War damages and economic conditions during WWI caused many Jews to flee S., a large number of whom did not return. The period between the World Wars was marked by efforts at economic recovery, which were hampered at times by antisemitism. Politically, the community was split between the Zionists, the ultra-Orthodox Agudat Israel, and the socialist Bund. In the 1924 community elections the Zionists won control of the council, but in 1931 Agudat Israel took over. In city council elections in 1925, the Jews won eight of the 33 seats and similar numbers in the 1935 and 1939 elections. In 1931 the J. pop. was 5,811 (27% of the total). The Germans entered S. on 9 Oct. 1939 and began kidnaping Jews for forced labor. In Nov., some 3,000 succeeded in fleeing to Lithuania, where most were killed in June 1941; 3,000 went to various places in the Soviet Union and 2,000 were expelled to Lublin. The fate of the last group was the same as that of other Jews there: most perished. After the war, a few dozen returned to S. In 1957, 11 Jews remained.

SVALAVA (Hung. Szolyva) Carpatho-Russia, Czechoslovakia, today Ukraine. Jews probably settled in the early 19th cent., numbering 45 in 1830 and 319 (total 1,664) in 1880. The community appointed its own rabbi in the 1880s and later opened a *talmud torah* and elementary school. Among the many charitable institutions maintained by the community was a

Bikkur Holim society. In 1921, after the establishment of the Czechoslovakian Republic, the J. pop. rose to 1,099, increasing to 1,423 (total 8,400) in 1941. Most Jews earned their livelihoods in trade (about 60 business establishments) and crafts (26 workshops). Seven factories and a bank were also in J. hands. There were professionals (a doctor and pharmacist) as well as public officials, clerical workers, and commercial agents. The Zionists and the J. National Party were very active, with Hashomer Hatzair, Bnei Akiva, and Betar influential among the young. The Hungarians occupied S. in March 1939, persecuting the Jews and undermining their livelihoods. In 1940, 150 Jews were drafted into labor battalions, some for forced labor, others for service on the eastern front, where many were killed. In late July or early Aug. 1941, a number of J. families without Hungarian citizenship were expelled to Kamenets-Podolski and murdered. On 22 May 1944, over 1,000 Jews were deported to Auschwitz. Some Jews joined the Czechoslovakian army organized in the Soviet Union and fought against the Germans. After the war a few dozen survivors returned but most subsequently left for Czechoslovakia.

SVATOVO (until 1923, Svatovo Luchka) Voroshilovgrad dist., Ukraine. Jews probably arrived in the early 20th cent., numbering 120 (total 10,799) in 1939. The Germans arrived on 9 July 1942, murdering

The Suwalki soccer team, Poland, 1917–18

the few remaining Jews along with 33 confined in the local insane asylum.

SVATY BENADIK   Slovakia, Czechoslovakia, today Republic of Slovakia. Jews numbered over 100 in the 1880s, maintaining a synagogue and cemetery. Sixty-two remained in 1940, most of them deported to the death camps in 1942.

SVATY JUR   (Hung. Szentgyorgy; Yid. Yergen) Slovakia, Czechoslovakia, today Republic of Slovakia. There is evidence of J. settlement in the Middle Ages. In 1529, the Jews were expelled following a blood libel in nearby Pezinok. They were present again in the late 17th cent. and in 1784 reached a pop. of 50 families. A synagogue was erected c. 1790. R. Moshe Schick, one of the leaders of Orthodox Jewry in the Austro-Hungarian Empire, served the community in 1837–61 and also headed a yeshiva there. The Jews reached a peak pop. of 400 in the 1840s. Many left for the big cities starting in the 1870s, reducing the J. pop. to 200 (total 3,500) in the early 20th cent. The Zionists became active after WWI, with Mizrachi the leading party. In May 1939, after the establishment of the Slovakian state, German youth vandalized the synagogue. In early 1942, 77 Jews remained. Most were deported to the death camps in March–June 1942. Two hundred young Jews were brought in to a local labor camp in 1943. Many managed to join the partisans. After the suppression of the Slovakian national uprising in 1944, the Germans deported the rest to Auschwitz and other concentration camps.

SVATY KRIZ   (Hung. Garamszentkereszt) Slovakia, Czechoslovakia, today Republic of Slovakia. Jews probably arrived in the 1860s, forming an organized Neologist community in the 1880s with a pop. of 30–50 (3–4% of the total) up to WWII. A synagogue was consecrated in 1888 and the community's only rabbi, Avraham Tiroler, had about 30 small communities under his jurisdiction. Most of the 65 Jews present in 1942 were deported on 9 June via Novaky to death camps in the Lublin dist. (Poland).

SVEDASAI   (Yid. Svadushtsh) Utena dist., Lithuania. By the 18th cent. there existed an established J. community in S. The J. pop. in 1897 was 528 (37% of the total). Relations with non-Jews were good

thanks to the local priest. When Jews left during WWI their homes were not looted. Between the World Wars the community was divided between Habad Hasidim and opponents of Hasidism. Zionist groups were active and many of the young emigrated to Palestine. The J. pop. in 1940 was about 400 (33% of the total). Under the Soviets (1940–41) businesses were nationalized and Zionist activity outlawed. All the Jews were killed after the German occupation of 26 July 1941.

SVEKSNA   (Yid. Shvekshne) Taurage dist., Lithuania. Jews first settled in the 17th cent. In the 1880s many emigrated, mainly to the U.S.. The J. pop. in 1897 was 974 (53% of the total). The community maintained two *hadarim*, a *talmud torah* and a yeshiva. In municipal elections after WWI, two of 21 council members were Jews. The 1930s were characterized by the boycott of J. businesses, antisemitic vandalism, and a blood libel. Although the community was ultra-Orthodox, many of the young were Zionists. The J. pop. in 1940 was about 500 (25%). After the German invasion in June 1941, the Jews were subjected to various abuses. Some were taken to the Silute labor camp while the remainder were confined to a ghetto in S. On 22 Sept. 1941 they were murdered. Those who survived the labor camp were taken in the end of July 1943 to Auschwitz and Warsaw and then later to the Dachau concentration camp.

SVERDLOVKA   Dnepropetrovsk dist., Ukraine. S. was a village with 115 J. families (total 130) in 1934 and attached to a J. rural council (soviet) with jurisdiction over another four kolkhozes. A regional elementary school was in operation there. The few Jews who had neither fled nor been evacuated prior to the German occupation of mid-Aug. 1941 perished in the Holocaust.

SVERZHEN   Gomel dist., Belorussia. The J. pop. was 405 in 1847 and 635 (total 1,056) in 1897. Most Jews were engaged in petty trade and crafts. In 1925, under the Soviets, five J. families formed an agricultural cooperative. A J. kolkhoz was founded near the town in 1927 and employed 19 families in 1930. The Germans occupied S. in late Aug. 1941, probably murdering the Jews in Dec.

SVETLA NAD SAZAVOU   Bohemia, Czechoslovakia. Jews probably settled at the turn of the 17th cent,

Jews of Sveksna welcoming president of Lithuania on his visit to the town, 1926 (Beth Hatefutsoth Photo Archive, Tel Aviv)

building a synagogue in 1889 and reaching a pop. of 107 (total 2,261) in 1921. In 1930, 79 remained. In 1942, the Jews were deported to the Theresienstadt ghetto together with the Jews of Prague and from there transported to the death camps of Poland.

SVETLOVICHI Gomel dist., Belorussia. The J. pop. was 114 (total 717) in 1897. In 1930, under the Soviets, 29 J. families were employed at a nearby kolkhoz. In 1939, the J. pop. was 173. The Germans arrived in Aug. 1941, probably murdering all the Jews in late Nov.

SVIATSK Oriol dist., Russia. A J. community existed in the late 18th cent. Its pop. was 290 (total 2,389) in 1897, rising to 588 in 1926 under the Soviets. The Germans occupied S. in Aug. 1942, murdering the town's 158 Jews on 3 Oct. 1941 and 25–26 Jan. 1942, most at an old brickyard.

SVIERZEN-NOVY Nowogrodek dist., Poland, today Belarus. Jews were probably present in small numbers in the second half of the 17th cent. Until

WWI Jews were in the habit of renting farm land in eastern Prussia from the spring to the fall (between Passover and Sukkot) and raising vegetables for sale there. After WWI, with most homes destroyed, the J. pop. dropped to 425 (total 1,195), from an 1897 peak of 732. Between the World Wars most children studied at the Tarbut Hebrew school in Stolowicze and the Zionists were active locally. The Germans arrived on 27 June 1941, instituting a regime of forced labor and extortion. In Oct., 31 Jews were murdered and the rest confined to a ghetto. In Nov., 380 women, children, and old people were executed at the J. cemetery. The 220 workers left alive were joined by 130 young Jews from Turzec. On 29 Jan. 1943, 200 escaped while the others were being murdered; of these, 130 joined the Zhukov partisan brigade and the rest other groups; 140 survived the war.

SVISLOCH Mogilev dist., Belorussia. Jews settled in the 17th cent. An independent community with its own rabbi and rabbinical court developed in the 18th cent. The J. pop. was 107 in 1766 and 1,120 in 1897, dropping to 742 in 1926 under the Soviets. J. tailors and shoemakers formed their own cooperatives in 1925 and 200 Jews were employed at a glass factory. Six families earned their livelihoods in agriculture. A J. elementary school was in operation. The Germans captured the town in July 1941, apparently murdering the Jews in Oct. with the aid of local police.

SVITAVY   Moravia (Sudetenland), Czechoslovakia. Jews settled after 1848 when the residence ban was lifted. Most were peddlers or traded in cloth and yarn. A synagogue was consecrated in 1902. In 1930 the J. pop. was 168 (total 10,466). Most Jews fled to the Czech Republic after the annexation of the Sudetenland to the German Reich in Sept. 1938. Many later emigrated, mainly to England and Palestine. The Nazis destroyed the synagogue and J. cemetery around the time of *Kristallnacht* (9–10 Nov. 1938). The remaining Jews were deported, together with the Jews of the Altreich, to the death camps of Poland in late 1942. A few survived in the Theresienstadt ghetto.

SWARZENDZ   Poznan dist., Poland. A group of poor Jews from Poznan was invited to settle by the local nobility in the first half of the 17th cent. The generous privileges, including tax exemptions and the endowment of a synagogue, school, and hospital, led the Poles to dub the town a "J. paradise." From the early 17th cent. to the mid-18th cent. the Jews constituted over half the pop., numbering 1,644 in 1840. Subsequently the J. pop. declined sharply through emigration, particularly after WWI. Others fled with the approach of the Germans in Sept. 1939, leaving 23, who were expelled to General Gouvernement territory to share the fate of the Jews there. The synagogue was blown up.

SWIECIE   Pomerania dist., Poland. A community was organized in the 19th cent., reaching a peak pop. of 497 (total 6,348) in 1885 and dropping sharply after WWI to 171. A synagogue and cemetery were opened in 1899. In Sept. 1939 the Germans executed the few Jews attempting to flee. The remaining 73 were murdered at the J. cemetery on 7–8 Oct., making S. one of the first cities in Pomerania to be declared "free of Jews" (*judenrein*).

SWIENCIANY   Vilna dist., Poland, today Lithuania. The J. settlement developed after the Lithuanian expulsions of 1496–1503, when Jews found refuge on the

large estates in the area. By 1765 they numbered 462, embroiled in external conflict and internal friction owing to R. Shneur Zalman of Lyady's proselytization on behalf of Habad Hasidism. In the 19th cent., Jews were active in the lumber, flax, and grain trade and supplied meat to the Russian army. In the second half of the cent. Jews opened a number of factories, including the only one in Poland for manufacturing felt boots. In 1881, R. Yitzhak Yaakov Reines, rabbi of S. in 1869–85 and future founder of the Mizrachi movement, started a modern yeshiva in the face of Habad opposition. The Zionist idea began to spread in S. in the 1880s. Avraham Solomiak of the Bilu movement left for Eretz Israel in 1885 and was among the founders of Gedera. In the early 20th cent., a number of families from S. settled in Nes Ziona. The Bund was especially influential among J.

Program for Zionist evening dedicated to Chlenov, Swienciany, Poland, 16 July 1920

laborers, craftsmen, and the intelligentsia. In 1887 a fire left 600 J. families homeless and after a second, smaller fire in 1891, J. homes were rebuilt in brick. The J. pop. was 3,272 in 1897 (total 6,025). In WWI, many Jews left, reducing the J. pop. to 2,750 in 1925 after a period of political instability and economic stagnation. Between the World Wars the Jews suffered from discriminatory government measures and anti-J. boycotts along with the loss of their traditional markets because of the new borders. The J. boot factory continued to grow and Jews developed a trade in medicinal plants. Two rival J. schools were in operation. A CYSHO school enrolled 170 students in 1929–30 and through a sister organization promoted Yiddish culture. The Tarbut Hebrew school, supported by all the Zionist groups, developed out of the *talmud torah* founded in 1891 as a continuation of the Reines yeshiva that had closed in 1885. After two years of Soviet rule the Germans arrived in late June 1941. On 15 July they shot 100 Jews in the Branowy forest; the rest, excluding

skilled workers, were sent to the notorious Poligon camp on 27 Sept. and executed on 7–8 Oct. with 8,000 other Jews from the region. The remaining 500 Jews were concentrated in a ghetto, augmented by 2,300 refugees. On 5 April 1943 they were transported toward Vilna and detoured to the Ponary woods where all those not murdered in flight were systematically executed. A group of 25 managed to join the partisans.

SWIENTA WOLA Polesie dist., Poland, today Belarus. The J. pop. in 1921 was 185 (total 615). The Jews were presumably murdered by the Germans in the beginning of Aug. 1941, by an SS cavalry unit.

SWIERZE Lublin dist., Poland. Jews are first mentioned in 1550. They numbered about 120 in 1769 and 294 (total 355) in 1921. In Sept. 1939, the Germans introduced a regime of severe persecution and subsequently established a *Judenrat* and ghetto. The J. pop. then stood at 800, possibly including refugees.

The Swienciany string orchestra before WWII, Poland

Additional refugees soon arrived and in summer or fall 1942 all were deported to the Sobibor death camp via Wlodawa.

SWIETOCHLOWICE Silesia dist., Poland. Jews numbered 48 in 1861 (total 3,818) and 100-115 in the early 20th cent. and were probably expelled by the Germans in fall 1939. A branch of Auschwitz operated as a forced labor camp in the area from June 1942 to Jan. 1945, averaging 1,300 inmates.

SWINEMUENDE (Pol. Swinoujscie) Pomerania, Germany, today Poland. A J. community developed in the 19th cent., comprising nine Jews in 1819 and 130 in 1887. It maintained a synagogue and a cemetery. The hotels in this health resort were characterized as antisemitic in 1904. In 1919-20, increased antisemitic agitation led to the formation of a Central Union (C.V.) branch. When the Nazis came to power in 1933, there were 70 Jews living in S. From 1933, there was rioting directed at J. clientele at the health resort as well as against the J. owners of boarding houses and spa facilities. On *Kristallnacht* (9-10 Nov. 1938), the synagogue was burned down, the cemetery was desecrated, and three Jews were arrested. By May 1939, there were only 29 Jews and 21 persons of partial J. origin (*Mischlinge*) in S. The remaining Jews were deported to the Lublin dist. (Poland) on 12-13 Feb. 1940 together with the Jews of Stettin. The one Jew who was still living in S. in Oct. 1942 was probably protected by marriage to a non-Jew.

SWINIUCHY Volhynia dist., Poland, today Ukraine. Jews are first recorded in the second half of the 16th cent. The J. pop. in 1897 was 629 (total 1,780). Most left during the nearby fighting in WWI, leaving 173 in 1921. The J. pop. grew to 498 in 1936. Most were Olyka and Tuczyn Hasidim. Under the German occupation from July 1941, they were persecuted by the Ukrainian local government and police. In Oct. 1941 they were expelled to the Lokacze ghetto and were executed on 13 Sept. 1942.

SWIR Vilna dist., Poland, today Belarus. Around 300 Jews were present in 1766. More arrived after being expelled from their villages in 1882, bringing the J. pop. up to 1,114 (total 1,686) in 1897. The Bund and the Zionists became active in the early 20th cent. The community recovered from the rigors

of WWI with the aid of J. relief organizations, but between the World Wars their economic situation remained difficult and unemployment was high. In 1925 the J. pop. was 820. Most children attended a Tarbut school, were fluent in Hebrew, and belonged to the Zionist youth movements. The Germans captured the town in late June 1941. A ghetto was set up in late 1941 and on 5 Dec., 21 young Jews were executed. In March 1943 the Jews were transferred to the Michaliszki ghetto. Most were soon after brought to the Ponary woods near Vilna for execution.

SWIRZ Tarnopol dist., Poland, today Ukraine. Jews are first mentioned in 1563. S. was famous for the magnificent multi-story candelabrum (*menorah*) housed in its synagogue, its origins shrouded in legend. The J. pop. stood at 381 in 1880 (total 1,948), declining to 184 in 1921, mainly through emigration to the U.S. Good relations with the Christian pop. prevailed in all periods. The Germans entered S. in July 1941, persecuted the Jews, and appointed a *Judenrat*. The Jews were expelled to the Bobrka and Przemyslany ghettoes in Nov. 1942 and shared the fate of the local Jews.

SWISLOCZ Bialystok dist., Poland. An organized community existed by 1713. The first settlers were lumber and grain merchants attracted by the fairs instituted by the local count. After the failure of the Polish rebellion in 1831, many Jews lost their livelihoods and consequently were drawn to the new hide-processing industry and the tanneries that began to develop. With the completion of a railway line in 1906, J. prosperity reached its peak, with the J. pop. standing at 2,086 in 1897 (total 3,099). Hovevei Zion became active in the late 19th cent., joined by an illegal Bund group agitating among J. workers in the factories. During WWI the Jews suffered from the depredations of the Cossacks. With the loss of the Russian market after WWI, the J. economic position deteriorated and the community was assisted by the Joint Distribution Committee. A Tarbut Hebrew school was founded and the Hehalutz organization became active. In 1921 the J. pop. was 1,959 (total 2,935). The Soviets occupied the town in 1939-41, introducing a Communist regime. The Germans arrived on 26 June 1941, giving the Polish mobs free rein to attack Jews. In July they set up a ghetto and instituted forced labor. On 2 Nov. 1942 the ghetto was liquidated when 300 of the sick and old and women with young children were taken to the Wishnik forest and murdered. The 2,000 that remained were transferred to Wolkowysk and kept under inhuman conditions until deported to the Treblinka death camp on 6 Dec.

SYCHEVKA Smolensk dist., Russia. Jews probably arrived in the late 19th cent. Their pop. was 327 (total 7,646) in 1926 and 138 in 1939. The Germans occupied the town on 10 Oct. 1941. On 7 Jan. 1943, they murdered 35 J. families and on 27 Nov., Jews from the neighboring village of Mitino.

SYKE Hanover, Germany. Numbering 23 in 1796, the community grew to 35 (4% of the total) in 1810. It had a burial ground, a religious school, and a prayer house, but services only took place on the major festivals. The community's membership, which included Jews in Brinkum, Leeste, and Kirchweyhe, numbered 37 after WWI. The community was secular and very assimilated. Relations between Jews and non-Jews deteriorated after the Nazis came to power, resulting in one suicide and the community's disposal of the synagogue in 1937. Jews feared for their lives after *Kristallnacht* (9–10 Nov. 1938) and seven emigrated in 1939. At least 20 perished in Nazi concentration camps.

SYNOWODZKO-WYZNE Stanislawow dist., Poland, today Ukraine. Jews were leasing land from the second half of the 16th cent. and later found employment mainly around the local sawmill. The J. pop. in 1921 was 341 (total 3,894). With the Soviet withdrawal in June 1941, the Ukrainians went on a rampage, murdering 147 Jews. The community was liquidated by the Germans in Aug. or Sept. 1942.

SYRTE Tripolitania dist., Libya. An ancient J. settlement was apparently founded by exiles from Jerusalem after the destruction of the Second Temple and perhaps earlier. Some of their descendants are believed to have settled in Yidder and Messurata. In the 19th cent., movement in the opposite direction took place when the Turkish government offered building lots in S., attracting merchants from Messurata who helped build the town's large marketplace and the modest J. quarter nearby. Economic and blood ties between the two distant communities persisted until WWII. Jews from Cyrenaica, particularly from Orpola and Benghazi, also arrived in the 19th cent. as S. became an important com-

mercial crossroads. A small synagogue was built in 1910. Most Jews fled after the outbreak of the Arab Revolt in 1915, seeking refuge in Khoms. Returning after the stabilization of Italian rule in the early 1920s, they found their homes and property in ruins. The construction of an Italian army base in the area brought renewed prosperity with Jews finding employment as builders and suppliers. Jews also earned their livelihoods as fishermen and cafe operators and owned flour mills. In 1931, the J. pop. was 262 (total 10,741). J. children attended an Italian public school in the mornings and a *talmud torah* in the afternoon. R. Moshe Balulu, who officiated from 1932 after serving two years in Messurata, had a great impact on the community. In 1936, a modern new synagogue was built with Italian aid. Relations with the Italians took a turn for the worse in WWII, when the proximity of their military installations made them wary of J. loyalties. R. Balulu was arrested in Dec. 1940 for alleged British sympathies and the entire community was deported on 5 Feb. 1941, destined for Khoms or Tripoli but in the end allowed to stay with their kinsmen in Messurata. The community was partially rehabilitated during the British occupation. Avraham Hadad, barely 20 and a student of R. Balulu, became rabbi and J. soldiers with the British army set up a Ben-Yehuda club. The riots of 1945 and 1948 in Tripolitania bypassed S. without bloodshed. In 1950–51 the Jews left for Israel, many to Moshav Sedeh Uzziyya.

SZABADSZALLAS Pest–Pilis–Solt–Kiskun dist., Hungary. Jews were only allowed to settle in S. in 1850. Consecrating a synagogue in 1860, they numbered 154 in 1880 and 120 in 1930. From the end of WWI to the racial laws of 1938, they were subject to considerable antisemitic hostility. Zionism was not popular. The men were rounded up in 1942 and sent to forced labor in the Ukraine. In spring 1944, the remaining Jews were detained at Kiskoros and Kecskemet and then deported to Auschwitz on 23 June.

SZABOLCSBAKA Szabolcs dist., Hungary. Jews arrived in the late 18th cent., encouraged by estate owners to market their produce, mainly wheat, corn, tobacco, and cabbage. They also established factories for producing alcoholic beverages, vinegar, and sauerkraut. The J. pop. was. 92 in 1880 and 83 in 1930. The community maintained a synagogue and *heder*. After WWI, it suffered from antisemitism encouraged by the local Protestant and Catholic clergy. On 30 May 1944, the Jews were deported to Auschwitz via Kisvarda.

SZACK   Volhynia dist., Poland, today Ukraine. Jews numbered 238 in 1921 (total 1,752) and some 200 families in the 1930s. Most were murdered by the Germans in Aug. 1942 while others, escaping to the forest, established a family camp in early 1943 that was discovered and liquidated. Some of the young joined the partisans.

SZADEK   Lodz dist., Poland. Jews first settled in the early 18th cent. In 1897 the J. pop. was 495 (20% of the total). When the Germans entered S. early in WWII they expelled many J. families and in May–June 1940 ghettoized the remaining 410 Jews. On 14 Aug. 1942 they were deported to Chelmno.

SZAKOLY   Szabolcs dist., Hungary. Jews settled in the late 18th cent,, constructing a synagogue in 1890 and numbering 76 in 1930. In spring 1944, the Jews were first confined to the Nyiregyhaza ghetto. When they protested at the crowded conditions, they were dispersed to nearby farms in Simpapuszta and Harangod. On 22 May 1944, they were brought back to Nyiregyhaza prior to deportation to Auschwitz.

SZAMOSSALYI   Szatmar dist., Hungary. Owing to opposition from estate owners, Jews were only allowed to settle in S. in the late 19th cent. They numbered 144 in 1900 and 84 in 1930. In spring 1944, they were taken to Mateszalka and in late May deported to Auschwitz.

SZAMOSSZEG   Szatmar dist., Hungary. Jews probably settled in the late 18th cent., maintaining two cemeteries, a school, and a synagogue. They numbered 96 in 1880 and 94 in 1930. In late May 1944, they were deported to Auschwitz via Mateszalka.

SZAMOTULY   Poznan dist., Poland. Jews first settled in 1403. Most left after the J. quarter burned down in 1634. The community was reestablished in 1714 under a charter according freedom of worship and internal autonomy along with qualified trade and residence rights. The community grew to 949 (total 4,214) in 1871 as Jews expanded their trade and opened factories, including a large furniture factory and three mechanized flour mills. S. was the birthplace of the scholar and bibliographer Akiva Barukh Posner (1890–1962). Emigration increased sharply after WWI, encouraged by growing antisemitism under Polish rule. The 88 Jews remaining in Sept. 1939 were soon expelled by the Germans to General Gouvernement territory.

SZANY   Sopron dist., Hungary. Jews arrived in the late 18th cent. On 5 July 1944, the village's Jews, about 50, were deported to Auschwitz via Sopron.

SZARKOWSZCZYZNA   Vilna dist., Poland, today Belarus. A community of 472 existed in 1847. J. tradesmen relied on the weekly market day for their incomes and many Jews were employed in warehouses, cleaning and packing flax, which was then taken to the distant railroad station by J. carters. J. tailors and shoemakers circulated through the surrounding villages. Until WWI, all earned respectable livings, with the J. pop. reaching a peak of 1,007 (total 1,151) in 1897. Most J. homes were burned down by rampaging Polish soldiers in 1920 and a severe epidemic followed. The J. pop. in 1921 was 1,036. In the economic crisis between the World Wars, the relief organizations and relatives abroad helped 35 J. families set up farms. Children studied at CYSHO and Tarbut schools, the latter promoting Zionist activity. Under the German occupation from 27 June 1941, J. property was confiscated and forced labor instituted. In Oct. 1941 the town's 1,900 Jews including refugees were confined to two ghettoes. On 17 July 1942, apprised of a coming *Aktion*, the Jews set the ghettoes on fire and tried to flee. Seven hundred succeeded. The rest were massacred the next day. Those reaching the Glembokie ghetto met their end there; others remained in the forest. Few survived.

SZARVAS   Bekes dist., Hungary. Jews settled in 1842, splitting into Neologist and Orthodox congregations in 1870. A J. school was established in 1852. The J. pop. was 820 in 1880 (4% of the total), dropping in 1941 to 636. In 1941, young Jews were seized for forced labor in the Ukraine, many perishing while clearing minefields there. On 15 May 1944, the Jews of S. were confined to a ghetto together with Jews from nearby settlements. In June, they were all transferred to the Szolnok ghetto and from there on 25–27 June to Auschwitz, with most deported to Austria. Nearly 500 returned to form the postwar community, which gradually dwindled.

SZATMARCSEKE Szatmar dist., Hungary. Jews arrived in the early 18th cent., contributing to the town's economic life as merchants, artisans, and factory owners. A synagogue was consecrated in 1884. The community suffered in the White Terror attacks (1919–21) after WWI. Under the racial laws of 1938, almost all males were seized for forced labor. A J. estate owner in S. sponsored a Zionist training farm for J. youngsters from all over Hungary. In late May 1944, the Jews were transferred to Mateszalka en route to Auschwitz.

SZATMAROKORITO Szatmar dist., Hungary. Jews settled in the late 18th cent. and numbered 170 in 1900 and 126 in 1930. In late April 1944, they were expelled to Mateszalka and from there deported to Auschwitz on 15–16 May.

SZCZAKOWA Cracow dist., Poland. Jews first arrived in the late 18th cent., reaching a peak pop. of 469 (total 3,362) in 1910. In 1918 and 1919, J. property was looted by rampaging peasants and factory and mine workers. Between the World Wars the Zionists expanded their activity and the community took under its wing the J. soldiers (numbering 80 in 1939) serving in the town's garrision. In fall 1939 the town was annexed to the Third Reich and the Germans instituted a regime of forced labor, deporting 200 children and old people to Auschwitz in Nov. 1941. The last Jews were sent to Auschwitz in summer 1942.

SZCZAWNICA-WYZNA Cracow dist., Poland. The J. settlement began to grow from the 1880s with the development of S. as a health resort attracting a J. clientele and numbered 199 (total 1,671) in 1921. The existence of a local Gestapo station under the German occupation in WWII brought severe persecution. On 28–30 Aug. 1942, after the old and sick were murdered, all the Jews were expelled to Nowy Targ, mainly for deportation to the Belzec death camp.

SZCZEBRZESZYN (Yid. Shrebshin) Lublin dist., Poland. Jews are first mentioned in the early 16th cent., forming an independent community at the end of the cent. and consecrating a cemetery and a beautiful synagogue in the Renaissance style. Most were killed in the Chmielnicki massacres of 1648–49. R. Meir ben Shemuel of S. described the massacres in *Tzok ha-Ittim*, published in 1650. Hasidic influence was

dominant. Haskala was introduced by R. Yaakov Reifmann when he took up residence in S. in 1836. The J. pop. grew from 1,083 in 1827 to 3,965 (total 6,122) in 1913. The Bund became active during the 1905 revolution but many of the young emigrated to the west in the subsequent reaction. J. political life revived under the Austrian occupation of WWI as the Zionists formed their first groups. In 1921 the J. pop. was 2,644. Between the World Wars, Yavne and CYSHO schools were in operation. The Germans occupied S. permanently on 9 Oct. 1939, instituting a regime of forced labor and persecution. A *Judenrat* and ghetto were soon established as refugees increased the J. pop. to 3,000 by April 1942. On 8 May, the Germans rounded up the J. pop. and randomly opened fire, killing 100 and demanding that the Jews pay for the bullets. At the end of May, 300 Jews were deported to the Belzec death camp. On 8 Aug., another 400 were sent to Belzec and 200 of the elderly murdered outside the town. Seven hundred were sent to forced labor in Chelm and murdered there. On 23 June 1942, many were arrested and sent to Bilgorai. Their fate is unknown. The remaining Jews were deported to Belzec on 21–24 Oct. 1942. Many escaped to fight as partisans but few survived.

SZCZEKOCINY Kielce dist., Poland. Jews are first mentioned in the late 15th cent. but the hostility of the local pop. kept the community from growing until the 18th cent. The wealthier Jews lent money to the estate owners and bought up their produce (grain and alcoholic beverages). In the late 18th cent. the Jews formed an organized community with a synagogue and cemetery. A separate J. quarter was established in 1822. The J. pop. grew to 2,305 (total 3,393) in 1897. At the turn of the 19th cent., Jews opened a number of factories (for paper, bricks and roof tiles, and honey and mead). Many J. homes were destroyed in fires in 1895 and 1910. In this period, Hasidism began to spread under the influence of R. Lipa, a follower of the "Seer of Lublin," and R. Yisrael of Kozienice. Gur Hasidim were the dominant group. During WWI, the Jews suffered from severe food shortages but community life continued unabated with Agudat Israel, Mizrachi, and Ha-No'ar ha-Tziyyoni becoming active. Agudat Israel later opened a Beth Jacob school for 200 girls. In 1921, the J. pop. was 2,532. In the 1930s, economic boycotts undermined J. livelihoods as antisemitism intensified. The Germans captured S. on 4 Sept.

1939, their bombardments destroying half the city. Rioting Poles immediately looted J. property and the Germans murdered over 20 Jews within a week. Many Jews fled, leaving 1,500 out of a prewar pop. of about 2,800. A *Judenrat* was set up under a regime of forced labor and severe persecution. On 20 Sept. 1942 (Yom Kippur eve), the sick and old were executed and the rest deported to the Treblinka death camp. About 200 local Jews returned to Poland from the Soviet Union after the war, 130 settling in Sosnowiec, but most eventually left for the U.S. and Israel.

SZCZERCOW   Lodz dist., Poland. Jews lived there from 1790 and in 1897 numbered 962 (35% of the total). In Sept. 1939 the town was destroyed and the Jews fled to Zelow and Belkhatow, where they shared the fate of the local Jews.

SZCZERZEC   Lwow dist., Poland, today Ukraine. Jews are recorded from 1629, reaching a pop. of 1,385 (80% of the total) in 1880 with a majority on the municipal council as well as J. mayors from 1878. The J. pop. fell to 712 after WWI with the Joint Distribution Committee providing relief and Zionist influence increasing. In Aug. 1942, 180 Jews were expelled by the Germans to Bobrka and the rest were deported to the Belzec death camp at the end of Nov.

SZCZODROHOSZCZE   (Yid. Sedrovich) Volhynia dist., Poland, today Ukraine. The J. pop. was approximately 100 in the 1930s. In the Holocaust, the Jews were brought to the Ratno ghetto for liquidation.

SZCZUCIN   Cracow dist., Poland. Jews settled in the late 18th cent. and engaged in the Russian-Austrian transit trade in the 19th cent. The Jews numbered 566 (half the total pop.) in 1880, their growth retarded by fires in 1888 and 1912 and the devastating flood of 1934 as well as by the virtual destruction of the town by the Russians in 1914. The Germans arrived on 8 Sept. 1939 and four days later executed 40 Jews along with 70 Polish prisoners of war. The community was liquidated in the second half of 1942 when the majority was sent to Domrowa Tarnowska to share the fate of the Jews there.

SZCZUCZYN (I)   Bialystok dist., Poland. A few J. families were present in the 18th cent. as leaseholders and distillers. By 1857 the J. pop. reached 2,268 and

3,336 by 1897 (total 5,043), with most now engaged in petty trade. From the late 19th cent. S. became known as a resort area, attracting mainly J. vacationers. The Zionists became active in 1898. The J. pop. dropped to 2,506 in 1921 as economic conditions deteriorated. Community activity continued unabated. A Tarbut school founded in 1921 enrolled 350 children. The community maintained pioneer training facilities, libraries, a drama circle, and a Maccabi sports club. In the shortlived German occupation of Sept. 1939, 350 J. men were sent to Germany for forced labor; 30 survived. After two years of Soviet rule, the Germans bypassed the town in June 1941, leaving the Jews in Polish hands. Three hundred were murdered in a brutal massacre by axe-wielding mobs on 28 June. Another 100 were executed on 24 July. On 8 Aug. the Germans murdered 600 Jews at the J. cemetery and packed the rest into a ghetto. On 2 Nov. all were sent to Bogusze and from there deported to the Treblinka death camp around the end of the year.

SZCZUCZYN (II)   Nowogrodek dist., Poland, today Belarus. The Jews of S. and environs numbered 401 in 1766. They constituted an organized community with an ancient synagogue and two stone *battei midrash*. In 1897 their pop. was 1,356 (total 1,742). R. Yehuda Leib Hassman served for 20 years from 1906 and founded a branch of the Slobodka yeshiva in 1909, with a peak enrollment of 300. After WWI, stiff competition undermined the livelihoods of J. tradesmen and numerous charitable organizations were in operation. The J. pop. grew to around 2,000 in 1930. Tarbut and CYSHO schools were opened in the 1920s. The Germans captured the city on 26 June 1941, appointing a *Judenrat* in July and setting up a ghetto in Aug. Jews brought in from neighboring towns swelled its pop. to 3,000, living under a regime of severe persecution. In Sept. 1941, dozens of the community's leading figures were executed near the village of Topiliszki. Another few dozen sent to Ejszyszki as workers were murdered later in the month. All but 500–600 of the rest were executed near the J. cemeteries on 9 May 1942. The others were sent to labor camps and gradually killed off, the last in the Majdanek concentration camp in Sept. 1943.

SZCZUROWA   Cracow dist., Poland. The J. pop. in 1921 was 132 (total 1,971). The Jews were deported to the Belzec death camp via Brzesko in Sept. 1942.

Squad of Jewish soldiers, Szczuczyn, Nowogrodek dist., Poland

SZCZUROWICE Tarnopol dist., Poland, today Ukraine. Jews are first mentioned in 1570, living without restrictions. In the 19th cent. they worked as innkeepers and distillers as well as leasing parcels of the surrounding forests. Most were Hasidim (Belz, Olesko, Husyatin-Ruzhin. In 1880 the J. pop. reached 752 (total 1,705). After WWI, the Jews numbered 100. The community was liquidated by the Germans in the fall of 1942 when the Jews were expelled to Sokal or Brody.

SZECSENY Nograd dist., Hungary. Jews settled in the early 18th cent. The Orthodox congregation exercised jurisdiction over numerous smaller communities in the late 19th cent. The J. pop. fell from 564 in 1840 to 280 in 1941. At the outset of WWII, J. businessmen and professionals were detained in a concentration camp and others were seized for forced labor. On 1 June 1944, the Jews were transferred to Balassagyarmat and on 10 June deported to Auschwitz.

SZEDRES Tolna dist., Hungary. Jews settled in the mid-19th cent., praying in a small synagogue until 1944, when they numbered 90. On 19 May, they were expelled to the Tolna ghetto. On 29 June, they were sent to Pecs, and then on 4 July deported to Auschwitz.

SZEGED Csongrad dist., Hungary. Jews first settled in 1781. The community became one of the largest and strongest in Hungary as residence and trade restrictions were lifted. In 1869 the J. pop. was 3,628 and 6,903 (6% of the total) in 1910. In 1869, the community formed a Neologist congregation. The community continually outgrew the various synagogues it built until, in 1903, a magnificent synagogue designed by Lipot Baumhorn was consecrated. The Reform leader R. Leopold Loew, a chaplain in the rebel army during the Hungarian revolt of 1848-49, officiated in S. between 1850 and 1875. He was also an historian and the first of the city's rabbis to preach in Hungarian. His son, Dr. Immanuel Loew (1878-1944), was a renowned lexicographer. A J. public school was founded in 1820, reaching an enrollment of 574 in 1902-03. A J. hospital opened in 1856 was another of the community's many welfare institutions. Most Jews were merchants and tradesmen but many also owned and operated major factories. Jews were also active

Synagogue in Szeged, Hungary

in public life, serving in the Hungarian parliament and as district judges and heads of professional associations. Between the World Wars, the Zionists became active under the inspiration of R. Jeno Frenkl, forming Hashomer Hatzair, WIZO, and Hehalutz groups. In this period, the J. pop. dropped sharply, by about 40%, owing to conversion, a declining birthrate, and rising mortality rates. In 1941 the J. pop. was 4,161. From 1939 the Jews were subjected to forced labor in an atmosphere of increasing antisemitism, many being sent to the Bor coal mines in Yugoslavia in 1943 under German jurisdiction. In May 1944, the Jews were confined to a ghetto. The Catholic Church, both at the local and national level, managed to save about 200 Jews. Deportations to Auschwitz, where 3,000 of S.'s Jews perished, commenced on 25–28 June 1944. Two transports were erroneously routed to Strasshof in Austria. The postwar community numbered 2,124 in 1946 and 927 in 1958, maintaining a synagogue, a school, and an orphanage for 400 Budapest children who lost their parents in the Holocaust.

SZEGHALOM   Bekes dist., Hungary. Jews from Devavanya settled in the first half of the 19th cent., forming a Neologist congregation in 1869 and opening a synagogue and school in 1889. The J. pop. was 343 (4% of the total) in 1890 and 220 in 1930. On 26 June 1944, the Jews were expelled to Szolnok; most were then deported to Auschwitz and the rest to Austria. Those in Austria returned after the war, but the general hostility and a blood libel forced most to leave by 1955.

SZEGI   Zemplen dist., Hungary. The J. pop. was 72 in 1930. At the end of May 1944, the Jews were deported to Auschwitz via Satoraljaujhely.

SZEGVAR   Csongrad dist., Hungary. The J. pop. was 63 in 1930. Between 23 and 28 June 1944, the Jews were deported to Auschwitz via Mindszent.

SZEKESFEHERVAR   Fejer dist., Hungary. Jews arrived in the 13th cent., forming a prosperous community augmented by Jews from Turkey and Buda during the Ottoman period (1544–1688). Expelled with the Turks, Jews only settled again in 1840, reaching a pop. of 2,689 (10.5% of the total) in 1880. Separate Neologist and Orthodox congregations had their own synagogues (erected in 1862 and 1876, respectively). A J. school founded in 1843 was attended by 190 children in 1895–96. The Orientalist Yitzhak (Ignaz) Goldziher was born in S. in 1850. In 1941, the J. pop. was 2,075 after many left for Budapest in the wake of Hungary's 1938 racial laws. In 1939, some richer members of the community established Zionist training farms at nearby Enying and Bodajk. S. became a mobilization center for forced labor, with 12,000 Jews from the region put to work on nearby farms. Others were sent to the Ukraine. In May 1944, all the Jews were confined to a ghetto. In mid-June, they were deported to Auschwitz along with 3,000 other Jews from the district. After the war, 250 survivors reestablished the community.

SZEKSZARD   Tolna dist., Hungary. Jews settled in the first half of the 19th cent. and formed a Neologist congregation in 1869. A J. school was opened in 1853. S had a high percentage of mixed marriages. Local Jews were severely victimized in the White Terror attacks of 1919–21. The J. pop. fell from 847 (6% of the total) in 1890 to 675 in 1920 and 437 in 1941 (3%). Although city officials sought to ensure that forced labor battalions remain in S., an antisemitic bureaucracy issued secret orders directing the units to the Ukraine and ordering commanders to see to it that the Jews never returned to Hungary. Following the arrival of the Germans in spring 1944, S. became the only district city in Hungary where Jews were not forced to enter a ghetto. Jews, working with influential Christians, nearly prevented deportations until Endre Laszlo, dist. commissioner and a leading antisemite, made the destruction of the J. community in S. a personal matter. The Jews were dispersed to Bonyhad, Tamasi, Pincehely, and Dombovar. From Bonyhad they were brought to Pecs and deported to Auschwitz on 5 July; from Dombovar they were taken to Kaposvar and deported to Auschwitz on 1 July, the women being transferred to Hess-Lichtenau in Thuringia for forced labor.

SZELKOW NOWY   Warsaw dist., Poland. The J. pop. in 1921 was 107 (total 408). The Jews were ex-

pelled by the Germans to the Makow Mazowieckie ghetto in Sept. 1940, sharing the fate of the other Jews there.

SZENDRO   Borsod dist., Hungary. Under Count Csaky's patronage Jews from Germany settled in the late 18th cent. to take over local trade. A synagogue was established in 1780. R. Binyamin Ze'ev Tannenbaum officiated in 1820–47 and founded a popular yeshiva in 1830. The J. pop. rose to 221 in 1880. In the 20th cent., the Mizrachi movement was active. Antisemitism intensified after 1933. The J. pop. was 277 in 1941. On 10 June 1944, the Jews were deported to Auschwitz via Miskolc. Survivors reestablished the community but all left by 1956.

SZENTENDRE   Pest–Pilis–Solt–Kiskun dist., Hungary. Jews arrived with the Romans in the third cent. The modern community was founded in the early 19th cent. Jews engaged mostly in the marketing of local fruit. A synagogue was established in 1850 and a school was operating by 1860. The J. pop. was around 200 from the late 19th cent. until WWII. In 1940, S. became a forced labor center and many were sent to the Ukraine, where they perished. In late April 1944, the Jews were confined to a ghetto, where they were terrorized by Arrow Cross gangs. On 7–8 July they were deported to Auschwitz. Survivors reestablished the community.

SZENTES   Csongrad dist., Hungary. Twenty J. families settled in 1742. A J. school was opened in 1841 and a Neologist congregation was formed in 1869, when the J. pop. reached 919. The community displayed strong assimilationist tendencies. In 1944, 450 Jews remained. They were expelled to Szeged on 25–28 June and a week later deported to Auschwitz and Austria. After the war, survivors, primarily those in Austria, reestablished the community.

SZENTGAL   Veszprem dist., Hungary. Jews were present by 1735 and numbered 88 in 1930. A synagogue was established in 1897. No further details are available.

SZENTGOTTHARD   Vas dist., Hungary. A few families were present throughout most of the 18th and 19th cents. A J. school was established in 1904. The J. pop. numbered 178 in 1930. In mid-June

1944, the Jews were expelled to Szombathely and in early July deported to Auschwitz. Survivors reestablished the community, but left after 1956.

SZENTLORINC Baranya dist., Hungary. Jews settled in the late 18th cent., numbering 42 in 1880 and 210 in 1929. In June 1944, they were expelled to Pecs and from there deported to Auschwitz.

SZERENCS Zemplen dist., Hungary. In 1770, 215 Jews were present in S. and environs. In the 19th cent., the Jews became prominent as wine merchants. They numbered 407 in 1880 and 955 in 1930. In early June 1944, they were confined to the Miskolc ghetto and on 10 June 1944 deported to Auschwitz.

SZERESZOW Polesie dist., Poland, today Belarus. Jews are first recorded in 1583. In the first half of the 19th cent. some engaged in smuggling as S. be-

Jewish family store, Szerencs, Hungary

came a border town between Russia and Poland. Many J. merchants left when the border was opened in 1851. In 1897 the J. pop. was 2,553 (half the total). Under the German occupation in WWI the Jews were put to forced labor and persecuted, their pop. dropping to 1,341 in 1921, supported by Jews from the U.S. A Hebrew school existed. The Germans occupied S. on 24 June 1941 and instituted a regime of forced labor and extortion and appointed a *Judenrat*. On 25 Sept. 1941 the community was brought to Antopol and then transferred to Drohiczyn. In Oct. the Jews were dispersed, most to Chomsk, where they were murdered in April 1942. A small group was brought to Pruzhana for deportation to Auschwitz in Jan. 1943.

SZIGETVAR Somogy dist., Hungary. Jews were present in the 17th cent., erecting synagogues in 1821 and 1857 and forming a Neologist congregation in 1869. A J. school was opened in 1879. In 1898, R. Mendel converted to Christianity and paralyzed the S. rabbinate for years. The J. pop. was 713 in 1880 and 263 in 1941. In the beginning of July 1944, the Jews were deported to Auschwitz after being detained in the Barcs ghetto.

SZIKSZO Abauj–Torna dist., Hungary. Jews are mentioned in 1702. R. Shemuel ben David Ehrenfeld (1868–74) and his grandson R. Shaul Ehrenfeld (c. 1875–1905) attracted students from all over Hungary to the local yeshiva. A splendid synagogue was consecrated in 1914. The J. pop. reached a peak of 824 in 1920. In the 1930s, Zionist activity intensified via Hashomer, Betar and Mizrachi groups. The J. pop. was 703 in 1941. In 1942, 175 Jews aged 18–48 were seized for forced labor, most perishing in the Ukraine. The rest were expelled to Kassa in April 1944 and from there deported to Auschwitz between 12 and 15 June. By 1960, most of the 92 survivors who had reestablished the community were living in Israel.

SZIL Sopron dist., Hungary. Jews settled in 1784 and numbered 50 in 1944. On 5 July 1944, they were deported to Auschwitz after being detained in Csorna and Sopron.

SZOB Hont dist., Hungary. Jews settled after 1840 and numbered 100 in 1930. A synagogue was established in 1922. In late June 1944, the Jews were deported to Auschwitz after being detained in Vamosmikola and Ipolysag.

SZOLNOK   Jasz–Nagykun–Szolnok dist., Hungary. Jews settled after 1840, erecting a synagogue in 1858 and forming a Neologist congregation in 1869. A J. public school was opened in 1855, reaching an enrollment of 179 in 1927–28. The J. pop. rose from 1,101 in 1880 to 2,590 (6% of the total) in 1941. In 1935, a cultural center with a library was opened alongside the synagogue. Hungary's 1938 racial laws undermined J. life and from 1941 many perished in the Ukraine under forced labor. Despite protests by the local rabbi, Zionist activists established a center for Hebrew study (*ulpan*) and a training farm. On 16 April 1944, the 1,800 remaining Jews were confined in a ghetto. On 16 June they were brought to the local sugar refinery with 4,000 Jews from surrounding settlements and on 26 and 29 June, respectively, deported to Austria and Auschwitz. About 600 returned from Austria to form a postwar community that numbered 180 in 1963.

SZOMBATHELY   Vas dist., Hungary. Jews settled after 1840, founding a J. school in 1846 and consecrating a Great Synagogue in 1880, when the J. pop. reached 1,678 (13% of the total). Zionist sentiment was strong from the start. In 1869, Yehoshua Stampfer set out for Eretz Israel, becoming one of the founders of Petah Tikva. Between the World Wars, Mizrachi and Hashomer Hatzair were active despite Orthodox opposition and Neologist apathy, with 25 Jews reaching Palestine in 1933–39. During the White Terror attacks of 1919–21, several Jews were killed. The J. pop. reached a peak of 3,482 in 1900 and then dropped to 3,088 in 1941. In 1942, the young were seized for forced labor, many perishing. In early May 1944, the Jews were herded into a ghetto with Jews from the neighboring settlements. All were deported to Auschwitz on 13 July although several managed to escape to Budapest. The postwar community reached a peak of 342 in 1948 before dwindling through emigration, many leaving for Israel.

SZRENSK   Warsaw dist., Poland. The J. settlement was one of the oldest in the Masovia region, originating in the late 17th cent. An organized community existed from the 1820s, growing to 865 (total 1,750) in 1857 but then declining through emigration

Neologist synagogue in Szombathely, Hungary, 1880 (Jewish Museum, Budapest/photo courtesy of Beth Hatefutsoth, Tel Aviv)

to 613 in 1921. Zionist activity commenced in 1902 and a Hebrew school enrolling about 80 children was founded in 1917. The Germans captured the town in Sept. 1939, instituting a regime of forced labor, property expropriations, and arbitrary fines. The synagogue and *beit midrash* were destroyed in late 1939. All 600 Jews were expelled to the Mlawa ghetto in Nov. 1941. They were sent to the Treblinka death camp and Auschwitz in three transports during Nov. 1942.

SZUBIN   Poznan dist., Poland. Jews settled in the first half of the 18th cent. The community developed after the Prussian annexation in 1772. A synagogue and elementary school were opened and the J. pop. grew to an 1873 peak of 418 (about 12% of the total). Emancipation and higher education brought the young closer to German culture and many left for the big German cities to pursue professions. In 1910, 139 Jews remained and 27 in 1939. The Jews were then expelled by the Germans to General Gouvernement territory by the end of the year.

SZUMOWO NOWE Bialystok dist., Poland. Jews were present in the early 19th cent. and numbered 125 (total 364) in 1921. Eight hundred Jews from S. and the neighborhood were shot in Aug. 1941 in the nearby forest. All the rest were sent to the Zambrow transit camp on 1 Nov. 1942 and deported to Auschwitz in Jan. 1943.

SZUMSK Volhynia dist., Poland, today Ukraine. Jews were present from the first half of the 18th cent. In 1745 a Jew relocated his brickyard in the area and built a *beit midrash*, bath house, and stores for rental to other Jews in the town. In 1897 the J. pop reached a peak of 1,962 (total 2,258) in an atmosphere of economic prosperity. Most merchants dealt in grain and Jews owned small factories while J. tailors produced readymade wear. After WWI the lumber industry also became an important source of income but was cut back in the 1930s as the Polish authorities undermined J. economic life. The Zionists were active between the World Wars. Five days after the arrival of the Germans on 5 July 1941, the Ukrainians staged a pogrom. A *Judenrat* was established and in March 1942 the Jews were confined to a ghetto. On 18 Aug., 1,792 were murdered outside the town; all but 15 of the rest were killed on 9 Sept.

SZYDLOW Kielce dist., Poland. Jews are first mentioned in 1494 and from 1663 were living under a royal privilege as merchants trading mainly in grain, lumber, and hides. Numbering about 100, they built one of the most magnificent synagogues in Poland in the Renaissance style at the turn of the cent. The J. pop. reached a peak of 1,139 in 1827, falling off to 660 (total 2,246) in 1921. Under the German occupation from Sept. 1939, the Jews were subjected to severe persecution. A *Judenrat* was established in May 1940, charged with furnishing forced labor. A ghetto was set up on 1 Jan. 1942 and in Oct. 1942, after 150 of the able-bodied were selected for labor camps, the remaining 1,000 including refugees were deported to the Treblinka death camp via Chmielnik.

SZYDLOWIEC Kielce dist., Poland. When exactly the Jews settled in S. is unclear, but in 1663 they were living under a royal privilege. By the 1770s they comprised 90% of the pop. In the early 19th cent., S. became an important center of Hasidism. R. Natan David Rabinowicz (d. 1865), son of Yerahmiel of Przysucha (Pshischa), founded a hasidic dynasty that attracted thousands of followers. In 1876, most of the town was destroyed in a fire and not until the late 1880s did the community fully recover. In 1910, the J. pop. was 6,433 (total 8,597). In the late 19th cent., Jews entered new fields of employment, operating 14 shoemaking and hide-processing shops and ten quarries. The Bund became active in the early 20th cent. and Haskala followers started a cultural society (*Kultur Farayn*) in 1910–11. After WWI, the garment industry became the major source of J. employment, with 1,400 Jews working in 150 workshops. J. trade unions were highly influential and Zionist activity was extensive but Agudat Israel, supported by Gur Hasidim, controlled the community council for many years. In 1939, the J. pop. was about 7,200. The Germans entered the city on 9 Sept. 1939, burning down the synagogue and executing 23 community leaders. A ghetto was established in Dec. 1941 as refugees increased the J. pop. to over 10,000. On 23 Sept. 1942, most were deported to the Treblinka death camp. Six hundred found in hiding were shot immediately, as were 52 patients in the J. hospital. The 600 Jews remaining in the ghetto were sent to the Skarzysko-Kamienna labor camp around early Oct. 1942. A new ghetto was then set up for 6,000 surviving Jews in the district. On 8 Jan. 1943 about 1,000 were selected for work at the Hassag munitions factory in Skarzysko-Kamienna and the rest were sent to Treblinka.

T

TAB Somogy dist., Hungary. Jews arrived in the early 18th cent. A J. public school was opened in 1862 and a synagogue in 1897. The J. pop. was 646 in 1869 and 495 in 1941. After the Germans arrived in spring 1944, the Jews were confined in a ghetto. The men were subjected to forced labor on nearby farms. On 3 July, the Jews were transferred to Kaposvar and in early July deported to Auschwitz. Survivors reestablished the community, but many left in 1956. In 1960, there were five J. families in T.

TABOR Bohemia, Czechoslovakia. Jews are first mentioned in 1548. A community was founded in 1621 and a synagogue was erected in the late 1630s. In the 17th cent., Jews traded in wool, hides, salt, meat, and cheese and in the 18th cent. they were employed as butchers, bakers, farmers, glaziers, soap manufacturers, distillers, carters, and knitters of socks. A new synagogue, a second cemetery, and a J. elementary school were opened in the late 19th cent. as the J. pop. rose to 455 in 1884. In 1933, 265 Jews remained. The synagogue was closed down in Oct. 1941. The Nazis subsequently destroyed the two J. cemeteries. In 1942 they used T. as a staging area for deportations from the region to the Theresienstadt ghetto. Most Jews were sent on to Auschwitz in Jan., Sept., and Oct. 1943. Seventy survived in the two transports sent to Theresienstadt on 12 Nov. 1942 and 206 Jews married to non-Jews were still present in the city at the end of 1944. Three labor camps attached to the Flossenbuerg concentration camp operated in the area in 1943–45 as well as three detention camps including one at Plana nad Luznici for Jews in mixed marriages and one for their children.

TACHOV Bohemia (Sudetenland), Czechoslovakia. Jews were apparently present in the 13th cent. After the 1848 revolution, they played leading roles in establishing the wood and glass industries in T. A well-known yeshiva was maintained in T. in the 18th–19th cents. and the town also served as the seat of the dist. rabbinate. A new synagogue was erected in 1912 after the old one was destroyed in 1818 by fire. The J. pop. was 310 in 1900 and 179 in 1930 (total 7,075). Most Jews left the town during the Sudetenland crisis. The rest were deported directly to the death camps in 1942. The Nazis destroyed the synagogue on *Kristallnacht* (9–10 Nov. 1938). Hundreds of victims of death marches and transports were buried in the area, including 200 massacred at the local train station.

TACOVO (Hung. Tecso; Yid. Tetsch) Carpatho-Russia, Czechoslovakia, today Ukraine. Eight Jews were living in T. in 1728. After abandoning the town, Jews apparently returned in the 1820s, numbering nine in 1830 and 350 (total 3,524) in 1880. In the mid-19th cent., the community was given the right to appoint a rabbi. The first was R. Yaakov Klein. In 1921, under Czechoslovakian rule, the J. pop. rose to 1,266. In 1941 it was 2,150 (total 10,371). In this period, Jews owned 47 business establishments, five small factories, a flour mill, and a bank. About 30 families earned their livelihoods from crafts and some Jews belonged to the professional class (two doctors, two lawyers). Agudat Israel was especially active among the young and Zionist youth organizations like Betar and Hashomer Hatzair also exerted much influence. The J. National Party had representatives on the municipal and county councils. Hungarian policy seriously affected J. livelihoods after the occupation of the town in March 1939. In 1940–41, young Jews were drafted into labor battalions, most being sent to the eastern front, where they perished. In July 1941, a number of

J. families without Hungarian citizenship were expelled to the German-occupied Ukraine and murdered. A ghetto was established in April 1944, with about 8,000 Jews from the area transferred there. In late May, all were deported to Auschwitz. A few local Jews volunteered for the Czechoslovakian army in the Soviet Union and fought against the Nazis.

TAGANROG Rostov dist., Russia. Jews are first mentioned in the first half of the 19th cent. In 1897, their pop. was 2,960 (total 50,000). The old synagogue in the city was erected in the late 1860s or early 1870s. In the early 20th cent., the community maintained a number of traditional welfare institutions, private schools, and *hadarim*. In the Soviet period, the J. pop. dropped to 2,633 in 1926 but rose again to 3,124 in 1939 (total 188,781). The well-known Russian actress of J. extraction F. Ranievskaya-Feldman was born in T. in 1896. The Germans captured the city in mid-Oct. 1941 and on 26 Oct. murdered about 1,800 Jews from T. and its environs.

TAJURA (also Tadjoura) Tripolitania dist., Libya. Little is known of the medieval community. The small modern community dates from the mid-19th cent. Unlike other Jews in the Tripoli and coastal area, most Jews in T. engaged in farming, mainly growing dates and selling them in the market. The dates were mainly used to produce arrack. J. women also wove woolen robes and a few wealthy Jews were wholesalers. Others were artisans and enjoyed a reputation for the knives they produced. The J. pop. numbered about 100 in 1886 and 189 (total 14,610) in 1931. Boys attended an Italian public school for five years from the age of seven and a *talmud torah* in the afternoons. Community life centered around the ancient synagogue. In the transition to Italian rule, rioting Arabs murdered Jews and pillaged and vandalized the synagogue. The Arabs borrowed money from wealthy Jews and utilized the services of J. brokers to buy and sell livestock. Like the Arabs, the Jews maintained minimal contact with the Italian authorities. During WWII, the community continued to live in relative isolation, barely affected by events. J. soldiers arriving with the British in early 1943 revived the connection with Palestine. The Arab riots of Nov. 1945 in Tripolitania spread to T. as well. In the community of 230 Jews seven Jews were killed and dozens hospitalized, with homes, businesses, and the syna-

gogue destroyed. The entire community left for Israel in 1950, most settling in Moshav Biriyya near Safed and Moshav Alma in Upper Galilee to continue their lives as farmers.

TAKTAHARKANY Zemplen dist., Hungary. Jews are mentioned in 1812 and numbered 72 in 1930. Jews dominated commerce in T. In 1938, 20 young people from 16 families were sent to forced labor. At the end of May 1944, the remaining Jews were deported to Auschwitz via Satoraljaujheny.

TALHEIM Wuerttemberg, Germany. Few Jews resided in T. until the second half of the 18th cent., when a few families were allowed to occupy the demolished western wing of a local castle and erect baking and *mikve* facilities. The settlement developed under Wuerttemberg rule after 1806 and reached a peak pop. of 122 in 1860, with some emigrating, mainly to the U.S. Jews were fully integrated in the town's social life but were not active politically. In 1933, 82 remained (total 1,512). Nazi pressure brought about the social and economic isolation of the Jews. On 11 Nov. 1938, the day after *Kristallnacht*, SA troops wrecked the synagogue and beat and pillaged Jews in their homes. The community was subsequently forced to "sell" the synagogue and J. school building to the municipal council at a nominal price. In 1940–41, J. men were put to forced labor paving a street; in 1941 farm land still in J. hands was impounded. Thirty-eight Jews managed to emigrate, 26 of them to the U.S. Of the others, 38 perished after expulsion to the east in 1941–42.

TALKA Minsk dist., Belorussia. The Germans captured the town in early July 1941 and murdered about 300 Jews (222 according to another source) in late Sept. or early Oct.

TALLINN Estonia. Jews were present in the early 14th cent. under Danish rule and continued to maintain a presence afterwards under the Order of Teutonic Knights despite the ban on J. residence in Baltic lands. Jews were also present in the period of Swedish rule (1621–1710) as merchants benefiting from trade relations between Sweden and Poland. Under Russian rule, all the Jews were expelled from the city in 1742, returning only in the 1780s, though subjected to various restrictions through local pressure. The large com-

The Old City of Tallinn, Estonia

munity that began to develop was curtailed by a new wave of expulsions that commenced in 1804 and left 36 Jews in the city in 1820. The modern community was founded in the 1830s by Cantonists serving there, joined in 1865 by a few dozen Lithuanian craftsmen under Czar Alexander's relaxation of residence restrictions outside the Pale of Settlement. Economic conditions improved as the pop. grew during the 1870s, with the port and army bases providing sources of livelihood and J. contractors active in construction and railroad work employing J. laborers and skilled workers. During the 1880s the J. pop. fell from 963 to 647 after new expulsion orders were directed against settlers coming from the Pale of Settlement and after emigration to the U.S. commenced. There were also a number of antisemitic incidents. However, with the publication of renewed residence privileges in 1894, the J. pop. rose again to 1,193 in 1897 (total 58,810) and continued to grow thereafter, doubling by the 1930s. The Cantonists and Lithuanians constituted two social classes in the community, the former cut off from their Jewishness and the latter imbued with

J. values and experience but relatively unlearned. Friction between the two led to the establishment of a separate Lithuanian synagogue in 1870. To unite them, community leaders saw to the construction of a single central synagogue in 1885 which remained standing until 1941. In the 1870s a private *heder* was converted into a J. public school, but the well-to-do preferred to send their children to general schools or Lithuanian *yeshivot*. Zionism took hold in the late 19th cent., while most of the young Jews who took part in the revolutionary events of the early 20th cent. joined the Social Democrat Party. During WWI, about 2,000 J. refugees reached the city, benefiting from its economic prosperity to earn a livelihood and at the same time furnishing the community with activists and religious teachers. The Feb. 1917 Revolution further stimulated national and social awakening, with the Zionist Organization playing a central role. A relatively large number of Jews were factory workers (most in a J. textile plant) while over half the artisans were tailors and hatmakers. The community operated extensive welfare services. The cultural autonomy accorded to the Jews from

1926 in independent Estonia (more extensive than anywhere else in Europe) allowed full control of education, which became a bone of contention between Zionist and Yiddishist circles. From the 1926–27 school year, Hebrew began to replace Russian as the language of instruction in the J. public school. In 1928 a rival Yiddish-language school was founded, which, in a form of compromise, operated parallel classes in the Hebrew-language school through the 1930s. Though the Zionists controlled the community's autonomous culture council by 1929, the leading cultural institute remained the Yiddishist Bialik Farein, putting on plays from the classic Yiddish repertoire and sending its choir on tour and to appear on Estonian radio. Among its many distinguished literary guests was Bialik himself in 1931. Through the 1930s the Zionist youth movements were active, with Hehalutz offering pioneer training on Estonian farms prior to *aliya*. Antisemitism rose in the late 1930s under Nazi influence. The Soviets arrived in June 1940. The process of sovietization affected J. businessmen and shortly before the Soviet withdrawal in June 1941 hundreds of J. property owners and Zionist activists were exiled to the the interior of the Soviet Union. Over half the J. pop. left by choice with the Soviets. The Germans took the city in Aug. 1941, finding around 1,000 Jews there and immediately instituting a regime of persecution, carrying out mass arrests with the assistance of the Estonian Omakaitse "self-defense" organization. Some Jews were held in the city's main jail, while the able-bodied were sent to forced labor on Estonian farms and the peat bogs. From mid-Sept. 1941 the Jews began to be killed off systematically in small groups in Kalevi-Liiva, joined by Jews brought in from the Theresienstadt ghetto and Germany. The killers were Omakaitse units under *Sonderkommando 1a* orders. By 19 Dec. 1941, 610 Jews had been murdered, the women tormented and humiliated. Most of the women and children previously deported to Paskow were executed there in Feb. 1942. The city was liberated by the Red Army on 22 Sept. 1944. Within a short time, 1,500 J. refugees assembled there, joined later by Russian Jews to constitute a peak pop. of 3,754 in 1970 (total 364,446). Thereafter the renewed community diminished through a process of emigration to Israel.

TALLYA Zemplen dist., Hungary. Jews settled in the late 18th cent., producing and selling wine. In 1840,

when they consecrated their third synagogue, they numbered 340. After WWI, the disturbances in T. were particularly severe and a J. defense group was sent from Budapest to assist the community. In 1941, 173 Jews remained. In Dec. 1942, all males between 18 and 48 were seized for forced labor. On 12–15 June 1944, the remaining Jews were deported via Satoraljaujhely to Auschwitz, where 140 perished.

TALNOE Kiev dist., Ukraine. Jews numbered 11 in 1765 and 5,452 (total 9,610) in 1897. In 1882, about 200 were employed as farm workers on local estates. Most Jews were Hasidim. A *talmud torah* and private school for boys were operating in the early 20th cent. On 12 Dec. 1917, Ukrainian soldiers passing through the town rioted in the market, robbing and destroying J. stalls and stores. J. soldiers from the same unit arrested the rioters. In further riots in spring 1919, gangs murdered 53 Jews. In the Soviet period, many Jews worked in a sugar refinery and in 1928, 12 cooperatives were opened, employing 204 workers, most of them Jews. A nearby J. kolkhoz had 840 members. A Yiddish-language elementary school was started in the 1920s and a clubroom and Yiddish library were also active in the town as well as a clinic whose 35 doctors and nurses were Jews. In 1939 the J. pop. was 1,866. The Germans captured T. on 29 July 1941 and on 19 Sept. murdered the Jews in groups near the village of Bielashki. On 17 April 1942 children of mixed marriages were murdered.

TALSI (Yid. Talsen) Kurzeme (Courland) dist., Latvia. Jews began settling in the early 19th cent. and reached a pop. of 1,411 in 1897 (total 4,113). Thereafter emigration across the sea curtailed growth. Among the J. upper class there was a marked degree of Germanization, with many children studying at the two German schools for boys and girls. J. education was based on private *hadarim*, some with modern tendencies. Both the Zionists and J. socialists were active from the late 19th cent., the latter playing a leading role in the 1905 revolution. In 1915 the Jews were expelled from T. by the Russian army. About a third returned after WWI, supported by assistance from the Joint Distribution Committee and American relatives. Economic conditions soon stabilized, with the Jews dominating trade (particularly in textiles, jewelry, wood products, and steel). A J. public school was opened in 1920 and Zionist activity expanded, some of the youth movement graduates leaving for Palestine. In 1935 the J. pop. stood at 499. J. communal life was extinguished under Soviet rule (1940–41) while businesses were nationalized. Some Jews left for the big cities to seek work or to study. A group of political activists and property owners with their families (50–60 in number) were expelled to the Soviet Union, most of the men perishing in labor camps. The Germans took the town on 1 July 1941. A regime of persecution and forced labor ensued. The community was liquidated around the end of Sept. 1941 when the Jews were taken outside the town and executed by a firing squad of Latvian "Arajs Commandos" and local police.

TAMASI Tolna dist., Hungary. Jews settled in the first half of the 19th cent., numbering 254 in 1880 and 211 in 1930. Most were merchants, farmers, and artisans. A synagogue was opened in 1851 and a J. school in 1880. The Jews did not suffer during the White Terror attacks (1919–21), mainly because many participated in the 1919 revolt against the Communists. On 30 June 1944, the Jews were deported to Auschwitz via Dombovar.

TAMEZRET Matmata district, Tunisia. The J. community dates from the end of the 19th cent., though Algerian responsa indicate a J. presence in the 13th–14th cents. T.'s J. community was small, never amounting to more than seven families. The J. pop. was 48 in 1936 and 55 in 1946. The Jews lived in caves and earned their living as tailors and petty tradesmen. South Tunisian Jews considered T.'s ancient synagogue holy, visiting it on Passover and Sukkot. In the late 19th cent., Matmata, 6 miles (10 km) distant, became T.'s commercial center and Gabes its spiritual center. In 1942, the Germans took the town. The Jews supplied them with food and goods, but were not mobilized for forced labor. Following liberation (March 1943) and especially after Israel's War of Independence began, relations with the Arabs deteriorated. In 1952, 39 Jews (five families) emigrated to Israel.

TANGERMUENDE Saxony, Germany. Jews lived in T. from the first half of the 14th cent. They suffered in the Black Death persecutions of 1348–49 and following the Host desecration trial in Berlin in 1510. A local Jew from T. was executed and finally, in 1573, the Jews of T. were expelled together with those of Brandenburg. The Jews settled again in the beginning

of the 18th cent. In 1765, the community of 90 individuals maintained a prayer room and a cemetery. In 1933, the J. pop. dropped to 20. Under Nazi rule most Jews left. By 1939, only seven Jews were still living in T. No information is available about their fate.

TANN Hesse–Nassau, Germany. Established in 1750, the community maintained an elementary school (1830–1930), opened a new synagogue in 1880, and numbered 140 (13% of the pop.) in 1885. Affiliated with the rabbinate of Fulda, it declined to 72 in 1933. Nazis demolished the synagogue on 7 Nov. 1938 (two days before *Kristallnacht*) when the local SA chief was killed by a falling beam. No Jews remained in Feb. 1940, 36 having emigrated (mostly to the U.S. and Palestine).

TAPIAU (Rus. Gvardeysk) East Prussia, Germany, today Russia. The community maintained a synagogue and a cemetery. In 1895, the J. pop. was 70 and in 1925 it was 40. In 1894, t he community provided religious instruction to 16 children. However, toward the end of the Weimar period, the local Jews could no longer afford this service. No information is available about the fate of the 28 Jews who were living in T. when the Nazis took over in 1933.

TAPIOBICSKE Pest–Pilis–Solt–Kiskun dist., Hungary. Jews settled in 1746 and numbered 220 in 1840, declining steadily to 61 in 1930. At the end of June 1944, they were deported to Auschwitz via Nagykata and Kecskemet.

TAPIOGYORGYE Pest–Pilis–Solt–Kiskun dist., Hungary. Jews arrived in the late 18th cent., numbering 108 in 1880 and 74 in 1930. At the end of June 1944, they were deported to Auschwitz via Nagykata and Kecskemet. In 1956, hooligans burst into a J. old age home in T. and were only prevented from massacring the residents by the arrival of soldiers.

TAPIOSULY Pest–Pilis–Solt–Kiskun dist., Hungary. Jews are known from the late 18th cent. and numbered 76 in 1930. In the beginning of June 1944, they were deported to Auschwitz via Nagykata and Kecskemet.

TAPIOSZELE Pest–Pilis–Solt–Kiskun dist., Hungary. Jews settled in the 18th cent., founding a synagogue in 1810 and a school in 1840, when they numbered 396 (14% of the total). In 1941, 243 remained. On 18 June 1944, all were deported to Auschwitz via Nagykata and Kecskemet.

TAPOLCA Zala dist., Hungary. A few families settled in 18th cent., mostly selling wine, both locally and abroad. Jews dominated the town's commerce and industry and owned a bank and daily newspaper. The pop. in 1850 was 51. A school was opened in 1855 and a synagogue in 1863. In 1868, the Jews formed a Neologist congregation. In the 1880s, the town submitted a petition against its Jews to parliament, which discussed and then rejected it. During the White Terror attacks of 1919–21, 17 Jews were killed. By 1930, they numbered 706. In the beginning of June 1944, they were deported to Auschwitz.

TARASHCHA Kiev dist., Ukraine. Jews numbered 134 in 1765 and 4,905 (total 11,250) in 1897. Most were Hasidim. On 23 April 1917, Ukrainian gangs pillaged and destroyed J. homes and stores and injured nine. New riots erupted in Dec. 1917. In July and Aug. 1919 the Petlyura gangs attacked the Jews. Under the Soviets, a Yiddish-language elementary school, night school, and kindergarten were opened. In 1939, the J. pop. was 1,140. The Germans occupied T. in July 1941. In Aug. they executed 109 people, most of them Jews; nearly all the rest were murdered in an *Aktion* in fall 1941.

TARCAL Zemplen dist., Hungary. Jews are first mentioned in 1746 as wine merchants. In 1896, they numbered 280; in 1930, 321; and in 1941, 299. A synagogue was opened in 1860 and a J. school in 1901. J. farms and vineyards were confiscated in 1939 under Hungary's racial laws, and Jews were seized for forced labor in 1942. The remaining Jews were deported to Auschwitz via Satoraljaujhely on 16 May 1944. A small group of survivors tried to reestablish the community, but most left after 1956.

TARCZYN Warsaw dist., Poland. Jews first settled in the early 19th cent., trading in cattle, grain, and lumber as well as engaging in crafts. The J. pop. grew to 630 in 1857 and 1,427 (total 2,526) in 1921. The Zionists, the Bund, and Agudat Israel were all active between the World Wars. The Germans captured T. in Sept. 1939, instituting a regime of forced labor. All the Jews were expelled to the Warsaw

ghetto in early 1941, meeting their end in the Treblinka death camp.

TARDOSKED (Hung. Tardoskedd) Slovakia, Czechoslovakia, today Republic of Slovakia. Jews settled in the early 18th cent. and again in the early 19th after their expulsion in the mid-18th cent. They numbered 165 (total 4,191) in 1869; 106 in 1930; and 58 in 1940, when they owned a few grocery stores, bakeries, butcher shops, and taverns. Under the Hungarians, they were seized for forced labor. On 13 June 1944, the Germans deported them to Auschwitz.

TARGOVISTE Walachia dist., Rumania. Jews first settled in the mid-17th cent., and in the early 19th cent Jews from Ploiesti fleeing the plague moved to T. The J. pop. in 1930 was 551 (2% of the total). In Nov. 1940 the Iron Guard ordered the J. merchants to close down their stores and on 5 Dec. to sell their goods and property at 10–15% of their value. Most of the Jews fled.

TARGOWICA Volhynia, Poland, today Ukraine. Jews are first recorded in 1569. The J. pop. was 891 in 1897 (total 907) and 660 in 1921 after the rigors of WWI and the civil war (1918–21). The German arrival on 25 June 1941 was accompanied by the murder of 20 Jews. On 1 Aug., 130 J. men were executed outside the town. The community was expelled to the Ostrozec ghetto in spring 1942. On 9 Oct. 1942, 900 were murdered with the local Jews; most of the 200 who fled were also caught and killed.

TARGU-FRUMOS Moldavia dist., Rumania. Jews settled here in the mid-18th cent. and were involved in municipal activities in the early 19th cent. In 1899 the J. pop. was 2,123 (46% of the total). In March 1907, peasants plundered J. homes and stores, and 59 J. families were left destitute. Antisemitism was widespread between the World Wars. In fall 1940 Jews aged 18–50 were sent to the Tudoreni-Rechita forced labor camp and then to work in quarries in Bessarabia. On 9 June 1944 Rumanian soldiers recaptured T. and killed 15 Jews. Only a third of the community remained after the war.

TARGU-GLODURI Moldavia dist., Rumania. Jews settled here in 1838. The J. pop. in 1930 was 86 (16% of the total). From 1911 communal affairs were directed by the U.E.P. (Association of Rumanian-born Jews). On the outbreak of the Soviet-Rumanian war (1941) the community's remaining 75 Jews were expelled to Bacau.

TARGU-JIU Oltania dist., Rumania. The J. community was founded in 1890 and numbered 100 in 1930 (19% of the total). An antisemitic periodical appeared between the World Wars. During WWII an internment camp for political dissidents was opened nearby for non-Jews and Jews who were later deported to Transnistria.

TARGU LAPUSULUI (Hung. Magyarlapos) N. Transylvania dist., Rumania. A J. community was founded c. 1820 and a synagogue built in 1885 still exists. R. Moshe David Teitelbaum served the community for almost 50 years (1885-1935) and established one of the largest *yeshivot* in the dist., with up to 140 students. An unusually large number of erudite rabbinical scholars lived and taught in T. until the end of the 19th cent. The J. pop. in 1920 was 804 (34% of the total). Zionist activity began after the establishment of the Transylvanian Zionist movement in 1920, and Zionists were among the leaders of the community. Young Po'alei Agudat Israel set up a training farm for its members. The situation of the Jews deteriorated from the time the Hungarians took the town in Aug. 1940. In June 1942, 20 men were drafted into labor battalions and sent to the Ukraine for forced labor where they all died. Up to 1944, males aged 21-40 were sent to forced labor within Hungary. After the occupation by the Germans on 19 March 1944, discriminatory regulations were imposed. On 6 May the community was transferred to the Dej ghetto and suffered the same fate as the local Jews.

TARGU-MURES (Hung. Marosvasarhely; Ger. Neumark am Maros; formerly Uj-Szekelyvasar, Ujvasar, Szekely-vasarhely) N. Transylvania, Rumania. Jews first settled in Naznan-Falva (a suburb of T.) in 1601 and its synagogue was one of the first in Transylvania. Permission for Jews to settle in the city itself was granted in 1843. In 1870 the community split into Orthodox and Status Quo congregations. The Orthodox community created a network of educational institutions including the Beth Jacob school for girls, a yeshiva with dormitories for 100 students from outside T., and adult education classes. Courts of most hasidic sects were active from the late 19th cent. and grew after WWI. The Status Quo community followed a western, modern way of life with assimilationist tendencies. It nevertheless supported the Zionist movement and many of its members immigrated to Palestine as pioneers. The community's last rabbi, Dr. Pinhas Levi, who served for 40 years, was also the founder of the Zionist movement in T. The J. Cultural Center was built in 1928 and served as the meeting place for all Zionist parties and communal activities. The Status Quo community also developed a network of educational institutions for children, youth, and adults. The Zionist movement in T. was founded in 1913 and was one of the most active in Transylvania. T. exceeded all other communities in its collections for the J. National Fund and the Keren Hayesod. The pioneer training farms of Hashomer Hatzair were based there, and over half of the adults and 60% of the youth were organized in the Zionist movement. The J. pop. in 1930 was 5,193 (15% of the total). In 1939, anti-J. regulations were introduced whereby thousands of Jews were ejected from official positions, businesses were transferred to non-Jews, and Jews were stripped of Hungarian citizenship. With the return of the Hungarian regime in 1940, J. merchants and industrialists were forbidden to trade; the activities of members of the professions were restricted; a *numerus clausus* was introduced for J. pupils in high schools and institutes of higher education; and J. artists were prevented from appearing on the stage and forbidden to contribute to the arts. In 1941-44, 1,200 J. males aged 21-48 were conscripted into labor battalions; over 50% of them died in the Ukraine, Poland, and Hungary. On 21 March 1944 the Germans occupied T. A *Judenrat* was set up and in April the Zionist leadership and members of leftist parties were arrested. All communal and Zionist activities were outlawed, J. shops were closed, and all valuables collected. On 3 May 1944, the ghettoization in three locations of the 8,648 Jews was begun. Youth movement members organized assistance to the sick and study groups for children, built primitive accommodations, and together with doctors and nurses provided sanitary facilities. From 29 May 1944, 6,953 Jews were deported to Auschwitz. Only 1,200 survived. A community was reestablished after the war but the majority of those who returned made their way to Israel.

TARGU-NEAMT Moldavia dist., Rumania. Jews

were granted the right to settle here in the late 15th cent. In 1579 they were expelled. They were permitted to return in the early 17th cent. In 1899 the J. pop. was 3,671 (42% of the total). A stone synagogue built in 1737 was gutted by fire in 1774 and rebuilt in 1856. R. Hayyim Mordekhai Roller, who served the community between 1895 and 1941, was a leading scholar in the region. Jews were subject to blood libels (the first in 1710) throughout the 18th and 19th cents. A modern *talmud torah* existed with 235 pupils in 1910. Between the World Wars Jews were involved in municipal politics and in 1931 a Jew was elected deputy mayor. The Iron Guard imprisoned and tortured the community's leaders, who were forced to forfeit their possessions. Toward the end of the Soviet-Rumanian war in 1941 the Jews were forced to flee to Buhusi. The community was reestablished after the war.

TARGU-OCNA   Moldavia dist., Rumania. Jews settled in the late 18th cent. following the development of salt mines in the area. In 1899 the J. pop. was 1,700 (20% of the total). Many of T's Jews were followers of the hasidic rabbi of Buhusi (Bohush). Between the World Wars a Jew served as deputy mayor and a number of Jews as municipal councilors. The Jews were persecuted by Antonescu and the Iron Guard. In June 1941, most of the men were imprisoned. On 10 July 1941, after the arrival of German soldiers, the Jews were expelled to Bacau. After the war, 100 J. families returned.

TARGU SACUIESC   (Hung. Kezdivasarhely) N. Transylvania dist., Rumania. A J. community was organized in the 1880s with the smallest J. pop. in Transylvania: 66 in 1920. In May 1944, the community was transferred to Sfantul Gheorghe and in June deported to Auschwitz.

TARHUNA   Tripolitania dist., Libya. J. settlement from neighboring towns, especially Gharian, commenced with the entrenchment of Italian rule in 1923. The Jews won a reputation for their metal work, particularly their agricultural implements. Two families owned a flour mill and Jews owned eight general stores. Most, however, were itinerant peddlers. Two synagogues operated in private homes, representing two factions contending for the presidency of the community. Children studied at an Italian public school in the mornings and a *talmud torah* in the afternoons.

The J. pop. was 79 (total 36,760) in 1931. Italy's restrictive racial laws of 1938 forced J. children to drop out of school after the fourth grade and prevented merchants from doing business with government offices. In 1942, some J. men were sent to a forced labor camp and Allied bombings caused the Jews to flee the city. On their return they found their homes looted. In the 1945 and 1948 riots, the Jews sought refuge in the army camp the British had taken over. About 150 refugees from Tripoli also stayed there in 1945. In 1949, 41 of the community's 45 families were receiving assistance from the Joint Distribution Committee as preparations for *aliya* began to be made. In 1950, all but five families left for Tripoli and in 1952 most emigrated to Israel.

TARLOW   Kielce dist., Poland. Jews settled in the late 16th cent. and in 1617 were granted wide-ranging privileges. In the mid-17th cent., most were tailors and furriers but toward the end of the cent. they went over to trade. As the local economy stagnated in the 18th cent., their numbers declined, standing at 658 (total 1,236) in 1857. Between the World Wars, the Orthodox controlled the community and its institutions. In 1921 the J. pop. was 1,052. The German occupation of Sept. 1939 established a *Judenrat* and introduced a regime of forced labor and "contributions." In Dec. 1941, a ghetto was established, its pop. swelling to 7,000 with the arrival of refugees. All were deported to the Treblinka death camp on 29 Oct. 1942.

TARNA MARE   (Hung. Nagytarna) N. Transylvania dist., Rumania. A J. community was organized here in the mid-19th cent. The J. pop. in 1930 was 349 (5% of the total). In May 1944 the community was transferred to the Nagyszollos ghetto and then deported to Auschwitz.

TARNAVENI   (Hung. Discoszentmarton) S. Transylvania dist., Rumania. A J. community was established in 1868 and was attached to the Adamus community. Among the early settlers were Sephardim from Alba-Iulia. At the end of the 19th cent., the J. pop. doubled when T. became the district capital. Jews played an important role in its economic development. In 1920, T. with a J. pop. of 490 was the only town in the area where Jews constituted over 10% of the total pop. A small hasidic community became entrenched between the World Wars. Zionist activity began in 1918, led by Dr. Erno Marton, editor of the *Uj Kelet* newspaper and later elected to the Rumanian parliament. In fall 1940, the Iron Guard stopped all J. commerce and J. shops were closed down. In 1941, the J. pop. of 796 was transferred to Blaj, but returned ten days later when T. became a center for J. refugees from the area. Many Jews were forced to vacate their homes and relocate to remote areas. The young were sent to forced labor and some were exiled to Transnistria. The community was reorganized after the liberation and the majority emigrated to Palestine.

TARNAWA NIZNA Lwow dist., Poland, today Ukraine. The J. pop. in 1921 was 115. The Jews were possibly deported to the Belzec death camp in the second half of 1942, directly or via Turka.

TARNOBRZEG-DZIKOW Lwow dist., Poland. Jews settled permanently in the second half of the 17th cent. and developed economic ties to the estates of the aristocratic Tarnowski family. The hasidic court of the Ropczyce (Ropshits)-Dzikow dynasty — whose founder Eliezer ben Naftali Tzevi Horowitz was rabbi of Dzikow in the 1840s — also contributed to the J. economy. While heavy taxation under Austrian rule took its toll, the J. pop. grew to form a large majority by 1880 (2,768 of a total 3,460) and a J. mayor was elected in 1878. A devastating fire in 1888 left many homeless. The Zionists became active in 1893 and until the outbreak of WWI relations with the non-J. pop. were for the most part satisfactory. Most Jews fled the city in the first days of the war. Arson, pillage, and typhoid were the fate of those who remained. Hundreds never returned, the J. pop. dropping to 2,146 in 1921 with the community now supported by the Joint Distribution Committee. While Agudat Israel controlled the community council, Zionist activity expanded and youth movements operated training farms. The late 1930s were marked by rising antisemitic agitation. The Germans took the town on 13 Sept. 1939, instituting a regime of severe persecution. In the fall (Sukkot) the entire community was expelled to the east, dividing itself among various E. Galician settlements, with those refusing to accept Soviet citizenship exiled to the interior of Russia in the summer of 1940. T. became a ghetto for J. refugees in the area and then a shortlived labor camp after the ghetto was liquidaed on 19 July 1942.

TARNOGORA Lublin dist., Poland. A 1743 residence ban retarded the growth of the J. community, which remained small even after the 1862 emancipation. In 1921, the community, attached to Izbica, numbered 107 (total 1,589). In WWII, many went eastward with the retreating Soviet army. The few who remained after the German occupation were presumably deported to the Belzec death camp in spring 1942.

TARNOGROD Lublin dist., Poland. Jews were among the town's first settlers, receiving a royal privilege of unrestricted residence in 1569. Many were murdered in the Chmielnicki massacres of 1648-49 but J. life revived and by the late 17th cent. an organized community, active in the Council of the Four Lands, existed with a synagogue and cemetery. Among its outstanding rabbis were Azriel ha-Levi, author of *Nahalat Azriel* (1691), Moshe Margoliot, and Aryeh Leib Teicher, who presided for 68 years until his death in 1935. The J. pop. rose from 1,673 in 1857 to 2,238 (total 4,768) in 1921. After WWI, many Jews operated stores and market stalls. A prosperous class of merchants dealt mainly in forest products while others marketed local farm produce in Lublin and Warsaw. Jews also ran two flour mills, a sawmill, and a plywood and shingle factory. Economic conditions deteriorated in the 1930s and many lost their businesses because of tax arrears. Though Zionist activity increased, Agudat Israel maintained community leadership throughout the period. T. fell to the Germans on 15 Sept 1939 and a *Judenrat* was established in early 1941. Refugees increased the J. pop. to about 3,000. A ghetto was set up in May 1942 and crowded, unsanitary conditions led to an unprecedented mortality rate. Many were sent to labor camps. On 9 Aug. 1942, 800 Jews were deported to the Belzec death camp by way of Bilgorai. On 2 Nov. 1942, the rest were sent there after 50 of the sick and old were murdered at the J. cemetery.

TARNOPOL Tarnopol dist., Poland, today Ukraine. J. settlement began with the founding of the town in 1540 and increased with the granting of unrestricted residence rights. After a fire the Jews were permitted to erect a fortified synagogue (completed in the 1640s) and to trade freely in everything but hides (to protect the local shoemaking monopoly). In 1625 they were allowed to manufacture and market mead, but disqualified from purchasing or cultivating land.

They were also allowed to practice crafts under contract with the Christian guilds. By the mid-17th cent. the well-established community numbered 300 families. Most of the Jews fled in the Chmielnicki massacres of 1648–49 and those who remained were killed. In the subsequent Cossack and Swedish wars Jews played an active part in the town's defense. The community only began to revive toward the end of the cent., when the grain and cattle trade was dominated by J. merchants and month-long trade fairs attracted buyers from all over the province of Rzeszow. In the early 18th cent. the community was served by Yehoshua Heshel Babad, the first of a long line of rabbis active in T. Economic conditions worsened under Austrian rule from 1772 and Jews were burdened by heavy taxes and restrictive measures while T.'s fairs lost their attraction when Brody became a free city and its merchants ceased to visit T. Failed efforts were also made by the Austrians to assimilate the Jews by forcing them to farm, attend secular J. schools (the Homberg system, closed down in 1806), and serve in the army. A central figure in the community was the eminent author and satirist Yosef Perl (1773–1839), who founded a J. school in 1813 combining modern and traditional elements and gathered around him a circle of Haskala adherents whose clash with the Orthodox defined community life for the coming generation. Among the Haskala figures active in T. were Menahem Mendel Levin (Lefin) of Satanov, Nahman Krochmal, Shemuel Leib Goldberg, and Bezalel Stern. In 1816 a ban was placed on the *maskilim* by R. Yaakov Ornstein of Lwow, followed by R. Tzevi Hirsch Eichenstein of the hasidic Zhidachov dynasty in 1822. The outstanding pioneer of Haskala and the Science of Judaism (*Wissenschaft des Judentums*), Shelomo Yehuda Rapoport, later rabbi of Prague, was forced out of rabbinical office in 1839 by Orthodox circles after two years of service. Nonetheless dominance of the community by Haskala leaders continued until the 1860s. By 1869 the J. pop. had grown to 11,000. The Perl school reached an enrollment of 656, but the *talmud torah* also underwent a process

Synagogue in Tarnopol, Poland

of modernization and had 300 students. Most of the Jews were employed in retail trade and crafts; 75 of the city's 76 big stores were J.-owned and most of the city's 884 merchants were Jews; many engaged in the liquor trade. A son of Yosef Perl opened the first J. pharmacy in Austria in 1832. In 1880 the J. pop. was 13,468 (total 25,819), showing virtually no change until the Nazi era as economic conditions worsened and many Jews emigrated to the U.S. Jews engaged more and more in petty trade and peddling and manufacturing was confined to small establishments while J. tradesmen met stiff competition from Ukrainian and Polish cooperatives. With the decline of assimilationist political influence, the Orthodox and the Zionists came to the fore, respectively controlling the community council and the J. seats on the city council from the early 20th cent. Under the Russian occupation in WWI, J. commercial life was almost entirely curtailed and as many as 500–600 Jews a day were mobilized for forced labor. On their withdrawal in summer 1917, the Russians left behind a trail of pillage and destruction. In the chaos and anarchy that followed the disintegration of the Austrian empire the Jews suffered depredations from all the rival parties. Economic recovery was slow, with inflation and arbitrary taxes compounding the difficulties. In 1930, 95% of J. artisans were not fully employed and a third of the community needed assistance for the Passover holidays. Among the wealthier Jews were about 60 restaurant and hotel owners and eight big flour mill operators. Community services were affected by underrepresentation on the city council (and in municipal jobs) and discriminatory allotments from the municipal budget. The Zionist youth movements were particularly active and hundreds of pioneers on their way to Palestine between the World Wars passed through Hehalutz training farms. The Hebrew supplementary school founded in 1902 joined the Tarbut network in 1924 and J. university students sometimes continued their studies at the Hebrew University in Jerusalem (36 in 1937). The J. pop. in 1931 was 13,999. When the Red Army entered the city on 17 Sept. 1939. J. property was nationalized and community leaders were exiled or expelled along with refugees unwilling to become Soviet citizens. With the annexation of Eastern Galicia to the Ukrainian Soviet Socialist Republic in Nov.-Dec. 1939, J. community institutions ceased to operate. On the arrival of the Germans on 2 July 1941, about 17,000 Jews were present in the city. Within two days a week-long pogrom com-

menced. Jews were dragged off the streets and out of their homes and shot. Some were tortured at the local jail, while others were hacked and bludgeoned to death by rampaging Ukrainians. About 5,000 Jews were murdered. A regime of extortion and forced labor was then instituted. A *Judenrat* was appointed in Aug., and a ghetto was sealed off by 1 Dec. 1941. The sick and poor died off rapidly while the skilled and able-bodied survived for a time, with clandestine commerce maintained inside the ghetto and Jews sent to labor camps to work on the roads, on farms, and in quarries. On 25 March 1942, 600–700 Jews were executed in the Janowka forest outside the city. Another 3,000–4,000 were deported to the Belzec death camp on 29–31 Aug. and another 600–750 on 30 Sept. In early Nov. a further 2,500 were sent there. The fittest of the 8,000 remaining Jews were concentrated in a labor camp at one end of the ghetto, set up as a branch of the Janowska Judenlager in Lwow, where relatively tolerable conditions prevailed. In the other part of the ghetto, executions continued, with 1,000 slaughtered in nearby fields on 8–9 April 1943. Many fled as final liquidation grew near. On 20 June, 500 Jews were murdered in the fields in a final *Aktion*. On 22 July 1943, the 2,000–2,500 Jews in the labor camp were taken out and executed. One group offered armed resistance and was cut down. Many of the hundreds who had escaped to the forests at one time or another were hunted down and murdered by local Ukrainians or handed over to the Germans. With the liberation of the city by the Red Army on 15 April 1944, 739 Jews from T. and environs came out of hiding. Most soon emigrated to Poland. In the late 1950s, there were about 500 Jews in T., only a few of them natives of the city.

TARNORUDA   Tarnopol dist., Poland, today Ukraine. Founded in the 19th cent., this community of tradesmen reached a pop. of 320 in 1880 (total 744). All the Jews, numbering 138, were shot and killed by the Germans in the winter of 1942–43.

TARNOW   Cracow dist., Poland. The first J. settlers were apparently among the Germans invited into the country in the 14th and 15th cents. to help raise the level of Polish economic life. They were accorded liberal residence and trade rights but were faced with unrelenting efforts by the local pop. to undermine their position. In 1670 a compromise agreement was signed with townsmen conceding privileges to the Jews in return for an increased tax burden, but friction continued. In 1708 and 1711 fires destroyed most J. homes and stores. Fires in 1732 and 1735 caused additional suffering. Originally Jews engaged extensively in money-lending but by the 17th cent. most were in trade and crafts. J. guilds existed from the second half of the 18th cent. An organized community with a synagogue and cemetery was established in the second half of the 16th cent, belonging to the Land of Lesser Poland and under the aegis of Szydlow until transferred to the province of Cracow in the late 17th cent. Under Austrian rule from 1772, the Jews suffered from a discriminatory tax burden. In 1848 they participated actively in revolutionary events, agitating for equal rights and allying themselves with liberal Polish nationalists. Nonetheless antisemitism intensified and anti-J. riots in 1870, 1897, and 1901 had to be suppressed by the army. The J. pop. grew from 1,914 in 1846 to 11,349 (total 24,627) in 1880. Economic conditions worsened from the 1890s in the face of anti-J. boycotts and the rise of competing Polish cooperatives. Efforts were

made to relieve economic distress through the establishment of loan funds and to strengthen community institutions. A. J. hospital was opened in 1842 and the cornerstone of a new synagogue was laid in 1864 (completed in 1908). A Baron Hirsch school enrolled 232 children in 1894, a Hebrew school was opened in 1896, and a Safah Berurah school for supplementary Hebrew education for 200 children started operating in 1902. The *talmud torah* had 150 students in 1906. During the 19th cent., both Hasidism and Haskala spread in the community as did the Zionist movement. The Jews suffered grievously under the Russian occupation at the outset of WWI and again in 1918–19 under General Haller, when his Polish soldiers and local mobs unleashed a reign of terror which led to the formation of a J. militia to protect the community. In 1921 the J. pop. stood at 15,608. Joint Distribution Committee aid organized by Henry Morgenthau, Sr., who visited the city in 1919, provided a measure of relief but economic distress continued between the World Wars. In 1931, 66% of the city's wholesalers and 80% of its retailers were Jews, with peddlers and stallkeepers providing a

Gymnastics in Tarnow, Poland, 1921

convenient target for anti-J. attacks. An extensive network of mutual aid societies and welfare agencies continued to operate. The TOZ public health organization provided children with medical attention and organized summer camps for the needy; an old age home was attached to the hospital. The Safah Berurah society expanded its activities, founding a kindergarten and elementary and secondary schools. Mizrachi opened a Yavne elementary school in 1926, reaching an enrollment of 250 in 1935, and Agudat Israel set up a Beth Jacob school for girls in 1926. The J. public library grew to 15,000 volumes. The Zionists became the dominant J. force in both the community and municipal councils, with Mizrachi and Hehalutz operating pioneer training facilities, while the Bund was active in the trade unions and in promoting Yiddish culture. Antisemitism increased during the 1930s as Jews were pushed out of jobs and attacked in the streets.

Many fled on the approach of the Germans in Sept. 1939 while at the same time thousands of J. refugees flooded the city. The Germans immediately instituted a regime of forced labor and persecution. J. bank ac-

counts were frozen on 18 Sept. and on 4 Nov. Jews in the public service were dismissed from their jobs. On 9 Nov., nearly all the synagogues and study houses in the city were burned down. During the fall, J. businesses were "Aryanized" and J. public institutions closed. A *Judenrat* was appointed around the beginning of Nov. and extortionate "contributions" were exacted from the community. In summer 1940, Jews were evicted from choice apartments, contributing to the housing shortage among a refugee-swollen pop. that now numbered around 40,000. Sporadic killing decimated the pop. until the first mass *Aktion* on 11 June 1942, when 3,500 Jews were deported to the Belzec death camp and hundreds of others were murdered in the city. The *Aktion* was continued on 15–18 June, when as many as 10,000 Jews were murdered at the J. cemetery and Zwilitowski Hill while perhaps another 10,000 were sent to Belzec. A ghetto was sealed off immediately afterwards, housing 20,000 survivors. On 10 Sept. 1942 the ghetto was surrounded by the German police and 8,000 were selected for shipment to Belzec. New refugees brought the ghetto pop. back

Jews in Polish Red Cross course, Tarnow, Poland, 1938

Street in Tarnow, Poland

to 15,000. Typhoid claimed many victims and on 15 Nov. another 2,500 were rounded up for deportation. The ghetto was now divided into separate sections for the able-bodied and the "unproductive." On 2 Sept. 1943 both sections were liquidated: 7,000 Jews were sent to Auschwitz, 3,000 to the Plaszow camp, and a small number to the Szebnie camp. The few hundred Jews left behind to clean up and those coming out of hiding were killed off or deported over the next few months. A J. resistance group was wiped out in a pitched battle with SS troops in the Tuchow forest and there were also unsuccessful instances of armed resistance during the *Aktions*. There were also attempts to cross the border into Hungary, but most failed. The city was declared "free of Jews" (*judenrein*) on 9 Feb. 1944.

TARNOWSKIE GORY (Yid. Tarnovich) Silesia dist., Poland. Jews are first mentioned in 1732 and by 1815 were organized as an independent community. J. settlers came from Germany and were people of means, among them proprietors of mines and merchants. Under the Prussian edict of 1847, J. children were enrolled in public schools. A J. school was set up in the 1890s. The J. pop. fell from 627 in 1890–91 (total 8,618) to about 300 in 1933. Between the World Wars, Polish Jews arrived in T. Already in Oct. 1939 the town was annexed by the Reich. All Jews were expelled east by Feb. 1940 and shared the fate of local Jews.

TARPA Bereg dist., Hungary. Jews arrived in the late 18th cent., numbering 195 in 1880 and 252 in 1944. The community maintained a school and other communal institutions. In April 1944, they were sent to Beregszasz and from there on 20 May deported to Auschwitz.

TARSOLT (Hung. Tartolcz) N. Transylvania dist., Rumania. Jews settled in the late 18th cent. The J. pop. in 1920 was 131 (8% of the total). In May 1944 the community was transferred to the Satu Mare ghetto and in June deported to Auschwitz.

TARTAKOW Lwow dist., Poland, today Ukraine. Most of the first settlers of the town, which became known for its yearly fairs, were apparently Jews. By the early 18th cent. they maintained an organized community, which came to be dominated by Belz Hasidism. The J. pop. stood at 770 in 1880 and 1,139 in 1921 (70–75% of the total). In WWI the Jews suffered at the hands of Cossack and Circassian army units as well as from typhoid epidemics. With the situation stabilizing, the Zionists became active. Most children went to Polish schools. Early in WWII the Soviet regime brought J. public life to an end. After heavy shelling, the Germans occupied the town, putting 173 Jews to death and instituting a regime of forced labor. The community of 900 was liquidated around Oct. 1942, sent partly to the Belzec death camp, partly to the Sokal ghetto.

TARTU Estonia. J. peddlers and merchants were present from the 16th cent. and a few dozen were apparently living there permanently at the beginning of Russian rule in 1704. In 1743, 18 Jews were expelled from T. by Czarina Elizabeth. In the 1830s Jews were permitted to stay in the town for the purpose of utilizing its health facilities and J. students at the university were permitted to live in T. during the period of their studies. The community was formally established in 1859 when the ten Cantonist families living there organized a *minyan* in one of their apartments. Another 30 families of artisans and others moved in from neighboring districts until the J. pop. reached a peak of 1,449 in 1897. The atmosphere was generally tolerant of the Jews. In 1884, one was elected to the municipal council. However, at the end of the 1880s many without certificates authorizing residence were forced to leave the town. Most of them, about 100 families, emigrated to North America. They were replaced by Jews expelled from other cities in the region. In 1902 a large and impressive synagogue was dedicated. In 1874 a J. elementary school was founded with volunteer teachers from among the J. students at the university. In the early 20th cent., the local *talmud torah* was incorporated into the school, J. studies received more emphasis, and Hebrew was taught in a national-Zionist spirit. In the 1880s the number of Jews at the university reached 240, or 15% of the student body, half coming from Germany and almost all studying medicine. Subsequently, under the *numerus clausus*, they were limited to 3%. The largest and most important student organization among the Jews at the university was the Academic Union, which sought to spread J. awareness through the study of J. history and literature. It also worked in the community, setting up a soup kitchen after a cholera epidemic in 1892, while its members formed a Hovevei Zion society in the early 1880s. Many joined the local branch of the Zionist Organization after the First Zionist Congress in 1897. The Bund made its appearance in 1904, inspiring accelerated social activity against a background of political rivalry with the Zionists, though the two organizations cooperated for self-defense. Public life awakened after the Feb. 1917 Revolution in Russia. Under the shortlived Bolshevik occupation of 1918, many Jews left the city and the J. pop. underwent a marked decline to 1,000 (constituting a quarter of Estonian Jewry) in 1925, with a further drop to 800 in the late 1930s (total pop. 60,000) despite new immigrants from Germany, Austria, Czechoslovakia, and the Nazi-annexed city of Memel. A later decline stemmed from emigration to Tallinn and *aliya* to Palestine. Economically the Jews maintained a sound position and only 5% requested welfare assistance. Jews worked as tradesmen, professionals, and salaried personnel and operated two large factories for plastic and aluminum products. In independent Estonia between the World Wars the Jews enjoyed autonomy as an independent legal body responsible for its own institutions. In the 1930s, 70% of J. children were enrolled in the J. elementary school, which went over from Yiddish to Hebrew as the language of instruction in 1933–34. The school served the community as a cultural center as well. Hebrew was also the language of instruction at the kindergarten set up in 1932. A J. high school was founded in 1925, but only 7% of J. students went there in its last year of operation (1934–35). A new secondary school was founded in 1937 with more emphasis on the Estonian language. Among the Zionists, Betar became the dominant youth movement in the 1930s while WIZO was an important focus of cultural and educational activity. Throughout the period, anti-Zionist tendencies were prominent in Yiddishist circles. A J. printing press was in operation from the end of WWI. After the war the number of J. students at the university rose again, reaching a postwar peak of 188 in 1926 (with 104 studying law). A chair for J. studies was established in 1934. Under Soviet rule (1940–41), J. businesses were nationalized and all the J. institutions operating within the framework of cultural autonomy were closed down. The chair for J. studies at the university was also eliminated. Around ten J. families (property owners and Zionist activists) were exiled to the Soviet Union, the men to labor camps in the Ural Mts., the women and children to Siberia and other distant places. Most of the Jews were able to escape to the interior of the Soviet Union as the Germans advanced. Only 40–50 Jews remained in T. when the Germans arrived on 10 July 1941. All were immediately arrested by the German *Einsatzkommando 1a* with the assistance of the Estonian "Omakaitse" and confined to a concentration camp. From there they were transported in small groups to the antitank ditches along the road to the Riga ghetto and executed, with women first raped and infants murdered separately. The city was liberated by the Soviets on 25 July 1944. Around 200 Jews returned from the Soviet Union, joined later by Russian-born Jews. After the Six-Day War in 1967 the renewed community began to diminish through emigration to Israel.

TARUTINO (Yid. Anciokrak) Bessarabia, Rumania, today Republic of Moldova. Jews first settled in 1832 and T. became the second largest J. community in southern Bessarabia. A community was established in 1917. Zionist activity also began in 1917 and the entire community was Zionist-oriented. The Jews set up a self-defense unit to counter attacks, especially during fairs. The Rumanian forces returning in 1918 disbanded the unit and imprisoned its members. The J. pop. in 1930 was 1,546 (27% of the total). Sixty youths emigrated to Palestine between the World Wars. From 1939, the situation of the Jews deteriorated under the antisemitic rule of Goga-Cuza's Fascist party. In 1941, after the Soviets left, the returning Rumanian forces attacked the Jews and plundered their property, following which they rounded them up and machinegunned them, killing all.

TASNAD N. Transylvania dist., Rumania. Jews settled at the end of the 18th cent. A synagogue built in 1867 existed until 1944. In the 1890s a school was established attended by most of the J. children, but closed in 1912. In WWI 55 Jews were conscripted for military service; nine fell in action. In 1930 the J. pop. was 823 (15% of the total). In 1919, R. Mordekhai Brisk established the largest yeshiva in Transylvania, enrolling up to 400 students in the 1930s. R. Leibush Levinger set up a press in the 1920s which printed textbooks in Hebrew prepared by R. Brisk. Zionist activity began in 1924. Antisemitism was widespread after the entry of Hungarian forces in Sept. 1940. The yeshiva was closed down and in 1942–43 Jews were drafted into labor battalions and sent to the Ukraine, where most died. On 6 May 1944 the community was transferred to the Simleul Silvaniei ghetto and on 29 May deported to Auschwitz. Survivors tried to reestablish a community but soon left.

TATAOUINE (also Foum Tatahouine) Tataouine dist., Tunisia. Jews settled after the establishment of the French Protectorate in 1881 as suppliers of the army base there and represented the only J. satellite community of Djerba to be founded by Jews from the Hara Saghira ("Little Quarter"), where most of the *kohanim* on the island lived. T. was the southernmost J. community of Tunisia. Most stores in the market belonged to Jews. Wealthy Jews traded in mutton, wool and leather products, cloth, and groceries. Some owned farm land worked by Arab sharecroppers. Among the artisans were tailors and jewelers. The community was fairly prosperous. The J. pop. numbered 369 in 1921 and 627 (total 1,244) in 1936. Rabbis were supplied by Djerba. The chief rabbi, David Kohen-Yehonatan (al-Maghrebi), served until his

death in 1943. Three synagogues were in use and boys first attended a *talmud torah* known for its high level. If gifted, they afterwards went on to study at a yeshiva. Girls remained at home, working to supplement the family income. When Allied bombardment in WWII led the Jews to flee for safety to cave-dwelling villagers in the area, local Arabs pillaged their homes and stores. The Germans occasionally seized young Jews for forced labor. Montgomery liberated the city on 17 Feb. 1943. The J. pop. was 770 in 1946. After the war, the Joint Distribution Committee helped the community recover. The Ateret Zion movement of Djerba became active in T. and modern Hebrew classes were organized for adults and children. Relations with the Arabs deteriorated with the outbreak of Israel's War of Independence. *Aliya* started only in 1952 when half the community emigrated to Israel. The rest of the Jews left in the early 1960s.

TATAROW Stanislawow dist., Poland, today Ukraine. The J. pop. in 1921 was 129. The 1,500 Jews there in WWII, including refugees mostly from Hungary, were executed locally in Oct. 1941.

TATARSK Smolensk dist., Russia. An organized community existed by the mid-18th cent., reaching a pop. of 621 in 1847. A J. colony was founded nearby in 1848 and numbered 20 families (56 people) in the early 20th cent. The J. pop. of T. was 1,378 (total 1,517) in 1897 and 864 in 1926 under the Soviets. After the arrival of the Germans in mid-Sept. 1941, the Jews were moved to a ghetto and killed off in a number of *Aktions* (75 in the first, 200 in the second). The final *Aktion* occurred in Feb. 1942. In all, the Germans murdered about 600 Jews from T. and its environs.

TATA-TOVAROS Komarom dist., Hungary. Jews were present in the 13th cent. Most were killed in the Turkish wars of 1529–70. The modern J. settlement was established in 1711 under the protection of Count Esterhazy and grew to 1,037 (10% of the total pop.) in 1880. A hospital was opened in 1838, but soon closed, and a school in 1840. Moritz Fisher Farkashazi founded Hungary's famous porcelainware industry (the Herend factory). Jews also ran a brickyard and leather and carpet factories. In 1869, Jews formed a Neologist congregation. The Zionists were active between the World Wars. In 1941, 527 Jews remained. In early June 1944, they were taken to Komarom and on 14 June they were deported to Auschwitz. Sixty-three survivors reestablished the community, but gradually left due to the hostile atmosphere.

TAUBERBISCHOFSHEIM Baden, Germany. Jews are first mentioned in 1235 but may have been among the victims of the Rhineland massacres during the first two Crusades in 1096 and 1146. They also suffered grievously in the Rindfleisch massacres of 1298, the Armleder massacres of 1336–39, and the Black Death persecutions of 1348–49. J. settlement was renewed in 1356 under the benign protection of Bishop Gerhard of Mainz. During the Thirty Years War (1618–48) the Jews were persecuted and pillaged by the Swedish army but continued to enjoy relative tolerance at the hands of local rulers. With Jews allowed to open stores and purchase land in the 18th cent., a period of accelerated economic growth commenced which brought prosperity to the town as a whole, but the Jews became fully integrated into local life only after the emancipation in 1862. The J. pop. grew steadily through the 19th cent. and reached a peak of 200 in 1880 (total 3,074). A J. elementary school was opened in the 1830s and a synagogue was built in 1845. In 1933, 106 Jews remained. Community life intensified and Zionism began to exert an attraction. On *Kristallnacht* (9–10 Nov. 1938), the synagogue was vandalized and Jews were detained in the Dachau concentration camp. Forty-nine Jews emigrated directly from T., mostly to the U.S., along with nine of the 25 Jews who left T. for other German cities. Of the latter, 16 ended up in the camps, as did the last 22 Jews in T., who were deported to the Gurs concentration camp on 22 Oct. 1942; six survived.

TAUBERRETTERSHEIM Lower Franconia, Germany. A J. community is known from the early 19th cent., numbering 63 (total pop. 697) in 1867 and ten in 1933. The synagogue was vandalized on *Kristallnacht* (9–10 Nov. 1938) and subsequently sold. Two remaining elderly women were respectively deported to Izbica in the Lublin dist. (Poland) and to the Theresienstadt ghetto in 1942.

TAURAGE (Yid. Tavrig) Taurage dist. Lithuania. Jews first settled in the 18th cent. In the mid-19th cent. the community's preacher, Natan Friedland, was the assistant of Tzevi Kalischer, one the founders of modern religious Zionism. In the 1880s there was a *talmud torah* with religious and secular studies. The Hovevei Zion movement, established in 1884, included Orthodox and Haskala adherents. The J. pop. in 1897 was 3,634 (55% of the total). During WWI all the Jews were expelled, half returning after the war. Jews served on the municipal council and there was a J. deputy mayor. In 1935 a blood libel claiming that Jews had killed an infant to make unleavened bread (*matzot*) for Passover led to attacks on Jews and their property. Thirty rioters were heavily fined. The J. educational system, supported by former residents of T. in the U.S., included a modernized *heder* and Hebrew elementary and secondary schools. A library housed thousands of Hebrew and Yiddish books. Most members of a pioneer training group emigrated to Palestine. In 1940 the J. pop. was about 2,000 (19% of the total). Upon Lithuania's annexation by the Soviet Union in 1940, all Zionist and Hebrew activities ceased. After the German invasion in June 1941, 300 J. men were taken to Visbuta, where they were shot. A group of 122 J. men was murdered on the way to Silale. In Sept. all the remaining Jews were put in a ghetto under subhuman conditions. After two weeks they were taken to a forest outside T. and executed.

TAURAGENAI (Yid. Taragin or Toragin) Utena dist., Lithuania. Jews first settled here in the 18th cent. Many emigrated to the west. The J. pop. in 1897 was 596 (56% of the total). Between the World Wars a *heder* and a religious school were in operation. The J. pop. in 1940 was 200 (18% of the total). Most J. institutions were shut down under Soviet rule (1940–41). After the German invasion in June 1941, the Jews were expelled by the Lithuanians to neighboring villages. On 11 July the Lithuanians forced the Jews into open pits and shot them.

TAUTENI Bukovina, Rumania, today Ukraine. In 1930 the J. pop. was 80. In 1941, the Jews were transferred to Ocna and almost all were killed there. The survivors were deported to Transnistria.

TCZEW Pomerania dist., Poland. J. merchants were present from the late 15th cent. but Jews were only allowed to settle after the annexation to Prussia in 1772. The first settlers traded mainly in grain and hides, later expanding into textiles, with many opening clothing stores. A synagogue was erected in 1835. The J. pop.

reached a peak of 515 (total 11,146) in 1887, declining through emigration to 18 in 1939. A Zionist youth movement was active in the 1920s. Most of the Jews were murdered by the Germans on the day of their arrival in the city on 7 Sept.

TEACA (Hung. Teke; Ger. Teckendorf) N. Transylvania dist., Rumania. Jews settled in the 1820s. The J. pop. in 1920 was 154 (6% of the total). Many belonged to the Dej hasidic sect. In May 1944 the community was transferred to the Reghin ghetto and in June deported to Auschwitz.

TEBOURBA Tunis dist., Tunisia. Jews from Tunis settled in the late 19th cent. Zionism made inroads in the small community through the proximity of the Alliance Israelite experimental agricultural school in Djedeida, which closed its doors after WWI. The community numbered 44 in 1909 and ended in the late 1930s.

TEBOURSOUK Teboursouk dist., Tunisia. Jews from Tunis settled in the early 20th cent. in search of new sources of employment. They maintained a community of about 50 (1% of the total) until after WWII, when most left.

TECUCI Moldavia dist., Rumania. Jews settled in the late 18th cent. In 1899 refugees from neighboring villages and hamlets settled here and the J. pop. grew to 1,606. Zionist activity began in 1870 and the Theodor Herzl Zionist Society set up in 1912 existed until the outbreak of WWII. Jews were involved in local politics after WWI and one was deputy mayor. In 1918 a Jew established the first factory (leather processing) in T. The local Zionist organization published two periodicals in Rumanian. The Jews did not suffer excessively in 1940–44 due to their good relations with the local authorities. Certain restrictions were imposed in June 1941 and some Jews were sent to forced labor. On the outbreak of the Soviet-Rumanian war in June 1941, 1,400 Jews from villages and towns of the district arrived in T. In 1947 the J. pop. was 2,600.

TEGLAS Hajdu dist., Hungary. Jews settled in the late 18th cent., numbering 174 in 1930. In WWII, many of the young perished in the Ukraine, where

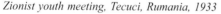

Zionist youth meeting, Tecuci, Rumania, 1933

they had been sent for forced labor. Under the German occupation in mid-July 1944, the Jews were deported to Auschwitz and Austria after being held in Bacsipuszta and Debrecen. Forty-seven survivors, primarily those from Austria, reestablished the community, but gradually left.

TEIUS   (Hung. Tovis) S. Transylvania dist., Rumania. A J. community existed in the 1870s and was attached to the Alba-Iulia community. The J. pop. in 1930 was 156 (3% of the total). In Sept. 1940, Jews were forced to hand over their shops to Iron Guard Legionnaires. At the outbreak of the Soviet-Rumanian war in June 1941, the J. pop. was transferred to Albia-Iulia, Dumbraveni, and Tarnaveni. The men were sent to forced labor and returned only in Jan. 1942 together with the rest of the J. pop. J. males were once again sent to forced labor in Focsani and returned in Aug. 1944. The majority emigrated to Israel after the war.

TEKOVSKE SARLUHY   (Hung. Nagysallo) Slovakia, Czechoslovakia, today Republic of Slovakia. Jews from the Nitra dist. probably settled in the 1830s. By 1900 they numbered 110 (total 2,584) with 14 communities affiliated to their congregation. A synagogue and regional school were opened c. 1900. The J. pop. rose to 180 in 1930 and then dropped to 154 in 1941. Under Hungarian rule, Jews were deprived of their livelihoods and subjected to forced labor. On 15 June, after the German occupation, about 110 Jews were deported to Auschwitz via the Levice ghetto.

TELC   Moravia, Czechoslovakia. A J. community existed in the first half of the 17th cent. A new synagogue was erected 1904 after a fire destroyed the old one in 1885. The J. pop. was 93 in 1921 and 78 (total 4,270) in 1930. The Jews were apparently deported to the Theresienstadt ghetto together with the Jews of Brno in late 1941–early 1942. From there they were sent to the death camps of Poland.

TELCIU   (Hung. Telcs) N. Transylvania dist., Rumania. Jews settled in the early 19th cent. The J. pop. in 1920 was 215 (7% of the total). In May 1944 the community was transferred to the Bistrita ghetto and in June deported to Auschwitz.

TELECHANY   Polesie dist., Poland. Jews settled in the first half of the 18th cent. The digging of a canal in 1776–1826 as part of the Pripet–Dnieper River link contributed to the community's growth. Haskala spread as J. experts and contractors arrived. The J. pop. reached 1,508 in 1897 (total 2,588). A glass factory built in 1895 employed many Jews. In 1915 the Russians expelled some Jews from the town, leaving a J. pop. of 463 (total 895) in 1921, with Jews continuing to return as Polish rule stabilized. Between the World Wars 80 families left for Palestine. The Germans arrived on 28 June 1941 and on 5–7 Aug. an SS cavalry unit murdered the J. pop. beside freshly dug pits.

TELEPINO   Kirovograd dist., Ukraine. Jews probably settled in the late 18th cent., numbering 191 in 1847 and 632 (total 3,199) in 1897 but dropping to 54 in 1926, conceivably as a result of a pogrom in 1919. After they occupied the town in Aug. 1941, the Germans murdered the few Jews who had neither fled nor been evacuated.

TELESNICA OSZWAROWA   Lwow dist., Poland, today Ukraine. The J. pop. in 1921 was 100. The Jews were possibly executed locally or expelled to Zaslawie for extermination in summer 1942.

TELSIAI   (Yid. Telz, Telzh) Telsiai dist., Lithuania. Jews first settled here in the 15th cent. In 1797 the J. pop. was 1,650 (66% of the total). In 1800 the municipal council had three J. representatives, but they were removed at the demand of Christian members. In the 1880s, young Jews emigrated to the U.S., Argentina, and South Africa. Many Jews subsisted from the Great Yeshiva (founded in 1880), which provided housing and food to its many students. By the end of the 19th cent., the T. yeshiva was one of the largest and best in Eastern Europe with 400 students and many graduates becoming leading rabbis throughout the world. In the 1880s, the poet Yehuda Leib Gordon founded a J.-Russian school, with separate classes for boys and girls, but had to leave after six years because of Orthodox opposition. Despite the strong influence of the anti-Zionist yeshiva, Zionist organizations, including Hovevei Zion, were founded at the end of the 19th cent. The J. pop. in 1897 was 3,088 (51% of the total). Between the World Wars Jews were elected to the municipal council. The difficult economic situation was ameliorated by social welfare organizations supported by former residents of T. living in the U.S. The focus of secular culture was the Hebrew-Yiddish library. Despite Agudat Israel's hegemony, many belonged to Zionist organizations. Pioneer training groups existed, including one sponsored by the Agudat Israel youth group. The J. pop. in 1940 was about 2,800 (48% of the total). When Lithuania was annexed by the Soviet Union in 1940, all Zionist organizations were closed, Hebrew education was stopped, and the yeshiva's buildings were confiscated. After the German invasion in June 1941, all Jews were evicted from their homes. The men were separated from the women and children, and then both groups were brought to nearby Rainiai and housed in cowsheds and barns. The men were taken to forced labor, including the exhumation of Lithuanian political prisoners killed by the Soviets. All the J. men were murdered in a grove near the camp. The women and children were taken to the Geruliai camp and housed in lice-infested, empty shacks. After 500 young women were selected to be taken to T., the others were shot. The children and some of the remaining women were buried alive. The women taken to T. were housed in a ghetto and taken to forced labor, some with farmers who raped them. On 24–25 Dec. 1941, the women were brought back to Rainiai and executed. Sixty-four women who had fled survived the war.

TEMERIN   Vojvodina dist., Yugoslavia. Jews first settled there in the 19th cent. In 1940 they numbered 80. In Jan. 1942 they were massacred by the Hungarians.

TEMIRGOYEVSKAYA   Krasnodar territory, Russia. The Germans occupied the village in summer 1942, murdering the few J. refugees they found there at the village of Petropavlovskaya in Sept.

TEMPELBURG   (Pol. Czaplinek) Pomerania, Germany, today Poland. Jews arrived here only in the early 19th cent., constituting nine households by 1812. By 1895, the J. community numbered 218, dropping to 69 in 1925. It maintained a synagogue and a cemetery. The antisemitic riots which broke out in Pomerania when the Neustettin synagogue was burned down in 1881 spread to T. When the Nazis came to power in 1933, there were 63 Jews in T. No further information about their fate is available.

TEOFIPOL   Kamenets-Podolski dist., Ukraine. Jews

settled in the 18th cent., numbering 516 in 1765 and 2,914 (total 4,484) in 1897. Two J. schools, for boys and for girls, were operating in the early 20th cent. About 300 Jews were murdered in pogroms in 1917 and 1919. In the Soviet period, a J. rural council (soviet) was active. In 1929, a J. kolkhoz was founded, numbering 94 families in 1936. In 1939, the J. pop. was 1,266. The Germans occupied the town on 6 July 1941. About 1,000 Jews were executed in Dec.

TEPLICE   (also Teplice-Sanov) Bohemia (Sudetenland), Czechoslovakia. Jews are first mentioned in 1414 and in the 16th cent. constituted one of the largest and most important J. communities in Bohemia. Other than a small number in 1667–68, Jews were never expelled from T. although they were confined to a ghetto and forced to wear a special collar for identification. In the 19th cent., under the protection of Count Clary, the Jews prospered and contributed to the development of the glass, ceramics, and mining industries. Thousands of needy Jews received free treatment at the city's well-known mineral baths under the supervision of Dr. Ignaz Hirsch. Jews also participated in public life and by 1861 had achieved full civil rights. Synagogue services followed Reform practice. An influx of East European Jews, organizing their own Orthodox community, increased the J. pop. to 1,718 (12% of the total) in 1880 and to 3,128 in 1921. The Zionists were active from 1904 and in the 1920s, T. became a regional center for the movement. Antisemitism provoked by local German residents intensified after the Nazis rose to power in 1933. Most Jews left during the Sudetenland crisis in summer and fall 1938. The synagogue was burned on 14 March 1939. A community of 500 existed in 1965.

TEPLIK   Vinnitsa dist., Ukraine. J. settlement commenced in the early 18th cent. The J. pop. was 289 in 1765 and 3,725 (total 7,044) in 1897. In 1919, as many as 400 Jews died as a result of Petlyura gang attacks. In the Soviet period, a J. council (soviet) was active and a J. elementary school had 262 students in 1929. Jews earned their livelihoods in 15 artisan cooperatives with a number of families engaging in agriculture. In 1939, the J. pop. was 1,233. The Germans arrived on 26 July 1941. A ghetto and *Judenrat* were subsequently established and dozens of the young sent to a forced labor camp. On 27 May 1942, 769 local Jews were murdered along with 520 Jews from

Bukovina. A small group of skilled workers was executed later.

TER APEL   Groningen dist., Holland. A J. community was formed in 1880. The J. pop. in 1938 was 75, with 115 in nearby Vlagtwedde. All the Jews were deported and perished in the Holocaust. In 1942 a J. labor camp was established close to nearby Sellingen. All 330 inmates were sent to the death camps via the Westerbork transit camp.

TERBORG   Gelderland dist., Holland. J. settlement began in the early 18th cent. and the community developed in the 19th cent., numbering 92 in 1901. The J. pop. in 1940 was 71. In the Holocaust 33 perished while 38 survived in hiding.

TEREBLA   (Hung. Talaborfalu) Carpatho-Russia, Czechoslovakia, today Ukraine. A number of Jews were present in the first half of the 18th cent. but they were forced to leave. Jews only settled again in the mid-19th cent. In 1880, their pop. was 116, rising to 123 in 1921 and 179 (total 2,928) in 1941. A new synagogue seating 80 was built in 1934. Some Jews were farmers. The Hungarians occupied the town in March 1939. In Aug. 1941, they expelled a few dozen J. families to Kamenets-Podolski, where they were murdered. The rest were deported to Auschwitz in late May 1944.

TEREKHOVKA   Gomel dist., Belorussia. In 1939, under the Soviets, the J. pop. was 101 (total 3,101). A four-year J. elementary school operated during the period. The Germans occupied T. on 25 Aug. 1941. Some Jews managed to flee to the Soviet Union. In Sept., 60 Jews and gypsies were arrested and a few days later executed.

TERESPOL   Lublin dist., Poland. Jews were present without restrictions in the early 18th cent. In the 19th cent., the vinegar and pickling plants which they operated were known for their fine products. In the wake of dislocations and instability following WWI, the J. pop. dropped from a peak of 2,884 in 1907 (total 3,385) to 1,200 in 1921. Between the World Wars, Zionist influence increased. Many young people fled with the Red Army as the Germans approached in Sept. 1939. The remaining 284 Jews were deported to the Treblinka death camp on 29 Aug. 1942.

Jewish shopkeeper in Teresva, Czechoslovakia, 1937

TERESVA   (Hung. Tarackoz; Yid. Tersif) Carpatho-Russia, Czechoslovakia, today Ukraine. J. settlement apparently commenced in the first quarter of the 18th cent. Four families were present in 1768. In 1880, the J. pop. was 155. In 1921, under the Czechoslovakians, it was 471 and in 1941, 983 (total 3,348). The community maintained a few *hadarim* and a *talmud torah* for children attending Czech schools. Jews owned a number of sawmills and a flour mill. The Zionists and Agudat Israel were active. The Hungarians occupied the town in March 1939 and in 1941 drafted dozens of young Jews into labor battalions, sending them out to work elsewhere and to the eastern front. In Aug. 1941, a few J. families without Hungarian citizenship were expelled to Kamenets-Podolski and murdered. About 700 were deported to Auschwitz in mid-May 1944.

TERLICA   Vinnitsa dist., Ukraine. Eight Jews were present in 1765 and 1,191 (total 2,304) in 1897. In 1926, their number was 1,054. The Germans captured the town on 22 July 1941. On 29 May 1942, 153 Jews from T. and the surrounding area were among the 5,000 the Nazis murdered in the Borklow (Poperechni) forest not far from Monastyrishche.

TERNOVKA   Vinnitsa dist., Ukraine. Four Jews were present in 1765. Their pop. rose to 2,823 (total

5,364) in 1897 and 3,081 in 1926. A private J. boys' school operated in the early 20th cent. and in 1924, under the Soviets, a J. elementary school with 300 students was founded. A J. council (soviet) was still active in the mid-1930s. The Germans occupied T. in late July 1941, soon setting up a ghetto for the Jews of the area. In late May 1942, the Germans executed 2,500 Jews, many from the region, in a nearby forest.

TESCHENMOSCHEL Palatinate, Germany. The J. pop. was 22 in the early 19th cent. and 56 (11 merchant families) at mid-cent. In 1932, the J. pop. was 21 (total pop. 200). The last six Jews were deported to the Gurs concentration camp in Oct. 1940. Five perished there. The synagogue was damaged on *Kristallnacht* (9–10 Nov. 1938), and razed in 1945.

TESTOUR Majaz al-Bab dist., Tunisia. The grave of R. Fraji Chaouat, a reputedly saintly miracle healer who died in the early 17th cent., is located in T. As a pilgrimage site for Jews, the grave was a source of tension with local Arabs down through the years. The J. pop. was 156 in 1909, 107 in 1936, and 91 in 1946. In 1910, T.'s J. community officially organized and formed a social welfare committee. During WWII many Jews left. After the war and the withdrawal of the French, the community declined until only one family remained to care for R. Chaouat's grave.

TET Gyor–Moson dist., Hungary. Jews probably arrived in the late 18th cent. They numbered 340 in 1840 and 159 in 1941, maintaining a synagogue and school. On 11 June 1944, they were deported to Auschwitz. In 1946, survivors reestablished the community, but left in 1956.

TETETLEN Hajdu dist., Hungary. Jews settled in the first half of the 19th cent. and numbered 61 in 1930. In mid-June 1944, they were deported to Auschwitz via Puspokladany.

TETERIN Mogilev dist., Belorussia. The J. pop. was 286 (total 602) in 1897 and 246 in 1923. The community maintained a *beit midrash*. The Germans occupied the town in July 1941, murdering all the Jews in spring 1942.

TETIEV Kiev dist., Ukraine. Jews numbered 708 in 1765 and 3,323 (total 3,493) in 1897. Most were Has-

idim. A private boys' school combining secular and religious studies was opened in 1910. Cossack gangs murdered 300 Jews and burned all J. homes in 1919 and 1920. J. self-defense forces brought the second pogrom to a halt. There were no Jews present here in the Soviet period.

THALA Thala dist., Tunisia. Jews moved to T. with its development in the beginning of the 20th cent. as a site for growing *alafa*, a plant particularly useful for papermaking. The Jews acted as agents in exporting the crop as well as providing services to the army outpost located there. The J. pop in 1909 was 12, rising to 52 (2% of the total) in 1936 and then dropping to 37 in 1946. The Germans did not occupy T. in WWII. After the war almost all the Jews left.

THALFANG Rhineland, Germany. Three to eight J. families were living in T. in the late 18th cent. The number of Jews grew to 77 in 1808 and a peak of 113 (a fifth of the total) in 1843. It then dropped to 85 in 1895 and 40–45 in 1932–33. Twelve Jews emigrated in the Nazi period and 19 moved to other places in Germany. The last nine were deported to the Lodz ghetto in Oct. 1942. Twenty-two perished in the Holocaust. The synagogue erected in 1822 was seriously damaged on *Kristallnacht* (9–10 Nov. 1938), and torn down in 1956. The 18th cent. cemetery was also desecrated in the rioting.

THALMAESSING Middle Franconia, Germany. Jews are first mentioned in 1531 and were expelled in 1560 and 1569. Though restricted to five families in 1618, the community thereafter grew steadily, numbering 227 in 1743 and being among the wealthiest and most important in the Ansbach principality. A cemetery was consecrated in 1832 and a new synagogue was erected in 1857. By 1880 the J. pop. had fallen to 112 (total 1,105). In 1933, when the Nazis came to power, there were 33 Jews left. The synagogue was vandalized on *Kristallnacht* (9–10 Nov. 1938). By May 1939 all Jews had left T., 13 emigrating and 20 moving to other German cities.

THANN Haut-Rhin dist., France. The J. community was established in the 19th cent. The synagogue was founded in 1862. By 1885 there were 630 Jews living in T., dropping to 551 in 1895 and 451 in 1910. In 1924, the synagogue, destroyed during WWI, was reconstructed. In 1926 the community consisted of 224 Jews and of 201 in 1931. On the eve of WWII, there were 81 Jews in T. All were expelled to the south of France with the rest of Alsace-Lorraine Jews.

THASOS (Thassos) North Aegean island, Greece. Jews lived in T. in the 14th cent. In WWII, 16 Jews were arrested on 4 March 1943 and deported to the Treblinka death camp.

THEILHEIM Lower Franconia, Germany. A J. community existed by the late 17th cent. A synagogue was built in 1751. Yitzhak Yehuda Rosenbaum of Hoechberg (d. 1810), founder of one of the largest J. families in Bavaria, was active there as a cantor. In the mid-19th cent. a new synagogue was built and 50 children were enrolled in the J. school. The J. pop. was 225 in 1867 (total 535) and 70 in 1933. Thirty-one Jews emigrated in 1933–41, including 24 to the U.S. The synagogue and J. homes were vandalized on *Kristallnacht* (9–10 Nov. 1938). Another thirty-one Jews were deported to Izbica in the Lublin dist. (Poland) via Wuerzburg on 25 April 1942 and nine to the Theresienstadt ghetto in Sept.

THEMAR Thuringia, Germany. There were Jews living in T. in the 13th cent. After the persecutions of 1298, there is no mention of J. settlement in T. until the mid-19th cent. In 1865 and 1867, the local J. pop. increased following an influx of newcomers from neighboring Bibra and Marisfeld. The community, numbering 93 in 1871, was officially constituted only in 1877 when a synagogue was dedicated. Burials were conducted in the J. cemetery in nearby Marisfeld. Of the 62 Jews living in T. when the Nazis came to power in 1933, only 48 remained in March 1938. On *Kristallnacht* (9–10 Nov. 1938), 18 J. men were arrested, abused, and deported to the Buchenwald concentration camp, where at least one died. The synagogue, which was adjacent to non-J. houses, was not destroyed. Fifteen of the 48 remaining Jews emigrated to the U.S., England, and Palestine. Those who remained were deported during the war years.

THEODOSIA (Rus. Feodosiya) Crimea, Russia, today Ukraine. A J. community existed in the tenth cent. The modern community was established in the late 18th cent. The Jews had two synagogues, an old one with a stone inscription from the 13th cent. and

a new Ashkenazi synagogue (closed in 1928). In 1897, the J. pop. was about 3,000 (total 24,000). A number of Jews were killed and injured in pogroms in Feb. and Oct. 1905. Three Zionists were elected to the municipal council in 1917. The Zionists also won the elections to the community council in the same year. Hashomer Hatzair was active until 1927. In the early 1920s, the local authorities transferred the J. hospital (founded in the 19th cent.) to the community council. In addition to the J. school operating in the town, there was a J. section in the local teachers' college. In 1939, the J. pop. was 2,922. The Germans occupied T. on 2 Nov. 1941. A ghetto was established and on 4 Dec. *Sonderkommando 10b* forces murdered over 1,700 Jews (according to another source, 2,500), not including 245 Krimchak Jews from T. and its environs. Another 200 Jews were murdered in Feb.–May 1942 after a short Soviet occupation.

THIONVILLE Moselle dist., France. Jews are recorded as living in T. from 1546, but 20 years later there were no Jews in the town. In 1780, there were about 20 J. families. The local synagogue was founded in 1805. The community grew, numbering 310 members in 1831 but dwindling to 183 in 1880. In 1909–40, T. was the seat of a rabbinate. In 1931 there were 281 Jews in T. During WWII, all were expelled to the south of France with the rest of the Jews of Alsace-Lorraine. Thirty families were deported and five Jews were shot. The synagogue was completely destroyed. A new synagogue was established in 1957. In 1964 there were 520 Jews in T.

THOLEY Saar, Germany. A J. butcher is mentioned in 1729. A hundred years later, the J. pop. was 23, growing to 91 (total 1,173) by 1895. By the Nazi era, the J. pop. dropped to 41. The community maintained a synagogue from 1864, a cemetery (probably from the 18th cent.), and an elementary school which operated from 1874 to 1916. Most Jews left under the Nazis. The last four were deported to the Gurs concentration camp on 22 Oct. 1940. The synagogue and school building were sold in 1937.

THUENGEN Lower Franconia, Germany. The J. settlement was started in the second half of the 17th cent. by Jews expelled from the Wuerzburg region. The J. pop. reached 350 in 1837 (total 880). A new synagogue was built in the 1860s. The J. pop. declined steadily to 152 in 1933, with the community known for its Orthodox way of life. Jews were attacked on the eve of the Austrian *Anschluss* (13 March 1938) and during the Sudetenland crisis in 1938. Most left in 1937–39. In all, 110 emigrated (86 to the U.S.) and 56 left for other German cities (34 to Wuerzburg).

TIARLEVO Leningrad dist., Russia. Jews probably settled in the early 20th cent., numbering 216 (total 5,794) in 1939. After their arrival in Sept. 1941, the Germans murdered the few Jews who had not fled or been evacuated.

TIBANA Moldavia dist., Rumania. Jews first settled in T. in 1859. The J. pop. was 122 in 1899 and 86 (12% of the total) in 1930. At the outbreak of the Soviet-Rumanian war in June 1941 the J. pop was transferred to Vaslui and never returned to T.

TIBAVA (Hung. Tiba) Slovakia, Czechoslovakia, today Republic of Slovakia. A number of Jews earning their living as distillers were present in the early 18th cent. By 1880, the J. pop. was 174 (total 419), dropping to 65 in 1941. In mid-May 1944 the Jews were deported to Auschwitz via Sobrance and Uzhorod.

TIBOLDDAROC Borsod dist., Hungary. Jews were present by 1747 and numbered 110 in 1880 and 70 in 1930. On 11–15 June 1944, they were deported to Auschwitz via Miskolc.

TIEL Gelderland dist., Holland. Jews lived there in the Middle Ages until expelled in 1570. Settlement was renewed in the late 17th cent. and a community was organized at the end of the 18th cent. In the 19th cent. the community grew significantly. A synagogue was inaugurated in 1839 and a school in 1841. In 1869 there were 317 Jews living in T. (4% of the total) but their number dwindled to 79 by 1940. In the Holocaust the non-J. pop. helped hide Jews. During the war 38 Jews were deported and perished; 41 survived.

TIENGEN Baden, Germany. Jews were probably present in the 14th cent. A Hebrew printing press operated there in 1559. In 1650, eight J. families received a letter of protection under which they could conduct trade but not open stores. Throughout the 18th cent. there was constant friction with the local pop. and only from the 1870s were Jews welcome in public

life. A synagogue was built in 1793 and a J. elementary school was opened in 1830 as the J. pop. grew steadily to a peak of 233 in 1880 (total 2,247). The pop. dropped to 106 in 1900 and 46 in 1933. Under the Nazis, local antisemitism again came to the fore and individual Jews were relentlessly persecuted. On *Kristallnacht* (9–10 Nov. 1938), J. stores were looted and J. homes were vandalized, as were the synagogue and cemetery, while five J. men were taken to the Dachau concentration camp, where two died. Twenty-seven Jews left T. by Nov. 1938 and another 12 after *Kristallnacht*, most emigrating. Five were subsequently deported to the camps from France and four from other German cities along with five directly from T. to the Gurs concentration camp on 22 Oct. 1940; all but one perished.

TIGANASI Moldavia dist., Rumania. T. was founded by Jews in 1856. The J. pop. was 78 in 1859 and 105 in 1930 (15% of the total). At the outbreak of the Soviet-Rumanian war in June 1941, the J. pop. was expelled to Iasi.

TIGHINA (Hung. Bendery) Bessarabia, Rumania, today Republic of Moldova. Jews first settled in the late 18th cent. A synagogue was opened in the local castle in 1770. The first hasidic court in Bessarabia was set up in T. by R. Arieh Leib Wertheim in the early 19th cent. In 1897 the J. pop. was 10,644 (34% of the total). The situation of the Jews after WWI deteriorated with the rise of antisemitism as T. became one of the centers of Cuza's Fascist movement. Under the Soviets (1940–41) the property of wealthy Jews was confiscated and J. community and Zionist leaders were exiled to Siberia. Before the arrival of the Rumanian and German armies, the local authorities arranged train transport for those wishing to flee to the Russian interior and many Jews escaped. On 4 July 1941, the Rumanian army returned, took the 700 remaining Jews to the castle, and shot them. In Sept. 1944, 800 Jews returned and reestablished the community and its institutions. Later most left T.

TIKHINICHI Gomel dist., Belorussia. Jews settled in the late 18th cent. Their pop. rose from 90 in 1789 to 687 (52% of the total) in 1897. An organized community existed with a prayer house and cemetery. In 1923, under the Soviets, a J. kolkhoz was set up nearby, employing 11 J. families in 1930. In 1926, the J.

pop. of T. was 420. Local residents rioted against the Jews in 1929, destroying homes. The courts sentenced the organizers of the riot to ten years in prison. The Germans occupied T. in late July 1941. The Jews were probably murdered in the fall.

TIKHORETSK   Krasnodar territory, Russia. Jews probably settled in the early 19th cent. The Germans occupied the town on 5 Aug. 1942, murdering about 220 Jews from T. and its environs in three groups. A few escaped from the execution site. In all, the Germans murdered 316 Jews.

TIKHVIN   Leningrad dist., Russia. J. settlement probably began in the late 19th cent. The J. pop. was 121 (total 6,000) in 1897, 176 in 1926, and 113 in 1939. The Germans occupied the town on 8 Nov. 1939 and murdered the few Jews who had not fled or been evacuated.

TILBURG   Noord-Brabant dist., Holland. Jews were living in the parent community of Oisterwijk from the mid-18th cent. and began settling in T. in the late 18th cent. Communal prayers were held by 1814. A synagogue was built in 1873-74. In 1883 the J. pop. was 153. The community continued to grow in the 20th cent. Zionism was introduced in 1907. In 1941 there were some 150 refugees in T. in a J. pop. of 333 with 45 living in Oisterwijk. Deportations began in Aug. 1942. Of the 133 deported, 105 perished. After the liberation (Oct. 1944) 175 Jews came out of hiding.

TILSIT   (Rus. Sovetsk) East Prussia, Germany, today Russia. Jews settled in T. at the beginning of the 19th cent. The J. pop. was 13 in 1811; 265 in 1843; and 780 in 1895. A cemetery was in use in 1825 and a synagogue was dedicated in 1842. In the early 20th cent., the Association of East Prussian Communities established an office to care for J. immigrants arriving from Eastern Europe. The realignment of national boundaries after WWI placed T. on the Lithuanian border and many Lithuanian Jews, especially butchers, brought their cheap goods to T., creating serious competition for local J. businessmen. Lithuanian Jews also joined the community in daily religious services. In 1928, the J. pop. was 797. The synagogue and the cemetery were desecrated several times in the early 1930s. In 1933, on the eve of the Nazi assumption power, there were about 640 Jews living in T. In July 1933,

a curfew was imposed on Jews during the evenings. The community prepared for emigration and a local branch of the German Zionist Organization was active. English and Hebrew language courses were organized and on the outskirts of the city a training farm for prospective emigrants to Palestine was established. On *Kristallnacht* (9–10 Nov. 1938), the synagogue was destroyed and Jews were arrested. In May 1939, 298 Jews were still living in T. Those still there in 1941 were brought to Koenigsberg prior to the German attack on Russia and presumably later deported. In July 1944, there were still 31 Jews in T., probably protected by marriage to non-J. partners.

TILZA   Latgale dist., Latvia. The J. pop. in 1935 was 61. Those Jews not fleeing to the Soviet Union were murdered by the Germans in summer 1941.

TIMISOARA   (Hung. and Ger. Temesvar; under the Nazis, Temeschburg) S. Transylvania dist., Rumania. J. exiles from Spain, arriving via Belgrade and Constantinople, settled c. 1515. In the early 18th cent., Ashkenazi Jews began to settle and a mixed community was founded in 1739. Synagogues and community institutions for both Sephardi and Ashkenazi Jews were built in 1762 in the "J. Court" at the Eugen gate. Jews participated in the 1848 revolt, but when the Austrians took control in Oct., their situation worsened. In the 19th cent. Jews founded banks and factories, contributing to making T. an important industrial center. A J. hospital was built in the early 19th cent. J. schools were opened in the city center (Belvaros) and in the Gyarvaros suburb in the 1840s. At this time, the J. pop. was 1,200. Schools for girls were opened in 1860. In the mid-19th cent., the J. communities in the suburbs expanded and the Belvaros community lost its hegemony over them. The Belvaros community defined itself as Neologist in 1868, but the Gyarvaros and Yosfaros communities remained Orthodox. In addition there were two Sephardi communities. Zionist activity began in 1908 in the Yosfaros community. The Neologist community became involved in Zionism during WWI. The Neologist community opened a commercial high school in 1918 with 220 pupils as well as a general high school with 70 pupils. The high level of studies attracted students from throughout Rumania and even from overseas. In 1927, an elementary school opened with 160 pupils and in 1932 a nursery school was added. The other communities had their own educational institutions, including a yeshiva (at Gyar-varos), and each had its own religious facilities. Between the World Wars, J. newspapers and periodicals were published, including the Zionist *Uj-Kor*. In 1923–24, antisemitic students at the Polytechnic College ejected J. pupils, and this developed into antisemitic demonstrations throughout the city. Manifestations of antisemitism continued between the World Wars and in 1939, 1,000 Jews were deprived of Rumanian citizenship. The J. pop. in 1930 stood at 9,368 (10% of the total). The situation of the Jews deteriorated under the Antonescu regime (Sept. 1940). J. shopowners were forced to sell their shops at prices well below their value and the majority of the J. pop. became impoverished. In July 1941, thousands of destitute Jews from surrounding villages arrived in T. and were assisted by the communities. On 4 Aug. 1941, men aged 18–50 were sent to forced labor camps. Community property was nationalized, but J. educational institutions continued to function. Over 100 Jews suspected of Communism were expelled to Transnistria; few returned. From 1943, the J. pop. assisted the "illegal" immigration of Polish Jews to Palestine via T. The community was reestablished after the war on a small scale.

TIMKOVICHI Minsk dist., Belorussia. Jews probably settled at the turn of the 18th cent., numbering 49 in 1811 and 1,523 (total 2,393) in 1897. In the Soviet period, some Jews engaged in agriculture, with 40 J. families working in two kolkhozes in the 1930s. A J. elementary school (apparently four grades) was active. In 1939 the J. pop. was 1,093. The Germans established a ghetto after occupying the town in late June 1941. In the second half of July 1942, they murdered the few hundred Jews still there.

TIMOSHEVTS (Sovkhoz) Krasnodar territory, Russia. On 17 Aug. 1942 the Germans murdered 21 Jews in the workers' settlement and another five at nearby Khutor Proletarskyi.

TINCA (Hung. Tenke) S. Transylvania dist., Rumania. Jews first settled in the late 19th cent. The community defined itself as Orthodox and the first synagogue was built in 1869. A J. school was opened in 1899, but closed after WWI. In 1930 the J. pop. was 201 (5% of the total). In Aug. 1940, the J. pop. was re-

moved to Beius and two months later deported to Ginta. After the war, 120 Jews returned.

TINNYE Pest dist., Hungary. A community of 216 existed in 1840, dwindling to 68 in 1930. On 30 June 1944, the Jews were deported to Auschwitz via Budafok.

TIRASPOL Moldavia, today Republic of Moldova. Jews settled in the late 18th cent. An organized community of 1,406 existed by 1847, growing to 8,668 (total 31,616) in 1897. The Jews suffered during pogroms in 1905 and 1917. With T. the capital of the Moldavian SSR in 1929–40, the J. pop. grew somewhat, standing at 11,764 in 1939. R. David Schapira, who served the community in the 1930s, was arrested sometime in 1937. German and Rumanian forces captured T. on 8 Aug. 1941. The Germans immediately massacred 10,000 Jews, burying them in a mass grave. A small number hid in the "Aryan" part of the city. In late 1941, Jews expelled from Rumania and on their way to Transnistria began arriving in the city. About 100 were confined to a ghetto in summer 1942; in 1944, their number reached 821. They were mobilized for forced labor outside the ghetto. The ghetto itself became a model of self-help and internal organization, aided substantially by the head of the local Rumanian gendarmerie. From Dec. 1943, the ghetto also received material assistance from the Bucharest Relief Committee. As a consequence of its exemplary organization, the ghetto was visited by foreign delegations, including representatives of the Vatican (summer 1943) and the Red Cross. With the fighting drawing near, the Rumanian authorities provided most of the deportees with papers allowing them to return home. However, between the Rumanian evacuation on 19 March 1944 and the liberation of the city, the Germans still there took another 1,000 lives, murdering prisoners in the local jail, most of them Jews.

TIRKSLIAI (Yid. Tirkshle) Mazeikiai dist., Lithuania. Jews first settled here in the 18th cent. From the end of the 19th cent. many emigrated to the west. In 1915 the Jews were expelled and only some returned after WWI. The J. pop. in 1923 was 119 (10% of the total). Despite its small size, the community maintained J. institutions and voted in Zionist Congress elections. All the Jews were killed in the Holocaust.

TIRSCHTIEGEL   (Pol. Trzciel) Posen–West Prussia, Germany, today Poland. A 1745 document pertaining to the history of the local Jews indicates that Jews had been living in T. earlier. With Prussian rule in 1772, the J. pop. stood at 253, with most Jews quite poor. A synagogue existed in 1770; a cemetery was consecrated in 1775; and a rabbi was employed from 1789 on. By 1880, the J. pop. was 162. The school set up in the 19th cent. had to be closed in 1910 because of a lack of pupils. In 1932, 22 Jews were living in T. J. businesses were demolished on *Kristallnacht* (9–10 Nov. 1938) and the synagogue set on fire. In March 1940, the remaining Jews were arrested, interned in the Buergergarten camp near Schneidemuehl, and shortly afterwards deported to the east.

TIRZA   (Yid. Tarzik) Courland dist., Latvia. The small 19th cent. community apparently ended in the early 20th cent.

TISOVEC   (Hung. Tiszolc) Slovakia, Czechoslovakia, today Republic of Slovakia. Jews settled c. 1850, building a synagogue in 1887 as their pop. reached a level of about 100 (2.5% of the total). Many of the young left for the big cities in the 1920s, causing the J. pop. to drop to 65 in 1930. In 1940, it was 89. In the Slovakian state, J. children were expelled from the public schools and Jews were forced out of their businesses. In March–April 1942, young J. men were deported to the Majdanek concentration camp and the women to Auschwitz. Families were deported to the Lublin dist. (Poland) on 9 June. Others fled to the forests when the Germans arrived in 1944. In all, 58 Jews perished in the Holocaust.

TISZABERCEL   Szabolcs dist., Hungary. Jews are first mentioned in 1770, numbering 188 in 1880 and 115 in 1930. The men were sent on forced labor to the Ukraine in 1938. On 16 April 1944, the remaining Jews were taken to Nyireghaza and on 12 May deported to Auschwitz.

TISZABEZDED   Szabolcs dist., Hungary. Jews are first mentioned in 1747. Engaging in trade and agriculture, they numbered 73 in 1930. In 1938, they were savagely attacked by rioters. In spring 1944, the 60 who remained were transported to Kisvarda and several weeks later deported to Auschwitz.

TISZABO   Jasz–Nagykun–Szolnok dist., Hungary. Jews probably settled in the early 17th cent., numbering 130 in 1914 and 27 in 1921. At the end of June 1944, the four remaining families were deported to Auschwitz via Torokszentmiklos and Szolnok.

TISZABUD   Szabolcs dist., Hungary. Jews were present in 1770. They numbered 73 in 1880 and 59 in 1930. Most were small tradesmen. They were deported to Auschwitz on 16 May 1944 after short periods of detention in Nyiregyhaza and Nyirjespuszta.

TISZACSEGE   Hajdu dist., Hungary. The J. pop. was 135 in 1930. In the beginning of July 1944, the Jews were deported to Auschwitz via Debrecen.

TISZADADA   Szabolcs dist., Hungary. Jews arrived in the late 18th cent., numbering 130 in 1851 and 175 in 1930. Forty were seized for forced labor in 1942. The remainder were deported to Auschwitz via Nyiregyhaza on 22 June 1944.

TISZADOB   Szabolcs dist., Hungary. Jews settled in the late 18th cent., numbering 162 in 1880 and 90 in 1930. Most were small merchants, artisans, and fishermen. On 17 May 1944, they were deported to Auschwitz via Nyiregyhaza.

TISZADOROGMA   Borsod dist., Hungary. Jews settled in the early 19th cent. and numbered 52 in 1930. They were deported to Auschwitz via Miskolc on 11–15 June 1944.

TISZAESZLAR   Szabolcs dist., Hungary. Jews settled in the early 19th cent. as tradesmen and sharecroppers. T. was the site of the infamous blood libel of 1882, in which 13 Jews were implicated, prior to Passover, in the murder of a Christian girl. After a 42-day trial in Nyiregyhaza which reverberated throughout the world, the Jews were finally exonerated. The J. pop. was 61 in 1930. The Jews were deported to Auschwitz via Nyiregyhaza and Simapuszta on 17 May 1944.

TISZAFOLDVAR   Jasz–Nagykun–Szolnok dist., Hungary. Jews are first mentioned in 1853 but probably arrived a few decades earlier. Most were merchants. In 1930, they numbered 35. At the end of spring 1944, they were deported to Auschwitz.

TISZAFURED Heves dist., Hungary. Jews settled in the late 18th cent. They founded a yeshiva in 1865, a J. school in 1876, and three synagogues, including a magnificent Great Synagogue in 1910. In 1900, the J. pop. reached a peak of 682, dropping to 442 in 1941. Under the German occupation, the Jews were held in the local brickyard with Jews from neighboring settlements under a regime of forced labor. On 8 June, they were deported to Auschwitz via Kerecsend. The community was reestablished by 70 survivors but few remained after 1956.

TISZALOK Szabolcs dist., Hungary. Jews were present in the early 17th cent. and were active as tradesmen as well as operating a knitting mill, brickyard, and shoe polish factory. A synagogue was built in 1840, a school in 1878. The J. pop. was 556 in 1880 and 362 in 1941, when the young were seized for forced labor, 40 perishing. The rest were deported to Auschwitz via Nyiregyhaza on 17 May 1944.

TISZALUC Zemplen dist., Hungary. Jews are known from the 17th cent., first selling lumber and then turning to farming. They numbered 174 in 1930. Under the 1938 racial laws, many without proper citizenship papers were deported to Kamenets-Podolski and murdered. The rest lost their farms and were excluded from trade. In 1942, 25 were sent to forced labor and on 12–15 June 1944, the remainder were deported to Auschwitz via Satoraljaujhely.

TISZAROFF Jasz–Nagykun–Szolnok dist., Hungary. Jews settled in the first half of the 19th cent. and numbered 113 in 1880 and 58 in 1930. On 26 June 1944, they were deported to Auschwitz and Austria after periods of detention in Torokszentmiklos and Szolnok.

TISZASZALKA Bereg dist., Hungary. Jews are first mentioned in the mid-19th cent. but were probably present in the 18th cent. They numbered 70 in 1944 and after a period of persecution and forced labor were deported to Auschwitz via Beregszasz in May.

TISZASZENTIMRE Jasz–Nagykun–Szolnok dist., Hungary. Jews arrived in the early 19th cent., building a synagogue in 1850. No pop. figures are available. The Jews suffered from attacks in the early 1920s and late 1930s. At the end of June 1944, they were deported, mostly to Auschwitz via Karcag and Szolnok and some to Austria.

TISZASZENTMARTON Szabolcs dist., Hungary. Jews are mentioned in 1770, numbering 66 in 1880 and 56 in 1930. They were deported to Auschwitz via Kisvarda at the end of May 1944.

TITEL Vojvodina dist., Yugoslavia. The J. community was established in the second half of the 19th cent. In 1940, the J. pop. was 47 (total 6,000.) In Jan. 1942, 36 of T.'s Jews were murdered by the Hungarians.

TIVROV Vinnitsa dist., Ukraine. Jews numbered 353 in 1765 and 1,051 (total 3,153) in 1897. In the Soviet period, Yiddish cultural activity continued through the late 1930s. In 1939, the J. pop. was 397. The Germans captured T. on 18 July 1941, immediately murdering 28 J. men in the Black Forest. Another 250–400 were executed there in Nov. The Germans murdered about 420 Jews from T. and another 721 from the surrounding region. Sixteen young Jews survived in the forests.

TLUMACZ Stanislawow dist., Poland, today Ukraine. Jews are first recorded in the late 16th cent. The community was destroyed in the 17th cent. but began to develop again in the 18th. In the Austrian period, with its heavy taxation, all trade was in J. hands. The laying of a branch of the main Stanislawow–Tarnopol railroad line at the end of the 19th cent. boosted the economy. Jews marketed agricultural produce to the Galician centers, owned stores, and opened stalls on market days. Home industries like knitting and embroidery occupied about 200, mostly young women. Despite a steady stream of emigration, the J. pop. leveled off at around 2,000 or some 40% of the total from the 1890s on. WWI brought considerable hardship. The Russians and Austrians vying for control of the town with the Cossacks contributed to the general destructiveness that left J. homes looted and half destroyed. Between the World Wars J. businesses faced competition from the Poles and Ukrainians. During the period Zionist youth movements were very active. The Soviet regime of 1939–41 brought nationalization of big businesses and the phasing out of trade. The Hungarian army arrived on 7 July 1941 and a month later over 1,000 J. refugees from Carpathia came to the town. The Ukrainians drowned a number of them as well as some local Jews. The Germans arrived in Sept. 1941. The following April, about 1,000 Jews were sent to Stanislawow and murdered at the Rodolf Flour Mill. At the beginning of May, stricken by hunger and disease, the Jews were herded into a ghetto. On 18 April, about 180 were murdered in the streets and 350 sent to forced labor. Final liquidation took place in Aug.–Sept. with many murdered on the spot and others sent to meet a similar fate at Stanislawow. Of the few dozen who survived the war, most emigrated to Palestine and the west.

TLUMACZYK Stanislawow dist., Poland, today Ukraine. The J. pop. in 1921 was 127 (total 1,965), facing severe antisemitism. It may have been decimated in a Ukrainian pogrom after the Soviet withdrawal in June 1941; the remainder was expelled to Kolomyja by the Germans in 1942.

TLUSTE (Yid. Toist) Tarnopol dist., Poland, today Ukraine. Jews first settled in T. in the late 17th cent. Many dealt in farm produce, trading particularly in grain. T. is associated with the beginnings of Hasidism, the Ba'al Shem Tov having resided there in the 1730s when he revealed himself as a healer and leader. From the end of the 19th cent. Chortkov, Vizhnitz, and Kopyczynce Hasidism with rival dynastic courts contended for domination in the community. J. textile factories were set up in the early 20th cent. and all the town's inns were in J. hands. The J. pop. stood at 2,157 in 1880 (total 3,199) but dropped to 1,196 in 1921 with the collapse of J. businesses in the course of WWI. Economic distress was again felt in the 1930s together with rising antisemitism. The Zionists expanded their activities between the World Wars. Soviet rule (17 Sept. 1939–6 July 1941) brought an end to J. commercial and community life. The Hungarian army entered the town on 7 July 1941. The Germans took over on 1 Sept., imposing forced labor and extortionate measures. Many of the Jews were sent to work in a network of rubber plant farms and found a measure of security there. In July 1942, 200 of the sick and aged were deported along with 75 girls seized from one of the farms to make up the deportation quota. Another 1,000 were deported to the Belzec death camp on 5 Oct., including Jews brought in from the surrounding villages. Of the hundreds murdered in the streets, many were infants. The winter of 1942–43 brought disease and starvation, with sporadic shootings. On 27

May 1943, with the J. pop. further swelled from the nearby settlements, 3,000 were assembled in the market square and led away to be shot at the J. cemetery in groups of 100–200. A week later, the remaining 3,000 Jews were packed into a few dozen buildings in a two-block ghetto. On 5 June another 1,000 were murdered at the cemetery and the remainder deported a few days later. Of those hiding out, some tried to link up with the partisans while others found refuge as farm workers. Many were nonetheless murdered as were those running into Russian and Ukrainian collaborators fleeing the advancing Soviets at the beginning of 1944 or Cossacks under German command. The hundred or so Jews who gathered in T. after the liberation soon emigrated to Palestine and the west.

TLUSTE WIES Tarnopol dist., Poland, today Ukraine. The J. pop. in 1921 was 185. The Jews were probably expelled to Tluste for liquidation in summer–fall 1942.

TLUSZCZ Warsaw dist., Poland. The J. settlement was founded in the early 20th cent., growing to 437 (total 1,102) in 1921. Gur Hasidim predominated in the community, which was served by R. Yaakov Yosef Brikman from 1912 until his murder by the Nazis in 1942. The Zionists and Agudat Israel were active between the World Wars, with Yavne and Beth Jacob schools in operation. The Germans took the city on 14 Sept. 1939, setting up a *Judenrat* in Oct. and instituting a regime of forced labor. Many fled east in winter 1939–40, leaving about 740 Jews including refugees in the town. Crowded into a ghetto in Sept. 1940 they suffered from starvation and a typhoid epidemic during the winter. On 27 May 1942, 600 were led toward Radzymin after 70 were shot in the town; about half were murdered along the way and the rest were sent to the Warsaw ghetto.

TOKAJ Zemplen dist., Hungary. Jews from Poland arrived in the first half of the 18th cent. They leased vineyards and developed a flourishing wine export trade. In the late 19th cent., Jews opened a match factory and a bank. In 1880, their pop. reached a peak of 1,161. A J. school was founded in 1856 and a new synagogue was built in 1889. Zionist activity was widespread between the World Wars. The local authorities refused to let White Terror gangs enter T. (1919–21) and the Jews remained untouched. The J. pop. was

958 in 1944. In May the Jews were brought to the Satoraljaujhely ghetto. On 18 May, deportations to Auschwitz commenced. The community was reestablished by 112 survivors but few remained by 1960.

TOKOL Pest–Pilis–Solt–Kiskun dist., Hungary. Jews settled in the late 18th cent. and numbered 74 in 1930. A synagogue was built in 1890. On 7–8 June 1944, the 59 remaining Jews were brought to Czepel and a month later deported to Auschwitz. Hundreds of leading Jews from Budapest were brought to the Horty-Ligat camp, near T., and deported to the death camps in Germany.

TOLCSVA Zemplen dist., Hungary. Jews are first mentioned in 1723 as winegrowers. The community maintained a synagogue and yeshiva and reached a pop. of 929 in 1890, declining to 363 in 1941. In 1941, several J. families without proper papers were taken to Kamenets-Podolski and shot. The young men were sent to forced labor in the Ukraine, where most died. On 19 March 1944, the Jews were brought to Satoraljaujhely and from 16–25 May deported to Auschwitz. Fifty survivors reestablished the community but most soon left for Israel.

TOLNA Tolna dist., Hungary. Jews apparently arrived with the Turks in the 16th cent. and subsequently left with them, the modern community beginning in 1735 and growing to a pop. of 392 in 1880. By 1864, the community maintained a synagogue and J. school. In the late 19th cent., two paprika factories founded by Jews enjoyed a national reputation. In 1930, 258 Jews remained. They were deported to Auschwitz via Paks on 4–6 July 1944.

TOLOCHIN Vitebsk dist., Belorussia. Jews are first mentioned in 1717. Their pop. was 648 in 1766 and 2,054 (total 3,415) in 1897. Most Jews earned their living in the cattle trade and in the industries associated with it. In the 1920s, under the Soviets, 106 Jews were artisans, most organized in cooperatives, while 37 J. families were employed in agriculture. The local J. elementary school closed in 1937. In 1939, the J. pop. was 1,292. The Germans occupied T. on 6 July 1941, setting up a ghetto in Sept. for 2,000 Jews from T. and the neighboring villages. On 13 March 1942 they were executed near the village of Raitsy.

TOMASHOW MAZOWIECKI Lodz dist., Poland. The first Jews came in 1815 to develop the textile industry. In 1911, 72 Jews were among the 109 manufacturers in the town. Many of the textile workers were Jews. A number of hasidic rabbis had their courts here and by 1892 the Hasidim had 17 prayer houses. In 1864 the community decided to build a synagogue, which took 14 years to complete. Jews were among the revolutionaries in the 1863 Polish uprising and three of them were awarded the country's highest military medal in independent Poland. Zionist political activity began in the 1880s and the community was well represented at the Zionist Congresses. In 1903 Bund activists from Lodz organized a workers strike. The Mizrachi movement became the strongest Zionist party, closely followed by the Revisionists. From 1931 to 1936, Agudat Israel dominated the community council. Afterwards the Zionists formed a majority. The J. pop. in 1931 was 11,310 (30% of the total). The J. merchants association set up its own bank. Among J. welfare institutions were a hostel, an orphanage, and an old age home. Between the World Wars three government (*szabasowki*) schools for Jews operated and a J. high school opened in 1920. Agudat Israel and other organizations ran their own schools. Following the occupation of T. on 5 Sept. 1939, Jews were rounded up and 90 J. males were sent to the Buchenwald concentration camp, where most died. In Oct. 1939 *Volksdeutche* and Hitler Youth burned down the synagogue. By June 1940, with the influx of refugees, the number of Jews reached 16,500 (13,000 in 1939). The *Judenrat*, organized in fall 1939, consisted mainly of the community council leadership. The ghetto was set up in Dec. 1940 and enclosed by a fence in Dec. 1941. In 1942 several hundred J. males were taken to work deepening the bed of the Wolberka River. The *Judenrat* set up a soup kitchen that in its peak period served 1,500 meals a day. Some schooling and concerts were organized clandestinely. In Oct.–Dec. 1941, 1,500 of the refugees as well as the inhabitants of the quarters across the river were expelled to small towns in the area. In April–May 1942 the Germans began killing Communists, members of the intelligentsia, and members of the *Judenrat*. On 30 Oct. 1942, Jews brought to T. from Biala Rawska, Rawa Mazowiecka, Ujazd, and surrounding villages were transported to the Treblinka death camp. On the following day the J. community was rounded up and the majority sent to the Treblinka death camp. In all, 15,000 Jews were sent to their deaths. The remaining 600–900 Jews were deported to Blizhyn at the end of May 1943. About 200 survivors returned to T. after the war, but by 1957 only five remained.

TOMASHPOL Vinnitsa dist., Ukraine. The J. pop. was 531 in 1765 and 4,515 (total 4,972) in 1897. During the civil war (1918–21), the Petlyura and other gangs attacked Jews on several occasions. In the Soviet period, most J. children attended a J. elementary school and J. cultural life centered around a local J. theater, library, and club. Most Jews were employed in artisan cooperatives, a sugar refinery, and a kolkhoz. A. J. council (soviet) was also active. In 1939, the J. pop. was 1,863. The Germans captured the town on 20 July 1941, murdering six Jews five days later and another 150 on 11 Aug. In early Sept., T. was attached to Transnistria and the Jews subsequently concentrated in a ghetto, where many died from starvation, the cold, and hard labor.

TOMASZGOROD Volhynia dist., Poland, today Ukraine. The J. pop. in 1921 was 159 (total 803). The community was liquidated on 28 Aug. 1942 after expulsion to Sarny.

TOMASZOW LUBELSKI Lublin dist., Poland. Jews are first mentioned in the late 16th cent. They maintained an organized community with a synagogue and earned their living dealing in cattle, knitted goods, alcoholic beverages, and crafts. The Chmielnicki massacres of 1648–49 virtually destroyed the community, leaving just 18 families at the end of the cent. By 1765 the J. pop. numbered 806, becoming a hasidic center (Kotsk-Gur, Trisk, Ruzhin, Belz, Zanz) and known for its Torah scholars. In the 19th cent., Jews owned half the town's factories, mainly in the textile industry. Many supplied goods and services to a Russian army unit stationed nearby. In 1897, their pop. reached 3,646 (total 6,077). In the early 20th cent, Haskala and Zionism began to make inroads among the young. A modern J. school for boys was opened in 1913 while 400 children still studied in the *heder* and *talmud torah* system. Under the Austrian and German occupation in WWI, the Jews suffered from heavy taxes and food shortages and in 1918, 325 J. families were left homeless after a devastating fire. A local Catholic priest, Julian Bogatek, provided Jews with shelter from Polish and Balakhovich brigade soldiers

Heder *in Tomaszow Lubelski, Poland*

who were attacking the community and later in the 1930s from antisemites. After the war, various credit and mutual aid societies helped the J. economy revive while Zionist influence expanded, with many of the young emigrating to Palestine in 1933–34 as part of the Fourth Aliya. Mizrachi opened a Yavne school and Agudat Israel a Beth Jacob school. On the German advance in Sept. 1939, about 2,000 Jews left with the Red Army, leaving 3,500 behind. The Germans appointed a *Judenrat* and instituted a regime of forced labor and extortionate "contributions," later establishing a ghetto. In Dec. 1939, the Nazis forced a group of handicapped and mentally ill Jews into a cellar and drowned them. In March 1942, all Jews over the age of 32 were deported to the Belzec death camp. The rest of the Jews were sent there on 27 Oct. 1942. Most of those in the Soviet Union survived the war and after repatriation emigrated to Israel.

TOPLITA (Hung. Marosheviz) N. Transylvania dist., Rumania. A J. community was organized in the 1830s. A large synagogue built prior to WWI still exists. The J. pop. in 1930 was 746 (9% of the total). T. had one of the most active Zionist groups in Transylvania during the 1930s. Beginning in Sept. 1940, Jews were deprived by the Hungarians of their lumber mills and forestry holdings. They were drafted into labor battalions and sent to the Ukraine, where they died. In May 1944 the Jews were transferred to the Reghin ghetto and in June deported to Auschwitz.

TOPOLCANY (Hung. Nagytapolcsany) Slovakia, Czechoslovakia, today Republic of Slovakia. Though J. merchants were present in the city in the 14th cent., permanent J. settlement commenced only in the 17th cent. under the protection of Count Porgacs. The Jews of T. were included in the general expulsion from the country's mining dist. in 1727 but soon returned, their number growing steadily in the latter half of the 18th cent. as Moravian refugees began to arrive. A synagogue was constructed c. 1780 and under R. Avraham Ulman (1810-25) the community's famous yeshiva, one of the first in Slovakia, was founded. With the J. pop. rising to 561 (total 2,500) in 1828, most trade was in J. hands. In 1848, rioting peasants pillaged J. homes and stores. A J. school for boys was opened in 1850, becoming a coeducational elementary school in 1858 with an enrollment of 150 children. A new synagogue seating about 500 was consecrated in 1898. In 1900, the J. pop. was 1,676. The community was a religious center and flourished economically with Jews running factories and estates and serving on the local council. The first Zionist society was founded in 1898 but Zionist activity declined somewhat after WWI owing to the vehement opposition of R. Avraham Eliezer Weiss, who served as chief rabbi for 17 neighboring settlements from 1921. He also headed Agudat Israel in Czechoslovakia, its local branch becoming a major influence in community life. Zionist activity intensified in the 1930s as hundreds of the young joined Hashomer Hatzair and Bnei Akiva and the Maccabi sports club continued to operate. Another synagogue, constructed in the 1920s, served mainly Polish, Hungarian, and east Czechoslovakian newcomers. An old age home was also opened in the 1920s. The J. elementary school now had 200-250 pupils as the J. pop. rose to 1,954 in 1920. Jews continued to hold public positions and dominate commercial life, controlling all wholesale trade, operating three banks, and manufacturing building materials, brushes, and beverages. Persecution intensified with the creation of the Fascist Hlinka Guard after Slovakia was granted autonomy

in Oct. 1938. Jews were removed from the municipal council and 67 J. aliens were expelled from the city. In Oct. 1939, 300 Jews were seized for forced labor and in 1940–early 1942 most J. businesses were closed down. In Oct 1941, 124 Jews were sent to the nearby Novaky labor camp but with 365 refugees arriving from Bratislava, the J. pop. reached a peak of 3,060 in late 1941 with nearly another 1,000 in the 51 settlements of the county. Deportations commenced on 22 March 1942, when 56 young J. men were sent to the Sered transit camp. Another 141 were sent to Novaky on 29 March and from there to the Majdanek concentration camp two days later; 155 young J. women were deported to Auschwitz via Patronka on 1 April. Families were deported through Sept.: 380 Jews to Auschwitz via Zilina on 15 April; 850 to Opole in the Lublin dist. (Poland) via Sered on 18 April; 560 in June; 837 in July; and a few dozen J. families sent to Auschwitz from the Vynhe and Novaky labor camps on 21 Sept. In all, about 2,400 Jews from T. itself were sent to the death camps in 1942. When the Germans occupied the city in early Sept. 1944, about 800 Jews were present. Most were deported to Auschwitz within a month. After liberation, about 500 Jews returned to T. and reestablished the community. Forty-seven Jews were injured and much J. property was damaged in a pogrom following a blood libel in Sept. 1945, the most serious postwar incident in Slovakia. In 1948, about 330 Jews remained, most leaving for Israel or other countries in 1949. The rest gradually moved to Bratislava.

TOPOROW Tarnopol dist., Poland, today Ukraine. Jews appeared with the founding of T. in 1603, receiving extensive residence and trade rights, including brewing and distilling licenses. In the 19th cent., many Jews also marketed locally produced pottery. Hasidism was the dominant force in the community. The J. pop. grew to 1,133 (a third of the total) in 1880 but after a series of fires and the tribulations of WWI it dropped to 689. Between the World Wars the Jews suffered severe economic hardship and with the arrival of the Soviets in 1939 all private initiative came to an end. Two days after the arrival of the Germans, on 26 June 1942, the Ukrainians murdered 180 Jews. Others were put to forced labor and hundreds were deported to the Belzec death camp in March and Sept. 1942 and Feb. 1943.

TORACENI Bukovina, Rumania, today Ukraine. The J. pop. of 61 in 1930 was a branch of the Putila community. In June 1941 the J. pop. was deported to Transnistria. Few survived.

TORCZYN Volhynia dist., Poland, today Ukraine. Jews settled in the 16th cent. The community suffered in the Chmielnicki massacres of 1648–49 as well as from fires and epidemics. Under Russian rule, the community began to grow, reaching a pop. of 2,629 in 1897 (total 4,507). Most factories and the grain trade was in J. hands. There were numerous hasidic sects and the Bund and the Zionists began operating openly after the Feb. 1917 Revolution. The Germans arrived on 25 June 1941 and established a *Judenrat*. On 2 Aug. they executed 276 Jews, mostly young, on the pretext of collaboration with the Soviets. In Feb. 1942, 3,000 Jews, including 1,500 refugees, were crowded into a ghetto; 150 sent to Kiev to work were murdered in May and the rest were executed beside open pits on 23 Aug. 1942.

TORGOVITSA Kirovograd, Ukraine. Jews probably settled in the late 18th cent., numbering 1,299 (total 3,679) in 1897 and 846 in 1926 under the Soviets. On 10 and 18 Dec. 1918, pogroms were staged. A J. elementary school was operating in the mid-1920s, with an enrollment of 118 in 1927. In the late 1920s, many Jews, stripped of their rights and living in straitened economic circumstances, left the town, some to work in agriculture. The Germans captured T. in early Aug. 1941, murdering 425 Jews at the beginning of 1942.

TORNALA Slovakia, Czechoslovakia, today Republic of Slovakia. Jews may have arrived in the mid-19th cent. A beautiful 300-seat synagogue in the Neo-Gothic style was built in 1890 and the J. pop. grew to 378 (total 1,793) in 1900. The community also maintained an elementary school and a *talmud torah*. The local rabbinate had jurisdiction over 15 neighboring settlements. The J. pop. reached a peak of 682 in 1930 with 100 children attending the J. school and others in a J. kindergarten. Seven Jews sat on the local council. The Zionists became active in the 1920s with most of the young belonging to such youth movements as Hashomer Hatzair, Betar, and Bnei Akiva. Agudat Israel was also active, with Orthodox girls in the Beth Jacob movement. After the annexation to Hungary in 1938, the Jews were subjected to persecution and forced to liquidate their businesses. Eight families were expelled to Kamenets-Podolski in the German-occupied Ukraine and others were seized for forced labor. In spring 1944, 620 Jews were confined to a ghetto, leaving behind 181 apartments and 185 businesses which the authorities sequestered. On 6 June, 800 Jews from T. and the surrounding area were deported to Auschwitz via Miskolc. Most of the postwar community of 179 emigrated to Israel in 1949.

TORNYOSPALCA Szabolcs dist., Hungary. Jews are mentioned in 1770 and numbered 103 in 1930. At the end of May 1944, they were deported to Auschwitz via Kisvarda.

TOROKBALINT Pest-Pilis-Solt-Kiskun dist., Hungary. Jews settled in the late 19th cent. and numbered 93 in 1930. The community maintained a school and synagogue. In late May 1944, the Jews were brought to the Budafok ghetto and in late June deported to Auschwitz via Budakalasz.

TOROKSZENTMIKLOS Jasz-Nagykun-Szolnok dist., Hungary. Jews were allowed to settle in T. in 1840, soon establishing a cemetery, a synagogue in 1848, and a school in 1858. The J. pop. grew to 821 (4% of the total) in 1900. A hospital was founded during WWI and a yeshiva in 1928. Three Jews were killed in the White Terror attacks (1919-21) and many sent to the Zalaegerszag concentration camp. Increasing antisemitism promoted conversion but also Zionist activity. The racial laws of 1939 destroyed J. economic life and many men were sent to forced labor in the Ukraine. In 1941, 520 Jews remained. On 16 May 1944, they were confined in two ghettos with Jews from neighboring settlements. In the beginning of June, they were brought to Szolnok and from there on 29 June deported to Auschwitz and Austria, most returning from the latter to renew the community. Most of the young men left for Israel after 1948 and in 1962, 90 Jews remained.

TOROPETZ Kalinin dist., Russia. Jews probably settled in the mid-19th cent. The J. pop. was 570 (total 7,000) in 1897, rising to 1,158 in 1926 under the Soviets and then dropping to 500 in 1939. A J. school and club were functioning in 1925. The Ger-

Synagogue in Torokszentmiklos, Hungary, before WWII

mans occupied T. on 29 Aug. 1941, moving the Jews into a ghetto. After two months of abuse, including murder, 95 were executed in late Oct.

TORUN (I) (Ger. Thorn) Pomerania dist., Poland. Despite a residence ban spanning hundreds of years, J. merchants frequented the town and by the 18th cent. a few J. families had settled. A large group arrived with special permits after the annexation to Prussia in 1793 but the residence ban was only officially lifted in 1846. Most Jews earned their living as petty traders and lived in crowded conditions and straitened economic circumstances. Their situation improved in the second half of the 19th cent. as peddlers became shopkeepers with a few entering banking and large-scale trade. A professional class of doctors, lawyers, and municipal bureaucrats also began to develop. A new synagogue was built in 1847 and a J. elementary school was opened in 1862. The Liberal rabbi Hermann Simon officiated for 50 years (1825–75), followed by Tzevi Hirsch Kalischer (1875–95), an early advocate of Zionism. He maintained, to the ire of strictly Orthodox

circles, that the redemption of Israel depended as much on human effort as divine intervention and thus preached the settlement of Eretz Israel. The Zionist movement itself became active in 1906. Liberal religious tendencies under Haskala influence were exemplified by confirmation exercises for girls with singing and music in the Protestant style. T. was also the birthplace of the scholar Hartwig Hirschfeld (1854–1934), famous for his edition of Yehuda ha-Levi's *Kuzari* and his studies on the Cairo Genizah. The J. pop. reached a peak of 1,371 (total 28,018) in 1890 but declined as Jews moved to the larger cities. After WWI, antisemitism reached virulent proportions, led by the right-wing Endecja (National Democracy) Party. Zionist activity consequently intensified, with Hashomer Hatzair prominent among the youth movements with a membership of 60 in 1935. The arrival of Jews from former Congress Poland partially offset the accelerated exodus of Jews, bringing the J. pop. up to 576 on the eve of WWII. Many fled on the approach of the Germans, leaving 285 in Oct. 1939. Most were soon expelled, ultimately perishing in the death camps.

TORUN (II) (Hung. Toronya) Carpatho-Russia, Czechoslovakia, today Ukraine. J. settlement apparently began at the turn of the 18th cent. The J. pop. was 67 in 1830 and 173 (total 680) in 1880. In 1921, under Czechoslovakian rule, the J. pop. grew to 298 and then to 310 in 1941. A Hebrew elementary school was opened in the 1920s, the first of its kind in the country. Zionist youth organizations such as Hashomer Hatzair were active. Jews owned 15 business establishments and four workshops while four families earned their livelihoods from agriculture. After the Hungarian occupation of March 1939, the Jews were cut off from their sources of income. In 1941, a few dozen were drafted into forced labor battalions, some being stationed on the eastern front, where many were killed. In late July 1941, dozens of Jews without Hungarian citizenship were expelled to the German-occupied Ukraine and murdered. The rest were deported to Auschwitz in May 1944.

TOTKOMLOS Bekes dist., Hungary. Jews settled in the late 19th cent., maintaining excellent relations with their Slovakian Hussite neighbors, who regarded themselves and the Jews as fellow refugees. A synagogue and school were opened in 1860. The J. pop. was 168 in 1880 and 192 in 1930. A Jew, Nandor Vas, headed the town's ruling political party until 1944. When the Jews were enclosed in a ghetto in April 1944, their Christian neighbors supplied them with food and J. clerks continued to receive their salaries from their employers. On 26 June, the 120 remaining Jews were taken to Auschwitz via Bekescsaba and Debrecen. They were accompanied by 52 Jews from a single family in neighboring Vegegyhaza. Eighty Jews included on Kasztner's list were saved.

TOULON Var dist., France. The J. community dates from the 13th cent. The community was destroyed during the Black Death persecutions in 1348-49 when the J. quarter was attacked, houses were pillaged, and 40 Jews were slain. The Jews returned to form a small community in the 19th cent. In 1941, there were between 30 and 35 J. families in T. (50, according to some sources.) All were from Alsace, two-thirds being refugees. A synagogue was built in 1945 after the liberation. In 1964, there were 1,280 Jews in T., mostly from North Africa.

TOULOUSE Haute-Garonne dist., France. The J.

presence dates from 1020. The Jews, mainly engaged in commerce and moneylending, established a flourishing community. In 1217 all were imprisoned and ordered to choose between baptism and death. Simon de Montfort released the adult Jews on payment of large ransoms, but their children, baptized by force, never returned. In 1306, when the Jews were expelled from the Kingdom of France, the local J. community was still numerous and economically important. It ceased to exist in 1320, when the Jews became victims of the Pastoureaux persecutions and the Inquisition produced new forced converts. After 1359, 15 families established a new community, but it too vanished after the final expulsion of 1394. Individual merchants, though, were allowed to trade four times a year in T. From the second half of the 18th cent., individual Jews tried to obtain official permission to settle. In 1808, 87 Jews were listed in T. Most were peddlers and merchants, originally from Avignon, Alsace, and Germany. Communal life was organized gradually. In 1816, a local cemetery was opened and in 1852, Leon Oury was nominated as rabbi of T. A synagogue was founded in 1857. In 1867, a local committee of the Alliance Israelite Universelle was established and Jews were well integrated in the community with Leon Cohn becoming governor of T. (1886-94). Prominent figures from T. include the philosopher Frederic Rauh (1861-1909). After 1871, the community absorbed Jews from Alsace-Lorraine; in the 1920s, Jews from Turkey; and later refugees from Eastern Europe (Poland, Rumania), western Germany (the Saar region after the annexation of 1935), and Austria. T. thus developed into the largest community in the south of France, numbering between 1,000-1,500 Jews in the 1930s. During WWII, many Jews found refuge in T., because it was situated in the unoccupied zone. In July 1940, the first relief committee for refugees in unoccupied France was established. During the last months of 1940 and the beginning of 1941, the J. resistance organization, Organisation Juive de Combat, was formed. It cooperated with the Zionist youth movement as well as the association of J. scouts. By 1941, T. was the seat of a regional rabbinate for about 560 families in ten settlements. The regional offices of the Commissariat Generale aux Questions Juives was located in T. In Aug. 1942, when 1,525 foreign-born Jews were destined for deportation, the Archbishop of T., Mgr. Saliege, protested. Following the German occupation of all of France in Nov. 1942, the persecution of the Jews increased and many were brutally arrested and deported. It has been estimated that 6,400 were deported from the T. region, with 97%–98% being killed. The high figures are due to the presence of several camps in the vicinity of T., such as the Gurs concentration camp and a labor camp (Service du Travail Obligatoire) at Noe where 211 foreign Jews were held. Another labor camp in T. held 254 J. prisoners in Nov. 1942, with only 120 remaining in April 1944. It is believed that one-third of the foreign Jews and one-tenth of the French Jews were deported from the region. After WWII, the community of T. was reconstructed. With the influx of Jews from Morocco and Algeria in the 1960s, it developed into one of the most important communities in France. It consisted of 20,000 Jews in 1964.

TOURS Indre-et-Loire dist., France. The J. community dates back to the sixth cent. During the Middle Ages, T. was renowned for its talmudists, such as Salomon de Tours, a contemporary of Rashi, David de Tours, and Yosef ben Elie in the 13th cent. The community ceased to exist in the 14th cent. as a result of expulsions. The modern community was reestablished around 1880 with the arrival of Jews from Alsace-Lorraine. The local synagogue was inaugurated in 1907. After WWI the Societe de la Jeunesse Israelite de Tours dedicated itself to encouraging education and philanthropy as well as establishing a library and organizing lectures for members. In Feb. 1942, arrests began in T. Twenty Jews were taken hostage and on 31 March 1942 they were deported. In Aug. arrests were renewed. In 1942 there were 77 Jews in T. There were arrests again in Jan. 1944. In 1964, the community consisted of 600 Jews.

TOUSTE Tarnopol dist., Poland, today Ukraine. Jews lived there from the early 18th cent. and increased to 671 residents in 1880 (total 2,139), but their number fell to 105 after WWI. With the withdrawal of the Soviets, the Ukrainian populace went on a rampage and murdered nearly all the Jews in early July 1941.

TOVACOV Moravia, Czechoslovakia. Jews were probably present in the mid-15th cent. By the mid-16th cent. they numbered 26 families. They maintained a synagogue and cemetery, both destroyed by the Swedish army in the Thirty Years War (1618-48). In 1736–83, 17 Jews (15% of the Jews) converted and in 1783–1807 four fires destroyed J. homes. The J.

pop. rose to 194 (total 1,697) in 1851. In 1930, 52 remained. The Nazis executed a Jew on 30 Sept. 1941 and on 26 June 1942 deported the remaining 47 Jews to the Theresienstadt ghetto via Olomouc. A few weeks later most were sent to Maly Trostinec (Belorussia) and the Treblinka death camp.

TOZEUR Tozeur dist., Tunisia. A J. community living in its own quarter is known from the early 20th cent. though it is possible that Jews were present earlier. Most came from Algeria to the west and Djerba and Tripolitania to the east. The J. pop. reached a peak of 181 in 1926 and dropped to 143 (total 11,698) in 1936. It was comprised of a small number of extended families. The Touitous and Sa'adons were the largest and most influential with 85 members. Another 64 members of the two families lived in Nefta 15 miles (24 km) away, making for close ties between the two. Jews were mainly engaged in the date industry, buying them from Arab farmers and marketing them to the coast and northern Tunisia. They also distilled and marketed the popular *bukha* drink as well as 5,000 quarts a year of date arrack. J. merchants imported silk fabrics and textiles from Europe. J. artisans also maintained a virtual monopoly on silver work, primarily for Arab customers. Tensions with the local pop. developed against the background of Arab nationalism and the J. aspiration to become French citizens. In WWII, shortly before the German occupation of 19 Feb. 1943, over half the Jews fled the city as T. was in the frontline of the war. They never returned and the remaining 63 Jews emigrated to Israel in an *aliya* operation organized by the J. Agency in the early 1950s.

TRABELSDORF Upper Franconia, Germany. Jews are known from the mid-18th cent. Around 60 Jews lived there in the 19th cent. (15% of the total pop.). The community was united with Walsdorf in 1907 and numbered 18 in 1933. The synagogue was vandalized on *Kristallnacht* (9–10 Nov. 1938), and nine of the last Jews were deported to Izbica in the Lublin dist. (Poland) on 25 April 1942.

TRABY Nowogrodek dist., Poland, today Belarus. A small J. settlement probably existed in the early 18th cent., growing to a pop. of 634 (total 1,183) in 1897. About 400 Jews were made homeless by a 1934 fire, compounding the distress of the community in the years of economic crisis. Under Soviet rule in 1939–41, most were employed in the new cooperatives. About 600 Jews were living there when the Germans entered T. on 25–26 June 1941. They were expelled to the Iwie ghetto in fall 1941. On 12 May 1942 most were executed near the village of Staniwicze with the other ghetto Jews.

TRACHENBERG (Pol. Zmigrod) Upper Silesia, Germany, today Poland. Jews were present in the 16th and 17th cents. but a permanent community was only founded in the modern period. The J. pop. was 90 in 1880 and 117 in 1875. The community established a cemetery in 1822, a school in 1855, and a synagogue in 1861. The J. pop. dropped to 85 in 1900, 38 in 1910, and 28 in 1933. Nineteen Jews remained in 1937. On *Kristallnacht* (9–10 Nov. 1938), the synagogue and J. stores were destroyed. No further information is available about the Jews under Nazi rule. Presumably those who failed to emigrate were deported and perished.

TRAKANY (Hung. Tarkany) Slovakia, Czechoslovakia, today Republic of Slovakia. The J. pop. was 188 in 1880 and 103 in 1941. All who remained were deported to Auschwitz in May 1944.

TRAPPSTADT Lower Franconia, Germany. Jews are first mentioned in 1686 and a community existed in the mid-18th cent., maintaining a pop. of 60–65 (10% of the total) throughout the 19th cent. and then declining steadily to ten in 1933. The 18th cent. synagogue building was sold in 1937. The last four Jews were deported to Izbica in the Lublin dist. (Poland) and Auschwitz in 1942–43.

TRAVNIK Bosnia-Hercegovina, Yugoslavia, today Republic of Bosnia. Sephardi Jews first arrived in T. at the end of the 17th cent. and a community was established in the mid-18th cent. During the Ottoman period (until 1878) most were traders and craftsmen. Under Austro-Hungarian rule (1878–1918), the community continued to prosper. In the late 19th cent. Ashkenazi Jews settled in T., many holding government positions, but most left with the end of Austro-Hungarian rule. During this period, J. children began to receive secular education and Zionism was introduced. During WWI the community suffered economic hardship and its numbers dropped from 472 in 1910 to 383 in 1921 (total 6,334). This situation continued under the new

Yugoslavian government (from 1918). In 1940 there were 261 Jews in T. In April 1941 the Ustase began terrorizing the Jews of T., who were seized for forced labor. They were required to wear the yellow badge and their possessions were confiscated. Restrictions were imposed on their movements. On 20 Oct. 1941, 25 Jan. 1942, and 24 March 1942 the Jews were sent to concentration camps. Only a few escaped to join the partisans or to reach Italian areas.

TRAWNIKI Lublin dist., Poland. Jews settled in the late 19th cent. and numbered about 100 before WWII. They were deported to the Belzec death camp via Lublin in spring 1942. T. served as a training facility for thousands of Ukrainian and *Volksdeutsche* death camp guards and also as a labor camp where 10,000 Jews, mostly from Warsaw, were confined. On 3 Nov. 1943, they were forced to enter pits and then shot.

TREBIC Moravia, Czechoslovakia. Tradition speaks of a synagogue dating to the tenth cent. A number of Jews were murdered in T. during the Pulkau blood libel of 1338 and King Matthias Corvinus destroyed the whole city in 1464. In the late 16th cent., Jews engaged in moneylending, traded in old clothes, and worked as tanners and distillers. They manufactured gloves, boots, and soap and supplied wool to weavers. In 1799, the J. pop. was 1,770 (total 3,012) with 92 Jews registered as merchants (grain and fodder, wool, hides, flax, and feathers). Floods, fires, and epidemics struck the community repeatedly in the 16th–19th cents. In 1849–1925, the community enjoyed political autonomy but from the late 19th cent., the J. pop. declined steadily as many left for Jihlava, Brno, and Vienna. The ghetto, established no later than the 16th cent., has been preserved to the present day. The J. cemetery contains about 11,000 graves. The Nazis deported the city's 281 Jews, together with the Jews of the Jihlava dist., to the Theresienstadt ghetto on 18 and 22 May 1942. Many were sent on to the Lublin dist. (Poland) in the same month or to the Treblinka death camp in Oct. The rest were deported to Auschwitz in 1943–44. Thirty-five survived.

TREBISOV (Hung. Toketerebes; Yid. Terebesh) Slovakia, Czechoslovakia, today Republic of Slovakia. Jews are mentioned in 1736. They numbered 77 in 1828 and 240 in 1880 (total 3,959). A J. school was opened in 1850. The synagogue burned down in

1900 and was subsequently rebuilt. Refugees from Galicia arriving before WWI founded a hasidic congregation of their own. A Zionist society was started in the 1920s and the J. National Party had three representatives on the local council. Hashomer Hatzair was the first Zionist youth movement to operate in the town. Jews owned most of the businesses in T. These were closed down under Slovakian rule and in 1941, with the J. pop. reaching a peak of about 700, dozens of Jews were seized for forced labor. Fifty-four young J. women were deported to Auschwitz on 25 March 1942 and 70 young men to the Majdanek concentration camp a few days later. Most of the others were deported in early May, the able-bodied to the Majdanek concentration camp, the others to Lubartow in the Lublin dist. (Poland). In a rare display of support, local residents opposed the deportations and the Hlinka Guard had to disperse them by force. Of the 140 Jews who remained behind, some found refuge in peasant homes while others were caught by the Germans after the Slovakian uprising of fall 1944.

TREBNITZ (Pol. Trzebnica) Lower Silesia, Germany. One Jew was present in 1346 and a Street of the Jews is mentioned in the late 14th cent. but an unbroken record of J. settlement exists only from the 19th cent. A synagogue was consecrated in 1830 and a J. cemetery was opened around the same time. The J. pop. grew from 54 in 1837 to 127 in 1871. In the late 19th cent., the J. pop. dropped, reaching 64 in 1925. The cemetery was desecrated in 1930: swastikas were painted on tombstones and the walls were defaced with Nazi slogans. The J. pop. was 42 on the eve of the Nazi rise to power in 1933. On *Kristallnacht* (9–10 Nov. 1938), the synagogue and three J. stores were destroyed and the J. school was damaged. Five Jews in mixed marriages remained in T. in Nov. 1942. No further information is available about the fate of the Jews under Nazi rule. Presumably those who failed to emigrate were deported and perished.

TREBON Bohemia, Czechoslovakia. Jews settled in the first half of the 19th cent. and established a community in the 1870s. In 1930 they numbered 43 (1% of the total). Under the Nazis, the remaining Jews were assembled at Ceske Budejovice and deported to the Theresienstadt ghetto on 18 April 1942. Half were sent to Warsaw, Lublin, and Zamosc in the same month and the rest to Auschwitz in 1943–44.

TREBUR Hesse, Germany. Founded in the 18th cent., the J. community numbered 100 (about 6% of the pop.) in 1871, dwindling to 12 in 1933 and disbanding three years later. Nearly all the remaining Jews left before WWII.

TREBUSANY (Hung. Terebesfejerpatak) Carpatho-Russia, Czechoslovakia, today Ukraine. Jews probably settled in the 1840s, numbering 165 (total 1,958) in 1880. A new synagogue (apparently built of stone) was consecrated in the early 20th cent. The J. pop. rose to 283 in 1921 under the Czechoslovakians and to 303 in 1941. Jews owned 22 business establishments, ten workshops, two sawmills, and a flour mill. The Hungarians occupied T. in March 1939 and in 1941 drafted Jews into forced labor battalions. In Aug. 1941, they expelled Jews without Hungarian citizenship to Kamenets-Podolski, where they were murdered. The rest were deported to Auschwitz on 22 May 1944.

TREIS (Mosel) Rhineland, Germany. In the first two-thirds of the 19th cent. the J. pop. was between 30 and 40, in the last third between 20 and 25, and 15 in 1925 (total 1,393). The synagogue built in 1865 was probably sold before *Kristallnacht* (9–10 Nov. 1938). Local Jews buried their dead in the cemetery belonging to the affiliated community of Luetz. Fourteen Jews perished in the Holocaust.

TREIS AN DER LUMDA Hesse, Germany. The community, dating from 1654, opened a synagogue (1829) and numbered 88 (4% of the total) in 1895. Four generations of the Wetzstein family were associated with its leadership. A pogrom was organized on *Kristallnacht* (9–10 Nov. 1938). Of the 59 Jews who lived there after 1933, 42 managed to escape (28 emigrating) before WWII. Nine others were deported in 1942.

TREMBOWLA Tarnopol dist., Poland. A small community was maintained from the mid-16th cent and was organized in the early 18th cent., growing to a pop. of around 2,000 in the late 19th cent. (around 25% of the total) but dropping to 1,486 in 1921. Between the World Wars the Jews suffered from straitened economic circumstances with antisemitic disturbances in 1937. During this period, the Zionist youth movements were very active. The Red Army arrived on 17 Sept. 1939, instituting a Soviet regime. The Germans took the town on 7 July 1941. Beginning in the fall, contingents of Jews were sent to labor camps in the vicinity. A ghetto including Jews from surrounding settlements was sealed off on 28 Oct. 1942. On 5 Nov., 1,400 were deported to the Belzec death camp. A typhoid epidemic claimed many lives in the winter of 1942–43. Another *Aktion*, on 7 April 1943, rounded up 1,000 Jews, who were shot in the nearby forest and buried in mass graves. Some offered resistance and some managed to escape in the melee. On 2–3 June, the last 1,000 Jews in the ghetto were also taken to the forest and murdered.

TRENCIANSKA TEPLA   Slovakia, Czechoslovakia, today Republic of Slovakia. Jews probably settled in the early 19th cent., founding a Neologist congregation with a small synagogue in the 1890s and reaching a pop. of 101 (total 1,884) in 1900 and 140 in 1919. The Zionists were active after WWI. Jews owned a large sugar refinery, a brickyard, and an alcohol factory. In 1941, J. businesses were closed down. In 1942 most of the remaining seven J. families were sent to the death camps.

TRENCIANSKE TEPLICE   Slovakia, Czechoslovakia, today Republic of Slovakia. Jews arrived in the isolated village in the early 18th and only began to increase in number in the late 19th cent. after the local mineral springs were commercially developed. The J. pop. reached 200 (about 13% of the total) in the early 20th cent. and remained somewhat above that level until WWII. J. livelihoods were mostly connected to the baths and tourist trade. After WWI, Zionist activity was extensive and local J. hotels hosted various Zionist conferences. In 1940, a J. elementary school was opened for J. children expelled from the public schools. In 1941 Jews were forced out of their businesses. In March–April 1942, young Jews were deported, the men to the Majdanek concentration camp and the women to Auschwitz. Shortly after, J. families were deported to the death camps of the Lublin dist. (Poland).

TRENCIN   Slovakia, Czechoslovakia, today Republic of Slovakia. The J. community was one of the oldest in Slovakia, dating back to the Middle Ages. No Jews were present in the 15th and 16th cents. In the 17th cent., local efforts were made to eliminate J. settlement, but by the 1720s there was an organized community. A J. school combining secular and religious studies was started in 1790 and a J. elementary school was founded c. 1857 with over 100 children attending. A Status Quo congregation was constituted after the 1869 split. The old synagogue (built in the 1790s) was renovated and enlarged in 1873 and a new one was built in 1913. The J. pop. rose from 419 in 1825 to 1,198 (total 5,100) in 1890. It was 1,448 in 1919 and 1,619 in 1940. A separate Orthodox congregation with its own synagogue was established in the 1930s. In the Czechoslovakian Republic, Jews were active in public and economic life, serving on the municipal council and operating 205 business enterprises, 71 workshops, a number of factories in the wood industry, and two banks. Prewar Zionist activity expanded with WIZO and Hashomer Hatzair among the more active organizations. In 1941, J. businesses were closed down or "Aryanized" by the Slovakian authorities and Jews seized for forced labor. With dozens of refugee families arriving from Bratislava, the J. pop. rose to 1,900 in Nov. 1941. Young J. men were deported to the Majdanek concentration camp and the women to Auschwitz in late March and early April 1942. Many families were deported to Auschwitz later in April. On 18 May, over 100 families from T. and its environs were sent to the death camps of the Lublin dist. (Poland). On 16 Oct., a few dozen Jews from the psychiatric ward of the local hospital were dispatched to Auschwitz. In Sept. 1944, the Germans rounded up many families who were left behind and sent them to the death camps. In all, 1,554 Jews from T. and its environs perished in the Holocaust. Over half the postwar community of 330 emigrated to Israel in 1949; a few dozen Jews remained in 1990.

TREPTOW AN DER REGA   (Pol. Trzebiatow) Pomerania, Germany, today Poland. The first Jew to receive a letter of proctection for T. is mentioned in 1695. By 1764, the J. pop. numbered seven families and in 1880 it comprised 212 individuals. The community maintained a synagogue and a cemetery. When the Nazis came to power in 1933, there were 50 Jews in T. At the beginning of 1934, Hebrew language courses were started. In May 1939, there were 41 Jews and five persons of partial J. origin (*Mischlinge*) in T. It may be assumed that those who did not manage to emigrate were deported. In Oct. 1942 only one Jew was still living in T., probably protected by marriage to a non-Jew.

TREST Moravia, Czechoslovakia. Jews expelled from Jihlava in 1426 probably founded the community. A ghetto was established by the late 17th cent. In the 17th–18th cents. Jews traded mainly in cloth, wool, hides, and wine and manufactured potash. A new synagogue was erected in 1825 and the J. pop. numbered 750 in 1830. A school was opened in 1860. In the first half of the 19th cent., Jews opened numerous factories (weaving, woodworking, candy). In 1930, 64 Jews remained (total pop. 5,012). Fifty refugees from the Sudetenland joined the 20 J. families present in 1938. Like the Jews of Brno, some emigrated, mainly to England and Palestine. The rest were deported to the Theresienstadt ghetto in late 1941–early 1942 and from there sent to the death camps of Poland.

TREUBURG (Pol. Olecko) East Prussia, Germany, today Poland. The J. presence dates from 1834. The J. pop. was 71 in 1847 and 103 in 1880. The community maintained a synagogue (established in the early 1840s) and a cemetery. In 1871, the town became one of the first localities in Prussia where a Jew was appointed judge. Kurt Blumenfeld (1884–1963), a native of T., served as chairman of the German Zionist Organization from 1924 to 1933. On the eve of the Nazi assumption of power in 1933, the J. pop. numbered about 70–80. The synagogue was destroyed on *Kristallnacht* (9–10 Nov. 1938). By May 1939, only 25 Jews were left in the whole T. region. Of those who emigrated, some of the younger Jews arrived in Palestine. Those who did not manage to leave were deported to Biala Podlaska, probably in Jan. 1940, in one of the first deportations of German Jews.

TREUCHTLINGEN (among Jews, also Troilingen) Middle Franconia, Germany. Jews were among the vic-

Synagogue in Treuchtlingen, Germany

tims of the Black Death persecutions of 1348–49. In the 17th and 18th cents. they lived under letters of protection and constituted one of the important communities in Bavaria. New synagogues were built in 1730 and 1819. A J. school was open from 1877 to the Nazi period. In 1837 the J. pop. was 282 (total 1,590), declining to 168 in 1867 and 119 in 1933 (total 4,237). In 1936, Jews were attacked on trains and J. children were expelled from the local school. On *Kristallnacht* (9–10 Nov. 1938), the synagogue was burned to the ground. By the end of the year, all but two of the Jews had left the town, most to other German cities.

TREYSA (now part of Schwalmstadt) Hesse–Nassau, Germany. Established in the 18th cent., the J. community preserved ancient liturgical traditions. It built a new synagogue in 1819 and maintained an elementary school (1835–1922). In 1895 the J. pop. was 193 (8% of the total). The temporary disappearance of a Christian maidservant in 1906 gave rise to anti-J. agitation. Jews prospered in commerce and during the Weimar Republic several were elected to the town council. Affiliated with the rabbinate of Marburg, the community numbered 130 in 1925. Its synagogue, renovated in 1929, was vandalized (though not destroyed) on *Kristallnacht* (9–10 Nov. 1938). By 1940 most of the Jews had left: 59 emigrated (21 to Palestine) and over 30 perished in the Holocaust.

TRIER (Treves) Rhineland, Germany. The J. community was probably founded in the time of the Franks. The first explicit reference to it dates from 1066. In 1096, during the massacres of the First Crusade, many (mainly women and children) drowned themselves and a few converted to save their lives. In the 11th and 12th cents., the community included doctors and Torah scholars. By the first half of the 14th cent. it numbered 30–50 families and was one of the most important in the Rhineland. The Jews inhabited a J. quarter open to Christian residence until it was closed off by three gates in 1338 following an agreement between Archbishop Baldwin and the municipality. Under the protection of Baldwin, the Jews flourished as moneylenders, serving him in various financial and administrative capacities in the manner of the future Court Jews. In the Black Death persecutions of 1348–49, the Jews were robbed, beaten, and murdered with a few escaping. Baldwin published a formal

order of expulsion in 1351 and together with his successor, Archbishop Boemund, made himself the beneficiary of their property and uncollected debts. A community of 15–25 J. families was reestablished in the late 14th cent., continuing to engage in moneylending. But in 1418, the community ended, not to be renewed until the 17th cent., when all were expelled from the archbishopric. In 1640, there were eight J. families (82 Jews) in the city, growing to 18–19 families by 1787. A cemetery was opened around the 1650s and a synagogue was erected in 1762. From the beginning of the 18th cent., the community was the most important in the Upper Trier dist. and the seat of the dist. rabbi. In the late 18th cent., Jews engaged in trade, with cattle dealing and its auxiliary activities becoming the central means of livelihood. The expanding activity of the Jews brought them into conflict with the Christian merchant guilds. From 1806, Shemuel Levi Marx, the grandfather of Karl Marx, served as dist. rabbi, participating in the Paris Sanhedrin and becoming the chief rabbi of the T. consistory in 1809. In the first half of the 19th cent., many of the established J. families converted, including R. Marx's son along with the six-year-old Karl. In 1817, the J. pop. reached 280. From the mid-19th cent., the J. pop. again grew rapidly, exceeding 800 in the 1880s (2.5% of the total) before dropping somewhat in the early 20th cent. Economic conditions continued to improve with Jews formerly engaged in petty trade and peddling becoming shopkeepers and sons of well-to-do families entering the professional class. Jews from Eastern Europe began settling in the city at the turn of the 19th cent. Reform made inroads under R. Yosef Khan, who even proposed that circumcision cease to be obligatory. A new synagogue was consecrated in 1859. The J. elementary school, which opened in 1825, had 70 pupils in four grades in 1869 and was recognized as a public school in 1890. A Jew was elected to the municipal council in 1877 and Jews joined various societies though some still excluded them into the 20th cent. There was also some Zionist activity at the time. In the Weimar period, Jews continued to be prominent in trade and the professions. They owned at least three factories (wallpaper, brushes, leather), department stores, restaurants, a printing press, and a private bank. In 1933, the J. pop. was 796 (total 76,692). From the outset of Nazi rule, Jews were persecuted, physically attacked, and arrested. According to Nazi lists, 99 J. businesses were active at the time, including 29 selling textiles and 17 selling food products. These were targeted for boycott. At the same time the community expanded its cultural and social activities. The Zionists had 78 members in 1936 and youth groups studied J. history and modern Hebrew. By 1938 the J. pop. had dropped to 400. On *Kristallnacht* (9–10 Nov. 1938), the synagogue was burned together with 24 Torah scrolls and J. homes and stores were vandalized. Another 165 Jews subsequently left but others arrived, so that in 1940–41, the J. pop. was about 450. On 16 Oct. 1941, 100 Jews were deported to the Lodz ghetto; 98 were then sent to the Lublin dist., Auschwitz, and the Theresienstadt ghetto on 26–27 July 1942; 69 were deported on 1 March 1942 and 22 on 15–16 March. The postwar community numbered 61 in 1984.

TRIESTE　Italy. Jews are first mentioned in 1236. Austria annexed T. in 1382 and Jews from Germany, involved in banking and commerce, settled in the city. Attempts to expel the Jews in 1583 failed. The Jews were confined to a ghetto in 1697. The liberal policy of Emperor Charles VI towards the Jews in 1717 was continued by his daughter Maria Theresa, who ascended to the throne in 1740. In 1747, the J. community numbered 30 families. In 1782, the Edict of Tolerance of Joseph II paved the way for improving the life of the Jews in T. and in 1784 Jews were free to reside in other parts of the city. Most, however, continued to live in the ghetto. In 1783, the first J. elementary school was opened. The first Hebrew printed work in T. was Shemuel Romanelli's Italian-Hebrew grammar published in 1799. Among the illustrious personalities of the 19th cent. were the great philologist and scholar Shemuel David Luzzatto; the poet and historian Giuseppe Revere; the writer and founder of a major insurance company Giuseppe Lazzaro Morpurgo; and the writer Italo Svevo (born Ettore Schmitz). The *Corriere Israelitico*, a J. newspaper in Italian, was published in T. from 1862 to 1915. During the 19th cent., the community absorbed J. immigrants from the Balkans and countries under the Hapsburgs as well as from Italian communities. In 1869, the community consisted of 4,421 members, growing to 5,070 in 1886. A large and impressive synagogue was inaugurated in 1912. In 1908, the Pro Emigranti Ebrei association was established to help Russian and Polish immigrants on their

Passport check in the Palestine Office, Trieste, Italy (Central Zionist Archives, Jerusalem/photo courtesy of Beth Hatefutsoth, Tel Aviv)

way to Palestine or the U.S. In the 1930s, T. was referred to as the "Port of Zion," because it was a central port of embarkation for J. immigrants from Central Europe to Palestine. When Italy annexed T. in 1918, decline set in. The port lost its importance and J. bankers and merchants suffered economically. According to the 1930 law reforming the J. communities in Italy, T. became one of 26 official districts and included under its jurisdiction Monfalcone (20 Jews in 1936) and Pola (40 Jews in 1936). In 1931, there were 5,025 Jews in T. By 1938 the J. community headed by R. Yisrael Zolli numbered 6,000 individuals. During WWII, the Germans established a camp at La Risiera di S. Sabba, near T. On 18 July 1942, the Fascists destroyed the synagogue. Between the end of 1943 and the beginning of 1944, 837 local Jews were arrested, taken to Risiera di S. Sabba and from there deported to Germany. Local Jews were active in the underground movement, among them Rita Rosani, born in 1922, who was killed in action near Verona on 17 Sept. 1944. In 1948, there were 1,600 Jews in the community. By 1965, the number had decreased to 1,052.

TRIKALA (Triccala, Trikkala, Tirhala) Thessaly, Greece. Jews probably lived in T. in ancient times. The Turks expelled the Jews to Istanbul in 1453. In 1506 there were some 90 Jews in T. The small Romaniot community (dating from the Byzantine period) absorbed exiled Spanish, Portuguese, and Sicilian Jews in the early 16th cent. and Hungarian Jews in 1526. The community became predominantly Sephardi and reached a peak pop. of about 1,000 towards the end of the 17th cent. There were three congregations (Romaniot, Sephardi, and Sicilian), each with its own synagogue. Two of the synagogues were destroyed by fire in 1749; one was rebuilt. Much J. property was pillaged during the abortive Greek revolt of 1770. In the 1870s, efforts were made to organize social welfare services for the community. The Orphans' Association assisted poor girls and supported various social causes. T. was annexed to Greece in 1881 and the community was granted religious freedom. There were blood libels in 1893 and 1898; the latter was followed by antisemitic riots. During this period the Jews fell into financial difficulties. In 1906 a Zionist organization was founded, the first of a number of Zionist clubs established in the following years. In 1911, there was again a blood libel; the police intervened before it

spilled over into violence. In the 1920s, the community maintained two synagogues, a school, two welfare organizations, and a theater company. The J. pop. in 1940 was 520. In WWII, T. was included in the Italian occupation zone and was able to take in refugees from Salonika. In Sept. 1943, when the Germans took over, 300 Jews went into hiding in neighboring villages and in Athens and its surroundings. Only about one-quarter of the J. pop. remained. In March 1944, a Greek citizen of T. warned the Jews of German plans to deport them. Many fled, but on 24 March the Germans surrounded the J. quarter and arrested 50 Jews, mainly women, children, and the elderly. They were then deported to the death camps. The Germans withdrew from T. in Oct. 1944 and the Jews slowly returned, numbering 267 in 1945. A small community was reestablished.

TRINEC Silesia, Czechoslovakia. Jews settled after 1848 following a long-standing ban on settlement. They never established an independent community but affiliated themselves with the Cesky Tesin congregation. In 1930, the J. pop. was 138. In Sept. 1938, the city was annexed to Polish Silesia following the Munich Agreement. The invading Germans burned the synagogue (erected in 1931) in Oct. 1939 and deported all J. males aged 16–65 to Nisko on 27 Oct. Women, children, and the elderly were sent to the Sosnowiec ghetto and from there to Auschwitz.

TRIP (Hung. Terep) N. Transylvania dist., Rumania. Jews settled at the end of the 18th cent. The J. pop. was 195 in 1930 (15% of the total). In May 1944 the community was transferred to the Satu Mare ghetto and in June deported to Auschwitz.

TRIPOLI Tripoli dist., Libya. Jews first arrived as merchants in the Phoenician period, in the ninth cent. B.C.E. In the Roman and Byzantine periods, a large J. community was present. In the late seventh cent. C.E., under Arab rule, T. was a stronghold against the Judaized Berbers ruled by the legendary Queen Kahina, who organized opposition to the Moslem conquest. An autonomous J. religious court, independent of the one in Eretz Israel, operated in the 10th–11th cents. and in the 12th cent. the famous J. physician R. Tuviyya lived there. As in other regions of Islamic hegemony, the Dhimma (Protection) Laws determined the judicial status of the J. community in T. Jews were subjected to certain restrictions and discrimina-

The first Keren Kayemet committee in Tripoli, Libya, 1915 (Beth Hatefutsoth Photo Archive, Tel Aviv/courtesy of Vaad Kehilot Luv B'Israel. Tel Aviv)

tory measures but their life and property were guaranteed and they were granted communal autonomy. In 1159, during the rule of the fanatical Almohad dynasty in the western part of North Africa, the Jews in the area were given the choice of conversion or death. Although little is known of the J. settlement until the arrival of the Spanish exiles in the early 16th cent, it is nonetheless probable that already by the second half of the 13th cent., with the conquest of North Africa by the Hafsid dynasty (1247–1510), Jews began to return to T. In 1549, R. Shimon Lavi (d. 1580) arrived in the city. R. Lavi was a learned Jew from Spain who had first come to Fez in Morocco on his way to Eretz Israel. When he saw the spiritual desolation of the Jews in T. he decided to settle there to teach Torah. According to tradition, R. Lavi laid the foundations of the modern J. community and its institutions and created educational frameworks for Torah scholars from among the social elite, preparing them to serve as *dayyanim* steeped in Halakha. The situation of the Jews improved under Ottoman rule (1551–1711) as community life took root. In the 16th cent., Jews began arriving in search of employment. The 17th cent. saw the arrival of the Leghornians or Gorni (Grana) – descendants of the Spanish and Portuguese exiles and *anusim* (forced converts) from Italy, particularly from Leghorn, where they had developed Italy's interurban commerce. J. merchants exported wool, rice, wheat, barley, oil, ostrich feathers,

spices (especially saffron and salt), gold nuggets, African slaves, and ivory. Imports included wood, luxury items, clothing, and preservatives. In the 17th cent., the Jews were acting as commercial agents and brokers for European consulates. In 1705, the Jews were saved from the despotic governor of Tunisia, Ibrahim al-Sharif (1702–05), who besieged T. In 1795, the Jews were freed from the yoke of Ali Burgul, a tyrannical Algerian pirate who succeeded in gaining control of T. for a year and a half. The days came to be celebrated as additional Purim festivals – known as "Purim of al-Sharif" and "Purim of Burgul." Under the rule of the Qaramanlis (1711–1835), J. influence in the city increased still further, especially after the defeat of Ali Burgul. Most of the Qaramanli rulers were sympathetic to the Jews and preferred working with J. merchants. Yusef Bey empowered his J. agent Leon Fanfara to conduct the negotiations with the United States that resulted in the establishment of diplomatic relations with Tripolitania. Also prominent as diplomatic agents serving the Qaramanli rulers was the Serusi family. During Napoleon's invasion of Egypt in 1799, when the British demanded that all the Frenchmen in T. be surrendered to them, Avraham Serusi, temporarily in charge of the French consulate, saved all the property of the French general consul. The return of the Ottomans to direct rule in T. (1835–1911) coincided with the reforms instituted under pressure from the European powers and intended in large measure to alleviate the condition of non-Moslem minorities within the Ottoman realm. Under these reforms, the internal organization of the J. community also underwent changes, becoming more centralized and better regulated. The head of the community vis-a-vis the authorities was given the title of *hakham bakshi* and was at once a Torah scholar and spiritual leader and a secular representative with powers similar to those possessed by the J. *qa'id* in the past. The first to hold the office, in 1874, was Eliyahu Hazzan of Eretz Israel. His book *Zikhron Yerushalayim* discusses questions of religion and faith in the light of European assimilation. In the field of traditional education, he encouraged the establishment of the community's first reformed *heder*. Following him in office were R. David Papo, R. Yehuda David Kimhi, and R. Hizkiyahu Shabbetai, who officiated until 1908 and was the last appointed by Constantinople. With the increasing influence of Italy in T., an Italian school for the Jews was established in 1875 and on J. initiative the Dante Alighieri Society for the Prop-

The Hatikva school, Tripoli, Libya, 1935 (Beth Hatefutsoth Photo Archive, Tel Aviv)

Jewish home in Tripolitania, Libya (Photo: Dr. T. Gidal, Jerusalem. Tim Gidal Collection, Jerusalem/photo courtesy of Beth Hatefutsoth, Tel Aviv)

agation of Italian Culture began operating. In 1890, the Alliance Israelite Universelle founded a J. vocational school and in 1893 a modern religious educational institute called Yagdil Torah was started at the initiative of three Torah scholars – R. Shaul Adadi, R. Tziyyon Tzaror, and R. Mas'ud Janah – and a family of wealthy merchants active in international trade and known for its generosity to the community under its head, Nissim ben Halafalla Nahum. In 1893, 330 students were studying there. The J. pop. was 8,509 (29% of the total) in 1911, up from about 3,000 in 1783. At the outbreak of hostilities between Italy and the Ottoman Empire in 1911, the Jews of T. supported the Italians, as was the case with most J. communities in Libya. Chief among the supporters were the Jews of Italian origin, the Gorni. Traditional Jews, especially from the lower classes, were in fact indifferent to the Italian conquest but force of circumstance brought them over to the Italian side. Because of the anarchy that reigned in the interior of the country, many refugees from the provincial towns arrived in T. and crowded the J. quar-

ter. During the Arab revolt against French rule in 1915, Jews acted as mediators between the Italians and the Moslem rebels. After the repression of the revolt, the city developed, particularly in the 1930s. Its new and modern neighborhoods began to take on a European look. At this time (1931) there were 3,000–4,000 wealthy Jews in the New City in an overall J. pop. of 15,358, representing a quarter of the general total. The larger businesses enjoyed continuous growth while the smaller ones (two-thirds of the total) tended to stagnate. Many Jews lived in near penury. A serious problem never resolved during the years of Italian rule was the appointment of an Italian chief rabbi to the community. Those favoring the appointment of an Italian chief rabbi were "modern" members of the community. However, the traditional segment of the community was in the majority and opposed an Italian rabbi. The first Italian rabbi invited to preside as chief rabbi, in 1921, was R. Elia Artom. He was forced to resign three years after his appointment and for the next seven years T. was without a chief rabbi. In 1933,

R. Gustavo Castelbolognesi was appointed. He only lasted two years, until the introduction of the Sabbath Laws of 1935, when he came into bitter conflict with the governor and had to resign. The last Italian chief rabbi was R. Aldo Lattes, who was appointed in 1937. He was an exception among the Italian rabbis in Libya in that he acceded to the demands of the Fascist Italian authorities. He remained in office until 1944. During the 1920s, a number of Jews joined the Fascist Party and especially the Fascist youth movements – the Balila for ages 8–14 and the Avanguardisti for ages 14–18. The beginning of the Zionist movement in T. was rooted in the effort to revive the Hebrew language within the framework of Yagdil Torah and to a lesser degree in the Alliance and J.-Italian schools. The pioneer of Zionist activity in the spirit of the Basle Program was Eliyahu Nehaisi, a young photojournalist working for *La Settimane Israelitica* ("The J. Week"). In 1913 he set up a Zion Society which also published a magazine (*Degel Tziyyon*) in Judeo-Arabic. The movement embraced a variety of social reforms and drew support from among the workers. However, after the rise of the Fascists to power in 1922, most Zionist activity was directed toward the revival of the Hebrew language, especially after the arrival in May 1928 of the Hebrew teacher Eliyahu Bohbut from Palestine and the founding of the Ben-Yehuda Association in 1928. The founders of the Association were young J. graduates of the public high school, especially two Zionist activists, Yaakov Fargion and Tziyyon Adadi. In 1932, the Association began publishing the weekly *Limdu Ivrit* with Hebrew lessons accompanied by a parallel Italian and Arabic translation. The most important adjunct of the Association was the Hatikva school opened in 1932. Already in its first year, it had an enrollment of 512 students and by 1938 attendance reached 1,200. Most of the anti-J. measures enacted by the Italian government from 1922 derived from its Fascist colonial outlook. The unwillingness of the Jews to assimilate disappointed the local authorities in general and Governor Badolio in particular, who wrote to Rome in July 1930 vilifying the Jews as inferior even to the Arabs. Italo Balbo, who succeeded him (1934–40), took an entirely different approach. He attempted to postpone the enforcement of Libya's racial laws in 1938–40, but, at the same time, he demanded that the community abandon a number of traditional customs, including Sabbath observance. On 5 Dec. 1936, a few dozen protesting J.

businessmen did not open their stores, almost all of which were located on the main street of the European quarter. In retaliation, business licenses were revoked and the more recalcitrant perpetrators were publicly flogged. Eventually the Jews found a way to get around the Sabbath Laws by hiring non-Jews to keep their businesses open and by arranging with the school principal that J. children not be made to write on the Sabbath. When Mussolini visited Libya in March 1937, he was enthusiastically welcomed in the J. quarter. A year later the king of Italy visited T. and was also warmly received.

Following the publication of the racial laws in Oct. 1938, 46 Jews were dismissed from the civil service in T. and thousands of J. students were left without an educational framework. The word "Jew" was stamped on official documents, such as identity cards, and local newspapers frequently published antisemitic articles. Violent incidents also increased as Jews were attacked in the market. J. foreign nationals were singled out, and many were forced to leave the country. In Sept. 1940, all enemy aliens were herded into quarantine camps, where Jews were kept through 1941. Like all of T.'s inhabitants, the Jews suffered from military operations, especially the Allied bombing. Four synagogues were totally destroyed and others damaged. The J. cemetery, used for anti-aircraft emplacements because of its location, was severely hit. Many Jews fled to the provincial towns and the nearby Arab villages. On 12 Feb. 1942, a German army force entered T. and all residents were required to attend a military parade through the city's main streets. On the same day, R. Lattes was ordered to hand over the keys to the Maccabi and Ben-Yehuda clubrooms. The Nazi officials applied unremitting pressure on the Italian authorities to toughen their stance against the Jews. The measures that were subsequently taken resulted in a greater loss of J. life than anywhere else in the Middle East and North Africa during WWII. J. property was "Aryanized" and Jews were prohibited from entering transactions involving real estate or agricultural facilities. In 1942, the Italians enacted forced labor and deportation measures, with Mussolini himself issuing the deportation decree on 7 Feb. 1942. Deportations were to a number of destinations: a) Jews of British nationality were sent first to a detention camp on Italian soil and after the German occupation of Italy in Sept. 1943 to concentration camps in Austria (Innsbruck) and Germany (Bergen-Belsen); b) French nationals were sent to Algerian and Tunisian camps, mostly at Sfax and Gabes. Of the approximately 300 Jews of British nationality in Libya, about two-thirds lived in T. In late June 1942 they were deported as enemy aliens and sent to Naples. In Italy they were mostly dispersed among three camps – Arezzo, east of the Siena River, Civitella del Tronto in central Italy, and Bagno a Ripoli, southeast of Florence. In these detention camps, the British Jews were held in public buildings or large private homes, in groups of up to 100. There was considerable overcrowding but families were not separated. As soon as the Germans seized power in Italy on 8 Sept. 1943, the situation of the Jews in these camps deteriorated. On 28 Oct. 1943, the German SS transferred J. males from the Civitella del Tronto camp to Crocetta and Chietti to work on fortifications on the Sangro River line. Women and children remained behind. The work was backbreaking and lasted from dawn to dusk; rations were meager, consisting mostly of bread and beans. In Jan. 1944, a Civitella del Tronto

group was sent to Bergen-Belsen. At about the same time, the rest of the Jews were transferred to the Italian Fossoli di Carpo concentration camp, north of Modena. In May 1944, they, too, were deported to Bergen-Belsen, as were the Jews incarcerated in Arezzo. Most of the British Jews held in Bazano were sent to Innsbruck. The Jews deported to Bergen-Belsen were sent in four transports, the first from Civitella del Tronto, two from Fossoli di Carpi, and one from Arezzo. The first transport arrived in Jan 1944 and the last in Aug. 1944. Most left Bergen-Belsen in Nov.–Dec. 1944. Conditions in the camp, which were tolerable in early 1944, when the Libyan Jews arrived, deteriorated in late 1944, when they left. In late 1944, the camp became a veritable hell. The bodies of tens of thousands of victims of starvation, exhaustion, and typhoid fever remained unburied for months. Some of the Jews were housed in the "privileged" wing, where families remained together and the prisoners were not tormented. Others were held at the Star camp under

Jewish soldiers in the Palestinian Jewish brigade praying in the Great Synagogue of Tripoli, Libya, Passover 1943

overcrowded conditions, where men and women were separated and SS men abused the inmates continuously. The Libyan Jews communicated with other Jews in the camp in Hebrew. Some of the Libyan Jews, about 83, were transferred in Nov. 1944 and sent to the Biberach-Riss prisoner-of-war camp in southern Germany, on the Swiss border. Another group was sent to the Wurzach camp for British prisoners of war, also in southern Germany, near Biberach, in Jan. 1945, when conditions were already extreme. Here they enjoyed relatively tolerable conditions until the liberaton. About 100 Libyan Jews of British nationality were imprisoned in the Innsbruck camp (part of Dachau). They suffered from the European winter and the abuse of the guards and some of the elderly died. Despite the terrible conditions and their hunger, they tried to observe the laws of *kashrut*. Most of the Libyans remained alive and in April 1944 they were transferred to the Vittel refugee center in France, where they enjoyed relatively tolerable conditions until the liberation. About 1,600 Jews of French and Tunisian nationality were deported from Tripolitania and Cyrenaica to Tunisia in early 1942. Some went to cities like Tunis or Gabes where there were J. communities but most were concentrated in a loosely supervised camp about 4 miles from Sfax. Even after the German withdrawal and the liberation, the lot of camp inmates did not improve. Over 400 Jews from T. and environs reached the town of La Marsa, not far from Tunis. They were housed in rickety shacks by the seashore. The J. community of La Mansa tried to help but conditions remained harsh — unbearable crowding, broken toilets and sewers, and insufficient food. On 28 June 1942, under German pressure, the Italian authorities published a forced labor edict pertaining to J. males aged 18–45. The plan called for a J. work force of 4,000–5,000.

Meeting of Mussolini and R. Lattes, chief rabbi of Libya, outside Tripoli (Beth Hatefutsoth Photo Archive, Tel Aviv/courtesy of Cultural Center of the Jews of Libya, Tel Aviv)

The German authorities also pressed the Italians to institute deportation for all the Jews of T. and not just the British nationals, as a first step toward the Final Solution. However, given the large number of Jews in T. and their economic importance, the Italian authorities defied the Germans in this matter, preferring to exploit the J. work force within the borders of Libya. The task set for the forced labor was, first and foremost, to build a road connecting Libya and Egypt in order to facilitate the transport of reinforcements to the front. In Aug. 1942, 3,000 of T.'s Jews were concentrated at the Sidi Azaz camp, about 7 miles from Homs and 95 miles east of T. Most, however, were sent back home owing to the lack of drinking water there. A thousand remained, mostly professional building workers. Another camp was established at Buqbuq in eastern Cyrenaica, on the Egyptian border. The Jews were given the task of building and improving roads on the Cyrenaican front. Responsibility for carrying out the work was placed on a J. engineer, Moshe Hadad, who selected his workers from the Sidi Azaz camp. A total of 350 Jews were taken to the desert camp and set to work from 7 a.m. to 5 p.m. In late Oct. 1942, Buqbuq was frequently bombed from the air. The last weeks of Axis rule in T. were particularly hard on the Jews, particularly in the J. quarter. The economy was in a shambles, prices were sky high, food and other basic items were in short supply. Worst of all were the Allied air attacks. Multitudes of refugees arrived in the city from Cyrenaica and from the villages. Food was distributed against ration cards, with the Jews discriminated against viv-a-vis the Italians and Arabs. The community council concentrated its efforts on one aim—to help the neediest.

The first year of the British occupation was a period of relief for the Jews of T. and all of Libya. Despite German and Italian bombardments in the first month of the occupation, the end of 1942 represented for the Jews the end of the war. Jews were allowed to join the police force for the first time. A source of particular joy for the J. community at the outset of the British occupation was the meeting with J. soldiers from Palestine arriving with the British army. By 1944, the Jews were beginning to feel disappointment in the British occupation. But despite British support for Arab national aspirations, most of T.'s Jews remained pro-British until the Nov. 1945 pogroms, sparked by deteriorating relations with the Arabs. The disturbances lasted four days, spreading outside the capital as

well. In T., 35 Jews were murdered and 265 injured. Five synagogues were burned along with the Maccabi club. Damage to property was estimated at 500,000 pounds sterling. A total of 736 J. business premises, stores, and workshops were destroyed in T. and 4,000 Jews in the area were left homeless. With the UN partition vote of 29 Nov. 1947 and the start of Israel's War of Independence, Arab-J. relations deteriorated further in T., with tensions rising daily until a second wave of riots erupted in June 1948. These were less violent than those in 1945, occurring only in T. and claiming fewer victims as well as damaging less property. This time the British were more effective in restoring order, acting after two days of rioting instead of after four as they had in 1945. Fourteen Jews and 30 Arabs were killed, 1,600 Jews were left homeless, and 300 J. families were left without a source of income. Many J. refugees made their way to T. Some crowded into the J. quarter and some into the Old City while others stayed in the vicinity of T. The influx of refugees increased when the British made it known that they would soon allow the Jews to leave Libya. Many Jews who still owned businesses in Libya hastened to liquidate them, sometimes at a loss, in order to be ready to leave. In early 1949, over a third of the J. pop. was living on charity and relief. The link to Palestine also strengthened religious education in T. In early 1946, R. Shelomo Yaluz of Tiberias arrived to serve as chief rabbi of Libyan Jewry. R. Yeluz promoted secondary religious education for boys completing *talmud torah* studies. In late 1947, R. Moshe Auerbach and his son R. Shemuel arrived to teach at the *talmud torah*, raising its level. Hebrew became the official language of instruction and by 1948 over 1,200 children were in attendance. R. Yeluz also established the Neve Shalom yeshiva high school, which continued to expand until the mass *aliya* of Libyan Jewry. In 1947 the yeshiva, in cooperation with the *talmud torah*, began publishing *Semadar*, a Hebrew journal of history and literature. Illegal immigration had commenced from T. in 1943 with the help of J. soldiers in the city. In 1944, with the founding of Hehalutz in T., the shortage of immigration certificates was felt. The Palestine emissary Yisrael Gorelik, known as "the Uncle," put together a self-defense group and also started a group for illegal immigration (*ha'pala*). Some Jews were sent to Italy on forged passports. Others were sent without passports, in fishing boats, arriving at an Italian base from where *aliya* emissaries smuggled them into Palestine. Subsequently Gorelik opened a second route, via Tunis and Marseille. By 1947, 1,700 "illegals" had been smuggled into Palestine. Following the riots of 1948, the Joint Distribution Committee began aiding the community, opening first aid stations, schools, and soup kitchens. In Feb. 1949, the British permitted all those who wished to leave Libya to do so. Immediately, Barukh Duvdavani, Israel's official *aliya* emissary for Libyan Jewry, arrived and began organizing an accelerated mass exodus to Israel. He remained in T. until Jan. 1950. He was replaced by Dr. Meir Vardi and in Sept. 1951 Meir Shilon arrived to complete the work of getting Libya's last Jews to Israel.

TRITTENHEIM Rhineland, Germany. Jews are mentioned in 1702 and a number of protected Jews were accorded residence rights up through the late 18th cent. A permanent settlement of 46 existed in 1808, growing to a peak pop. of 65 (total 1,026) in 1871 and then dropping to 31 in 1932. The community maintained a synagogue from 1857 and a cemetery (1898–99). In the Nazi era, a few Jews emigrated and some left for other places in Germany. In 1936, the synagogue was sold for lack of a prayer quorum (*minyan*). A year later, the community was dismantled and attached to Neumagen-Niederemmel together with other shattered communities. On *Kristallnacht* (9–10 Nov. 1938), the homes of the remaining Jews were vandalized and in 1943 the last two Jews were deported to the camps, where they perished together with eight other local Jews.

TRNAVA (Hung. Nagyszombat; Ger. Tyrnau) Slovakia, Czechoslovakia, today Republic of Slovakia. The J. settlement dates from the 12th cent. and was one of the oldest in Slovakia. Jews lived in a J. quarter as wine merchants and moneylenders, suffering from the unremitting hostility of the mainly German local residents. R. Yitzhak Tyrnau, compiler of a famous book of customs and rites and head of what was perhaps the first yeshiva in Hungary, was active in the early 15th cent. In 1494, 14 Jews were burned at the stake in the wake of a blood libel and in 1539 they were expelled from the city. Jews settled again in 1783, encountering the same hostility as in the Middle Ages. Their pop. began to grow in the 19th cent., to 524 in 1857 and 1,751 (total 12,422) in 1900. A small synagogue was erected in 1831 and a J. elementary school

Jewish farmer and his geese, Trnava, Slovakia, 1936

was opened in 1855. A Status Quo congregation was formed after the split in 1869 and in 1880 Orthodox families established a separate congregation with its own yeshiva, *talmud torah*, and elementary school. A Zionist society, the second largest in Slovakia, was founded in 1899. In new riots after WWI, 30 J. stores were looted. The J. pop. grew to 2,728 in 1930. In the Orthodox community, R. Shemuel David Unger headed a yeshiva with about 230 students. Agudat Israel began operating in 1919. All the Zionist movements were also active. Jews were prominent in the economy, owning 184 businesses, 64 workshops, and 23 factories. In the Slovakian state, Jews were seized for forced labor and their businesses liquidated or "Aryanized." In fall 1941, 1,166 refugees from Bratislava arrived, pushing the J. pop. up to 3,611. Deportations commenced in March 1942, when 61 J. girls were sent to Auschwitz and about 200 young men to the Majdanek concentration camp. Family deportations began in April with nearly 1,300 sent to Sered by 11 April, most to be deported to Majdanek and Lubartow in the Lublin dist. (Poland). Another 509 were deported to Auschwitz on 14 April and 212 to Opole on 21 April. In all, 82% of the Jews were deported in 1942. In early 1944, 631 Jews remained in T. under certificates of protection. The Germans rounded up those still there in Sept. for deportation, increasing the number who perished in the camps to 2,000. Over half the postwar community of 250 emigrated to Israel and other countries in 1949.

TRNOVEC (Hung. Tornoc) Slovakia, Czechoslovakia, today Republic of Slovakia. Jews numbered about 120 in the 1880s in an independent community with a synagogue and cemetery. Fifty-four remained in 1930.

TROKI Vilna dist., Poland, today Lithuania. Karaites settling in the late 14th cent. and defined as Jews by the Polish authorities received the status of free residents with broad rights which later became a bone of contention between themselves and Rabbinate Jews. The friction between the two groups, including competition in trade, set the tone for Karaite-J. relations wherever they lived together. Under Russian

rule (1795–1914), the Jews engaged mainly in petty trade. J. merchants provided the villages with essential goods and owned a few larger stores selling tools, jewelry, cosmetics, sewing accessories, and metal products. They also held distillation and fishing concessions. In 1897 the J. pop. was 425 (total 3,240). Of the community's rabbis, R. Hayyim Gruenhaus supported the Zionists and was among the founders of Mizrachi in the early 20th cent. Under the German occupation in WWI, commerce came to a halt, harvests were impounded, and residents put to forced labor. The community was afterwards helped by the J. relief agencies but remained in dire economic straits, exacerbated by the collapse of the Polish farm sector and anti-J. government measures. The Zionists remained active, with the youth movements sending 50 pioneers to Palestine between the World Wars. The community had a library, choir, orchestra, drama circle, and Maccabi sports club. On the arrival of the *Wehrmacht* in late June 1941, there were 300 Jews in the town. They

Talmud class in Trnava, Slovakia, 1937

were immediately confined to a ghetto and on 30 Sept. 1941 they were among the 2,500 Jews in the area brought to an island in the local lake, where they were executed by shooting or drowning. The Karaites were spared and their community continues to exist. A Karaite museum was established in the 1990s.

TRONDHEIM Norway. The first Jews arrived in the 1890s and a community known as the Mosaic Religious Congregation was organized in 1905. In 1923, the J. community purchased the local railroad station building and turned it into a synagogue which opened in 1925 to become the northernmost synagogue in the world. Prior to WWII, the community consisted of 150 members. In April 1941, the Germans seriously damaged the synagogue and subsequently used it as a warehouse and barracks. In fall 1941, in a second wave of anti-J. operations, the Jews of T. as well as of other cities in the north and west of the country were subjected to arrests, property confiscations, and executions. In Jan. 1942, four local Jews were arrested on false charges and three days later executed. In Oct. 1942, all J. males over the age of 14 were arrested. Mass arrests by the Norwegian police began on 26 Oct. The Jews were brought to the Bredtvedt concentration camp, run by Norwegian *hirdmenn*. On 25 Feb. 1943, 158 prisoners, most from T., were put aboard the *Gotenland* and shipped to Stettin. From Stettin they were transported to Auschwitz via Berlin in sealed freight cars. The names of 60 J. war victims are inscribed in the J. War Victim Memorial in T. In 1955, a J. community center, including a Hebrew school, was added to the synagogue building. In 1984, the community consisted of 150 members.

TROSKUNAI (Yid. Trashkon) Panevezys dist., Lithuania. The J. community began to organize at the end of the 18th cent. It had a hasidic synagogue and one for *Mitnaggedim*. The J. pop. in 1897 was 779 (64% of the total). During WWI the Jews were expelled, most returning after the war. The J. pop. in 1940 was about 90 families. Under the Soviets, Zionist activity

Tombstone over mass grave of pogrom victims, Trostyanets, Ukraine, 1919

was forbidden. After the German conquest of 1941, the Jews were taken to Pajuoste near Panevezys and murdered on 23 Aug.

TROSTYANETS   Vinnitsa dist., Ukraine. Jews numbered 119 in 1765 and 2,421 (total 4,421) in 1897. In the late 19th cent., most of the town's 47 stores were in J. hands and a large number of its 153 artisans were Jews. About 370 Jews were murdered and many seriously injured in a pogrom on 10 May 1919. In the early 1920s, most Jews were still tradesmen but their number gradually declined under the Soviets. A J. school was opened in the mid-1920s and a J. council (soviet) was active for many years. In 1939, the J. pop. was 878. The Germans captured T. on 25 July 1941. Most of the Jews were murdered in the first months of the occupation and the rest sent to the Ladyzhyn ghetto in Transnistria. Hundreds of Jews from Bukovina and Bessarabia were expelled to T.; 95 were still there on 1 Sept. 1943. The Germans murdered 504 Jews in the area, most from T.

TROYANOV   Zhitomir dist., Ukraine. Jews settled in the 18th cent. Thirteen perished in an epidemic in 1788. In 1897, the J. pop. was 1,469 (total 7,224). Aharon David Gordon, a leader of the Zionist pioneer movement and a founder of Deganya Alef, was born here in 1856, giving his name to the Gordonia youth movement. Over 20 Jews were killed in a 1905 pogrom amid widespread looting. The J. pop. dropped between the World Wars, standing at 581 in 1939. Those Jews who neither fled nor were evacuated were murdered in the Holocaust.

TROYANOWKA   Volhynia, Poland. Jews settled in the second half of the 17th cent. and numbered 212 (total 647) in 1921. On 11 Aug. 1941, under the German occupation, they were able to fight off a gang of 200 Ukrainian attackers. On 3 Sept. 1942 they were taken to the Maniewicze ghetto to meet their end.

TROYES   Aube dist., France. One of the most important centers of medieval Judaism, T. is the birthplace of Rashi (1040–1105), the Bible and Talmud commentator. He founded a yeshiva, which later was headed by his grandson, Rabbenu Tam (1100–71). The yeshiva attracted students from all over Europe. In 1288, as a result of a blood libel, 13 Jews were burned at the stake. Several elegies commemorate this incident. Following the banishment of the Jews of France in 1306, Jews returned after 1315, but left after the expulsion of 1322. In the second half of the 19th cent., the community, consisting largely of Jews from Alsace, was reorganized. A synagogue was founded in 1877. On the eve of WWII there were about 200 Jews in T. During the war, a camp was established where the Germans interned a large number of non-French Jews as well as Jews who came from "prohibited" departments. In Feb. 1944, the Germans arrested 52 Jews in T. In 1964, the community consisted of 460 members: 70% from North Africa, 20% from Eastern Europe, and 10% from Alsace.

TROYITSKOYE   Odessa dist., Ukraine. The J. pop. was 587 (total 3,028) in 1897 and 220 in 1939. In the 1920s, under the Soviets, a J. library and club were active. The Germans arrived on 8 Aug. 1941 and murdered 74 Jews on 27 Sept.

TRSTENA   Slovakia, Czechoslovakia, today Republic of Slovakia. Jews probably settled in the 1770s. They formed a Neologist congregation after the split in 1869 and built a synagogue in the 1880s, also operating a J. elementary school. The J. pop. rose from 72 in 1828 to 257 (total 2,168) in 1919. After WWI, Jews owned 25 business establishments and 14 workshops. The Zionists and WIZO were active. Most of the young joined Hashomer Hatzair and the Maccabi sports club had a few dozen members in the 1930s. Emigration of the young to the big cities reduced the J. pop. to 143 in 1940. In late March 1942, young J. men were deported to the Majdanek concentration camp and the women to Auschwitz. Families were deported to the Lublin dist. (Poland) on 2 June. In all, 88% of the Jews in the area were sent to the death camps in 1942.

TRUBCHEVSK   Oriol dist., Russia. Jews probably settled in the mid-19th cent. Their pop. rose from 47 in 1873 to 166 (total 7,000) in 1897 and then dropped in the Soviet period to 137 in 1939. The Germans occupied T. on 9 Oct. 1941, murdering in Feb. 1942 the few dozen Jews who had neither fled nor been evacuated.

TRUDOLUBOVKA   Zaporozhe dist., Ukraine. Jews from the Kovno (Kaunas) region founded T. as a J. colony in 1848. In 1858, 32 J. families were present and in 1897 the J. pop. reached 496 (total 564). Residents of

Gaychur, the neighboring village, staged a pogrom on 6 May 1881 and destroyed much J. property. On 24 Dec. 1918, there was another pogrom in which as many as 250 Jews lost their lives. Under the German occupation from Oct. 1941, the few Jews who remained in T. perished in the Holocaust.

TRUDY Vitebsk dist., Belorussia. The J. pop. was 123 (total 1,463) in 1926. The Germans occupied T. in July 1941, forcing its 78 Jews to live in three houses. On 7 Feb. 1942, they were murdered near the village of Zheltsy.

TRUSKAWIEC Lwow dist., Poland, today Ukraine. In 1880 the J. pop. stood at 58 (5% of the total). With the development of T. as a health resort, Jews found employment at the bath houses and mineral springs as well as in the oil industry. The Germans, who ruled from 1 July 1941, burned the synagogue and murdered the assembled Jews in the nearby forests in Aug. 1942. The last 40 Jews employed in the oil facilities were murdered in mid-1943.

TRUSKOLASY Kielce dist., Poland. Jews were present from the early 18th cent. and grew in number with the development of the tourist industry in the late 19th cent. Most left in WWI, leaving 266 (total 1,714) in 1921. During the 1930s, the antisemitic atmosphere led to riots against the Jews. They were deported to Auschwitz by the Germans on 22 June 1942.

TRUTNOV Bohemia (Sudetenland), Czechoslovakia. Jews are mentioned in 1545. The modern community was founded in 1870, its pop. rising to a peak of 478 in 1910 with a synagogue consecrated in 1885. Jews were active in trade and local industry. Most spoke German and the young joined the local Zionist youth movement. In 1930, the J. pop. was 369 (total 15,923). Most Jews left after the annexation of the Sudetenland. The synagogue was burned on *Kristallnacht* (9–10 Nov. 1938) and the last Jews were deported to the Theresienstadt ghetto on 5 Dec. 1942.

TRYBUCHOWCE Tarnopol dist., Poland, today Ukraine. The J. pop. in 1921 was 138. The Jews were probably deported to the Belzec death camp via Buczacz in Sept. 1942.

Group of Orthodox Jews at the Truskawiec spa, Poland, 1938

TRYPOLE Kiev dist., Ukraine. Jews settled in the late 16th cent. They were murdered during the Chmielnicki massacres of 1648–49 and only resettled in the 19th cent. In 1897, their pop. was 1,238 (total 5,637). In Oct. 1905, rioting peasants extorted large sums of money from wealthy Jews and on 7 Dec. 1919 the Zeleny gang murdered several Jews in an outbreak of violence. By 1926, under the Soviets, there were no Jews there.

TRYSKIAI (Trishik) Siauliai dist., Lithuania. Jews first settled at the end of the 17th cent. An organized J. community did not exist until the end of the 18th cent. In the 1890s the economic situation was difficult and many emigrated to the west. Despite the situation, a large number contributed to Zionist funds. The J. pop. in 1897 was 681 (34% of the total). A boycott by Lithuanian businessmen in the 1930s forced many Jews to emigrate to the west. The J. pop. in 1940 was 200 (12.5% of the total). After the German invasion in June 1941, 70 men were murdered. The women and children were left in an open field for a week in Aug. On 2 Oct. 1941 they were executed in Zagare.

TRZCIANKA Bialystok dist., Poland. The J. pop. in 1921 was 129 (total 1,143). The Jews were presumably expelled by the Germans in fall 1939.

TRZCIANNE Bialystok dist., Poland. Jews were present in the three villages that amalgamated to form the town in the 18th cent. and in 1897, with 2,226 residents, represented the highest concentration of Jews (98% of the total) of any settlement in Polesie. Their pop. dropped considerably after WWI under difficult economic conditions and numbered 1,401 in 1921, which was still almost the entire pop. The Germans arrived on 23 June 1941 and on 28 July brought the 600 remaining Jews outside the town, holding them in a large pit without food and water while executing them in groups over a period of eight days.

TRZEBINIA (Yid. Chabin) Cracow dist., Poland. Jews first settled in the late 17th cent. The community expanded with the development of mines and other industries in the second half of the 19th cent., reaching a pop. of 634 in 1880 and 915 (total 1,317) in 1921. Polish independence brought anti-J. riots in Nov. 1918 and again in 1919. The economic hardship that followed

Study group, Trzebinia, Poland

was alleviated by the establishment of a hasidic court in 1932 by R. Ben-Zion Halberstam of the Bobow dynasty. Another illustrious rabbi active in the town between the World Wars was Dov Berish Weidenfeld, known for his responsa and founder of a yeshiva there. The Zionists too were active. With the approach of the Germans in Sept. 1939 many tried to flee but their escape routes were blocked and some were murdered on their return. A regime of persecution ensued, with J. stores and factories transferred to "loyal Aryans" and Jews put to forced labor. In 1941 the Jews were confined to a ghetto and in June 1942, after the able-bodied were selected for forced labor in Germany or factory work in Chrzanow, the rest were deported to Auschwitz.

TSEBRIKOVKA (also Tsebrikovo; until 1900, Govnunstal) Odessa dist., Ukraine. During the Soviet period, dozens of J. families earned their livelihoods in a new colony nearby, Frayberg, where 25 J. families were residing in the late 1920s and a J. elementary school was still in operation in the mid-1930s. The J. pop. of T. was 210 (total 3,036) in 1939. The Germans captured T. on 8 Aug. 1941 and by the end of the month, 185 of the region's inhabitants, mainly Jews, were murdered. The Rumanians expelled hundreds of Jews from Bessarabia to T. after it was annexed to Transnistria in early Sept. During Sept. about 60 Jews from T. and 68 from Frayberg were murdered.

TSURIUPINSK (until 1928, Aleshki) Nikolaiev dist., Ukraine. Jews settled in the early 19th cent. and numbered 744 (total 8,000–9,000) in 1897. In 1939, under the Soviets, 472 remained. On 10 Oct. 1941, a month after capturing the city, the Germans murdered over 800 Jews from T. and its environs.

TUBRUQ (also Tobrouk) Cyrenaica dist., Libya. Jews began to arrive from Barce and Derna after the Italian occupation of 1911. Others came in the 1920s, attracted by the city's prosperity after the Italians built a port and army camp there. The Jews continued in traditional occupations as tradesmen with a few also working as bank or postal clerks. The wealthier Jews were wholesalers and controlled the community council. The community maintained a modest synagogue and sent its children to the Italian public school. The J. pop. was 175 in 1931 and 42 (total 17,591) in 1936. After the Arab Revolt (1915–

22) the Italian authorities tended to discriminate against the Jews in their effort to reconcile the Arabs. In the late 1930s, violent incidents involving Arabs increased. There were no Zionist organizations in T., but Keren Kayemet fundraising took place at the synagogue. Jews suffered under Italy's 1938 racial laws and from food shortages in WWII. Allied bombing attacks led many to flee the city. In 1942, the Jews were deported to the Jado, Yefren, and Gharian concentration camps. When the British liberated T. in Jan. 1943, the Jews returned to find the city in ruins and their homes and stores pillaged. Their Arab neighbors helped them to repair the damage. In 1949, the Jews left for Tripoli, coming under Joint Distribution Committee and OZE care until emigrating to Israel in 1951.

TUCHOLA Pomerania dist., Poland. Jews settled after the annexation to Prussia in 1772 and contributed significantly to the development of the town, trading in grain, lumber, and hides. The J. pop. rose to 959 (total 2,764) in 1876 and then declined through emigration to 118 in 1932, dropping still further during the decade. The last Jews were expelled by the Germans to General Gouvernement territory in Nov. 1939.

TUCHOW Cracow dist., Poland. Residence restrictions severely limited J. settlement until 1865, the J. pop. reaching a peak of 455 (total 2,667) in 1910. When all but 40 Jews fled with the Austrian army at the outset of WWI, the community was left impoverished. Zionist activity was widespread. The Germans burned down the synagogue on their arrival in Sept. 1939. In Dec., 15 Jews were executed outside the town and the following year a group caught praying in a private home was also murdered. Refugees swelled the pop. of the ghetto set up in June 1942 to 3,000. All but a few were deported to the Belzec death camp in Sept.; the others were executed or transferred to Tarnow on 18 Aug.1943.

TUCZYN Volhynia dist., Poland, today Ukraine. Jews probably arrived in the early 17th cent. and numbered 2,535 (total 3,753) in 1897. There were five synagogues in the community, two of which belonged to Turzysk Hasidim. Ten yearly fairs, some light industry, and a large Russian army camp augmented J. livelihoods. After the Oct. 1917 Revolution, the Zionists and the Bund became active. In 1921 the J. pop.

stood at 2,159. The community maintained a Hebrew school, kindergarten, and small yeshiva. The Germans entered T. on 6 July 1941 and the Ukrainians immediately staged a pogrom, murdering 70 Jews. The next day an *Einsatzkommando 4a* unit executed another 30. A *Judenrat* was established and a regime of extortion ensued with 3,000 Jews including refugees confined to a ghetto in Sept. 1942. With intimations of an *Aktion*, the ghetto organized resistance, gathering small arms. On 24 Sept. 1942, as the German and Ukrainian police moved in, 60 young Jews opened fire and the ghetto houses were set ablaze as prearranged. In the confusion, 2,000 Jews were able to escape to the forest; half were caught and murdered and 300 women and children returned of their own accord. Few of those who remained behind or returned or reached the forest survived.

TUEBINGEN Wuerttemberg, Germany. Jews were present in the 13th cent., 30 of their houses being preserved to this day and indicating a pop. of 100–150 families. They were expelled in the Black Death persecutions of 1348–49, again in 1456, and again with the opening of the university in 1477. J. students were first enrolled in the university in the early 19th cent. and numbered 54 in 1842. The settlement was renewed in 1848 by Jews from neighboring Wankheim. The J. pop. of T. rose from 34 in 1869 to 139 in 1910 (total pop. 19,076). While Jews participated actively in the town's public and economic life they were not accepted socially, which accounts for the unusually high rate of conversion. While 82 Jews remained in T. prior to the Nazi rise to power, another 43 were converts or offspring of mixed marriages. Antisemitism was already felt at the university in the 1920s and J. lecturers were dismissed in 1933. In the city, synagogue windows were smashed in 1928 and the SA often attacked Jews in the streets. The economic boycott introduced in 1933 destroyed J. business. By 1938 all J. establishments had either been closed or "Aryanized." On *Kristallnacht* (9–10 Nov. 1938), the synagogue was burned. By 1940, 68 Jews had emigrated, of whom 34 went to the U.S. and 15 to Palestine; 21 were deported to their deaths in the Riga and Theresienstadt ghettoes and in Auschwitz in late 1941 and in 1942–43. Six of the 11 Jews in neighboring Rottenburg, whose medieval community was now attached to T., were also deported (three emigrated).

TUKUMS Zemgale (Courland) dist., Latvia. Jews began arriving from the surrounding villages after the commencement of Russian rule in 1795 and constituted half the town's pop. by the mid-19th cent., growing to 2,858 in 1881 and 5,500 in 1910. A fire in 1865 destroyed much J. property and in 1883 Latvian army conscripts attacked J. homes and stores in a drunken riot. In 1877 a group of "illegal" Lithuanian J. settlers was expelled from the town. The Lichtenstein family provided the community with rabbis from the early 19th cent. through WWII, setting a tone of strict observance but showing Zionist sympathies after WWI. Zionist influence began to spread among the young and the educated from the early 20th cent. and J. socialists played an active role in the 1905 revolution. In 1915 the Jews were expelled from T. by the Russian army. After WWI the J. pop. shrank to around 1,000 (about 13% of the total) but the Jews continued to exert economic influence, owning half the town's larger business establishments and a quarter of its factories. A J. public school was opened in 1919, expanding to include a kindergarten and library. The Maccabi organization was active in sports and culture and the Gordonia movement operated a pioneer training farm for members all over Latvia, sending many of its graduates to Palestine. Under Soviet rule (1940–41) J. communal and commercial life was closed down. About a third of the community was able to leave with the Russians on the approach of the Germans in June 1941. The Germans entered T. on 1 July 1941. The Latvian "self-defense" unit operating with German approval commenced a regime of persecution. All the town's Jews were expelled from their homes and either imprisoned in the synagogues or sent to forced labor on neighboring farms. A few were executed by the Germans as "collaborators" after being convicted in a show trial. In mid-July the systematic liquidation of the community began. Most were trucked to Lake Valgums 7 miles (11 km) outside the town and shot beside open pits. Some were burned alive inside one of the synagogues. After the war, J. survivors began to return, numbering 250–300 by 1950 and reviving community life. However, repressive Soviet measures were instituted at the end of the 1950s and the community dwindled as members emigrated or died.

TULCEA Dobruja dist., Rumania. Jews settled in the early 19th cent. The community expanded with Jews arriving from southern Bessarabia in 1878 when T. was

The Great Synagogue of Tulchin, Ukraine

annexed to Rumania. Many women from the Judaizing Russian Subbotniki ("Sabbath Observers") sect settled, converted to Judaism, and married Jews. Zionist activity began in the 1880s. In 1896 a number of Jews were expelled. The J. pop. in 1899 was 1,903 (10% of the total). Many Jews left when T. was occupied by Bulgaria during WWI (1916–17). Zionist activity continued between the World Wars and a Zionist youth movement was established. The J. pop. in 1930 was 824. The situation of the Jews worsened after Antonescu's antisemitic regime took over in 1940. In Jan. 1941 J. merchants were ordered to hand over their stores to the Iron Guard and their merchandise was looted. About 120 J. males aged 18–50 were sent to forced labor in Transnistria and returned only after the war when normal communal life was resumed.

TULCHIN   Vinnitsa dist., Ukraine. Jews are first mentioned as victims of the Chmielnicki massacres of 1648–49, when 1,500 of the 2,000 living there were killed. Their pop. was 452 in 1765 and 10,055 in 1897 (total 16,245). In the late 19th cent., the community maintained a synagogue and 18 prayer houses.

Most shopkeepers and artisans were Jews. A pogrom was staged in Jan. 1918 and again on 11 July 1919, when Ukrainian gangs murdered 519 Jews. Under the Soviets, most Jews earned their livelihoods in artisan cooperatives or in the town's old sugar refinery. A separate J. council (soviet) was active until 1930; a J. law court with deliberations in Yiddish operated in the late 1920s; and a J. elementary school was open throughout most of the 1930s. In 1939, the J. pop. was 5,607. The Germans captured the town on 23 July 1941. In early Sept., it was annexed to Transnistria and soon after a ghetto and *Judenrat* were established. On 10 Nov. 1941, the Rumanians expelled 3,005 Jews to the Pechera forced labor camp where most perished. Over 100 skilled laborers remained in the ghetto. They were joined by Jews from Mogilev-Podolski and other places. In mid-1944, after the liberation, 1,303 Jews remained in the town and the region.

TULGHES   (Hung. Gyergyotolgyes) N. Transylvania dist., Rumania. Jews settled in the early 19th cent. and engaged in the lumber industry. The J. pop. in 1920 was 242 (7% of the total). The Jews were ex-

Election rally for the Jewish candidate Elie Samama, Tunis, Tunisia (Beth Hatefutsoth Photo Archive, Tel Aviv/courtesy of Gaston Cohen-Solal, Marseille)

pelled from this border town by the Hungarians in summer 1941 and dispered throughout Rumania.

TULISZKOW   Lodz dist., Poland. Jews first settled early in the 19th cent. The J. pop. in 1897 was 200 (11% of the total). In Dec. 1939, a *Judenrat* was established and the next month the Jews were ghettoized. In Oct. 1941, the inhabitants of the ghetto were transported to the rural ghetto at Kowale Panskie, where they shared the fate of the local Jews.

TUNIS   Tunis dist., Tunisia. A J. settlement existed at nearby Carthage in the first cent. C.E. According to tradition, settlement in T. probably commenced in the tenth cent. The conquest of North Africa by the fanatical Almohads in 1159 put an end to the J. community in both T. and the surrounding area. When the city became the capital of Tunisia under the Hafsids in the 13th cent., Jews were again permitted to settle, enjoying communal autonomy and freedom of worship granted by the Islamic Dhimma (Protection) Laws. A *qa'id* or *sheikh al-Yahud* stood at the head of the com-

munity. The situation of the Jews improved owing to their knowledge of languages and the diplomatic services they rendered in their commercial ties with the cities of Europe, particularly those in Italy. The number of Jews increased with the arrival of *hakhamim* from among the Spanish exiles. With the Ottoman conquest in 1574, Christians and their "collaborators" were massacred, among them 32 Jews from T. The Jews constituted an important body within the city: they were a source of money and the *qa'id* was coopted into the administrations of the Tunisian beys ruling on behalf of the Ottomans. Commercial ties with the European cities strengthened the J. standing in the bey's court still further. In the 17th cent., there was an influx of descendants of the Spanish and Portuguese exiles who had been living for a number of years in Italy, particularly in Leghorn and Palermo. Some were descendants of forced converts (*anusim*) who had sought a place where they could practice their religion openly, finding it under Duke Toscana in the port of Leghorn. These Jews were called Leghornians or Gorni (also Grana). After their emigration, relations between Leghorn and

The Jewish Quarter, Tunis, Tunisia (Photo: Bernard Allali, Paris. Bernard Allali Collection, Paris/photo courtesy of Beth Hatefutsoth, Tel Aviv)

T. became closer. The Gorni established large business enterprises and grew rich ransoming Christian captives from Moslem pirates. They maintained close ties with their families in Italy and refused to become part of the local J. community, the "Touansa" (natives of Tunisia). The rift deepened during the 18th cent, until it was decided in 1741 to formulate a community regulation (*takkana*) that in effect drew the two communities further apart, with each maintaining its own synagogues, treasurers, butchers, religious courts, and cemeteries. The renowned Tunisian-born talmudist R. Yitzhak Lombroso (d. 1752) was, despite his Leghornian parentage, a student of R. Avraham Tayeb (of the "Touansa" sages) and thus accepted in both communities. He served as a *dayyan*, rabbi, and teacher and corresponded with the sages of Leghorn. His *Zera Yitzhak* (1768) was the first Hebrew book to be published in Tunisia. The era of reform in Tunisia, touching upon the status of the Jews as well, commenced with the rise to power of Ahmed Bey (1837–55). Among his J. intimates were his minister of finance, the *qa'id* Nissim Samama, the physicians Avraham Lombroso and Jacomo Castel Nuevo, and Avraham Memmi, who served as Dr. Lombroso's interpreter. In 1823, Muham-

mad Bey, the ruler of Tunisia, was forced for the first time to accede to the pressure of the Great Powers when Great Britain sent a naval squadron to the Gulf of Tunis and forced the Bey to rescind regulations regarding the wearing of turbans after the flogging of a Jew from British Gibraltar. In 1857, when Muhammad Bey executed a Jew accused of blaspheming Islam, the French sent a fleet of warships to T. The Bey backed down and promised to carry out a program of liberal reforms. On 10 Sept. 1857, he indeed published a charter of rights (Pacte Fundamental) for Tunisians. The document stipulated that all the Bey's subjects were equal before the law and entitled to freedom of worship. In 1861, the Bey Muhammad al-Sadiq published an amendment to the Pacte called the Loi Organique, which is considered the first modern constitution in a Moslem state. These two documents freed Jews from the exorbitant collective tax reserved for non-Moslems. Now they only had to pay regular taxes, like all other citizens. For the first time, they were allowed to purchase real estate in the cities and villages. The general rise in taxes and the granting of equal rights to the Jews produced much dissatisfaction among the Arabs, leading to a revolt in 1864 which forced the Bey to suspend

Law school graduates, University of Tunis, Tunisia (Beth Hatefutsoth Photo Archive, Tel Aviv/courtesy of Charles Haddad, Marseille)

the implementation of the new constitution. On 24 April 1881, the French invaded Tunisia but French citizenship was not extended to the Jews of Tunisia. Until 1910, not a single one of the Bey's J. subjects received French citizenship; even after 1910, when standards were relaxed, it was not conferred on Tunisian Jews on a large scale. During the early days of the French Protectorate, there was anti-J. rioting in T. against the background of the public debate in France surrounding the Dreyfus Trial (1894–1905). Most incidents occurred in 1898, with pillaging in the J. quarter. The victory of Dreyfus and his supporters in France symbolized the triumph of justice and tolerance in the eyes of Tunisian Jews and encouraged them to present their own demands to the authorities for the first time. The first to fight for J. rights in Tunisia was the journalist Mordecai Smaja, who founded the weekly *La Justice* in 1907. The journal appeared without a break until 1914. On 3 Oct. 1909, Smaja organized a demonstration attended by 5,000 Jews prepared to disavow their legal status. At the same time, the Arabs held a meeting attended by 20,000 protesting against Smaja and his group. The results of the struggle were disappointing to the Jews. Nonetheless, French rule

brought economic, social, and especially educational benefits to the Jews. The Alliance Israelite Universelle pioneered modernization in J. education in T., founding its first school for boys in the city. At first the school had 750 students, all of them from the old *talmud torah*; by 1892, attendance was up to 1,318. A girls' school was founded in 1882. A particularly noteworthy Alliance project in vocational education was an agricultural boarding school founded in 1895 in Djedeida, not far from T. It remained open, under great difficulties, almost to the end of WWI. In 1907, the Alliance founded a rabbinical seminary in T. Alongside the improvement of economic and social conditions for individual Jews, the French authorities attempted to limit the community's autonomy, beginning with burials. The next step in circumscribing J. autonomy concerned the sensitive issue of ritual slaughter. In an 1888 decree, the French authorities issued new regulations for slaughterhouses and butchers, published tax schedules for kosher meat, and stipulated how the tax receipts were to be used. Finally, the French dealt with the *qa'id*, publishing in 1899 an official edict over the Bey's signature abrogating the office. At the same time, the chief rabbi of Tunisia was given broader powers in the realm of communal organization and religious affairs. The new title of the community council reflected the change. Now called the Caisse de Secours et de Bienfaisance (J. Welfare Fund), this body was charged with cooperating with the chief rabbi in administering the community's religious life. Its income derived mainly from taxes on meat and wine, gifts and contributions, and earnings from its funds and property. The Gorni and Touansa congregations continued to operate a number of their services and institutions separately. The authority of the religious court in T. was extended over all of Tunisia. In 1893, some of the community's leaders founded a J. Hospital Society whose funds were used to build a hospital. In WWI, serious antisemitic incidents occurred simultaneously in T. and in other towns in northern Tunisia during the week of 21–26 Aug. 1917. A further exacerbation was the agitation of the French and the Moslem mayor of T. The French policy of turning the anger of the mob against the Jews made things worse and explained the slowness of the French response to the riots. The incidents in T. left two dead, a few seriously injured, dozens with minor injuries, and 25 J. stores looted. There were also a few outbreaks of antisemitism the following year.

Owing to the improvement in medical and sanitation services and the control of epidemics, the growth of the J. pop. reached 1.5% per annum after WWI. The percentage of Jews in T. and its suburbs rose from 47% of the total J. pop. of Tunisia in 1921 to 54% in 1936. The number of Jews in T. rose from 19,029 in 1921 to 27,345 in 1936 (total 219,578 for the city). Jews arrived in T. from the provincial towns and from other countries. During the 1920s, Jews arrived from Turkey, leaving in the wake of Kemal Ataturk's reforms. Many came from Algeria, especially after the anti-J. riots in Constantine in 1934, and from Libya in the wake of Italo Balbo's Sabbath Laws of the late 1930s. Finally, on the eve of WWII, J. refugees from Germany and Poland arrived. A gradual exodus from the J. ghetto of T. commenced. The ghetto dwellers were the poorer class and more tradition-oriented while residents in the European part of the city comprised a higher socio-economic class with weaker religious ties. Between the World Wars, the French influence outside the ghetto reached a peak. Because of the rise of Fascism, Italian cultural ties began to weaken in this period even among the Gorni. Also contributing decisively to this phenomenon were the proximity to Algeria, the

A Jewish lawyer (Maitre Perone), Tunis, Tunisia (Beth Hatefutsoth Photo Archive, Tel Aviv/courtesy of Annie Goldmann, Paris)

Alliance schools, and the French public school system. Between the World Wars, almost all the J. children of T. attended modern elementary schools with French as the language of instruction. Consequently most J. children received at least six years of schooling, either in Alliance or in public schools. In 1931, only 22% of J. children studied in Alliance schools and the rest in the French public schools. The percentage of girls in the Alliance schools was even lower than for boys. Parents preferred to send their daughters to the public schools. The *talmudei torah* attached to the synagogues did not disappear entirely, but their prestige declined in the now westernized society of T. Boys attended in the afternoon, after finishing their public school classes, mainly to get some basic J. knowledge before their bar mitzva. Many Jews proceeded with secondary school, some even reaching university level. In 1914, 27 of the city's 90 high school graduates were Jews; 12 became doctors and nine were lawyers.

Jewish artists, Tunis, Tunisia (Bernard Allali Collection, Paris/photo courtesy of Beth Hatefutsoth, Tel Aviv)

Knowledge of French became universal in the J. community. After WWI, the French instituted organizational reforms within the J. community. In 1921, they decided to allow the Jews to elect democratically a Council of Sixty in place of the previously appointed community council. The vote was given to all local J. subjects 21 years of age and paying FF 5 into the community treasury. The Council of Sixty chose a Council of Twelve as an executive committee, from which the president of the community was selected. Unlike the Welfare Fund's committee, which had run community affairs for the first 40 years of the Protectorate's existence, the new body was explicitly designated as the J. Community Council (Conseil de la Communaute Israelite). However, its freedom of action remained strictly limited and it was empowered to deal only with religious affairs and traditional education. Despite the new decree, no effort was made to unite the Touansa and Gorni congregations. They continued to exist separately, each with its own communal organization, synagogues,

rabbis, *talmudei torah*, *yeshivot* and even burial societies (*hevrot kaddisha*). In the new J. cemetery in Borgel, a wall separated the burial plots of the two communities. In the Council of Sixty, it was determined that 46 members would be chosen from among the Touansa and 14 from the Gorni; in the executive committee, there were nine and three, respectively. After the Balfour Declaration in 1917, there was an upsurge of Zionist feeling in T. All the parties were represented, from the General Zionists and Hashomer Hatzair to the Revisionists. The Revisionists were the strongest group between the World Wars. From the outset, the founders of the Zionist movement in Tunisia assumed an activist political stance. The connection between Jabotinsky and such leaders of Tunisian Zionism as Alfred Valensi and Felix Allouche served to strengthen the Revisionist cause. In late 1926, with the distribution in T. of *Le Reveil Juif*, edited by Allouche, Revisionist ideas from the southern periphery of Tunisia began to filter through to T. The outstanding representative of Jabotinsky's thought in T. was Robert Brunschvig, a native of Bordeaux and product of French culture who had emigrated to T. and was employed as a teacher (later becoming an outstanding Orientalist at the Sorbonne). He gathered around him a circle of Zionist activists prepared to disseminate the Revisionist idea in the community. The first success of the movement came in the elections to the 15th Zionist Congress in 1927. The Revisionist ticket won a surprisingly overwhelming victory against the General Zionists. Zionist youth movements were also active in T., such as Betar, Hashomer Hatzair, the Zionist-oriented scouts, and an organization unique to T. – the Keren Kayemet Brigade, which several youngsters founded in 1937. The Keren Kayemet office in T. operated through occasional volunteers, the synagogue treasurer, and some of the scouts, collecting money, mostly on holidays. Keren Kayemet activists organized themselves into a brigade, which included former members of Hashomer Hatzair like Albert Memmi, who later became a well-known writer, producing *La statue de sel (Pillar of Salt)*. The Brigade published the journal *La Jeunesse*, which had a literary and intellectual character. It was active

for seven years and filled the vacuum created by the demise of Hashomer Hatzair, until the founding of the Tze'irei Tziyyon movement after WWII. Between the World Wars, T. became a hothouse of J. cultural activity. and dozens of J. periodicals were published in French and Judeo-Arabic.

The dramatic events in Europe in the late 1930s had a direct effect on the Gorni. These Jews were fired from their jobs at the Italian Embassy after the publication of Italy's racial laws in 1938 and many exchanged their Italian citizenship for French. Already from the early days of Sept. 1939, when the French declared war on Nazi Germany, Jews with French citizenship were inducted into the army. In T. there were also volunteers among Jews with Tunisian citizenship. With the establishment of the Vichy regime in France, the position of the Jews in T. worsened. The decree authorizing community council elections was rescinded and a J. Council was appointed. The new French anti-J. laws (Statut des Juifs) were applied to Tunisia just a few months after they came into force in France. The first basic law concerning the status of the Jews was drafted in France (by Raphael Alli-

Synagogue in Tunis, Tunisia

bert) on 3 Oct. 1940 and published in T. on 30 Nov. as a decree of the Bey signed by the French general commissioner, Admiral Astoi. The law defined the term "Jew" while subsequent measures went on to remove them from civil offices, from educational positions, and from professional positions in newspapers, radio, the theater, and motion pictures. A *numerus clausus* was fixed for Jews in other professions such as law and medicine. The application of these measures in Tunisia was less strict than in other places under Vichy rule, both in France itself and in North Africa. Admiral Astoi and a number of his aides opposed the anti-J. legislation on moral grounds, many of them feeling that it did not serve France's interests in Tunisia. Italy too had interests within Tunisia. Thus, with the publication of the first decree of the Statut des Juifs in Tunisia, the Italian Armistice Commission protested against the application of the laws to Italian Jews. The Italians did not relax their efforts to protect their interests in Tunisia, even during the German occupation. At the same time, for reasons of their own, the Italians commenced expelling French citizens and subjects from their colony in Libya, including 1,600 Jews. In summer 1942, some of these refugees arrived in T. The J. community received them warmly and extended whatever aid it could. About 400 of the Libyan refugees were housed in a school building. The German occupied Tunisia in response to the Allied invasion of Algeria and Morocco on 8 Nov. 1942. On 23 Nov., SD units under the command of Walter Rauff arrested several Jews. Rauff also demanded that the community supply him with 3,000 Jews for forced labor. The body on which the task devolved was styled the Council for Mobilizing J. Manpower, calling to mind the East European *Judenrat*. The head of the Council, Paul Ghez, volunteered his services in order to help the community in its hour of crisis. In addition to maintaining the forced laborers at a cost of FF 31 million, the community was forced to pay out another FF 32 million to the Germans in fines. The Jews of T. were sent to work in various places and were more widely dispersed than Jews from the provincial towns. The number of forced laborers in Tunisia eventually came to 4,000–5,000, of which the Jews of T. constituted 90%. There were two main groups of labor camps: a) those in T. and its environs; b) those set up for T.'s Jews in more distant places, stretching from Bizerta in the north to Kairouan in the south. Some of the camps were under German command and some

under Italian command. The ones with the harshest conditions were at Bizerta and Mateur in the north, under German command. On 15 Feb 1943, 30 Frenchmen were arrested for their political ideas and activity in leftist organizations, among them a number of Jews. They were brought to German concentration camps, some never to return. Dozens of Jews from T. and other Tunisian communities living in Europe during WWII perished in the Holocaust. Many were seized around Paris, sent to Drancy, and from there transported to Auschwitz, the Sobibor death camp, and other camps. T. was liberated by the Allies on 7 May 1943. With Tunisian independence, there came a change in the status of the Jews, who numbered 34,193 in T. (total 364,593) in 1946. Those of European origin returned home, while those of Tunisian origin received Tunisian citizenship with equal rights. The rights enjoyed under President Habib Bourguiba did not include autonomy for the J. community. Accordingly, about 40% of the Jews—those with strong J. national feelings—emigrated to Israel in the early 1950s. The rest emigrated to France or left for Israel at a later date.

TUNYOG Szatmar dist., Hungary. Jews settled in the early 19th cent. and numbered 87 in 1930, subjected to increasing antisemitism. Twenty-two perished under forced labor in the Ukraine and the rest were deported to Auschwitz via Mateszalka at the beginning of June 1944.

TURA Pest-Pilis-Solt-Kiskun dist., Hungary. Jews arrived in the mid-18th cent. and numbered 94 in 1930. They were deported to Auschwitz via Rakoscsaba and Monor on 8 July 1944.

TURA LUKA Slovakia, Czechoslovakia, today Republic of Slovakia. The J. pop. was over 150 in 1880. The 11 Jews remaining in 1940 were deported to the death camps in 1942.

TURANY Slovakia, Czechoslovakia, today Republic of Slovakia. The J. pop. grew from 59 in 1828 to 161 in 1880, maintaining a synagogue, cemetery, and community center. In 1940, 37 Jews remained.

TURBOV Vinnitsa dist., Ukraine. Eighteen Jews were present in 1863. A pogrom was staged on 9 July 1919. In 1939, the J. pop. was 217 (total 4,576). The Germans occupied T. on 20 July 1941, murdering the 97 Jews who had not fled or been evacuated.

TURCIANSKY SVATY MARTIN (Hung. Turocszentmarton) Slovakia, Czechoslovakia, today Republic of Slovakia. Jews settled by the early 18th cent. They erected a synagogue in the 1820s and formed a Neologist community after the 1869 split. J. homes and stores were looted in the 1848–49 riots. Economic conditions improved in the late 19th cent. with the J. pop. growing to 433 in 1880 and a peak of 604 (total 4,113) in 1910. A J. elementary school was opened in the 1860s and a big, new synagogue was built around the turn of the cent. In the Czechoslovakian Republic, Jews served on the municipal council and owned 48 business establishments, 14 workshops, and two factories. The Zionists engaged mainly in fundraising but Hashomer Hatzair was also active among the young and the Maccabi sports club offered a wide range of activities. In 1940, 434 Jews remained. In the Slovakian state, Jews were forced out of their businesses and mobilized for forced labor. By late 1941, the J. pop. was down to 270. In late March 1942, young J. men were deported to the Majdanek concentration camp and women to Auschwitz. In subsequent months, J. families were sent to Auschwitz and the death camps in the Lublin dist. (Poland). In all, nearly two-thirds of the Jews were deported in 1942. In fall 1944, the Germans murdered another 50, including 21 children, in the city.

TURDA (Hung. Torda) S. Transylvania dist., Rumania. Jews from N. Transylvania and Hungary settled in 1780–1800. In 1900, 29 Jews were registered as owners of estates. Others played a leading role in commerce and industry prior to WWI. In 1932–33, a new synagogue was built which is still extant. T. was one of the leading Orthodox communities in Transylvania. The rabbi, R. Ben-Zion (Albert) Wesel, was chairman of the Organization of Orthodox Communities in Transylvania. A number of Zionist organizations were active between the World Wars. The J. pop. in 1930 stood at 852 (4% of the total). In Nov. 1940, J. enterprises and communal property were seized by the government and the situation of the J. pop. became the worst in Transylvania in 1941. In June 1941, 1,000 refugees from the area were brought to T. and together with Jews from other areas the J. pop. reached 2,000. During 1941–44, 300 J. men were sent to forced labor in the surrounding mountains; a small group was deported to Transnistria. They all returned in 1944. During 1941–43, J. organizations succeeded in rescuing 1,200 Jews escaping from Hungary and N. Transylvania as well as from Poland and Slovakia. When Hungarian and German troops entered T., 85% of the J. pop. escaped to the Munti Apuseni mountains, to Alba-Iulia, and to other towns. After the liberation at the end of Oct. 1944, the community was renewed and provided aid to Jews passing through. During 1945–47 many local Jews left for other towns and emigrated to Palestine.

TUREK Lodz dist., Poland. Jews lived there from the 19th cent. The J. pop. in 1897 was 2,072 (25% of the total). In the 1920s, 138 textile workshops were owned by Jews. Zionist activity began in 1912 and the Bund was active. In Nov. 1939, the Germans sent 700 Jews to hard labor in Bochnia. In July 1940, the 1,750-member community was ghettoized and in Oct. 1941 expelled to Kowale Panskie, suffering the fate of the Jews of the region.

TURIN (Ital. Torino) Piedmont province, Italy. The presence of the Jews, who were mainly engaged in moneylending, is first recorded in 1424 and again in 1430. Duke Amedeo VIII of Savoy issued statutes that regulated their position in the duchy for 400 years. The Jews were forced to wear a badge on their clothes. In the 16th–17th cents., they were also increasingly involved in producing and trading in textiles. High taxes threatened to undermine their position. Both in 1560 and 1566 there were attempts to expel the Jews, but since their economic role was vital, the decrees were not carried out. In 1624, there were nine J. banks operating in T. In 1662, a *talmud torah* was established. The ghetto was established in 1678 and by 1702, 800 Jews were living there. Their number increased to 3,200 by 1840. In 1723 and 1729, the statutes of 1430 were renewed. Hebrew printing commenced in the second half of the 18th cent. With the French Revolution, T. Jews were emancipated after the annexation to France in 1798. They were no longer compelled to reside in the ghetto. But with Napoleon's fall in 1814, former restrictions were reinstituted. Some restrictions, though, were abolished, and in 1828 the local Jews were allowed to reside outside the ghetto. Local Jews participated in the Italian Risorgimento. Full emancipation was achieved in 1848. With T. becoming the center of Italian unification and J. emancipation, more Jews were attracted to the city and the J. community grew to 4,500 members in 1871. The central synagogue of T. was inaugurated in 1880. Leading J. personalities in T. were Giacomo Bolaffio, Dario Disegni, and Sergio Joseph Sierra. The 20th cent. writer and Holocaust survivor Primo Levi (1919–87) was also from T. In the 1920s, the community maintained an orphanage, *talmud torah*, nursery and elementary schools, an old age home, and a charitable society. According to the 1930 law reforming the J. communities in Italy, T. was recognized as one of 26 district communities. The T. district included Aosta, Carmagnola (90 Jews in 1873; 12 in 1936); Cherasco (40 Jews in 1873; ten in 1936); Chieri (80 Jews in 1873; six in 1936); Cuneo (320 Jews in 1873; 45 in 1936); Fossano (110 Jews in 1873; six in 1936); Ivrea (160 Jews in 1873; 30 in 1936); Mondovi (140 Jews in 1873; ten in 1936); and Saluzzo (250 Jews in 1873; 50 in 1936). In 1910, the J. pop. was 4,500. Its spiritual leader was Dr. G. Bolaffio. In 1935, Ettore Ovazza organized a J. group which was anti-Zionist and Fascist, and published a J. newspaper, *La Nostra Bandiera*. He and his family were subsequently murdered. In 1943, there were 3,000 Jews in the community. During the war, the British bombed and destroyed the community archives and offices and the Nazis deported 875 Jews to the death camps. The Jews were active in the resistance movement. At the end of the war there were 1,060 Jews in T., of whom 94 were not of Italian nationality. In 1971, the community consisted of 1,560 members.

TURKA Lwow dist., Poland, today Ukraine. Jews arrived in 1729 when T. received the status of a proprietary town. Real development occurred with the coming of the railroad in the early 20th cent. The J. pop., which doubled from an 1880 figure of 2,368 to 4,887 in 1910, constituted nearly half the total pop. and provided a J. mayor. With the town changing hands in WWI and the brutality of Russian soldiers, nearly all the Jews fled, only returning with the Austrian reconquest at the end of 1915. Between the World Wars a large number of newly established sawmills provided employment and the Jews enjoyed a period of normalization, though set back by a fire that raged through the town in 1927. Most children were enrolled in Polish schools, with a few hundred receiving traditional education. The Soviet regime of 1939 brought J. commerce to an end. The German occupation in July

1941 unleashed a spate of Ukrainian attacks and a regime of forced labor, with hunger mounting through the winter of 1941–42. On 7 Jan. 1942, around 500 Jews were rounded up and murdered beside mass graves near the town's brick factory. Another 150, mostly children, were executed in June and in a four-day *Aktion* commencing on 4 Aug. 1942, after Jews from the surrounding villages had been brought to T., between 2,000 and 4,000 were deported to the Belzec death camp. Many of those trying to escape to Hungary or the forests were murdered or turned in by the local pop. The last Jews were sent to the Sambor ghetto in Dec. 1942 to await their fate. About 30 survivors greeted the town's Soviet liberators in Sept. 1944.

TURKEVE Jasz–Nagykun–Szolnok dist., Hungary. Jews from Abony settled after 1848 and were active in local life, displaying assimilationist tendencies. In 1869, they formed a Neologist congregation and in 1900 numbered 338. Zionist representatives were welcomed, but no branch offices were established here. In 1941, 179 Jews remained. In 1942, 21 were sent to the Ukrainian front, most perishing under forced labor. On 25–27 June 1944, the rest were deported to Auschwitz via Szolnok.

TURNA NAD BODVOU Slovakia, Czechoslovakia, today Republic of Slovakia. Jews probably arrived in the early 19th cent. Their pop. grew to 96 in 1880 and 320 (total 1,692) in 1910. A synagogue was built in 1934 and dozens of youngsters belonged to the Agudat Israel youth movement. In 1941, 215 Jews remained. Under the Hungarians, dozens were seized for forced labor, some perishing on the eastern front. The Germans deported most of the others to Auschwitz on 19 May 1944.

TURNOV Bohemia, Czechoslovakia. An organized community is first mentioned in 1526. Most Jews were peddlers and moneylenders in the 16th cent., living in straitened economic circumstances. The new synagogue erected in 1719 was in use until WWII. In the 19th cent., Jews were distillers and polishers of glass and precious stones. Their pop. rose to 478 (3% of the total) in 1910 and then dropped steadily to 104 in 1930. Most of the Jews were deported to the Theresienstadt ghetto in 1942 and from there to the death camps of Poland. In all, 93 Jews perished in the Holocaust.

TURNU-MAGURELE Walachia dist., Rumania. Jews settled here in 1367 but left for Bulgaria. In the late 19th cent. Jews settled and traded in grain. The J. pop. in 1899 was 264 (3% of the total). In fall 1940, when the Green Shirts forced Jews to hand over their shops, most left.

TURNU-SEVERIN Oltania dist., Rumania. Jews, mainly Sephardi from Cerneti, settled in 1829. T. was a center of the Eretz Israel Settlement movement, which published periodicals in Ladino and Hebrew (1894). The J. pop. in 1899 was 839 (4% of the total). In 1921, the local Zionist youth movement organized the first Zionist youth convention in Rumania. Between the World Wars a strong antisemitic movement existed. J. shops were taken over by the Green Shirts on 10 Jan. 1941. The 413 Jews of T. provided 600 J. refugees from Darabani with clothing and accommodations when they arrived in 1941.

TUROBIN Lublin dist., Poland. Jews may have settled in the late 16th cent. Subsequently granted liberal privileges to build houses and to engage in unrestricted trade by the town's proprietor, they made a name for themselves as furriers. An organized community active in the Council of the Four Lands existed from the early 17th cent. The J. pop. rose to a peak of 1,509 (total 2,377) in 1897, dropping to 965 in 1921. Zionist and Haskala influence began to spread in the early 20th cent. During WWI, the Jews were attacked by the local pop. as well as by Russian and Polish soldiers. The economic crisis between the World Wars, with the loss of traditional markets and the competition of Polish cooperatives, undermined J. livelihoods, necessitating assistance from the Joint Distribution Committee and relatives abroad. Nonetheless, community life flourished as Agudat Israel, deriving its strength from Gur Hasidim and founding a Beth Jacob school for 150 girls, contended with the Zionists for dominance. On the eve of WWII, the J. pop. was about 1,400. The Germans occupied the town permanently in early Oct. 1939, establishing "order" after rampaging Poles staged violent anti-J. riots. A *Judenrat* was set up in early 1940 as refugees flowed into the town. Hundreds were sent to labor camps. On 15 May 1942, about 60 Jews were murdered by SS men. On 17 May, the remaining 2,700 Jews were deported to the Sobibor death camp.

TUROV Polesie dist., Belorussia. In 1623 the Jews

Monte de Sinay, *Hebrew literary journal published by A. Krispin, the Sephardi rabbi of Turnu-Severin, Rumania, 1895*

of T. were under the jurisdiction of the Pinsk community. In 1765 their pop. was 316, rising to 2,253 (total 4,290) in 1897. In a 1920 pogrom staged by the Balakhovich brigade, 71 Jews from T. and its environs were murdered, about 60 J. women raped, and numerous J. homes looted. A J. council was established in 1925 and in 1930, 285 children attended the local J. elementary school. In 1929 about 60% of the Jews were artisans and 10% engaged in trade. That year all synagogues were closed down, though two private *minyanim* continued to exist. The J. school and J. council were eliminated in the late 1930s. In 1939, the J. pop. was 1,528. The Germans captured the town on 6 Aug. 1941. On 18 Aug. they murdered about 100 J. families at the village of Rydcha. The rest were murdered near the village of Starozhevtsy in late Aug., making a total of 500 Jews executed by the Nazis.

TURT (Hung. Turcz) N. Transylvania dist., Rumania. Jews from Galicia organized a community in the early 19th cent. A stone synagogue was built in the

1880s and existed until 1944. The J. pop. in 1920 was 339 (10% of the total). In May 1944 the community was transferred to the Nagyszollos ghetto and then to Auschwitz.

TURULUNG (Hung. Turterebes) N. Transylvania dist., Rumania. Jews settled in the late 18th cent. The J. pop. in 1920 was 254 (7% of the total). Most spoke Hungarian. In May 1944 the community was transferred to Halmeu and in June deported to Auschwitz.

TURYANREMETY (Hung. Turjaremete; Yid. Remit) Carpatho-Russia, Czechoslovakia, today Ukraine. Jews probably settled in the early 19th cent., numbering 45 in 1830 and 162 (total 1,371) in 1880. In 1921, under the Czechoslovakians, the J. pop. was 177, dropping to 168 in 1941. Sixteen Jews engaged in trade, ten in crafts, and some farmed. Jews also operated a distillery and a few belonged to the professional class. After the Hungarian occupation of March 1939, Jews were drafted in 1941 into forced labor battalions. In Aug. 1941, a number of J. families without Hungarian citizenship were expelled to Kamenets-Podolski and murdered. The rest were deported to Auschwitz in the second half of May 1944.

TURZA WIELKA Stanislawow dist., Poland, today Ukraine. The J. pop. in 1921 was 201. The Jews were expelled to Bolechow for liquidation in Aug. 1942.

TURZE Lwow dist., Poland. The J. pop. in 1921 was 179. The Jews were deported to the Belzec death camp in Aug. 1942, directly or via Sambor.

TURZEC Nowogrodek dist., Poland, today Ukraine. A J. community is known from the mid-16th cent. The J. pop. numbered 737 (total 1,616) in 1897, dropping to around 500 between the World Wars as a result of emigration. The Germans captured T. on 27 June 1941. In Oct. 1941, 55 young Jews were murdered. On 14 Nov., after 150 were sent to the Nowy-Swierzen labor camp, the rest were executed at the J. cemetery. On 20 Jan. 1943, 105 Jews from the labor camp escaped to the forest and joined the Soviet partisans.

TURZOVKA (Hung. Turzofalva) Slovakia, Czechoslovakia, today Republic of Slovakia. Jews are mentioned in 1746. The community grew to 150 (total 6,569) in 1828, serving as a center of religious services for numerous settlements in the area. A Neologist congregation was founded after the 1869 split. In 1895, a synagogue was erected. A J. elementary school was also opened during this period. All J. homes and stores were looted in riots in 1918 and a number of houses burned. Seventy Jews remained after WWI. These were persecuted and forced out of their businesses under Slovakian rule (from March 1939). On 29 April 1942, ten J. families were deported to Auschwitz via Zilina; others were sent from Zilina to the Lublin dist. of Poland on 6 June.

TURZYSK (Yid. Trisk) Volhynia dist., Poland, today Ukraine. Jews settled in the mid-16th cent. In the 1830s R. Avraham Twersky (the "Maggid of Trisk") set up a famous hasidic court including housing facilities, meeting halls, a bath house, and synagogue which thousands of followers visited, creating a major source of income for local Jews operating hostels. The J. pop. reached 1,713 (total 2,938) in 1897 but dropped to 1,173 after WWI when the court was moved to Kowel. Despite hasidic opposition, the Zionists became active before WWI. A Tarbut school enrolling 200 at its peak was founded in 1922 and there was also a Yiddish school. The Zionist youth movements included Hashomer Hatzair, founded in 1930, with 100 members. The Germans arrived on 28 June 1941, subjecting the Jews to forced labor and extortion until murdering them outside the town on 23 Aug. 1942.

TUSZYN Lodz dist., Poland. Jews lived there from the 17th cent. and from the 18th cent. were involved in the production and sale of liquor. The J. pop. in 1897 was 589 (36% of the total). Between the World Wars Jews made their living by supplying summer visitors who came to take the baths in the town's mineral waters. In Dec. 1939, the Nazis forced the approximately 1,500 Jews to march to the Piotrkow Trybunalski ghetto. They shared the fate of the rest of the local Jews.

TUZLA Bosnia-Hercegovina, Yugoslavia, today Republic of Bosnia. A Sephardi community was established in 1890. Ashkenazi Jews arrived later. In 1931 the Jews numbered 340 (total 16,708). Most perished in the Holocaust.

TUZSER Szabolcs dist., Hungary. Jews arrived in the first half of the 18th cent. and numbered 68 in

1930. On 25 May 1944, they were deported to Auschwitz via Kisvarda.

TVERAI (Yid. Tver) Telsiai dist., Lithuania. The J. pop. in 1923 was 102 (18% of the total). The community had neither a school nor a cemetery. The J. pop. in 1940 was 15–20 families, mostly engaged in agriculture. All the Jews were murdered in Viesvenai after the German occupation in 1941.

TVRDOSIN Slovakia, Czechoslovakia, today Republic of Slovakia. Jews settled in the early 17th cent and by the 1830s numbered about 200. After the split in 1869 they formed a Neologist congregation, building a synagogue in the 1880s, when their pop. rose to over 270 (15% of the total). Subsequently their number declined, dropping to 133 in 1919 and 87 in 1940 as a result of emigration to the big cities. The Zionists were active, with WIZO providing a cultural framework for dozens of women and most of the young joining Hashomer Hatzair. A J.-owned button factory employed about 60 workers and exported to Europe. In the Slovakian state, J. children were expelled from the public schools and J. businesses were closed down. Young J. men were deported to the Majdanek concentration camp and the women to Auschwitz, in March–April 1942. Most of the others were sent to the death camps in the Lublin dist. (Poland) on 2 June.

TWIERDZA Lwow dist., Poland, today Ukraine. The J. pop. in 1921 was 148 (total 512). The Jews probably shared the fate of nearby Frysztak's Jews in the Holocaust.

TWISTRINGEN Hanover, Germany. By 1833, there were 31 Jews living in the town and a community was established in 1845, when members (some recruited from Heiligenloh and Ehrenburg) opened a synagogue. They numbered 41 (2% of the pop.) in 1895, declining to 34 (1%) in 1925. In 1933, the community numbered 28 Jews. Many Catholics at first ignored Nazi boycott regulations, but relations between Jews and non-Jews deteriorated in 1935. Children were released from school on the morning after *Kristallnacht* (9–10 Nov. 1938) to watch the synagogue burn. Stormtroopers raided J. homes, confiscated valuables, and dispatched Jews to the Buchenwald concentration camp. J. property was thereafter sold at a loss or

"Aryanized." Most Jews managed to emigrate before 1940. Those who remained perished in the Holocaust.

TYCZYN Lwow dist., Poland. Jews settled in the 15th cent. Economic conditions picked up with the establishment of a hasidic court by R. Shelomo Aryeh-Leib Weinshallbaum in the second half of the 18th cent., which became the center of local J. life. The J. pop. stood at 999 in 1890 (a third of the total) and maintained nearly that level until WWI. After the war, J. villagers driven from their homes by economic hardship and anti-J. agitation replaced emigrating J. townsmen. The community declined when the hasidic court moved away in 1927 and only then were the Zionists able to gain a foothold. Under the Germans the Jews were ghettoized with the many refugees pouring in mainly from Lodz. Most were expelled to Rzeszow in June 1942 and from there deported to the Belzec death camp in July.

TYKOCIN (Yid. Tiktin) Bialystok dist., Poland. Ten J. families from Grodno settled in 1522 under a charter of privileges enabling them to trade and open a synagogue and cemetery. Despite friction with the local pop., including a blood libel in 1657 that led to the execution of two Jews, the community flourished and in time broke away from the jurisdiction of Grodno. When the Lithuanian Council was established in 1623, the community chose to affiliate itself with the Council of the Four Lands and consequently a dispute raged between the two councils for many years. The community also had a longstanding dispute with Grodno concerning jurisdiction over the smaller communities in the area, including Bialystok, which only left T.'s auspices in 1771. Among T.'s illustrious rabbis was R. Shemuel Edels ("Maharsha"), known for his Talmud commentary and serving in the 1620s. The synagogue built in 1642 was one of the most beautiful in Poland. The J. pop. grew to 3,457 (total 4,947) in 1857, declining to 1,461 in 1921. Between the World Wars, most Jews were poor, engaging in petty trade and crafts, while merchants had commercial ties with Bialystok and a few were active in light industry (small textile factories, flour mills, hide-processing plants, and a beer brewery). The Zionist movement was the most important social and cultural force in the community. Agudat Israel had 200 members, sending a few to Palestine, and ran a Beth Jacob school for 100 girls. Under Soviet rule from Sept. 1939 to June

An old synagogue in Tykocin, Poland

Elijah's Chair, Tykocin synagogue, Poland

1941, the Jews worked in the new cooperatives and nationalized factories as well as in the Soviet bureaucracy. The Germans liquidated the community on 25–26 Aug. 1941, executing all but 150 of the 1,400 Jews of T. in the Lopuchowow forest. The rest, fleeing, were mostly turned in by Polish peasants and also murdered, while those reaching Bialystok shared the fate of the Jews there.

TYLICZ Cracow dist., Poland. Jews settled in the late 18th cent., numbering 139 in 1921 (total 1,253). They were expelled by the Germans in Oct. 1940, probably to Nowy Soncz, where they shared the fate of the local Jews.

TYN NAD VLTAVOU Bohemia, Czechoslovakia. Jews are mentioned in 1569 and maintained a synagogue, cemetery, and school in the early 17th cent. In 1684, they were expelled but were again present in the late 18th cent., most dealing in wool, hides, and alcoholic beverages. Their pop. was 60 in 1886 and 23 in 1930. In 1942, the Jews were deported to the Theresienstadt ghetto via Tabor. In Jan., Sept., and Oct. 1943, they were all sent to Auschwitz.

TYRAWA WOLOSKA Lwow dist., Poland, today Ukraine. Jews settled in the 18th cent., with many farming. The pop. reached 415 in 1900 (40% of the total) and declined to 299 in 1921. In WWII, following a regime of persecution and forced labor, the Jews were sent by the Germans to Zaslawie in March and July 1942 and subsequently to the Belzec death camp.

TYSHKOVKA Kirovograd dist., Ukraine. The J. pop. in 1939 was 138 (total 6,122). The Germans captured T. in Aug. 1941, murdering the 72 remaining Jews in May 1942.

TYSMIENICA Stanislawow dist., Poland, today Ukraine. Jews are mentioned in the 15th cent., with an organized community in the late 17th cent. By the second half of the 18th cent. Jews controlled the town's trade, arriving at Breslau for the fairs. Up to WWI they were particularly active as furriers and textile workers and even in the coral trade. During the war, the suffering of the Jews was particularly severe as the town changed hands time and again between the Russians and Austrians, with many fleeing or expelled and heavy bombardments wreaking havoc. Tribulations continued under the Ukrainians and at the beginnings of Polish rule, but J. commercial life was able to recover slowly. The pop. dropped from its 1880 high of 2,529 (total 6,953) to 1,090 in 1921. Under Soviet rule from Sept. 1939 to June 1941, J. commercial and communal life suffered. The Hungarian army entered the town on 2 July 1941 in the wake of the retreating Soviets and were able to restrain the rioting Ukrainians. The Germans instuted a regime of repressive measures. Expulsions to Stanislawow commenced in Sept. 1941 with subsequent execution there or deportation to the Belzec death camp. There were 56 survivors and around 30 reached Israel.

TYSZKOWCE Stanislawow dist., Poland. The J. pop. in 1921 was 129. The Jews were possibly expelled to Horodenka for liquidation in April 1942.

TYSZOWCE Lublin dist., Poland. Jews were present in the late 16th cent., enjoying wide-ranging royal privileges. T. was one of the principal communities in the Chelm–Belz region with meetings of the Council of the Four Lands convened there in 1583, 1742, and 1744. From 1866 until the Holocaust, the Wahl–Glanz family provided the community with rabbis while Belz, Trisk (Turzysk), Ruzhin, and Husyatin Hasidim all operated *shtiblekh*. The J. pop. was 940 in 1856 and 2,451 (total 4,420) in 1921. Zionist influence spread in the 1920s, with a Tarbut Hebrew school founded in 1926. Agudat Israel derived its strength from the Hasidim and the Bund was active among working-class Jews. About 1,000 Jews fled with the Red Army prior to the final German occupation of the town in late Sept. 1939. In spring 1940, a *Judenrat* was established to organize forced labor and meet extortionate demands. A labor camp was set up in T. where local Jews were confined with hundreds of Jews from Lublin and other localities. On 25 May 1942, 800 Jews were deported to the Belzec death camp. In Sept. 1942, 49 were executed and in the final *Aktion* in Nov. another 70 were sent to Belzec while 22 were shot resisting. Most of those escaping to the forest were hunted down and killed by the Germans or by Polish and Ukrainian antisemites. A few managed to organize a partisan unit and engage in effective anti-German action. Because the mayor of T., Zarbemski, made strenuous efforts to protect the Jews and to help them with funds and food, he was arrested in 1942 and sent to the Dachau concentration camp.

TYTUVENAI (Yid. Tzitevyian) Raseiniai dist., Lithuania. Jews first settled in the 19th cent. After WWI, many emigrated, mainly to South Africa, some to Palestine. The community maintained a synagogue and *beit midrash*. Most of the Jews were farmers. The Zionist movement enjoyed widespread support. Zerah Barnett, one of the founders of Petah Tikva, came from T. The J. pop. in 1940 numbered about 50 families. After the German invasion in June 1941, Lithuanian nationalists took control of the town. On 12 Aug. 1941, the Jews were taken to a forest outside the town and murdered. One Jew returned to T. after the war.

TYUKOD Szatmar dist., Hungary. Jews settled in the late 18th cent., most as peddlers and shopkeepers. In 1930, the J. pop. was 98 and in 1941 there were 80 Jews. The authorities ignored the racial laws but could not avoid the demand for forced labor and 16 J. men were sent to the Ukraine. In the beginning of June 1944, all the Jews were deported to Auschwitz via Mateszalka and Budakalasz. Ten survivors found the synagogue, Torah scrolls, and cemetery preserved by neighbors but were unable to reestablish the community.

U

UBLA Slovakia, Czechoslovakia, today Republic of Slovakia. Jews settled in the early 19th cent. and Galician refugees formed an Orthodox congregation towards the end of the cent. The J. pop. grew to 136 (total 1,090) in 1930. About 100 Jews were sent to the Uzhorod ghetto on 16 April 1944 and from there to Auschwitz in mid-May.

UCHANIE Lublin dist., Poland. Jews as grain merchants are mentioned from 1640. In 1897, they numbered 1,386 (of a total 1,980). Many left during and after WWI and in 1921 the J. pop. was 1,010. The Germans occupied U. in Sept 1939 and on 10 June 1942 deported the town's 2,025 Jews including refugees (among them 680 from Horodlo) to the Sobibor death camp.

UCKANGE Moselle dist., France. A small J. community was established in 1730. The community inaugurated a new synagogue in 1848. During WWII, the Jews were evacuated with the rest of Alsace-Lorraine Jewry to the south of France. After WWII the synogogue was destroyed.

UDEN Noord-Brabant dist., Holland. A community existed from 1859 and numbered 50 in 1892. It dwindled to seven in 1941. Six Jews were deported and one survived.

UDINE Italy. The J. presence in U. dates from the end of the 13th cent. Local Jews, mainly engaged in moneylending, were permitted to purchase land for a cemetery in 1405. In 1424, Jews were forced to wear the J. badge. In 1500, all privileges were canceled. In 1543, the Jews were confined to a ghetto. U. was the birthplace of Shelomo Natan Ashkenazi, private physician to Sigismund II of Poland. After the battle of Lep-

anto in 1571, Ashkenazi negotiated with the Venetian Republic on behalf of the Turkish Grand Vizier Sokollu Mohammed Pasha. Due to his mediation, the expulsion of the Jews from Venice was rescinded. In 1556, the Jews of U. were expelled, charged with causing a plague that killed 827 inhabitants. In 1631, Jews are once again mentioned as residing in U. and burying their dead in the old cemetery. In 1777, Jews received permission to work in the silk industry, but a year later it was revoked. Expelled from the ghetto, most relocated in Gorizia and Trieste. In 1881, there were 64 Jews in U. and in 1901 there were 71. The synagogue was reopened in 1928, when the community of S. Daniele del Friuli was united with that of U. According to the 1930 law reforming the J. communities, U. was included in the district of Gorizia, one of the 26 formally recognized communities in Italy. The local synagogue was inaugurated in 1932. In 1936, 60 Jews resided in U. Among those deported by the Germans was Elio Morpurgo, the former mayor of U. and senator. In 1948, 37 Jews were listed as living in U. By the 1980s, one family was left.

UDOBINSKYI (county) Krasnodar territory, Russia. The Germans murdered 19 Jews at the Boyevik kolkhoz on 16 Sept. 1942. In early Oct. the remaining Jews in the county were brought to the Molotov kolkhoz and from there they were transferred to the First of May kolkhoz, where 370 people were murdered, most of them probably Jews.

UEBERLINGEN Baden, Germany. Jews were present in the 13th cent., maintaining a prosperous community based on moneylending and inhabiting a special quarter with a synagogue and cemetery. In 1332, over 300 were burned alive in the synagogue in a blood libel. In the Black Death persecutions of

1348–49, Jews were murdered and in 1429 Jews were again burned to death. The five Jews present in 1933 emigrated to the U.S

UEDEM   Rhineland, Germany. The 19th cent. J. community numbered 67 (of a total 1,707) in 1871 and then dropped to 20 in the 20th cent. Eleven Jews perished in the Holocaust and the rest emigrated. The Nazis desecrated the cemetery, dating back to at least 1835.

UEHLFELD   Middle Franconia, Germany. A J. community existed in the first half of the 16th cent. The Jews were expelled in 1583 and present again in 1619. A synagogue was built in 1696 and a cemetery was consecrated in 1732. In 1813 a J. public school was opened. The J. pop. grew to 300 in 1837 (total 1,015), with many Jews farming or working as artisans. A new synagogue was erected in 1889. From the early 1920s the Jews suffered persecution at the hands of local Nazis. In 1933, 49 Jews remained. On *Kristallnacht* (9–10 Nov. 1938), the synagogue was burned to the ground and the last 15 Jews were expelled from the town. In all, seven are known to have emigrated and at least 31 went to other cities in Germany.

UELZEN   Hanover, Germany. Two J. families were living there in 1828 and a district community – which also included the Jews of Bevensen, Bienenbuettel, Ebstorf, Niendorf, Oldendorf, Oldenstadt, and Bergen/ Dumme – was established between 1842 and 1855. The Jews of U., whose number grew to 35 in 1858 and to 90 in 1907, maintained a prayer hall and cemetery. When the Nazis came to power in 1933, there were 34 Jews left. After *Kristallnacht* (9–10 Nov. 1938), their number dropped to 16, four of the eight emigrants having left for Palestine. The last 11 Jews were deported, mostly to the Theresienstadt ghetto.

UERDINGEN   Rhineland, Germany. Jews were victimized in the Black Death persecutions of 1348–49. In 1822–23 they numbered 61. In 1933, 31 remained, attached to the Krefeld congregation.

UFFENHEIM   Middle Franconia, Germany. Jews were present in the second half of the 13th cent. and were among the victims of the Rindfleisch and Armleder massacres in 1298 and 1336, respectively. In the late 14th cent. they were under the protection of

Count Friedrich von Hohenzollern and from the 16th cent. they were subjected to expulsions and residence restrictions. The modern community was founded in 1870 by Jews from nearby Ermetzhofen, Weigenheim, and Welbhausen. In 1890, when a synagogue was built, the J. pop. reached 102 (total 2,378). In 1906 a J. educational institution was opened. In 1933 the J. pop. was 50, most earning a livelihood as cattle and horse traders. All the Jews left by 1939, at least 19 emigrating from Germany.

UGALE   Courland dist., Latvia. The J. pop. in 1930 was 24. The Jews were murdered by the Germans with the aid of local Latvian nationalists in summer or fall 1941.

UHERSKE HRADISTE   Moravia, Czechoslovakia. Jews are mentioned in 1342. They were expelled in 1514, returning only in the mid-19th cent. A synagogue was erected in 1875 as the J. pop. rose to 488 in 1880. After WWI, most Jews belonged to Zionist groups. In 1939, the J. pop. was 325. The synagogue was destroyed on 22 June 1941 and in early 1942 the Jews were expelled to Uhersky Brod. From there they were deported in Jan. 1943, to the Theresienstadt ghetto and then to the death camps of Poland.

UHERSKY BROD   Moravia, Czechoslovakia. Jews probably settled in the region around 1270 and are first mentioned as living in U. in 1470 in an atmosphere of tolerance. The community suffered in the Thirty Years War (1618–48). In 1683, 438 died in an epidemic and another 103 were massacred by the Kuruc peasant army. Again the community recovered and in 1857 reached a peak pop. of 1,068 (26% of the total). In 1891, Moritz Jung founded the first modern J. high school, attracting hundreds of students from a number of countries. In 1939, 489 Jews remained. The synagogue was burned in late 1941. U. then became a concentration point for deportations. In Jan. 1943, there were 2,837 Moravian Jews in U. All were sent to the Theresienstadt ghetto in three transports and from there to death camps in Poland.

UHLA   (Hung. Uglya; Yid. Igle) Carpatho-Russia, Czechoslovakia, today Ukraine. J. settlement probably dates from the early 19th cent. The J. pop. was 379 in 1880 and 707 in 1910 with Jews earning their livelihoods in trade and crafts. Jews owned about 20 business establishments, and also operated two flour mills. Between the World Wars, various youth groups were active, including Betar, Hehalutz, and Tze'irei Mizrachi. After the occupation of the town by the Hungarians in March 1939, dozens of Jews were drafted into labor battalions. By 1941, the J. pop. had dropped to 669. In Aug. 1941, dozens of J. families without Hungarian citizenship were expelled to Kamenets-Podolski, where they were murdered. In the second half of May 1944, the rest of the town's Jews (about 250) were deported to Auschwitz.

UHLIRSKE JANOVICE   Bohemia, Czechoslovakia. Jews are first mentioned in 1686. A J. school was opened in 1849. In 1904 and 1913 fires destroyed J. homes, including the synagogue in the latter conflagration. A new synagogue was built in 1914 and in 1921 the J. pop. stood at 187, dropping to 59 (of a total 2,012) in 1930. The Jews were deported to the Theresienstadt ghetto together with the Jews of Prague in 1942 and from there sent to the death camps of Poland.

UHNOW   (Yid. Hivnov) Lwow dist., Poland, today Ukraine. A small J. community dates from the 16th cent. but it only began to grow in the late 18th cent., reaching a pop. of 2,140 (50% of the total) by the end of the 19th cent. Relations between the Jews and their Ukrainian neighbors were always strained and marked by antisemitic incidents. The Cossack occupation of the town in WWI produced further hardship. In 1915 a cholera epidemic claimed many J. lives. From the mid-19th cent. Hasidism was the predominant spiritual force among the Jews, but after WWI the Zionists made significant inroads. The economic situation of the Jews in these years was extremely difficult, with heavy taxation and stiff competition in trade from the Ukrainian cooperatives. Since the Jews constituted more than half the pop., they were well represented in the city council. Between 26 Sept. 1939 and the end of June 1941, U. was under Soviet rule. When the Germans took over, they instituted a regime of terror and forced labor. The community was liquidated in Oct. 1942 with the Jews expelled to the Rawa Ruska ghetto.

UHORSKA VES   (Hung. Magyarfalu) Slovakia, Czechoslovakia, today Republic of Slovakia. Jews were present in the early 18th cent., possibly before. They formed a Status Quo congregation after the 1869 split and numbered 118 (total 2,370) in 1900 and 68 in 1940. Most were deported to the death camps of Poland via Sered in spring 1942.

UIOARA   (also Ocna Muresului; Hung. Marosuyvar) S. Transylvania dist., Rumania. Jews first settled in the mid-19th cent. The majority worked in the salt mines and in businesses connected with the mines. The first synagogue was built of wood and a permanent stone structure was erected in the 1830s. The first rabbi, R. Yehezkel Paneth (1870-1930), opened a yeshiva that functioned up to the Holocaust and published its own periodical. The majority of the J. pop., 514 in 1930 (10% of the total), belonged to the Dej hasidic sect. Zionist youth movements were active. In summer 1941, the J. pop. was transferred to Aiud. In winter 1942, it was permitted to return.

UITHOORN-MIJDRECHT   Noord-Holland-Utrecht dist., Holland. Jews first settled there in the late 18th cent. and numbered 106 in 1860. In 1938 there were 29 community members. In April 1942 they were transferred to the Westerbork transit camp and from there to the death camps. Only a few survived.

UJAZD   Lodz dist., Poland. Jews settled in the second half of the 17th cent. The discovery of iron ore in the area in the late 18th cent. was a source of employment for Jews. In the early 19th cent. they became involved in the weaving industry. Between the World Wars their situation deteriorated due to a devasting fire (1923), an economic boycott, and manifestations of antisemitism. In 1939 the J. pop. was 800, swollen by refugees to 2,000 in 1941-42. All were sent to their deaths in the Treblinka death camp on 1 Jan. 1943.

UJFEHERTO   Szabolcs dist., Hungary. Jews settled in the early 18th cent., most trading in farm produce. Hasidism led by R. Shalom Eliezer Halberstam of Zanz was dominant. A J. school opened in 1870 and the J. pop. reached 1,303 (11% of the total) in 1920. The 400 J. families in U. were deported to Auschwitz via Nyirjes and Sima on 17 May 1944.

UJKECSKE   Pest-Pilis-Solt-Kiskun dist., Hungary. Jews apparently first settled in 1770 and formed an organized community c. 1816, its pop. reaching 115 in 1869 and 160-180 (about 2% of the total) from 1890 to WWII. Jews suffered grievously during the

Communist Revolution (1919) and the White Terror attacks of 1919–21. Their land was nationalized after the publication of the racial laws of 1940 and several weeks after the German occupation in March 1944 they were expelled to Kompoc and then Szeged (at the beginning of June) and then from 24–26 June deported to Auschwitz.

UJLAK (Hung. Bodzasujlak) Slovakia, Czechoslovakia, today Republic of Slovakia. Jews arrived by the mid-18th cent. and probably formed an independent community with a synagogue and cemetery in the 1840s. They owned stores and traded in livestock and farm produce, their pop. growing to 101 (of a total 1,093) in 1880 and 125 in 1941. On 20 April 1944, after the German occupation of Hungary, the Jews were moved to the central Satoraljaujhely ghetto and from there deported to Auschwitz.

UJPEST Pest–Pilis–Solt–Kiskun dist., Hungary. J. settlement began when Yitzhak Loewy of Nagysurany set up a factory on estate land in 1835 and a synagogue in 1839. He obtained various religious rights from the estate owner. Numerous J. factories followed, making U. one of the country's most important industrial centers. Jews also played a major entrepreneurial role in U., establishing banks and export facilities. As their pop. grew to 3,915 in 1890 and 10,140 (18% of the total) in 1910, Jews entered the professional class. A J. school was opened in 1840; a second one, opened after WWI, enrolled 250 students in 1929. Among the community's rabbis, Albert Stern-Szterenyi (1867–84), was notable for his controversial anti-traditional stance. His son, Joseph Szterenyi, became minister of commerce and industry under Francis Joseph I and was made a baron. After WWI, workers within the local Social Democrat Party prevented the White Terror gangs from harming Jews. From the outset of WWII, the city's 11,000 Jews were persecuted by the provincial Hungarian administration under Endre Laszlo. Many were sent to Yugoslavia for forced labor. After the German occupation of 20 March 1944, the Jews were confined in a ghetto. On 2 July, they were transferred to Begesmegyer amid random shooting that left many dead. After being kept for days without food or shelter in pouring rain, they were deported to Auschwitz. Zionist organizations helped about 300 who evaded the deportation to escape to Budapest, where they survived the war. Some Jews in U. were rescued by underground groups, but 150 children hidden in a monastery were murdered on the banks of the Danube. Many in the postwar J. community emigrated to Israel after 1948.

UKMERGE (Yid. Vilkomir) Ukmerge dist., Lithuania. Jews began settling in the 17th cent. Lord Nathaniel Rothschild contributed to the community's rehabilitation after a fire in 1877. For centuries U. was a center of Torah learning. By 1860 it had 20 synagogues, including the main synagogue, the oldest and most magnificient in the city and serving as a refuge in pogroms, a jail, and a detention center for those kidnapped to serve in the Russian army. In addition to the traditional *heder*, a Hebrew school was established in 1868. A *talmud torah*, mainly serving orphans and needy children, provided meals and clothing. The J. pop. was 10,810 in 1891 (66% of the total) and 7,287 in 1897 (54%). Haskala took hold among the youth of U. despite the opposition of the ultra-Orthodox, who also fought against Zionism. In the early 20th cent. many of U.'s Jews emigrated to South Africa and the U.S. When in 1915, early in WWI, all the Jews were expelled, the local police protected J. property and provided transportation for the deportees. Most returned during the German occupation later in 1915. After Lithuania's independence, disturbances broke out against Jews in 1919. Many rioters were arrested but due to pressure were freed and the police chief was fired. A community council was elected and succeeded in its work despite the continuing controversy between Zionists and anti-Zionists. In the 1921 municipal elections, 17 Jews were elected to the 35-member council and a Jew was elected mayor. The J. pop. in 1930 was 3,885 (37% of the total). Educational and social welfare institutions also operated along Zionist–anti-Zionist lines. There were Yiddish and Hebrew high schools, though in 1933 the two schools were united as a Hebrew school. All the Zionist parties had branches in U. After Germany's invasion of the USSR in June 1941, the Germans immediately murdered several Jews, including rabbis, lawyers, and public servants. Two hundred suspected J. Communists were killed in the Pivonija forest. After the Jews were taken to a ghetto and forced labor in Aug., they were executed in groups in the Pivonija forest from Aug. through 26 Sept. 1941.

ULANOV Vinnitsa dist., Ukraine. Jews probably

Exhibition of children's projects in the Ukmerge (Vilkomir) Jewish school, Lithuania, 1928

settled in the early 18th cent., numbering 201 in 1784 and about 2,000 (of a total 2,047) in 1897. Under the Soviets, a few Jews worked in kolkhozes. A J. council was active from the late 1920s. J. children attended a J. elementary school reaching an enrollment of about 290 in 1931. In 1939, the J. pop. was 1,188. The Germans arrived on 15 July 1941 and on 10 July 1942 executed 3,235 Jews from U. and the surrounding area at the Polish cemetery.

ULANOW   Lwow dist., Poland. The first J. settlement was wiped out in the Chmielnicki massacres of 1648–49 but the Jews soon reestablished themselves. Under the Austrians they suffered from heavy taxation. Economic conditions were alleviated by the town's position as a hasidic center, attracting hundreds of Sabbath and holiday visitors to the courts and bringing business to local enterprises. The J. pop. reached a peak of 1,947 (half the total) in 1880 but subsequently declined radically through emigration as economic conditions worsened in the absence of a railroad link. Antisemitic incidents were also a periodic occurrence

and in WWI the Russians burned and pillaged J. houses as well as exiling the J. populace on their retreat, causing the J. pop. to drop to 861 by 1921. Between the World Wars the Joint Distribution Committee supported the community and the Zionists came to the fore after the earlier suppression of their activities by the Hasidim. When the town changed hands between the Germans and Russians in Sept. 1939, many Jews were able to leave with the retreating Red Army. The German occupation was marked by mounting persecution and a regime of forced labor. A *Judenrat* was established early in 1940 and a ghetto in Jan. 1942. Most were expelled to Zaklikow on 3 Oct. 1942 (Simhat Torah). The majority of those who remained were hunted down and murdered.

ULASZKOWCE   (Yid. Lashkavitz, Lashavitz) Tarnopol dist., Poland, today Ukraine. The J. community began to develop in the 19th cent. and in 1900 numbered 489 (total 2,280). J. livelihoods revolved around the yearly fair, which brought an influx of Jews from all over Galicia. With the Russian evacuation in June

1941, the Jews were attacked and plundered by the Ukrainian pop., 68 were murdered, and the rest fled to other towns in the environs.

ULAZOW Lwow dist., Poland, today Ukraine. The J. pop. in 1921 was 180. Most Jews fled to Soviet-held territory in Sept.–Oct. 1939. Those who remained were probably deported to the Belzec death camp in summer–fall 1942 via Lubaczow or Rawa Ruska.

ULIANOVKA Odessa dist., Ukraine. In the 1930s, under the Soviets, many Jews worked in a sugar refinery. The J. pop. was 186 (total 4,474) in 1939. The Germans captured U. on 1 Aug. 1941. On 16–22 Feb. 1942 the Jews of the surrounding Grushka region were brought to O. and 219, including 86 from the town, were murdered with the active assistance of local German settlers.

ULLA Vitebsk dist., Belorussia. Jews settled in the early 18th cent. Their pop. was 129 in 1765 and 1,539 (62% of the total) in 1897. In 1924, under the Soviets, a J. council (soviet) was established. A J. elementary school was also in operation. Two kolkhozes set up near the town in the late 1920s employed 24 J. families. In 1939, the J. pop. was 516. The Germans arrived in July 1941. An open ghetto housing the 200 remaining Jews was established in Dec. On 17 Jan. 1942, they were among the 350 Jews from the area executed outside the town.

ULM Wuerttemberg, Germany. Jews settled in the first half of the 13th cent., engaging mostly in moneylending and occupying a J. quarter where a synagogue was maintained. In 1349 the quarter was stormed by rioters after a well-poisoning libel and throughout the 14th cent. J. life was undermined by restrictive measures under pressure from the Christian guilds. The small community was expelled in 1499. Settlement was only renewed in 1782, but anti-J. feeling kept it from developing until after the 1848 revolution. In 1857 it was recognized as an independent community and in 1873 a splendid synagogue was inaugurated. Jews engaged in the textile trade and were represented in the professional class. They were also active in public life, with representatives in the chamber of commerce, city council, and Wuerttemberg parliament. Albert Einstein was born there in 1879. By 1880 the J. pop. stood at 694 (total 32,773). A reading society founded in 1855 became a vital center of J. social life, organizing various functions and accumulating a 7,000-volume library. Under the Weimar Republic, antisemitism was rekindled, becoming virulent in the Nazi era as persecution intensified. In Oct. 1938, 17 Jews with Polish citizenship were deported. On *Kristallnacht* (9–10 Nov. 1938), the synagogue was burned, Jews were beaten, and J. stores were looted. Of the 530 Jews in U. in 1933, 331 emigrated by 1941, 169 to the U.S., 55 to Palestine, and 49 to England. The rest were expelled, many ending their days in the Theresienstadt ghetto. After the war a refugee camp for 1,000–1,200 Displaced Jews was set up near the city and a small J. community reestablished.

ULMBACH (now part of Steinau) Hesse–Nassau, Germany. Numbering 61 (5% of the total) in 1885, the J. community dwindled to 36 in 1933 and disbanded three years later.

ULMENI (Hung. Sulelmed) N. Transylvania dist., Rumania. Jews settled in the late 18th cent. The J. pop. in 1920 was 102 (12% of the total). In May 1944 the community was transferred to the Simleul Silvaniei ghetto and in June deported to Auschwitz.

ULRICHSTEIN Hesse, Germany. Jews first settled there in 1347. The community, numbering 107 (11% of the total) in 1861, was affiliated with Giessen's Liberal rabbinate. By Sept. 1938 the community had disbanded, 41 Jews emigrating (27 to the U.S.) and 13 moving to other German towns before May 1939.

ULRUM-LEENS Groningen dist., Holland. A J. community existed from the 18th cent. and numbered 57 in 1889. All 17 Jews (total pop. 7,594) were sent to the Westerbork transit camp in 1941 and then to the death camps in Eastern Europe in 1942.

ULUCZ Lwow dist., Poland. The J. pop. in 1921 was 210. Some Jews were engaged in agriculture. All were probably killed in 1942.

UMAN Kiev dist., Ukraine. Jews settled in the 17th cent. In 1729, all the Jews were murdered in a Haidamak raid. By 1765, 405 Jews were living there again but in 1768 the Haidamaks under Zheleznyak again massacred the Jews. In 1897, the J. pop. was 17,945 (of a total 31,016). The Jews earned their livelihoods in petty trade, wholesaling, and crafts. U. was a center of Hasidism, particularly Bratslav, since R. Nahman of Bratslav was buried there. A modern J. school was founded in the city in the late 19th cent. in the face of hasidic opposition. The Zionists also became active at the time. On 21 Oct. 1905, 73 J. homes and a similar number of J. stores were looted in a pogrom. J. self-defense prevented loss of life. New riots in Aug. 1917 claimed 28 J. lives and on 12 May 1919, J. homes and stores were looted and burned, women raped, and 400 men, women, and children murdered. In 1923, ORT opened two J. vocational schools and in 1925, under the Soviets, a J. law court was established in the city. In 1927–28, 105 J. families resettled in the Crimea and Krivoi Rog area; another 20 families and ten bachelors moved to Birobidzhan. Local cooperatives were organized with a J. membership of 70%, including many Jews deprived of their rights by the Soviets. Two Yiddish-language schools with an enrollment of 500 were opened and a Yiddish section was inaugurated in the local building trades school and attended by many. R. Twersky officiated in the community and religious institutions continued to operate until 1937. In 1939, the J. pop. was 13,233. The Germans occupied the city on 1 Aug. 1941. On 13 Aug., a number of Jews belonging to the educated class were murdered. In early Sept., over 1,000 Jews were locked into a cellar and suffocated to death. On 9 Oct., about 10,000 Jews were murdered in a mass *Aktion*. The remaining 1,800 were confined in a ghetto and subjected to a regime of forced labor under conditions of starvation and overcrowding. All were murdered in a final *Aktion* in April 1942.

UNETCHA Oriol dist., Russia. J. residence was banned in 1882 but allowed again in 1903. The J. pop. was 1,409 in 1926 and 1,708 (of a total 13,955) in 1939. Following the German occupation of 17 Aug., 1941, 342 Jews were murdered at the local train station.

UNGEDANKEN (now part of Fritzlar) Hesse–Nassau, Germany. Established according to tradition by refugees from the Chmielnicki massacres (1648–49), the community numbered 78 (22% of the total) in 1871. Its district school, built in 1864, had 36 pupils (1869). Only one J. family remained there in 1937.

UNGURMUIZA Latgale dist., Latvia. The J. pop. in 1930 was 16. The Jews were murdered by the Germans with Latvian assistance after their occupation of late June 1941.

UNIEJOW Lodz dist., Poland. Jews lived here from the mid-18th cent. and in 1897 numbered 960. Some were industrialists, but after a boycott in 1936 the community issued a call to Polish Jewry for aid. In 1940, the Germans enclosed the 130 families into a ghetto. On 20 Oct. 1941 they were expelled to the Kowale Panskie region and murdered with other Jews on 20 July 1942.

UNNA Westphalia, Germany. The first J. family is mentioned in 1304, marking the beginning of unbroken J. settlement. A prayer house and cemetery were in use in the late 18th cent. In 1846, 18 J. families were present, most engaged in trade. In 1848, the community purchased a building that formerly housed a Catholic church and converted it into a synagogue (dedicated in 1851). The community was officially recognized in 1854. A J. school was in operation in the early 19th cent., becoming a public school in 1895. The cemetery was desecrated in 1900, with 28 tombstones damaged. In 1905, an old age home for the Jews of Westphalia was opened. The community reached a peak pop. of 240 in 1909. Jews were active in public and social life, with one Jew serving on the municipal council in 1913. In June 1933, their pop. was 156. Jews began to emigrate and five families of Polish origin were expelled to Poland in Oct. 1938. By Nov. 1938, 89 Jews remained. On *Kristallnacht* (9–10 Nov. 1938), the three remaining J. stores were vandalized, windows of J. homes were smashed, and the synagogue was partially burned (and razed a few days later by the municipality). Twenty-five J. men and women were taken into "protective" custody; some of the men were sent to the Sachsenhausen concentration camp. The J. pop. rose to 108 in 1940 after Jews from surrounding settlements arrived. A few still managed to leave, but in 1942, 84 were deported to the death camps, including those in the old age home.

UNSLEBEN Lower Franconia, Germany. Jews are mentioned in 1571 and numbered 26 families in 1749 with a synagogue constructed in 1753. A J. public school was opened in 1840 as the J. pop. reached 225 (of a total 930). Many were farmers and craftsmen.

Between 1834 and 1853, 48 Jews emigrated to the U.S. A second synagogue was built in 1855 and a cemetery was opened in 1856. Around 140 remained in the Nazi era. Up to Nov. 1938, 59 left the village, 30 of them to the U.S. Soon after the *Kristallnacht* riots (9–10 Nov. 1938), another 19 left for Cuba, as did 29 of the 39 Jews emigrating in 1939. Of the last 17, ten were deported to Izbica in the Lublin dist. (Poland) on 25 April 1942 and four to the Theresienstadt ghetto on 23 Sept.

UNTERALTERTHEIM   Lower Franconia, Germany. Jews were present in the first half of the 17th cent. In 1890 the J. pop. reached 94 (of a total 653), dropping to 34 in 1933. The day after the *Kristallnacht* disturbances (9–10 Nov. 1938), the synagogue and J. homes were vandalized. The remaining Jews were herded into a single house. In 1934–40, nine Jews emigrated from Germany. The last 15 were expelled to Wuerzburg on 24 April 1942 and deported to Izbica in the Lublin dist. (Poland) the next day.

UNTEREISENHEIM   Lower Franconia, Germany. The J. pop. in 1897 was 48 (total 620). Of the seven present under Nazi rule, five emigrated and the last two were expelled in 1940.

UNTERERTHAL   Lower Franconia, Germany. A J. community is known from the first half of the 17th cent. Some fled to Hammelburg during the Thirty Years War (1618–48) and others were expelled in 1671. In 1837 the J. pop. numbered 68 (total 845). In 1933, 20 remained, most reduced to penury under Nazi rule. On *Kristallnacht* (9–10 Nov. 1938), the synagogue was vandalized. Five Jews emigrated by 1939. Of the last 12, eight were deported to Izbica in the Lublin dist. (Poland) on 25 April 1942.

UNTERGROMBACH   Baden, Germany. Jews were present during the Thirty Years War (1618–48). Most left the region under the severe restrictions imposed by Bishop August Karl Philip in the 1770s. A new settlement was organized in the early 19th cent. A synagogue in 1815 and J. public school were opened. The J. pop. grew to a peak of 124 (total 2,070) in 1895 and then dropped steadily to 32 in 1933. Fifteen emigrated by 1938, including the Meerapfel family, one of the largest cigarette wholesalers in Germany. Of those who remained, five were deported to the Gurs concen-

tration camp on 22 Oct. 1940 and from there to Auschwitz in 1942.

UNTERMERZBACH   Lower Franconia, Germany. Jews from U. frequented the Leipzig fairs in 1685–1762 and constituted an important community with a cemetery and public school in the first half of the 19th cent. and a peak pop. of 122 in 1837 (total 530). The last two families there suffered violence in the 1920s. Six Jews were living in U. in 1933 and one family emigrated to Argentina in 1937.

UNTERRIEDENBERG   Lower Franconia, Germany. A J. community was present from at least the late 18th cent., numbering 84 in 1867 (of a total 298) and 32 in 1933. Under Nazi rule, J. cattle traders were forced to sell off their stock. Twenty Jews left before *Kristallnacht* (9–10 Nov. 1938), 15 for other German cities. On *Kristallnacht* SA troops wrecked J. homes. The remaining 11 Jews left for Frankfurt on 10 Dec.

UPYNA   Taurage dist., Lithuania. Prior to WWII, there were 20–30 J. families in U. They were petty traders or farmers. On 23 June 1941, the German army entered U. and immediately began to persecute the Jews. On 22 July 1941, males from the age of 13 were murdered. Women were taken to a forest in Batakiai, together with J. women and children from other towns in the area, and were all shot.

URBERACH   Hesse, Germany. Numbering 44 (3% of the total) in 1880, this small community disbanded before *Kristallnacht* (9–10 Nov. 1938). No Jews remained in 1939.

URETCHE   Minsk dist., Belorussia. Jews apparently settled at the turn of the 18th cent., numbering 92 in 1811 and 483 (of a total 509) in 1897. In mid-July 1920, retreating Polish soldiers went on a rampage of rape, murder, robbery, and arson. In the Soviet period, a J. elementary school (four grades) founded in 1924 was still open in 1935 with 160 students. A number of Jews worked in a kolkhoz. In 1939, the J. pop. was 979. The Germans occupied the town on 28 June 1941. In 1942, 900 people were murdered. Most probably nearly all were Jews from U. and the surrounding area.

URISOR   (Hung. Alor) N. Transylvania dist., Rumania. Jews first settled in the mid-18th cent. A community was organized in the early 19th cent. and a synagogue built in 1807. The J. pop. in 1920 was 103 (19% of the total). From 1920 the community expanded with the influx of Jews from neighboring villages. Under Hungarian rule from Aug. 1940, restrictions were imposed on the Jews. Some were drafted into labor battalions in the Ukraine where most died. On 3 May 1944 the community was transferred to the Dej ghetto from where they were sent to labor camps and death camps in Germany.

URITSK Leningrad dist., Russia. U. was founded in 1925 under the name of Ligovski Posiolok and had a J. pop. of 43 in 1925. In 1939, the Jews numbered 316 (of a total 19,772). The few Jews who had not fled or been evacuated were murdered after the German occupation of 19 Sept. 1941.

URMIN Slovakia, Czechoslovakia, today Republic of Slovakia. Although in 1727 this mining region was closed to Jews and they were expelled from the area, they soon returned. A synagogue was built c. 1820 and the local rabbi served Jews in 12 neighboring settlements. In 1869, the J. pop. reached a peak of 414 (total 2,842). A new synagogue was built in 1870 and a J. elementary school was opened. The J. pop. then declined with the young leaving for the bigger cities. In 1919, 170 Jews remained and 119 in 1940. Most engaged in trade. With Slovakia a satellite of Germany in WWII, Jews were pushed out of their businesses in a process of "Aryanization." In March and April 1942, young men were deported to the Majdanek concentration camp and the women to Auschwitz. Families (over 50 members) were dispatched via Nitra on 15 April to the Rejowiec ghetto in the Lublin area, where most perished.

URSPRINGEN Lower Franconia, Germany. The first Jews settled in the early 17th cent. after their expulsion from Wuerzburg. A new synagogue was built in 1803 and a J. public school was subsequently opened. The J. pop. reached 220 in 1837 (total 1,060) and thereafter declined steadily to 78 in 1933. Thirteen left in 1935–38. On *Kristallnacht* (9–10 Nov. 1938), the synagogue and J. homes were vandalized by local SA troops and a few Jews were sent to the Dachau concentration camp. Another 13 Jews left by late 1939. Of the remaining 44 Jews, 42 were deported to Izbica in the Lublin dist. (Poland) via Wuerzburg on 25 April 1942.

URYCZ Stanislawow dist., Poland. The J. pop. in 1921 was 151 (total 1,219). All were murdered by the Ukrainians and/or Germans in 1941–42.

URZENDOW Lublin dist., Poland. Though J. residence was officially banned until 1862, Jews were present from the 18th cent., mostly leasing inns. In 1886, the J. pop. was 153, rising to 509 in 1929. By 1905 the community had a synagogue. Between the World Wars the Zionists were active. Most Jews barely earned a living and with the intensification of antisemitism in the 1930s, J. peddlers were attacked in the villages. After the Germans took U. in Sept. 1939, Jews lived relatively normal lives for a few years in the absence of a permanent occupation force. Refugees brought the J. pop. up to 549. In Oct. 1942, the ablebodied were sent to the Budzyn labor camp and the rest to the Belzec death camp via the Krasnik ghetto.

URZICENI Walachia dist., Rumania. Jews settled from 1865 but a J. community was founded only in 1915 with a J. pop. of 112. Before WWI most Jews belonged to the Rumanian Cultural Association. The Iron Guard persecuted the Jews and in Nov. 1940 all were forced to leave, for Budapest or Ploesti.

USCIECZKO Tarnopol dist., Poland, today Ukraine. A small community existed in the 18th cent., growing to nearly 1,000 (40% of the total) in 1880 but subsequently declining to around 250 in the face of economic hardship. The Jews were expelled by the Nazis to Tluste at the end of 1942.

USCIE ZIELONE Tarnopol dist., Poland, today Ukraine. Jews are first mentioned in 1552, with an organized community in the 17th cent. and the J. pop. leveling off at around 600 (a quarter of the total) at the end of the 19th cent. Most of the town's craftsmen were Jews. The community endured much suffering after WWI at the hands of armed bands. It was liquidated in the German *Aktions* at the end of 1942 after being expelled to Buczacz.

USCILUG (Yid. Ustilla) Volhynia dist., Poland, today Ukraine. Jews were present in the 17th cent. By 1897 their pop. reached 3,212 (total 3,590) with the Hasidim worshiping at 12 synagogues and the town a transit point for the Bug River grain and lumber traffic. Most Jews left with the Russian withdrawal in summer 1915 but returned under the Austro-German military government to face stringent economic regulation. The Balfour Declaration of 1917 was greeted by a huge parade and nearly all the Zionist parties were active between the World Wars. Cultural life revolved around the Yiddish and Hebrew libraries founded under Austrian rule. The German bombardment of 22 June 1941 took a heavy toll in life and property. A *Judenrat* was appointed in July 1941. In Oct. 1941 the Germans executed 890 of the community's leading figures. Sporadic killing continued until a ghetto for the 2,000 survivors was set up in March 1942. Most were taken to the Wlodzimierz-Wolynski ghetto in Sept. 1942 and murdered.

USHACHI Vitebsk dist., Belorussia. Jews are first mentioned in the late 17th cent. Their pop. was 611 in 1765 and 1,129 (78% of the total) in 1897. A J. council was established in 1924 and a J. elementary school was in operation. In 1930, 17 J. families were employed at two nearby kolkhozes. In 1939, the J. pop. was 487. The Germans arrived on 3 July 1941. A few Jews managed to flee. A ghetto was set up in Oct. and on 12 Jan. 1942 its 464 residents were murdered outside the town.

USHOMIR Zhitomir dist., Ukraine. Jews are first mentioned in 1750 with reference to the transfer of the Ovruch region from Pinsk to the Volhynia dist. They numbered 1,754 (total 2,381) in 1897. In March–May 1919, the Petlyura gangs robbed and murdered Jews as well as exacting a tribute from them. The J. pop. was 1,749 in 1926, probably dropping by 1941. The Germans arrived on 6 Aug. 1941. Some Jews managed to flee. The Germans first murdered all the J. men in U. When four J. youngsters burned 48 houses in retaliation, they murdered the women and children as well.

USINGEN Hesse–Nassau, Germany. Although Jews lived there from the 17th cent., numbering 31 in 1801 and opening their third synagogue in 1886, they only won recognition as an independent community in 1868. Affiliated with the rabbinate of Bad Ems, the community – which also had members in five neighboring villages – grew to 126 in 1933. Its synagogue

lay in ruins and the community had virtually disbanded prior to *Kristallnacht* (9–10 Nov. 1938), when SA troops and Hitler Youth organized a pogrom. No Jews remained in U. by 1940, 28 having emigrated (mostly to the U.S.).

USLAR Hanover, Germany. Belonging to a regional community centered in Bodenfelde (1843), the Jews of U. numbered 42 in 1913. They dedicated a new synagogue in 1920. Most earned prosperous livings in the textile and furniture trade. Jacob Freudenthal (1839-1907), a prominent German J. philosopher, taught philosophy at the J. Theological Seminary in Breslau. When the community disbanded in 1937, some Jews emigrated, but most perished in Nazi camps.

USPENSKOYE Krasnodar territory, Russia. On 25 Aug. 1942, the Germans murdered 46 Jews near the village and another 85 toward the end of the month.

USTEK Bohemia (Sudetenland), Czechoslovakia. Jews were permitted to reside on a local estate from 1327 but are only mentioned from the 16th cent. From 1649 to 1848 they lived under a wide-ranging charter granted by Ferdinand III. A new synagogue was built in 1774. A Reform service was practiced from 1851. Many traded in beer hops. The J. pop. rose to 172 in 1880, dropping steadily to 53 (total 2,061) in 1930. When the Sudetenland was annexed to the German Reich in Sept. 1938, the Jews fled to the Czech Republic. Most subsequently emigrated to England and Palestine. The synagogue was burned on *Kristallnacht* (9–10 Nov. 1938).

USTI NAD LABEM Bohemia (Sudetenland), Czechoslovakia. Jews were probably present before 1556 but were subsequently expelled and only returned in the late 19th cent. A cemetery was consecrated in 1866 and a synagogue in 1880. In the 20th cent., the J. pop. maintained a level of nearly 1,000. Jews were active in the coal industry and ran the largest battery factory in Central Europe. Most left during the Sudetenland crisis of summer and fall 1938. The synagogue was destroyed on 1 Jan. 1939. The remaining Jews were put to forced labor and afterwards sent to the Theresienstadt ghetto. Of the 366 Jews who were deported, 224 perished, most in the death camps of the Zamosc, Riga, and Lodz areas.

UST-LABINSKAYA Krasnodar territory, Russia. The Germans occupied the village on 8 Aug. 1942, murdering a few hundred inmates of the local prison in Dec., many of them J. refugees from the western part of the Soviet Union.

USTRON Silesia dist., Poland. Never exceeding much more than a hundred Jews (total 4,000), the community was apparently expelled in the summer of 1942 and sent to Auschwitz and labor camps in Silesia.

USTRZYKI DOLNE (Yid. Istrik) Lwow dist., Poland, today Ukraine. The Jews were among the first settlers of the town when it was founded in the early 19th cent. and constituted around 60% of the pop. until WWI (2,328 out of 3,919 in 1910). Two wealthy J. landowners provided livelihoods to newcomers and the community prospered. Hasidism also flourished. The largest school was Agudat Israel's Beth Jacob for around 100 girls. Most of the Jews fled with the Russian occupation at the beginning of WWI, only returning at the end of 1915 when the Austrian army liberated the town. Between the World Wars antisemitism and Ukrainian competition led to a deterioration in the J. economic position. More than 150 Jews immigrated to Palestine. Jews were severely persecuted during the short German occupation in Sept. 1939. Some 40–60 Jews trying to flee were seized by the Ukrainian police and murdered. Under Soviet rule (Sept. 1939–June 1941) J. institutes were dismantled. The return of the Germans on 24 June 1941 brought a series of repressive measures. J. homes were plundered and food was confiscated. Forced labor was stepped up in April 1942 and on the eve of Shavuot (5 May) all Jews over 65 years of age (about 300) were murdered. The Gestapo rounded up and murdered Jews in the surrounding villages, and the influx of refugees swelled the town's J. pop. to nearly 3,000. On 8 Sept. all were deported to the Zaslawie camp and from there to the Belzec death camp.

USVIYATY Smolensk dist., Russia. Jews probably settled in the late 18th cent. Their pop. was 1,016 in 1847 and 956 (total 2,679) in 1897. In the Soviet period, a number of Jews belonged to a J. agricultural cooperative which became a multinational kolkhoz in the 1920s. The number of Jews in U. dropped to 136 in 1939. During the German occupation of 14 July 1941–28 Jan. 1942, 160–170 Jews from U. and its environs were held in a ghetto: 100 were murdered immediately after the Germans arrived; 30 towards the end of July; and 20 young men in Jan. 1942, shortly before the German withdrawal.

USZNIA Tarnopol dist., Poland, today Ukraine. The J. pop. in 1921 was 120. The Jews were probably expelled to Zloczow for liquidation in Nov. 1942.

UTENA (Yid. Utiyan) Utena dist., Lithuania. Graves from the 16th cent. attest to a J. presence. By 1765 the J. pop. was 565. Devasting fires in 1879 and 1890 caused considerable suffering to the community. The J. pop. in 1897 was 2,405 (74% of the total). Many Jews fled in WWI. Those who remained suffered as did the rest of the pop. from German measures, including forced labor. When the Germans retreated in 1918, leaving an administrative vacuum, the Jews formed a public committee to take care of their needs. Under Lithuanian independence, J. autonomy was granted and a community council with powers of taxation was established. The community maintained a Hebrew elementary and junior high school as well as a Yiddish school. Two Jews served as mayors of U. and after the 1931 elections, seven of the 12 city council members were Jews. The Lithuanians began to curtail J. economic activity, refusing to parcel out land to Jews and moving the market day to the J. Sabbath. Zionism was deeply rooted from the beginning of the cent. and all the Zionist parties were represented. When the USSR annexed Lithuania in 1940, the Zionist organizations and Hebrew school were closed down. In June 1941 a number of Zionist leaders and property owners were exiled; others were imprisoned and killed. Before the Germans entered U. on 25 June 1941, local Lithuanian nationalists took control, harassing Jews and killing some. Lithuanians painted the word "*Jude*" on J. houses and together with German soldiers abused Jews, who were ordered to wear the yellow badge. On 14 July, all Jews were taken from the town. From 31 July through the end of Aug. most were murdered in the Rase forest and buried in large pits. In the early 1990s, a three-story tower was erected with a plaque in Yiddish saying: "At this place on 8.8.1941 Hitlerite murderers and their local helpers murdered approximately 8,000 Jews, men, women and children."

UTRECHT Utrecht dist., Holland. The first record of a J. presence in U. dates back to 1231. In 1444

Children of the Utena Hebrew school in the play "Jeremiah," Lithuania

Jewish prisoners of war, Utena, Lithuania, Passover eve, 1915

The Jewish mayor of Utena, Lithuania

the Jews were expelled, but from 1736 they were permitted to work in U. during the day, leaving at night. Between 1730 and 1740 a number of J. Portuguese traders lived in U. In 1788 Jews were officially permitted to settle and a community was founded. Under the French Empire (1795–1813), U. was the seat of the region's chief rabbi. By 1792 there were 24 J. families in U. A building for a synagogue was purchased in 1796, and from 1814, when the Kingdom of Holland was established, the community flourished (although the chief rabbinate was then transferred to Amersfoort). At the end of the 19th cent. a branch of the Alliance Israelite was opened. In 1901, 10% of the community (70 out of 700 Jews) were considered needy and supported by the community and its welfare organizations. In 1917 the seat of the chief rabbi returned to U. During this period nationwide J. organizations were founded, including Agudat Israel and the Zionist Organization. Zionist youth movements were also established. In the 1930s, many J. refugees from Germany reached U. and in Sept. 1940 the Germans transferred some 400 German refugees from the coastal regions to U. In Nov. the Jews were dismissed from government positions and J. professors from the universities. The mayor of U. refused to cooperate in the registration

of Jews and in the distribution of anti-J. propaganda. In 1941 the J. community of U. proper numbered over 2,000 (total 168,253) while some 1,300 Jews from the surrounding areas also belonging to the community. In Sept. 1941 J. children were expelled from the public schools and most entered J. schools. Between Feb. 1942 and April 1943 most of the Jews were deported, the majority to the Westerbork transit camp. Community activities – cultural, educational, and religious – continued until the last deportations. Two J. families received permission to remain in U. while hundreds of Jews managed to hide (thanks to various organizations that refused to cooperate with the Germans, notably the *Kindercomite*, which saved J. children). After the Holocaust, some 500 Jews returned to U. from hiding and a few from the camps. A community was reestablished after the war.

UVAROVICHI   Gomel dist., Belorussia. The J. pop. was 622 (total 2,046) in 1897. The Hebrew writer Shaul Gurevich was born in U. In 1924–25, under the Soviets, 40 J. families earned their livelihoods in agriculture and an agricultural cooperative founded at the time had 11 J. members. Over half the Jews were artisans (tailors, bakers) organized in cooperatives. In

1930, 53 J. families were employed in two kolkhozes. In 1927–28, 81 J. children attended a four-year J. elementary school. In 1939 the J. pop. was 517. The Germans occupied the area in Aug. 1941. In Sept., all the Jews in the region were brought to U. and on 15 Nov., SD forces and local police executed the Jews outside the town. The 247 who survived were brought to a nearby kolkhoz and murdered there.

UVAROVO Moscow dist., Russia. Jews probably settled in the early 20th cent. The Germans arrived in Nov. 1941 and immediately murdered the few remaining Jews. A number of Jews were also murdered in the neighboring villages of Federovskoye, Vlasovo, and Selischivo.

UZDA Minsk dist., Belorussia. J. settlement probably commenced in the first half of the 18th cent. The J. pop. was 263 in 1765 and 2,068 (total 2,756) in 1897. On 12–13 July 1920, retreating Polish soldiers staged a pogrom, burning dozens of J. homes and exacting a heavy tribute. In the early 1930s, a J. council (soviet) and J. elementary school were still active. In 1930 a few dozen J. families farmed, 31 in a kolkhoz and ten outside it. In 1939, the J. pop. was 1,143. After the Germans occupied the town in late June 1941, Jews from U. and its environs were confined in a ghetto. On 16–17 Oct., a major *Aktion* took place and 1,740 Jews were murdered. Small groups of Jews were executed before and after the *Aktion*. A few were sent to the Minsk ghetto in late Feb. 1942, sharing the fate of the Jews there.

UZHOROD (Hung. Ungvar) Carpatho-Russia, Czechoslovakia, today Ukraine. Jews are mentioned in the late 17th cent. Ten families were present in 1747. The J. pop. then rose to 762 in 1830 and 4,497 (of a total 12,187) in 1880. A famous yeshiva with about 250 students was founded in the first half of the 19th cent. It was headed by one of the great halakhists in the Austro-Hungarian Empire, R. Meir Eisenstadt, the town's rabbi. The community also maintained a J. hospital, an old age home, and a school system that included a *talmud torah, heder,* elementary school, and Beth Jacob school for girls. In the period of the Czechoslovakian Republic, the J. pop. continued to grow, reaching 7,357 in 1930 and 9,576 (total 32,215) in 1941 under the Hungarians. Several Zionist organizations operated in U.

Synagogue in Uzhorod, Czechoslovakia, 1937

and the national executive of the J. National Party was located there. Some of its members served on the municipal and dist. councils. A J. elementary school and Hebrew secondary school were opened in the city. Many Jews belonged to the professional class: 24 doctors, 19 lawyers, and a number of senior officials in public and business administration. U. was annexed to Hungary in Nov. 1938. Under the new regime, J. livelihoods were hard hit. In 1940–41, hundreds of Jews were drafted into labor battalions, some under conditions of forced labor, others stationed on the eastern front, where most died. In late July and early Aug. 1941, dozens of J. families without Hungarian citizenship were expelled to Kamenets-Podolski and murdered there. After the German occupation of Hungary, a *Judenrat* and improvised ghetto were set up. Another 18,000 Jews were brought in from the district and in May 1944, all were deported to Auschwitz in seven transports. A few hundred survivors returned to U. after the war, most subsequently leaving for Czechoslovakia.

UZOK (Hung. Uzsok) Carpatho-Russia, Czechoslovakia, today Ukraine. Jews probably settled in the first half of the 19th cent. The J. pop. was 70 (total 572) in 1880 and 125 in 1910, dropping again to 76 in 1941. The Hungarians occupied the town in March 1939. In the second half of May 1944, the Jews were deported to Auschwitz.

UZPALIAI (Yid. Ushpal) Utena dist., Lithuania. Jews settled in the 18th cent. By 1897 the J. pop. was 691 (93% of the total), but by 1923 it was 551 (36%). All Zionist parties were active until the Soviet annexation of 1940. When the Germans entered U. on 26 June 1941, the Jews were forced into a ghetto. Groups of Jews were murdered. On 29 Aug. 1941 the remaining Jews in U. were taken to the Rase forest and executed.

UZVENTIS (Yid. Uzshvent) Siauliai dist., Lithuania. The first Jews arrived in the 18th cent. By 1897 the J. pop. was 330 (35% of the total); by 1923 it had dropped to 173 (22 %). In June 1939 a fire started by antisemites destroyed the main J. institutions. After Germany's invasion on 22 June 1941, J. refugees fled to U. Between 30 July and 8 Dec. 1941 all but a few of U.'s Jews and its refugees were murdered.

UZVIN Vinnitsa dist., Ukraine. Jews numbered 40 in 1765 and 445 (total 1,921) in 1897. In 1926, in the Soviet period, the J. pop. was 395. The Germans occupied U. on 18–19 July 1941. On 2 March 1942 they murdered 97 Jews, apparently all those who had not succeeded in fleeing.

Wedding in Uzpaliai, Lithuania (synagogue in background)

V

VABALNINKAS (also Abolnik; Yid. Vavolnik) Birzai dist., Lithuania. Jews began settling here in the 17th cent. A few of V.'s Jews emigrated to Eretz Israel before the Hovevei Zion period in the 19th cent. In 1897 the J. pop. was 1,828 (78% of the total). During WWI, Cossack soldiers staged a pogrom. Jews then were ordered to the interior of Russia and the town's four synagogues were burned. The J. pop. in 1940 was 500 (30%). After Germany's invasion of the USSR in June 1941, Lithuanian nationalists arrested many Jews. They were taken to Kupiskis and shot. The remaining Jews were ordered into a ghetto. Forty escaped and the rest were taken to the Zadeikiai forest, where they were shot and buried in pits.

VAC Pest dist., Hungary. A J. settlement existed under Turkish rule in the 16th cent., abandoned with the destruction of the town in 1684 and renewed in the mid-19th cent. Many Jews were wine and grain merchants and Jews dominated local trade. Two J.

Jewish mandolin and guitar orchestra, Vabalninkas, Lithuania, 1932 (The Jewish Museum, Lithuania/photo courtesy of Yad Vashem, The Holocaust Martyrs' and Heroes' Remembrance Authority, Jerusalem)

*Yeshiva students, Vac, Hungary, 1937 (Dr. Abraham Fuchs, Israel/photo courtesy of Yad Vashem, The Holocaust Martyrs' and Heroes'
Remembrance Authority, Jerusalem)*

printing presses produced some of the most important
Hebrew periodicals in Hungary, including *Tel Talpiot*
(1892–1938). A Status Quo community was founded
in 1875. A J. elementary school was opened in 1857,
augmented by junior high schools for boys and girls
in 1922. The J. pop. was 1,543 (12% of the total) in
1880 and 1,854 in 1941. In May 1944, the Jews
were brought to Monor and then deported to Auschwitz on 7–8 June.

VACHA   Thuringia, Germany. Jews settled in V. in
the first half of the 14th cent. They were expelled during the Black Death persecutions of 1348–49. A community began to develop in modern times and by 1841
there were 68 Jews in V. The community maintained a
synagogue and a cemetery dating back to the 17th cent.
The J. pop. was 121 in 1913. Of the 71 Jews who lived

in V. on the eve of the Nazi takeover in 1933, seven
died of natural causes and 33 emigrated, most to safe
havens in Palestine, England, and the U.S. On *Kristallnacht* (9–10 Nov. 1938), the synagogue was completely destroyed. No further information is available
about the fate of those who remained in V.

VACHNOVKA   Vinnitsa dist., Ukraine. The J. pop.
was 2,404 (total 5,371) in 1897. In an 1884 fire, 120
J. homes were destroyed. The synagogue in V. is believed to be one of the oldest in the region. Jews
were attacked in a pogrom on 8 July 1919. In 1926,
the J. pop. was 2,091. The Germans occupied V. between 20 and 22 July 1941. In early June 1942, the
Germans murdered hundreds of Jews in the Lipovets
area. On 3 June they murdered 413 from V., apparently
representing most of the Jews there.

VAD (Hung. Farkasrev) N. Transylvania dist., Rumania. Jews settled in the early 19th cent. The J. pop. in 1920 was 190 (9% of the total). In summer 1941 non-Hungarian Jews were handed over to the Germans and were murdered in Kamenets-Podolski. In April 1944 the rest were transferred to the Berbesti ghetto and in June deported to Auschwitz.

VADOKLIAI Panevezys dist., Lithuania. The J. pop. in 1923 was 79. All the Jews were killed in the Holocaust.

VADU RASCU (Yid. Rashkev) Bessarabia, Rumania, today Republic of Moldova. Jews settled after the Russian conquest of 1812 and grew tobacco and traded in hides and furs. In 1930 the J. pop. was 1,958. The majority of the J. pop. fled to the Russian side of the Dniester River after 22 June 1941.

VAIGUVA (Yid. Vaigeve) Siauliai dist., Lithuania. Jews began settling in the 19th cent. In 1897 the J. pop. was 193 (36% of the total). Famine caused much of V.'s pop. to leave. Ten J. families were present in 1939. After Germany's invasion of the USSR in June 1941, Lithuanian nationalists transferred all the Jews to nearby Kelme, where they were executed on 29 July 1941. The children, who had been separated from their parents, were murdered on 2 Oct.

VAINODE Kurzeme (Courland) dist., Latvia. A small community existed before WWI in the newly founded town, growing to 125 (total 1,416) in 1935 and operating a J. school. All the Jews were killed in late summer 1941 under the German occupation.

VAINUTAS (Yid. Vainute) Taurage dist., Lithuania. Jews began settling in the 17th cent. Prior to WWI there were about 80 J. families there. In the 1921 municipal elections, two Jews were elected to the 19-member city council. Many of V.'s Jews participated in Zionist activities. In the years prior to WWII, Lithuanian antisemitism culminated in a blood libel and pogrom in 1940. The J. pop. in 1940 was about 55 families. After Germany's invasion in June 1941, J. males aged 12 and up were taken to forced labor. The community's religious books were burned. Ninety J. men were executed in the Siaudvyciai forest; the other 30 were taken to the Haidekrug camp. Some were murdered, others died at Auschwitz and the Da-chau concentration camp. The women and children were murdered in the Gerainiai forest.

VAJA Szabolcs dist., Hungary. Jews are mentioned in 1770, trading in farm produce and operating most of the local estates. They later developed food-processing plants. The Jews numbered 123 in 1880 and 220 in 1930. The men were seized for forced labor in 1942 and the rest were sent to Kisvarda after the German occupation of spring 1944. From there, at the end of May, the Jews were deported to Auschwitz. Survivors failed to reestablish the community and most arrived in Israel.

VAJDACSKA Zemplen dist., Hungary. Jews probably arrived in the early 19th cent. and numbered 62 in 1930. In spring 1944, they were sent to Satoraljaujhely and from there, on 16–26 May, deported to Auschwitz. Those not gassed immediately were transferred to Bergen-Belsen as laborers.

VALASSKE MEZIRICI Moravia, Czechoslovakia. The J. community was established in 1891 with the J. pop. numbering 170 in 1921 and 135 (total 5,281) in 1930. The Zionists with their Tekhelet Lavan youth movement were active from 1923. Most Jews were deported to the Theresienstadt ghetto via Ostrava in Sept. 1942 and almost immediately thereafter to Maly Trostinec (Belorussia). A few managed to emigrate earlier, mostly to England and Palestine.

VALCAUL DE JOS (Hung. Alsovalko) N. Transylvania dist., Rumania. Jews settled in the late 18th cent. In 1920 the J. pop. was 106 (12% of the total). In May 1944, local and neighboring Jews were transferred to the Simleul Silvaniei ghetto and in June deported to Auschwitz.

VALDEMARPILS Kurzeme (Courland) dist., Latvia. Jews were present in the first quarter of the 18th cent. and numbered 1,197 in 1897 (total 1,774). Thereafter the J. pop. declined steadily, leveling off at around 160 between the World Wars. The Jews were supported by the Joint Distribution Committee and by relatives in the U.S. and South Africa until economic circumstances stabilized somewhat. All were murdered under the German occupation in summer or fall 1941.

VALEA LUI MIHAI (Hung. Ermihalyfalva) N. Transylvania dist., Rumania. Jews from Galicia settled around 1780 and engaged in agriculture and commerce. A junior high school was opened in 1873 and attended by most of the community's children. In 1898, 50 Hungarian hasidic rabbis convened in V. to protest against the critical attitude of the Orthodox rabbis in Budapest. In the late 19th cent., Anschel Bak opened a Hebrew printing press. The J. pop. in 1930 was 1,430 (20% of the total). Between the World Wars Jews were the leaders of local industry, employing hundreds of workers. Zionist activity began in the 1930s with the establishment of youth groups and in 1935 V. was the site of the Ha-No'ar ha-Tziyyoni national convention. In summer 1941, ten families were expelled across the border and murdered in Kamenets-Podolski. In May 1944 the community was transferred to the Oradea ghetto and then deported to Auschwitz. After the war some survivors returned but soon left.

VALEA LUI VLAD Bessarabia, Rumania, today Republic of Moldova. This J. settlement dates from 1836. Its settlers engaged in agriculture and in the wheat trade. In 1930 the J. pop. was 1,355, with a J. school in operation. The fate of the community during WWII is unknown. It is thought that some were killed in the village; others fled or were deported to Balti, the dist. capital.

VALEA-REA Moldavia dist., Rumania. Jews settled here in the early 19th cent. The J. pop. in 1895 was 250 (82%). In June 1941 all the Jews were expelled to Bacau; about half returned after the war.

VALEGOTSULOVO (after 1944, Dolinskoye) Odessa dist., Ukraine. Jews settled in the early 19th cent. A pogrom was staged in 1882. V. was the birthplace of the well-known J. composer Lazare Saminsky (1882–1959), who published studies on the history of J. music. In the 1920s, the Jews suffered from widespread unemployment despite the efforts of J. artisan cooperatives to solve the problem. The J. pop. grew from 1,865 (total 9,301) in 1897 to 2,549 in 1926 but dropped to just 541 in 1939. German and Rumanian forces captured V. on 7 Aug. 1941. Local Jews shared the fate of the other Jews in the area.

VALENCIENNES Nord dist., France. A small J. community was established in the 19th cent., inaugurating a synagogue in 1863. The community included

Jews of French origin and immigrants. During WWII, the Nord dist. came under the jurisdiction of the military commander of Belgium. On 13 June 1942, he ordered all the Jews to wear the yellow badge. Shortly afterwards 327 Jews were registered in V. Some were arrested but others were helped by their neighbors and acquaintances and thus escaped deportation. In 1964 there were 240 Jews in V., originating from Alsace, Poland, and North Africa.

VALGA Estonia. The community was founded in 1859 by three J. soldiers in the Russian army and grew to 784 (4% of the total) on the eve of WWI. Public life received a boost after the Feb. 1917 Revolution when J. soldiers in the Russian army set up Zionist and Bund organizations and published magazines in Russian and Yiddish. The J. school founded in 1926 was the only one in Estonia's provincial towns. It utilized Hebrew as the language of instruction and served as the community's cultural center. Economic conditions were satisfactory, with Jews working as tradesmen, laborers, teachers, and clerks. Emigration abroad and to Tallinn reduced the J. pop. to around 50 families in the 1930s (total 10,000). Under Russian rule (1940–41), J. community life came to a virtual end. On the approach of the Germans, some Jews managed to escape to the Soviet Union. The rest were murdered in summer or fall 1941 by the German *Sonderkommando 1a* with the assistance of the Estonian Omakaitse "self-defense" organization.

VALKA Vidzeme (Livonia) dist., Latvia. The community was established in the 1860s and numbered 380 in 1897. Most went over to the Estonian side of the town after it was divided in 1920. The J. pop. in 1935 was 57. Those not fleeing to the Soviet Union were murdered by the Germans and Latvians by the end of 1941.

VALKENBURG Limburg dist., Holland. A community existed by 1792. Its numbers increased from 1900 and reached 48 in 1924. In 1941, 33 refugees from Germany were living in V. The J. pop. in 1941 was 68 (total 8,913). In the Holocaust 46 perished and 16 survived in hiding.

VALLENDAR Rhineland, Germany. Jews were present in the 15th cent. The modern community was formed in the 18th cent. and included four protected

Jews (*Schutzjuden*) in 1781. Officially constituted in 1865, the community reached a peak in 1895 with 181 Jews. A new synagogue was erected in 1857 and a cemetery was opened in 1862. In 1933, 125 Jews remained, many emigrating by Nov. 1938. On *Kristallnacht* (9–10 Nov. 1938), the synagogue was burned, J. homes and stores were vandalized, and J. men were arrested. The last 40 Jews were deported to the death camps in 1942.

VALMIERA Vidzeme (Livonia) dist., Latvia. The first Jews were Cantonists conscripted into the Russian army under Nicholas I. In 1897 the J. pop. reached 166 (total 5,056) and was reduced by a third after WWI, with most engaged in trade. Economic conditions were satisfactory. The Germans arrived on 4 July 1941 and gave the Latvians a free hand to "purify" the town. The Jews, including refugees from Riga and other places, were executed in the forest, with the area declared "free of Jews" (*judenrein*) in Nov. 1941.

VALPOVO Croatia, Yugoslavia, today Republic of Croatia. The J. pop. was 157 in 1931 (total 3,730). Most perished during WWII.

VAMA (I) (Hung. Vamfalu) N. Transylvania dist., Rumania. Jews settled in the late 19th cent. The J. pop. in 1930 was 213 (8% of the total). In May 1944, the community was transferred to Satu Mare and in June deported to Auschwitz.

VAMA (II) Bukovina, Rumania. Jews settled in the late 19th cent. The J. pop. in 1930 was 392. In Oct. 1940, antisemites forced the J. pop. to flee to Gura–Humorului, from where, a year later, they were deported to Transnistria. Less than half returned.

VAMOSMIKOLA Bars–Hont dist., Hungary. Jews settled in the early 19th cent. Most were merchants and artisans, but several produced and exported kosher wine. Jews also established electricity and steam plants in V. A synagogue was erected in 1901. In 1930, the J. pop. was 133. In May 1944, the 113 remaining Jews were transferred to the Ipolysag ghetto and from there in mid-May to Auschwitz via Illesipuszta.

VAMOSPERCS Hajdu dist., Hungary. Jews settled in the first half of the 19th cent., controlling the area's trade in farm produce. The community maintained a synagogue and public school and grew to a pop. of 166 in 1880 and 294 in 1941. After WWI, J. property was looted and in 1939 Jews were seized for forced labor, many perishing in the Carpathian Mts. Most were deported to Auschwitz via Debrecen on 25–28 June 1944.

VANDZIOGALA (Yid. Vendzigole) Kaunas dist., Lithuania. Jews first settled here in the 17th cent. The J. pop. in 1897 was 374 (57% of the total). From the 1880s until WWI, many emigrated to the U.S. In WWI the Russian army expelled the Jews, many of whom returned later. In the 1920s the community's rabbi encouraged religious Zionism. When Germany invaded the country in June 1941, antisemitic decrees were promulgated. In July, 68 Jews were executed in the Borekas grove. On 9 Aug. 100 men were taken from the synagogue and murdered in Babtai, where the remaining Jews were shot at the end of Aug. 1941.

VAPNYARKA Vinnitsa dist., Ukraine. Eight Jews were present in 1784. In 1897, the J. pop. was 370 (total 760). On 20 Oct. 1905, 150 members of the Black Hundreds, an antisemitic organization that enjoyed government support, staged a pogrom against the Jews. A number of Jews were killed in another pogrom in May 1919. By 1939 the J. pop. was 711. The Germans occupied V. on 22 July 1941. After it was attached to Rumanian-administered Transnistria in early Sept., a camp was set up to which thousands of Jews from Rumania and from Chernovtsy (Cernauti) were expelled in 1941–42. Over a thousand were still alive there on 1 Sept. 1943.

VARAKLANI (Yid. Varaklian) Latgale dist., Latvia. The community was established in the late 18th cent. and grew to 1,365 (total 1,810) in 1897. Jews traded in farm produce and were also craftsmen who eked out a living by traveling from village to village. In this period emigration to the U.S. was stepped up but the J. pop. remained stable through WWI. In 1915, hundreds of J. refugees were accommodated in the town. About 50 J. homes were destroyed in the war. In the postwar period help from American relatives and the U.S. *Landsmannschaften* kept the community on its feet. Economic conditions worsened in the 1930s. In 1935 the J. pop. was 952 (total 1,661). The Jews led an active public and cultural life throughout the period, with almost all the political parties represented and the anti-Zionists predominating in the 1920s. From 1920 to 1934, J. mayors served the town and municipal council meetings were sometimes conducted in Yiddish. Antisemitic disturbances and Baptist missionary activity disturbed the community, which the right-wing press accused of organizing a pogrom against the Latvians. Twenty-two Jews were arrested in 1925 for complaining about attacks by local students, 13 being sentenced to two- to eight-month jail terms. Under Soviet rule (1940–41), J. property was nationalized and community life terminated. A few hundred Jews succeeding in fleeing to the Soviet Union on the approach of the Germans in June 1941. Those remaining were subjected to severe persecution by the Germans and Latvians and soon restricted to a ghetto under a regime of forced labor. On 4 Aug. 1941, 540 were taken to the J. cemetery and shot beside a pit that they themselves had been forced to dig.

VARAZDIN Croatia, Yugoslavia, today Republic of Croatia. Jews settled at the end of the 18th cent. and founded one of the first communities in Croatia (officially established in 1825 and including neighboring villages). Antisemitism was marked during the early period but was not present in the modern era until

the Holocaust. The J. pop. in 1931 was 486 (total 14,612). In May 1941 the Jews were sent to the Gospic, Jadovno, and Jasenovac camps, where most perished.

VAREL Oldenburg, Germany. Jews arrived in the late 17th cent., under Danish rule. Their number rose to 15 families in 1760 and reached a peak of about 85 Jews in the mid-19th cent. A J. cemetery was opened in the mid-18th cent. and a synagogue was consecrated in 1848. In June 1933, there were 39 Jews living in V. Many left the city and in Nov. 1938 only 20 remained. On *Kristallnacht* (9–10 Nov. 1938), the synagogue was almost completely destroyed, many Jewish businesses were looted, and J. men were sent to the Sachsenhausen concentration camp. Several Jews managed to leave, and six remained in May 1939. Their number rose to over 30 when elderly Jews from Oldenburg and Ostfriesland were brought to the city in 1941 and kept in one of the houses there. On 23 July 1942, all the remaining Jews were deported to the Theresienstadt ghetto. Some who left the city before the outbreak of WWII also perished in the death camps.

VARENA (Yid. Aran) Alytus dist., Lithuania. A few Jews lived in V. in the mid-18th cent. The J.

Market in Varena, Lithuania

pop. in 1897 was 1,473 (56% of the total). Prior to WWII, there were about 60 J. families with a Hebrew school and a *talmud torah*. The German army entered V. on 23 June 1941. On 28 June all J. men were ordered to report for forced labor, which they performed under difficult conditions, including abuse by Lithuanian nationalists. J. members of the Komsomol (Communist youth movement) were shot. A *Judenrat* was established. After incidents of murder and rape, the remaining Jews were murdered in a nearby forest on 9 Sept. 1941.

VARIN (Hung. Varna) Slovakia, Czechoslovakia, today Republic of Slovakia. Jews settled around the turn of the 18th cent., building a synagogue in the early 19th cent. and forming a Neologist community after the split in 1869. A J. elementary school with a few dozen students was in operation as the J. pop. grew from 242 in 1828 to 261 (total 1,390) in 1880. Thereafter it declined steadily as the young emigrated, mainly to Zilina. In 1940, the J. pop. was 67. The Zionists and the J. National Party were active between the World Wars. In the Slovakian state, J. men were seized for forced labor in 1941 and on 3 June 1942, the community was deported to the Lublin dist. (Poland) via Zilina, the able-bodied men to the Majdanek concen-

tration camp, the others to the Sobibor death camp where most perished.

VARNIAI (Yid. Vorne) Telsiai dist., Lithuania. Jews began settling in the 17th cent. The J. pop. in 1897 was 1,226 (39% of the total). The community maintained synagogues and a *heder*. Prior to WWI, a reformed *heder* was established where J. and secular subjects, including Hebrew, were taught. Its principal, Yeshayahu Ben-Zion Friedman, was a Zionist and his son, Mordekhai Ish-Shalom, served as mayor of Jerusalem (1960–65). Another native was Boris Schatz (1867-1939), founder of the Bezalel art school in Jerusalem. When Germany occupied V. during WWI, Jews were mobilized for forced labor. After the war, German deserters helped train Jews to defend themselves against the Lithuanians. Antisemitic acts between the wars led to emigration. The J. pop. in 1940 was 700 (32% of the total). In July 1941, after Germany's invasion in June, all of V.'s Jews were sent to nearby Viesvenai, where the men were executed. The women and children were then sent to Giruliai to be killed.

VARNSDORF Bohemia (Sudetenland), Czechoslovakia. Jews apparently settled only in the late 19th cent. and numbered 226 (total 22,621) in 1930. The

Jews of Varniai at social gathering

Zionists were very active at this time. Most left just before the Sudetenland was annexed to the German Reich in fall 1938. The others were deported to the death camps of Poland in 1942, with a few surviving the war in the Theresienstadt ghetto. Three labor camps for J. women operated nearby in 1943–45 (two in Jiretin pod Jedlovou, one in Dolni Podluzi). An unknown number of J. victims of the death march from the Schwarzheide concentration camp were buried in nearby Horni Chribska.

VARPALOTA Veszprem dist., Hungary. The J. settlement dating from the early 18th cent. enjoyed the protection of the counts of the Zichy family until 1848. The discovery of coal mines boosted the economy and in 1869 the J. pop. reached a peak of 695. A splendid new synagogue was consecrated in 1840 and a Status Quo community was formed in 1878. A J. elementary school was established. Jews set up a hospital for all residents of V., one of the few cities in Hungary where Jews remained untouched by the White Terror attacks (1919–21). In 1941, 211 Jews remained. All were deported to Auschwitz via Szekesfehervar on 17–21 June 1944.

VARVAROVKA Nikolaiev dist., Ukraine. Jews probably settled in the early 19th cent. and numbered 781 (total 2,532) in 1897. In 1905 they were attacked in a pogrom. In 1939, 135 remained. The Germans arrived on 14 Aug. 1941 and in Sept. murdered 117 Jews.

VARY (Hung. Vari) Carpatho-Russia, Czechoslovakia, today Ukraine. Jews probably settled in the mid-18th cent., with two J. families present in 1768. The J. pop. only grew in the 20th cent., reaching 179 under Czechoslovakian rule between the World Wars (total pop. 2,839 in 1941). Seventeen Jews engaged in trade, seven in crafts, and a few farmed. A Zionist youth group was active, sending a few of its members to Palestine before WWII. The Hungarians annexed the town in Nov. 1938 and in 1941 drafted a number of Jews into labor battalions for forced labor or assignments on the eastern front. The rest were deported to Auschwitz in the second half of May 1944.

VASAROSNAMENY Bereg dist., Hungary. Jews settled in the early 18th cent. as fishermen and barge operators. Galician Jews arrived in the 19th cent.

Many were active in the lumber industry and others opened factories. The J. pop reached 764 in 1930. From 1934, there was considerable Zionist activity. In 1941, those who could not prove Hungarian citizenship were sent to the Ukraine. The remaining Jews were deported to Auschwitz via Beregszasz on 22 May 1944. After WWII, 174 survivors reestablished the community, most leaving shortly afterwards.

VASILAU Bukovina, Rumania. A J. community existed in the late 19th cent. The J. pop. in 1930 was 231. The Zionist were active between the World Wars. In 1941, the J. pop. was transferred to Ocna-Bucovinei and shared the fate of the local Jews and other refugees. Few survived.

VASILEVICHI Polesie dist., Belorussia. A small number of Jews were apparently present in the 19th cent. Despite the residence ban introduced in 1882, Jews numbered 229 (total 1,968) in 1897. Residence was officially allowed only in 1903. In 1939, the J. pop. was 216. The Germans arrived on 25 Aug. 1941. In Feb. 1942 they murdered the 89 Jews who had not fled or been evacuated.

VASILEVKA Zaporozhe dist., Ukraine. In 1939, the J. pop. was 97 (total 5,620). The Germans captured the town on 4 Oct. 1941 and murdered the 42 remaining Jews in the same month.

VASILKOV Kiev dist., Ukraine. Jews numbered 1,478 in 1799 and 5,156 in 1897. Many Jews were employed as production workers and clerks in the city's brickyard or at one of its nine factories. In 1900, a new building was constructed for the *talmud torah* and secular studies were incorporated in the curriculum. A Zionist society was also founded around that time and in 1906–08 a number of families emigrated to Eretz Israel. In a pogrom staged by Anton Denikin's White Army soldiers on 7–13 April 1919, 110 Jews were murdered. Women and young girls were raped and J. stores and homes set on fire. In Sept. 1919, the Petlyura gangs attacked the Jews. In the Soviet period, a J. club and a Yiddish library were opened. In 1939, the J. pop. was 1,736. The Germans arrived on 31 July 1941 and murdered 220 Jews in Sept. Many Jews were also murdered in a second *Aktion* in 1942.

VASKAI (Konstantinovo) Birzai dist., Lithuania.

The Vasilkov Jewish school under construction, Poland (The Central Archive for the History of the Jewish People, Jerusalem/photo courtesy of Yad Vashem, The Holocaust Martyrs' and Heroes' Remembrance Authority, Jerusalem)

The first Jews settled here in the 17th cent. In 1897 the J. pop. was 440 (50% of the total). In WWI the Jews were expelled, some returning later. In the 1920s many emigrated to South Africa and the U.S. The J. pop. in 1940 was 340 (34%). After Germany's invasion in June 1941, alleged J. Communists were executed. In Aug. 1941 the remaining Jews were taken to Pasvalys and murdered.

VASKOVICHI   Zhitomir dist., Ukraine. Jews settled in the early 19th cent and numbered 198 (total 1,877) in 1897 and 234 in 1926 under the Soviets. After the arrival of the Germans on 8 July 1941, the few Jews perished.

VASLUI   Moldavia dist., Rumania. Jews first settled in the early 18th cent., mainly from Galicia and Buko-

vina. Merchants and artisans had their own community organization, hospital, school, burial societies, and ritual slaughterers. Zionist activity began already in 1880 and Hovevei Zion was established in 1894. The J. pop. in 1899 was 3,747 (31% of the total). In 1909 R. Shalom Halpern founded the V. hasidic dynasty. The J. pop. in 1941 was 2,904 (25% of the total). On 1 July 1941 all J. males up to age 60 were imprisoned in the synagogue and sent to forced labor in the area. Other Jews from the region were concentrated in V. From Sept. 1941 Jews were required to wear the yellow badge. Jews of Bessarabian origin were deported to the Caracal internment camp while others were expelled to Transnistria. The community continued to exist and resumed normal life after the war.

VASVAR   Vas dist., Hungary. Jews were present in

the 13th cent., resettling in the late 17th cent. after the Turkish destruction of V. in the 16th cent. They later founded an electricity company, brickyard, flour mill, and bank. An elementary school was established in 1860 and a synagogue in 1865. The Jews numbered 223 in 1930. In early July 1944, they were deported to Auschwitz.

VATRA-DORNEI Bukovina, Rumania. Jews first settled in the 17th cent. and monopolized the lumber trade. They also helped develop V. as a vacation and health resort. Zionist activity began in 1900. A J. school was opened prior to WWI where Hebrew was the language of instruction. In 1921, a vocational school was founded in which courses were taught in Yiddish. Antisemitism was widespread between the World Wars, especially under the Goga-Cuza regime. The J. pop. in 1930 was 1,737 (22% of the total). In Aug. 1941 the J. pop. was ghettoized and on 11 Oct. it was expelled to Atachi. One group was deported to Transnistria and the other to Lucavat, where the Jews were persecuted by the Ukrainian militia and sent to forced labor. Others were taken to Copaigorod, where the majority died of starvation and disease. When the survivors returned in March 1944 they found many J. refugees from elsewhere in Bukovina in the town.

VATRA-MOLDOVITEI Bukovina, Rumania. Jews settled in the mid-19th cent. In 1930 the J. pop. was 136. In Sept. 1940, the J. pop. was forced to move to Gura-Humorului and Campulung. In Oct. 1941 the Jews were deported to Transnistria. Almost all perished.

VCHERAISHE Zhitomir dist., Ukraine. Jews were present in the area but not in the town in the mid-19th cent. In 1897, the J. pop. was 1,108 (total 3,324), dropping to about 500 after the pogroms of the civil war (1918–21) and internal migration. The Germans captured V. on 16 July 1941, murdering 300 Jews, a third of them children, in a nearby forest.

VECA (Hung. Vagvecse) Slovakia, Czechoslovakia, today Republic of Slovakia. Jews settled in the 1740s, building a synagogue late in the cent. Their number rose rapidly in the 19th cent. to a peak of 500 (total 1,200) in 1869, thereafter declining steadily as many moved to neighboring Sala. R. Hillel Lichtenstein (1815–91), one of the great halakhists of Hungary,

was born in V. In 1941, 48 Jews remained. After the annexation to Hungary, they were persecuted and subjected to forced labor. The remaining 30 or so were deported by the Germans to Auschwitz via the Sala and Nove Zamky ghettoes in June 1944.

VECSES Pest–Pilis–Solt–Kiskun dist., Hungary. The organized community dates from 1904 and numbered 160 in 1930. All were deported to Auschwitz via Monor at the beginning of July 1944.

VEENDAM EN WILDERVANK Groningen dist., Holland. Jews lived in V. and W. from the late 17th and early 18th cents. The community grew significantly throughout the 19th cent. and reached a peak pop. of over 600 in the early 20th cent. A J. school had 89 pupils in 1858. In 1941 there were 105 Jews in V. and 122 in W. All were deported in the Holocaust; only four returned from the camps.

VEENENDAAL Utrecht dist., Holland. Jews were present in the mid-17th cent. and a community was probably established in the 1740s. It reached a peak pop. of 109 in 1860. In 1941 the J. pop. was 22 (total 12,321). In the Holocaust, 11 Jews were deported and perished; eight survived in hiding.

VEGERIAI (Yid. Veger) Mazeikiai dist., Lithuania. The J. pop. in 1940 was 50 (6% of the total). On 5 Aug. 1941 all of V.'s Jews were taken to Mazeikiai, where they were shot and buried in mass graves.

VEGHEL Noord-Brabant dist., Holland. Jews lived in V. from the 18th cent. and a community was established in the late 1820s, numbering 75 in 1900. The J. pop. in 1941 was 28 (total 8,818). In the Holocaust nine fled to other countries, four went into hiding, and 19 were deported and perished.

VEISIEJAI (Yid. Vishai) Seinai dist., Lithuania. Jews began settling here in the 18th cent. The J. pop. in 1897 was 974 (63% of the total). During WWI the Russian army expelled all the Jews, half of whom returned after the war. Between the World Wars emigration continued, with most of the young going to Lithuania's cities, the west, and Palestine. Zionist activity, which began in the late 19th cent., continued until WWII. The community's choir was famous throughout Lithuania. After Germany's invasion in June 1941, J.

males were seized for forced labor. All the Jews were transferred to the Katkiskes ghetto in Sept. and murdered on 3 Nov. 1941.

VEITSHOECHHEIM (in J. sources, Hechi) Lower Franconia, Germany. Jews numbered 105 in 1837 (total 1,346) and 36 in 1933, with a synagogue dating from 1730. In 1935–40, 31 left, 18 of them emigrating from Germany; the rest were deported to Izbica in the Lublin dist. (Poland) and to the Theresienstadt ghetto in 1942.

VEIVIRZENAI (Yid. Verzhan) Kretinga dist., Lithuania. A small group of Jews was living here in 1662. The J. pop. was 281 in 1847 and 259 in 1923 (28% of the total). Antisemitism increased in the 1930s. There was a Hebrew school and Zionist youth groups were active. After Germany's invasion in June 1941, 150 J. men were taken to the Silute labor camp. Fifty others were murdered. The women and children were taken outside the town and executed on 21 Sept. 1941 (Rosh Hashanah eve).

VELATIN (Hung. Velete) Carpatho-Russia, Czechoslovakia, today Ukraine. Jews probably settled at the turn of the 18th cent. and numbered 45 in 1840 and 267 in 1880. In 1921, under Czechoslovakian rule, their pop. reached 414 and in 1941, 436 (total 3,670). Such political groups as Tze'irei Mizrachi, Hehalutz, and Agudat Israel were active between the World Wars. The Hungarians occupied the town in March 1939 and in 1940 drafted a few dozen Jews into forced labor battalions. In Aug. 1941, six J. families without Hungarian citizenship were expelled to Kamenets-Podolski, where they were murdered. The rest were deported to Auschwitz in the second half of May 1944.

VELBERT Rhineland, Germany. The J. pop. was 38 in 1871 and reached a peak of 80 (total 19,730) in 1909. The V.-Heiligenhaus community was affiliated with the Orthodox Adass Jisroel congregation of Elberfeld. Jews were attacked at a funeral in 1894 and the J. cemetery was desecrated in 1905, in 1910, and again in 1928. In 1933, the J. pop. was 58. At the outset of Nazi rule, the mayor advised local residents to break off business relations with the Jews. On *Kristallnacht* (9–10 Nov. 1938), the synagogue was burned (though the building had been sold in 1934); J. homes

and stores were destroyed; the cemetery was vandalized; and six Jews were sent to the Dachau concentration camp. Between Sept. 1939 and April 1940, 30 Jews emigrated. Eighteen Jews were sent to their deaths in the concentration camps between Sept. 1941 and late 1944.

VELEDNIKI Zhitomir dist., Ukraine. The local proprietor Count Potocki permitted J. tailors and furriers to form a guild in 1757, extending the right to all J. artisans in 1783. The J. pop. was 152 in 1765 and 569 (total 1,143) in 1897. Between the World Wars, the J. pop. dropped to about 400. The Germans entered V. on 24 Aug. 1941. Some Jews presumably fled to safety. Those who remained were murdered in the first days of the occupation.

VELIKA DOBRON (Hung. Nagydobrony; Yid. Groys Dobron) Carpatho-Russia, Czechoslovakia, today Ukraine. Jews probably settled in the early 19th cent, numbering six in 1830 and 123 (total 2,087) in 1880. In 1921, in the Czechoslovakian Republic, their pop. reached 227, with 17 engaged in trade and 12 in crafts. Jews owned a flour mill and a farm where a number of J. families worked. The Hungarians annexed V. in Nov. 1938, expelling a few dozen Jews without Hungarian citizenship to Kamenets-Podolski, where they were murdered. In 1941, the J. pop. was 275. The last 17 or so Jews were deported to Auschwitz in the second half of May 1944.

VELIKA KOPANA (Hung. Felsoveresmart; Yid. Groys Kopanie) Carpatho-Russia, Czechoslovakia, today Ukraine. Jews probably settled in the mid-18th cent. Three J. families (16 people) were present in 1768. The J. pop. then rose to 112 in 1830 and 226 (total 1,292) in 1880. In 1921, in the Czechoslovakian Republic, the J. pop. rose to 273 and in 1941 to 314. During this period, 16 Jews were tradesmen, three were artisans, a few were farmers, and a few engaged in the building trades. Jews also owned a flour mill. The Zionists were active. The Hungarians occupied V. in March 1939 and in 1941 drafted a few dozen Jews into forced labor battalions, sending some to the eastern front, where most died. In Aug. 1941, a number of J. families without Hungarian citizenship were expelled to Kamenets-Podolski and murdered. About 300 were deported to Auschwitz in the second half of May 1944.

VELIKE GEJOVCE (Hung. Nagygejoc; Yid. Gevits) Carpatho-Russia, Czechoslovakia, today Ukraine. Jews probably settled in the late 18th cent., numbering 52 in 1830 and 183 (total 1,105) in 1880. In 1921, in the Czechoslovakian Republic, their pop. was 120 and in 1941 it was 69. The Hungarians annexed the town in Nov. 1938 and in 1941 about half the Jews were expelled to Kamenets-Podolski and murdered. The rest were deported to Auschwitz on 28 May 1944.

VELIKE KOMNATY (Hung. Magyarkomjat; Yid. Komyat) Carpatho-Russia, Czechoslovakia, today Ukraine. Jews are first mentioned in the late 17th cent. Apparently they abandoned the town in the late 18th cent., returning in the mid-19th. In 1880, their pop. was 296 (total 2,230), rising to 416 in 1921. Many were farmers, 11 were tradesmen, and seven were artisans. The Hungarians occupied V. in March 1939, drafting a few dozen Jews into forced labor battalions and expelling others without Hungarian citizenship to Kamenets-Podolski, where they were murdered. In 1941, the J. pop. was 413. The remaining Jews were deported to Auschwitz in the second half of May 1944.

VELIKE LOUCKY (Hung. Nagylucska; Yid. Groys Litshik) Carpatho-Russia, Czechoslovakia, today Ukraine. Jews probably settled in the late 18th cent., numbering 20 in 1830 and 130 (total 3,283) in 1880. In 1921, in the Czechoslovakian Republic, the J. pop. rose to 156 while in 1941 it was 339. Most Jews (25) engaged in trade; 15 were artisans and two flour mills were in J. hands. The Hungarians occupied V. in March 1939 and in 1941 drafted dozens of Jews into labor battalions for forced labor on the eastern front, where many perished. In late July 1941, a few J. families without Hungarian citizenship were expelled to Kamenets-Podolski, where they were murdered. About 300 were deported to Auschwitz in the second half of May 1944.

VELIKII ZHVANCHIK Kamenets-Podolski dist., Ukraine. Jews arrived in the 18th cent., numbering 22 in 1765 and increasing to 638 (21% of the total) in 1897. In 1923, in the Soviet period, the J. pop. stood at 556. A J. council (soviet) was active in the 1920s and 1930s. The Nazis arrived in mid-July 1941 and on 1 Sept. executed 1,224 people from V. and its environs in the Sokoletz forest.

VELIKIYE LUKI Kalinin dist., Russia. J. settlement probably began in the mid-19th cent. Only 19 Jews were present in 1861. In 1869, Jews from Nevel whose homes had burned down were given permission to reside in V. The principal occupation of the Jews was sewing. In 1897, their pop. was 669 (total 8,466). A synagogue was functioning in the early 20th cent. In 1905, a number of Jews were killed in a pogrom. In the Soviet period, the J. pop. was 1,627 in 1926 and 1,519 in 1939. The Germans first captured V. on 19 July 1941. They were driven out within a few days but returned on 24 Aug. to occupy the city until Jan. 1943. By German count, only 59 Jews remained in Sept. 1941; they were murdered shortly thereafter.

VELIKY BOCKOV (Hung. Nagybocsko; Yid. Bychkev) Carpatho-Russia, Czechoslovakia, today Ukraine. Jews settled in the early 18th cent., with two families living there in 1728. The town was then abandoned and Jews only returned in the mid-19th cent. Their pop. rose to 520 (total 3,605) in 1880 and the community supported a rabbi and a number of welfare and charity organizations, such as Bikkur Holim. The growth of the community continued in the Czechoslovakian period, reaching a figure of 1,092 in 1921. In 1941, the J. pop. was 1,708. About 30 J. families earned their livelihoods in trade and 16 in crafts. Jews also owned a sawmill, flour mill, and brickyard and a number were professional people and government officials. The Zionist youth organizations were active. The Hungarians occupied V. in March 1939, forcing Jews out of their occupations and in 1940–41 drafting dozens into forced labor battalions and sending some to the eastern front where they perished. In late July 1941, a few J. families were expelled to Kamenets-Podolski and murdered. The rest were deported to Auschwitz in late May 1944. After the war, a few dozen survivors returned but most left for Czechoslovakia. A small community existed until 1950.

VELIKY PALAD (Hung., Nagypalad; Yid. Groys Palad) Carpatho-Russia, Czechoslovakia, today Ukraine. About 40 J. families were living in V. between the World Wars. The young were members of Tze'irei Mizrachi. The Hungarians occupied the town in March 1939. In the second half of May 1944, the remaining Jews (134 in April) were deported to Auschwitz.

VELIKY RAKOVEC (Hung. Nagyrakoc; Yid.

Groys Rakovits) Carpatho-Russia, Czechoslovakia, today Ukraine. Six J. families were present in 1728. The J. pop. was 35 in 1830 and 286 (total 2,074) in 1880. In 1921, under the Czechoslovakians, the J. pop. rose to 399. Jews owned 11 business establishments, two flour mills, and a distillery. A number of Jews were engaged in crafts and agriculture. The Hungarians occupied the town in March 1939 and in 1941 drafted several dozen Jews into forced labor battalions. The J. pop. was 374 in 1941. In Aug., a number of J. families without Hungarian citizenship were expelled to Kamenets-Podolski and murdered. The remaining 50 families were deported to Auschwitz in the second half of May 1944.

VELIUONA (Yid. Velon) Kaunas dist., Lithuania. The first Jews arrived here in the 15th cent. In WWI the Russians expelled all the Jews, some of whom returned after the war. In the 1920s a secular J. community existed in V. In 1923 the J. pop. was 335 (71% of the total). Many emigrated to the west and to larger Lithuanian cities. Yiddish culture was well represented, though there was a Zionist camp also. The J. pop. in 1940 was about 40 families. After Germany's invasion in June 1941 the Jews were abused, first by the Lithuanian nationalists, then by Germans. Most of the Jews were murdered in July 1941. Those who survived (mostly women and children) were executed in Sept.

VELIZH Smolensk dist., Russia. Jews probably settled in the mid-18th cent. Their pop. rose from about 300 in 1797 to 3,080 in 1847 and 5,989 (total 12,193) in 1897. In 1823–35, a number of Jews stood trial in a blood libel. They were finally exonerated but not before a few died in prison. In the 1880s, the community maintained a synagogue and seven prayer houses. A state J. school for 100 students with a vocational-training department was opened in 1883. A private J. school for boys was opened in the early 20th cent. Most of the 650 artisans in the town were Jews while hundreds of J. families earned their livelihoods in petty trade. During the Soviet period, the J. pop. declined to 3,274 in 1926 and 1,788 in 1939. During the 1920s a few J. cultural institutions were still in operation, including a kindergarten, J. school, and small library and reading room. The Germans captured V. on 13 July 1941, confining the Jews to a camp under a *Judenrat*. On 21 Sept., they murdered about 150 young Jews outside the town and in early Nov. transferred

1,000, including Jews from the surrounding area, to a ghetto. In late Jan. 1942, the Germans set the ghetto on fire. Hundreds perished in the flames and others were shot to death trying to escape. Twenty, including five children, succeeded in fleeing and survived.

VELKA BYTCA (Hung. Nagybicscse) Slovakia, Czechoslovakia, today Republic of Slovakia. A few Jews were present in the early 18th cent. with an organized community apparently established in the early 1770s. In 1776, Count Esterhazy gave the community land for a synagogue and cemetery against a yearly payment and extended his protection over the Jews. A J. school was opened in 1850 and the congregation embraced Neoligism in the late 19th cent. The J. pop. grew from 147 in 1828 to a peak of 619 (total 3,122) in 1910. A new synagogue was built in 1886 and the Zionists became active in the early 20th cent., continuing to operate extensively after WWI. The J. pop. dropped sharply between the World Wars, standing at 316 in 1940. Jews were active in public life, serving on the local council. They owned 58 business establishments (16 groceries, ten taverns and restaurants),14 workshops, and seven factories, including a beer brewery, sawmill, and match factory. The Slovakian authorities closed down most J. businesses in 1941. In late March 1942, dozens of young J. men were deported to the Majdanek concentration camp and the women to Auschwitz. Through the summer, families were sent to the death camps via Zilina, increasing the total deported in 1942 to two-thirds of the community. Others fled before the Germans arrived in Sept. 1944. Those caught were murdered by the SS or sent to Auschwitz.

VELKA IDA (Hung. Nagyida) Slovakia, Czechoslovakia, today Republic of Slovakia. Jews probably settled in the late 18th cent. A modest synagogue was erected in the early 19th cent. and the community reached a peak pop. of 210 (total 1,706) in 1880. Yitzhak Bilitzer served as rabbi (1835–87) and headed a yeshiva and *talmud torah* and R. Tzevi Reichman served from 1887 to 1937. In 1941, 109 Jews remained. After the annexation to Hungary, they were persecuted and seized for forced labor. In April 1944, the last 100 or so were transferred to a ghetto and on 15 May deported to Auschwitz.

VELKE KAPUSANY (Hung. Nagykapos) Slovakia, Czechoslovakia, today Republic of Slovakia. Jews settled in the 18th cent. The community began to grow when the town became a county seat in 1848, reaching a pop. of 268 in 1869. A synagogue was consecrated in 1891. After WWI, in the Czechoslovakian Republic, the Zionists and Agudat Israel became active and Jews served on the municipal council. In 1921 Jews owned 42 business establishments and ten workshops. The J. pop. grew to 464 (total 2,668) in 1941. In 1940–41, after the annexation to Hungary (Nov. 1938), dozens of Jews were seized for forced labor, many dying on the eastern front. On 16 April 1944, after the German occupation, the Jews were transferred to the Uzhorod ghetto and from there deported to Auschwitz in mid-May. Most of the postwar community of 224 left for Israel and other countries in 1949.

VELKE KOSTOLANY (Hung. Nagykosztolany) Slovakia, Czechoslovakia, today Republic of Slovakia. Jews probably settled in the early 18th cent., most of them Moravian refugees. A new influx of Jews from Moravia further increased the pop. in the mid-18th cent. As economic conditions improved in the 19th cent., the growth of the J. pop. accelerated to 151 in 1828 and 200 (total 1,343) in 1869. A J. elementary school was opened in the mid-19th cent. The J. pop. declined steadily in the 20th cent. as many left for neighboring Piestany. In 1940, 76 Jews remained. A Zionist group was active and Jews owned a number of groceries and butcher shops. In the Slovakian state, the J. school was reopened to accommodate J. children expelled from public schools. J. businesses were closed down in 1941 and in spring 1942 most Jews were deported to the east, where they perished.

VELKE MEZIRICI Moravia, Czechoslovakia. Jews probably arrived after the expulsions from Jihlava (1426) and Brno and Znojmo (1454). A new community, founded after the depredations of the Thirty Years War (1618–48), numbered 32 families in 1710. Three synagogues existed side by side in the J. ghetto along the banks of the Oslava River, the oldest dating from the early 16th cent. and the most recent from 1867. Fires and floods repeatedly devastated the community in the 18th–19th cents. Most Jews were peddlers in the first half of the 18th cent. In the late 19th cent., Jews operated factories (cloth, glue). Their number reached 1,116 in 1857 but subsequently dropped steadily to 650 (total 5,623) in 1880, 289 in 1900, and 76 in

1930. The Jews were apparently deported to the Theresienstadt ghetto together with the Jews of Brno in late 1941–early 1942 and from there to the death camps of Poland.

VELKE RIPNANY (Hung. Nagyrepeny) Slovakia, Czechoslovakia, today Republic of Slovakia. J. settlement probably began in the 1830s. The J. pop. reached a peak of 131 (total 699) in 1880. A J. elementary school was opened in the 1870s and a handsome synagogue was erected in 1904. Emigration of the young caused the J. pop. to decline to 70–80 in the 20th cent. After the establishment of the Slovakian state in March 1939, J. children were expelled from the public schools and J. businesses were closed down. About 50 Jews were deported to the Lublin dist. (Poland) on 16 April 1942 and perished. Others hid or were rounded up by the Germans in 1944.

VELKY BEREZNY (Hung. Nagyberezna; Yid. Groys Berezna) Carpatho-Russia, Czechoslovakia, today Ukraine. J. settlement apparently commenced in the first half of the 18th cent. Two families (eight Jews) were present in 1746. The J. pop. then grew to 159 in 1830 and 492 (total 1,683) in 1880. In 1921, under the Czechoslovakians, it rose to 979 and again to 1,237 in 1941. In this period, Shelomo Yehoshua Schreiber served as the community's rabbi, also running a yeshiva for 70 students. The community maintained a number of welfare and charity organizations, such as Bikkur Holim and Gemilut Hasadim. The young belonged mainly to Zionist groups. Jews owned 42 business establishments, a distillery, a bank, and a few small factories. Thirty-one Jews were artisans and several were professionals (including four doctors, and three lawyers). The Hungarians occupied the town in March 1939, cutting the Jews off from their livelihoods. In 1940–41 a few dozen were drafted into forced labor battalions, some perishing on the eastern front. In late July 1941, a number of J. families without Hungarian citizenship were deported to Kamenets-Podolski, where they were murdered. The rest were deported to Auschwitz in May 1944.

VELKY MAGER (Hung. Nagymagyar; Yid. Magendorf) Slovakia, Czechoslovakia, today Republic of Slovakia. According to tradition, J. refugees from Vienna settled in 1670. In the 1770s, the community purchased land to erect a modest synagogue and other facilities. A *talmud torah* operated from the early 19th cent. and a J. school from 1859. In 1888 a *beit midrash* and yeshiva were added. The J. pop. reached a peak of 379 (total 1,275) in 1880 but then declined somewhat as the young left for the big cities. Before WWI, 23 settlements were under the auspices of the local rabbinate. Agudat Israel became active in the 1920s and the Zionist Organization in the 1930s. In 1941, under Hungarian rule, the J. pop. was 251. Dozens of J. men were seized for forced labor. On 11 June 1944, after the German occupation, about 350 Jews from V. and its environs were transferred to the Dunajska Streda ghetto; on 16 June they were deported to Auschwitz.

VELKY MEDER (Hung. Nagymegyer) Slovakia, Czechoslovakia, today Republic of Slovakia. Jews settled around the mid-18th cent., apparently in limited numbers owing to local opposition. In the 19th cent. the community maintained a synagogue, cemetery, elementary school, *beit midrash*, and *talmud torah*. The J. pop. increased to 217 in 1869 (total 2,831) and 416 in 1919. Under Czechoslovakian rule after WWI, Jews owned most of the town's commercial establishments (14 of 18 groceries; all 12 cloth and clothing outlets; and all eight lumber and heating fuel businesses). The Zionists and Agudat Israel were active, with Hashomer Hatzair operating from the 1930s and Orthodox girls organized in the Beth Jacob movement. In 1941 the J. pop. reached a peak of 522. Persecution commenced with the annexation to Hungary in Nov. 1938. Jews were seized for forced labor and deprived of their sources of livelihood. After the arrival of the Germans in 1944 the Jews were rounded up and in mid-June they were deported to Auschwitz via Komarno. Most of the postwar community of 100 left by 1949.

VELKY SARIS (Hung. Nagysaros) Slovakia, Czechoslovakia, today Republic of Slovakia. Jews were probably present in the late Middle Ages and returned in the 18th cent. after being expelled in the 16th. They built a *beit midrash* c. 1820 which was later converted into a synagogue. The J. pop. reached a peak of 202 (total 2,792) in 1828 before emigration to the cities from the late 19th cent. reduced it to 136 in 1900 and 76 in 1940. Between the World Wars, Jews owned a few shops and taverns. Most were deported to the Rejowiec ghetto in the Lublin dist. (Poland) on 23 May 1942 and most perished.

VENCSELLO Szabolcs dist., Hungary. Jews arrived in the late 18th cent. and numbered 55 in 1930. Most were small merchants. On 17 May 1944, they were deported to Auschwitz via Nyiregyhaza.

VENDERSHEIM Hesse, Germany. Numbering 49 in 1828, the community dwindled to six in 1933 and by 1938 no Jews remained.

VENEV Tula dist., Russia. Jews probably settled in the early 20th cent. Twenty-one were present in 1926. During the short German occupation of 25 Nov.–11 Dec. 1941, the few who had not been evacuated or had not fled were murdered.

VENICE Veneto, Italy. There is evidence of Jews in V. as early as the 11th–12th cents. V. was a necessary stopover for merchants on their travels between east and west and J. merchants traveling from Germany and France to the Byzantine Empire and the Middle East made business contracts to reside in Venice, called *condotte*. Temporary residence often ended in permanent settlement. Acting primarily as wholesale merchants and moneylenders, the Jews were not allowed to reside in the city proper but only on the nearby island of Spinalunga. According to a decree from 1290, they were obliged to pay a special tax of 5% on all their export and import transactions. At first, loan banks were opened at Mestre, a small town near V., but in 1366, Jews were allowed to reside in the city itself and open loan banks. Although permitted to live in V., they had to wear a yellow badge in the form of a circle on their clothing, later altered to a yellow hat, and finally to a red hat. In March 1516, a decision was made to separate the Jews from the rest of the community and they were ordered to reside in a separate quarter, known as the "Ghetto Nuovo." The area added in 1541 was called "Ghetto Vecchio," the Old Ghetto, while the "Ghetto Nuovissimo," Newest Ghetto, the small northeastern section, was added in 1633. In 1589, many Portuguese Marranos were allowed to come to V. and since they had returned to Judaism, they settled in the Ghetto Vecchio. They developed the international trade of the city. Levantine Jews enjoyed special consideration from the city authorities. These Jews conducted a flourishing trade in expensive cloth, jewels, and precious objects. The Jews of German origin, the Ashkenazim, also prospered, establishing a synagogue, the Scola Grande Tedesca, in 1528–

29 in the Ghetto Nuovo. A second Ashkenazi synagogue, the Scola Canton, was built in 1531–32 in a corner of the Ghetto Nuovo and renovated in 1736 and 1859. The Scola Levantine (Levantine Synagogue) was built in 1538 and the Scola Spagnola (Spanish Synagogue), the largest synagogue in V., was built in 1555 and rebuilt a century later. The Italian Synagogue was built in 1575. In the early 16th cent., Daniel Bomberg, a Christian from Antwerp, established a Hebrew printing press. In 1545, Marco Antonio Giustiniani, a nobleman, also established a Hebrew press. In 1549, another nobleman, Alvise Bragadini, began printing Hebrew books. In 1553, Pope Julius III ordered the public burning of the Talmud and related books. Economic prosperity led to the emergence of many cultural and educational societies and associations. Among the community's illustrious scholars and rabbis were Yehuda Katzenellenbogen, who served as rabbi for over 50 years and died in 1597, Leon da Modena (1571–1648), Simone Luzzatto (1583–1663), and Shemuel Aboab (1616–94). In 1655, the J. pop. of V. was approximately 4,800. In the 17th and 18th cents., the role of the Jews in the economic and commercial sphere declined with the Republic. The threat of the Ottoman Empire's growing power led the authorities to seek additional sources of finance. They imposed heavy taxes and borrowed large amounts of money from the Jews. Many Jews of Levantine and Portuguese origin left V. for places with more active commerce. In 1737, the J. moneylenders went bankrupt. Many Jews in V. were peddlers, merchants of used clothing, and tailors. With Napoleon's victory in 1797, a democratic government was established and the Jews were granted equality. The ghetto gates were demolished and the street leading to the ghetto was renamed "Contrada dell Unione," the Street of the Union. Following the 1797 Treaty of Campoformio, V. came under Austrian rule and the Jews lost their rights, but they were no longer confined to the ghetto. A 1797 census listed 1,626 Jews in V. In 1806, Napoleon, as ruler of Italy, including V., reinstated the rights of the Jews. In the Paris Sanhedrin, the community of V. was represented by three rabbis: Yaakov Emmanuel Cracovia, Aharon Lattes, and Avraham Tedesco. In 1815, V. was again conquered by Austria and the restrictions on the Jews were reinstated. The Second Republic established following the 1848 revolution was headed by a citizen of J. origin, Daniele Manin, and two of the ministers were also Jews: Isacco

Pesaro Maurogonato and Leone Pincherlee. In Aug. 1849 the Austrians returned and once again the rights of the Jews were annulled, to be restored only in 1866, when V. became part of the Kingdom of Italy. In 1869, the J. community of V. consisted of 2,430 Jews; in 1900, 2,800. According to the 1930 law reforming the J. communities of Italy, V. was declared one of 26 recognized communities. Its jurisdiction included Conegliano (ten Jews in 1936), Belluno Treviso (35 Jews in 1873; 30 in 1936), and Vittorio Veneto (50 Jews in 1873; ten in 1936). By 1938, the community included 2,000 Jews. During WWII, on 17 Sept. 1943, Giuseppe Jona, the president of the J. community, committed suicide to avoid giving the Germans a list of Jews in the city. During the night of 5–6 Dec. 1943, 150 Jews were arrested. At first they were held at the Marco Foscarini College, then transferred to the S. Maria Maggiore prison, and finally to the Fossoli concentration camp. On 22 Feb. 1944, they were deported to Auschwitz. In summer 1944, 90 Jews were arrested in V. and taken to the La Risiera di S. Sabba camp. Among the deportees, 20 were taken from the J. convalescence home and 29 from the J. hospital. Chief Rabbi Adolfo Ottolenghi was also deported at this time. Several died in the camp and the rest were deported to death camps in Poland and Germany. Altogether, 205 Jews were deported to death camps between 9 Nov. 1943 and 17 Aug. 1944. After liberation in 1945, there were 1,050 Jews in the community. In 1965, there were 844 Jews in V., dropping to 600 in 1987.

VENLO Limburg dist., Holland. Jews lived in V. in the 14th, 15th, and 16th cents. but the settlement ended in 1546. The settlement was renewed in the early 19th cent. and numbered 123 Jews in 1855. A synagogue and social welfare organizations were established during the cent. In 1931 a pro-Zionist cultural association (De Joodsche Vriendenkring) was founded, which organized all social and cultural activities. By 1938 there were 89 German refugees in V. The J. pop. in 1941 was 139 (total 39,286). In the Holocaust 70 Jews were deported; 64 of them perished in the camps, six survived, another 39 Jews survived by hiding in Christian homes, and a few left for other countries. A small J. community was active after the war.

VENNINGEN Palatinate, Germany. Twelve families (55 Jews) were present in the mid-19th cent., half of them farming, the other half in trade. A synagogue was consecrated in 1847 and a cemetery in 1887. In 1875, the J. pop. was 78 (total 914), dropping to 53 in 1900 and 29 in 1932. Most Jews left after *Kristallnacht* (9–10 Nov. 1938), about half emigrating and the other half moving to other places in Germany. The last two Jews were deported to the Gurs concentration camp in Oct. 1940.

VENTSPILS (Yid. Venden, Vindoy) Kurzeme (Courland) dist., Latvia. There was a J. presence from the 17th cent. but the community only began to develop under Russian rule from 1795, reaching a pop. of 1,407 (total 5,872) in 1881. Thereafter emigration across the sea curbed the growth of the community until a new wave of settlers, including most of the Jews of Piltene, arrived in the early 20th cent. and brought the J. pop. up to around 5,000 on the eve of WWI. Jews owned most of the stores and workshops in the town, while J. merchants were prominent in the lumber trade and J. bankers and contractors were central figures on the local stock exchange commission. The Bund took an active part in the 1905 revolution. In 1915 the Jews were expelled from V. by the Russian army. Most settled in Orsha in Russia's Mogilev province and with a relatively small percentage returning, the J. pop. stood at 1,276 in 1925 (total 16,384). J. life was rehabilitated between the World Wars with the aid of the Joint Distribution Committee, while political life came under the dominance of the Zionists. The Betar branch founded in the 1920s was among the earliest in Latvia and the Maccabi sports club operating from 1920 was one of the largest in Latvia with hundreds of members. A J. grade school enrolled 200 of the town's 300 J. children and a J. high school had 40 students in 1929. Other children studied at a *talmud torah*. The Jews continued to dominate trade and owned seven of the town's 12 sawmills. The Soviets annexed V. in Aug. 1940 and brought J. communal and commercial life to an end. The Germans entered V. on 1 July 1941. The thousand or so Jews in the town were herded into the synagogues and a few dilapidated buildings near the Wenta River and subjected to severe persecution and forced labor. Towards the end of July 1941 a few hundred J. men were executed in the Kazin forest by German and Latvian firing squads; another 200 Jews were murdered there in Sept. and 533, mostly women and children, on 3–17 Oct. 1941.

VERBOVETS Vinnitsa dist., Ukraine. Jews settled in the early 18th cent., numbering 202 in 1765 and 661 (total 2,311) in 1897. In 1926, under the Soviets, the J. pop. was 165. In WWII the Jews were expelled to Murovanye Kurilovtsy, where they were murdered.

VERCELLI Piedmont, Italy. The J. presence in V. dates back to 1446, when Abramo della Vigneria and his son Angelo established a loan bank there. In 1448, the local Jews were compelled to reside in a separate quarter. They were expelled in 1556, but were readmitted on payment of a large sum. In 1597, the community absorbed the Jews expelled from Milan. In 1624, there were eight loan bankers in V. Planning of the ghetto began in 1727, but the J. community, consisting of 29 families (159 individuals), only moved in in 1740. They were forced to live there until 1798. In 1740, a new synagogue was inaugurated in the ghetto. Elia Emanuele Foa (1750–96), a renowned figure in V., bequeathed his fortune to the community and the funds were used to establish the Collegio Foa in 1829, where many Italian rabbis and teachers were trained. With the arrival of Napoleon, in Dec. 1798, the four gates of the ghetto were torn down. R. Giosue (Salvador) Segre of V. was one of the eight Italian rabbis present at the Paris Sanhedrin in 1806. He and R. Abram Vita Cologna of Mantua were also members of the Central Consistory established in 1808 in Paris. With Napoleon's downfall, former restrictions were once again reintroduced. By 1816, however, many restrictions were abolished, including the obligation to wear the J. badge. In 1848, the 600 Jews of V. were granted citizenship. In 1853, Giuseppe Levi and Esdra Pontremoli founded the journal *L'Educatore Israelitica*. It was superseded in 1878 by the *Vessillo Israelitico*. In 1873, the J. community numbered 500. In 1878, a new synagogue was inaugurated. By 1882, the community reached a peak pop. of 580 individuals, dwindling to 360 in 1910. Its spiritual leader was R. I. C. Cingoli. According to the 1930 law reforming the J. communities, V. was a recognized community among the 26 communities of Italy. Its district included Novara (95 Jews in 1873; eight in 1936), Biella, and Trino (95 Jews in 1873; eight in 1936). In 1931, the J. pop. of V. was 275, decreasing to 165 in 1936. During the Holocaust, 26 local Jews were deported to death camps. After the war, there were 130 Jews in the V. dist. and 75 in 1969.

VERDEN AN DER ALLER Hanover, Germany.

The first reliable evidence of the presence of Jews dates from 1571, but a permanent J. settlement only developed at the end of the 18th cent. The J. pop. was 54 in 1836 and 120 in 1875. The community established a synagogue in 1858 and a cemetery in 1834. By 1933, there were still 78 Jews living in V., but by autumn 1938, their number had shrunk to 41. The teacher for religious studies was deported to Poland in the deportation of Polish Jews in Oct. 1938. On *Kristallnacht* (9–10 Nov. 1938), the synagogue was burned down, J. businesses were wrecked, and 13 J. men were arrested and detained for several weeks. On 11 Nov. 1941, the 22 Jews who remained in V. were deported to Minsk (Belorussia). Only one survived. At least 29 Jews from V. perished under Nazi rule, including those who were deported from neighboring countries where they had hoped to find shelter.

VERESHCHAKI   Mogilev dist., Belorussia. V. was founded as a J. colony in the first half of the 19th cent. In 1851, the J. pop., numbering about 64 people or nine families, was engaged in farming. In 1898, the J. pop. was 168, working 300 acres of land. In 1924, under the Soviets, all but ten of the settlement's 47 J. families still worked the land. The others engaged in crafts. A clandestine *heder* operated in the local prayer house. A J. school opened in 1924 was attended by 30 children in 1927. During the German occupation, many J. refugees arrived. In March 1942, about 400 Jews were murdered outside the town A number of Belorussian peasants risked their lives in hiding escaping Jews.

VERHOVKA (I)   Vinnitsa dist., Bar county, Ukraine. The J. pop. was 251 (total 1,344) in 1897 and 148 in 1926. The Germans captured V. in mid-July 1941 and in the early fall expelled the Jews to the Yaltushkov ghetto, where they shared the fate of the local Jews. Hundreds of Jews from Bessarabia and Bukovina were then brought to V., about 530 dying from disease and the cold.

VERHOVKA (II)   Vinnitsa dist., Obodovka county, Ukraine. The J. pop. was 105 in 1765 and 1,094 (total 3,091) in 1897, dropping to 420 in 1926. In fall 1941, under the Nazi occupation, over 1,000 Jews from Bukovina and Bessarabia were transferred there, 536 dying from starvation and the cold. On 1 Sept. 1943, 69 of them were still alive. Most of the local Jews died together with the refugees.

VERIA   (Verea, Karaferia, Verroia) Greece. Jews from V. are mentioned in the New Testament, dating their presence to 49–50 C.E.. In 1453, the Ottoman conquerors expelled the J. community to Istanbul, but in the first half of the 15th cent. Spanish immigrants joined the small Romaniot community left there. In 1597, the Jews numbered 737 and constituted an organized, predominantly Sephardi (Spanish and Portuguese) community that was highly influenced by the Salonika community. In the 17th cent., the Jews suffered economic difficulties. Most worked in the textile industry and many in trade. A number of Jews converted to Islam with the emergence of the Shabbatean movement. In the 18th cent., the synagogue was built (or extended) in the style of Salonika's Sephardi synagogues. V. constituted a holiday retreat for Salonikian Jews well into the 20th cent. The J. pop. in 1880 was 149. When antisemitism increased in Thessaly following the Turkish-Greek war in 1898, many Jews from the region settled in V. In 1900, the Jews numbered some 500–600. In the following years public organizations for the welfare of the community were established and, with assistance from the Alliance Israelite, a J. school was opened. Following the Balkan wars (1912–13), V. was annexed to Greece. While some V. Jews then emigrated to Turkey and Bulgaria, Jews escaping epidemics in Salonika settled in V. In 1925, a blood libel was spread, falsely accusing a Jew of kidnapping a Christian child. The police intervened before violence erupted. Zionist activity was minimal and unorganized in V. On the eve of WWII, the community numbered 850. Many refugees from war-torn areas reached V. and during the famine of winter 1941 in Greece, 170 Jews from Salonika escaped to V. When the Germans arrived in 1941, anti-J. decrees were imposed. Before deportations began, 144 Jews went into hiding in the surrounding villages and in the Bulgarian occupation zone. On 31 March 1943, 680 Jews were arrested and held in the synagogue; the wealthy were tortured to reveal the whereabouts of their valuables. After three days they were sent to Auschwitz via Salonika. About 130 survived the Holocaust, but by the 1990s only two families remained in V.

VERJACIA   (Hung. Verecze; Yid. Veryiats) Carpatho-Russia, Czechoslovakia, today Ukraine. Jews probably settled at the turn of the 18th cent., numbering 47 in 1830 and 148 (total 801) in 1880. In 1921, under the Czechoslovakians, the J. pop. fell to 118 and again to

103 in 1941. Jews owned six stores and also engaged in agriculture. In 1941, after the Hungarian occupation, Jews were drafted into labor battalions and a number of J. families without Hungarian citizenship were deported to Kamenets-Podolski and murdered. The rest of the Jews were deported to Auschwitz on 24 May 1944.

VERKHNEDNEPROVSK Dnepropetrovsk dist., Ukraine. Jews settled in the early 19th cent. and numbered 2,058 (total 6,701) in 1897. A pogrom was staged in 1905. By 1939, under the Soviets, the J. pop. had dropped to 282. The Germans captured V. on 17 Aug. 1941. During the occupation, 51 of the 70 Jews who had neither fled nor been evacuated were murdered.

VERKHNEYE Voroshilovgrad dist., Ukraine. The J. pop. in 1939 was 331 (total 34,221). After their arrival on 10 July 1942, the Germans murdered the Jews still there.

VERKHOVNIA Zhitomir dist., Ukraine. Jews numbered 316 (total 2,440) in 1897 and 104 in 1926 under the Soviets. The Jews who neither fled nor were evacuated perished under the German occupation (from 9 July 1941).

VERNIKOVSKY (county) Krasnodar territory, Russia. The Germans murdered 72 Jews in the village of Dziginka and another seven in the village of Pervomaysk.

VERONA Veneto, Italy. The J. presence dates back to the Roman period. Jews were expelled in 965 and resettled in the 12th cent. By the 13th cent., several renowned scholars lived in the city, among them the tosafists Eliezer ben Shemuel of Verona and Yeshayahu ben Mali di Trani. In 1408, when V. was transferred to the Republic of Venice, Jews were legally permitted to reside in the city, to trade, and to establish loan banks. In 1422, the J. badge was introduced. In 1600, the Jews of V. were confined to a ghetto. For 200 years, the Jews maintained an active social and religious life. At first, V. was an Ashkenazi community, but soon Jews expelled from the Duchy of Milan as well as Marranos and Sephardi Jews began to settle. Separate communities were established, each with its own charitable institutions. In 1600, there were 400 Jews in V. As bank-

ing diminished, local Jews engaged in trade and crafts. In the 16th and 17th cents., several Hebrew books were printed in V. The community maintained several charitable and social welfare institutions. After the French conquered V. in 1796, the ghetto was abolished and Jews were granted civil rights. In 1806, when Napoleon convened the Sanhedrin in Paris, there were two representatives from V. among the 16 from Italy. When V. came under Austrian rule in 1814, the Jews were not required to return to the ghetto, but they were only fully emancipated when V. was incorporated into the Kingdom of Italy in 1866. In 1873, there were 1,240 Jews in V and in 1886, 975. According to the 1930 law reforming the J. communities, V. was among the 26 recognized communities. The V. district included Vicenza (50 Jews in 1869, ten in 1936). In 1936, there were 500 Jews registered in the V. community, which was headed by R. Dr. E. Friedenthal. During WWII, the community numbered about 340 Jews. An office of the Committee for Assistance to Jewish Emigrants (DELASEM: Delegazione Assistenza Emigrati Ebrei) was active. A concentration camp for Jews was established in Caprino, in the province of V. Thirty Jews were deported during WWII. In 1948, there were 119 Jews registered as living in the community.

VERPELET Heves dist., Hungary. Jews probably arrived in the late 18th cent. and maintained a synagogue, school, and yeshiva. They numbered 174 in 1880 and 146 in 1931. In May 1944, they were brought to the Bagolyuk coal mines and in June deported to Auschwitz.

VERSAILLES Yvelines dist., France. Jews originating from Alsace, Germany, and Comtat-Venaissin settled in this royal city in the 18th cent. The modern community was founded in 1883. A synagogue was dedicated in 1886. Louis Kahn (1895–1967), French general, naval engineer, and a leader of French Jewry, was a native of V. as was the great rabbi Julien Weill (1873–1950). In 1941, there were 321 Jews (107 families) in V. The community numbered 800 members in 1964 following the influx of North African Jews,.

VERSMOLD Westphalia, Germany. One J. family was present in the late 17th cent. By the mid-19th cent., the J. pop. was 30–40. A synagogue was consecrated in 1900. In 1933, the J. pop. was 31. Most left by Nov. 1938, half to the U.S. and England, half to

Yeshiva students, Verpelet, Hungary

other places in Germany. The synagogue was burned on *Kristallnacht* (9–10 Nov. 1938) and the last three Jews were deported to the Theresienstadt ghetto in July 1942.

VERTES   Bihar dist., Hungary. Jews are mentioned in 1774. When Jews were allowed to live in Debrecen, many left V. after 1840, reducing the J. pop. from 152 in 1830 to 105 in 1860 and 89 in 1930. All were deported to Auschwitz via Nagyvarad from 20 May to 3 June 1944.

VERTUJENI (Vartajeni) Bessarabia, Rumania, today Republic of Moldova. Jews founded V. in 1838 and engaged mainly in growing wheat. Refugees from the pogroms in Russia in 1917 passing through V. were killed by antisemites. The J. pop. in 1930 was 1,843 (91% of the total). In 1941 the J. pop. fled to the Russian side of the Dniester River. A camp was set up in V. by the Rumanian army for the few survivors of the massacres in the Soroca area. Most of them were killed there. Others were expelled to Transnistria.

VESELINOVO   Odessa dist., Ukraine. Jews settled at the turn of the 19th cent. In 1939 they numbered 58 (total 1,912) and 189 in the region as a whole. The Germans entered V. on 11 Aug. 1941 and murdered 40 Jews on 5 Sept. The Rumanians expelled thousands of the Jews from Bessarabia and Odessa to the area after it was annexed to Transnistria. Most perished within a year.

VESOLYIA   Zaporozhe dist., Ukraine. Jews from the Vitebsk and Mogilev region founded V. as a J. colony in the mid-19th cent. The J. pop. was 424 in 1858 and 436 in 1897, dropping to 134 under the Soviets in 1922. A J. school was in operation in 1909. New J. settlers arrived from Podolia in the 1920s, founding a J. kolkhoz in the area. The Germans arrived in early Oct. 1941 and probably murdered the remaining Jews of V. at the kolkhoz in the same fall.

VESOUL   Haute-Saone dist., France. Jews are mentioned in V. before the end of the 13th century and an important community was established there. The Jews of V. suffered during the Black Death persecutions of 1348–49. After expulsion they returned for a short time only. Individual Jews returned to V. at the time of the French Revolution, but a community was only established in the 19th cent. After a cholera epidemic in 1830, the Jews succeeded in acquiring their own cemetery, which was later expanded. A synagogue was inaugurated in 1873. V. served as the seat of the consistory and the rabbinate. Between the World Wars there was a small community in V. In the middle of the 1930s, religious life in the community was revived. In 1944, 96 Jews from V. and the surrounding areas were arrested in one day. Their fate is unknown. During WWII, the community came to an end.

VESZPREM Veszprem dist., Hungary. Jews were probably present during the Ottoman occupation and in 1723 were accorded residence rights by Bishop Esterhazy. The J. pop. was 1,689 in 1880, declining after 1860 when the new railroad bypassed the town. A J. school, one of the first in Hungary, was opened in 1805, with an enrollment of 308 children in 1877. A splendid new synagogue was completed in 1865. Jews contributed to the town's commerce and industry, founding a number of factories (soap, vinegar, cement). In 1941, the J. pop. was 887. On 15 April 1944, Jews from surrounding settlements were brought into the town and two ghettoes set up. All were deported to Auschwitz at the end of June.

VESZTO Bekes dist., Hungary. Jews arrived in the late 19th cent as peddlers, later opening stores, workshops, and a few factories. The J. pop. reached 197 in 1900. A J. school was founded in 1894 and a new synagogue in 1934. In 1941, the J. pop. was 130. The local pop. opposed Hungary's racial laws of WWII. On 21 June 1944, the Jews were brought to Szolnok. Most were deported to Auschwitz and the rest to the labor camps in Austria. Survivors renewed the community, but after the 1956 revolt many left for Israel.

VETKA Gomel dist., Belorussia. Jews settled in the late 18th cent., reaching a pop. of 984 in 1847 and 3,726 (total 7,204) in 1897. Most Jews engaged in petty trade but there were also lumber merchants among them. J. property was damaged in riots in 1905. In 1926, under the Soviets, the J. pop. was 2,094. In 1925, about 600 Jews did not have the right to vote. In 1930, 160 J. artisans (of a total 230) organized themselves into eight cooperatives. Forty-five J. families worked at kolkhozes founded near the town in 1925-30. The local J. elementary school was closed in 1937. In 1939, the J. pop. was 944. The Germans occupied V. on 18 Aug. 1941. Many Jews were

evacuated beforehand. In Sept., those remaining were moved to a ghetto and remained there until 2 Dec. under a regime of forced labor, starvation, and overcrowding. On 2 Dec., 448 were executed beside a ditch. A few managed to escape.

VETRINO Vitebsk dist., Belorussia. Eighteen J. families were present in V. in 1924, six of them engaged in agriculture. A four-year J. elementary school was in operation. In 1939, the J. pop. was 61. The Germans arrived on 3 July 1941. A ghetto was established in Oct. 1941 and 59 Jews were murdered in Jan. 1942.

VETTWEISS Rhineland, Germany. A J. butcher settled in 1791 and in 1812 three Jews were present. Their pop. grew to 30-35 in the late 19th and 20th cents. A cemetery was opened in 1860-70 and a synagogue was erected in 1890. Its interior was destroyed on *Kristallnacht* (9-10 Nov. 1938). At least six Jews perished in the Holocaust.

VIAREGGIO Tuscany, Italy. In 1910, there were 31 Jews residing in V. In 1917, proposals to establish a community were rejected by the Jews residing in the town. By 1927, the number of Jews was 45. With the reform of the J. communities in Italy in 1930, V. was included in the Pisa dist. In 1938, 150 Jews resided in V.; in 1948, 125. A synagogue was erected in 1954.

VIAZOVKA Zhitomir dist., Ukraine. Jews settled in the 19th cent., numbering 239 (total 1,178) in 1897 and 165 in 1926 under the Soviets. The few Jews who had neither fled nor been evacuated perished after the arrival of the Germans on 21 Aug. 1941.

VICHY Allier dist., France. There was a J. community in the 13th cent. A small J. community existed between the World Wars and a synagogue was inaugurated in 1933. V. was the site of a regional rabbinate for three communities in the department. In 1938 and 1939, refugees from Alsace joined the community. In 1941, there were 950 J. families in V., numbering 4,000-5,000 Jews. In 1964, the community numbered 750 members.

VICOVUL DE SUS Bukovina, Rumania. There were 42 Jews here in 1782. The J. pop. in 1930 was 334. The Zionists were active between the World Wars. In 1940, Rumanian soldiers transferred much of the J. pop. to Suceava and then to Bacua and other towns. Another group was deported in 1941 to Transnistria.

VIDISKIAI (Yid. Vidishok) Ukmerge dist., Lithuania. The J. community began early in the 19th cent. The J. pop. was 151 in 1897 (31% of the total) and 50 in 1940 (12%). All of V.'s Jews were killed in Ukmerge on 5 Sept. 1941.

VIDUKLE Raseiniai dist., Lithuania. Jews began settling in the 17th cent. Germany's entry into V. in April 1915 preempted Russia's planned expulsion of the Jews. The J. pop. in 1940 was about 160 (about 21% of the total). After Germany's invasion in June 1941 Lithuanians began persecuting Jews. On 24 July, elderly men were marched naked to a prepared pit and shot. On 22 Aug. 1941, women who had been detained in the *beit midrash* and had not succeeded in escaping, as others had, were ordered to strip and then shot. The children were thrown alive into the pit. The men were also ordered into a pit and shot.

VIEKSNIAI (Yid. Vekshne) Mazeikiai dist., Lithuania. Jews first settled here in the 17th cent. A conflagration in 1886 caused many Jews to emigrate to South Africa, the U.S., and Eretz Israel. The J. pop. in 1897 was 1,646 (56% of the total). The Hovevei Zion movement flourished in V. In WWI the Russian army expelled the Jews, only some of whom returned after the war. In the 1920s the economic situation caused many to emigrate. The community supported several social welfare organizations and two schools, one Orthodox, the other secular-Zionist. The library had 1,200 Hebrew and Yiddish books. The J. pop. in 1940 was 600. After Germany's invasion in June 1941, Lithuanian nationalists assembled all the J. men and sent them to forced labor. After abusing and torturing the Jews for weeks, the Lithuanians took all the Jews to Mazeikiai. Together with Jews from several other towns, the men dug mass graves and were then shot.

VIENNA (Ger. Wien) capital of Austria. Jews first settled here in the 12th cent. They maintained a synagogue and owned houses. During the Third Crusade

Preparing matza *for distribution to the poor, Vienna, Austria, 1921*

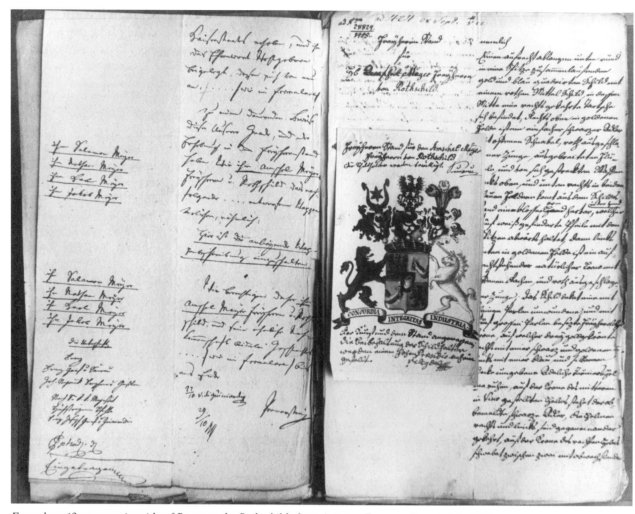

Formal certificate granting title of Baron to the Rothschilds from Austrian Emperor Francis I in 1822

(1196) Jews were murdered. By 1204 a second synagogue was erected and by the end of the cent., there were 1,000 Jews living in V. in a J. quarter. At the time of the Black Death persecutions (1348–49), the community served as a refuge for Jews from other towns. In 1421, the year of the Wiener Gesera persecutions, the community was destroyed and J. property confiscated. In 1512, Jews resettled in V., numbering about 15 families. During the Thirty Years War (1618–48) the community suffered as result of the occupation of the city. In 1624, Ferdinand II confined the Jews to a ghetto which included 500 families in 136 houses. Jews mostly engaged in trade, some of them on an international scale. During the Chmielnicki massacres of 1648–49 Jews found refuge here, among them the rabbis Yom Tov Lipmann Heller and Shabbetai Sheftel Horowitz. In 1669, Leopold I expelled all the Jews from V. and converted the synagogue into a Catholic church, the present-day "Leopoldskirche." When the city ran into financial difficulties Jews were allowed to resettle, but had to pay high taxes. Among the founders of the new community were the Court Jews Samuel Oppenheimer (1630–1703) and Samson Wertheimer (1658–1724). In 1696, Oppenheimer built a hospital. In the 1740s the community supported the poor in Eretz Israel. In 1777, there were 520 Jews in V., their number still restricted by the legislation of Maria Theresa. From the end of the 18th cent. to the beginning of the 19th cent., V. became a center of the Haskala movement. Among its adherents were Peter Peretz Beer and Naftali Herz Homberg (1749–1841), who tried to introduce religious reform. At the time of the V. Congress (1815), the salons of such J. hostesses as Fanny von Arnstein were quite popular,

The Jewish quarter of Vienna, Austria, 1915 (Oester. Staatsarchiv/Kriegsarchiv, Wien/photo courtesy of Yad Vashem, The Holocaust Martyrs' and Heroes' Remembrance Authority, Jerusalem)

providing entertainment and a meeting place for Congress participants. Noah Mannheimer (1793–1865), a leading preacher and creator of a moderate, compromise Reform ritual, served as head of the Seitenstetten Synagogue in V. Together with the cantor Salomon Sulzer, he tried to introduce liturgical music during services, which became a model for all countries in Central Europe. Among Mannheimer's successors were Adolf Jellinek, Moritz Guedemann, and Zwi Perez Chajes, all of whom served as chief rabbis in V. In 1857, the J. pop. was 6,217, rising rapidly to 40,230 in 1869 and 118,495 in 1890. After WWI, about 50,000 refugees from Galicia and Bukovina settled in V. and the J. pop. rose to 201,513 in 1923. By 1934, there were 176,034 Jews in V., constituting 8% of the total pop. V. maintained 59 synagogues, representing various religious rites. There was also a widespread educational network. In 1893, a rabbinical seminary was founded and V., together with Berlin and Breslau, became one of the European centers for the study of Jewish literature and history. V. was also a scientific and cultural center and personalities such as Arthur Schnitzler, Franz Werfel, Stefan Zweig, Gustav Mahler, Arnold Schoenberg, Richard Beer-Hofmann, and Sigmund Freud gained international recognition here. V. was also a city of national awakening, where Peretz Smolenskin, Nathan Birnbaum, and Theodor Herzl published their first Zionist writings. But Zionism gained strength in V. only after WWI. In 1919 the Zionist Robert Stricker was elected to the Austrian Parliament. In the community elections of 1932, the Zionists won a majority. Jews were engaged in trade and were

Jewish soldiers in a Vienna synagogue, Austria, before WWI

represented extensively in the professional class. About 60% of the doctors and lawyers in V. were Jews. The community supported many charity and relief organizations, including the Rothschild Hospital and three orphanages. In March 1938, there were 165,946 Jews in V. Immediately after the *Anschluss* (13 March 1938), the leaders of the community were arrested and sent to the Dachau concentration camp, where some were murdered. J. organizations and activities were outlawed. The chief rabbi, Dr. Israel Taglicht, and other prominent Jews were forced to sweep the streets with their bare hands. Big property owners were arrested and sent to Dachau. The Nazis murdered those who refused to hand over their property. In March 1938, 311 Jews committed suicide; in April, 267. As result of persecution in other towns, Jews from the provinces began to arrive. In May 1938, the religious corporation (*Kultusgemeinde*) was allowed to open its offices again. The Zionist Palestine Office was permitted to organize

legal and illegal emigration. From July to Sept. 1938, 8,600 Jews emigrated every month. Vocational courses served as preparation for emigration. Until the end of 1939, 31,306 Jews participated in these courses. In Oct. 1938, antisemitic riots erupted. J. families were thrown out of their homes and housed in certain districts of V. In the same month Jews of Czech nationality were expelled to Czechoslovakia while thousands of Jews holding Polish passports were deported to the no man's land on the German-Polish border. On *Kristallnacht* (9–10 Nov. 1938), 42 synagogues were burned and 4,000 stores looted. The interior of the famous Seitenstettengasse Synagogue was damaged but not set on fire since there were other buildings nearby. In Sept. 1939, with the outbreak of WWII, 17,000 Jews holding valid visas were not allowed to use them. In Oct. 1939, 1,000 Jews were sent to Nisko in the Lublin dist. (Poland), only 152 returned in April 1940. During the first months of the war, about 11,000 Jews emigrated to neutral countries. By the end of 1939, the community numbered 53,403, with 45,140 on relief. A total of 5,017 children attended the various educational facilities organized by the community. Of the approximately 131,000 Jews who succeeded in emigrating with the help of the V.J. community, 31,050 went to England, 38,340 to other European countries, 29,860 to the U.S., 15,200 to Palestine, and 6220 to China. Between Feb. 1941 and Oct. 1942, about 43,000 Jews were deported, 11,200 of them to ghettoes in Poland; 5,400 to the Lodz ghetto; 13,150 to ghettoes in Minsk and Riga; and 13,600 to the Theresienstadt ghetto. In Nov. 1942, the community officially ceased to exist. After the war it was reestablished with an estimated 12,000 members.

VIERNHEIM Hesse, Germany. Jews lived there from the 17th cent. and established a community numbering 60 in 1828. Jews prospered in the tobacco and livestock trade. The community became affiliated with the Liberal rabbinate of Darmstadt. By 1900 the J. pop. had grown to 123 (2% of the total). In the wake of the Nazi boycott campaign, Jews started leaving before *Kristallnacht* (9–10 Nov. 1938), when stormtroopers burned down the synagogue and organized the looting or destruction of J. property. During the years 1933–39, at least 28 of the 69 Jews in V. emigrated (17 to the U.S.). Those who remained were mostly deported in 1942.

VIERSEN Rhineland, Germany. The first J. family settled in 1712 and the community reached a peak pop. of 157 in 1925. A synagogue was consecrated in 1862 and the community also maintained a J. school which was closed on the eve of the Nazi rise to power in 1933. In that year, the J. pop. was 141. By Nov. 1938, 36 had emigrated and 35 had moved to other German cities. On *Kristallnacht* (9–10 Nov. 1938), J. homes were vandalized and J. men were jailed in Anrath. Other Jews subsequently left V., leaving 48 in May 1939. Those who remained were deported in 1941–42.

VIESINTOS (Yid. Vishinte) Panevezys dist., Lithuania. The J. community began in the early 19th cent. The synagogue, completed in 1882, was the community's religious and cultural center. The J. pop. in 1897 was 400 (54% of the total). In WWI the Jews fled V. when the Russian army destroyed their

homes. Most returned after the war. The J. pop. in 1926 was 25 families. When the Soviets took over V. in the summer of 1940, Hebrew and Zionist institutions were closed down. After the German invasion of June 1941, Jews were abused by Germans and Lithuanian nationalists and all were killed in Kupiskis at the end of Sept. 1941.

VIESITE Zemgale (Courland) dist., Latvia. On the eve of WWI Jews constituted a majority of the new town's 462 residents. During the war they were expelled and in 1935 numbered 193 (total 1,340). Shortly after the German occupation, on 19 July 1941, all the Jews were taken outside the town by the Latvians and shot beside two open pits. Many of the women were raped beforehand.

VIEVIS (Yid. Vevie) Troki dist., Lithuania. Jews began settling at the end of the 18th cent. The J. pop. in 1897 was 647 (89% of the total). The Jews left V. in WWI when Cossacks set their homes on fire. Some returned after the war. The J. pop. in 1940 was 350 (39% of the total). After Germany's invasion in June 1941, Jews who had fled were forced to return to be persecuted and murdered by the Lithuanians. On 6 Oct. 1941 most of V.'s Jews were executed in Semeliskes.

VIJNICIOARA Bukovina, Rumania, today Ukraine. There were 339 Jews living in V. in 1880 (25% of the total) and 227 in 1930. In fall 1941, the J. pop. was deported to Transnistria. Few survived.

VIJNITA Bukovina, Rumania. A J. community existed in the mid-18th cent. In the late 19th cent., many Jews from Russia and Moldavia settled. Jews engaged in the lumber industry and were known for their bookbinding expertise. Under Austrian rule, most of the officials were Jews, as were the mayor and the entire municipal council. After R. Menahem Mendel Hager set up his court in 1850, V. became a center for adherents of the Kosov and Maramures dynasties. The J. pop. in 1890 was 4,247 (90% of the total). During WWI, the town was destroyed and the majority of the J. pop. fled to Vienna. The J. pop. in 1930 was 2,666. Between the World Wars, Zionist youth movements were active. On the eve of WWII, eight prayer houses, a *heder, talmud torah*, yeshiva (opened in 1918), and Hebrew high school were in operation. In

June 1941, local Ukrainians and Rumanian soldiers plundered J. houses and murdered 21 Jews; another 14 were shot in the nearby forest. In Oct. 1941, 2,800 Jews were deported to Transnistria. Most of the 800 survivors emigrated to Palestine.

VILAKA (Yid. Viliaki) Latgale dist., Latvia. Jews began to settle after the Russian annexation in 1772 and reached a stable pop. of 540 in 1903 after the settlement received municipal status in 1892. The majority *Mitnaggedim* and the Hasidim prayed separately in the town's two synagogues. Many J. homes were damaged in the fighting between the Bolsheviks and Latvians at the end of WWI. After the war economic conditions were satisfactory, with a third of the J. pop. defined as wealthy and just 10% as needy. Despite restrictions instituted by the Ulmanis regime in 1934, Jews maintained their control of trade with 77 of the town's 92 retail establishments and three of its four factories in their hands. The Zionists were active between the World Wars and a J. public school with teaching in Yiddish was founded in 1921. In 1935 the J. pop. was 465 (total 1,582). The Germans arrived in early July 1941 and almost immediately confined the Jews to a ghetto. In early Aug. the men were separated from the women and children and the two groups executed separately in the forest with Latvians joining the firing squads.

VILANI (Yid. Vilon) Latgale dist., Latvia. The community was established after a large tanning factory was set up in 1873 by a wealthy Jew. The community numbered 300–400 (30% of the total) for most of its existence. All J. children attended a J. school founded in 1922. The Zionists were active between the World Wars and a few families emigrated to Palestine. In 1935, 56 of the town's 71 business establishments were in J. hands, but the creation of a Latvian cooperative cut into J. business. Throughout the period there were manifestations of antisemitism, occasionally violent. The J. pop. in 1935 was 396. Under Soviet rule (1940–41), J. businesses were nationalized and community life was phased out. The Germans arrived in early July 1941 and confined all the Jews to a former school building, instituting a regime of forced labor marked by rape and beatings by Latvian guards. On 4 Aug. all were murdered outside the town.

VILBEL (now Bad Vilbel) Hesse, Germany. Established in the 18th cent., the community opened a synagogue in 1813 and developed a vigorous social and cultural life. Affiliated with Giessen's Orthodox rabbinate, it numbered 113 (3% of the total) in 1880. After *Kristallnacht* (9–10 Nov. 1938), only nine of the 75 Jews living there in 1933 remained. At least 21 had emigrated (nine to Palestine); those who did not leave Germany mostly perished in the Holocaust.

VILJANDI Estonia. The community was founded by Cantonists in the 1860s, soon maintaining a synagogue and cemetery and reaching a pop. of 241 in 1881. After WWI the J. pop. averaged around 25 families (in a total pop. of 12,000 people). About 40% of the J. working pop. was salaried, mainly as sales personnel, while the rest were tradesmen, professionals, and factory operators. After the annexation of Estonia to the Soviet Union in Aug. 1940, J. businesses were nationalized. Most Jews left with the Red Army on the approach of the Germans in June 1941. The few who remained were murdered in fall 1941 by Estonian Omakaitse ("self-defense") units operating on orders from the German *Sonderkommando 1a*.

VILKAVISKIS (Yid. Vilkovishk) Vilkaviskis dist., Lithuania. Jews began settling here in the beginning of the 16th cent. when Queen Bona allotted wood to all of V.'s residents to build houses of worship, including a magnificent three-story synagogue which remained intact until WWII. When Napoleon's army encamped in V. in 1812, it took over the synagogues for lodging, but on the request of a J. delegation returned them on the eve of the Ninth of Av, the traditional day of mouring for the destruction of the Temples in Jerusalem. The J. pop. in 1897 was 3,480 (60% of the total). Zionist activity began in the 1880s and the Zion Society had 400 members in 1899. During WWI, many Jews fled; some returned after the war. During the German occupation (1915–18) V. had a J. mayor. Between the World Wars at least half the city council consisted of Jews and Jews served as deputy mayor, city treasurer, chairman of the dist. council, and dist. engineer. A Hebrew school system was established, including religious and secular high schools. Training facilities in V. prepared pioneers for *aliya* to Palestine; several helped found kibbutzim. The J. pop. in 1939 was 3,609 (41%). On 22 June 1941, the Germans bombed V., destroying most J.-owned houses and the ancient synagogue. Lithuanian nationalists immediately began to

The Vilkaviskis old age home and hospital, Lithuania

pillage J. homes and seize Jews for forced labor. The Germans introduced anti-J. measures, established a ghetto outside the city, and appointed a *Judenrat*. On 27 July 1941, 250 men were ordered to dig pits in the ghetto and on the next day 800 men, including 65 non-J. Communists, were shot and buried in one of them. The J. women and children remaining in V. were taken to the ghetto and shot and buried in another pit on 24 Sept. 1941, the day after Rosh Hashanah.

VILKIJA (Yid. Vilki) Kaunas dist., Lithuania. Jews began settling here in the 18th cent. In 1859, V. had a synagogue and a yeshiva. The J. pop. in 1897 was 1,431 (71% of the total). During WWI, Russian soldiers rioted against the Jews, abusing men and raping women. The Russians expelled the Jews, 60% of whom returned after the war. In the 1930s the economic crisis and boycott of Jews led to emigration to west-

ern countries and Palestine. The community maintained a Hebrew school, two synagogues, and social welfare organizations. Many Jews belonged to the Zionist camp. The J. pop. in 1940 was 500 (25% of the total). After Germany's invasion in June 1941, Lithuanian nationalists executed suspected Communists, Jews and non-Jews. The Germans and Lithuanians crowded the Jews into a ghetto, mobilizing them for forced labor. On 28 Aug. 1941, all of V.'s Jews were taken to the Pakarkle forest and shot.

VILLANY Baranya dist., Hungary. Jews settled in the late 18th cent. establishing a Neologist congregation in 1891. They numbered 81 in 1930. They were deported to Auschwitz via Barcs at the end of June 1944.

VILLINGEN Baden, Germany. The medieval community was wiped out in the Black Death persecutions of 1348–49 and a new community was expelled in 1510. The community was reestablished after emancipation in 1862 and numbered 75 in the Nazi era, affiliated with the Randegg congregation. Forty-two emigrated, ten left for other German cities, and 11 were deported. At least 18 perished in the camps.

VILLMAR AN DER LAHN   Hesse–Nassau, Germany. Established in 1772, the community opened a synagogue in 1846 and numbered 71 (4% of the pop.) in 1871, declining to 35 in 1933. The Jews were mostly dealers in cattle and farm produce, and the community was affiliated with the rabbinate of Bad Ems. Until 1911 a separate, much older community existed in nearby Runkel, where Shelomo Zalman Runkel (d. c. 1400) – the teacher of Yaacov Moellin ("Maharil") – was born. On *Kristallnacht* (9–10 Nov. 1938), the interior of V.'s synagogue was destroyed. A third of the Jews emigrated and another 12 perished in the Holocaust.

VILNA   (Pol. Wilno; Lith. Vilnius) Vilna dist., Poland, today Lithuania. Individual Jews were present sporadically from the late 15th cent. to the mid-16th

cent., settling on lands outside municipal bounds that belonged to the bishop and nobility. In 1573 they were allowed to construct a synagogue and by the 1590s an organized community was in existence with freedom of worship and the right to engage in trade and crafts. The opposition of townsmen to the J. presence led to a pogrom in 1592, when J. stores and homes were pillaged and the synagogue was burned down. A new synagogue was built of brick in the West European style and in 1633 the Jews received a charter of privileges from King Wladyslaw IV confirming their rights and establishing a J. quarter. With the establishment of the Council of Lithuania, V. was granted special status and in 1652 became a principal community like Brest, Pinsk, and Grodno. With V. the capital of the Lithuanian Duchy, Jews were active as lobbyists (*shtadlanim*) in the royal court. Most Jews fled when the Cossacks captured the city in 1655, while those remaining were killed. Those who returned suffered from hunger and disease and the community was forced to take large loans to recover. Among the prominent rabbis in this period were R. Shabbetai ha-Kohen ("Shakh"), Aharon Shemuel Koidanover, and Moshe Rivkes. Economic conditions deteriorated as

The Jewish quarter in Vilna, Poland (today capital of Lithuania)

wars, epidemics, and devastating fires racked the community in the first half of the 18th cent. Nonetheless the J. pop. continued to grow, reaching nearly 4,000 in 1765 as J. commerce expanded into foreign trade with Germany, Russia, and Turkish-controlled Walachia. Among the striking personalities in the community were R. Yekutiel Gordon, a physician, kabbalist, and talmudic scholar, and the wealthy R. Yehuda ben Eliezer "Safra ve-Dayyan" ("Yesod"), who initiated a long controversy lasting until 1791 when he forced his son-in-law R. Shemuel ben Avigdor on the community as rabbi. In the second half of the 18th cent., V. became a center of Torah learning. The outstanding figure of the age—and one of the most erudite and influential of post-medieval scholars—was R. Eliyahu ben Shelomo Zalman (1720–97), known as the "Gaon of V." He spearheaded the struggle of the *Mitnaggedim* against the Hasidim and in 1772 pronounced a ban against them. Groups of his followers settled in Eretz Israel in 1808 and 1809. Under Russian rule, the number of J. merchants in V. rose to 86% (2,752 in number) of the total in 1876, while J. artisans comprised 56.5% (5,962), organized into 25 guilds according to trade. All carters and 60% of coachmen were

Jews. Jews also owned 43 small factories. At midcent. the J. pop. stood at around 40,000 and in 1897 it was 63,841 (total 154,532). V. became an important center of Haskala, producing such figures as Adam ha-Kohen Lebensohn and his son Mikhah Yosef Lebensohn, Mordekhai Aharon Ginzburg, Kalman Schulman, Yitzhak Meir Dick, Avraham Mapu, and Yehuda Leib Gordon. The first Hebrew weekly, *Ha-Karmel*, appeared in 1860–80. Vilna was known for its Hebrew printing presses, producing many standard texts and the famous 1886 edition of the Babylonian Talmud by the Romm house. A government-sponsored rabbinical seminary was opened in 1847, enrolling 463 in 1871–72. There were also three *yeshivot* in V., one of them started by R. Yisrael Lipkin (Salanter), founder of the Musar movement. According to the 1897 census, nearly half the 26,745 J. breadwinners worked in industry, crafts, and transport and Jews ran 125 factories, most of them small (paper, printing, woodworking, tanning, flour milling, beer brewing). Two-thirds of the city's artisans and merchants were Jews (the latter numbering 6,117 and engaging mostly in petty trade and peddling), 7,952, including 2,600 women, worked in the services, and 1,206 in the professions (45% of

Students at the Jewish Polytechnic in Vilna, Poland

the city's total). In the same year there were 698 J. educational institutions in operation, mostly *hadarim*, with an enrollment of 15,000 children. The number of *hadarim* dropped to 275 in 1907 while the number of J. children attending public schools rose to 12,847. A J. vocational school founded in 1892 produced 500 graduates by the early 20th cent. In 1910 there were 104 recognized prayer houses in the city. In addition to a J. hospital treating 1,000 patients in 1908 (but under municipal management) the community ran a medical service employing 35 doctors, ten nurses, and ten midwives and operating the largest pharmacy in the city. The famed Strashun library, opened in 1892, was transferred to a special building in the main synagogue courtyard in 1901. Zionist activity commenced in the late 19th cent. The founding convention of Mizrachi was held in V. in 1902 and Theodor Herzl visited the city in 1903, receiving an ecstatic welcome. Various Zionist parties and movements had their headquarters in V. At the turn of the 20th cent., R. Hayyim Ozer Grodzinski initiated the Orthodox Keneset Israel organization which grew into Agudat Israel in 1912. The Bund held its founding convention in the city in 1897. In the early stages of WWI, some 200,000 J. refugees passed through the city, about 3,500 remaining. The Germans captured the city on 18 Sept. 1915, confiscating goods and subjecting the Jews to forced labor. Under wartime conditions, J. mortality rates doubled and tripled. On the withdrawal of German troops in 1918, democratic elections were held for the community council, with the Zionists and the Bund equally dividing the majority of seats. The arrival of the Polish army in April 1919 was accompanied by severe persecution and the arrest of hundreds of Jews, 70 of whom were murdered. A commission sent to investigate by Woodrow Wilson under Henry Morgenthau, Sr., in July 1919 determined that 2,000 J. homes and stores had been looted. Of the 46,265 Jews in the city, half required financial support from the Joint Distribution Committee. Among those active in organizing relief was R. Yitzhak Rubinstein, who was later a member of the Polish senate. In the slow recovery that followed, the J. pop. reached a stable level of 55,000–60,000 between the World Wars. The J. economy was adversely affected by the loss of the Russian market and the introduction of government monopolies in the tobacco, alcoholic beverage, salt, and match industries. Many J. stores closed down (22% in 1929) and Jews now opened smaller factories, but

they also entered new fields, such as the manufacture of radios. About 20 small establishments manufactured chocolate and candy and a preservative industry began to develop as did factories manufacturing leather gloves, socks, furs, and galoshes. In the early 1930s, 10,027 of the city's 23,215 J. breadwinners (27% of the city's total) were engaged in industry and crafts, 7,729 in commerce, 2,363 in the professions, and 964 in transport. However, 80% barely earned a living. Between the World Wars a wide variety of Hebrew and Yiddish schools were in operation. From the early 20th cent. V. was an important center of J. literature and journalism. Among those active were Simon Dubnow (1903–06) and the Zionist leader Shmarya Levin (1904–06). Many Hebrew and Yiddish peridicals appeared in V., including the Hebrew daily *Ha-Zeman*. In 1925 the YIVO Institute for J. Research was centered here. The sculptors Mark Antokolski and Boris Schatz (founder of Bezalel) were associated with the city and the violinist Jascha Heifetz was born there. The famous theatrical Vilna Troupe was founded during WWI. Hehalutz became active in 1919, sending 28 pioneers to Palestine in 1920. By 1931 it had 1,062 members. The local Betar branch was opened in 1925 and in the 1930s, when Vladimir Jabotinsky frequently visited the city, had 2,000 members together with the Revisionists. In 1922–30, Dr. Jacob Vigodski served in the Sejm. There was an extensive Hebrew and Yiddish secular and religious educational system. In the 1930s it included kindergartens and *hadarim*, 16 elementary schools, eight secondary schools, including a vocational school for training mechanics and electricians, and two teachers' colleges. Three libraries operated in Vilna: the Strashun library with 33,134 volumes, YIVO with 40,000, and the Mefitzei Haskala library with 46,234.

The Red Army entered V. on 19 Sept. 1939, ceding the city to Lithuania on 28 Oct. Anti-J. disturbances immediately followed, as gangs of marauding Poles, abetted by Lithuanian police, looted J. stores and injured 200 Jews Only the arrival of Soviet tanks put an end to the rioting. Large numbers of J. refugees began to arrive, 10,000 by the end of the year, including such leaders of Polish Jewry as Moshe Kleinbaum (Sneh), Zerah Warhaftig, and Menahem Begin, all of whom became prominent in Israel's political life. Organized groups from such movements as Po'alei Zion, Betar, and the Bund along with some 2,500 yeshiva students and rabbis also found refuge. With Lithuania

Front page of Hebrew newspaper Tarbut, *Vilna, Poland, 1935*

annexed to the USSR in June 1940 as a Soviet Socialist Republic, a process of sovietization commenced. All J. public and political institutions were closed down and J. banks, factories (265 of the city's 370), wholesale establishments, and real estate holdings were nationalized. Shopkeepers and peddlers were heavily taxed and thus forced to liquidate their businesses while artisans were pressured into organizing themselves into cooperatives. The J. educational system went over to a Soviet curriculum with Yiddish as the language of instruction. International pressure enabled around 7,000 Jews holding papers to continue to emigrate, over half reaching Palestine and the others the U.S., China, Japan, and elsewhere. Many Zionists and Bundists were exiled to the interior of the Soviet Union as "enemies of the people." On the approach of the Germans in June 1941, fewer than 3,000 Jews were able to flee with the Soviets. Thus, when the Germans entered the city on 24 June, 57,000 Jews were present. Immediately J. men were seized for forced labor and of a group of 60 held as hostages all but six were murdered. J. homes were looted by Germans and Lithuanians and Jews were dismissed from their jobs and thrown out of food lines. Jews were also banned from public transportation facilities and the main streets of the city and the Lithuanian pop. began expropriating the small J. businesses still in operation. On 4 July, the Germans ordered a *Judenrat* to be set up. On that same day the German *Einsatzkommando 9* with the assistance of an *Ordnungspolizei* unit and about 150 Lithuanian police and anti-Soviet "partisans" commenced mass executions in the Ponary woods about 7 miles (11 km) from the city. Jews were pulled off the streets and out of their homes and held for a few days at the Lukiszki prison before being taken to the killing site—big Soviet fuel storage pits surrounded by earthworks. Victims were "registered," stripped naked, blindfolded, marched to the edge of the pits, and executed at the rate of 100 per hour. By 20 July, 5,000 Jews had been murdered. Killing on a smaller scale continued through Aug. but on 31 Aug.–3 Sept., 8,000 men, women, and children were murdered at Ponary after two Lithuanians shot at some German soldiers from a Jew's house. On 6 Sept. the Jews were divided into two ghettoes—30,000 in one and 9,000–11,000 in the other. Another 6,000 were murdered at Ponary. Two new *Judenrats* were appointed, a hospital was set up in the larger ghetto, and infirmaries and schools in both. On 15 Sept. the sick and old together with orphans were transferred from the first to the second ghetto and Jews with work permits and their families from the second to the first. Another 2,400 Jews without work permits were seized from the first ghetto and brought to Ponary for execution. On 1 Oct. (Yom Kippur), 1,700 from the second ghetto were taken to the Lukiszki prison. The next day, 2,200 permit holders from the first ghetto were taken to Lukiszki with most murdered at Ponary. The second ghetto was liquidated in the course of the month: 2,000 on 4 Oct., 3,000 on 16 Oct., over 2,500 on 21 Oct.—all murdered in Ponary's "valley of death." About 28,000 Jews remained in the first ghetto, 12,000 of them—including their families—holding work permits. Prominent among the places of J. employment was the Keilis fur factory, where 1,000 J. workers and their families were registered, living in a few houses near the plant, which was in effect a labor camp. It was managed by Oskar Glueck, a Jew posing as a German who was later found out and murdered with his wife. On 23 Oct., another 5,000 Jews without permits were rounded up in the ghetto and murdered at Ponary in the next two days. Roundups and executions continued through Nov. and Dec. By the end of the year, 34,000 Jews had been murdered. All this while, members of the youth movements had kept in contact. Seventeen members of Hashomer Hatzair, among them Abba Kovner, were able to find shelter in a monastery not far from V. and Mordekhai Tenenbaum (Tamaroff), one of the leaders of Hehalutz Hatzair-Deror, hid out in the city disguised as a Karaite. A large group from the latter movement made its way to Bialystok and Warsaw in Jan. 1942. Kovner, who maintained that the larger ghettoes were as dangerous as V. since German policy was to murder all the Jews everywhere, issued a proclamation in Dec. 1941 exposing Nazi aims and calling for revolt. On 21 Jan. the FPO (Unified Partisan Organization) was founded with the aim of organizing armed resistance and participating in partisan activities. By fall 1943, the FPO had 300 members, mostly armed and constituting two 100–120-member fighting battalions and special forces. Apart from the FPO, there were two small groups, one led by Yehiel Sheinboim and the other called Ma'avak, which joined later. From early 1942 to spring 1943 ghetto life was relatively quiet, creating the illusion that economic usefulness to the Germans might save the community. The number of J. workers was thus pushed up to a peak of around

Private entrance to the study of Eliyahu ben Shelomo Zalman, the Gaon of Vilna (1720–1797), Vilna, Poland, 1937

14,000 in June 1943. The *Judenrat* ran four soup kitchens and in 1942 over 3,000 Jews were treated in the ghetto hospital. Two elementary schools now had an enrollment of 700–900 5–12-year-old children and 100 children attended a secondary school. About 100 teachers were active. Concert and theater performances were also organized within the ghetto and a public library numbering 45,000 volumes had 2,500 regular readers. It also housed an archive documenting the atrocities of the Nazi occupation. Three synagogues continued to operate as well. In July 1942, Yaakov Gens, chief of the J. police, was named the new head of the *Judenrat*, becoming a controversial figure as he pursued a policy of meeting German demands during their *Aktions* in the hope that by sacrificing part of the community the rest might be saved. During July, the J. police handed over groups of the sick and old to the Germans for execution at Ponary. Another 406 of the aged were brought to Oszmiana, where 4,000 Jews from neighboring settlements had been concentrated for liquidation. On 6 April 1943, 3,800 Jews told that they were being brought to Kovno to join their families were taken instead to Ponary and executed. At the same time the Germans began to liquidate the labor camps in the area. Hundreds of Jews being held outside were murdered in June and July. Flight from the ghetto to the forests increased and contact with Soviet partisans was stepped up. On 6 Aug., about 1,000 J. workers were sent to Estonian concentration camps; another 1,500 were sent on 24 Aug. In July 1943, owing to the failure of the Communist underground outside the ghetto, the Germans learned about Itzik Wittenberg, one of the leaders of the FPO and its link to the outside underground. They demanded his surrender and Gens turned him in, but he was freed by the FPO. After a German threat that the ghetto would be destroyed, Wittenberg gave himself up and committed suicide. On 1 Sept. the FPO published a call to resist the expulsions, but the majority of ghetto inhabitants did not respond and expulsions continued. In all, around 7,000 Jews were deported to Estonia. During this time another 200 Jews escaped to the forests. After the last expulsions to Estonia in Sept. 1943, 12,000 Jews remained in the ghetto. Of these, the 3,000 still working outside the ghetto were removed to labor camps near their places of employment. On 14 Sept., Gens was executed by the Germans. On 23–24 Sept. the ghetto was liquidated. Families were separated and members sent their separate ways: 2,000 men to Estonian camps, 1,500 young women to

Latvian camps, and 4,500 non-working women with their children to the Majdanek concentration camp. A few hundred of the sick and old were murdered at Ponary. The last resistance fighters in the ghetto made their way to the forests. During their retreat on the eastern front the Germans had the bodies at Ponary disinterred and burned – over 60,000 in number. On 2–3 July 1944, all 2,200 Jews in the labor camps were murdered at Ponary. The J. men being held in Estonia were thinned out through selections and the remainder sent to the Stutthof concentration camp in East Prussia in Aug. 1944 together with some of the J. women at the Kaiserwald camp in Latvia. In Jan. 1945, as the Red Army approached, they were marched to the interior of Germany, hundreds dying on the way of starvation and the cold. The Jews in the forests fought with the partisans and formed family camps. Over 100 were killed in the Narucz forest in fall 1943 when the Germans made their big anti-partisan sweep. A group led by Abba Kovner fought in the Rudniki forest, some being murdered by the Polish partisans of the Armia Krajowa. V. was liberated by the Red Army on 13 July 1944. Within a short time, 6,000 J. survivors gathered there and the community was reestablished. Large numbers soon left, many for Palestine through the Beriha organization. In 1970 the J. pop. of V. was 16,491 (4% of the total), many of them newcomers. Most left in the exodus of the early 1970s and late 1980s and 1990s, many reaching Israel.

VILSHOFEN Lower Bavaria, Germany. Jews are first mentioned in 1331–32 and were murdered in the disturbances following the massacre of the Jews in the nearby community of Deggendorf in 1338. The modern community never exceeded two dozen Jews (total pop. 3,000–4,000). Sixteen emigrated in 1934–39; six left for other German cities.

VIMPERK-CKYNE Bohemia, Czechoslovakia. Jews were present in both settlements in the first half of the 17th cent. C. had a J. pop. of nearly 240 in the mid-19th cent., with a synagogue, cemetery, and school, but only 11 in 1930. Community facilities were transferred to V. in 1897, its pop. standing at 57 (1% of the total) in 1930. The Nazis destroyed the synagogue in the Holocaust and in 1942 deported the Jews to the Theresienstadt ghetto and then on to the death camps of Poland. A total of 108 J. girls and women, victims of death marches, were buried in the area.

VINCENNES Val-de-Marne dist., France. A small J. community was established at the beginning of the 20th cent., inaugurating a synagogue in 1907 and a cemetery in 1927. Before WWII, the J. pop. numbered 976, dropping to 778 in 1941. In July 1942, 153 Jews were arrested. More arrests followed in Nov. 1942. The Jews were deported to Auschwitz via Drancy. Altogether 171 Jews (including 40 foreign Jews) were deported.

VINKOVCI Croatia, Yugoslavia, today Republic of Croatia. J. settlement began at the end of the 19th cent. Intense communal and Zionist activity began in the 1910s. In 1923 a conference of Yugoslavian rabbis was held there. The J. pop. in 1931 was 995 (total 13,267.) In WWII most of the Jews died in Croatian death camps and Auschwitz.

VINNE Slovakia, Czechoslovakia, today Republic of Slovakia. Jews arrived in the early 18th cent. and renewed the community in the 1730s after abandoning it. Galician refugees settled in the 19th cent., creating a hasidic atmosphere. The J. pop. reached a peak of 272 (total 1,325) in 1880, then dropped rapidly to 60 in 1919 and 32 in 1940. A yeshiva and *talmud torah* were maintained. The Jews were deported to the Lukow ghetto in the Lublin dist. (Poland) on 6 May 1942 and perished.

VINNITSA Vinnitsa dist., Ukraine. Jews are first mentioned in 1532. In 1648 they were murdered in the Chmielnicki massacres and in 1750 the Haidamaks attacked them. The J. pop. was 348 in 1765 and 11,689 in 1897. In the 19th cent., Jews owned the majority of light industry factories as well as wholesale warehouses (wine, grain, lumber) in the city. Most of the city's 212 stores as well as its inns and restaurants were also in J. hands. The community maintained one large synagogue and 16 prayer houses. R. Natan Rubinstein gained a reputation through the 13 halakhic works he wrote. In 1901 two reformed *hadarim* were opened along with a private girls' school. Jews were attacked in a 1905 pogrom; several were killed and property was damaged. They were again attacked, by the Petlyura gangs, on 3 Aug. 1918, with damage to homes and stores. There were no fatalities owing to the quick response of J. self-defense units. In the Soviet period, J. artisans organized themselves into cooperatives and ORT sponsored vocational training for the young. Many Jews were factory or white-collar workers and about 1,500 remained unemployed, mostly those deprived of rights. In the 1930s, new factories were opened, employing many additional J. production workers and clerks. Three Yiddish secondary schools were founded as well as a teachers' college graduating 1,000 teachers by 1938. A theater group was also active. The J. pop. of V. grew to 33,150 in 1939. The Germans captured the city on 11 July 1941. Until then, 17,500 Jews managed to escape to the east. On 29 July, the Germans executed 25 Jews and the next day another 146 belonging to the educated class. In Aug., they shot 350 people, most of them probably Jews, and on 19 Sept., in a mass *Aktion*, about 8,000 Jews were murdered. A closed ghetto was established in Oct. where about 7,000 Jews were confined. Shortly thereafter, 2,000 of the sick and old were removed and killed. In early 1942, J. experts and skilled workers still in the ghetto were put to work constructing a forward command post for Hitler. In Aug. 1942, their families were executed along with some of the workers. The rest were transferred to a labor camp; few survived the war.

VINOGRAD   Kiev dist., Ukraine. A small number of Jews were present in the 18th cent. In 1897, the J. pop. reached 1,523 (total 4,064). Seven Jews were murdered in a pogrom on 13 Nov. 1918. In 1926, under the Soviets, the J. pop. was 1,108. Nearly all the Jews were murdered during the German occupation of WWII.

VINTUL DE JOS   (Hung. Alvincz) S. Transylvania dist., Rumania. Jews settled in the early 18th cent. One of the oldest synagogues in Transylvania was located here. The Jews were attached to the Alba-Iulia community. The majority were employed on the estate of Mor Glick, the head of one of the richest J. families in the region. He received a royal title in 1879. After WWI, the J. pop. declined to 67 (2% of the total) in 1930. In summer 1941, the J. pop. was transferred to Dumbraveni and Alba-Iulia. After the war, the Jews did not return to V.

VIRBALIS   (Yid. Virbaln or Verzhbelov) Vilkaviskis dist., Lithuania. Jews began settling here in the 17th cent. On the Shavuot holiday in 1790, a rabbi was executed in the wake of a blood libel. Antisemitism in the 1870s and 1880s caused many of V.'s Jew to emigrate. Two reformed *hadarim* were established in the late 19th cent. where boys and girls learned together. The

noted Bible scholar Shemuel Leib Gordon taught in one of these schools prior to his emigration to Palestine. Eliyahu Warshavski, the grandson of the Gaon of Vilna, was very active in the field of social welfare. Hovevei Zion began fundraising activities in V. in 1884. Shelomo Bloomgarden ("Yehoash"), a V. native and a noted writer, translated the Bible into Yiddish. The J. pop. in 1897 was 1,219 (37% of the total). A Hebrew high school existed from 1918 through 1934, closing because of a lack of students and the inability of parents to pay tuition. Many of its graduates emigrated to Palestine. The J. pop. in 1939 was 600 (13%). Under the Soviets (1940–41), J. commercial and community life suffered. After the Germans occupied V. on 22 June 1941, the new civil administration kept Jews from working or having contact with non-Jews. On 7 July, all J. males aged 16 and up were taken by the Lithuanians to antitank ditches outside the town and shot. The rest of the Jews were transferred to a ghetto. On 11 Sept. 1941 the women and children were forced into the ditches and also shot.

VIRISMORT   (Hung. Tiszaveresmart) N. Transylvania dist., Rumania. Jews settled in the mid-18th cent. In 1920 the J. pop. was 120 (15% of the total). In April 1944 the community was transferred to the Sighet ghetto and then deported to Auschwitz.

VIROVITICA   Croatia, Yugoslavia, today Republic of Croatia. Jews first settled in the mid-18th cent. and an organized community was established in the mid-19th cent. Following WWI, deserters from the Austro-Hungarian army plundered the Jews. The J. pop. numbered 233 (total 10,654) in 1931 and reached 350 before the Holocaust. During the Holocaust the Jews were persecuted by the Ustase and then sent to Auschwitz and the Dachau concentration camp. Only a few survived the war.

VISAKIO-RUDA   (Yid. Visoke-Rude) Marijampole dist., Lithuania. The J. pop. in 1923 was 80. The Jews were killed in the Holocaust.

VISEGRAD   Bosnia-Hercegovina, Yugoslavia, today Republic of Croatia. In 1879 there were 37 Jews in V. By 1940 they numbered 110 (total pop. 5,000). Only about 40 survived the Holocaust; the rest perished in the German and the Croatian Fascist concentration camps.

The Beit Yisrael yeshiva, Viseul de Sus, Rumania

VISEUL DE SUS (Hung. Felsoviso; Yid. Ober Vishoi) N. Transylvania dist., Rumania. Jews from Galicia settled here in the late 18th cent. and engaged mainly in the lumber industry. In 1859 the first wooden synagogue was built, and another in stone in 1859; another three large synagogues were constructed up to the early 20th cent. Most of the rabbis were erudite scholars and wrote and published numerous tractates. R. Shemuel Shmelke Ginzler served the community for 45 years (1866–1911) and established a yeshiva that became one of the largest in Transylvania. The Jews were mainly members of the Vizhnitz hasidic sect. The majority of the children did not receive a general education but were educated in *heder*-type classes. The J. pop. in 1920 was 3,912 (34% of the total). Between the World Wars the J.-owned lumber mills employed several hundred J. and non-J. workers. J. lawyers, engineers, and officials were employed in public service. R. Menahem Mendel Hagar served the community during 1921–40 and expanded the yeshiva to 300 students. The situation of the Jews declined in Sept. 1940 when the Hungarians took control. Economic sanctions were imposed and Jews were sent to concentration camps in Hungary. In 1942 young Jews were drafted into labor battalions in the Ukraine, where most died. R. Barukh Hager was arrested and tortured for forging certificates for J. inhabitants born before WWI. He was also falsely charged with being a Communist. During 16–23 April 1944, 13,000–17,000 Jews from the V. dist. were ghettoized together with the 4,000 Jews of the community. The physical and sanitary conditions were unbearable and many suffered from hunger. All the Jews were deported to Auschwitz on 17–23 May 1944. In 1947, 800 survivors were living in V., but by 1972 the community no longer existed.

VISKI   Latgale dist., Latvia. The community was established at the turn of the 18th cent. and lived in straitened economic circumstances although constituting the town's majority (668 of 959 residents in 1897 and 423 of 750 in 1935). In the 1930s, the young left for the big cities and some emigrated across the sea. With the arrival of the Soviets in 1940, most J. stores (50 of the town's total of 58 in 1935) were nationalized and J. public life was ended. The German expelled the Jews to the Daugavpils (Dvinsk) ghetto on 28 July 1941 and executed them a few days later in the Pogulianka forest together with Jews from other provincial towns.

VISOKO Bosnia-Hercegovina, Yugoslavia, today Republic of Bosnia. Jews first settled at the end of the 18th cent. The J. pop. in 1931 was 113 (total 4,709). In WWII the Germans murdered most of the Jews.

VISTUPOVICHI Zhitomir dist., Ukraine. The J. pop. was 109 (total 1,032) in 1897 and 204 in 1926 under the Soviets. The Jews who had neither fled nor been evacuated perished in the German occupation (from 22 Aug. 1941).

VISTYTIS (Yid. Vishtinetz) Vilkaviskis dist., Lithuania. By 1758 there was an organized J. community. In 1878 a J. high school, in the spirit of Haskala, was founded. In 1897 the J. pop. was 799 (32% of the total). In the beginning of the 20th cent. many Jews emigrated to the U.S., Argentina, and Palestine. Many were Zionists. There was an ancient and magnificent synagogue. In 1940 the J. pop. was about 150. After Germany's invasion of the USSR in June 1941, the men were separated from the women and children. In July the men were forced to dig mass graves and

then murdered. The women and children were murdered on 9 Sept. 1941.

VITEBSK Vitebsk dist., Belorussia. Jews are first mentioned in 1551. In 1597, King Sigismund III of Poland banned their residence in the city but they nonetheless managed to lease inns under the auspices of the local nobility. In 1627, the local ruler allowed them to erect a synagogue and in 1633 King Wladyslaw IV granted permanent residence rights to the Jews and confirmed all previously accorded rights. The Jews were placed under the jurisdiction of Voyevoda. After the Russians captured the city in 1654, they expelled the Jews, who had participated in its defense, to Novgorod and afterwards to Kazan in southern Russia. They were only permitted to return after a peace treaty was signed with Poland. In 1679, King John III Sobieski confirmed previous J. rights, including the right to build their own houses, maintain a synagogue and ritual bath, and trade freely. This charter of privileges was renewed by the Polish kings in 1729 and 1759. In the war between Poland and Sweden in the early 18th cent., the J. quarter was destroyed. The Jews of V. came under the jurisdic-

High school for Jewish girls, Vitebsk, Belorussia

tion of the Brest-Litovsk community in the Lithuanian Council. In 1765, the J. pop. was 667, rising to 1,227 (22% of the total) after the First Partition of Poland in 1772. During the 19th cent., the J. pop. in V. grew rapidly, from 5,940 in 1811 to 34,420 in 1897. The causes of this growth were the expulsion of Jews from villages and from Moscow (in the 1890s), increased river traffic to Riga via small craft on the Dvina River, and the establishment of a railway link between the interior of Russia and the Baltic ports. Jews played a leading role in the industrial and commercial development of the city. They controlled the trade in lumber, flax, and tobacco and were prominent as tailors. Hundreds worked for the Russian market as manufacturers of plows, furniture, and bricks and as beer brewers. V. was a stronghold of Orthodox Judaism. The first Hasidim in Lithuania, R. Menahem Mendel of V. and Shneur Zalman of Lyady, were active here while the influence of the *Mitnaggedim* was also great. Among the city's well-known state-appointed rabbis were Yitzhak Behard, who officiated from 1803 to 1860; Yekutiel Zalman Landau, who succeeded him and also headed the famous V. yeshiva; and from 1901, the Zionist leader Dr. Tzevi Hirsch Bruck, who had a great influence on public life, particularly as a delegate to the first Duma. As the community grew, the number of synagogues increased, from just two in the first half of the 19th cent. to 17 in the 1890s. There were also dozens of prayer houses, most serving the Hasidim. Hovevei Zion became active in the city in the 1880s and the socialist movement took root in the late 1890s, with V. becoming one of the first centers of the Bund. In the late 19th cent, 72% of school-age J. children attended 73 *hadarim* and two or three *talmudei torah*. At the initiative of the Po'alei Zion party, one of the *talmudei torah* became a regular school, combining religious and Hebrew-language secular studies. Other children studied at two state J. schools, at two private schools for boys, and at three private schools for girls. In the 1890s, 41 J. children attended a boys' secondary school (10% of the total enrollment) and 60 a girls' secondary school (total enrollment 278). The artist Y. Pen opened an art school in the early 20th cent. Among its students were Marc Chagall (b. 1887) and Shelomo Yudovin (b. 1894). Prominent figures born in V. include the Russian-Yiddish writer S. An-Ski (Shelomo Zainwil Rapaport; b. 1863) and various members of the wealthy Ginzburg family (mainly from its banking branch) who were active as financiers and philanthropists among the Jews of Russia in the second half of the 19th cent. and the early 20th. In 1887 and 1901, great fires destroyed hundreds of J. homes. During WWI, V. was a transit point for tens of thousands of J. refugees from Lithuania. Some (3,500 in 1916) settled in the city. In 1927, the Habad yeshiva of Polotsk moved to V. with its 150 students and continued to operate under R. Avraham Dreizin until 1930, when most of the students were arrested; the rest were dispersed throughout the Soviet Union or managed to flee the country. In the Soviet period, the J. pop. remained fairly stable: 37,013 in 1926 and 37,095 (total 167,299) in 1939. A number of Yiddish newspapers were published in the city, including *Der Royter Shtern* (early 1920s) and the weekly *Vitebsker Arbeter* (from 1925). After the closure of religious and private J. schools and a staged trial "against the *heder*" in 1921, the Soviet authorities opened a network of Yiddish-language schools. In the 1920s, the network included eight elementary schools (including a few with boarding facilities), eight kindergartens, and a J. teachers' college founded in 1922 and attended by over 150 students in 1927. In 1937, the latter was combined with the J. sec-

The Great Synagogue of Vitebsk, Belorussia

Витебскъ.

Marc Chagall, Paris, 1922. Chagall studied at the Y. Pen art school opened in Vitebsk in the early 20th cent.

tion of the Belorussian College of Minsk and reached an attendance of 225. Of the city's five vocational schools, one was exclusively for Jews while at the others Jews comprised 50% of the student body. A J. library with thousands of volumes was started in 1922 or 1923 and in the early 1920s the first J. law court in Russia with deliberations in Yiddish was opened. In the mid-1920s, 38% of the members of the local council (soviet) were Jews. In the late 1920s and early 1930s the number of J. industrial workers increased. The Vestchevoi factory employed over 1,400 in 1929 (82% of its work force). On the other hand, J. representation at the local textile plant dropped from 86% (246 of 286 workers) in 1927 to 62% (467 of 755) in 1929 and the downward trend continued in the 1930s. In the late 1920s, Jews comprised over 90% of the city's artisans. Despite the size of the city, there were a few kolkhozes in its environs, some J., where a number of J. families worked in agriculture. Of the Zionist parties, only Hehalutz (which founded a farm cooperative in the early 1920s) managed to hold its own with a few dozen members in a

hostile Soviet environment until liquidated in a wave of arrests in the mid-1920s.

The Soviet authorities evacuated many Jews together with non-J. residents prior to the German occupation of the city on 11 July 1941. However, the rapidly advancing German army cut off many evacuees in the Smolensk area, forcing them to return to V. Shortly after their arrival, the Germans established a ghetto around the bombed-out railway station and in a few alleyways, sealing it off with barbed wire and crowding 20–30 Jews into a room. Executions commenced on 24 July. Many J. refugees were arrested and sent to an unknown destination from which they never returned. On 12 Aug., 332 young Jews, supposedly chosen to work outside the city, were murdered at the village of Tcherkovschina. In late Aug., 300 (according to another source, 500–600) educated Jews were murdered outside the city near the Ilov River. Another 800 were also murdered in a single day during the summer. Most of the executions were carried out by *Sonderkommando 7a* and *9* units under the command of Dr. Filbert. The Germans set up a *Judenrat*, which, in addition to organizing the J. labor force, helped carry out a census of the Jews, who now numbered 16,000. In early Sept. another 397 were murdered and on 1 Oct., 52 J. refugees from Gorodok were killed. A few Jews succeeded in escaping to the forests but many were subsequently caught and put to death. Some, however, managed to join the partisans. The mass murder of the Jews began on 8–11 Oct. 1941. About 4,000 Jews (according to another source, 8,000) were transported to the Ilov River, near the village of Miskhury, and executed. In the same month, 207 Jews in the prisoner-of-war camp near the city were murdered. In early Nov., another 8,000–10,000 from V. and its environs were murdered near Miskhury. The last 500 Jews in the ghetto were murdered in March 1942. A few "essential" Jews were kept alive until the fall. In addition to those shot, about 5,000 died of starvation and disease, mainly in the summer and fall of 1941. In the late fall of 1943, the Germans began obliterating the traces of their crimes by digging up the mass graves and burning the bodies of their victims. Two years after the liberation of V. the J. pop. of the city was just 500.

VITKA Zemplen dist., Hungary. Jews settled in the mid-18th cent. under the protection of Count Karoly. They numbered 270 in 1880 but left in large numbers after WWI when much of their trade was curtailed by the Czech annexation of northern Hungary. On 18 April 1944, the remaining 72 Jews were brought to Mateszalka and on 2 June they were deported to Auschwitz.

VITRY-LE-FRANCOIS Marne dist., France. The J. community dates from the 16th cent. Simha ben Shemuel, a contemporary of Rashi and believed to be the author of *Mahzor Vitry*, was born in V. (in the 11th cent.). After 1870, families from Alsace and Lorraine settled in the town and the community was reconstituted. A synagogue was inaugurated in 1855. During WWII, children from the UGIF children's home in Paris found refuge here. The Germans completely destroyed the synagogue in 1944. The synagogue was reconstructed in 1957. In the mid-1960s the community numbered 60 members.

VITTEL Vosges dist., France. The J. community was established around 1925–26. Many community members originated from North Africa. The local synagogue was inaugurated in 1928. V. served as a summer resort for Nancy Jews. During WWII, several hotels were used to form a labor camp. One of the inmates was the Yiddish poet Itzhak Katzenelson, who was deported to Auschwitz, where he perished. From July 1944, 39 Jews were arrested.

VIZSOLY Abauj–Torna dist., Hungary. Jews settled in 1848 and never exceeded 50 in number. The last four J. families were deported to Auschwitz via Kassa in mid-May 1944.

VLACHOVO (Hung. Olyvos; Yid. Lahyf) Carpatho-Russia, Czechoslovakia, today Ukraine. Jews probably settled in the early 19th cent. Their pop. was ten in 1830 and 90 (total 943) in 1880. A few were farmers. In 1921, under Czechoslovakian rule, the J. pop. rose to 179, dropping to 171 in 1941. The Hungarians occupied the town in March 1939 and in 1940–41 drafted a number of Jews into forced labor batallions. In late July 1941, a few J. families without Hungarian citizenship were expelled to German-occupied territory in the Ukraine and murdered. The rest were deported to Auschwitz in mid-May 1944.

VLASENICA Bosnia-Hercegovina, Yugoslavia, today Republic of Bosnia. Jews settled there in the 19th cent. and in 1931 numbered 51 (total 4,904). The Jews perished in the Holocaust.

VLASIM Bohemia, Czechoslovakia. Jews are mentioned in 1570 and there was a small community in 1724. Most Jews were distillers and some were active in the phosphorus industry until the 1848 revolution, when they were integrated into the economy. Their pop. rose to 210 in 1893 and then dropped steadily to 67 (total 3,625) in 1930. In 1942, the Jews were deported to the Theresienstadt ghetto together with the Jews of Prague. From there they were sent to the death camps of Poland.

VLISSINGEN Zeeland dist., Holland. Jews were present in the 16th and 17th cents. but a stable community was established only in the 19th cent., numbering 129 in 1870. In 1941 the J. pop. was 38 (total 19,699). In March 1942 the Jews were evacuated to Amsterdam and from there deported to death camps; only two survived in hiding.

VLOTHO   Westphalia, Germany. Jews were present by the late 17th cent. and reached a peak pop. of 137 in 1855. The 17th cent. cemetery was replaced by a new one in 1854 and a synagogue was consecrated in 1851. In 1933 the J. pop. was 87. On *Kristallnacht* (9–10 Nov. 1938), the synagogue was vandalized and J. property destroyed. In May 1939, 59 Jews remained. The 25 still there in 1941–42 were deported.

VOCIN   Croatia, Yugoslavia, today Republic of Croatia. Jews lived there from the end of the 19th cent. The J. pop. in 1921 was 39 (total 6,437). The Jews perished in WWII.

VODNANY   Bohemia, Czechoslovakia. Jews were present in 1500 but the few there were expelled in 1541, returning only after 100 years. A new synagogue was built in the 1837–52 period. In 1884, the J. pop. was about 60 families. In 1930, 114 Jews remained (total 4,229). The synagogue was closed in Oct. 1941 and most of the Jews were deported to the Theresienstadt ghetto in 1942. From there they were sent to the death camps of Poland.

VOEHL   Hesse–Nassau, Germany. The community, which also had members in Marienhagen and Basdorf, dedicated a synagogue in 1829, maintained an elementary school (1835–1924), and numbered 86 (11% of the total) in 1885. Most of the 25 Jews still living there in 1933 had left (seven emigrating) by 1940; at least six perished in the Holocaust.

VOELKERSLEIER   Lower Franconia, Germany. A J. community is known from the mid-18th cent., with a synagogue erected in 1762. In 1830–54, 28 Jews emigrated to the U.S. The J. pop. in 1867 was 95 (total 602) and 33 in 1933. The economic boycott under the Nazis reduced many to penury and J. homes were looted on *Kristallnacht* (9–10 Nov. 1938). By Feb. 1939, 17 Jews had emigrated, including 14 to the U.S.; another nine left for other German cities by 1941. The last six Jews were deported to Izbica in the Lublin dist. (Poland) and the Theresienstadt ghetto in 1942.

VOELKLINGEN   Saar, Germany. The J. pop. was nine in 1895; 103 in 1927 (0.3% of the total); and 76 in 1935. The eight Jews who remained in Sept. 1939 subsequently perished in the Holocaust.

VOERDEN   Westphalia, Germany. Five J. families were present in the early 19th cent. The community numbered 38 (total 690) in 1871 and 18 in June 1933. It maintained a prayer room and from the late 19th cent. a cemetery. Nine Jews emigrated in the Nazi period and another four moved to other localities in Germany. On *Kristallnacht* (9–10 Nov. 1938), the windows of two J. stores were smashed. The last five Jews were deported to the Riga ghetto in Dec. 1941.

VOIO-NOVO   Crimea, Russia, today Ukraine. V. was founded in the late 1920s as a J. agricultural commune by 94 pioneers of the J. Labor Battalion (*Gedud ha-Avoda*), some of whose members were among the founders of Kibbutz Ramat Rahel in Palestine. The Soviet authorities encouraged the founders of the commune, returning from Palestine and disillusioned with the Zionist dream, to build their settlement as "proof" of the bankruptcy of Zionism. Their main source of income was farming. Having brought back a tractor and truck, they grew wheat and a variety of vegetables. A J. elementary school was opened in the early 1930s. In 1932, the J. pop. totaled 100 families. During the period of Stalinist terror, 43 of the founding "Palestinian" members were arrested; only 11 survived. When the Germans arrived in late Oct. 1941, they murdered the other Jews. A few escaped earlier to the Caucasian mountains. One J. family was handed over to the Germans by its non-J. neighbors and drowned in a well. A number of survivors returned after the war. A few of the settlement's founders were among the many Russian Jews who emigrated to Israel in the 1990s.

VOLCHANSK   Kharkov dist., Ukraine. Jews settled in 19th cent., numbering 40 in 1897 and 210 (total 20,435) in 1939. The Germans held the city on 6–11 Nov. 1941, killing all the Jews there before occupying it again in June 1942.

VOLKMARSEN   Hesse–Nassau, Germany. Established in the 17th cent., the community, which maintained a synagogue and an elementary school, numbered 169 (about 6% of the total) in 1855. Affiliated with the Kassel rabbinate, it dwindled to 34 in 1933. The Jews mostly emigrated, disposing of their synagogue in 1937; the last eight perished after they were deported to the east in 1942.

VOLKOVINTSY   Kamenets-Podolski dist., Ukraine. Jews are first mentioned in 1737 and numbered 98 in 1784 and 1,168 (56% of the total) in 1897. In 1939, under the Soviets, the J. pop. was 764. The Germans occupied the town on 17 July 1941. In the 1941–43 period, they executed 369 Jews at the J. cemetery. In Sept. 1942, 280 Jews were sent to Derazhnya, where they were executed. The last *Aktion* occurred in early 1943.

VOLLMERZ (now part of Schluechtern) Hesse-Nassau, Germany. Dating from the 18th cent., this J. community numbered 103 (23% of the pop.) in 1861 and 22 in 1933. Its wooden synagogue had an interior design and Hebrew inscriptions executed by a Christian artist in 1812. The interior was destroyed on *Kristallnacht* (9–10 Nov. 1938) and by 1941 all the remaining Jews had left.

VOLNOVAKHA Stalino dist., Ukraine. The J. pop. in 1939 was 174 (total 15,261). During the German occupation, which began on 11 March 1941, 283 Jews from V. and its environs were murdered.

VOLOCHISK Kamenets-Podolski dist., Ukraine. Jews arrived in the 18th cent and numbered 774 in 1767. Jews were attacked in riots on 5 May 1881. With the town located on the Russian-Austrian border, Jews engaged in some smuggling and traded in farm produce, particularly eggs and geese. In 1897, the J. pop. was 3,295 (49% of the total). Most Jews were expelled in WWI, returning to find their homes and stores pillaged. In the 1920s and 1930s, a J. council (soviet) was active in the town. By 1939 the J. pop. had fallen to 521. The Germans arrived in V. on 5 July 1941. In Aug. 1942, about 5,000 Jews were murdered, including about 600 from Kupel, Voitovetz, and other towns in the area.

VOLODARKA Kiev dist., Ukraine. Jews numbered 475 in 1765 and 2,079 (total 4,490) in 1897. V. was the birthplace of the well-known J. mathematician Salomon Loewenstein. Ukrainian gangs attacked the Jews in fall 1917 and in another pogrom on 3 Aug. 1918, nine Jews were murdered. On 23 June 1918, the Petlyura gangs staged a new pogrom. In 1926, under the Soviets, the J. pop. was 209. Five families left for Kalinindorf in the 1930s in the framework of agricultural resettlement. The Germans occupied V. on 14 July 1941 and immediately murdered ten Jews. Two more

were murdered the next day and nearly all the rest — about 200 — a short while afterwards.

VOLODARSK VOHLINSKII (Horoshki, Kutuzovo, Volodarskoye) Zhitomir dist., Ukraine. The J. pop. in 1897 was 2,018 (total 3,228). In 1929, under the Soviets, the J. pop. included 251 artisans, 149 laborers, and 34 merchants. In 1939, the J. pop. was 988. The Germans captured V. on 12 Aug. 1941 and soon afterwards murdered the 143 Jews who had neither fled nor been evacuated.

VOLODARSKYI Leningrad dist., Russia. J. settlement probably began in the early 20th cent. In 1939, the J. pop. was 153 (total 13,820). The Germans murdered 60 Jews after occupying the town in mid-Jan. 1942.

VOLOS (Volo) Thessaly, Greece. A small Romaniot (Byzantine) community existed in V. from the 14th cent. In the early 19th cent., 35 J. families from the Peloponnesus settled there and established a community. The Alliance Israelite opened a J. school in 1864 and a new synagogue was built in 1865. Due to lack of funds and corrupt administration, the school was closed in 1878. The J. pop. in 1869 was 190. The community became renowned for its hospitality to the many who passed through V.'s port. In the 1870s, the community experienced financial hardship, exacerbated by the arrival of 30–40 destitute J. families from Janina. In 1881, Thessaly came under Greek rule and the community gained rights as a religious body. A new Alliance school was opened in 1888 and operated until 1926. In the last decade of the cent., the community suffered from a blood libel, anti-J. propaganda, and widespread poverty. In 1892, R. Moshe Pesach was appointed community rabbi and held the position until his death in 1955. He worked diligently and selflessly for the benefit of the community. The J. pop. in 1896 stood at about 500 (total 16,788). In the early 20th cent., many Jews contributed to the economy and development of V. A J.-owned textile factory employed 600 workers. In 1908 a Zionist organization was established and a few others followed in the 1920s. In 1921 the Pan-Hellenist Zionist Congress, attended by representatives of all Greek communities, took place in V. By 1939 there were 14 charity associations alongside a number of cultural and youth organizations. In 1930, the J.

pop. reached a peak of about 2,000, but with the increasing financial difficulties many left for Athens and Salonika as well as overseas for England, Italy, and France. The J. pop. in 1940 was 882. In April 1941, the Italian army entered V. In 1943, many J. refugees fleeing the atrocities in Salonika and eastern Macedonia reached V. Their accounts led many to flee to Athens and the villages in the surrounding hills. In Sept. 1943, the Germans entered. With the assistance of the underground movement, Bishop Joachim of Dimitrias, the mayor, and the chief of police, most of V.'s Jews were able to escape to the surrounding villages with false identity cards. Many joined the underground movement and took part in anti-German activities. About 100, mostly those without means, remained in V. On 24–25 March 1944 the remaining Jews in V. were sent to Larissa and from there to the death camps. In all, 117 Jews from V. perished in the death camps, 12 were murdered in the area, and about 30 died of starvation and disease. After the war the community numbered about 700 Jews, some of whom were refugees from other communities. The community was rehabilitated and grew to be one of the largest in Greece after Athens and Salonika.

VOLOVE (Hung. Okormezo) Carpatho-Russia, Czechoslovakia, today Ukraine. Jews probably settled in the mid-18th cent., numbering 11 in 1768, 130 in 1830, and 269 (total 2,097) in 1880. In 1921, under Czechoslovakian rule, the J. pop. grew to 766. J. children attended a Czech school after an attempt to start a J. one in the 1920s failed. A few dozen Jews attended a yeshiva run by the community's rabbi, Aharon Teitelbaum. Most of the town's businesses were in J. hands, including 39 of its 45 stores. There were 23 Jews working as artisans. Jews owned a bank and a number of factories (producing alcoholic beverages and furniture). A few Jews were doctors or lawyers and a few were administrative officials. Betar, Bnei Akiva, and Hashomer Hatzair were active among J. youth. In 1941, the J. pop. was 952. The Hungarians occupied the town in March 1939 and in 1940–41 drafted dozens of Jews into labor battalions, sending some to the eastern front, where most perished. Others were subjected to forced labor in Hungary itself. In late July or early Aug. 1941, a few J. families without Hungarian citizenship were expelled to the German-occupied Ukraine and murdered. About 600 were deported to Auschwitz in May 1944.

VOLOVEC (Hung. Volocz) Carpatho-Russia, Czechoslovakia, today Ukraine. One J. family was present in 1768. In 1880, the J. pop. was 71 (total 679) while in the Czechoslovakian period it grew to 329 (in 1921). A few Jews farmed. Hashomer Hatzair was the most prominent among the youth groups. The Hungarians occupied the town in March 1939, drafting dozens of Jews into labor battalions. In 1941, the J. pop. was 388. In late July, a number of J. families without Hungarian citizenship were expelled to the German-occupied Ukraine and murdered. The remaining 300 were deported to Auschwitz in mid-May 1944.

VOLYNE Bohemia, Czechoslovakia. Jews are mentioned from the late 15th cent., with a ghetto established in the 17th or 18th cent. The J. pop. was 92 in 1724. The nearby Hostice community with its synagogue and 17 families was attached to the V. congregation in 1899. The J. pop. of V. was 63 in 1921 and 51 (total 3,083) in 1930. In 1942, 55 Jews were deported to the Theresienstadt ghetto together with the Jews of Prague and from there to the death camps of Poland.

VOLYNETS Vitebsk dist., Belorussia. The J. pop. was 602 (total 985) in 1897 and 457 in 1926. A kolkhoz founded in 1929 supported 11 J. families. The Germans arrived in early July 1941. The remaining 84 Jews were murdered in Feb. 1942.

VONIHOVO (Hung. Vajnag; Yid. Vinif) Carpatho-Russia, Czechoslovakia, today Ukraine. Jews settled in the mid-18th cent., numbering 19 in 1768, 67 in 1830, and 190 (total 774) in 1880. A few J. families farmed small plots of land. In 1921, the J. pop. rose to 342. During the Czechoslovakian period, a number of Zionist organizations were active, with Betar opening a club. The Hungarians occupied the town in March 1939 and in 1941 drafted a few dozen Jews into labor battalions. In 1941, the J. pop. was 354. In Aug., a few dozen J. families without Hungarian citizenship were expelled to Kamenets-Podolski, where they were murdered. The remaining 120 Jews were deported to Auschwitz in late May 1944. A few survivors returned after the war. One was murdered by a local resident and the rest left for Czechoslovakia.

VONKOVTSY (from 1946, Vinkovtsy) Kamenets-Podolski dist., Ukraine. A J. community was founded in the 18th cent., reaching a pop. of 305 in 1784 and

1,768 (56% of the total) in 1897. In 1939, under the Soviets, the J. pop. was 1,745. The Germans captured the town on 11 July 1941 and executed 1,875 Jews on 14 April 1942. Another 450 from V. and its environs were murdered at the village of Stanislavovka on 9 May. An anti-Nazi underground movement active during the occupation numbered six Jews among its 11 members. On 12 April 1942, they were arrested and on 5 June executed at Dunayevtsy.

VORONEZH Voronezh dist., Russia. Jews probably settled in the early 19th cent. In 1862, the J. pop. of the region was 337, including 245 in V. The J. pop. grew, reaching 1,708 (total 80,599) in 1897, after the railroad linked V. to the big cities. A number of Jews were killed in a pogrom that began on 21 Oct. 1905 and lasted a few days. A synagogue was operating in 1908. In the Soviet period, the J. pop. rose to 4,589 in 1923 and 8,358 (total 326,932) in 1939. V. was the birthplace of Soviet WWII hero General Jacob Kreiser (1905–69) and the poet and translator Shemuel Marschak (1887–1964). The Germans occupied the western part of the city in July 1942 after heavy fighting. Many Jews escaped to the Soviet side and were saved but a number were trapped by the Germans and murdered on 10 Aug.

VORONIECHI Vitebsk dist., Belorussia. Jews numbered 65 (total 163) in 1920. Of the 26 J. families there in 1925, seven were engaged in agriculture. The Germans occupied V. on 4 July 1941 and murdered all its 60 Jews in Jan. 1942.

VORONIZH Sumy dist., Ukraine. The J. pop. in 1939 was 96 (1% of the total). After the arrival of the Germans on 27 Aug. 1941, they murdered the Jews still there.

VORONOK Oriol dist., Russia. Jews probably settled in the mid-19th cent. In 1897, their pop. was 371 (total 3,707), dropping in the Soviet period to 93 in 1926. Following the German occupation in Aug. 1941, 26 Jews were murdered.

VORONOVITSA Vinnitsa dist., Ukraine. J. settlement commenced in the mid-18th cent., with the J. pop. growing to 115 in 1765 and 1,411 (total 3,013) in 1897. Most of the town's 72 self-employed artisans were Jews. In the 1930s, under the Soviets, when the town suffered from famine, nearly 300 Jews died. In 1939, the J. pop. was 860. The Germans occupied V. on 27 July 1941. Some Jews fled but the large majority were killed off in a number of *Aktions*: 200 in Oct. 1942; 150 in Jan 1943; and the rest on 24 May 1943.

VOROSHILOV Dnepropetrovsk dist., Ukraine. V. was a J. farm settlement in the Stalindorf J. Autonomous Region. The jurisdiction of the V. rural council (soviet) extended over more than 3,000 Jews in 1932 and the pop. of V. itself was 710 in 1934. The few Jews who had neither fled nor been evacuated at the time of the German occupation of Aug. 1941 were probably murdered in May 1942.

VOROSHILOVGRAD (until 1935, Lugansk) Voroshilovgrad dist., Ukraine. Jews probably settled in the early 19th cent. and numbered 1,502 (total 20,404) in 1897. Three J. schools were open in 1910. In 1912, Y. Lerner, editor of the newspaper *Ha-Perahim*, was chosen as chief rabbi of the community. During WWI, the community aided J. refugees who arrived in the city in 1915–16. In the 1920s, under the Soviets, most Jews were unemployed because of their status as declassed members of the bourgeoisie. In the 1930s, they began working in the city's railroad and tractor industries. The J. pop. reached 10,622 in 1939. Prior to the German occupation of the city on 17 July 1942, most of the Jews were evacuated. Of the 1,038 who remained behind most were murdered at Ivanishchev Yar on 1 Nov. 1942 and 21 Jan. 1943. Jews from other localities in the region were also murdered at V. In all, 1,966 Jews were executed.

VOROSHILOVKA Vinnitsa dist., Ukraine. Jews settled in the late 17th cent. and numbered 116 in 1765 and 1,592 (total 3,180) in 1897. A stone synagogue was erected in the mid-19th cent. After the civil war (1918–21), the J. pop. dropped, to 1,079 in 1926. A J. elementary school was still operating in the early 1930s. The Germans captured the town in mid-July 1941, immediately murdering the Jews who had not fled. V. was attached to Transnistria in the early fall and a ghetto and *Judenrat* were established. Hundreds of Jews from Mogilev and its environs were brought there in 1942. About half died; the rest were sent back in fall 1942. Hundreds more arrived from Bessarabia and Bukovina; 278 Jews were still there on 1 Sept. 1943.

VOROSHILOVO (I) Nikolaiev dist., Ukraine. A rural council (soviet) operated in the settlement in the Soviet period. The Germans arrived in Aug. 1941 and murdered 130 Jews from nearby villages, 78 of them from V. Another 150 J. deportees from Bessarabia were murdered at the neighboring village of Krasnoye.

VOROSHILOVO (II) (after WWII, Klimovo) Crimea, Russia, today Ukraine. Jews probably settled in the 1920s, numbering about 130 in 1932. V., as a J. farm settlement, was included in the J. county of Larindorf when it was established in 1935. The Germans occupied V. in late Oct. 1941 and murdered the Jews there on 24 Nov. A few survivors returned after the war but soon left.

VOROSHILOVSK (I) (until 1935 and from 1943, Stavropol) Stavropol territory, Russia. Ashkenazi Jews first settled in the 1830s. In time, the categories of Jews permitted to settle were expanded (artisans in 1865, for example) and the J. pop. grew to about 600 in 1879 and 1,236 (total 41,000) in 1897. In the early 20th cent., two modernized *hadarim* functioned and the community had the right to collect taxes from local Jews. During WWI and its aftermath, the J. pop. was augmented by hundreds of Mountain Jews (Tats) fleeing their villages in the area because of fear of the local pop. In the mid-1920s, the J. pop. was about 3,500, including 300 of the Mountain Jews, who left V. between the World Wars. The Germans occupied V. on 5 Aug. 1942 and gassed the remaining Jews in vans on 15 Aug.

VOROSHILOVSK (II) (until 1931, Alchevsk; from 1961, Komunarsk) Voroshilovgrad dist., Ukraine. J. settlement began in the early 20th cent. after the development of the town's iron mines and metal industry. In 1939, the J. pop. was 1,363 (total 54,531). The Germans captured V. on 12 July 1942 after most of the Jews were evacuated. The 100 remaining Jews were murdered on 24 Sept. 1942.

VORU Estonia. Cantonists founded the community in the 1860s and established a synagogue and cemetery. The J. pop. numbered 176 in 1881 (total 2,697). During WWI, J. refugees from Riga and Courland arrived as well as around 250 J. soldiers from the Russian army. Emigration reduced the J. pop. to 122 in

1922 and 55 in 1939 (total 5,000). Cultural life revolved around a politically unaffiliated social club, while most Jews identified with the Zionists. Some Jews escaped to the Soviet Union with the approach of the Germans in June 1941. The rest were murdered in summer or fall 1941 by the German *Sonderskommando 1a* with the assistance of the Estonian Omakaitse ("self-defense") organization.

VORZEL Kiev dist., Ukraine. The J. pop. in 1939 was 174. After their arrival on 23 Aug. 1941, the Germans murdered the Jews.

VOTICE Bohemia, Czechoslovakia. Jews probably arrived in the 14th cent. and by 1538 constituted one of the six largest communities in Bohemia. They traded at first mostly in wool, feathers, and flax and later in cattle and jewelry. Fires destroyed the J. quarter in 1661, 1693, and 1724. A new synagogue was built in the latter year. After the 1848 revolution, Jews entered fully into the social and economic life of the city. They joined the professional class while also operating a distillery and *matza* (unleavened bread) factory. Their pop. was 340 (total 2,492) in 1869; 163 in 1910; and 76 in 1930. The synagogue was closed down in Oct. 1941 and most of the Jews were deported to the Theresienstadt ghetto via Tabor in Nov. 1942. From there, in Jan., Sept., and Oct. 1943, they were sent to Auschwitz. In nearby Olbramovice, 82 Jews were executed and buried in May 1945. At neighboring Krestice, another 27 were murdered on a death march in 1945.

VOYKOVDORF Dnepropetrovsk dist., Ukraine. As a J. farm settlement, V. numbered 3,067 Jews in 1930 when it became part of the Stalindorf J. Autonomous Region. V. had a J. school with boarding facilities for children from about ten neighboring settlements. Two buildings for 70 of the children were built in 1934. The few Jews who had neither fled nor been evacuated at the time of the German occupation of Aug. 1941 were probably murdered in May 1942.

VOZNESENSK Odessa dist., Ukraine. The J. pop. was 778 in 1860 and 5,931 (total 15,748) in 1897. Two government schools for J. children and a *talmud torah* were operating in 1909. A J. elementary school was open in the mid-1920s under the Soviets. The J. pop. in 1939 was 2,843. The Germans arrived on 6

Aug. 1941. By the end of the year, they had murdered 67 local Jews and 174 from the surrounding area (another source has 300 murdered in Sept. 1941 alone). In Feb. 1942, 2,500 Jews from Odessa were murdered along the road leading to the village of Yastrebinovo. In all, 3,174 inhabitants of the region were murdered during the war, most of them Jews.

VRABLE Slovakia, Czechoslovakia, today Republic of Slovakia. Jews were apparently present by the early 17th cent. and probably expelled in 1727, returning only in about the 1830s. From 1880 until WWII, their pop. was 200–300 (9–10% of the total). A J. school was opened in the late 1850s and a synagogue was consecrated in 1872. The first rabbi, Feivel Jungreis, had jurisdiction over 23 neighboring settlements. The first J. store, a grocery, was opened in 1849 and soon most stores were in J. hands. In 1872, Jews founded the town's first factory (manufacturing vinegar). The Zionists became active after WWI. Expulsions and severe persecution accompanied the annexation to Hungary in Nov. 1938. Dozens were seized for forced labor in 1941. In March 1944, the J. pop. was 252. On 10 June the Jews were sent to the Levice ghetto and three days later deported to Auschwitz. Most of the postwar community of 87 left for Israel in 1949.

VRADISTE Slovakia, Czechoslovakia, today Republic of Slovakia. The J. pop. was over 400 in 1850. The community included eight affiliated settlements and maintained a synagogue, cemetery, community center, and *beit midrash*. Fifty Jews remained after WWI.

VRANOV (Hung. Varanno) Slovakia, Czechoslovakia, today Republic of Slovakia. Jews arrived in the early 18th cent. They numbered 683 (nearly half the total) in 1828, but in 1831 a cholera epidemic decimated the community, which was subsequently attacked in riots. The emperor levied heavy fines after Jews participated in the revolutionary events of 1848–49. This further undermined the community, causing many to leave. In the late 19th cent., a J. elementary school was opened and hasidic families arrived as the community began to recover economically. The J. pop. grew to 783 in 1919 and 1,010 in 1940. A magnificent synagogue was erected in 1928. The Zionists also became active in the 1920s. Jews served on

the municipal council and owned 75 business establishments, 34 workshops, and two factories. In the Slovakian state, J. children were expelled from the public schools and J. businesses were closed down while men were seized for forced labor. About 100 young J. women were deported to Auschwitz in March 1942. Young men were dispatched to the Majdanek concentration camp in early April; dozens of families were deported in mid-April; and on 19 May, 410 local Jews were included in a transport of 1,005 from the area bound for Nalenczow in the Lublin dist. (Poland). Altogether about 90% of the town's Jews were deported to camps in 1942. Most of the 125 Jews left behind were evacuated to western Slovakia in May 1944 and escaped the Germans.

VRBAS Vojvodina dist., Yugoslavia. Jews first lived in V. in the early 19th cent. and numbered 250 by 1840. The community took pride in its liberal school established in 1838. The Yugoslavian authorities suppressed the antisemitic attacks that followed WWI. In the 1930s Zionism developed and won over most of the community. The J. pop. in 1931 was 209 (total 8,361). In 1941 Hungarian-instituted anti-J. laws led more than a third of the Jews to leave for other towns. There were arrests and then all the men were mobilized for forced labor. Many died as a result. In March 1944, the Germans arrived and on 20 April all the remaining Jews were sent to concentration camps, most to Auschwitz in June. Some were later sent to the Theresienstadt ghetto. In all, 176 died in the Holocaust.

VRBOVCE (Hung. Verboc) Slovakia, Czechoslovakia, today Republic of Slovakia. Jews settled in the early 18th cent., possibly beforehand. Their number grew to 345 (total 3,982) in 1869 and then declined steadily. A J. elementary school was opened in the 1850s. In 1940, the J. pop. was 62. The Jews were deported to the death camps of the Lublin dist. (Poland) in spring 1942.

VRBOVE (Hung. Verbo) Slovakia, Czechoslovakia, today Republic of Slovakia. Jews were present as merchants and moneylenders in the late Middle Ages, possibly earlier. The modern community is thought to have been founded by refugees fleeing Uhersky Brod after the disturbances of 1683. In 1787, the J. pop. was 560, making the community the second largest in the

Nitra dist. after Nove Mesto. R. Yaakov Koppel Alt-konstatt served in 1793–1836, founding an important yeshiva. In the 19th cent., economic conditions improved with Jews trading in farm produce and the community reaching a peak pop. of 1,320 (total 4,629) in 1869. The V. community was known for its educational system, which included an elementary school founded in 1855 and a *talmud torah* in addition to the yeshiva. Emigration from the 1880s on reduced the J. pop. to 717 in 1919. In the postwar period, both the Mizrachi movement and Agudat Israel were active. Jews owned most of the town's commercial establishments and workshops. In 1940, 559 Jews remained. J. children were expelled from the public schools in 1940 and J. businesses were closed down or "Aryanized" in 1941. In fall 1941, 212 J. refugees from Bratislava arrived, bringing the J. pop. up to about 780. On 1 April 1942, 27 J. girls were deported to Auschwitz, followed by a few dozen young men sent to the Majdanek concentration camp. On 26 April, dozens of families were deported to the Lublin dist. (Poland) via Piestany and on 8 May, about 250 Jews were sent to Poland and the death camps via Sered. Eighteen families were sent to Zilina with most proceeding to Auschwitz in Sept. After the repression of the Slovakian national uprising in fall 1944, the Germans seized about 40 surviving Jews and sent them to Auschwitz.

VRCHLABI   Bohemia (Sudetenland), Czechoslovakia. Jews numbered 129 in 1900; 187 in 1910; and 105 (total 7,000) in 1930. Most Jews left in fall 1938 after the annexation of the Sudetenland. Those who remained in the Protectorate were ultimately deported to the Theresienstadt ghetto and the death camps. Few survived.

VREDEN   Westphalia, Germany. Jews are first mentioned in 1306 and lived under the protection of the Archbishop of Cologne and the Bishop of Muenster. The small community was destroyed in the Black Death persecutions of 1348–49. Jews again settled after the Thirty Years War (1618–48), reaching a pop. of seven families in 1784. In the late 18th cent., students from the local Franciscan school attacked the Jews a number of times. A synagogue was consecrated in 1808 and in 1810, ten children attended the attached J. school. The J. pop. grew to a peak of 111 in 1852 with nine of the community's 21 wage earners in trade (seven shopkeepers and two peddlers) and

seven working as servants. In 1857, the community was attached to the Ahaus regional congregation, maintaining an Orthodox religious orientation. The J. pop. declined in the late 19th cent. through emigration to the big cities. In 1933, it was 43 (total 4,571). On *Kristallnacht* (9–10 Nov. 1938), J. homes and stores were destroyed and the 130-year-old synagogue was seriously damaged. J. men, women, and children were arrested, beaten, and tormented. In all, 44 Jews emigrated (37 in 1938–39), 16 of them to Holland. Nineteen other Jews joined the community in the Nazi period. Of the last 11 Jews, seven were deported to the Riga ghetto in mid-Dec. 1941 and four were deported on 3 Feb. 1942. At least 23 perished in the Holocaust.

VRSAC   Vojvodina dist., Yugoslavia. The first Jews settled there in 1760. Community records exist from 1850 and in 1869 its members numbered 756 (total 21,437). In 1931 there were 404 Jews. They all perished in the Holocaust.

VRUTKY   (Hung. Ruttka) Slovakia, Czechoslovakia, today Republic of Slovakia. Jews lived in V. for a time in the late 18th cent., with new families arriving in the 1820s. The J. pop. rose to 212 in 1880 and 497 (total 6,262) in 1910. A Neologist congregation was formed in 1891 and a magnificent 300-seat synagogue in the Moorish style was completed in 1910. A large community center was dedicated in 1929. Jews were active in public life with one serving as deputy chairman of the local council for 48 years. The Zionists became active after WWI with most of the young belonging to Hashomer Hatzair. Jews owned seven groceries, six textile and fancy goods stores, and six taverns and hotels. In 1940, their pop. was 380. In the Slovakian state, J. children were expelled from the public schools and the authorities liquidated or "Aryanized" J. businesses. The young were deported to Auschwitz and the Majdanek concentration camp in late March 1942 where most perished. Families were sent to the Lublin dist. (Poland) in early June — able-bodied men to the Majdanek concentration camp, the rest to the Sobibor death camp. A few dozen were able to evade the German roundups in fall 1944.

VSETIN   Moravia, Czechoslovakia. Jews are mentioned in 1669. In 1823, they were expelled by Count Stefan Illehazy. They returned after the 1848 revolution with the Kohen family becoming active as lumber merchants and furniture manufacturers as well as establishing a glass factory. A synagogue was erected in 1898 and the J. pop. reached 165 in 1900. In 1899, J. property was destroyed in violent riots connected with a blood libel springing from the murder of a Czech seamstress. In 1930, the J. pop. was 101 (total 7,229). The Germans burned the synagogue immediately after entering the country on 15 March 1939. The factories were taken over and the community dismantled. In Sept. 1942, the Jews were deported to the Theresienstadt ghetto via Ostrava. Nearly all were then sent to Maly Trostinec (Belorussia). In all, 67 Jews are known to have perished in the Holocaust.

VUKOVAR Croatia, Yugoslavia, today Republic of Croatia. Jews first settled there in the early 19th cent. and a community was organized in the second half of the cent. Zionist activity began after WWI. The Jews numbered 306 in 1931 (total 10,862) and 213 in 1940. None survived the Holocaust.

VULCAN (Hung. Vulkan) S. Transylvania dist., Rumania. Jews first settled in the late 19th cent. and engaged in work connected with the coal mines. In 1905–06, the Orthodox community was organized. The J. pop. in 1930 was 516 (5% of the total). During the 1930s, the pop. dwindled by 30% owing to the economic crisis and antisemitism. In summer 1941, the remaining 301 Jews were expelled to Deva, Hateg, Ilia, and Paclisa. Only about 75 returned after the liberation, with many leaving during the 1940s.

VULCHOVCE (Hung. Irhoc) Carpatho-Russia, Czechoslovakia, today Ukraine. Jews probably settled in the 1730s, with 11 J. families present in 1768. In 1880, their pop. was 409 (total 2,421), increasing to 727 in 1921 and 851 in 1941. Most of the town's business establishments and workshops were in J. hands, with 21 families earning their livelihoods in trade and 27 in crafts. Jews also owned four flour mills. The Hungarians occupied V. in March 1939 and in 1941 expelled a few dozen J. families without Hungarian citizenship to Kamenets-Podolski, where they were murdered. The rest were deported to Auschwitz in late May 1944.

VYAZMA Smolensk dist., Russia. J. settlement apparently dates back to the 18th cent. A fire in 1882 burned down dozens of houses, most belonging to Jews. In 1897, the J. pop. was 504 (total 15,645). Permission to open a prayer house was granted in 1900. In fall 1905, the Jews were attacked in a pogrom. At the outset of Soviet rule the J. pop. remained stable at 506 in 1926, rising to 641 in 1939. The Germans captured the city on 7 Oct. 1941 and murdered the few remaining Jews at the J. cemetery.

VYCAPY-OPATOVCE (Hung. Vicsapapati) Slovakia, Czechoslovakia, today Republic of Slovakia. Jews were probably present in the early 18th cent., returning in the 1740s after being expelled in 1727. A synagogue was erected in the mid-19th cent. and a J. elementary school was opened towards the end of the 19th cent. The J. pop. reached a peak of 122 (total 581) in 1869 and then declined steadily to 66 in 1940. Deportations were carried out in March–April 1942: first the young were taken and afterwards the others were dispatched to the Rejowiec ghetto in Poland where they perished. In Sept. 1944, the Germans rounded up and deported several more.

VYLOK (Hung. Tiszaujlak) Carpatho-Russia, Czechoslovakia, today Ukraine. Jews probably arrived at the turn of the 17th cent. Two J. families were present in 1737. Apparently in the mid-18th cent., the Jews abandoned the town, returning only in the early 19th cent. They numbered ten in 1830 and 773 in 1880 (total 2,588). In 1921, under Czechoslovakian rule, the J. pop. rose to 1,115. In the 1930s, Shelomo Yitzhak Scheinfeld became the community's rabbi, running a yeshiva for a few dozen students. The community also maintained a J. school and a *talmud torah*. Most Jews engaged in trade with about 55 business establishments in their hands. Fifteen Jews were artisans and Jews owned two flour mills. A few were officials or professional people (including six doctors). Some also farmed. Zionist organizations, such as Mizrachi and Hashomer Hatzair, were active in the late 1920s and early 1930s. The Hungarians annexed the town in Nov. 1938, canceling J. business licenses. In 1941, with the J. pop. at 922, dozens of J. men were drafted into labor battalions, most being sent to forced labor on the eastern front, where some perished. In Aug. 1941, a few J. families without Hungarian citizenship were expelled to Kamenets-Podolski and murdered. The remaining 950 Jews were deported to Auschwitz in late May 1944.

VYRITSA Leningrad dist., Russia. J. settlement probably began in the early 20th cent. The J. pop. was 49 in 1926 and 138 (total 11,494) in 1939. The Germans occupied the town on 31 Aug. 1941. In Oct., they murdered the remaining Jews in a nearby forest.

VYSKOV Moravia, Czechoslovakia. Jews were apparently present in the first half of the 15th cent. and perhaps during the Thirty Years War (1618–48) but afterwards are not mentioned until the mid-19th cent. A synagogue was consecrated in 1885 and the J. pop. reached 263 in 1890. In 1930 it was 44 (total 5,400). The Jews were probably deported to the Theresienstadt ghetto together with the Jews of Brno in late 1941–early 1942 and from there sent on to the death camps in the east.

VYSKOVO NAD TISOU (Hung. Visk) Carpatho-Russia, Czechoslovakia, today Ukraine. J. settlement apparently commenced in the early 18th cent., with one J. family present in 1728. In 1768, the J. pop. was 19. After being expelled from the town, the Jews returned in the mid-19th cent., their pop. growing to 185 (total 3,016) in 1880. A local rabbi, Yitzhak Grinwald, was only appointed after WWI. He also ran a yeshiva for 50 students. In this period, 19 Jews engaged in trade, 15 were in crafts, a few were professionals, and one owned a flour mill. A number of J. families also farmed. In 1921, under Czechoslovakian rule, the J. pop. rose to 418. In 1941 it was 571. The Hungarians occupied the town in March 1939, drafting dozens of Jews into forced labor battalions. In late July 1941, the Hungarians failed in an attempt to expel Jews without Hungarian citizenship to German-occupied territory in the Ukraine for execution. Nearly 600 were deported to Auschwitz in late May 1944.

VYSNI APSA (Hung. Felsoapsa; Yid. Oyber Apsa) Carpatho-Russia, Czechoslovakia, today Ukraine. Jews probably settled in the mid-18th cent. One family of ten Jews was present in 1768. By 1880, the J. pop. was 312 (total 1,912) while in 1921, in the Czechoslovakian Republic, it rose to 1,283. Jews owned a few dozen stores and 15 workshops. A number of families farmed small plots of land. The Hungarians occupied the town in March 1939 and in 1940–41 drafted dozens of Jews into forced labor battalions, sending some to the eastern front, where they perished. In 1941, the J. pop. was 1,289. In late July, a few dozen J. families lacking Hungarian citizenship were deported to Kamenets-Podolski and murdered. About 500 were deported to Auschwitz on 26 May 1944.

VYSNI NERESNICE (Hung. Felsoneresznice; Yid. Oyber Nerysnica) Carpatho-Russia, Czechoslovakia, today Ukraine. Jews probably arrived in the early 19th cent., numbering eight in 1840 and 156 in 1880. Their number rose under the Czechoslovakian Republic, reaching 523 (total 1,948) in 1930 but then dropping to 443 in 1941. The Hungarians occupied V. in March 1939. On 28 May 1944, the Jews were deported to Auschwitz.

VYSNI SARD (Hung. Felsosarad; Yid. Groys Sard) Carpatho-Russia, Czechoslovakia, today Ukraine. Jews probably arrived in the mid-19th cent. Their pop. was 84 (total 1,304) in 1880; 111 in 1921 under the Czechoslovakians; and 105 in 1941. A number of Jews were farmers. The Hungarians annexed the town in March 1939 and in Aug. 1941 expelled a few Jews without Hungarian citizenship to Kamenets-Podolski, where they were murdered. The rest were deported to Auschwitz in mid-May 1944.

VYSNI STUDENY (Hung. Felsohidegpatak; Yid. Studniya) Carpatho-Russia, Czechoslovakia, today Ukraine. J. settlement probably began in the mid-19th cent. The J. pop. was 138 (total 770) in 1880; 189 in 1921; and 155 in 1941. A few Jews were farmers. The Hungarians occupied the town in March 1939. On 3 June 1944, the Jews were deported to Auschwitz.

VYSNI VERECKY (Hung. Felsovereczke) Carpatho-Russia, Czechoslovakia, today Ukraine. Jews probably settled in the late 18th cent. One family was present in 1768 while in 1880, the J. pop. was 141 (total 943), rising to 218 in 1921. The Hungarians arrived in March 1939 and in 1941 drafted Jews into forced labor battalions. The J. pop. in 1941 was 227. In late July, a few families without Hungarian citizenship were expelled to Kamenets-Podolski, where they were murdered. The rest were deported to Auschwitz in mid-May 1944.

VYSNY SVIDNIK (Hung. Felsoszvidnik) Slovakia, Czechoslovakia, today Republic of Slovakia. Jews settled in the early 18th cent., their number growing slowly in the remote town to about 30 in the 1820s. Most of the settlers were of Galician origin, giving the community a hasidic character. The J. pop. reached 113 (total 745) in 1900. A synagogue was built around that time. After WWI, Jews owned 23 business establishments and a factory. In 1940, their pop. was 148. The community opened a school in 1940 after J. children were expelled from the public schools. In 1941, Jews were forced to liquidate or "Aryanize" their businesses. Young men were deported to the Majdanek concentration camp and the women to Auschwitz in March–April 1942. About 275 Jews were deported to Rejowiec in the Chelm dist. of Poland on 24 May. Others were sent to the Lublin dist. (Poland) on 30 May where most perished. To evade the Germans, the few dozen survivors were evacuated to western Slovakia in May 1944.

VYSOKII ZIELONY GAI Kharkov dist., Ukraine. The J. pop. in 1939 was 124 (total 5,512). The Ger-

mans took the city on 22 Oct. 1941 and again on 2 March 1943, killing all the Jews there.

VYSOKOPOLE (until 1915, Kronay) Nikolaiev dist., Ukraine. Jews probably joined the original German settlers of the village in the 1870s. In 1897, they numbered 139 (total 744). In early fall 1941, the Germans murdered the few remaining Jews.

VYZUONOS (Yid. Vizhun) Utena dist., Lithuania. The J. community began here in the 17th cent. when a wooden synagogue was built. The J. pop. in 1897 was 445 (79% of the total). During WWI all of V.'s Jews were expelled to Russia's interior; most returned after the war. The community was hard hit in the economic crisis of the 1930s. In 1940 the J. pop. was about 50 families. Under the Soviets (1940–41) businesses were nationalized and Zionist and Hebrew activity banned. After Germany's invasion in June 1941, Lithuanian nationalists persecuted and then murdered all the Jews within a few weeks.

The Jewish People's Bank in Vyzuonos, Lithuania

W

WAALWIJK Noord-Brabant dist., Holland. A J. community already existed in the 18th cent. and reached a peak pop. of 90 in 1854, dwindling thereafter. In 1941 the J. pop. was 36 (total 11,630). Ten Jews perished in camps during the Holocaust while 14 survived.

WABZEZNO Pomerania dist., Poland. A community of 400 existed in 1709, growing to 589 (total 4,654) in 1885, with most engaged in trade. Emigration reduced the J. pop. to 92 in 1932. Those remaining in Sept. 1939 were expelled by the Germans to General Gouvernement territory.

WACHBACH Wuerttemberg, Germany. The permanent J. settlement dates from the 16th cent., reaching a peak. pop. of 215 (total 1,248) in 1843. In the second half of the 19th cent. the economic circumstances of the Jews improved but antisemitic incidents were a constant factor. Just eight Jews remained in 1933; three managed to emigrate.

WACHENBUCHEN (now part of Maintal) Hesse-Nassau, Germany. Numbering 38 (7% of the pop.) in 1835, the community maintained an elementary school from 1852 to 1933 and built a synagogue in 1880. Its pop. grew to 111 (10%) in 1905. Affiliated with the rabbinate of Hanau, it numbered 83 in 1933, dwindling to around 40 by *Kristallnacht* (9–10 Nov. 1938), when its synagogue and the one in nearby Hochstadt were vandalized. All the remaining Jews fled; 17 emigrated, while others perished in the Holocaust.

WACHENHEIM Hesse, Germany. Numbering 58 (about 12% of the total) in 1861, the J. community declined to 27 in 1933. Only four Jews remained in 1939.

WADOWICE Cracow dist., Poland. Residence restrictions delayed the development of a J. community until the 1860s. The first settlers came from Austrian Silesia and brought with them what they considered enlightened and progressive ways as opposed to Galician Orthodoxy. Towards the end of the cent. a Galician influx tipped the scales and a traditional way of life began to prevail. Growing steadily, the community numbered 722 (total 5,374) in 1880 and 1,437 (total 6,862) in 1921. Jews were an important economic factor, particularly in the food and flour trade, and among the pioneers of industrial development at the turn of the cent., setting up factories for the manufacture of fertilizers, shoemakers' nails, malt products, paper, whiskey, and candy. A luxurious synagogue seating 700 was built in 1885–89 on the Silesian model. Among the Galicians, Hasidism — primarily Bobowa — was the dominant force. During WWI, the community cared for the Jews among the Russian prisoners of war housed in a local camp. These were among the first to bring the Zionist idea to the town, spreading it especially among the youth. The depressed economic conditions prevailing between the World Wars impoverished many. Anti-J. agitation and calls for economic boycotts were also damaging. To alleviate the situation the community operated wide-ranging welfare services. The Zionists expanded their activities and there were also two hasidic *yeshivot* (Bobowa and Radomsk). The Germans entered W. on 4 Sept. 1939 and shortly thereafter razed the synagogue and other houses of prayer. Widespread pillaging by the Germans and the local pop. followed. Three hundred refugee families arrived in 1940 and Jews were sent to labor camps. Over 1,000 were employed in local shops in early 1942, making *Wehrmacht* uniforms, raincoats, belts, and shirts. On 2 July 1942, a large contingent of Jews was deported and the next day the rest were confined to a ghetto, which numbered 1,400 with the influx of refugees, all living in conditions of hunger, disease, and overcrowding. The ghetto was liquidated on 10 Aug. 1942 when the entire pop. was transported to Auschwitz.

WAECHTERSBACH Hesse–Nassau, Germany. Established before 1690, the J. community dedicated its third synagogue in 1895 and was affiliated with the rabbinate of Hanau. Its pop. remained constant (about 5% of the total) for many years—62 in 1835 and 55 in 1925. Jews played a dominant role in the cattle trade and after Nazis attacked them in July 1935 the market closed down. By Aug. 1938 all the Jews had left, some emigrating, and the community disbanded.

WAGENINGEN Gelderland dist., Holland. Jews first settled in the 16th cent. They were expelled in 1570–71 and resettlement began in the mid-17th cent. Welfare societies were founded in the 19th cent. The J. pop. in 1860 was 85. An agricultural school trained pioneers for immigration to Palestine in the 1920s and 1930s. The J. pop. in 1941 was 58 and 80 in nearby Ede. Most of the Jews perished in the Holocaust. Twenty-five survived in hiding and one in the camps.

WAGROWIEC Poznan dist., Poland. J. settlement was banned by the Church until the late 18th cent. The community grew in the 19th cent. under Prussian rule, maintaining a synagogue, an elementary school, and supplementary religious classes. In the latter half of the 19th cent. a process of emigration set in, reducing the J. pop. from 812 (total 2,876) in 1847 to 348 in 1913 and 206 in 1932. After the German arrival in Sept. 1939, four Jews were executed and a month later the rest were expelled to General Gouvernement territory.

WAIBSTADT Baden, Germany. A J. settlement is first mentioned in 1337 and was destroyed in the Black Death persecutions of 1348–49. Jews were again present in the mid-17th cent., with the community growing slowly to 67 in 1884 (total 2,012) as Jews

Group of young Jews before emigration to Palestine, Wadowice, Poland, 1934

engaged in the cattle and horse trade. The J. pop. in 1938 was eight. In the Nazi period, five Jews emigrated and the last five were deported to the Gurs concentration camp on 22 Oct. 1940.

WAIDHOFEN A. D. THAYA   Lower Austria, Austria. Jews first settled in 1617 and maintained a continuous presence. They were particularly active in the grain trade. In 1882, the community was recognized as a religious association (*Kultusverein*) and a synagogue as well as a cemetery was consecrated. In 1934, there were 300 Jews in W., declining to 80 in 1938. During this period antisemitic agitation was intense and most Jews emigrated. In June, the synagogue was handed over to the municipality and shops and private property were confiscated. In Nov. 1938, approximately 20 Jews still living in W. were sent to Vienna. Some managed to emigrate from there; others were deported to camps in the east.

WALDBREITBACH   Rhineland, Germany. The J. community numbered 20 families in the early 19th cent. and about 50 Jews (total 1,200–1,330) from the mid-19th cent. to WWI. A synagogue was consecrated in 1825 and a cemetery in 1830. In 1932, the J. pop. was 39. At least two Jews perished in the Holocaust. The fate of the others is unknown. On *Kristallnacht* (9–10 Nov. 1938), the synagogue was vandalized. The cemetery was also desecrated in the Nazi period.

WALDENBURG   (Pol. Walbrzych) Lower Silesia, Germany, today Poland. J. settlement commenced in 1830. The J. pop. grew from 32 in 1849 to 198 in 1871 and 300 in 1880. A synagogue was consecrated in 1882 and a J. cemetery prior to that time. In the late 19th cent., the J. pop. began to drop. The cemetery was desecrated in the early 20th cent. In 1930, the J. pop. was 219. In 1932, a Nazi youth gang attacked a J. merchant. On the eve of the Nazi rise to power, the J. pop. was 240. Among the organizations active in the community were the synagogue choir, the J. Youth League, Zionist groups, WIZO, and the Central Union (C.V.), all doing intensive cultural and welfare work even in the Nazi era. With many Jews leaving the city, their number fell to 100 in 1937. On *Kristallnacht* (9–10 Nov. 1938), the synagogue was burned and three J. stores were destroyed. Twenty-four Jews remained in 1939 and nine Jews in mixed marriages in Nov. 1942. Nothing more is known about the community under Nazi rule but it may be assumed that those unable to emigrate were deported and perished.

WALDENRATH   (formerly Waldenberg) Rhineland, Germany. Jews numbered 66 (total 2,047) in 1871 and 30 in 1925. Ten are known to have perished in the Holocaust.

WALEWSKIE   Warsaw dist., Poland. The J. pop. in 1921 was 149 (total 725). The Jews were expelled by the Germans to the eastern part of the Warsaw dist. in late 1939.

WALLAU   (now part of Hofheim am Taunus) Hesse-Nassau, Germany. Established in 1701, the community renovated its synagogue in 1885 and numbered 15 in 1905, with another 120 or so members in Nordenstadt, Diedenbergen, Delkenheim, Massenheim, and other villages nearby. Affiliated with the rabbinate of Wiesbaden, the united community dwindled from 109 in 1925 to 60 in 1938. The synagogue's Torah scrolls were destroyed on *Kristallnacht* (9–10 Nov. 1938), although the building survived. Fifteen members of the community emigrated in 1933–38, 40 were deported in 1942, and 34 perished in the Holocaust.

WALLDORF   Baden, Germany. Two J. families were present in 1422 and seven in 1743, monopolizing most of the trade in farm produce. Jews were attacked during the revolutionary disturbances of 1848. The J. pop. stood at 169 in 1852 (total 2,417). In the early 20th cent. Jews were active in the tobacco industry. In 1933, 67 remained. Thirty-one left the town by 1939, 21 emigrating. The synagogue and J. homes were vandalized on *Kristallnacht* (9–10 Nov. 1938) and the last 21 Jews were deported to the Gurs concentration camp on 22 Oct. 1940, 15 of them eventually perishing at Auschwitz.

WALLDORF AN DER WERRA   Thuringia, Germany. Jews lived in W. in the first half the 14th cent. They were persecuted and expelled during the Black Death disturbances of 1348–49. In the beginning of the 19th cent., Jews from the surrounding villages joined together to form a community which by the mid-19th cent. included more than a third of the entire J. pop. of the Duchy of Saxony-Meiningen and was the largest in the area. The community built a synagogue in 1790. In 1849, the J. pop. was 562, approximately a third of the total. By the end of the cent. there were 98 Jews in W. and 32 in 1933, when the Nazis came to power. On *Kristallnacht* (9–10 Nov. 1938), the synagogue was desecrated and destroyed. No further information is available about the fate of the Jews of W. during the Nazi period.

WALLERSTEIN Swabia, Germany. A community was formed around the end of the 13th cent., suffering from persecution in 1358. A new community existed in the first half of the 15th cent. R. Yom Tov Lippman Heller (1579–1654), the famous Mishna commentator, was born and educated there. The Jews of W. found temporary refuge in Noerdlingen during the Thirty Years War (1618–48) and again in 1672. They fled there during the fighting in 1701–04 as well. The Jews maintained a stable pop. of around 40 families from the late 17th cent. to the mid-18th cent., with W. the seat of the state rabbinate for nearly 200 years until 1809. Jews engaged in moneylending and the horse and cattle trade as well as real estate brokerage. A new synagogue was built in 1807. By 1867 the community numbered 78 (total 1,372); in 1933, 16. Six Jews left in 1936–39 and the last five were deported to Piaski (Poland) and the Theresienstadt ghetto in 1942.

WALLERTHEIM Hesse, Germany. Jews lived there from 1690 and established a community numbering 61 (about 6% of the total) in 1861. By 1933 it had declined to 36, the Jews in Gau-Bickelheim and Armsheim forming part of its membership. After SA troops and Austrian legionaries burned the synagogue to the ground on *Kristallnacht* (9–10 Nov. 1938), villagers helped them loot and destroy J. property. By 1940 all the Jews had left, 18 emigrating to the U.S.

WALSDORF Upper Franconia, Germany. The J. cemetery known from the 16th cent. served numerous communities. The community numbered 155 in 1812 and was united with Trabelsdorf in 1907. Twenty-three Jews remained in 1933 (total 602); 11 emigrated and four left for other German cities in 1933–38. The synagogue was vandalized on *Kristallnacht* (9–10 Nov. 1938) and six Jews were deported to Izbica in the Lublin dist. (Poland) on 25 April 1942.

WAMPIERZOW Cracow dist., Poland. In 1921 the J. pop. was 101 (total 1,596). The Jews were expelled

to Radomysl in July 1941 and most were deported to the Majdanek concentration camp in July 1942.

WANDSBEK Schleswig-Holstein, Germany. A J. community existed around 1600, establishing a synagogue in 1634 and a cemetery in 1675. At the end of the 17th cent., the Jews of W. were allowed to live in Hamburg, which offered better professional opportunities, if they continued to pay *Schutzgeld* (protection money) in W. The Hamburg community soon had more members than W. In 1671, W. merged with Altona and Hamburg into the community of three known by the acronym AHW, which existed until 1810, when Hamburg came under French rule. In 1840, the W. community, now independent again, consecrated a new synagogue building and in 1858 it engaged a rabbi. In 1887 the J. pop. was 285. The community maintained a number of associations, including a branch of the German Zionist Organization (1907). In 1919, cremations were authorized, a sign of Liberal tendencies. In 1932–33 the community numbered 170, most earning their livelihood as businessmen and traders. As a result of the boycott measures of 1 April 1933 and "Aryanization" most were forced to sell their businesses by 1937–38. On 1 Jan. 1938, W. merged with the communities of Altona, Harburg-Wilhelmsburg, and Hamburg to form the J. Religious Association of Hamburg. On *Kristallnacht* (9–10 Nov. 1938), the synagogue was completely wrecked, the cemetery was desecrated, and J. stores were looted. Fewer than half the Jews who were living in W. in 1933 managed to emigrate to safe countries. Those who remained in the town were included in the deportations from Hamburg which began in 1941. Altogether, 92 Jews perished under the Nazis.

WANFRIED Hesse–Nassau, Germany. Dating from 1610, this J. community was one of the largest in the area, numbering 102 in 1744 and 139 (7% of the total) in 1861. Affiliated with the rabbinate of Kassel, it maintained an elementary school from 1869 to 1904 and opened a new synagogue in 1890. The J. pop. declined to 44 in 1925. By Aug. 1937 no Jews remained.

WANGEN Baden, Germany. The 14th cent. community was destroyed in the Black Death persecutions of 1348–49. A new community was apparently established in the late 16th cent., growing steadily in the 18th cent. and reaching a peak pop. of 224 in 1825 (total 570). Most Jews engaged in the cattle trade across the Swiss border. A new synagogue was built in 1825 and a cemetery was consecrated in 1827. After 1875, the J. pop. dropped rapidly and numbered 20 in 1933. On *Kristallnacht* (9–10 Nov. 1938), the synagogue was blown up, the cemetery was desecrated, and Jews were severely beaten before being sent to the Dachau concentration camp. Nine left in 1933–40 and the last seven were deported to the Gurs concentration camp on 22 Oct. 1940.

WANIOWICE Lwow dist., Poland, today Ukraine. The J. pop. in 1921 was 172. The Jews were probably expelled to Sambor for liquidation in Aug. 1942.

WANNE-EICKEL Westphalia, Germany. The first traces of a J. presence in W. and E. date back to the mid-18th century. The few J. families in the two towns (nine by 1860) were affiliated with the Bochum J. community. However, they had their own cemetery and towards the end of the 19th cent. they developed their own associations and school. Finally, in 1907, the independent W. community was founded, dedicating a synagogue in 1910. It reached a peak pop. of 316 in 1925, partly owing to the influx of East European Jews. Virtually all the latter belonged to the working class and, being mostly Orthodox, held separate religious services. On the eve of the Nazi assumption of power, there were still 270 Jews in W. As early as 1933 they suffered from the Nazi terror and by the end of the year nearly 40% of the community had left. By 1937, there were 124 Jews in W. On *Kristallnacht* (9–10 Nov. 1938), the synagogue and several stores were set on fire and a number of J. homes were completely wrecked. J. men were arrested and deported to the Sachsenhausen concentration camp. Although no details are known, deportations from W. must have begun in 1941, because in 1942 only six Jews were still living in the town, probably protected by marriage to non-J. partners.

WARBURG Westphalia, Germany. Jews are first mentioned in 1559. A community served by a rabbi was established in the course of the 17th cent., becoming an organizational and religious center for the Jews of the Paderborn bishopric. The community numbered ten families in 1678, consecrating a cemetery in 1687 and a synagogue in 1697. In 1802, the J. pop. was 197 (10% of the total), reaching a peak of 295 in 1909. A school building was erected in the same year. In 1932, the J. pop. was 150. The Jews at the time were well integrated in the city's social and economic life. Nazi persecution began early. In Aug. 1933 a J. member of the Social-Democratic Party was arrested and shot to death "while attempting to escape." In 1934, the chairman of the local branch of the Central Union (C.V.) was sent to the Esterwagen concentration camp. In 1933, the Propaganda Ministry ordered the J. school to close down. By Nov. 1938, 16 Jews had moved to other German cities and six had emigrated. On *Kristallnacht* (9–10 Nov. 1938), the synagogue was vandalized and the old school building, where J. families were now housed, was seriously damaged. J. men were sent to the Dachau and Buchenwald concentration camps. Another nine Jews subsequently left for other German cities and six more emigrated from Germany. In May 1939, 91 Jews remained, of whom at least 53 were deported to the death camps and ghettoes during the war.

WARENDORF Westphalia, Germany. Jews were present without a break from the mid-16th cent. and reached a peak pop. of 99 in 1833. A cemetery was opened in 1772 (replaced in 1810) and a synagogue was consecrated in 1817. In June 1933, the J. pop. was 43. The synagogue was vandalized and the cemetery desecrated on *Kristallnacht* (9–10 Nov. 1938). Five Jews were hospitalized and about a dozen men arrested. Most Jews left by late 1939, 23 of them to havens across the sea. The last eight Jews were deported during the war.

WARENZ Lwow dist., Poland. Jews lived there from the 16th cent. and maintained an organized J. community from the late 18th cent. W. became a center of Belz Hasidism, which dominated the community and strongly opposed the Zionists when they came to the fore after WWI. The J. pop. of 1,486 (65% of the total) dropped to 520 after WWI. Most fled to Soviet territory at the outset of WWII.

WARKA Warsaw dist., Poland. Jews settled in W. in the mid-18th cent. It was the seat of a hasidic dynasty founded by Yitzhak Kalish which attracted many followers and provided livelihoods for the J. pop. (2,548 in 1897). Secular J. movements were founded after the outbreak of WWI. In 1921 the Jews numbered 2,176 (total 4,306). The Germans occupied W. in 1939.

Many Jews had already fled to Soviet-occupied Poland. The synagogue – one of the most beautiful in Poland – was burned, and Jews were put to forced labor. Among those murdered was R. Menahem Mendel Kalish, the last of the W. dynasty. Ghettoized in the fall of 1940, many died of illness. From 21 Feb. 1941 the survivors were sent to the Warsaw ghetto and from there to the Treblinka death camp.

WARKOWICZE Volhynia dist., Poland. A community existed after W. was accorded urban status in 1725, growing to 1,199 (total 1,926) in 1897. J. trades included tanning and brewing. Olyka and Turzysk (Trisk) Hasidism were active, as was the Zionist Organization and youth movements between the World Wars, when the J. pop. fell to 886. Under the Soviet occupation of 1939–41 a J. kolkhoz was set up on J. land. The Germans entered W. on 27 June 1941. The Jews

were confined to a ghetto. On 3 Oct 1942 they were taken to the forest and murdered. About 200 survived the war, some sheltered by Czech families in the area.

WARSAW (Pol. Warszawa) capital of Poland. Permanent J. settlement is thought to have commenced in the 13th cent. and an organized community existed in the 14th and 15th cents. under the protection of the nobility. Jews were permitted to reside in a special quarter and engage in trade and moneylending while enjoying freedom of worship. J. merchants dealt in grain, lumber, and livestock and in the face of the limited local market and competition, they were forced to broaden their horizons, doing business in Grodno, Brest, and Danzig. J. craftsmen, excluded from the Christian guilds, were active as furriers and ropemakers. Most of the Jews came from Germany or Bohemia and Moravia, bringing with them a German cul-

In the Jewish quarter of Warsaw, Poland, 1917 (Bundesarchiv/photo courtesy of Yad Vashem, The Holocaust Martyrs' and Heroes' Remembrance Authority, Jerusalem)

tural heritage. From the outset they faced the hostility of the local pop., which sought to undermine their economic position and bring about their expulsion from the city. These efforts bore fruit and already in the 1480s Jews were being excluded from W. In 1527 the town received a *de non tolerandis Judaeis* privilege from King Sigismund I and the next year all the Jews were expelled. However, Jews were able to settle on the nearby estates of the nobility and continue to do business in W., their presence increasing after W. became the capital of the country in 1595. The struggle to regain residence rights and expand trade continued through the 18th cent. Jews were allowed into the city during Sejm sessions, on official business on behalf of the Council of the Four Lands, or as holders of special passes. Outstanding among the 17th cent. Court Jews representing J. interests (lobbying for the Council of the Four Lands) and residing permanently in W. was Mordekhai Neckel. In the late 18th cent. a substantial number of Jews filtered into the city and a total of 892 (in 1782) were legally established in the suburb of Praga across the Vistula River. There the Jews maintained an organized community with its own rabbi and a cemetery, *beit midrash*, slaughterhouse, and ritual bath. Refugees from the Haidamak massacres in the Ukraine introduced Hasidism into the community. In W. itself efforts were still being made by townsmen, and particularly the Christian guilds, to remove the J. presence and in 1790 Jews were attacked and their stores looted. Nevertheless, by the time of the Third Partition of Poland in 1795 and the beginning of Prussian rule there were at least 6,000 Jews (8% of the total pop.) in W. and its environs. About a quarter of them were engaged in trade, often combined with banking activities. J. merchants shipped grain, lumber, and potash through the Baltic ports and sent livestock, tallow, hides, and cloth to Prussia and Silesia. The big merchants employed hundreds of agents buying up produce in Poland, Lithuania, and the Ukraine. They were also major importers of metals, precious stones, tea, spices, and tobacco, maintaining commercial ties with Jews in the west, particularly in Holland. Others were army suppliers. Most, however, engaged in petty trade, including peddling, and barely eked out a living. Of the 500 J. craftsmen active in 1792, 410 were tailors. Despite the official residence ban within the city, the authorities were forced to recognize a J. council of elders to regulate internal affairs and collect taxes. In Kosciuszko's 1794

rebellion against the Russians that had preceded the Prussian takeover, Jews and Poles joined hands for the first time against a common enemy. Berek Joselewicz raised a J. battalion of 500 cavalry, the first J. national fighting unit in modern European history. On 4 Nov. 1794 the Russians entered Praga and in a bloody battle wiped out the entire battalion before proceeding to massacre the civilian pop. of around 1,000 Jews. Under the Prussians the J. pop. doubled within ten years to 12,000 in 1805 (17% of the total). Jews arrived from the provinces as well as from Prussia and Lithuania. They were allowed to build houses on lots that the Christians did not want, restricted to doing business only in their stores, and ordered to adopt family names. In 1799 a J. hospital was authorized and in 1802 a cemetery opened. Hasidim and *Mitnaggedim* gathered in numerous prayer and study houses. A small number of *maskilim* were also present, characterized by European dress and ways and opening their own synagogue where sermons were given in German. Hebrew books were printed on Christian presses from 1796 while J. antiquarians and bookdealers made significant contributions to Polish culture. In 1804, J. homes and stores were attacked and Jews beaten in two days of anti-J. rioting. J. expectations were disappointed when civil rights for the Jews were postponed for ten years in the Grand Duchy of Warsaw set up by Napoleon after the Peace of Tilsit in 1807. Despite heavy taxes and a decree forcing the Jews off the main streets of the city and into a special quarter, the community became the largest in Europe in this period and its council the main spokesman for all the J. communities in the country. In Congress Poland (from 1815) residence restrictions remained in force, with the system of fees and "daily tickets" restricting the presence of nonresident Jews reintroduced and discriminatory taxation sometimes accounting for 50% of the municipality's income. Jews now became pioneers of local industry. The J. banker Leopold Frankel ran the city's first steam-operated textile plant, employing 600 workers. More significant than the operation of factories was the role Jews played as suppliers of raw materials and marketers of their products. The wool trade was largely in J. hands as was the supply of farm produce to the food industry. Jews were also granted concessions in government monopolies (salt, tobacco, alcoholic beverages) as efforts to replace them failed for want of suitable Polish candidates. On the other hand, J. craftsmen constituted just 5%

"The strike is our weapon" – Bundist May Day parade in Warsaw, Poland, 1936 (Sifriat Poalim/photo courtesy of Yad Vashem, The Holocaust Martyrs' and Heroes' Remembrance Authority, Jerusalem)

of the total, excluded from the guilds and unable to receive adequate apprentice training. Jews were also prevented from participating in public tenders or holding jobs in the public service. The leaders of the Polish revolt of 1830–31 were ambivalent towards the Jews. Some Jews joined the rebel ranks but others were murdered by them, including 13 from an old age home accused of "spying." The rebels were primarily interested in receiving financial support from the Jews. In 1841 a measure was introduced to outlaw traditional J. dress and replace it with the short Russian jacket and cap. The latter in fact were to become recognized as a particularly J. style of dress. Despite anti-J. measures the J. pop. rose to 42,639 in 1862. Two years later, in the wake of the abrogation of residence restrictions in the Polish kingdom by imperial decree, it increased to 72,776 (total 222,906). In the 1840s, as the Polish economy recovered from the revolt of 1830–31 and entered a period of relative prosperity, J. horizons expanded. In 1849, 231 of the city's 441 bigger mer-

chants were Jews and Jews ran 11 banks. Of the 15,168 J. breadwinners recorded in 1861, 56% were tradesmen, now comprising half the city's artisans and apprentices and 69% of its commercial class. In this period the state operated six public schools for J. children, under the supervision of the *maskil* Yaakov Tugendhold (later chief censor for Hebrew books). The schools combined secular and religious studies. In 1826 a rabbinical seminary was opened with most of its graduates advocating Polish acculturation. Shelomo Zalman Lipshitz, previously the rabbi of Praga, served as rabbi of W. in 1819–39. He was followed by Hayyim Dawidsohn (1839–54), Dov Berush Meisels (1854–70), and Yaakov Gesundheit (1870–73). The last was forced out of office by the Hasidim and *maskilim*, leaving W. with a rabbinical committee under revolving chairmanship instead of a chief rabbi. By 1867 Jews comprised 10% of the student body in institutes of higher education. J. attendance in high schools and business schools also increased.

In 1860 the J. publisher Shemuel Orgelbrand began publishing the Great Polish Encyclopedia. He also produced an edition of the Babylonian Talmud in a press run of 10,000 sets. In 1862 the first number of the Hebrew periodical *Ha-Tzefira* appeared. In the revolt of 1863 J. participation was particularly high: of the 10,000 who joined the partisans, 2,000 were Jews and 1,000 of them from W. In the following period, depite the decree lifting residence restrictions, the municipality continued to make efforts to confine the Jews to the J. quarter. In 1881 the pogroms that spread through Russia after Alexander II's assassination reached W. as well. Jews were beaten and robbed in their homes and shops in Dec. as the police stood idly by. However, the less favorable conditions in the provincial towns, including expulsions in the Russian empire, along with the industrial development of W. and its job opportunities, acted as a magnet for Jews and even some on their way to the west stayed on in the city. In the late 19th cent., when the J. pop. reached 212,900, a growing J. proletariat was employed in factories (half of them women and children), mostly in the tobacco industry. The J. bourgeois class also grew significantly. Jews owned 200 factories employing over 30 workers each. Jews also had controlling interests in stockholding companies that owned large factories in the food, clothing, textile, and metalworking industries, with up to 1,000 workers. In the same period the community council became a major institution with an extensive range of activities. In 1902 it dedicated a 559-bed hospital with modern equipment and prominent doctors. The Praga community was now attached to the Warsaw community and its synagogue (founded in 1808) was renovated. In 1878 the community consecrated the Great Synagogue and in 1899 opened a third synagogue. In addition there were around 340 prayer houses, mostly hasidic *shtiblekh*. Most children studied in the private *heder* system—11,056 boys in 206 *hadarim* and 1,157 girls in 19 *hadarim* in 1905. At the turn of the cent. the community council lost something of its centrality as private philanthropists increasingly took over charity and welfare work and political parties and societies increased their influence along with the press. The first Zionist groups were organized in 1883. Nahum Sokolow, editor of *Ha-Tzefira*, became one of the leading proponents of Zionism. In 1905 a group breaking away from the Ha-Tehiyya movement founded the W. Po'alei Zion under the leadership of Yitzhak Tabenkin and Ben-Zion Raskin, soon reaching

a membership of 400. A Bund office was opened in 1897, spreading its influence among J. workers throughout the city. Yiddishist circles gathered around the writer Y. L. Peretz (1852–1915). W. was the great center of the J. press. Among the Yiddish newspapers, *Haynt* maintained its position as the outstanding J. daily in the Diaspora until WWII, reaching a circulation of 100,000 with such contributors as Peretz, Shalom Aleichem, and Sholem Asch. The second leading daily (founded in 1910) was *Der Moment*, whose contributors included Hillel Zeitlin and Vladimir Jabotinsky. *Ha-Tzefira* was the leading Hebrew paper. By the eve of WWI the J. pop. had grown to 306,000. These were joined by 70,000 refugees at the start of the fighting. The Germans occupied W. in Aug. 1915. During the war J. tradesmen had their goods impounded at nominal prices and Jews were subjected to forced labor on defense works. Thousands were unemployed. However, political life was allowed to continue in a relatively liberal atmosphere. A branch of Mizrachi was organized in 1916 and Agudat Israel became active. After the War thousands emigrated to Palestine and the West as economic conditions worsened. The J. birthrate declined sharply from a prewar level of 30.5 per 1,000 to 13.7 in the 1930s while the mortality rate dropped from 21.0 to 11.0. Between the World Wars, W. Jewry represented about 11% of Poland's total as opposed to 22% on the eve of WWI. About

Jewish stores in Warsaw, Poland, 1937

90% of the Jews continued to reside in the J. quarter while those living outside were virtually indistinguishable from their Polish neighbors in terms of language, dress, and way of life. Recovery from the war was made more difficult by the severance of the city from its traditional Russian markets. This was compounded for the Jews by their exclusion from trade in government monopolies (alcoholic beverages, tobacco, matches, salt, lotteries) or entry into government-supported fields, such as transportation and heavy industry, including arms and chemicals. Nonetheless the Jews made a major contribution in trade, both foreign and domestic. In the textile industry commercial ties were forged with England and the Jews were the first to trade with Soviet Russia. The situation of the Jews improved somewhat in the 1926–29 period as political stability returned to the country but in the decade that followed, economic crisis along with discriminatory government measures brought J. economic life to a standstill. These included heavy taxation and the encouragement of non-J. cooperatives with the aim of cutting out the J. middleman. Consequently the share of J. merchants in the city dropped from 74% in 1921 to 54% in 1926 and the share of big J. business establishments from 40% in 1926 to 30% in 1928. By 1933, only 2,105 of the 16,204 J. business establishments in the city were officially classified as large-scale; the rest were mainly retail outlets. Jews comprised 84% of the city's peddlers, stallkeepers, and petty traders. In the late 1930s the situation was compounded by an economic boycott. Jews were also cut off from sources of credit and were forced to develop a central credit union with support from the Joint Distribution Committee that ultimately had 624 branches throughout Poland along with 53 cooperative societies. In 1931 the J. pop. stood at 352,700; 43% worked, indicating that more than one family member characteristically joined the labor market. Of these 151,153 workers, 70,574 earned their livings in crafts and industry and 49,496 in trade; in the same year, 34% were unemployed. Most of the Jews belonged to the lower middle class and lived in a closed J. world in the J. quarter, working for J. employers and shopping in J. stores. This closed community was supported by an extensive network of social welfare services, some through big centralized agencies like TOZ (public health), ORT (vocational training), CENTOS (orphans and abandoned children), and HIAS (refugees and emigres). The leading welfare organization in Poland between the World Wars was the American J. Joint Distribution Committee, which contributed $75 million to Polish Jewry up to 1930. In addition, the community itself provided numerous welfare services. Between the World Wars all the J. political parties active in Poland were represented in W. The central bloc in the World Zionist Organization were the General Zionists under the leadership in W. of Yitzhak Gruenbaum, who was also the leading J. figure in the Polish Sejm and later Israel's first minister of the interior. Mizrachi operated its extensive Yavne educational system. Po'alei Zion split into left- and right-wing groups in 1920. The former, leaving the Zionist Organization, cooperated with the Bund in operating 20 Yiddish CYSHO schools in the 1920s (reduced to four in the late 1930s). The latter united with Tze'irei Tzyyion (Zionist Socialists) in 1926 and became a mass movement in the 1930s, second only to the Bund in its influence in the J. labor movement. Also in the socialist camp was Hashomer Hatzair, active in the Zionist Tarbut school system and sending its pioneers to kibbutzim in Palestine. The Revisionists were also active in W. Betar had its first national convention in the city in 1928 and was active in pioneer training from 1929 in association with Hehalutz, which ran a 90-acre training farm for the youth movements at nearby Grochow. *Aliya* was organized by the Palestine Office. In 1920–23, 13,000 Jews made their way to Palestine via W.,

Licenses of Jewish porters, Warsaw, Poland, 1937

representing 40% of the Third *Aliya*. Another 32,000 (77% of the total) left through W. in 1924–26 and 25–38% of the immigrants in 1933–36 left from W. The Bund continued to agitate for cultural autonomy and the primacy of Yiddish as the national language alongside its involvement in the labor movement. Its W. branch was the largest in Poland and W. was the seat of the party's central committee. It set up workers' soup kitchens and consumer cooperatives and as part of its cultural program ran Yiddish libraries, choirs, and drama circles. In the late 1930s it was in the forefront of the struggle against antisemitism and constituted the largest bloc in the community council with 15 of 50 representatives. Many Jews in W. were also members of the illegal Communist Party. At its second congress in 1923, 30% of the delegates were Jews. Agudat Israel in W. and all of Poland was under the sway of Gur Hasidism and its leader R. Avraham Mordekhai Alter, who was president of the Polish rabbinical council. It pursued a policy of loyalty to the ruling regime and until the 1930s led the other J. parties in elections to the community and municipal councils. Jews were particularly active in the first three Polish Sejms, with 11 representatives in the first (1919), 35 in the second (1922), and 22 in the third (1928). In W.'s first two municipal councils (1919–27, 1927–34), 27 of the 120 members were Jews and one of them was a deputy mayor. No chief rabbi presided in W. since the 1870s. Of the dozens of rabbis serving the community, R. Menahem Zemba was one of the outstanding halakhists of the time, R. Shelomo David Kahana was later rabbi of the Old City of Jerusalem, R. Professor Moshe Schorr was a distinguished Assyriologist, and R. Shemuel Posnanski was an expert on the Karaites. The J. educational system included schools imbued with a Zionist spirit (Tarbut, Yavne), the traditional network (Horev, Beth Jacob, the *heder*, and the *talmud torah*), and the Yiddishist-socialist schools (CYSHO). Among the Zionist institutions was the state-recognized network of bilingual secondary schools founded by Dr. S. Z. Broida and Dr. Aryeh Tartakower. While the language of instruction was Polish, Hebrew and J. subjects were also taught. In the Tarbut schools, where Zionist and pioneering values were taught, the language of instruction was Hebrew. Mizrachi ran two Yavne schools and the Bund's four CYSHO schools enrolled 1,088 children in 1936–37. The number of children in Agudat Israel's Horev system exceeded those in all the others combined.

The community operated J. public schools – six elementary schools in 1936–37 for 1,565 children, six *talmud torah* schools for 2,200, four kindergartens, and business and vocational schools. On the establishment of independent Poland after WWI, 30% of the students at the W. medical faculty were Jews and 15% at the polytechnic institute. Later the number of Jews studying medicine, law, and engineering was restricted and J. students became targets of abuse and persecution. The J. Hapoel sports organization, founded in 1930, had over 1,000 members. One of the community's more important cultural institutions was the Library for J. Studies, founded in 1819, which accumulated 23,787 volumes in Hebrew and Yiddish and 10,260 in other languages. Between the World Wars, Yiddish, the language of the masses, remained the principal vehicle of J. literature. Sholem Asch (1880–1957) was known for his historical novels. I.J. Singer (1893–1944), author of *Yoshe Kalb*, wrote in the realistic tradition while his younger brother, Nobel Prize laureate Isaac Bashevis Singer (1904–91), published his first stories in W. in 1926–27. Among those writing in Hebrew were Nahum Sokolow (1859–1936), the poet David Frishman (1859–1922), Uri Tzevi Greenberg (1896–1981), one of the great stylistic innovators of the new Hebrew poetry, and Hillel Zeitlin (1871–1942), who wrote in Hebrew and Yiddish and was attracted to mysticism. In theater, the leading Yiddish company was the Vilna Troupe, which won international acclaim for its production of An-Ski's *Dybbuk* in 1920 and was active in W. in 1917–22 and 1928–32. Jews were also pioneers in the Polish film industry. The first talking nondocumentary J. film, *For the Sin*, was produced by the Sektor company in 1935 with the comedians Dzigan and Schumacher. A number of Yiddish stage classics were adapted for the cinema. Most of Poland's J. musicians were graduates of the W. Conservatory. Among the leading cantors (*hazzanim*) were Gershon Sirota and Moshe Koussevitzky.

The years immediately preceding WWII were marked by increasing antisemitism. Government policy was consciously aimed at undermining the economic position of the Jews while occasional violence erupted in the street. In 1938 the J. pop. of W. was 368,000 (total 1,265,000). The doors to countries of emigration had been shut, including Palestine, leaving the Jews of Eastern Europe to their fate. The first week of fighting in WWII at the beginning of Sept. 1939 brought the German army to the gates of W. The Poles were deter-

Nalewki St. in the Jewish quarter of Warsaw, Poland, 1938

mined to make a stand in the city, promptly fortifying it with antitank ditches and throwing up roadblocks. However, panic soon took hold and mass flight ensued. On 28 Sept. 1939, W. surrendered and the next day the Germans entered the city. A quarter of its houses had been destroyed and an estimated 50,000 people killed and wounded. Jews remembering the relatively tolerant German occupation of WWI were quickly disillusioned. Even before the publication of official orders by the Nazis, they became a target of abuse: J. homes and stores were pillaged, Jews were thrown out of food lines, seized for forced labor, and generally tormented, especially the religious. On 26 Oct. the General Gouvernement was established as a territorial entity meant to embrace the majority of ethnic Poles, with W. included. The first anti-J. measures were officially instituted in Nov. The Jews were instructed to wear white armbands, put up signs in their business establishments for identification, and hand in their radios. In Jan. they were prohibited from using the trains, the only means of public transportation in the city. At the same time, non-Jews were prohibited from buying or renting J. businesses without special licenses. Money owed to Jews was to be placed in escrow and the Jews allowed to withdraw the equivalent of a few dollars a week from such accounts. All payments of pensions and state allowances to Jews were stopped. With normal economic activity thus curtailed the Jews were now forced to barter whatever goods or valuables remained in their possession for the necessities of life in clandestine transactions. While up to tens of thousands of Jews had fled the city on the approach of the Germans, these were replaced by as many as 90,000 refugees, from Lodz and Wloclawek, from Kalisz and the western districts of Poland. All J. institutions ceased to operate and a *Judenrat* was set up in Oct. 1939, headed by Adam Czerniakow, an engineer by training who had been active in community affairs. In Nov., when a Polish policeman was killed by a J. against a criminal background, 53 Jews were seized by the Germans and murdered. Another 208 Jews were murdered after a member of the Polish underground escaped from jail. In Jan. 1940, Polish gangs began to roam the streets, beating up and robbing hundreds of Jews. During the Passover week (15–21 April) a virtual pogrom was staged. The only outside relief available to the community was through the Joint Distribution Committee, which, as an American organization, was still deferred to by the Germans. The Joint helped 250,000 Jews meet

the requirements of the Passover season in 1940. The most direct instrument of assistance were the soup kitchens, over a hundred of which were in operation. Nearly two million food rations were issued in March 1940. Another instrument of mutual aid, organized by the historian Emmanuel Ringelblum, were tenant committees, which by Sept. 1940 covered 2,000 J. buildings. In addition to material aid, they organized kindergartens, clubrooms for youth, and cultural activities. In Oct. 1940 the Jews were ordered into a ghetto, necessitating the uprooting of 138,000 Jews and the evacuation of 113,000 Poles from the designated area. On 16 Nov. the ghetto was closed off, with the J. refugees brought there as well. The ghetto held 350,000 Jews, 30% of the city's pop., and comprised just 2.4% of its total area. It included 73 of the city's 1,800 streets and was sealed off by 11 miles of walls 10 ft. high and crowned with barbed wire. There was an average of 13 people per room with thousands homeless. Economic life now came to an almost complete standstill. Those marched out of the ghetto to work for the Germans were not paid, receiving only a meager meal for their labor. By June 1941, 4,000–5,000 Jews a month were dying and the streets were strewn with the bodies as they succumbed to starvation. Epidemics, especially typhoid, were rife. In Dec. 1941 it was calculated that over 200,000 Jews had no means of support. Recognition of the cheap source of labor available in the ghetto soon led German firms to seek to exploit it by setting up factory branches there. Polish firms, too, finding they were incapable of meeting orders without skilled J. workers, were clandestinely supplied by J. artisans, as was the German army. Such clandestine ghetto production, particularly by carpenters and brushmakers, reached immense proportions. Those working outside the ghetto were able to smuggle in food as well. About 2,000 were employed regularly at menial labor in German army barracks, as porters at the railroad station, and in a variety of other demeaning tasks. Many more were sent to labor camps and put to work digging drainage ditches and paving roads. In summer 1941, 11,300 Jews were sent to labor camps in the W. area, in Lublin, and in Cracow. Food smugglers, including women and children, moved through connected buildings from the "Aryan" side of the city, over and under the walls of the ghetto and through hidden passages, and through the main gates after bribing successively German, Polish, and J. guards. (According to Czerniakow, the head of the *Judenrat*, most of the food available in W. was smuggled.) Apprehension generally resulted in death. In Oct. 1941 permission was granted to open the school year in the ghetto. Nineteen schools representing the old educational systems were operated, enrolling 6,700 children. Vocational schools under the auspices of ORT had 2,454 students by mid-1941. Cultural activity centered on clandestine groups and included illegal libraries. A symphony orchestra, however, was permitted. Together with such underground activity the seeds of future resistance were being sown, with the participation of all the political parties active in W. before the war. Underground newspapers proliferated and an archive was kept by Ringelblum documenting the life of the ghetto with thousands of items. By the summer of 1942, it was estimated that 100,000 Jews had died in the ghetto. Mass deportations commenced on 22 July 1942 and were meant to exclude the able-bodied and their families but these were included as well to fill daily quotas. Jews were seized at the rate of 6,000-7,000 a day, packed into transports – 100 to a railroad car – and taken away to be put to death in the Treblinka death camp. After ten days, 65,000 Jews had been thus deported. The second stage commenced on 31 July and lasted until 14 Aug. Now the actual work of rounding up the Jews was taken over from the J. police by the German police and their Ukrainian, Latvian, and Lithuanian auxiliaries and took on more brutal proportions. In addition to those seized, an estimated 10,000-20,000 were lured into reporting for deportation at the assembly point (*Umschlagplatz*) by the promise of food. Among the deportees was the educator Janusz Korczak, with the 200 children of his orphanage. Czerniakow, the head of the *Judenrat*, committed suicide on 23 July. The third stage of the deportations lasted from 15 Aug. to 6 Sept. and included Jews from the towns surrounding W. All were seized to meet quotas. Workers' families were seized in their homes and then the workers themselves, some of whom had taken to keeping their children with them at work. The final stage commenced on 6 Sept., when all the remaining Jews were ordered to gather in a few streets. About 35,000 tags were handed out to skilled workers, representing 10% of the ghetto pop. before the deportations. Another 20,000-25,000 managed to hide. Thus around 300,000 had been sent to their deaths. The ghetto was now divided into three parts, on a smaller scale: the central section contained the "shops" still in operation, the *Judenrat* building, and the dwellings of workers employed outside the ghetto; a second, smaller section contained two large factories and the third another shop. The ghetto took on the nature of a labor camp. Those who remained were mostly men and young women who had already lost their families. Though the expulsions had not come as a surprise they caught the underground groups unprepared and without a plan of action. On 28 July representatives of the youth movements – Hashomer Hatzair, Deror, and Bnei Akiva – created the J. Fighting Organization (ZOB). The first weapons – five pistols and eight handgrenades – were obtained from the Communist underground. On 20 Aug. an attempt was made to assassinate the head of the J. police, who escaped with just a wound. On 3 Sept., Josef Kaplan, one of the ZOB's leaders, was arrested by the Gestapo; another, Shemuel Breslav, was shot after pleading for his release and on the same day the Germans seized the organization's arms when they were being transferred from Mila Street to a new hiding place. In Oct. all the factions other than the Revisionists united in the ZOB under the command of Mordekhai Anielewicz. The Revisionists, under Pavel Frankel, operated independently. On 18 Jan. 1943 the second wave of deportations commenced. Many of the Jews ordered out of their homes for document checks refused to appear, hiding instead. In the first convoy of 1,000 deportees put together by the Germans in the early hours of the *Aktion*, a number of armed Jews from Hashomer Hatzair, led by Anielewicz, filtered through and opened fire on the guards. Most of the J. fighters were cut down. Anielewicz escaped and the deportees fled. Resistance was also offered in the streets. By 22 Jan. only 5,000-6,000 Jews had been rounded up, the Germans no longer daring to move freely. After the *Aktion*, arms purchases continued until all underground members were equipped with a handgun and a limited quantity of bullets in addition to the few rifles and machineguns at their disposal. The ZOB was divided into 22 units, each comprising 15 fighters. The Revisionist group was much smaller but had some heavy arms. Many in the ghetto felt that armed resistance combined with concealment could save lives until the Red Army, victorious at Stalingrad, arrived. Underground bunkers were prepared as Jews worked through the nights to secure hiding places. These were provided with food and water, medicines, bunkbeds, electricity, and air vents. Some were designed for a stay of months. The final liquidation of the ghetto commenced on 19 April 1943 (Passover eve). The Germans, under the command of SS General Jurgen Stroop, entered the ghetto at 3 a.m. with a force of 850 soldiers and 18 officers in two columns. The first was attacked from a house on Nalewki Street and thrown into confusion, retreating under fire. The main battle took place at the corner of Zamenhof and Mila Streets. Molotov cocktails were hurled at the tank and armored cars brought in by the Germans. The tank caught fire twice and the Germans retreated with 12 casualties. The Germans took the Na-lewki Street position and advanced to Moranow Square, where they encountered machinegun fire from Revisionist forces flying a blue and white flag from their position. A second tank went up in flames and the Germans broke off fighting for the day. The second day's fighting centered around the smallest ghetto sec-tion near the Vistula River (the brush shop area), where six J. units, including one belonging to the Revision-ists, were dug in under the command of Marek Edel-man. The explosion of a landmine and sniper fire again kept the Germans from advancing. The Germans now adopted a scorched earth policy and began destroying the ghetto house by house and street by street. Despite the unbearable heat in the bunkers beneath the ruins of the houses above ground, the Jews in hiding refused to give themselves up, forcing the Germans to use hand-grenades and tear gas or poison gas to flush them out. Armed resistance continued into May. In his report, Gen. Stroop claimed around 60,000 Jews killed or de-ported and 16 dead and 85 wounded from his own forces. Of the deportees, Jews from the small shop area were sent to the Poniatowa and Trawniki concentration camps and many from the central ghetto were sent to the Majdanek concentration camp and Bendzin and murdered in Nov. 1943. Thousands of others were sent on to Auschwitz and labor camps in western Poland. In all, up to 2,000 of these survived. Another 20,000 man-aged to hide out in the "Aryan" part of the city and in other places, some escaping from the ghetto through the underground sewers. Hundreds fought during the Polish uprising of summer 1944. After the war, thou-sands of Jews began to gather in W., their number ul-timately reaching 15,000-20,000, most not belonging to the prewar community. After a long process of em-igration, mainly to Israel, only about 2,000 remained. W. was the center of postwar J. life in Poland with a community center, research and documentation center, and Yiddish theater. Many J. tourists visited the monu-ments in the former ghetto, the *Umschlagplatz*, and the resistance headquarters.

WARTA (Yid. Dvart) Lodz dist., Poland. The com-munity, one of the first in the district, was founded by Jews from Moravia and other towns in Poland in the first half of the 16th cent. In 1671, the king granted the Jews a "privilege" protecting their rights and this was reaffirmed by all succeeding rulers. The J. pop. in 1897 was 1,772 (about half the total pop.). At the outbreak of WWI, Cossack units plundered, raped, and killed Jews. After the Germans recaptured the town, the Jews suffered from economic deprivation. Between the World Wars, the Zionists were the domi-nant force in the community. In 1939 bombing de-stroyed the J. quarter. A ghetto was set up in Feb. 1940, housing the local Jews and refugees. About 250 tailors and furriers worked in German workshops making clothes for the German army. Jews sent to forced labor camps reduced the community from 1,500-2,000 in 1939 to about half in summer 1942. Ten community leaders including the *Judenrat* chair-man and the rabbi were publicly hanged in 1942 for il-legally sending bread to the labor camps. In Aug. 1942 the remaining 1,000 Jews were deported to Chelmno.

WARTENBURG (Pol. Barczewo) East Prussia, Ger-many, today Poland. There was a small J. community in 1825. The J. pop. was 111 in 1880 and 70 in 1925. The community maintained a synagogue and a cemetery. No information is available about the fate of the 40 Jews who were living in W. in June 1933, about four months after the Nazi takeover.

WASILISZKI Nowogrodek dist., Poland, today Be-larus. The first Jews probably arrived in the early 18th cent. after the second Swedish war. The community grew to 719 in 1847 and a peak of 2,081 (total 2,781) in 1897. A few wealthy J. merchants dealt in flax, pig bristles, grain, and horses. Many Jews were carters, also buying up farm produce in the neighbor-ing villages. At the turn of the 19th cent. a large num-ber of the young belonged to socialist political parties, some emigrating for fear of arrest. After the Balfour Declaration in 1917, Zionist activity intensified. Fol-lowing WWI, Jews ran shops and market stalls as well as an electrically operated flour mill and two pitch factories. The J. pop. in 1925 was 1,800. In the 1930s, J. livelihoods were undermined by eco-nomic boycotts. A Tarbut Hebrew school was opened in 1925, reaching an enrollment of 105 in 1929-30. A Yavne school was opened in 1927. Under Soviet rule in 1939–41, stores were closed after selling off their stock and artisans were organized into cooperatives. The Germans entered the town on 25 June 1941, murdering alleged J. Communists while local police looted J. homes. A *Judenrat* was set up in July and the Jews were subjected to forced labor and frequent "contributions." In Nov. 1941 a ghetto was established, crowded with refugees from neighboring settlements. On 10–11 May 1942, after 200 skilled workers were selected, 2,200 Jews were brought to the J. cemetery in groups of 60–80 and murdered. The rest were sent to the Szczuczyn ghetto and later killed off. A few dozen managed to join the partisans, but few survived the war.

WASILKOW Bialystok dist., Poland. Jews arrived in 1566 and probably formed an organized community by the 17th cent., with a pop. of 144 in 1799. In the 19th cent. Jews pioneered the textile industry, operating five factories in 1870 with 140 J. workers. At the end of the cent. they were also active in the lumber industry, exporting wood for fuel and building and setting up a large sawmill on the river bank. About 90% of W.'s industrial production was in J. hands as the J. pop. reached 1,470 in 1897 (total 3,880). Many Jews left during WWI, bringing the J. pop. down to 950 in 1921. A new J. textile plant with dyeing and pressing departments employed 500 workers including non-Jews. A J. packing industry also developed, manufacturing crates for textile and hide exports. J. political life was highly active between the World Wars, with the Zionists prominent and the Bund sponsoring a Yiddish CYSHO school. Jews also founded a string orchestra and drama group. During the short German occupation in Sept. 1939, J. stores were looted by the *Wehrmacht*. After two years of Soviet rule, the Germans returned on 27 June 1941. An open ghetto was set up in Jan. 1942, crowding together about 1,250 Jews. They were put to forced labor in the peat bogs, doing roadwork, moving rocks, and loading trains with Nazi booty. On 2 Nov. 1942 all the Jews were brought to an old Polish army camp near Bialystok and from there deported to the Treblinka death camp on 19 Nov.

WASNIOW Kielce dist., Poland. Jews probably settled in the first half of the 19th cent. They numbered 191 (total 580) in 1921 and 250 on the eve of the German occupation of Sept. 1939. Refugees increased the J. pop. to 3,000. In May 1942, all were expelled to Za-wichost and then deported to the Belzec death camp on 29 Oct. 1942.

WASSELONNE Bas-Rhin dist., France. The J. community was established here in the 19th cent. In 1936 there were 79 Jews in the town. During WWII the community's synagogue was destroyed and all the Jews were expelled to the south of France with the rest of Alsace-Lorraine's Jews. Six Jews were deported. In the mid-1960s, the community consisted of 45 members.

WASSERTRUEDINGEN Middle Franconia, Germany. Jews were among the victims of the Rindfleisch massacres of 1298 and constituted an important community in the 17th and 18th cents., furnishing religious judges (*dayyanim*) to the chief rabbinate of the principality. A new synagogue was constructed in 1860 and the J. pop. numbered 122 in 1867 (total 1,763). Thereafter it declined steadily, dropping to 29 in 1933. By 1938, six Jews had emigrated and 14 left for other German cities. The last eight Jews left after the vandalization of the synagogue and J. homes on *Kristallnacht* (9–10 Nov. 1938).

WASYLKOWCE Tarnopol dist., Poland, today Ukraine. The J. pop. in 1921 was 141. The Jews were probably expelled to Kopyczynce for liquidation in spring–fall 1942.

WATTENSCHEID Westphalia, Germany. One J. family lived in W. in the 15th cent. Evidence of a J. presence ends in 1511. A community began to develop in the 17th cent. In 1652, Jews bought land for a cemetery and by 1734 the community numbered 43. At the beginning of the 19th cent., the J. pop. was 40 and in 1925 it was 202. A synagogue was dedicated in 1829 and in 1875 the community, which had until then been affiliated to Hattingen, became independent. In June 1933, about four months after the Nazis came to power, there were 148 Jews in W. Under Nazi pressure, 70 Jews left before *Kristallnacht* (9–10 Nov. 1938), when the synagogue was burned down, J. stores were damaged, and many Jews were arrested. By May 1939, there were only 44 Jews in W. Most left W. before the outbreak of WWII, but only about 50 made it to safe havens abroad. Those who did not manage to leave Germany or Nazi-occupied countries in time were deported to the ghettoes in the east and the death camps.

WATZENBORN-STEINBERG Hesse, Germany. The community, including Jews from Garbenteich and Steinbach, dated from the early 19th cent. At least 16 of the 28 Jews remaining in 1933 perished in the Holocaust.

WAWERN Rhineland, Germany. The J. pop. was 37 in 1808 and 98 (a quarter of the total) in 1871. A synagogue was erected in 1840 and a J. elementary school was opened in 1868, operating for six decades despite the small number of pupils. At the beginning of the Nazi era, 45 Jews remained. About half left before *Kristallnacht* (9–10 Nov. 1938) and the rest left before the outbreak of war. Eighteen remained in Germany and two Polish Jews were expelled in Nov. 1938. On *Kristallnacht* (9–10 Nov. 1938), the synagogue was vandalized.

WEENER (Ems) Hanover, Germany. The first Jews in W. arrived under a letter of protection from Count Ulrich in 1645. In 1749, the community was conducting public prayer and by the early 19th cent. it was receiving a full range of religious services. Its old cemetery had tombstones dating from the 16th cent. New cemeteries were opened in 1849 and 1850 and a synagogue was consecrated in 1829. A J. school was opened in 1853. By 1861, the J. pop. was 138, reaching a peak of 231 (total 3,724) in 1885. Most Jews engaged in trade, dealing mainly in cattle and meat products. Though efforts were made to impede the process of J. naturalization after the town was annexed by Prussia in 1866, relations with the local pop. were for the most part satisfactory and in 1894 a Jew was named chairman of the municipal council. The community was officially recognized in 1874 with a number of other communities coming under its jurisdiction. In 1921, in the Weimar Republic, it was given the status of a corporate body. Antisemitism began to develop in the early 20th cent. By 1933, the J. pop. was down to 131 after declining steadily from its 19th cent. peak. Boycotts and anti-J. pressure under the Nazis destroyed the J. economy in the town and by the end of 1937 almost all J. property had been "Aryanized." On *Kristallnacht* (9–10 Nov. 1938), the synagogue was set on fire, J. stores and homes were vandalized, and 12 J. men were arrested and sent to the Oranienburg concentration camp, where they were held until the following spring. During the Nazi era, 68 Jews moved to other German cities and at least 48 emigrated, 27 of them

to Holland. At least 43 Jews perished in the Holocaust, including 14 in Auschwitz.

WEESP Noord-Holland dist., Holland. A J. community in W. dates back to 1774 with 129 Jews in 1860. The J. pop. in 1941 was 84. In 1941, 66 Jews were deported, only seven of whom returned.

WEHEN (now part of Taunusstein) Hesse–Nassau, Germany. Founded in the 18th cent., the community built a synagogue in 1800 and numbered 43 (4% of the total) in 1871, dwindling to 12 in 1925. In 1937 a member of the community led a group of 20 German-J. farmers who emigrated to Argentina. Only one family remained when the synagogue was destroyed on *Kristallnacht* (9–10 Nov. 1938).

WEHLAU (Rus. Znamensk) East Prussia, Germany, today Russia. The community maintained a synagogue and a cemetery. Religious services were held only on holidays. The J. pop. was 56 in 1880 and 18 in 1925. No information is available about the fate of the 26 Jews who were living in W. when the Nazis assumed power in 1933.

WEHRDA (now part of Haunetal) Hesse–Nassau, Germany. The J. community dedicated a synagogue in 1804, maintained an elementary school from 1837 to 1919, and numbered 130 (16% of the total) in 1861, dwindling to 34 in 1933. The Jews of nearby Langenschwarz (numbering 116 in 1861) had disappeared by 1925 and Nazi pressure forced the W. community to disband in 1936. On 5 Sept. 1942 the last two Jews were sent to death camps.

WEHRHEIM Hesse–Nassau, Germany. Jews lived there from about 1650, engaging in the cattle trade and numbering 30 in 1744. Affiliated with the Bad Ems rabbinate, they opened a new synagogue in 1850 but dwindled to 15 in 1933. By Oct. 1938 the remaining Jews had emigrated to the U.S.

WEIDEN Upper Palatinate, Germany. Jews are mentioned in the 14th cent. and maintained a limited presence on a J. street (*Judengasse*), still in existence in 1930, until their expulsion in 1640. The modern community dates from the second half of the 19th cent. A J. school was opened in 1884 and a synagogue was dedicated in 1889. Jews dealt in real estate, textiles, pitch, hops, and glassware. In 1933 the J. pop. numbered 168 (total 22,775). On *Kristallnacht* (9–10 Nov. 1938) the synagogue was vandalized and dozens of Jews arrested. Between 1933 and 1939, 87 Jews emigrated and 53 moved to other German cities. Of the 12 Jews remaining in 1941, nine were sent to Piaski in the Lublin dist. (Poland) on 2 April 1942 and three to the Theresienstadt ghetto via Regensburg on 23 Sept. 1942.

WEIKERSHEIM Wuerttemberg, Germany. Jews were victimized in the Rindfleisch (1298) and Armleder (1336) massacres and the community was destroyed in the Black Death persecutions of 1348–49. Subsequently J. settlement was banned for three cents. The renewed community developed in the 18th cent. and numbered 158 (total 1,871) in 1807, thereafter declining through emigration. Most prominent in this period was the Pfeiffer family of Court Jews serving the kings of Wuerttemberg. The first synagogue was dedicated in 1678 and a J. school was opened in 1835. Jews numbered 82 in 1900 and just 16 in 1933; ten managed to emigrate.

WEILBURG Hesse–Nassau, Germany. The J. community, established after 1700, was the seat of a district rabbinate (1843–1924) and numbered 220 (6% of the total) in 1885. Shemuel Hirsch Margulies, its fifth incumbent (1887–90), became chief rabbi of Florence and head of Italy's rabbinical college. Jews earned their living in the cattle and textile trade, and opened an elegant synagogue in 1845. Jews served on the town council. Affiliated with the rabbinate of Bad Ems, the community numbered 81 in 1933. Nazi persecution, attaining its height on *Kristallnacht* (9–10 Nov. 1938), forced all the Jews to leave by mid-1939. In all, 58 emigrated, three committed suicide, and 38 perished in Nazi camps.

WEILERSWIST Rhineland, Germany. Jews are first mentioned in 1698. Four J. families were present in 1774. By 1869, the J. pop. rose to 54, with a synagogue erected in 1848 and a cemetery opened a few years before that. From the late 19th cent. until WWI, the J. pop. was 30–40 (total 1,100–1,300). At the beginning of the Nazi era, there were 24 Jews in W. The synagogue was set on fire on *Kristallnacht* (9–10 Nov. 1938). The last four Jews were deported to the camps during the war.

WEIMAR Thuringia, Germany. The first mention of Jews in W. dates back to the beginning of the 14th cent. They were probably expelled from the city in the course of the Black Death persecutions (1348–49), but returned before the end of the cent. The modern J. community begins with the settlement of the Court Jew Jacob Elkan and his son Julius Elkan, the founder of a famous banking house. In 1878, there were 22 J. taxpayers or family heads in Weimar. By 1925 there were 105 Jews in W. and 91 in 1933 at the outset of Nazi rule. The fact that approximately 30% were married to non-Jews helped protect them to some extent from anti-J. measures and possibly may account for the disproportionately large number of survivors in W. On *Kristallnacht* (9–10 Nov. 1938), 12,500 Jews from all over Germany were brought to the newly erected Buchenwald concentration camp on the outskirts of W. The Jews who still remained in W. after July 1941 were forced to vacate their apartments and crowded into a few "J. houses." In 1942, all were deported.

WEIMARSCHMIEDEN Lower Franconia, Germany. Jews numbered 85 (total 236) in 1816, with a cemetery from the mid-18th serving a number of nearby communities until 1909. The community ended after WWI.

WEINGARTEN Baden, Germany. Four J. families settled in 1346 but Jews do not seem to have been present again until the 16th cent. The community expanded in the early 19th cent. A synagogue was built in 1830 and the J. pop. reached 177 in 1871. The J. pop. declined steadily to 60 in 1933 (total 5,056). During the *Kristallnacht* disturbances (9–10 Nov. 1938), the synagogue was destroyed. Thirty-two Jews emigrated. The last 24 were deported to the Gurs concentration camp on 22 Oct. 1940 and another seven to other camps after leaving W. In all, 20 perished in Auschwitz and four survived the Holocaust.

WEINHEIM Baden, Germany. J. communities existing during the 13th and 14th cents. were destroyed in the Rindfleisch massacres of 1298 and the Black Death massacres of 1348–49. Subsequently J. refugees from Worms and Speyer settled under the protection of Rupert I, earning their livelihood as moneylenders. All were expelled by Rupert II in 1391 with the rest of the Jews of the Palatinate. A new J. community was formed in the late 17th cent. During the 19th cent. the Rothschild, Kaufmann, and Hirsch families became prominent in the city. Jacob Rothschild started a textile business in 1856 and was head of the community for many years. Sigmund Hirsch (1845-1908) operated what became the largest horsehide-processing plant in Europe. The community reached a peak pop. of 188 (total 14,170) in 1910. In 1933, 168 Jews remained, operating 19 business establishments and the Hirsch shoe and leather factory with its 400 workers. By Nov. 1938, 43 Jews had emigrated (a third to the U.S.) and 21 had left for other German cities. After the synagogue was blown up on *Kristallnacht* (9-10 Nov. 1938), J. homes and stores were damaged and most J. men detained in the Dachau concentration camp. Twenty-four emigrated and 15 left for other German cities. On 22 Oct. 1940, 46 were deported to the Gurs concentration camp, most perishing. Another 26 Jews from the local insane asylum were put to death at Heppenheim.

WEISENAU   Hesse, Germany. Established by refugees from Mainz in 1473, the J. community numbered 124 (7% of the total) in 1861. By 1937 it had disbanded and its Gothic synagogue was destroyed on *Kristallnacht* (9-10 Nov. 1938).

WEISKIRCHEN   Hesse, Germany. Jews from nearby Dudenhofen, Hainhausen, and Juegesheim formed part of the community, which numbered 51 (7% of the total) in 1871. It dwindled to 29 in 1933 and disbanded before *Kristallnacht* (9-10 Nov. 1938). Most Jews left W. (17 emigrating) by 1940.

WEISSENFELS   Saxony, Germany. The first reference to Jews in W. refers to their immolation in 1350 in the Black Death persecutions. The renewed late 14th cent. community came to an end in 1440, probably after an expulsion order. Jews returned at the beginning of the 19th cent. They first belonged to the Halle community, but after their number had grown to 70 in 1883, they set up an independent community with a prayer room and a cemetery. When the Nazis assumed power in 1933, the community numbered 165. At this time, the first families began to emigrate and community activities intensified. A local branch of the German Zionist Organization was set up in mid-1933 and a cultural association in 1935. The Central Union (C.V.) became more active. Three J. families

with non-German citizenship were deported to Poland in Oct. 1938. On *Kristallnacht* (9-10 Nov. 1938), the synagogue was destroyed and several Jews were arrested and taken to the Buchenwald concentration camp. In May 1939, there were only 40 Jews still living in W. and 24 in 1941. By 1943, four of them had died (three by suicide) and the others had been deported to the east.

WEISSWEILER   Rhineland, Germany. Jews are mentioned in 1546. The modern J. community began to develop in the late 17th cent. A synagogue was apparently dedicated in 1760. In 1854 the J. pop. numbered 72 and in 1930, 24. The community was affiliated to Dueren. On *Kristallnacht* (9-10 Nov. 1938), the synagogue – which had already been confiscated in 1935 – was vandalized, J. houses were wrecked, and the cemetery was desecrated. At least three Jews were deported. No further information is available on the fate of the others.

WEJHEROWO   Pomerania dist., Poland. The first Jews settled in 1812, mainly from the neighboring village of Bolszewo. Most were petty traders and shopkeepers while a few of the bigger merchants exported lumber and farm produce. The J. pop. reached 168 in 1871 (total 3,493), declining through emigration to 62 in 1921 but rising again to 218 in 1931 with the influx of Jews from the surrounding area. The few dozen Jews remaining in Sept. 1939 were executed by the Germans in the Piasnica forest.

WELDZIRZ   Stanislawow dist., Poland, today Ukraine. The J. pop. was 220 in 1921. The Jews were expelled to Bolechow for liquidation in Aug. 1942.

WENGROW   Lublin dist., Poland. Jews were present in the first half of the 16th cent. The Chmielnicki massacres of 1648-49 were followed by an epidemic in 1660. The community began to prosper economically in the late 18th cent. and the J. pop. numbered 2,130 in 1840 and 5,150 (total 8,268) in 1898. Many were artisans while others helped develop the city's light industry, operating flour mills, a hide-processing plant, and a knitting mill. Numerous other communities in the area were under W.'s jurisdiction. W. was also a hasidic center (including Kotsk-Gur, Aleksandrow, Warka, and other dynasties). After WWI, many young people emigrated in the face of looting and persecution by the Poles. In the period of postwar recovery, Jews operated 376 workshops and small factories, nearly half in the garment industry. Zionist influence spread, with a Tarbut Hebrew school founded in 1921. In the late 1930s, the Endecja Party provoked attacks on Jews in the market and public places and the anti-J. boycott left many without a livelihood. The German occupation of Sept. 1939 was accompanied by severe persecution, including the fatal stabbing of R. Yaakov Mendel Morgenstern in the synagogue on Yom Kippur (10 Sept.). The building was destroyed afterwards. In late 1939, a *Judenrat* was appointed, charged with supplying forced labor and collecting "contributions." It also opened a soup kitchen and a school for 450 children. Refugees brought the J. pop. up to 8,000. On 22 Sept. 1942, they were marched to the railroad station and deported to the Treblinka death camp. The 200–300 Jews left behind, primarily artisans, were sent to Treblinka in spring 1943.

WENINGS Hesse, Germany. Established in the 18th cent., the community built a new synagogue in 1875–78, numbered 126 (14% of the total) in 1880, and was affiliated with Giessen's Orthodox rabbinate. All of the remaining 47 Jews had left, many emigrating, by WWII.

WENKHEIM (in J. sources, Wenshtheim) Baden, Germany. Jews were present in the 14th–15th cents. The community grew to 160 (total 930) in 1875 and subsequently declined to 46 in 1933. Twenty-two emigrated to the U.S. and eight to Palestine. On *Kristallnacht* (9–10 Nov. 1938), the synagogue was vandalized and the last 13 Jews were deported to the Gurs concentration camp on 22 Oct. 1940; five survived the Holocaust.

WERBA Volhynia dist., Poland, today Ukraine. The J. pop. in 1921 was 228 (total 402). The Germans set up two ghettoes on 20 May 1942. The larger, containing 285 Jews, was liquidated on 30 May, the smaller one with 82 Jews at the end of summer.

WERCHRATA Lwow dist., Poland, today Ukraine. The J. pop. was 159 in 1921. The Jews were probably deported to the Belzec death camp in Sept.–Oct. 1942, directly or via Rawa Ruska.

WERL Westphalia, Germany. Jews were already present in the 16th cent. but a community was established only much later. A synagogue was consecrated in 1811 and the community reached a peak pop. of 131 in 1885. In June 1933, 52 Jews were registered. On *Kristallnacht* (9–10 Nov. 1938), the synagogue was burned but the ritual objects which had been kept by a friendly Christian neighbor remained unharmed. J. property was vandalized and looted and J. men were sent to the Buchenwald concentration camp. Thirty-seven Jews remained in May 1939 and 28 were deported to the Theresienstadt ghetto and to the Zamosc camp in the Lublin dist. (Poland) in 1942.

WERNE Westphalia, Germany. Jews were present without a break from the late 16th cent. and reached a peak pop. of about 80 in 1837. The community maintained a cemetery, opened in 1779, and a synagogue established in 1820. From the late 19th cent., the J. pop. began to drop, standing at 47 in 1932. The synagogue was destroyed on *Kristallnacht* (9–10 Nov. 1938) and J. men were rounded up and abused in the town square. Some Jews managed to leave beforehand. No futher information is available on the fate of the others.

WERTHEIM Baden, Germany. The J. settlement was one of the oldest in Baden and one of the few existing almost continuously from the turn of the 12th cent. to the Nazi era. Jews were victims of the Rindfleisch massacres of 1298 and in the 14th cent. were living in a J. quarter with a synagogue and the oldest J. cemetery in Baden at their disposal. During the Black Death massacres of 1348–49, many were murdered over a well-poisoning libel and the rest fled. By 1381 the community had revived but in 1447 the synagogue was destroyed at the instigation of a Capuchin monk. In the 15th–17th cents. the Jews lived under the burden of heavy taxes and discriminatory "Jew Laws" (from 1528). In 1640, seven J. families remained in W. The Wertheimers, prominent as Court Jews, originated there. The community grew steadily in the 19th cent., reaching a peak pop. of 201 in 1900 (total 3,915). In 1827, W. became the seat of the district rabbinate with jurisdiction over 16 communities. Violent anti-J. riots took place during the revolutionary disturbances of 1848. In 1933, 92 Jews remained, operating a variety of business establishments under growing economic isolation. By 1938, 29 Jews had emigrated from Germany and another 21 had left for other German cities. Community life was kept up throughout the period, with the Zionists active from 1934. On *Kristallnacht* (9–10 Nov. 1938), the last J. stores were looted. On 22 Oct. 1940, 19 Jews were deported to the Gurs concentration camp. Seven survived, but all 13 sent to the camps from other places after leaving W. perished.

WESEL Rhineland, Germany. Jews lived in W. at least from the beginning of the 13th cent. on. They were persecuted at the time of the Black Death in 1348–49. It is not clear whether there was a continuous J. presence in the town until the development of a modern community at the beginning of the 17th cent. This community maintained a synagogue and subsequently established two cemeteries (1693–96 and 1767). In the mid-19th cent., the community became Reform. The J. pop. reached a peak of 248 in 1905 following an influx of Jews from Eastern Europe. By 1933, the J. pop. had dropped to 161. On *Kristallnacht* (9–10 Nov. 1938), the synagogue and the school (closed in 1935) were burned down, the older cemetery was desecrated, and J. businesses were wrecked. In 1939, only 46 Jews were still living in W. The 30 Jews in H. who did not manage to emigrate were deported in 1942, with the exception of one Jew who was probably protected by marriage to a non-J. Several Jews who had hoped to find shelter in other German towns or in neighboring countries were also deported. Altogether the Nazis murdered 94 Jews from W.

WESERMUENDE Hanover, Germany. The roots of the J. community of W. are to be found in the Lehe community. Having established a cemetery in 1804 and numbering 63 members in 1816, the Lehe community included in the following decades those Jews who settled in the newly founded towns of Bremerhaven (around 1830) and Geestemuende (1845). Since most community members were soon living in Geestemuende, the community's synagogue was built there in 1878. When the amalgamation of Lehe and Geestemuende created the town of W. in the 1920s, the J. community became the community of W. Since the Jews of Bremerhaven were citizens of Bremen, they did not share equally in the community's leadership. A leading community member in the Weimar years was Joseph (Julius) Schocken, brother of Salman Schocken, the founder of the Schocken publishing house. Joseph and Simon Schocken founded a chain of department stores, including branches in W. and

Bremerhaven. When the Nazis came to power in 1933, the number of Jews in the W. community was 346, 99 of them living in Bremerhaven. By 1935, there were 226. On *Kristallnacht* (9–10 Nov. 1938), the synagogue was set on fire and J. businesses – particularly the Schocken department stores – and apartments were looted and wrecked. A number of Jews were maltreated and the men were arrested and taken to the Sachsenhausen concentration camp. Most of the remaining Jews were billeted in "J. houses" and deported in Nov. to the Minsk ghetto or in July 1942 to the Theresienstadt ghetto. As a result of J. immigration from the former Soviet Union, a community was reestablished in Bremerhaven in 1991.

WESSELING Rhineland, Germany. Although individual Jews were living in W. earlier, a community only started to develop from the 18th cent., with the presence of two families in 1717. It maintained a synagogue (first mentioned in 1822) and a cemetery. In 1885, the J. pop. was 92. When the Nazis came to power in 1933, 61 Jews were living in the town. By 1938, 22 had managed to emigrate. On *Kristallnacht* (9–10 Nov. 1938), the synagogue was set on fire and J. stores and homes were looted and wrecked. The remaining Jews were billeted in "J. houses," 23 of them being transferred in June 1940 to such houses in Cologne, from where they probably were deported. By Oct. 1942 only two Jews remained in W., probably protected by marriage to non-J. partners. In all, 29 Jews from W. lost their lives under the Nazis.

WESTERBURG Hesse–Nassau, Germany. The community grew from 60 in 1760 to 135 (9% of the total) in 1871. It was affiliated with the Bad Ems rabbinate. Jews prospered in the 19th cent., opening stores and a cigar factory which the Nazis later "Aryanized." On *Kristallnacht* (9–10 Nov. 1938), the synagogue's interior was destroyed. By 1939 most of the 85 Jews registered there in 1933 had left; 26 perished in the Holocaust.

WESTHEIM BEI HAMMELBURG (in J. sources, Venshteim) Lower Franconia, Germany. Jews fled the town in the Thirty Years War (1618–48). A synagogue was built in 1768 and the J. pop. reached 206 (total 582) in 1816. In 1830–54, 82 Jews emigrated overseas and the community continued to dwindle, numbering 39 in 1933. The J. public school closed in 1924.

Under Nazi rule, the Jews suffered from the economic boycott. Most were cattle traders operating auxiliary farms. The synagogue was sold off in 1938. In 1933–40, 20 Jews left for other German cities. Another 20 emigrated from Germany in 1935–39. The last three were deported to Izbica in the Lublin dist. (Poland) on 25 April 1942.

WESTHEIM BEI HASSFURT Lower Franconia, Germany. The Jews maintained a pop. of 100–110 (around 15% of the total) throughout the 19th cent. and numbered 43 in 1933. A synagogue was built in 1913. On *Kristallnacht* (9–10 Nov. 1938), it was severely vandalized along with J. homes. Nine Jews are known to have emigrated in 1938–41 (seven to the U.S.). Fifteen were deported to Izbica in the Lublin dist. (Poland) via Wuerzburg on 25 April 1942. The last five were sent to the Theresienstadt ghetto in Sept.

WESTHOFFEN Bas-Rhin dist., France. There was a J. community here in the Middle Ages and a cemetery from the 15th cent. In 1784, the J. community numbered 280 members. A synagogue was inaugurated in 1868. On the eve of WWII there were 63 Jews in W. All were expelled during WWII to the south of France with the rest of Alsace-Lorraine's Jews. The synagogue was looted and the cemetery damaged. Altogether 23 Jews from W. perished in the war. In 1965, there were 19 Jews in W.

WETTER Hesse–Nassau, Germany. Affiliated with the rabbinate of Marburg, the community built a synagogue in 1897 and numbered 83 (5% of the total pop.) in 1933, excluding members in Gossfelden and Sterzhausen. The synagogue's interior was destroyed on *Kristallnacht* (9–10 Nov. 1938) and most Jews left (43 emigrating) before 1939; 11 perished in the Holocaust.

WETZLAR Hesse–Nassau, Germany. The medieval J. community, established around 1295, fell victim in Sept. 1348 to the Black Death massacres. Jews returned in 1360 and once again (after banishment) in 1604. A 1626 law restricted their number to 12 families, but in return for paying heavy taxes they obtained freedom of worship and other concessions. Some engaged in the cattle trade and later owned stores or entered the professions. Wealthy Court Jews who moved elsewhere often adopted W. as their surname: Karl

Abraham W., an 18th cent. apostate, founded the Wetzlar von Plankenstern dynasty in Vienna. The community built a new and larger synagogue in 1756, affiliated itself with the rabbinate of Marburg in 1815, and numbered 210 (3% of the total) in 1880. By 1933 the J. pop. had declined to 132, excluding members from Ehringshausen and other villages. On *Kristallnacht* (9–10 Nov. 1938), the interior of the synagogue was destroyed. Altogether, 41 Jews from the district emigrated and 68 perished in the Holocaust. J. Displaced Persons made temporary use of the synagogue after WWII.

WEVELINGHOVEN Rhineland, Germany. Jews numbered 82 in 1843. Of the nine remaining in 1935, six were deported to the Riga ghetto in Dec. 1941 (five perishing).

WEYER (I) (now part of Villmar) Hesse–Nassau, Germany. Established around 1750, the community numbered 44 in 1843 and opened a synagogue in 1875. Affiliated with the rabbinate of Bad Ems, its 48 members included 30 from Muenster, Oberbrechen, and Wolfenhausen in 1933. They disposed of the synagogue and most left the area before 1940; the last seven Jews were deported to the east in 1941.

WEYER (II) (Loreley) Hesse–Nassau, Germany. In 1841 the Jews of Lierscheid, Nochern, and W. (W. ueber Sankt Goarshausen) founded one small community with a synagogue in W. Most Jews left before WWII; nine were deported in 1941.

WIAZYN Vilna dist., Poland, today Belarus. Jews were present by the 17th cent. and reached a pop. of 234 in 1897 (total 604). Most lost their property in WWI and those who managed to open stores and workshops after the war were saddled with heavy taxes that undermined their livelihoods. Under the Soviet occupation of 1939–41, Jews received estate land which they were able to farm successfully. The 60 Jews of W. were executed by the Germans in June 1942.

WICKRATHBERG Rhineland, Germany. In 1700, W. was the religious center for Jews who had been living in the surrounding villages since about 1600. The community numbered 75 members in 1808 and 240 members in 1885, including W., Wickrath, and Beckrath. The community maintained a cemetery and dedicated a synagogue in 1860. In 1933, the community numbered 94 individuals. On *Kristallnacht* (9–10 Nov. 1938), the synagogue was burned down and J. businesses and homes were looted. J. men were arrested and deported to the Dachau concentration camp. The remaining Jews were billeted in "J. houses" in W. and Wickrath in 1939. They were deported in Dec. 1941 and July 1942. Altogether, 43 community members perished under Nazi rule.

WIDAWA   Lodz dist., Poland. Forty-three J. families lived here in 1764. The community grew to nearly 1,000 during the 19th cent. but in 1897 only 530 were left (32.5% of the total). In 1939 the majority of the 728 Jews moved to Belkhatow.

WIDZE   Vilna dist., Poland, today Belarus.. Jews probably settled in the 16th cent. and formed an organized community by the late 18th cent. They leased forest land and estate production facilities and traded in flax, lumber, wild berries, and grain. In the 19th cent. they expanded into shopkeeping and crafts as their pop. grew to 3,480 (total 5,103) in 1897. Only 1,100 remained after the depredations of WWI. The collapse of the Polish farm sector in the 1930s along with heavy taxes and the competition of the Polish cooperatives further undermined J. livelihoods. Many of the young joined the Zionist youth movements. Prior to the entry of the German *Wehrmacht* in June 1941, the Polish and Lithuanian-Polish militia murdered 200 Jews outside the town. Random killing continued under the Germans, who set up a *Judenrat* to supply forced labor. All but 200 were soon expelled to Braslaw, Opsa, and Glembokie. In July 1942 the ghetto pop. rose to 2,000 with an influx of refugees. They were sent to the Swienciany ghetto in late 1942 and executed at the Ponary extermination site near Vilna in April 1943.

WIECBORK   Pomerania dist., Poland. The J. community numbered 312 in 1865 (total 1,612). Most left after WWI. In 1932, those remaining were attached to the Sempolno community. The last 15 were expelled by the Germans to General Gouvernement territory in late 1939.

WIELEN NAD NOTECIA   Poznan dist., Poland. A J. community is first mentioned in the 16th cent., growing to 1,593 (total 3,209) in 1831. A synagogue was built in the 1850s under Liberal domination. Most Jews engaged in petty trade, brokerage, and crafts. Many Jews emigrated in the late 19th cent. The 26 remaining in Sept. 1939 were expelled by the Germans to General Gouvernement territory.

WIELICZKA   Cracow dist., Poland. Despite a ban on J. settlement lasting until 1867, Jews were active in the town from the 14th cent., with an organized community in neighboring Klasno from the late 18th cent. coming to constitute in effect a suburb of W. The J. pop. of W. grew to 981 in 1900 (15% of the total), despite setbacks caused by a devasting fire in 1887. Rival factions kept the community leaderless until the eve of WWI. Virulent antisemitism was a constant factor with notable outbursts in 1889 and 1906 as well as at the end of WWI. In 1921, there were 1,135 Jews in W. with another 400 in Klasno, where they formed the majority and pioneered light industry. Zionist activity developed between the World Wars, as youth movements were organized and wide-ranging cultural programs offered. Young Jews were also attracted to the illegal Polish Communist Party. The economic situation deteriorated, leaving a quarter of the J. pop. on welfare in 1931. Most fled with the approach of the Germans in Sept. 1939. The Gestapo combed the town and murdered 32 men in the forest. In the absence of males the town became the only one with an all-female *Judenrat*. Women also performed the forced labor until the men began to return. In 1940–41 thousands of refugees streamed into W., mainly from Cracow. To forestall executions and expulsions the *Judenrat* set up a factory for 700 workers. In Aug. 1942 thousands of additional refugees were packed into the town, living 30 and 40 to a room. On 26 Aug. a large-scale *Aktion* commenced. After 11 Jews were murdered at dawn, 113 patients were dragged out of their hospital beds and brought to the forest for execution, along with 40 doctors and nurses. Hundreds fled to labor camps to save themselves, but 8,000–9,000 reported as instructed and after a selection of artisans and young laborers, 700 of the aged were weeded out for immediate execution. The rest were transported to the Belzec death camp. The artisans among the workers (280 with their families) were dispatched to Skawina for liquidation when their workshops burned down; the 600 or so laborers were sent to the Plaszow and Rozwadow camps.

Members of Hashomer Hatzair, Wieliczka, Poland, May 1939

WIELKIE OCZY Lwow dist., Poland, today Ukraine. Jews were apparently among the town's first settlers in the late 17th cent. The J. pop. reached 985 (half the total) in 1880 but fell to 487 by 1921 after much emigration. Longstanding tensions with the Ukrainians erupted in a pogrom in July 1910. The German occupation of July 1941 started with a Ukrainian pogrom, which claimed J. lives. Most of the Jews were expelled to Jaworow; others to the Janowska camp in Lwow.

WIELOPOLE SKRZYNSKIE Cracow dist., Poland. The first Jews arrived in the late 17th cent. The impoverished backwater community never grew much beyond 500 residents (half the pop.). On their arrival in Sept. 1939, the Germans instituted a regime of forced labor and extortion, while Gestapo units periodically sowed terror by individual murders. The community was expelled to Ropczyce on 26 June 1942 and then to the Belzec death camp.

WIELUN Lodz dist., Poland. In the 15th and 16th cents. Jews were involved in the grain, wool, and textile trade with Silesia, but were expelled in the 1720s. They began to return and built a synagogue in 1855 and at the end of the 19th cent. a yeshiva was established. The J. pop. in 1897 was 2,732. Jews participated in the uprising against the Russians in the 1860s as well as in the 1905–07 revolutionary activities. During WWI several hundred J. workers from Lodz settled here. Jews constituted 65% of the city's artisans. Some made their living transporting people and goods and in the 1930s twelve J.-owned buses plied between W. and Lodz. Yavne and Beth Jacob schools provided J. education for about 500 pupils (about 30% of J. school-age children). At the outbreak of WWII, W. was destroyed by heavy bombardments and many Jews fled. By Dec. 1940 there were 4,053 Jews in the town (including 450 refugees). Men were sent to forced labor camps in the Poznan area and in the Reich itself. Ten Jews were hanged publicly at the beginning of 1942 and in April some 2,000 Jews were transported from the city to an unknown destination. On 22 Aug., 10,000 Jews were deported from W. and the surrounding area to Chelmno; 922 were sent to forced labor in the Lodz ghetto. Some survivors returned to W. after the war, but in the face of antisemitism and murders, left the town.

WIENER NEUSTADT Lower Austria, Austria. Jews first settled in 1192. In spite of many anti-J. restrictions, the community flourished and maintained a synagogue, *mikve*, and cemetery. During the 13th cent., there were many famous rabbis living in W., including Hayyim ben Moshe and Yisrael Isserlein, known throughout Germany for their halakhic works and responsa. An important yeshiva was established during the 15th cent. Jews were engaged in moneylending. Some were government officials involved in financial affairs. In 1496, Maximilian I. expelled all the Jews from W. In the early 18th cent., J. refugees from Sopron (Hungary) settled in W. for a short period, but were forced to leave because of clerical anti-J. ag-

itation. Until 1848, Jews were not allowed to stay overnight, but they could attend fairs in the city. In 1862, the J. community was recognized as a religious association (*Kultusverein*). A cemetery was opened in 1899 and a new synagogue was inaugurated in 1902. In 1869, the J. pop. stood at 173, increasing rapidly to 1,059 in 1923. In the beginning of the 1930s, there were approximately 1,300 Jews in W., making it the fourth largest J. community in Austria at the time. In the 1920s, Agudat Israel and a local Zionist group were active. Jews engaged in trade, especially in cattle. Between 1933 and 1937, over 1,000 Jews emigrated. After the *Anschluss* (13 March 1938), there was an unsuccessful attempt to burn down the synagogue. By the end of April 1938 no Jews were allowed to attend the local cattle market and J. shops were "Aryanized." On *Kristallnacht* (9–10 Nov. 1938), J. homes, together with the furniture, and all J. bank accounts were seized by the local SA. On 2 May 1938, there were 347 Jews still living in W. Most managed to emigrate; others were forced to leave for Vienna and from there were deported to the east.

Bar Kochba athletes, Wierushzow, Poland, 1932

WIERUSHZOW Lodz dist., Poland. Jews expelled from Wielun settled here in 1586. Despite its proximity to the border and the 1823–25 laws restricting Jews from settling, the community expanded. By 1897 the 1,587 Jews constituted 36% of the inhabitants. Gur and Aleksandrow were the largest hasidic sects in the town. Zionist activity began in 1904 and Mizrachi and Po'alei Zion groups were soon established. In June 1918, shelling by the retreating German forces was the signal for widespread attacks on the Jews by local residents.. The community rallied after the war but during the 1928–31 economic crisis most Jews suffered from poverty. Zionist parties and their youth movements flourished after the war and a strong group of J. Communists existed within the general trade union. The community council was dominated by Agudat Israel, four of whose members represented the community on the nine-member municipal council. When German troops entered the city in 1939, they persecuted the Jews and murdered some of the leaders. A group of 80 J. males in their traditional garb were forced into railroad cars carrying goods and sent to Nuremberg. Signs on the cars claimed that the Jews inside had shot Germans. The weeklong journey was filmed for propaganda purposes. They were eventually returned to their homes. The Germans appointed a *Judenrat* with a J. police force. Heavy taxes were imposed on the Jews and males were sent to forced labor camps in the Poznan area. On 1 Jan. 1939 there were 2,400 Jews in W., but a year later only 1,740 remained. In Sept. 1941, 1,200 Jews were concentrated in a ghetto and on 11–23 Aug. 1942 they were rounded up and deported to Chelmno.

WIERZBNIK-STARACHOWICE Kielce dist., Poland. Despite an official residence ban until 1862, a J. community established itself by the mid-19th cent., growing to 975 in 1897. After the discovery of local iron deposits, Jews played a leading role in the town's industrial development, setting up one of its first foundries. Jews were also active in the lumber industry and ran a felt factory that attracted buyers from Russia and Germany. By 1921, the J. pop. was 2,159, with three J. banks in operation. Zionist activity was extensive, including the opening of a Tarbut elementary school, and local J. sportsmen participated in the 1935 Maccabiah Games in Palestine. The Germans captured the city on 9 Sept. 1939, soon burning down the synagogue. A *Judenrat* was established on

23 Nov., charged with furnishing forced labor and tributes. Refugees increased the J. pop. to about 4,000. On 27 Oct. 1942, 2,000 Jews, primarily women, children, and older people, were deported to the Treblinka death camp and the rest dispersed among the labor camps, mostly working at the nearby munitions factory. In 1945, several survivors returned, but after the murder of a J. family by Polish partisans, most left for Lodz.

WIERZBOWIEC Stanislawow dist., Poland. The J. pop. in 1921 was 131. The Jews were possibly executed locally in April 1942, or expelled to Kosow for extermination in Oct. 1942.

WIESBADEN Hesse–Nassau, Germany. A health resort dating from Roman times, W. had a J. community in 1573. Though subject to various restrictions (1638), it provided visitors with kosher facilities, maintained a district rabbinate from 1708, and opened a synagogue accommodating 200 worshipers in 1826. Avraham Geiger served as communal rabbi in 1832–38 and introduced changes in public worship; he also

Synagogue in Wiesbaden, Germany, consecrated in 1869

made W. the venue for the first conference of Reform rabbis in Germany in 1837. Religious issues came to a head during the rabbinate of Samuel Suesskind (1844–84). At the imposing new Moorish synagogue, dedicated in 1869, services were accompanied by an organ and choir. Orthodox Jews, who already attended a separate *minyan*, established a breakaway community which was recognized in 1879 under the Prussian law of secession. Its rabbinate was headed by Leo Kahn and subsequently by Jonas Ansbacher. The Jews of W., numbering 152 in 1825, played a leading role in commerce and the professions, especially medicine. By 1905 their number had increased to 2,656 (3% of the total). The historian Adolf Kober served as Liberal district rabbi (1909–18) and Jews from Eastern Europe (*Ostjuden*) boosted the community's final growth to 3,463 in 1925. A *Juedisches Lehrhaus* was established in 1921 to promote J. adult education in the Liberal community. A conference of the German Zionist Organization held in W. in 1924 was attended by WZO President Chaim Weizmann. Branches of the Central Union (C.V.), J. War Veterans Association, Mizrachi, Agudat Israel, WIZO, and several Zionist youth movements were active during the Weimar Republic. Anti-semitism made little headway before WWI, but the deteriorating economic situation led to a rapid increase in anti-J. violence from 1930. Once Hitler came to power in 1933, Nazi boycott measures afflicted the community (then numbering 2,713). Jews were dismissed from public office, at least two were murdered, and the "Aryanization" of their stores (over 250) began. Doctors were among the first to leave, 33 out of 54 emigrating by 1938. The community's welfare workers fed and aided the distressed while the rabbi opened a district school in 1936 and valiantly sought to sustain J. morale. On *Kristallnacht* (9–10 Nov. 1938), SS troops burned the Liberal synagogue to the ground and partly destroyed the Orthodox synagogue; 23 Jews died in the riots, after which hundreds were imprisoned in the Buchenwald concentration camp. The number of Jews declined to 1,125 by 1939; 500 were deported to the east in March–June 1942 and 600 to the Theresienstadt ghetto in Sept. 1942. Nearly 40 Jews committed suicide before the last transport and many of the 600 converts or part-Jews (*Mischlinge*) died in Nazi camps. The postwar community of Holocaust survivors, mainly from Eastern Europe, dedicated a new synagogue in 1966 and grew to about 400 in 1990.

WIESECK Hesse, Germany. Jews lived there from the 17th cent., opened a synagogue in 1872, and numbered 82 (3% of the total) in 1880. Though nominally independent, they became part of Giessen's Liberal J. community after WWI. On *Kristallnacht* (9–10 Nov. 1938), the synagogue's interior was badly damaged. By 1939, 21 of the remaining 39 Jews had emigrated. The last nine were deported in 1942.

WIESENBRONN Lower Franconia, Germany. Jews are first mentioned in 1548 and a community is known from the 17th cent. A synagogue was built in the late 18th cent. R. Seligmann Baer Bamberger ("the Wuerzburger Rav"), founder of the Wuerzburg teachers' seminary and chief rabbi of the Wuerzburg region in 1840–70, was born in W. in 1807 and founded a yeshiva there. The J. pop. reached 160 in 1837 (total 1,080) and then declined steadily to 22 in 1933. Nine left in 1933–37 and another six in 1939–40 in the wake of the *Kristallnacht* riots (9–10 Nov. 1938). Three remaining women were deported to Izbica in the Lublin dist. (Poland) and the Theresienstadt ghetto in 1942.

WIESENFELD Lower Franconia, Germany. A J. community is known from the mid-17th cent. The J. pop. declined from 160 in 1837 to 66 in 1900 (total 1,092) after many left for nearby Karlstadt in the last third of the 19th cent. In 1933, 55 Jews remained. On *Kristallnacht* (9–10 Nov. 1938), the synagogue and J. homes were vandalized and Jews arrested and held for six weeks. In 1933–40, 23 Jews emigrated, including 14 to the U.S. Of the 25 remaining in 1942, mostly aged 50–70, 19 were deported to Izbica in the Lublin dist. (Poland) via Wuerzburg on 24 April and six to the Theresienstadt ghetto in Sept.

WIESLOCH (in J. sources, Vietzenlich) Baden, Germany. The 14th cent. community was destroyed in the Black Death persecutions of 1348–49 and Jews settling later were expelled by Rupert I in 1391. After being limited to a few families in the 16th–18th cents., the community began to grow in the 19th cent., reaching a pop. of 119 in 1875. A synagogue was built in 1840. In the early 20th cent., Jews were active in the cattle trade and tobacco industry and played an important part in the city's commercial life, though not active politically. In 1933, 101 Jews remained. On *Kristallnacht* (9–10 Nov. 1938), the synagogue was vandalized, windows of J. homes were smashed, and J. men were detained in the Dachau concentration camp. At least 39 Jews emigrated from Germany. Eighteen were deported to the Gurs concentration camp on 22 Oct. 1940 and six were sent to other places, 15 perishing. Another 12 Jews from the local psychiatric hospital were put to death.

WILDUNGEN, BAD   see BAD WILDUNGEN.

WILEJKA   Vilna dist., Poland, today Belarus. The J. community grew rapidly in the late 18th cent., numbering 926 in 1797, but in the wake of floods and fires, the J. pop. dropped to 257 in 1847 before rising again to 1,328 in 1897 (total 3,560) as economic conditions improved. In the second half of the 19th cent. Jews began to expand from trade into crafts. In the pre-WWI years J. wholesalers were financed by a merchant bank and engaged in large-scale lumber exports. Jews also ran ten hostels for traveling businessmen. Most of the Jews were Habad Hasidim, with a minority of *Mitnaggedim*. In WWI, most J. homes were destroyed and the Jews suffered from food and fuel shortages. In the 1920s, Jews built two flour mills and a sawmill as well as operating a printing press, three small soap factories, and a beer brewery. The J. pop. in 1921 was 1,100. In the late 1930s the anti-J. economic boycott took a heavy toll. A Hebrew school was founded in 1918, later joining the Tarbut network. The young organized drama groups and a string orchestra. Most of the young belonged to the Zionist youth movements and some left for Palestine in the framework of the Fourth *Aliya*. Under Soviet rule (Sept. 1939–June 1941), J. businesses were nationalized and a number of wealthy Jews exiled to Siberia. The Germans captured the town on 25 June 1941. Local hoodlums immediately began breaking into J. homes. On 12 July 1941 the Germans executed a group of 150 J. men and boys in the nearby forest. A *Judenrat* was then appointed and on 29 July more Jews were rounded up and executed at a mass grave. The third *Aktion* took place on 2 March 1942 when all but a few skilled workers were also executed beside a mass grave outside the town. Of the 1,300 Jews of W., 26 now remained alive. These were confined to the local labor camp, where 300 young Jews were gathered. Most were subsequently executed or rounded up and murdered after fleeing. A group of J. partisans operated in the vicinity of W.

WILHELMSHAVEN   Hanover, Germany. Built on territory acquired from Oldenburg in 1853 and named in honor of William I, W. soon became one of Germany's most important naval bases. The ten Jews living there in 1876 grew to 47 in 1885, 131 in 1910, and 239 in 1925. A new synagogue was dedicated in 1910. During and after WWI, the community's religious teacher served as chaplain to J. sailors. There were anti-J. incidents, often involving navy personnel, and in 1922, two ultra-nationalists made an attempt on the life of Maximilian Harden, a prominent J. writer who edited *Die Zukunft*. In June 1933, there were 191 Jews in W. The J. community responded to Nazi pressure by intensifying its communal and Zionist activity. Nearly 100 Jews left before *Kristallnacht* (9–10 Nov. 1938). During the pogrom the synagogue was destroyed and J. businesses were looted. After Jews had been driven through the streets and pelted with rocks, 34 were transported to the Sachsenhausen concentration camp. By May 1939, a total of 45 Jews had emigrated from W. (nearly 30 to England and other safe havens); one joined the International Brigade in Spain and, later, the French Resistance. At least 16 of those who remained after 1939 perished in the Holocaust.

WILHERMSDORF   Middle Franconia, Germany. A community with a synagogue and cemetery is known from the early 15th cent. It became noted in the 17th and 18th cents. for its Hebrew printing presses, the first licensed to R. Yitzhak ha-Kohen Juedels of Prague in 1669 and the second founded by R. Tzevi Hirsch ben Hayyim in 1712. The J. pop. was 180 in 1867 and 35 in 1933 (total 1,737). In 1933–38, 23 Jews left the town. Eight more left after beatings in Sept. 1938.

WILLMARS   Lower Franconia, Germany. Jews from W. visited the Leipzig fair in the 18th cent. A new synagogue was built in 1901 and a J. public school operated until 1920. The J. pop. declined steadily from 161 in 1816 (total 574) to 35 in 1933. In Oct. 1938 the Jews were forced to dismantle the interior of the synagogue with their bare hands and were afterwards beaten. Of the 22 who left W. in 1936–41, 14 reached the U.S.

WINDECKEN   (now part of Nidderau) Hesse–Nassau, Germany. Expelled during the Black Death persecutions of 1348–49, Jews returned and built a synagogue in 1429 that was maintained for over 500 years. Numbering 192 (11% of the total) in 1850, the community was the birthplace of eminent individuals such as Lassa Francis L. Oppenheim (1858–1919), an authority on international law at Cambridge University. Socialists led the battle against antisemitism from 1891 until 1933, when the community (affiliated with the Hanau rabbinate) dwindled to 44. The Nazis burned the ancient synagogue on *Kristallnacht* (9–10 Nov. 1938) and by July 1941 no Jews remained. Thirteen had emigrated and at least 12 perished in the Holocaust.

WINDSBACH   Middle Franconia, Germany. A J. settlement is known from the 14th cent. and Jews lived there in small numbers until the late 17th cent. under periodic expulsions and letters of protection. The early 18th cent. community was subjected to numerous restrictions (including a ban on music during weddings) and attained a peak pop. of 97 in 1867 (total 1,525). Most were active in the cattle trade. A new synagogue was built in 1849. In 1933 the J. pop. was 42. Twenty remained in Nov. 1938, when local SA troops vandalized J. homes and the synagogue during *Kristallnacht* (9–10 Nov. 1938). All but one left the town by 17 Dec.

WINDSHEIM   Middle Franconia, Germany. Jews are first mentioned in 1274, living in a special quarter. In the Rindfleisch massacres of 1298, 55 were murdered. In the Black Death persecutions of 1348–49 the community was destroyed. The reestablished community was accorded a letter of protection by King Sigismund in 1416 but expelled at the end of the cent. The modern community was officially founded in 1877 when 12 J. families were present. In 1933 it numbered 58 Jews (total 3,900). Twenty-two remained in Nov. 1938. After the synagogue was partially burned on *Kristallnacht* (9–10 Nov. 1938), all left, 13 immediately and the rest by Jan. 1939.

WINGERSHEIM   Bas-Rhin dist., France. A small J. community was established in the 19th cent. and a synagogue was inaugurated in 1876. By 1936 there were 53 Jews in the town. During WWII, all were expelled to the south of France, together with the rest of the Jews of Alsace-Lorraine. Four or six Jews were deported.

WINNIKI   Lwow dist., Poland, today Ukraine. The J. community of 40–50 families (less than 10% of the total) increased to about 500 people with the arrival of Jews expelled from Lwow by the Soviets in 1940. The German occupation of 29 June 1941 ignited Ukrainian rioting. A few weeks later males above the age of 13 were led out of the town and murdered. The women and children were taken away in early 1942 and murdered probably in Piaski near Lwow.

WINNWEILER   Palatinate, Germany. The J. pop. was 40 in 1804, 165 (28 families) in 1848, 81 in 1900, and 30 in 1932. The synagogue, consecrated in 1901, was destroyed on *Kristallnacht* (9–10 Nov. 1938). In Oct. 1940, the last nine Jews were deported to the Gurs concentration camp, where six perished.

WINSCHOTEN   Groningen dist., Holland. J. settlement began after the mid-18th cent. and a community was organized by 1778. The J. pop. grew rapidly in the 19th cent., reaching 628 in 1860. The J. pop. in 1940 was 520. Some 500 were deported from Aug. 1942 to early 1943. About 20 survived the Holocaust.

WINSUM   Groningen dist., Holland. The community dates from the early 19th cent. and numbered 143 in 1854. The J. pop. in 1941 was 48. All but one perished in the Holocaust.

WINTERSWIJK   Gelderland dist., Holland. J. settlement began at the outset of the 18th cent. In 1800 a community was established and grew throughout the 19th cent. The J. pop. in 1892 was 151. In the 1930s many German-J. refugees reached W. The J. pop. in 1941 was 283 (total 19,668). From Nov. 1942 to April 1943, 235 Jews were deported, eight of whom survived. A few others survived in hiding.

WINTZENHEIM   Haut-Rhin dist., France. The J. community was established in the 18th cent. There were seven families in 1689 and 51 in 1766. By 1784, there were 88 families (430 individuals) living in the area. The synagogue was inaugurated in 1870. Before WWII, there were 97 Jews in W. In WWII, all Jews were evacuated to the south of France, together with the rest of the Jews of Alsace-Lorraine.

WINZIG   (Pol. Winsko) Lower Silesia, Germany. A J. family was present by 1815 and in 1821 the J. pop. was 21, rising to 51 in 1862. A synagogue and cemetery were consecrated in 1871 but in the latter half of the 19th cent., the J. pop. began to decline. In 1925, there were 30 Jews and in 1931, 23 (six families) in W. and its environs. Twelve Jews remained in 1937. On *Kristallnacht* (9–10 Nov. 1938), the synagogue and two J. stores were destroyed. One Jew in a mixed marriage remained in Nov. 1942. No further information is available about the fate of the community under Nazi rule. Presumably those Jews who failed to emigrate were deported and perished.

WIONZOWNA Warsaw dist., Poland. J. settlement in W. developed in the second half of the 19th cent. The J. pop. in 1921 was 272 (total 734). In Feb. 1941 the Jews were expelled to the Warsaw ghetto.

WISKITKI Warsaw dist., Poland. Jews lived there from the early 18th cent. In 1897 there were 1,138 Jews in a total pop. of 3,060. During WWI the J. pop. dwindled. Between the World Wars, J. organizations were founded. W. was occupied by the Germans on 8 Sept. 1939. Jews were persecuted and sent to forced labor. Refugees from neighboring towns increased the J. pop. to about 2,000 in Jan. 1941. In Feb. all were taken to the Warsaw ghetto and from there to the Treblinka death camp.

WISLICA (Yid. Wislic) Kielce dist., Poland. Jews are first mentioned in 1514. In 1566 they were forced to live outside the town walls and 50 families were massacred there by Stefan Czarniecki's irregular Polish troops in the mid-17th cent. Swedish war. Jews were subsequently allowed back into the town, building a synagogue and maintaining their own quarter. In 1765, the J. community numbered 256. Such hasidic leaders as R. Elimelekh of Lyzhansk and his brother Zusya of Hanipoli (Annopol) frequented the town and when the former's student, R. Moshe David Lida, served as rabbi W. became a hasidic center. In 1858, Jews numbered 1,370 (total 1,993) as economic conditions improved. In 1889, 200 children were studying in six private *hadarim*. After WWI, a new railway line helped economic recovery as Jews built warehouses near the station and started a gypsum factory and a burgeoning stocking industry. During this period, Zionist influence spread and J. public life flourished. Upon the German invasion of Sept. 1939, 1,437 Jews were present in W. Many fled eastward to Russian-controlled territory. The Germans immediately burned down the synagogue, exacting a "contribution" from

the community and beginning to seize J. men and women aged 15–60 for forced labor. A *Judenrat* was set up and with the arrival of refugees from Warsaw, Lodz, Cracow, and other places, the J. pop. rose to 2,200 in 1940. In 1941, 200 families from Plotsk and Radom arrived. Twenty Jews were executed for "illegal" trade. Many fell victim to a typhoid epidemic in winter 1941–42 as well as suffering from hunger and cold. On 3 Oct. 1942, as the Germans commenced an *Aktion*, hundreds fled, some to survive, others to be apprehended and murdered by the Poles or Germans. About 2,000 were deported to the Treblinka death camp via Jendrzejow. Members of a Gordonia training kibbutz in the area fled to the forests and linked up with Polish Armia Ludowa partisans.

WISNICZ NOWY (Yid. Vishnitsa) Cracow dist., Poland. A large part of the 200-family J. community fled during the mid-17th cent. disturbances. In the 18th cent. the community was one of the largest and most important in Lesser Poland, with 151 neighboring villages under its aegis. Restrictive Austrian rule from 1772 retarded its development and a devasting fire in 1863 left hundreds homeless. The founding of a large hasidic yeshiva by Shelomo Halberstam of Bobowa breathed new life into the community, which reached a pop. of 2,278 (total 3,791) in 1890, but the removal of his court in 1892 again set off a downward trend, with just 1,273 (total 2,691) remaining after WWI. Internecine strife brought members of the ousted community council to complain in Nov. 1918 to the Polish garrison commander of a budding rebellion and as a result large-scale executions almost resulted; in the end, 130 Jews aged 12–70 were publicly whipped. Zionist activity was suppressed through vehement rabbinic opposition, only making inroads between the World Wars, when depressed economic conditions prevailed and the Joint Distribution Committee provided extensive aid. Antisemitic incidents continued throughout the period. With the arrival of the Germans in Sept. 1939, a regime of forced labor and persecution was introduced. In 1940, refugees swelled the J. pop. to 3,000. All were expelled to Bochnia on 22 Aug. 1942, falling victim to the *Aktions* there.

WISNIOWIEC Volhynia dist., Poland, today Ukraine. The J. settlement dates from the second half of the 16th cent. It suffered greatly in the Tartar attack of 1653 but recovered quickly. The J. pop. was 2,825 in 1897. During the Russian civil war (1918–21), the Jews suffered from roving gangs. About 400 emigrated with the inception of Polish rule. Between the World Wars, J. cultural life centered around the Zionist youth movements. Jews exported large quantities of farm produce to Galicia and operated small factories. After the arrival of the Germans on 2 July 1941, nearly 600 Jews were murdered with active Ukrainian participation. A ghetto was set up in March 1942, housing 3,500 Jews including refugees. A *Judenrat* was established under the chairmanship of a refugee after local Jews refused to participate. Many died as their diet was reduced to 2 ounces of bread a day. On 8 Aug., 2,669 Jews, mainly women and children, were led out of the town and murdered.

WISSENBOURG   Bas-Rhin dist., France. The community dates from the Middle Ages. In 1260, community members were massacred in a blood libel. A new community was established in the 19th cent. Its synagogue was inaugurated in 1872. In 1885, there were 1,750 Jews living in W. and in 1895 there were 1,341. In 1905 the community set up a joint committee of Jews and non-Jews to raise money for the J. victims of the pogroms in Russia. On the eve of WWII, there were 146 Jews in W. All were expelled to the south of France in the beginning of the war together with the other Jews of Alsace-Lorraine. Eight were deported. The synagogue was completely destroyed. In the mid-1960s, the community numbered 56 Jews.

WISZNICE   Lublin dist., Poland. Jews settled in the late 18th cent. In the late 19th cent., Jews became active as food manufacturers and also operated a steam-powered flour mill and a hide-processing plant. The J. pop. rose from 696 in 1857 (total 1,465) to 811 in 1921. The Bund and Po'alei Zion were active in the early 20th cent. After WWI, control of community institutions passed from the Gur-dominated Hasidim to the Zionists. Violent anti-J. riots occurred in 1934 and 1936 and a fire in 1939 destroyed many J. homes. The Germans arrived in early Oct. 1939, setting up a *Judenrat* in Nov. 1939 and a ghetto crowded with refugees in late 1940. In Sept. 1942, as some 1,000 Jews were being marched to the Miendzyrzec Podlaski ghetto, several young people attacked and killed the gendarmes accompanying the marchers, with many escaping in the commotion. On 27 Oct. 1942, the Jews were deported from the ghetto to the

Treblinka death camp. The last 120 Jews were executed in W. on 17 Nov.

WISZNIEW   Nowogrodek dist., Poland, today Belarus. Jews settled in the late 18th cent., becoming active in the lumber industry as well as leasing a dairy and distilleries from the local estate. In the late 19th cent., when the J. pop. reached 1,463 including the neighboring villages (total pop. 2,650), J. merchants also dealt in grain, flour, and flax. A yeshiva was opened in 1910, headed by R. Yehuda Isser Unterman, who became chief rabbi of Israel in 1964. In 1915 a devasting fire left most of the Jews homeless. After flight and expulsion in WWI they returned, suffering from hunger and disease in the ruined town. The community recovered with the assistance of the YEKOPO relief committee and through employment at the J.-owned Chirinski lumber company. After the company's bankruptcy in 1926, Jews began buying up farm land to produce fodder for the Polish army. They also owned warehouses for farm and building supplies. However, the collapse of the Polish farm sector in 1931 undermined the economic position of the Jews. The Zionists were active between the World Wars, sending pioneers to Palestine through the youth movements. Yehoshua Rabinowitz (1911–79), future mayor of Tel Aviv and minister of finance in the Israeli government, was born there, as was Nahum Goldmann (1895–1982), later president of the World Zionist Organization and the World J. Congress. A Tarbut Hebrew school enrolled 150 children in 1929–30. After two years of Soviet rule, the Germans entered W. on 26 June 1941. Jews holding public positions under the Soviets were murdered. In early 1942 the Jews were confined to a ghetto and subjected to forced labor. On 22 Sept. 1942, over 1,000 were led out of the town, 20 at a time, put up against a wall, and executed. Those escaping joined the partisans and helped blow up a train full of *Wehrmacht* troops and later burned down the town of W. itself in a raid encompassing 300 fighters.

WITKOW NOWY   Tarnopol dist., Poland, today Ukraine. Jews lived there from the early 18th cent. with substantial growth in the 19th, the J. pop. leveling off at around 1,000 (half the total) at the turn of the cent. The J. homes along with the synagogue and *beit midrash* were destroyed in a fire in June 1904. By the outbreak of WWI the community had recovered, but suffered from the Russian occupation and Cossack looting. The Zionists became active between the World Wars. After Soviet rule (Sept. 1939–June 1941) the Germans occupied W. on 25 June 1941 and persecution commenced. In an *Aktion* in Oct. 1942, 160 Jews were deported to the Belzec death camp. The last Jews were expelled in March 1943.

WITTELSHOFEN Middle Franconia, Germany. An important J. community existed from the 18th to the mid-19th cent., known as one of the wealthiest in the region. A new synagogue was built in 1842. Most Jews traded in livestock. The J. pop. numbered 104 in 1867 and 17 in 1933 (total 512). The last eight Jews were expelled after the synagogue was burned to the ground on *Kristallnacht* (9–10 Nov. 1938).

WITTEN Westphalia, Germany. One J. family was present in the early 19th cent. and the J. pop. maintained a steady rate of growth over the next hundred years, reaching a peak of 521 in 1910. A community center housing a synagogue and school was erected in 1860 and a cemetery was opened in 1867 (replaced by a new one in 1891). The congregation was Liberal, introducing the Reform prayer service and a mixed choir into the synagogue. A small Orthodox group split off and opened its own synagogue and school. In June 1933 there were 400 Jews in W. By June 1934, 84 Jews, mainly of East European origin, had sold their property and left Germany. Emigration continued in subsequent years, primarily to other cities within Germany. On *Kristallnacht* (9–10 Nov. 1938), the synagogue was burned, J. property was vandalized and looted, and Jews were marched through the streets and abused. In May 1939, 97 Jews remained in W.; 86 were subsequently deported to the death camps of the east. Only a handful survived.

WITTENBERG Saxony, Germany. Jews were living in W. in the 14th cent.. Resettlement did not occur until the 19th cent. There were 33 Jews in 1880 and about 70 in 1898. They were first members of the Halle community, using the cemetery there, but eventually established their own prayer room. They finally set up their own community, which was affiliated to the Halle community. When the Nazis came to power in 1933, there were about 70 Jews in W. On *Kristallnacht* (9–10 Nov. 1938), which coincided with the celebrations commemorating the 450th anniversary of the birth of Martin Luther, to whom

the city owes its fame, J. homes and stores were wrecked, and J. men were deported to the Buchenwald concentration camp. In 1939, the last 22 Jews were forcibly billeted in a "J. house." Most were finally deported and perished. Four Jews who were married to non-Jews managed to survive in W.

WITTENBERGE Brandenburg, Germany. There was a J. settlement in the 19th cent. The J. pop. was 30 in 1880. The Jews belonged to the Perleberg community and only set up a community of their own in 1923. It had 56 members in 1925 and maintained a prayer room and a cemetery. On *Kristallnacht* (9–10 Nov. 1938), Jews were abused, their stores and homes were wrecked and looted, and the cemetery was desecrated. Thirty-one Jews managed to emigrate; three committed suicide and 18 were deported, three directly from W. to the Warsaw ghetto and the others from the places where they had hoped to find shelter. By Oct. 1942, only three Jews were still living in W., probably protected by marriage to non-Jews. Of the deportees, only three survived.

WITTLICH Rhineland, Germany. Jews arrived under the protection of Archbishop Baldwin in the first half of the 14th cent. and engaged in moneylending. All were killed in 1349 during the Black Death massacres, with their property expropriated by Baldwin and his successor, Boemund. Jews again settled around 1620. They traded in horses, wine, fruit, silver, and jewelry and were again active as moneylenders. In the 19th cent., their pop. grew steadily, from 68 in 1808 to 204 (total 3,085) in 1871. The majority dealt in livestock and from the beginning of the 19th cent., the majority of livestock traders in the town were Jews, with Yiddish the language of the livestock market and Yiddish expressions entering local speech. In the mid-19th cent., newcomers with capital also began operating successful stores, bringing in merchandise from the Leipzig, Frankfurt, and Berlin fairs, and becoming the first to open department stores and hold holiday and end-of-season sales. J. women worked as seamstresses. Between 1850 and 1864, Jews also opened three cigar factories. The shopkeepers came to represent the wealthier class amongst the Jews vis-a-vis the old-time livestock traders. In 1808, the community was attached to the Trier consistory. A synagogue was consecrated in 1833, its congregation reflecting the community's class structure, with the wealthier merchants tending toward Orthodoxy and the poorer livestock dealers embracing Liberalism. A private J. elementary school was founded in 1858 and recognized as a public school in 1891. From the late 19th cent. through the Weimar period, the J. pop. maintained a stable level of 200–230 despite a rapidly falling birthrate, which dropped from 6.56 children per family in 1830–60 to 4.2 in 1860–90, 2.63 in 1890–1920, and 1.5 in 1920–37. By 1912, the percentage of livestock dealers among J. breadwinners had dropped to 41%. The Frank textile outlet and the Wolf shoe store were the leading commercial enterprises. Gottfried Hess was a city assemblyman from 1900 to 1925 and Jews were active in local cultural organizations. Gustav Adolf Mueller, who served in the Bavarian Landtag from 1899 to 1918, was afterwards Germany's ambassador to Switzerland. At the same time there were manifestations of local antisemitism throughout the period. A new synagogue was consecrated in 1910. After WWI, the remaining cigar manufacturer expanded into match, candle, oil, and shoe polish production. Jews continued to engage primarily in trade and were represented in a wide variety of cultural organizations (theater, music, sports). Nazi antisemitism intensified from the mid-1920s. In June 1933, the J. pop. was 268. Under Nazi rule, Jews immediately became objects of abuse, attacked in the streets and isolated economically and socially. The few Germans who kept up their formerly friendly relations did so clandestinely. In 1933, income in J. stores dropped by 30%. Knives were confiscated from J. butchers even before the nationwide ban on ritual slaughter. J. dealers were also banned from the livestock market. In 1933–38, 155 Jews left W., 86 emigrating and 69 moving to other German cities, including 19 to Cologne. Zionist activity expanded, with 59 in the local branch in 1936 and 19 youngsters undergoing pioneer training in various localities prior to *aliya*. The Maccabi sports club was active in 1935. On *Kristallnacht* (9–10 Nov. 1938), the synagogue, J. school, and J. homes were wrecked. From 1939, Jews were held in two "J. houses," the men subjected to forced labor. By summer 1941, another 54 Jews left the town (46 in 1939), 21 emigrating and 33 moving to other German cities (26 to Cologne). Of the total 133 Jews who emigrated directly from W. or via their new homes in Germany, 30 reached Palestine, 13 South America, and ten Luxembourg. Deportations commenced in fall 1941 when 11 Jews were loaded onto a transport of 500 bound for the Lodz ghetto. Two were deported to the Riga ghetto on 7 Dec., seven to an unknown destination on 23 April 1942, and nine to the Theresienstadt ghetto on 22 July 1942. In all, 80 perished in the Holocaust.

WITTMUND Hanover, Germany. Eight J. families lived here in 1676 and at its peak, in 1878, the community numbered 115. The Jews built a synagogue in 1816 (replaced by a new one in 1910) and maintained an elementary school between 1846 and 1928. In June 1933, there were 41 Jews registered in W. Sixteen moved to other German cities and 23 emigrated (19 to the U.S.) The synagogue had already been disposed of before *Kristallnacht* (9–10 Nov. 1938). At least six Jews perished in the Holocaust.

WITZENHAUSEN Hesse–Nassau, Germany. The community opened a synagogue in 1622 and then became the seat of a chief rabbinate between 1665 and 1772. Its first incumbent, Mordekhai Suesskind Rothenburg, founded the duchy's only yeshiva; Moses Witzenhausen-Fraenkel, a district rabbi, served as advisor to the head of Westphalia's consistory (1807–13). After building a new synagogue in 1810, the Jews converted their *talmud torah* into an elementary school in 1863. They numbered 201 (6% of the total) in 1871. Originally peddlers and petty traders, they now owned stores and factories and participated in civic affairs. The community, which was affiliated with Kassel's rabbinate, still numbered 134 (3%) in 1925 but closed its J. school in 1933. Shortly before *Kristallnacht* (9–10 Nov. 1938) the synagogue was burned down and 49 Jews emigrated. In all, 55 deportees perished in the Holocaust.

WIZAJNY Bialystok dist., Poland. Jews were present from 1646. In 1921 they numbered 332 (total 1,396). In Oct. 1939, the 200 Jews there were expelled by the Germans to Lithuania. In the following years almost all met their death.

WIZNA Bialystok dist., Poland. In 1765 W. had 16 J. families; in 1890 the community numbered 567 (total 2,984). In the late 1930s, there was an increase in antisemitism. The Germans arrived on 24 June 1941 and in July ordered the Jews to leave W. Most reached Jedwabne, where they were burned in a barn; others reached the Lomzha ghetto and shared the fate of the Jews there.

WLADYSLAWOW-RUSSOCICE (Yid. Riseshitz) Lodz dist., Poland. Jews settled here in the late 18th cent. and numbered 293 in 1921. In 1940, the 115 remaining Jews were concentrated in a ghetto and on 20 Oct. 1941 they were transported to the Kowale Panskie dist. where they shared the fate of the Jews of the region.

WLOCLAWEK Warsaw dist., Poland. Jews did business at trade fairs here as early as the 16th cent. and settled after the residence ban was lifted in 1802. As the town expanded rapidly (in the latter half of the 19th cent.), the J. pop. grew to 4,248 in 1897. Most Jews were merchants and craftsmen, some were in the professions, and J. investors started up printing, metal, building, chemical, and food industries, modernized the port facilities, and opened banks. In the 1880s, Hovevei Zion laid the foundations for both secular and religious acceptance of Zionist aims and activity in the future. The community was directed by well-to-do and assimilated Jews until the end of the 19th cent., when its leadership was taken over by Zionists and religious groups. However, strong secular educational trends gained impetus at this time. Antisemitism, including violence against Jews in the early 20th cent., led to J. emigration. In 1906 R. Yehuda Leib Kowalsky, a disciple of the Sochaczew Rebbe, founded the Etz Hayyim yeshiva in W. The economy was severely affected in WWI and after the war, antisemitism rose and pogroms broke out repeatedly (1918-20, and more violently in the 1930s). Many Jews left for the West or Palestine. Zionists led the community and represented it on the city council. The J. pop. in 1931 was 10,209 (total 55,966). Yiddish and Hebrew culture flourished with libraries, newspapers, a theater, a choir, an amateur orchestra, and sports clubs. J. employment in the 1930s was severely affected by the antisemitic boycott of J. businesses. On 14 Sept. 1939 (Rosh Hashanah) the German army entered W. Aided by local sympathizers, the soldiers plundered J. property. On Yom Kippur, the SS caught and shot Jews, burned synagogues, and demanded huge sums to free 800 Jews taken hostage. Numerous Jews went to Warsaw and other places where the situation at the time was less severe. Many young Jews fled to Soviet-held territory. At the end of 1939, the remaining Jews were sent on to other ghettoes except for about 4,000 who were moved in Oct. 1940 to a local ghetto. In June 1941 and again in the spring of 1942, the Germans con-

signed able-bodied Jews to forced labor in Poznan. On 24-27 April 1942 the ghetto was liquidated when the remaining Jews, mostly the elderly, women, and children, were sent to their death in Chelmno. A number of Jews from W. joined the Polish army, the Red Army, and the resistance. Some of the youth joined the Warsaw ghetto fighters.

WLODAWA Lublin dist., Poland. Jews are mentioned in the 16th cent. and formed an independent community in 1623 with a representative on the Council of the Four Lands. Large numbers were killed in the Chmielnicki massacres of 1648-49 and the Swedish invasion of the mid-17th cent. In the 18th cent., the Jews received a royal privilege to engage in commerce. W. became known as a center of Torah learning and in 1765, 630 Jews were there. Their number grew to 2,236 in 1827 and 6,706 (total 8,955) in 1907. In the late 19th cent., they became active in industry, operating a steam-powered flour mill, a hide-processing plant, and a soap factory in 1894. They also owned 177 of the city's 184 stores. Zionist activity commenced in 1898 and Bund and Po'alei Zion members participated in the revolutionary events of 1905-07. After WWI, the community operated numerous credit facilities and welfare services. Most of the Zionist parties and youth movements were also active. The Gur Hasidim were represented by Agudat Israel, which operated a Beth Jacob school for girls. The Zionists founded a Tarbut Hebrew school in 1923. Anti-J. boycotts instigated by the Endecja Party marked the 1930s, with occasional attacks on J. peddlers. The Germans captured W. on 18 Sept. 1939, finding about 6,500 Jews there. The last J. businesses were seized in early 1940 and on 5 Jan. 1940 local Jews were sent to the nearby woods to bury 400 Polish-J. prisoners of war massacred there by the Germans. In April 1940 a *Judenrat* was established and on 17 Jan. 1941 the Jews were ordered into a ghetto. In March 1941, 1,014 J. refugees were brought there and in March-April 1942 another 800 from Mielec and 1,000 from Vienna. Many were deported to the Sobibor death camp on 23 May. Subsequent *Aktions* on 24 Oct. and 6 Nov 1942 brought the rest to Sobibor. Those in hiding were lured into labor camps, described by the Germans as "J. sanctuaries." The one in W., containing 500 workers and their families, was liquidated in April 1943 and its inmates deported to the Sobibor death camp.

WLODAWKA Polesie dist., Poland, today Belarus. The J. pop. in 1921 was 271 (total 292). The Jews were probably brought to the Domaczewo ghetto and liquidated there on 20 Sept. 1942.

WLODIMIERZEC Volhynia dist., Poland, today Ukraine. Jews were present in the 17th cent., reaching a pop. of 1,024 (half the total) in 1897. The Shalita family provided the community with its rabbis and the Hasidism (Turzysk, Stolin-Karlin, Stepan) operated small houses of prayer. A J. militia protected the community after the Feb. 1917 Revolution as public life under Zionist dominance awakened. A few hundred joined the youth movements by the 1930s, Betar being the largest. The economy picked up with the holding of weekly trade fairs but the competition of Polish stores in the late 1930s undermined J. livelihoods. In June 1941 the Germans executed local Jews taken as prisoners of war while fighting for the Red Army and in W. itself the Ukrainians staged a pogrom. A ghetto for 3,000 Jews including refugees was set up in April 1942 and a *Judenrat* was established. Most were murdered on 28 Aug. 1942. A few hundred succeeded in fleeing; those not caught were helped by Ukrainian Baptists and Polish villagers.

WLODZIMIERZ WOLYNSKI (Yid. Ludmir) Volhynia dist., Poland, today Ukraine. Jews are first recorded in 1171 and came to constitute a prosperous community trading as far away as the Rhine and enjoying extensive privileges except for a short period of expulsion (1495–1503). Annexation to the Kingdom of Poland in 1569 brought further development, with the community's rabbis and *parnasim* representing Volhynia on the Council of the Four Lands. Among its illustrious rabbis was Yom Tov Lippman Heller (1634–43). The community suffered grievously in the Chmielnicki massacres of 1648–49 but recovered quickly. The dissolution of the Council of the Four Lands in 1764 left J. settlements saddled with debts,

Poor quarter in Wlodzimierz Wolynski, Poland (Oester. Staatsarchiv/Kriegsarchiv, Wien/photo courtesy of Yad Vashem, The Holocaust Martyrs' and Heroes' Remembrance Authority, Jerusalem)

Synagogue in Wlodzimierz Wolynski, Poland

but under Russian rule, conditions stabilized. Jews dominated trade and the crafts and constituted two-thirds of the town's pop. Notweworthy among the community's figures was Hannah Rachel Werbermacher (1805–92), the "Maid of Ludmir," who attracted a large following as a visionary preacher. Among the Hasidim, the Trisk (Turzysk) sect predominated, while the Zionists and the Bund became active in the 1890s. By 1897 the J. pop. reached 5,869 (total 9,883). The manufacture of readymade wear and trade in farm produce were mainstays of the J. economy, which was boosted by the inauguration of a railway link with the Kowel junction in 1906. During WWI the city filled with refugees and on the Russian withdrawal in 1915, a cholera epidemic struck the community, which also suffered at the hands of the Cossacks. The community recovered from the war with assistance from the Joint Distribution Committee, growing to 10,665 in 1931 (total 24,591). Jews were engaged in light industry and also dominated the cattle, grain, and retail trade. A Tarbut school served 500 J. students and a yeshiva enrolled another 138. The Red Army occupied the town on 17 Sept. 1939. The Germans arrived after a heavy bombardment on 23 June 1941 killed many Jews. A *Judenrat* was set up on 7 July to regulate the supply of forced labor under a regime of periodic executions: 200 on 31 July, 300 on 29–30 Aug., 250 on 29 Sept., and then in Oct. two groups of 500 and 600 workers as well as a group of

120 from the educated class. On 24 Feb. 1942 another 250 were sent as laborers to Kiev, where they all perished. On 13 April, all who remained were herded together with refugees into a ghetto, which was divided in May into sections for productive and "nonproductive" Jews. On 1 Sept 1942, 4,000 of the latter were murdered beside open pits at the local prison; 14,000 of the former were led to the village of Piatydni and likewise murdered in an *Aktion* lasting until 15 Sept. Of the 4,000 remaining in the ghetto (skilled workers and those coming out of hiding), the majority were liquidated on 13 Nov. 1942 and the rest by 13 Dec. 1943. Some Jews managed to fight as partisans and others joined the Polish underground Armia Krajowa, mainly as artisans.

WLOKI MALE Warsaw dist., Poland. The J. pop. in 1921 was 144 (total 993). The Jews were expelled by the Germans to the east of the Bug River between Dec. 1939 and Feb. 1940.

WLOKI PIASKI Warsaw dist., Poland. The J. pop. in 1921 was 111 (total 751). The Jews were expelled by the Germans to the eastern part of the Warsaw dist. between Dec. 1939 and Feb. 1940.

WLOSZCZOWA Kielce dist., Poland. Jews are first mentioned in the 17th cent. but a J. community only developed in the 19th cent., growing to a pop. of 2,528 (total 3,722) in 1897. A synagogue was built in 1860 and in the early 20th cent. the Zionists and the Bund became active. Banned by the Russian authorities, they revived during the German occupation in WWI. In 1918, J. youth organized against General Haller's Polish troops and their depredations. After WWI, Jews operated 364 workshops and small factories, mostly family enterprises. Agudat Israel was influential but the Zionists dominated the community's leadership, opening a training farm and sending a group to Palestine. Until 1938, Jews occupied half the seats on the municipal council. Growing antisemitism and the anti-J. boycott of the 1930s added to the economic hardship of the Jews between the World Wars and many were forced to close their stores and market stalls. The Germans captured W. in early Sept. 1939, seizing Jews for forced labor and looting their homes and stores. A *Judenrat* was soon appointed and a ghetto was set up on 10 July 1940. Refugees increased the number of Jews in W. and environs from about 2,700 to 4,277 in April 1942. Crowded conditions led to an outbreak of typhus and the *Judenrat* opened a hospital and infirmary in 1940. With assistance from the Joint Distribution Committee, the *Judenrat* was able to operate a soup kitchen providing 700 meals a day and distributing flour and *matza*. The ghetto was liquidated in Sept. 1942, when 5,000 Jews were deported to the Treblinka death camp.

WODZISLAW   Kielce dist., Poland. Jews may have been present as early as the 11th cent. but J. settlement only became significant in the early 17th cent. Most Jews fled in the mid-17th cent. Swedish invasion but afterwards returned to form a community of 200 families. By the end of the cent., the J. community in W. was one of the largest and most important in the Sandomierz-Cracow region. Most of the Jews were Hasidim. In the 19th cent., some opened hide-processing plants while others engaged in the grain trade. The J. pop. grew from 1,463 in 1857 to 2,899 (total 3,622) in 1897. After WWI, most of the wealthier Jews left the town. Although economic conditions deteriorated, community life flourished as the Zionists became active, with Mizrachi founding a Hebrew school and a library being started in 1928. The Germans captured W. in Sept. 1939, appointing a *Judenrat* and proceeding to confiscate J. businesses. In late 1940, the Jews were confined to a ghetto. Refugees increased the J. pop. from 2,400 to 3,550. In anticipation of an *Aktion* in Sept. 1942, the Jews fled or hid, but within a short while, without food or water, gave themselves up. Most were deported to the Treblinka death camp in Nov. and the ghetto was then burned down by the Germans.

WOELFERSHEIM   Hesse, Germany. Established in the 18th cent., this small J. community numbered 31 (about 3% of the total) in 1871, declining to 15 in 1933. On *Kristallnacht* (9–10 Nov. 1938), a pogrom was organized, and by the summer of 1939 no Jews remained.

WOELLSTEIN   Hesse, Germany. Established in 1820, the J. community numbered 95 (about 5% of the total) in 1895, including members from nearby Siefersheim. Only 16 of the 45 Jews who lived there in 1933 managed to emigrate.

WOERRSTADT   Hesse, Germany. Banished in

1576, the community was reestablished around 1750. Despite efforts by the local authorities to prevent further J. settlement, the community opened a new synagogue in 1835, promoted religious education, and numbered 118 (6% of the total) in 1861. During the Weimar Republic era, Jews were active in social and commercial life. A vicious Nazi pogrom was organized on *Kristallnacht* (9–10 Nov. 1938), and by May 1939 all the Jews had left, 21 emigrating. Most of the 23 who settled in other German towns were eventually deported.

WOERTH A. MAIN   Lower Franconia, Germany. A J. community is known from the early 18th cent., numbering 36 in 1837 and 18 in 1933 (total 2,020). Six emigrated and nine left for other German cities in 1934–39. The synagogue and J. homes were vandalized on *Kristallnacht* (9–10 Nov. 1938) and Jews beaten.

WOHYN   Lublin dist., Poland. Two J. families were present in 1566. Royal privileges extended J. rights over the next 80 years and the J. pop. grew to 805 in 1857. The synagogue and many J. homes were destroyed in an 1881 fire. After WWI, economic conditions worsened. The J. pop. stood at 1,025 in 1921 (total 2,579). A few of the Zionist parties and youth movements were active. The Germans arrived in Sept. 1939. Little is known of the occupation beyond the fact that the last 150 Jews were deported to the death camps in summer 1942. At the end of the war, six of the survivors who returned were murdered by the Polish underground.

WOISLAWICE   (Yid. Voslovichl) Lublin dist., Poland. Jews are mentioned in the 15th and 16th cents. In a 1760 blood libel, the community's rabbi was tortured to death and two other Jews were executed. When a fire in 1778 destroyed most J. homes and property, the town's proprietor granted the Jews extensive privileges to help them recover. The J. pop. grew to 841 (total 1,557) in 1857. Alongside the synagogue and *beit midrash*, Trisk (Turzysk), Belz, and Gur Hasidim ran *shtiblekh*. At the outset of WWI, the Jews suffered at the hands of the Cossacks; in its aftermath they were abused by General Haller's Polish troops. Despite the poverty between the World Wars, J. public life was dynamic and the Zionists were active. The German arrived on 11 Sept. 1939, seizing Jews for forced labor, confiscating property, and setting up a *Judenrat* and ghetto. In fall 1942, most of the Jews were taken to Wolodawa and from there deported to the Sobibor death camp.

WOJNICZ Cracow dist., Poland. Jews apparently settled in the 18th cent., reaching a peak pop. of 200 (total 1,683) in 1880. In WWII the Germans imposed forced labor and other abuses. In July 1940 the Jews were joined by refugees from Cracow. All were expelled in Aug. 1942, most reaching the Zakliczyn ghetto, where they shared the fate of the Jews there.

WOJNILOW Stanislawow dist., Poland, today Ukraine. The community, dating from the late 17th cent., reached a pop. of 1,115 (total 2,726) in 1900. It was liquidated in WWII through a series of expulsions, the last in the spring of 1942 to Stanislawow, where the remaining Jews were murdered.

WOJTKOWA Lwow dist., Poland, today Ukraine. The J. pop. in 1921 was 113. The Jews were expelled to Dobromil or Zaslawie for liquidation in summer 1942.

WOLA KZHYSHTOPORSKA Lodz dist., Poland. Sixty-two Jews lived here in 1921. In Oct. 1942, all 60 J. inhabitants were deported to Piotrkow and from there to the Treblinka death camp.

WOLA MICHOWA Lwow dist., Poland, today Ukraine. The J. pop. in 1921 was 148. Of the 200–220 Jews there in 1939, 150 were murdered locally in 1942 and the rest deported to Zaslawie via Lesko, where they were killed or sent to the Belzec death camp.

WOLANOW Kielce dist., Poland. Jews first settled in the early 19th cent, numbering 232 (total 376) in 1857 and maintaining a synagogue. After WWI, the J. pop. rose to 313 with many engaged in the wholesale trade (flour, grain, and livestock). In the 1930s, among the Zionists, Betar ran the largest youth group. The Germans arrived on 5 Sept. 1939. Refugees increased the J. pop. to 500 in spring 1941. In July, a ghetto was set up. In July 1942, most were expelled to Szydlowiec, sharing the fate of local Jews. The able-bodied were sent to a nearby labor camp. About 700 Jews supplied services to the local airforce base. By 1943, most had been deported or murdered.

WOLA ZARCZYCKA Lwow dist., Poland, today Ukraine. The J. pop. in 1921 was 101 (total 3,398). The Jews were deported to the Belzec death camp via Tarnobrzeg in Sept. 1942.

WOLBECK Westphalia, Germany. The small J. community numbered 40–50 (total pop. 1,100–1,200) in the last third of the 19th cent. and 29 in June 1933. It maintained a synagogue and a cemetery (from before 1818). In the late 19th cent., it also ran a J. elementary school. Eight Jews emigrated to Holland and one to France in the Nazi era and six moved to other places in Germany. The synagogue was burned on *Kristallnacht* (9–10 Nov. 1938). Twelve Jews were deported to the camps in Dec. 1941 and Aug. 1942.

WOLBOZH Lodz dist., Poland. The community was organized when the hasidic court of R. Yissakhar Dov Baer ha-Kohen Tornheim was established in the 1830s. The rabbi was a gifted writer and composer who founded a choir and an orchestra. The community numbered 437 in 1897, but owing to a lack of educational institutions and antisemitism, only 250 Jews remained by 1939. Over 400 Jews, including refugees, were deported to Piotrkow in Oct. 1942 and from there to the Treblinka death camp.

WOLBROM Kielce dist., Poland. Jews are mentioned in the early 18th cent. but may have been present before that. After R. Yitzhak Menahem Rotenberg (d. 1874) settled in the town, it became an important hasidic center. The J. pop. rose from 724 in 1827 to 2,901 (total 4,815) in 1897. Jews traded in farm produce, manufactured and sold alcoholic beverages, and owned a number of factories. Zionist activity commenced in the early 20th cent., with Mizrachi operating a branch by the eve of WWI. During the war, economic activity came to a standstill and a typhoid epidemic claimed many J. lives. Economic hardship continued after the war, necessitating assistance from relief organizations and relatives abroad. In 1921, the J. pop. was 4,276. Jews ran 356 workshops and small factories, two-thirds of them in the textile industry. Most of the Zionist parties were represented while Hashomer Hatzair was the leading youth movement. Agudat Israel and the Bund were also active, the former running a Beth Jacob school for girls. A yeshiva was founded in 1929. Antisemitism intensified in the

1930s, leading to occasional violence. The Germans captured the city on 5 Sept. 1939, subjecting the Jews to unrelenting persecution. A *Judenrat* was immediately appointed, charged with furnishing forced labor and meeting extortionate demands. The city's J. pop. of 5,000 was increased by numerous refugees, including 3,000 from Cracow. In summer 1941, groups of Jews were sent to labor camps, mainly near Cracow. The last J. stores were impounded in late 1941 and in April 1942 the Jews were confined to a ghetto, where a typhoid epidemic broke out. On 5 Sept. 1942, after the sick and old were murdered, 6,000–7,000 Jews were transported to the Belzec death camp while 2,000–2,500 able-bodied men were selected and dispersed to various labor camps. In a second *Aktion* in Nov. 1942, the small number of remaining Jews were executed. The Jews in the labor camps slowly died under the inhuman conditions there, the last being transferred to camps in Germany on the approach of the Red Army in 1944. A few Jews managed to join the Polish partisans.

WOLCZYN   Polesie dist., Poland, today Belarus. Jews numbered 588 in 1897 and 180 (total 190) in 1921 after evacuation in WWI. Presumably they were expelled by the Germans to the nearby Wysokie Litewskie ghetto and murdered there on 2 Nov. 1942.

WOLDENBERG   (Pol. Dobiegniew) Brandenburg, Germany, today Poland. Jews were living in W. in the 14th cent. The modern community grew from 47 members in 1801 to 174 in 1880, dropping to 65 in in 1910. It maintained a synagogue and a cemetery. When the Nazis came to power in 1933, there were 51 Jews in W. No information about their fate under Nazi rule is available. During WWII, J. prisoners of war were interned – separately from the Polish prisoners of war – in a camp which the Germans set up in W.

WOLFENBUETTEL   Brunswick, Germany. Marcus Gumpel, the first Jew to settle in W. in 1697, headed a dynasty of bankers; Gotthold Ephraim Lessing (1729–81), the dramatist and philosopher who championed religious toleration and befriended Moses Mendelssohn, served as the duke's librarian there (1770–81). In 1781, Philipp Samson, a grandson of Marcus Gumpel, built a synagogue accommodating 81 worshipers and in 1786 founded a *talmud torah* for poor boys. Under the influence of Israel Jacobson, a

pioneer of Reform Judaism, the *talmud torah* was transformed in 1806 into the Samson School, an institute promoting educational and religious reform. Leopold Zunz (1794–1886), architect of the "Science of Judaism" (*Wissenschaft des Judentums*), was the first pupil confirmed there in 1807. Members of the local J. community, numbering 62 in 1831, at first disagreed with the school's radical line. In 1898, however, the community, which numbered 265 Jews, installed an organ in its new synagogue which reflected a Liberal stance. In June 1933, there were 112 Jews registered in W. Most left for larger cities or went abroad in the ensuing six years. The Nazis destroyed the synagogue on *Kristallnacht* (9–10 Nov. 1938), and the remaining 60 Jews were deported to Warsaw, Auschwitz, and the Theresienstadt ghetto in 1942–43. At least 52 perished in the Holocaust.

WOLFHAGEN   Hesse–Nassau, Germany. After the slaying of 18 Jews in 1235, no community was organized until the 17th cent. Members opened a religious school in 1788 and dedicated a new synagogue in 1859. The community numbered 258 (8% of the total) in 1861 and was affiliated with the rabbinate of Kassel. Since Jews handled most of the town's commerce, Nazi propaganda was able to foster latent antisemitism in the 1920s. On *Kristallnacht* (9–10 Nov. 1938), townspeople helped SS troops from Arolsen destroy the synagogue and loot J. property. The burgomaster, dissociating himself from the "vandalism," saw to it that stolen cash and valuables were returned to their owners. By Nov. 1939, however, the remaining 70 Jews had left. Eleven emigrated and about 30 perished in the Holocaust.

WOLFISHEIM   Bas-Rhin dist., France. The J. presence in W. dates from the Second Crusade in the 12th cent. The modern community was established in the 18th cent. In 1784, the community numbered 80 members. A synagogue was inaugurated in 1868. In 1936, there were 114 Jews in W. During WWII all were expelled to the south of France with the rest of Alsace-Lorraine's Jews. Sixteen were deported. The synagogue was looted and partly destroyed. In 1965, there were only 65 Jews in W.

WOLKOWYJE   Volhynia dist. Poland. The J. pop. in 1921 was 112 (total 2,533). The Jews were probably taken to Dubno and murdered there.

Memorial ceremony at monument made from desecrated and broken tombstones, Wolfhagen, Germany, 5 April 1948

WOLKOWYSK Bialystok dist., Poland, today Belarus. Jews first settled in the 16th cent. By 1847 they numbered 1,429 and in 1897 reached 5,528 (total 10,323). Jews were active as wheat, fruit, and lumber exporters and pioneered light industry, opening hide-processing and tobacco-processing plants, a weaving mill, brickyard, beer brewery, and steam-powered flour mills. The community was typically characterized by Zionist sympathies in religious circles. A yeshiva founded in 1887 reached an enrollment of 300. In 1898 a J. hospital was endowed and in 1908 an old age home. A Bund-organized strike put an end to Saturday night work for J. factory hands. Under the German occupation in WWI the Jews suffered from severe food shortages and the shutdown of commerce while subjected to forced labor. In its aftermath they suffered from attacks by Polish soldiers. J. tradesmen recovered with the help of money from relatives abroad. In the absence of transportation facilities, J. carters and porters formed a company to transport goods, saving the town from isolation. The big J. Kolontai Co. owned flour mills, fruit orchards, a dairy,

and timber land. The Barash family ran an iron foundry and machine assembly plant and until 1929 Jews dominated the trade in oil, sugar, and salt and the entire tobacco industry. However, discriminatory government measures led many Jews to emigrate to North and South America and by the 1930s, when their pop. stood at 7,347, their prominent position in the city's economy was in decline as many shut down their stores. Between the World Wars, both Yiddish and Hebrew schools were in operation. The TOZ organization provided health care for children, free meals and summer camps for the needy, and counseling for expectant mothers. The Zionists dominated the community's political life. Two J. weeklies appeared in H. Under Soviet rule in 1939–41, J. businesses were nationalized and artisans organized into cooperatives. The Germans captured W. on 29 June 1941. In Sept., 200 Jews were executed in the forest. On 14 Oct. 1942, 27 J. doctors were murdered for allegedly treating partisans. In Nov., the Jews were transferred to 15 big bunkers in a nearby camp where Jews from the entire province were being held and where starvation and disease claimed 600 lives a day. On 6 and 8 Dec. 1942 all but 1,700 were deported to the Treblinka death camp. The latter were sent to Auschwitz on 26 Jan. 1943.

WOLLENBERG   Baden, Germany. Few Jews were present in the 16th–17th cents. The community reached a peak pop. of 150 in 1830 (total 410) and then declined steadily to 21 in 1933. The synagogue built in 1825 was vandalized on *Kristallnacht* (9–10 Nov. 1938), and the last 11 Jews were deported to the Gurs concentration camp on 22 Oct. 1940. All perished.

WOLLIN   (Pol. Wolin) Pomerania, Germany, today Poland. Jews only arrived in W. in the 19th cent. In 1812 the J. pop. was five; in 1849, 90; and in 1880, 141. The community maintained a synagogue and a cemetery. When the Nazis came to power in 1933, there were 25 Jews in W. and by May 1938 only two J. businesses remained. The Jews who did not manage to emigrate were deported to the Lublin dist. (Poland)

together with the Jews of Stettin on 12–13 Feb. 1940. By Oct. 1942, one Jew was still living in W., probably protected by marriage to a non-Jew.

WOLMA   Nowogrodek dist., Poland, today Belarus. The J. pop. was 149 in 1921 and approximately 250 in 1939. The Jews were expelled by the Germans to the Rubiezhowicze ghetto and shared the fate of the Jews there.

WOLMIANKA WIELKA   Volhynia dist., Poland, today Ukraine. The J. pop. in 1930 was 189 (total 364). The Jews were probably taken to the Rozyszcze ghetto and murdered there.

WOLOMIN   Warsaw dist., Poland. Jews settled towards the end of the 19th cent. They dealt mainly in leasing property, innkeeping, commerce, and crafts. With the outbreak of WWI a lack of food and industrial supplies led to widespread destitution and the community opened a kitchen for the poor and refugees. In 1921 the J. pop. numbered 3,079 (out of 6,248). Be-

The Young Pioneers, Wolomin, Poland, March 1934

tween the World Wars, community leadership was divided between the Zionists and Agudat Yisrael. W. was occupied by the Germans on 13 Sept. 1939. The Jews were tortured, seized for forced labor, and their property plundered. Many fled to Soviet areas of eastern Poland. In Nov. 1940 all Jews were moved into a ghetto in the village of Sosnowka, where they ran a kitchen, orphanage, and hospital. Anyone trying to escape was executed. On 4 Oct. 1942 they were sent to the Treblinka death camp, via Radzymin.

WOLOSKA WIES Stanislawow dist., Poland, today Ukraine. The J. pop. in 1921 was 216. The Jews were expelled to Bolechow for liquidation in Aug. 1942.

WOLOZYN (Volozhin) Nowogrodek dist., Poland, today Belarus. A community of 383 existed in 1766, growing to 2,452 in 1897 including the surrounding villages (total 4,534). W. was famous for its Etz Hayyim yeshiva, founded in 1802 by R. Hayyim Volozhiner on the initiative of his teacher "the Vilna Gaon." Its other well-known head was R. Naftali Tzevi Hirsch Berlin ("Ha-Natziv"). It introduced the system of study partners (the *hevruta*) and by the late 1880s had 500 students. Its students included H.N. Bialik, who immortalized the study atmosphere in his poem *"Ha-Matmid."* Providing room and board to the students was a source of additional income to community members, who also found employment in the lumber and brick industries and as tanners. Most of the town's stores and taverns were in J. hands as well the majority of trade. The temporary closure of the yeshiva by the Russian authorities in the 1890s struck hard at the J. economy and led to the emigration of about 100 J. families up to WWI. A number of major fires in the 1880s was another debilitating factor that contributed to the community's decline. The Zionists became active in 1902 and a Tarbut Hebrew school was opened in 1925. During WWI the yeshiva was moved to Minsk and when it returned to W. in 1921 it was reduced in size and had only 55 students in 1929–30. In 1931 the J. pop. stood at 3,663 including the neighboring villages. Under the Soviet occupation of 1939–41 the yeshiva was nationalized and converted into a restaurant. The Tarbut school was sovietized and J. artisans were organized into cooperatives. The Germans captured the town on 25 June 1941. On the same day a local mob murdered a number of Jews and burned down two synagogues. A ghetto was estab-

Ha-Hayyim, *the Hebrew newspaper of the Etz Hayyim yeshiva, Wolozyn, Poland*

lished in Aug. and Jews were regularly murdered. On 4 Nov. 1941, 250–300 were executed in a sports field next to an old Polish army camp. On 10 May 1942, 1,500–2,000 were stripped naked and shot at the J. cemetery, after which their bodies were burned. On 29 Aug. 1942 the last few hundred were murdered. The students at the yeshiva in 1941 were among the victims of the killings.

WOLPA Bialystok dist., Poland, today Belarus. J. settlement commenced in the second half of the 16th cent. The community prospered owing to W.'s position as a commercial center and built a wooden synagogue famous for its design. It survived the destruction of the town by the Swedes in 1656 and was declared an historic building by the Polish Sejm in 1781. Trade declined when the railroad bypassed the town in the 19th cent. In 1897 the J. pop. was 1,151 (total 1,976). After WWI, government monopolies and heavy taxes further undermined J. commerce.

Interior of 17th cent. wooden synagogue in Wolpa, Poland

Most children attended a Hebrew school and graduates of the Zionist youth movements made their way to Palestine. After two years of Soviet rule, German bombardments in June 1941 destroyed all J. homes and the old synagogue. The Jews built bunkers in which to live and were subjected to forced labor. On 2 Nov. 1942, 66 of the sick and elderly were murdered at the J. cemetery and the rest of the town's 900 Jews were brought to the notorious Wolkowysk transit camp, from where they were deported to the Treblinka death camp.

WOLSZTYN Poznan dist., Poland. The first Jews arrived in 1530 and by the time of Prussian rule in 1793 numbered 561 (nearly a third of the total). Many were in the shoe trade and a few were grain mer-

chants. A new synagogue was completed in 1842. In the late 19th cent. emigration among the young and educated increased, intensifying after WWI to reduce the J. pop. from a high of 834 in 1846 to 64 in 1931 and 18 in 1939. Those remaining were expelled by the Germans to General Gouvernement territory.

WONCHOCK Kielce dist., Poland. A few dozen families were present in the 19th cent. The J. pop. was 468 in 1921 (total 2,389). On 20 Sept. 1942, three years after the German occupation, 600 Jews, less those selected for labor, were executed in the nearby woods.

WONSEWO Bialystok dist., Poland, today Belarus. In 1765, 95 Jews lived in W. The J. pop. in 1921 was

269 (total 809). During WWII the Jews were probably executed along with those of the neighboring areas.

WONSOSZ   Bialystok dist., Poland, today Belarus. The J. community grew in the 19th cent. to 453 in 1857. In the 1930s the Jews suffered antisemitic upheavals. From Sept. 1939 the Soviets controlled W., which was taken by the Germans on 22 June 1941, when 400–600 Jews were living there. On 5 July Polish police brutally massacred the Jews. The 15 survivors were sent to the Treblinka and Auschwitz death camps in 1942.

WONWOLNICA   (Yid. Vanovlitch) Lublin dist., Poland. J. settlement commenced in the 17th cent. and expanded despite local opposition. Many traded in farm produce. The J. pop. rose from 404 in 1857 and 836 in 1897 to 1,043 (total 3,003) in 1921. The post-WWI economic crisis undermined J. livelihoods and reduced the J. pop. In 1927, a fire left 200, mostly Jews, homeless. Though the community was initially dominated by Orthodox circles, the Zionists soon gained control of community institutions. Agudat Israel remained active primarily in charity work and religious education. After the German occupation of mid-Sept. 1939, refugees brought the J. pop. up to 2,000. A *Judenrat* was established in early 1941 and Jews were sent to distant labor camps. In Feb. 1942 a ghetto was set up. On 22 March 1942, 120 Jews were executed at the J. cemetery, suspected of murdering a Pole of German origin. On 31 March, a selection, sent the able-bodied to the Opole ghetto and to labor camps in the Lublin dist. (Poland). The remaining Jews were deported to the Belzec death camp.

WORMDITT   (Pol. Orneta) East Prussia, Germany, today Poland. Jews settled in W. c. 1800. By 1871, the J. pop. was 174, dropping to 109 in 1905 and to 45 in 1925. The community maintained a synagogue and a cemetery (established in 1806). By June 1933, about four months after the Nazis assumed power, the J. pop. still numbered 45. The last community official left in summer 1937. On *Kristallnacht* (9–10 Nov. 1938), the synagogue was set on fire, but the flames were extinguished. No further information about the fate of the community under Nazi rule is available.

WORMS   (in J. sources, Vormayza, Vermes, Garmayza) Hesse, Germany. Jews lived there in Roman times and by 960 had established a community that gained spiritual as well as numerical importance during the 11th cent. Built in 1034, its synagogue was the oldest in Central Europe until 1938. Emperor Henry IV's charters exempting "Jews and other inhabitants of W." from customs duties in 1074 and granting freedom of worship and other rights in 1090 indicate the vital role played by J. merchants in the Rhineland. Within this hospitable environment the community flourished, maintaining a yeshiva that attracted preeminent scholars and students. The "Sages of W." included Eliezer ben Yitzhak the Great, Ya'akov ben Yakar, Yitzhak ben Eliezer, and Shelomo ben Shimshon – all of whom taught Rashi, the great Bible and Talmud commentator, while he studied there. Kalonymus ben Shabbetai and Meir ben Yitzhak Sheli'ah Tzibbur were among the leading liturgical poets. When the Crusaders invaded the J. quarter (*Judengasse*) and the bishop's palace, however, 800 Jews perished (18–26 May 1096). Survivors, including forced converts who had reverted to Judaism, were permitted to restore the community in 1097. During the Second Crusade (1146), W. Jews took refuge elsewhere and during the Third Crusade (1187–88) Emperor Frederick I Barbarossa prevented another massacre. The *"Shum"* communities (Speyer, W., and Mainz) secured rabbinical authority over all the Jews of "Ashkenaz" (1150). The synagogue was rebuilt in 1175 and a new generation of scholars arose, headed by the revered mystic Eleazar ben Yehuda Roke'ah (1165–1230), last great representative of Hasidei Ashkenaz. Simha ben Yehuda compiled the W. *Mahzor* (prayer book) for festivals in 1272. Meir ben Barukh ("Maharam") of Rothenburg (1215–93), the greatest halakhist of his time, was born and buried in W. (where his tombstone can still be seen). From 1312 a council of 12 members, with a *Judenbischof* ("J. bishop") or *parnas* at its head, regulated communal affairs. When the Black Death struck W. in March 1349, a mob destroyed the *Judengasse* and slaughtered about 400 Jews. Having transferred the "ownership" of his J. chattels to W. in 1348, Emperor Charles IV allowed the city to confiscate the murdered (or exiled) Jews' property. However, financial losses impelled the authorities to recall the surviving Jews in 1353. They restored the synagogue and observed a fast day on the anniversary of the Black Death massacre (10 Adar). Confined to a ghetto and numbering about 180 in 1376, they had to contend with a blood libel in 1410, riots in 1431, and the en-

Interior of Rashi Chapel, Worms, Germany

forcement of a humiliating "Jew's oath" in 1490. Several members of the Bacharach family held rabbinical office in W. from 1506. Avraham Shemuel Bacharach was *av beit din* and Eliyahu Loanz, a famous kabbalist, headed the yeshiva when new riots broke out and the Jews were twice expelled in 1614–15. The Elector Palatine, Frederick V, banished troublemakers and then ordered the city to reimburse the Jews. After paying for the synagogue's renovation, David ben Yehoshua Oppenheim, first *parnas* of the restored W. community, built an adjoining study house known thereafter as the Rashi Chapel (1624). Two outbreaks of the plague (1635, 1666) claimed 336 J. lives. Moshe Shimshon Bacharach served as dist. rabbi (1650–70) and Aharon ben Moshe Teomim succeeded him in 1670–89. Yiftah Yosef Yozpa compiled a *Memorbuch* as well as *Sefer Ma'aseh Nissim*, tales and legends woven around the community (1696). During the 17th cent. Jews entered the wine trade and some became physicians. The office of *parnas* declined when notable incumbents chose to live far from W. Thus David ben Avraham Oppenheim

(1664–1736) became chief rabbi of Moravia (in Nikolsburg) and Bohemia (in Prague). Louis XIV's invading troops destroyed much of W., including the ghetto, and in 1689 most people fled. After the community's revival, Yair Hayyim Bacharach served as rabbi (1699-1702) and Samson Wertheimer, a W.-born Court Jew, gave practical support. No significant change occurred until the era of French revolutionary occupation (1792–1813). Jews obtained civil rights and the ghetto gates were demolished. Shemuel Levi, the French-speaking rabbi of W., attended the Paris Sanhedrin convened by Napoleon in 1807. Under the Grand Duchy of Hesse, however, J. disabilities were renewed and a campaign for their abolition only proved successful one year before the 1848 revolution. Although many Jews supported the republican cause, Ferdinand Eberstadt's election as burgomaster in 1849 was a rare achievement. The community grew to 985 (7% of the total) in 1861 and J. represenation among high school pupils reached 26% in 1857. Jews also gained renown in the professions, Friedrich Gernsheim as a

Interior of Worms synagogue, Germany, believed to be the oldest in Central Europe, 1924 (Bildarchiv Preussischer Kulturbesitz, Berlin/ photo courtesy of Yad Vashem, The Holocaust Martyrs' and Heroes' Remembrance Authority, Jerusalem)

composer and conductor, Ludwig Edinger as a neurologist. By 1842, advocates of Reform Judaism were modifying synagogue worship. Dr. Marcus Jastrow, the future lexicographer, deleted certain prayers and approved a mixed choir (1864–66). The installation of a harmonium (and then of an organ) by his successor impelled Orthodox members to found a breakaway congregation in 1877, with East European Jews (*Ostjuden*) later founding a synagogue of their own. Branches of the Central Union (C.V.), J. War Veterans Association, and German Zionist Organization were active after WWI. Growing interest in communal history led to the renovation of ancient monuments (such as the Rashi Chapel) and the opening of a J. museum (1924), but members of the Liberal congregation rarely attended Sabbath services. Numbering 1,306 (3%) in 1905, the community declined to 1,016 in 1933.

Nazi violence escalated after Hitler rose to power. On 7 March 1933, SA troops kidnapped and murdered Julius Frank, onetime head of the Social Democratic "Reichsbanner" organization in Dolgesheim. Many Jews were sent to the Osthofen concentration camp, and from 1 April the dismissal of J. professionals and the "Aryanization" of J.-owned stores accentuated the Nazi boycott campaign. In response, the community augmented its cultural program and established a central welfare bureau in 1934. Hebrew courses and talks or film shows about life in Palestine were arranged by the Zionist Organization, which advised those planning *aliya*. The W. synagogue's 900th anniversary on 3 June 1934 was a low-key event. A J. regional school, staffed mainly by teachers who had lost their jobs, operated from 1935 to 1941. By 31 Dec. 1937, only 525 Jews remained and at least 37 *Ostjuden* were expelled to the Polish border town of Zbonszyn in Oct. 1938. On *Kristallnacht* (9–10 Nov. 1938), Nazis burned the historic synagogue and adjacent Rashi Chapel, vandalized other communal property, and sent 46 J. men to the Buchenwald concentration camp. Great heroism was displayed by Herta Mansbacher, the J. school's former principal, who tried to prevent the main synagogue's destruction. Valuable documents and manuscripts, together with museum exhibits and half-burned Torah scrolls, were rescued by the city archivist, Dr. Illert, who kept them hidden until 1945; he also managed to preserve the ancient J. cemetery. Of the 1,345 Jews who lived in W. during the Nazi period, 802 emigrated by Sept. 1941. At least 435 perished as a result of deportation, torture, and suicide. When U.S. troops entered W. in March 1945, not a single Jew remained. Federal German authorities rebuilt the medieval *Judengasse* after WWII and the Rashi Chapel was also restored in Dec. 1961. Archive material was sent to Israel, where the J. National and University Library published a facsimile edition of its newly acquired W. *Mahzor* in 1984–85.

WORNIANY Vilna dist., Poland, today Belarus. Jews arrived apparently in the second half of the 18th cent. Until WWI, many earned their livelihoods in the lumber industry in an atmosphere of general prosperity. After the war economic conditions deteriorated and the Polish cooperatives undermined J. artisans. In 1921 the J. pop. was 240 (total 300). Under Soviet rule in 1939–41 J. businesses were nationalized and J. artisans organized into cooperatives. With the approach of the Germans in June 1941, local peasants looted J. homes. The Germans confined the Jews to a ghetto in fall 1941, instituting a regime of forced labor. In Aug. 1942 they were expelled to the Michaliszki ghetto and on 7 April 1943 they were executed at the extermination site of Ponary near Vilna.

WOROCHTA Stanislawow dist., Poland, today Ukraine. The J. pop. in 1921 was 196. Some of the Jews were probably executed locally by the Germans in Oct. 1941; the others were deported to Nadworna for liquidation in summer 1942.

WORONOWO Nowogrodek dist., Poland, today Belarus. A few J. families may have been present at the turn of the 18th cent. At the end of the 19th cent. when the J. pop. reached 1,432 (total 1,574), most engaged in trade, brokerage, and transportation services. Twenty-five J. families operated farms. R. Zalman Sorochkin (later chairman of Agudat Israel) and R. Shelomo Shleifer (rabbi of Moscow in WWII) served for a short while in N. After WWI the J. pop. dropped to 980, most eking out a living as shopkeepers and arti-

sans in the face of stiff competition from the Polish cooperatives. Four sewing shops employed 40–50 Jews. The Zionists were active between the World Wars. After two years of Soviet rule the Germans captured the town in late June 1941, setting up a *Judenrat* and a ghetto that reached a peak pop. of 3,000 with the influx of refugees. On 14 Nov. 1941, 250 Jews who had escaped from Vilna were executed in a nearby grove. Another 1,834 Jews were murdered in the Bilorowski forest on 11 May 1942. The remaining 600–700 Jews were brought to the Lida ghetto on 23 May, sharing the fate of the Jews there when the ghetto was liquidated in Sept. 1943.

WRIEZEN Brandenburg, Germany. Mention of the first protected Jew (*Schutzjude*) dates from 1677. The J. pop. was six families in 1750 and 117 individuals in 1848. A cemetery was established in 1730 and in 1821 a synagogue, which was replaced at the end of the 19th cent by an impressive new building. When the Nazis came to power in 1933, the community had grown to 127 members. On *Kristallnacht* (9–10 Nov. 1938), the synagogue was set on fire and J. men were arrested and abused. By Oct. 1942, only four Jews, probably protected by marriage to non-Jews, were still living in W. No further information about the fate of the other Jews is available. It may be assumed that those who did not manage to emigrate were deported to the east.

WRONKI Poznan dist., Poland. The first Jews probably settled in the late 16th cent., receiving a charter in 1607 allowing them to engage in trade and crafts and build a new synagogue. The J. pop. reached a peak of 813 in 1846 as a period of prosperity commenced and J. peddlers and petty traders began to open stores and artisans converted their workshops into factories. Zionism began to take hold in the late 19th cent. With increasing education, emigration increased, bringing local Jews to Berlin, Breslau, and New York. Some achieved fame, like Prof. Adolf Feiner in chemistry (in Berlin) and Profs. Bernhard and Hermann Zondek in medicine (in Jerusalem). Thirty-one Jews remained when the Germans entered the city in Sept. 1939; all were expelled to General Gouvernement territory.

WRZESNIA Poznan dist., Poland. Jews were present from the founding of the town in the mid-

14th cent. and contributed significantly to its economic development. The community suffered in the mid-17th cent. wars, murdered and pillaged by the troops of Stefan Czarniecki, who led Polish irregulars against the Swedes. The community subsequently recovered and built a synagogue in 1710. The J. pop. reached a peak of 1,352 (total 2,232) in 1846 as a period of prosperity set in, but emigration reduced the pop. steadily, leaving 150 in 1921. Antisemitism intensified between the World Wars. The 60 Jews remaining on the eve of WWII were expelled by the Germans to General Gouvernement territory in Oct. 1939.

WSIELUB Nowogrodek dist., Poland, today Belarus. Jews are believed to have arrived in the 16th cent. In the 19th cent. J. merchants were particularly active in the lumber trade. All Jews had auxiliary farms and many grew cereal crops on leased land. In 1897 the J. pop. was 645 (total 1,306). In WWI, 195 were made homeless when their houses burned down. The houses were rebuilt with assistance from YEKOPO but the J. pop. dropped to 286 in 1921 as many emigrated to Venezuela and Argentina and later to Palestine. After two years of Soviet rule, the Germans captured the town on 2 July 1941. On 7 Dec., 800 Jews including refugees were expelled to the ghetto in Nowogrodek and subsequently executed near the village of Skidelwo.

WUERZBURG Lower Franconia, Germany. Jews are first mentioned around 1100 and probably included refugees from the Rhineland massacres of the First Crusade (1096). The community grew in importance and prosperity in the first half of the 12th cent. but suffered with the rest of the J. communities in South Germany during the Second Crusade (1147) as Crusaders murdered 17 Jews, including the community's three rabbis. Jews were attacked in the Third Crusade as well (1188) but managed to escape to the local castle. Jews in W. were allowed to buy land and houses in the city. This was done on a large scale through the mid-13th cent. A synagogue is first mentioned in 1170. From 1247 the Jews were under the protection of a bishop, who vied with the local municipality for the right to impose taxes on them. Like most of the Jews of Germany at the time, the Jews of W. engaged primarily in moneylending and moneychanging, but because of the proximity of the J. quarter to the market they were also involved in other areas of economic

life, such as wine production and land transactions. W. was also an important spiritual center with many illustrious rabbis, attracting students from all over Germany and beyond. Among its outstanding figures were R. Eliezer ben Natan ("Raban") of Mainz (c.1090–1170), one of the first tosafists in Germany, and his grandson R. Eliezer ben Yoel ha-Levi ("Ravyiah"), R. Yitzhak ben Moshe of Vienna (author of *Or Zaru'a*), and R. Meir ben Barukh ("Maharam") of Rothenburg. The community ended in the Rindfleisch massacres of 1298 when 900 Jews, including 100 from neighboring settlements seeking refuge, were massacred in a single day. Survivors revived the community with the addition of Jews from Strasbourg, Cologne, and other places, but its position as a Torah center was lost. Jews were again threatened in a well-poisoning libel during the Black Death persecutions of 1348–49 and in the face of the impending pogrom chose to burn themselves alive in their homes. By 1377 the community was again established. In 1411 the Jews received new privileges, giving them greater freedom in trade. In 1422 local rulers confiscated promissory notes held by Jews in the principality and divided the proceeds among themselves; they also extorted large sums for the cancelation of an expulsion order. In the aftermath many Jews left W. Later in the cent. the community again achieved prominence as a spiritual center, with R. Moshe ben Yitzhak ha-Levi Mintz, one of the outstanding scholars of the age, officiating there. However, toward the end of the 15th cent. further restrictions and renewed persecution reduced the number of Jews in the community and in 1559 a general expulsion order for the principality was issued by Emperor Ferdinand I. Over the next cents. few Jews lived in W. The modern community was founded in the 19th cent. after the annexation of W. to Bavaria in 1803. The army contractor Moses Hirsch settled there and after him Jews from Heidingsfeld and Hoechberg arrived. In 1814 the state rabbinate was transferred there from Heidingsfeld by the chief rabbi, Avraham Bing. In 1819, university students provoked a series of anti-J. Hep! Hep! riots that spread beyond Franconia. J. stores were looted, Jews were beaten, and a few were killed. In the aftermath many Jews were expelled from the city. The Hirsch family maintained its prominence. Jacob Hirsch became court banker to Duke Ferdinand and was made a baron in 1818. His son Joel founded an important bank in the city and pioneered the development of Franconia's transportation system. The yeshiva headed by R. Bing attracted students from all over Germany and beyond, including Nathan Marcus Adler, chief rabbi of British Jewry from 1845. With the dismantling of the chief rabbinate in 1839 and the creation of six dist. rabbinates, R. Seligmann Baer Bamberger ("the Wuerzburger Rav") became rabbi of W., taking over the local yeshiva and founding a J. public school in 1856 and a teachers' seminary in 1864 that would furnish Germany with hundreds of J. teachers. New riots broke out in 1866, causing much damage to J. homes. In 1842 a new synagogue was opened, in 1892 a J. hospital, and in 1895 a geriatric ward. The J. pop. rose from 1,099 in 1867 to 2,567 (total 75,499) in 1900. A second synagogue for East European Jews residing in W. was consecrated in 1924. Despite the increasing antisemitism in Bavaria after WWI, four Jews were elected to the municipal council of W. in 1919 and one was elected mayor. J. social and cultural life was lively and a large number of Jews studied at the university. In 1930 Jews were attacked after a performance of *The Dybbuk* by Habimah and 14 severely injured as anti-J. agitation intensified. In 1933, the J. pop. was 2,145 (total 101,003), subsequently augmented by refugees. Most were engaged in commerce (65%) and various professions (17%). The W. dist. rabbinate encompassed 18 communities, seven charitable organizations were in operation, and the Zionists including Mizrachi, the Central Union (C.V.), and various youth movements were active. Attacks on Jews commenced in the first days of Nazi rule when Jews were beaten, cars impounded, and stores closed. The economic boycott quickly undermined J. livelihoods. In 1935, J. stores were looted and Jews again beaten while three big J. factories were "Aryanized." On *Kristallnacht* (9–10 Nov. 1938), nearly a thousand SA troops gathered in the city and proceeded to destroy J. homes, stealing valuables in the process. Stores were also pillaged and the two synagogues wrecked. Nearly 300 Jews were sent to the Buchenwald and Dachau concentration camps for detention. In early 1942, the remaining Jews were evicted from their homes and packed into a building at the J. cemetery. Jews transported to W. from other communities in Franconia were housed in the J. hospital. All adults were subjected to forced labor. Until the liquidation of the community commenced, 1,649 Jews managed to emigrate from Germany, half in 1938–39, including 667 to the U.S., 270 to Palestine, 208 to England, and 107 to Holland.

Another 667 left for other German cities. Deportations commenced on 27 Nov. 1941, when 202 Jews were sent to the Riga ghetto via Nuremberg; 1,191 Jews were sent to Izbica in the Lublin dist. (Poland) in March and April 1942 and 739 were sent to the Theresienstadt ghetto in Sept. A final seven were sent to Theresienstadt on 17 June 1943 with another 57 going to Auschwitz. Of the total 2,196 deported Jews, 1,494 were J. refugees from other localities. After the war, 52 Jews returned and reestablished the community.

WUESTENSACHSEN (now part of Ehrenberg) Hesse–Nassau, Germany. Dating from the 18th cent., the J. community numbered 137 (13% of the total) in 1871 and was affiliated with the rabbinate of Fulda. It maintained an elementary school from around 1860 until 1935. The 75–80 Jews living there in 1933 fell victim to Nazi persecution and the synagogue was destroyed on *Kristallnacht* (9–10 Nov. 1938). By Jan. 1939 no Jews remained; 22 emigrated (mostly to the U.S.) and 30 perished in the Holocaust.

WULKA MAZOWIECKA Lwow dist., Poland, today Ukraine. The J. pop. in 1921 was 136. The Jews were possibly expelled to Rawa Ruska for liquidation in Sept.–Oct. 1942.

WUNSTORF Hanover, Germany. Although Jews lived there previously, no community was established until the 19th cent. Numbering 88 (4% of the total) in 1861 and 72 in 1913, they maintained an elementary school, established a new synagogue in 1908, and founded a Central Union (C.V.) branch in 1920. In June 1933, there were 46 Jews registered in W. The synagogue was demolished on *Kristallnacht* (9–10 Nov. 1938). By 1940, 33 Jews had left, 18 emigrating (12 to the U.S.). The last ten Jews were deported in 1942.

WUPPERTAL-BARMEN Westphalia, Germany. Two J. families were present in 1812 and until 1895 B. was part of the Elberfeld regional congregation. Subsequently it formed an independent community though continuing to maintain close relations with the neighboring Elberfeld community. The J. pop. was 500 in 1895 and 721 in 1925. The community, which maintained a cemetery and a synagogue from 1897, was served by a rabbi. In 1932, the J. pop.

was 720, dropping to 415 in 1937. In March 1933, a Jew was arrested in the street by the SA; on the way to the SA's Duesseldorf headquarters, he was beaten, severely injured, thrown into the river near the Bever Dam, and drowned. On *Kristallnacht* (9–10 Nov. 1938), the synagogue was vandalized and its contents were burned. The building was later destroyed. The Jews still in the city after the outbreak of war were held in five "J. houses" and deported to the death camps together with the Jews of Elberfeld in 1941–42.

WUPPERTAL-ELBERFELD Westphalia, Germany. Although Jews were present by the 15th cent., the agitation of the guilds prevented them from residing there permanently until the French conquest in 1806. In 1809, they included nine families and in 1810 a cemetery was opened. In the mid-1840s, Moses Hess (1812–75), one of the future founders of Zionism, was active in the city together with Frederick Engels trying to further the Communist idea. When the J. pop. reached 92 in 1846, a united congregation was formed with neighboring Barmen. This sparked the rapid growth of the J. pop., which reached 450 in 1866, 1,249 in 1895, and a peak of 2,335 in 1925. A new synagogue was consecrated in 1865 and a new and larger cemetery was opened in 1867, augmented by a third cemetery, maintained together with Barmen, in 1895. At this time, Barmen split off and formed an independent community. The poetess Else Lasker-Schueler was born in E. in 1869, leaving Germany when the Nazis came to power and residing in Jerusalem during WWII until her death in 1945. With the growth of the J. pop., Jews became active in local life. They prospered economically, primarily from the textile trade. From the founding of the Second Reich in 1871, the Jews formed a class of well-to-do businessmen, including Leonard Tietz, who set up the second of the department stores in his chain in the city, and the Heimann and Alsberg brothers with their textile establishments. In 1903, the first Jew was elected to the municipal council. During the 1880s and 1890s, nationalistic antisemites tried to gain a foothold in the city but with limited success. In the early 20th cent., Orthodox Jews arrived from the east, forming their own congregations (the Ahdut congregation in 1906 and Mahzikei ha-Dat in 1913). Following WWI, the East European J. pop. grew significantly, altering the power structure of the community, which had heretofore been dominated by organizations like the Cen-

tral Union (C.V.) and the J. War Veterans Association with their German-J. orientation. The East European Jews were mostly Orthodox with a deep-rooted J. ethnic identity, reflected both in the maintenance of their religious Orthodoxy within a community of Liberal character and in the rise of local Zionism. In June 1933, the combined J. pop. of W. (E. and Barmen) was 2,471. Persecution of J. political activists commenced almost immediately after the Nazis came to power in 1933. A J. Social-Democrat was shot to death in the street in March 1933. On *Kristallnacht* (9–10 Nov. 1938), the Liberal synagogue (erected in 1865) was burned down and the Orthodox synagogue was vandalized. The funeral parlor at the J. cemetery was also vandalized and burned and 125 J. men and women were taken into "protective" custody, the men being sent to the Dachau concentration camp after the women were released. In May 1939, the combined J. pop. of W. was 1,129 according to the Nuremberg definitions (1,111 by actual religion). Of these, 766 were deported (202 to the Lodz ghetto on 26 Oct. 1941, 233 to the Minsk ghetto on 11 Nov., 22 to the Riga ghetto on 11 Dec, 61 to Izbica in the Lublin dist. (Poland) on 22 April 1942, and 248 to the Theresienstadt ghetto on 20 July 1942). Others were trapped in occupied Europe after emigration. At least 1,000 Jews were deported during the Holocaust.

WYBRANOWKA Lwow dist., Poland, today Ukraine. The J. pop. in 1921 was 101. The Jews were expelled to Bobrka for liquidation in the second half of 1942.

WYSMIERZYCE Kielce dist., Poland. Jews first settled in the 19th cent. and numbered 109 in 1921. In July 1942, after three relatively quiet years under the German occupation, 500 including refugees from Przytyk were deported to the Treblinka death camp via the Bialobrzegi ghetto.

WYSOCK Volhynia dist., Poland, today Ukraine. A community, attached to Pinsk, existed from the early 17th cent., growing to 880 (total 912) in 1897 and engaging in such trade as the export of wild berries and mushrooms to Kiev and Odessa. Economic conditions improved somewhat before WWI with the development of the food-processing industry (oil and cheese). Rampaging Petlyura gangs caused much suffering at the end of the war. In 1921 the J. pop. stood at 893 (total 2,978) and was supported by the Joint Distribution Committee. Stolin-Karlin Hasidism was the dominant spiritual force. The Bund and the Zionists were also active, the youth movements operating training farms and sending 150 pioneers to Palestine. Many fled with the Red Army on the Soviet retreat in July 1941. The Germans immediately established a *Judenrat* and instituted a regime of extortion. About 1,500 Jews including 300 refugees were packed into a ghetto on 20 July 1942. On 9 Sept. all were led to freshly dug pits outside the town to be murdered; about 100 escaped to the forests where they were helped by Polish villagers.

WYSOCKO NIZNE   Lwow dist., Poland, today Ukraine. The J. pop. in 1921 was 141. The Jews were probably deported to the Belzec death camp in the second half of 1942, directly or via Turka.

WYSOCKO WYZNE   Lwow dist., Poland, today Ukraine. The J. pop. in 1921 was 220. The Jews were probably deported to the Belzec death camp in the second half of 1942, directly or via Turka.

WYSOKIE   Lublin dist., Poland. A few dozen Jews were present in the mid-18th cent. The J. pop. fell from 352 in 1895 to 285 (total 1,041) in 1921, living in straitened economic circumstances. In fall 1942, three years after the German occupation, most of the Jews were deported to the Belzec death camp via the Izbica ghetto.

WYSOKIE LITEWSKIE   Polesie dist., Poland. Jews settled in the mid-16th cent. and numbered 2,876 in 1897 and 1,994 (total 2,395) in 1921. Most trade was in their hands. Fires in 1884, 1889, and 1904 struck the Jews particularly hard. Between the World Wars the Zionists and the Bund were active. The Germans captured the town on 22 June 1941 and confined the Jews to a ghetto. The community was liquidated on 22 Nov. 1942, with many of the young escaping to the forests.

WYSOKIE MAZOWIECKIE   Bialystok dist., Poland. Jews lived there from the 17th cent. and in 1897 numbered 1,910 (66%). At the beginning of the 20th cent. anti-J. incitement and economic boycott in-

Breakfast in Jewish elementary school for girls, Wysokie Mazowieckie, Poland, 1918 (Sonia Kilodny, Israel/photo courtesy of Yad Vashem, The Holocaust Martyrs' and Heroes' Remembrance Authority, Jerusalem)

creased. The community maintained an Orthodox character. Cultural and Zionist activity developed during WWI. During the war the community became more impoverished and a kitchen for the poor was established. In 1919–20, the Jews were persecuted by soldiers from General Haller's army and by local hooligans. In the 1930s, when antisemitic propaganda and violence increased, the community became mostly Zionist. The Germans arrived on 10 Sept. 1939. On 12 Sept. they took all the men to a forced labor camp. On 19 Sept. all the Jews were expelled to Soviet territory, but were released shortly after W. came under Soviet rule. The Germans occupied W. again on 23 June 1941, thereafter killing and maltreating Jews daily. In July a *Judenrat* was formed and Jews were forced to wear the yellow badge. In Aug. the Jews were forced into a ghetto. In Nov. 1942 they were sent to Zambrow camp and from there to Auschwitz.

WYSZKOW Warsaw dist., Poland. Jews probably first lived there in the 17th cent. Their numbers began to increase significantly in the 19th cent. In

Selling apples in Wysokie Mazowieckie, Poland, one of the main centers of Jewish urban settlement, early 1920s (Sonia Kilodny, Israel/photo courtesy of Yad Vashem, The Holocaust Martyrs' and Heroes' Remembrance Authority, Jerusalem)

1857 they numbered 1,067 (out of 1,590), most of whom were Hasidim. Zionist activity began in the early 20th cent. After the Polish army entered W. in 1918, violence against Jews began. The community experienced an economic crisis and was helped by the Joint Distribution Committee. In the 1930s most of the Zionist parties and youth movements, as well as Agudat Israel, were active. In Sept. 1939 the Germans entered W. and in the first four days over 1,000 Jews were killed. No Jews were left by 13 Sept., but some who had fled survived the pogrom in nearby villages. Most of them died later in death camps. Only several hundred Jews (out of some 5,000 – about 40% of the general pop.) survived the war, mostly in the Soviet Union. Mordekhai Anielewicz, leader of the Warsaw ghetto uprising, was from W.

WYSZOGROD Warsaw dist., Poland. J. settlement began in the 15th cent. A synagogue was built in the mid-18th cent., which survived until the Holocaust. Under Prussian and subsequent Polish rule (1793–1807) the number of Jews increased to constitute over 50% of the general pop. until the end of WWI (2,735 in 1897). During the 19th cent., J. communal life was strongly influenced by Hasidism. Zionist groups were organized on the eve of WWI. At the beginning of WWI, the Germans plundered J. homes and stores and most Jews fled. Between the World Wars various J. schools were in operation. On 9 Sept. 1939, W. was occupied by the Germans and Jews were murdered or seized for forced labor. In 1940, a ghetto was established. In Aug. 1940, the men were sent to a labor camp in Bielsk. In March 1941, 700 Jews were sent to Slupia Nowa, where they lived in cramped quarters. Some 400 managed to return to W. In July 1941 over 100 Jews were taken to an unknown destination. The remaining Jews were sent to Auschwitz in 1942. Approximately 2,450 Jews (out of 2,700–2,800) died in the Holocaust.

WYSZONKI KOSCIELNE Bialystok dist., Poland. In 1921, 177 Jews lived in W. (total 278). In the 1930s the community suffered antisemitic attacks and was probably liquidated in fall 1941.

WYZHGRODEK Volhynia dist., Poland, today Ukraine. The J. pop. stood at 1,078 (half the total) in 1897. Most identified with Turzysk (Trisk) Hasidism. Rampaging Ukrainian gangs caused many to flee during the Russian civil war (1918–21), leaving a J. pop. of 944 in 1921 (total 976). Between the World Wars the Zionists were the leading public force. The Germans arrived in July 1941, transferring the Jews in March 1942 to the Wisniowiec ghetto, where they were murdered on 11 Aug.

WYZWA   Volhynia dist., Poland, today Ukraine. Jews were present from the mid-16th cent. with extensive residence and trade rights. The J. pop. was 720 in 1870 (total 1,505) and 358 in 1921. Most were craftsmen serving the neighboring villages. The Germans took the town on 27 June 1941. On 5 Aug., 260 Jews were marched out of the town and murdered. In summer 1942, refugees were housed in an open ghetto and at the end of Aug. all the Jews were executed.

Y

YAGOTIN Poltava dist., Ukraine. Jews settled in the late 19th cent. and numbered 943 (total 4,409) in 1897. A four-year J. school operated in the 1930s under difficult conditions: the children learned Ukrainian in the first two years and were then taught in Yiddish in the last two, all without textbooks. In 1939, the J. pop. was 365. The Germans occupied Y. on 15 Sept. 1941 and on 5 Oct. murdered the 280 remaining Jews.

YALTA Crimea, Russia, today Ukraine. Jews settled in the early 19th cent., numbering 87 in 1847 and 1,025 (total 13,000) in 1897. A pogrom was staged against the Jews on 13–14 March 1905. The Zionists won the elections to the community council in 1917 and in the same year one Jew, also a Zionist, was elected to the municipal council among 26 representatives. Jews earned their livelihoods mainly from the tourist trade in the area's many vacation sites. A number of J. kolkhozes were set up nearby in the 1920s. In 1939, the J. pop. was 2,060. The Germans occupied Y. on 8 Nov. 1941. On 21 Nov. they murdered 11 Jews and on 18 Dec. about 1,500 from Y. and its environs.

YALTUSHKOV Vinnitsa dist., Ukraine. Jews numbered 192 in 1784 and 1,238 (total 3,533) in 1897. In early Dec. 1883, Jews were attacked in a pogrom. In 1926, under the Soviets, their pop. was 1,392. A J. elementary school (four grades) and J. council (soviet) operated from the 1920s. Most Jews worked in factories (sugar, textiles), in artisan cooperatives, and in a J. kolkhoz (19 families). The Germans arrived on 15 July 1941, establishing a ghetto and murdering a few hundred Jews on 19–20 Aug. 1942. The young and skilled workers were mobilized for roadwork and subsequently murdered as well. On 15 Oct. 1942, 1,194 Jews from Y. and the surrounding area were executed in a second *Aktion*.

YAMPOL (I) Vinnitsa dist., Ukraine. Jews probably settled in the late 17th cent. and by 1740 maintained a burial society (*hevra kaddisha*). The J. pop. was 664 in 1790 and 2,823 in 1897 (total 6,605). Many Jews became carters because of the distance from the railroad station; most local stores were in J. hands. On 6 Nov. 1917, rioting soldiers and peasants robbed and burned J. homes and killed four Jews. Under continuing anti-J. agitation, another pogrom broke out on 19 Dec. and in Dec. 1919 General Denikin's White Army troops carried out a further attack. In the Soviet period, Jews worked in a local sugar refinery, in various artisan cooperatives, and in a J. kolkhoz. In 1939, the J. pop. was 1,495. The Germans captured Y. on 18 July 1941 after some of the Jews managed to flee. In late July, the *Einsatzkommando 10a* murdered nine Jews. Another 38 were murdered in Aug. Others were apparently murdered in Aug. 1943 and in Feb 1944, just before the liberation of the town. A total of 136 were killed. Y. was also a transit station for thousands of Rumanian Jews expelled to Transnistria. About 350 were allowed to remain in Y., where they were confined in a ghetto under a *Judenrat*.

YAMPOL (II) Kamenets-Podolski dist., Ukraine. Jews probably settled in the early 17th cent. In 1705–08 (the Northern War), Russian, Polish, and Swedish soldiers attacked the Jews. In a 1766 blood libel, 15 leading figures in the J. community were tortured. The J. pop. was 476 in 1765 and 1,482 (58% of the total) in 1897. In 1939, under the Soviets, the J. pop. dropped to 1,058. The Germans occupied Y. on 6 July 1941. In 1941–42, 1,700 Jews from Y. and the neighboring towns were murdered.

YANOVICHI Vitebsk dist., Belorussia. The J. community dates from the late 17th cent. In 1897, the J.

pop. was 1,702 (total 2,359). During the Soviet period, a J. elementary school and J. council were in operation. Both were closed down in the late 1930s. In 1939, the J. pop. was 709. The Germans captured the town on 12 July 1941. Most Jews remained, their number increased by J. refugees from Liozno, Vitebsk, and other places. The first murders took place in mid-Aug. 1941 when 150 J. men were executed near the village of Okhryutka. Another 70 were murdered a week later. A ghetto and *Judenrat* were established on 25 Aug. The 1,500 Jews there were executed on 10 Sept. near the village of Zaitchevo.

YANOVKA Odessa dist., Ukraine. The J. pop. was 1,438 (of a total 1,898) in 1897 and 353 in 1939. A J. elementary school operated during the Soviet period. The Germans captured Y. on 10 Aug. 1941 and murdered 342 Jews from Y. and its environs in the same month. In all, 526 Jews from the area were murdered.

YANUSHPOL Zhitomir dist., Ukraine. Jews are first mentioned in 1569. Only a few dozen were present in the 18th cent. In 1897, the J. pop. was 1,251 (of a total 5,085). Many were artisans or worked in two J.-owned sugar refineries. In the civil war (1918–21), there were a number of pogroms staged against the Jews. In one pogrom, the Petlyura gangs killed 30 Jews, including the community's rabbi, Shemuel Brodski. In another instance, Red Army cavalrymen engaged in a spree of rape, robbery, and beatings. In the Soviet period, a J. elementary school operated until the mid-1930s. The J. pop. dropped between the World Wars, reaching 721 in 1939. The Germans captured Y. on 3 July 1941. Within a few days, 32 Jews were executed as alleged Communist activists. The Jews were confined to a ghetto. Placed under a regime of forced labor, they suffered from hunger and the cold,. On 20 May 1942, 80 J. males were sent to the Berdichev labor camp, where they perished. On 29 May, the 600 remaining Jews were taken outside the city and executed. Of the few who escaped, some later joined partisan units.

YARCEVO Smolensk dist., Russia. Jews probably settled in the late 19th cent. They were granted permission to erect a prayer house in 1898. The J. pop. was 520 (total 18,703) in 1926 and 454 in 1939. After their arrival on 5 Oct. 1941, the Germans murdered the few Jews who had not fled or been evacuated.

YARMOLINTSY Kamenets-Podolski dist., Ukraine. The J. pop. was 253 in 1765, dropping to 60 after a Haidamak attack in 1775. It rose again to 2,633 in 1897. The main source of J. livelihoods were the weekly market day and yearly fairs. The community maintained an ancient synagogue and a number of prayer houses. In 1939, under the Soviets, the J. pop. was 1,264. The Nazis occupied the town on 8 July 1941. A ghetto was established on 2 Sept. 1942. Jews from neighboring towns were brought there in early Oct. 1942 and housed in army barracks. During the year, 14,000 Jews were executed. One group of Jews offered armed resistance and in the battle that developed they killed 16 gendarmes and five German civilians.

YAROSLAVSKAYA Krasnodar territory, Russia. The Germans occupied the village in Aug. 1942 and murdered 25 Jews at the Labinskaya airport on 19 Nov. There were also a few Jews among the more than 200 people the Germans murdered at the Mikhizeyva Polyana workers settlement on 13 Nov.

YARUGHA Vinnitsa dist., Ukraine. Jews numbered 63 in 1765 and 1,271 (total 2,506) in 1897. In Dec. 1919 they were attacked by General Denikin's White Army soldiers. In 1926, under the Soviets, the J. pop. was 1,833. A J. school and J. rural council (soviet) were in operation from the mid-1920s to the late 1930s. Most Jews earned their livelihoods in a J. kolkhoz (151 families in 1939) which continued to exist for awhile after the liberation in March 1944. Wine production and tobacco cultivation were important sources of income there. The Germans captured Y. on 18–19 July 1941. Under Rumanian administration, a ghetto was established and over 1,000 Jews expelled from Bukovina and Bessarabia arrived there. Some Jews from Y. were murdered in late May 1942 while others were expelled to Mogilev-Podolski and shared the fate of the Jews there. The rest were sent to the Pechera death camp.

YARYSHEV Vinnitsa dist., Ukraine. The J. pop. was 438 in 1765 and 1,499 (total 3,642) in 1897. In the Soviet period, the J. pop. declined, reaching 509 in 1939. In 1930, 46 J. families (a third of the total) were employed in a J. kolkhoz and in the 1920s a J. school and J. council (soviet) were active. The Germans arrived on 15 July 1941, murdering 25 Jews the same day. According to another source, 40 J.

Synagogue in Yaryshev, Ukraine (The Central Archive for the History of the Jewish People, Jerusalem/photo courtesy of Yad Vashem, The Holocaust Martyrs' and Heroes' Remembrance Authority, Jerusalem)

men were murdered on 19 July and 175 Jews two weeks later. Another 212 Jews were murdered in Y. on 19–21 Aug. 1942 and 595 from the whole area on 21 Aug. 1942.

YASEN   Mogilev dist., Belorussia. Jews numbered 285 in 1923 and 119 in 1939. A four-grade J. school existed but many children studied in *hadarim*. In 1928, 12 J. tailors started a cooperative. Most Jews were artisans. The Germans arrived in early July 1941 and probably murdered the Jews in Nov. with the participation of their collaborators.

YASENEVO   Odessa dist., Ukraine. Jews numbered 573 (total 4,324) in 1897 and 610 in 1926. The Germans captured Y. in early Aug. 1941 and murdered about 150 Jews in the fall.

YASINOVATAYA   Stalino dist., Ukraine. Jews probably settled in the 19th cent. with the discovery of iron deposits and the development of the railroad industry. The J. pop. was 573 in 1897 (total 4,324) and 218 (total 16,432) in 1939. The fate of the Jews under the German occupation from 22 Oct. 1941 was the same as of all the Jews of the area.

YEFINGAR   Nikolaiev dist., Ukraine. Y. was founded as a J. settlement in 1807–09 and numbered 49 families in 1815. Its name derived from the Hebrew for "beautiful river" (*yefei nahar*) In 1897, the J. pop. was 2,038 (total 2,226), dropping to 1,528 in 1926. A pogrom was staged in early 1918. A number of J. kolkhozes were started up near Y. in the 1920s and a J. elementary school founded in the early 1920s was still open in the mid-1930s. The Germans captured Y. in mid-Aug. 1941 and on 10 Sept. murdered 519 Jews

YEFREMOV Tula dist., Russia. Jews probably settled at the turn of the 19th cent., numbering 129 in 1926. After the German occupation of 23 Nov. 1941, the few who had neither fled nor been evacuated were murdered.

YELETS Oriol dist., Russia. J. settlement began in the mid-19th cent. In 1897, the J. pop. was 764 and in 1900 the Jews were allowed to open a synagogue. In 1926, under the Soviets, the J. pop. rose to 1,017 (of a total 43,240) but then dropped in 1939 to 461. In WWII, the town was occupied by the Germans for a few days only (5–9 Dec. 1941). All the Jews who had not fled or been evacuated were immediately murdered.

YELSK Polesie dist., Belorussia. The J. pop. was 632 in 1923 and 1,231 (total 3,878) in 1939. The J. elementary school, opened in 1923, had an enrollment of 80 children in 1925. In the mid-1920s, about 40 J. families earned their livelihoods in agriculture; by the early 1930s, many Jews were tailors, shoemakers, and carters. The Germans occupied Y. on 23 Aug. 1941, murdering the 550 Jews still there.

YEVPATORIA Crimea, Russia, today Ukraine. The first J. families settled around 1810. In 1847, the J. pop. was 30 and in 1897 there were 1,592 Jews in the city (total 17,913) as well as 1,505 Karaites, Y. in fact being a Karaite center until the Oct. 1917 Revolution. One Jew was killed and a number injured in a pogrom on 20 Oct. 1905. A J. school for boys and two for girls were in operation before WWI. In elections to the community council in 1918, the Zionists won ten of 25 seats and the Bund five. Hashomer Hatzair continued to be active, partly underground, until 1927. From 1923 the county was earmarked for J. agricultural settlement. An agricultural federation including 40 J. families was founded. In the late 1920s, a J. hospital was opened in Y. to serve the thousands of Jews in the region. The J. Autonomous Region within the county accommodated six J. councils (soviets) with jurisdiction over several dozen farm settlements (dropping to ten in 1932 with a pop. of 935 J. families). In 1932, the

In the fields of a Jewish kolkhoz, Yevpatoria, Crimea, 1931 (YIVO Archive, New York/photo courtesy of Beth Hatefutsoth, Tel Aviv)

Joint Distribution Committee set up a textile factory for hundreds of J. workers in the area. In 1939, the J. pop. was 4,249 (total 47,300). The Germans captured the city on 31 Oct. 1941. On 24 Nov., 600–650 Jews were executed and on 29 Dec. a *Sonderkommando 11b* unit murdered about 150 Rabbanite Krimchaks. In the second half of Dec., 86 Jews from the Alchin, Kalinin, Ikor, and Molotov kolkhozes were murdered. Hundreds more were murdered in the area's kolkhozes in the first months of 1942.

YEZERISHCHE Vitebsk dist., Belorussia. The J. pop. in 1939 was 77 (total 1,152). The Germans occupied Y. on 17 Aug. 1941, setting up a ghetto for nearly 170 Jews including refugees in Oct. In Feb. 1942 all were murdered.

YEZIORANY (Ozierany) Volhynia dist., Poland, today Ukraine. Y. was founded in 1848 as a J. farm settlement and numbered 637 people in 1898. The Germans captured Y. on 26 June 1941 and expelled the Jews to the Warkowicze ghetto, where they were murdered with the local Jews on 3 Oct. 1942.

YITL (Seliba) Polesie dist., Belorussia. Y. was founded as a J. agricultural colony in 1833 on land leased by 13 J. families. In 1898, the J. pop. was 270. The Germans occupied Y. in early July 1941 and presumably murdered all the Jews.

YLAKIAI (Yid. Yelok) Mazeikiai dist., Lithuania. The J. community was established in the beginning of the 19th cent. The J. pop. was 775 in 1897 (57% of the total) and 409 in 1923 (41%). Between the World Wars many emigrated to the U.S., South Africa, and Palestine. All the Jews were killed after the German occupation of 1941.

YOCHANOV Smolensk dist., Russia. Jews probably settled in the late 19th cent. In 1897 they numbered 64 (total 2,000), their number dropping in the Soviet period to 34 in 1926 and 25 in 1939. The few who remained when the Germans arrived on 5 Oct. 1941 were murdered.

YUKHOVICHI Vitebsk dist., Belorussia. The J. pop. was 336 in 1897 (total 618) and 349 in 1926

under the Soviets. The Germans occupied the town in July 1941, transferring the remaining Jews to the Rossony ghetto, where they were murdered together with the local Jews.

YUREVICHI Polesie dist., Belorussia. Jews are first mentioned in the late 18th cent. Their pop. was 65 in 1811 and 1,287 (total 1,577) in 1897. A Musar yeshiva was active in the town until the Soviet authorities closed it down in 1922. In the same year a J. elementary school was opened. In 1926, the J. pop. was 1,139 and in the early 1930s, 60% of the Jews were artisans. Two J. kolkhozes near the town supported 50 J. families in 1930. The Germans occupied Y. on 22 Aug. 1941. A ghetto was established in Oct. On 19 Nov., 200–250 Jews were murdered on the banks of the Pripet River. The rest were murdered beside a pit near the town on 27 Nov. In all, the Nazis executed over 400 Jews.

YURKINO Nikolaiev dist., Ukraine. A J. kolkhoz operated in the settlement during the Soviet period. Under the German occupation, which began in late Aug. 1941, 178 Jews were murdered.

YUSKHOVO Kalinin dist., Russia. In early Feb. 1942, the Germans herded 44 Jews into a building and burned them alive.

YUSTYNGRAD-SOKOLKA Kiev dist., Ukraine. The J. pop. was 2,521 (total 3,194) in 1897 and 539 under the Soviets in 1926. With the German occupation in WWII, the Jews were immediately abused and on 19 Sept. 1941, 35 were murdered. The rest were subsequently executed.

YUZEFPOL (from 1944, Yosipovka) Odessa dist., Ukraine. Jews settled in the mid-18th cent. and numbered 66 in 1784. Their pop. increased to 872 (total 2,401) in 1897 and 1,041 in 1926. In the Soviet period, some Jews were employed in the J. kolkhozes in the area. The Germans captured Y. on 5 Aug. 1941. On 10 Aug. they arrested 50 Jews, murdering some, and on 22 Aug. murdered 100 more. The remaining Jews were murdered in Dec. 1942. In all, 481 Jews from Y. and from the nearby Kotovsky kolkhoz were murdered.

Z

ZAANDAM (Zaanstad) Noord-Holland dist., Holland. An organized J. community was already active in the early 19th cent. and numbered 186 in 1860. Towards the end of the cent. its numbers began to dwindle. By 1938, 46 German refugees reached Z. The J. pop. in 1940 was 225. Some 200 Jews were deported to Poland in Jan.–April 1942 from Z. and the surrounding areas. About 20 survived the deportations and 20 others survived in hiding.

ZABALJ Vojvodina dist., Yugoslavia. A J. community was established at the end of the 19th cent. In Jan. 1942 the Hungarians shot or beat all the Jews to death – about 100 in all.

ZABIE Stanislawow dist., Poland, today Ukraine. The Jews were organized as an independent community in the 1880s, numbering 654 (total 6,816) in 1890 and maintaining a stable pop., their livelihoods augmented by farming small plots of land for family needs. Relations with the Ukrainian villagers were good until the antisemitic recrudescence of the 1930s. With the German occupation of June 1941 many fled to Bukovina. The community was liquidated on 15 Dec. 1941 with the creation of a ghetto on the outskirts of Z. and the execution of the Jews beside a freshly dug pit a few days later.

ZABINKA Polesie dist., Poland, today Belarus. The J. pop. grew to 445 (total 610) in 1921, developing after the arrival of the railroad in the late 19th cent. In the Holocaust, the Jews were presumably expelled by the Germans to Brona Gora and murdered.

ZABLOCIE Volhynia dist., Poland. Jews numbered 20 families in the 1930s, mostly dealing in lumber.

ZABLOTOW Stanislawow dist., Poland, today Ukraine. Jews settled here in the early 18th cent. In the 19th cent. Z. became a hasidic center with rival courts and thousands of visitors. A pogrom was staged in 1903, fires broke out in 1905 and 1911, and during WWI a cholera epidemic struck the town. Many fled never to return and recovery was slow, the J. pop. dropping from the turn of the cent. figure of around 2,000 (half the total) to 1,070 in 1931. Soviet rule in 1939–41 brought J. communal life to an end and with the coming of the Hungarian army on 1 July 1941 a regime of confiscations and forced labor was instituted with the local Ukrainian pop. adding a dimension of violence. The Germans took over the town in early Sept. 1941, staging their first *Aktion* in Dec., when around 1,000 Jews were executed beside open pits and another 100 or so within the town. In the spring of 1942 another 400 Jews were deported to the Belzec death camp and the remainder sent to the Kolomyja ghetto. Of the 250 who managed to return to the town, 200 were rounded up on 7 Sept. and transported to Belzec while the others were later brought to Kolomyja, soon to meet their end.

ZABLUDOW Bialystok dist., Poland. Jews first arrived in the late 16th cent., making the community one of the oldest in the Bialystok area. Prince Radziwill accorded the Jews broad privileges, allowing them to put up public buildings, open shops and stalls in the market, and engage in wholesale trade and crafts. All this created friction with the local pop. Z.'s famous wooden synagogue with its rich decoration was built in the mid-17th cent. and rebuilt in 1756. In the 18th cent. Jews were prominent as textile importers and exported beer hops while J. tailors and furriers were organized in guilds. In the 19th cent. they expanded into light industry as cloth manufacturers and hide processors. The

17th cent. synagogue in Zabludow, Poland

first industrial strike in Z. was organized by J. girls exploited by the textile factories. In the late 19th cent. some factories closed down following a crisis in the textile industry. They were soon replaced by tanneries, also at J. initiative. In 1897 the J. pop. reached a peak of 2,621 (total 3,772). Z.'s yeshiva was known for its outstanding teachers. A Hovevei Zion society became active in the late 19th cent. and on the eve of WWI Po'alei Zion, Mizrachi, and the Bund also formed groups. At the same time the tanning industry declined and a number of factory owners emigrated to the U.S. In 1921, 1,816 Jews remained. Trade was affected by the loss of the Russian market and J. commerce in general was undermined by discriminatory government measures and economic crises. Consequently the J. pop. fell to 152 in 1931 through mass emigration. Most children studied at two Hebrew schools and the J. political parties remained active. Under Soviet rule in 1939–41 J. tradesmen were organized into cooperatives and many J. refugees began to arrive from Nazi-occupied territory. The Germans entered Z. on 26 June

1941, burning down most of the town. The homeless Jews were soon herded into a ghetto and a *Judenrat* was established. On 2 Nov. 1942 they were brought to an old Polish cavalry camp near Bialystok and on 21 Nov. were deported directly to the gas chambers of the Treblinka death camp.

ZABOKREKY (Hung. Nyitrazsambokret) Slovakia, Czechoslovakia, today Republic of Slovakia. The few Moravian J. families present in the early 18th cent. were expelled in 1727 with the rest of the Jews in the mining region of central Slovakia. Jews returned in the mid-18th cent. A synagogue was probably built in the 1770s. By the early 19th cent., the local rabbinate had jurisdiction over 37 neighboring settlements. A J. elementary school was opened in 1855 and the J. pop. reached a peak of 286 (total 742) in 1880. In the Czechoslovakian Republic between the World Wars, Jews were increasingly active in public life. The Zionist movement also became active after WWI, with Bnei Akiva the leading youth movement.

Jews owned most local stores, eight workshops, and three factories. In 1940, 139 Jews remained. In 1941 they were forced out of their businesses and in March 1942, young men were deported to Novaky and the women to Patronka, the latter then on to Auschwitz on 1 April. Dozens more were deported to Opole in the Lublin dist. (Poland) in April and June. In the course of suppressing the Slovakian national uprising in fall 1944, the Nazis murdered the last Jews from the area. A few managed to survive in hiding.

ZABOTIN Kiev dist., Ukraine. Five J. families were present in 1765. All were murdered in 1768 by the Zhelezniak gangs. In 1897, the J. pop. was 272 and in 1926, under the Soviets, 44 (total 4,498). Those who failed to escape were murdered by the Germans in WWII.

ZABRZEZ Vilna dist., Poland, today Belarus. The Jews were expelled in 1882 but despite the ban there were 40 J. residents in 1895. The J. pop. in 1921 was 97 (total 306). The Germans entered Z. on 22 June 1941 and expelled the Jews to the Szarkowszczyzna ghetto in late 1941, murdering them there on 18 July 1942 with 1,200 other Jews.

ZACHENTA Kielce dist., Poland. The J. pop. was 270 (total 423) in 1921. The last Jews were probably deported to the Treblinka death camp by the Germans in summer 1942.

ZADAR (Ital. Zara) Croatia, Yugoslavia, today Republic of Croatia. Jews first lived in Z. in the 14th cent. The attitude of the authorities towards them fluctuated: at times the Jews held influential positions, on other occasions they were expelled. At the end of the 19th cent. there was some antisemitism. In 1938 there were 49 Jews in Z. (2% of the total), but no organized community.

ZADNE (Hung. Zadnya) Carpatho-Russia, Czechoslovakia., today Ukraine. Jews probably settled in the first half of the 18th cent., with one J. family mentioned in 1746. The J. pop. then grew to 40 in 1830 and 118 (total 1,364) in 1880. In 1930, in the period of the Czechoslovakian Republic, it was 371, rising again to 409 in 1941. Twenty Jews earned their livelihoods in trade, nine as artisans, and a few as farmers. Jews also owned two flour mills. The Hungarians oc-cupied Z. in March 1939 and in 1940–41 drafted dozens of Jews into forced labor battalions. Jews lacking Hungarian citizenship were expelled to Kamenets-Podolski and murdered. The remaining Jews were deported to Auschwitz on 19 May 1944.

ZAGARE (Yid. Zhager) Siauliai dist., Lithuania. Jews first settled here in the 16th cent. Z. developed separately on the two banks of the Svete River, with two separate J. communities. The J. pop. in 1897 was 5,443 (60% of the total). In the 1880s many emigrated to South Africa and the U.S. and then helped support the community from abroad. Many were followers of R. Yisrael Salanter, founder of the Musar movement. There were also religious Jews influenced by Haskala. Many natives of Z. became leaders in their fields throughout the world, including Herzl's collaborator and noted ophthalmologist Max Mandelstamm and the U.S. trade union leader Sidney Hillman. In WWI most Jews were expelled; many did not return after the war. A considerable number emigrated to South Africa, the U.S., and Palestine. Jews served on the municipal council. The J. pop. in 1939 was about 1,000 (18% of the total). After Germany's invasion in June 1941 dozens of Jews were shot to death. All of Z.'s Jews were put in a ghetto where they were robbed and abused and women raped. Men were sent to forced labor. On 2 Oct. 1941 the Jews were taken to the market square. After a reassuring speech, the German officer signaled to armed Lithuanians to commence a massacre of the Jews. Some resisted but were killed. Those who fled were taken to a park and murdered beside previously prepared pits.

ZAGHOUAN Zaghouan dist., Tunisia. Jews apparently settled at the turn of the 19th cent., numbering 30 in 1909 and four in 1936. During WWII, a forced labor camp was established there under Italian command where 345 Jews were held. Two months before the end of the German occupation the camp was transferred to Djebibina. There was never an organized community in Z.

ZAGNITKOV Vinnitsa dist., Ukraine. Fourteen Jews were present in 1765. In 1897, the J. pop. was 560 (total 4,660), dropping to 251 in 1939 under the Soviets. The Germans arrived on 23 July 1941 and probably murdered the few dozen remaining J. families in the fall.

Maccabi committee, Zagare, Lithuania

The market square, Zagare, Lithuania

ZAGOROW Lodz dist., Poland. In 1897 the J. pop. was 658 (22% of the total). In 1940, with the influx of refugees, the 500-member community expanded to 2,000. All were ghettoized and some sent to forced labor. In Oct. 1941 the remaining Jews were murdered in the Kazimiezh Biskupi forest.

ZAGORZ Lwow dist., Poland. Jews began arriving from Sanok and neighboring Lesko in the second half of the 19th cent. when the railway line was laid. They operated bath houses for the railway workers along with grocery and building-supply stores. In 1880 the J. pop. stood at 207 (total 1,639). Villagers and local hoodlums wrecked J. stores in 1896 and after fleeing the Red Army in WWI the Jews returned to find the town in near ruins. In WWII the Germans severely persecuted the Jews. By Aug. 1942 all had been sent to the Zaslawie concentration camp, from which thousands were subsequently deported to the Belzec death camp, with many murdered on the spot.

ZAGORZE (I) Stanislawow dist., Poland, today Ukraine. The J. pop. in 1921 was 194. The Jews were probably expelled to Kalusz for liquidation in Aug. 1942.

ZAGORZE (II) Kielce dist., Poland. J. settlement commenced in 1880, including Aleksandrow Hasidim. Many left after WWI, leaving just 40 families, most of them supporters of Mizrachi. Further emigration reduced the J. pop. to 60 when the Germans arrived in early Sept. 1939. In Oct. 1940, the able-bodied were sent to labor camps in Upper Silesia and the rest to Dombrowa Gornicza. In 1942, the Jews of Z. were sent together with those from Dombrowa Gornicza to Auschwitz.

ZAGREB (Ger. Agram) Croatia, Yugoslavia, today Republic of Croatia. Jews lived in Z. from the 14th cent. but were expelled in the 16th cent. by King Ferdinand of Austria. Jews returned in the 18th cent. and

Zagorze congregation honoring aliya of its president, M. Lederman, to Eretz Israel, Poland

contributed to the development of trade, industry, and banking, receiving equal rights in 1873. The community was officially founded in 1806 and in the 19th cent. became the focus of J. culture in the region. The synagogue was inaugurated in 1867 but was destroyed by Croat nationalists in 1941. With the institution of Reform Judaism in the middle of the cent., the Orthodox formed a separate, small community. Jews were prominent in the modern industry and economy of Z., and the community grew from 234 Jews in 1835 to 1,924 in 1890 (5% of the total). Many Jews rose socially, some achieving titles of nobility. The community was able to engage in its extensive welfare and social activities freely until the Holocaust. The forerunners of Zionism in Z. were students who returned from Vienna in the first years of the 20th cent., and Z. soon became the region's Zionist center. Alexander Licht was the Zionist leader in Z. during the Yugoslavian period and served as the third chairman of the Yugoslavian Zionist Organization. The Zionist Organization in Z.

Synagogue in Zagreb, Yugoslavia, before WWII

ran pioneer training farms in various locations to prepare youth for immigration to Palestine. Z. was also the hub of J. publishing in Yugoslavia. In 1931 the community numbered 8,702 (total 185,581). With the rise of Nazi Germany, Yugoslavia – and Z. in particular – took in many German, Austrian, Czech, and later Hungarian refugees. By 1940 the number of Jews in Z. had reached 12,000. This provoked antisemitic reactions among the masses and the Jews gradually lost their civil rights. The J. refugees were cared for by a special committee established by the community and were assisted by the Joint Distribution Committee and the HICEM emigration association. On 10 April 1941, German forces entered Z. and the next day the community's administration was liquidated. The Nazis' Croatian accomplices – the Ustase – began to persecute Serbs and Jews and introduced anti-J. (and anti-Serb) laws that limited their movement, trade, and general activities. Some Jews escaped to Italian areas and were able to survive the war, albeit in concentration camps. Property was confiscated, arrests were made, and the Jews lived under inhuman conditions. They were exploited for forced labor in concentration camps from June 1941 and most were put to death over the following months. The community continued to function from a private home – even in times of great distress – in an effort to assist those taken to the camps. The Joint continued to assist those without means of support until Dec. 1941. From May 1941 many of the surviving Jews were active in the underground opposition to the Fascists and in partisan groups. Those who were still alive at the end of 1942 were taken to Jasenovac death camp. In March 1943, trains transported even more Jews who had been hiding to Auschwitz. It was only at this last stage of destruction that the Catholic Church intervened to save converted and intermarried Jews. Some of the survivors returned to Z. to revive the community after liberation. In the mid-1990s, 1,500 Jews were living there.

ZAKHARINO Smolensk dist., Russia. Z. was located in the J. Pale of Settlement. The J. pop. was 538 in 1847 and 566 (total 574) in 1897. During the Soviet period, there was a J. council (soviet). The Germans occupied Z. in July 1941 and on 9 May 1942 murdered 263 Jews, including 216 from the town.

ZAKINTHOS (Zakynthos, Zanthe, Zante) Ionian Islands, Greece. The earliest records of J. life in Z. date back to the late 15th cent. With the Spanish and Portuguese expulsions (1492–97) a large number of Sephardi Jews settled alongside the small Romaniot community. The Venetians who controlled Z. required the Jews to wear a yellow ribbon and hat. In 1522 there were 30 J. families. In the 17th cent. the community split into a number of congregations. Refugees from Crete established a congregation in 1699. The J. pop. peaked at around 1,000 in 1686. The community was active in the redemption of captives. The Jews lived in a ghetto and relations with the Christian inhabitants of Z. were tense, intensifying with the growth of the J. pop. in the 17th cent. and culminating in a blood libel in 1712. A few Jews were killed in acts of revenge. In 1728, many died in an epidemic and the distressed community suffered from poverty. The J. pop. in 1811 was 274. Under British rule (1815–64) the situation improved, but Jews still did not enjoy full citizenship. Refugees from the Greek mainland settled in Z. during the Greek war of independence (1820s) along with a number of Italian Jews. Full citizenship was granted to Jews when Z. was annexed to Greece in 1864, although antisemitism and poverty continued. Following rumors of a blood libel in Corfu in 1891, Christian rioters raided the J. quarter, destroying homes and property and killing four. Many fled to other towns, including Athens. Two years later many died in an earthquake. Other communities in Greece and Europe, as well as the Alliance Israelite in Paris, assisted the community during its devasting upheavals with donations and supplies. Avraham Constantini (d. 1918), born in Z., became a leader of the Athens community and a philanthropist and assisted the Z. community. Poverty continued and Z. suffered another earthquake in 1912. The J. pop. in 1940 was 275 (total 41,165). In WWII, persecution began when the Germans arrived in Sept. 1943. With the assistance of Z.'s archbishop and mayor, the Jews were protected and helped to go into hiding in the surrounding villages. In the course of moving from village to village, some 30 died of starvation. The Jews of Z. were the only community in Occupied Greece that survived destruction, thanks to the island's mayor, Lucas Karrer, and Archbishop Demetriou Chrysostomos, who were subsequently named Righteous among the Nations in 1978. After the war 70 Jews returned; most emigrated in the following decades.

ZAKLICZYN Cracow dist., Poland. Jews settled in the second half of the 17th cent., the community never

exceeding 300 (20–25% of the pop.). Zionist activity flourished from 1906 and there was a lively social and cultural life. Antisemitism was widespread, but Jews nonetheless continued to contribute to public life, helping the town recover after a devastating flood in 1934. Under the Germans, the Jews set up workshops in the hope of forestalling deportations to the labor camps. A ghetto housing 1,500 Jews, including many refugees, was established in July 1942. Most were deported to the Belzec death camp in Sept. 1942; the last 70 were murdered in April 1943.

ZAKLIKOW Lublin dist., Poland. Jews first settled in the late 16th cent. working as distillers. Their pop. rose from 355 in 1827 and 559 in 1867 to 1,403 (total 3,013) in 1921. In the late 19th cent., they initiated a large limestone-processing plant and a nail factory. After WWI, economic conditions deteriorated but community life flourished, dominated by the Zionists but with the Bund and Agudat Israel also active. The Germans arrived on 15 Sept. 1939, establishing a *Judenrat* and instituting a regime of forced labor. With the influx of refugees from Cracow and the Lublin area, the J. pop. reached 2,200 in fall 1942. Most were deported to Belzec on 3 Nov. 1942.

ZAKOPANE Cracow dist., Poland. Jews first settled in the late 18th cent. The harsh climate and bands of robbers kept the isolated Carpathian Mountain community from developing significantly, though a flourishing health and tourist industry provided Jews with jobs. The J. pop. stood at 198 in 1900 (total 5,298), growing to 533 (total 8,808) in 1921 with professional people, particularly doctors, arriving. The Zionist movement also utilized the tourist facilities to operate camps and hold sports events. However, J. tourism was discouraged by increasing antisemitic incidents in the 1930s, when J. businesses and institutes were attacked and J. entertainers fired from their jobs. When the Germans arrived on 1 Sept. 1939, they initiated a regime of forced labor, confiscations, and extortion. All the Jews were expelled, most to Nowy Targ, in mid-1940 and the town was subsequently utilized to house labor camps. The forced laborers, including Jews, came from other loctlities.

ZAKROCZYM Warsaw dist., Poland. A small community existed in the 15th cent., only developing significantly in the 18th cent. A synagogue and cemetery

Jewish high school students from Zakopane, Poland, on an excursion (Wiesenthal Institute/photo courtesy of Yad Vashem, The Holocaust Martyrs' and Heroes' Remembrance Authority, Jerusalem)

were consecrated in the 1820s. In the second half of the 19th cent. Jews engaged in light industry and were the principal distributors of agricultural produce, though faced with stiff Polish competition at the turn of the cent. The J. pop. rose to 2,211 (total 4,218) in 1897, dropping to 1,865 in 1921 after WWI. The Zionists became active in 1898 and between the World Wars contended with Agudat Israel for control of the community. Most of the Jews fled to Warsaw as a consequence of the fighting that destroyed 70% of the city at the outset of WWII. Afterwards at least 300 returned. Those without residence permits were expelled along with the elderly to Pomiechowek in July 1941; the rest were transferred to the Nowy Dwor ghetto in Nov. 1941, sharing the fate of the Jews there.

ZAKRZOWEK Lublin dist., Poland. The J. pop. was 169 in the late 19th cent. and 408 (total 2,216) in 1921. The German occupation of Sept. 1939 was followed by a regime of forced labor. In Oct. 1942, fol-

lowing an *Aktion* in which 50 children and old and handicapped Jews were murdered immediately, the 370 Jews remaining in Z., augmented by refugees from Lublin, were transferred to Krasnik, In Nov. 1942, they were deported to the Belzec death camp together with some 2,500 Jews from Krasnik and other nearby settlements.

ZALAEGERSZEG Zala dist., Hungary. Jews are first mentioned in 1711. A J. school was opened in 1820 and by 1904 two synagogues were in use. The J. pop. rose from 349 in 1840 to a peak of 1,659 (12.5% of the total) in 1920. Ten were murdered in the White Terror attacks (1919–21) and 215 were detained in concentration camps in 1922. The local priest, Yosef Mindszenty, later Cardinal and Archbishop of Hungary, was among those leading the antisemitic incitement. In 1941, 873 Jews remained. Many of the young perished in the Ukraine under forced labor. In May 1944, after the arrival of the Germans, the Jews were confined in a ghetto and from 4–6 July they were deported to Auschwitz. About 100 survivors reestablished the community but gradually most left.

ZALALOVO Zala dist., Hungary. The first Jews arrived in 1746. In 1869, they formed a Neologist congregation. They maintained a school and two synagogues. The J. pop. was 129 in 1880 and 100 in 1941. All were deported to Auschwitz via Zalaegerszeg on 6 July 1944.

ZALASZENTGROT Zala dist., Hungary. Jews settled in the early 18th cent. A synagogue was opened in 1796 and a school in 1849. In 1869, when the J. pop. reached a peak of 424, a Neologist congregation was founded. During the White Terror attacks (1919–21), some Jews were sent to the Zalaegerszeg concentration camp. In 1941, 151 Jews remained. On 4 July 1944, all were deported to Auschwitz via Zalaegerszeg. The community reestablished itself after the war, but in 1956 most left.

ZALAU (Hung. Zilah) N. Transylvania dist., Rumania. A J. community was organized in the late 19th cent. The J. pop. in 1920 was 552 (6% of the total). In 1942 several hundred Jews were drafted into labor battalions and sent to the Ukraine, where they died; others were sent to a camp in Ciuc. On 5 May 1944 the community was transferred to Simleul Silvaniei and in June to Auschwitz.

ZALESZCZYKI Tarnopol dist., Poland, today Ukraine. Jews were apparently among the founders of the town in the early 18th cent. The community grew to a peak of 4,513 (80% of the total) in 1890 but straitened economic circumstances and stiff competition in trade led to considerable emigration, much of it to the U.S., reducing the J. pop. by nearly half at the end of WWI with most families on relief. In the war itself, the Russian occupation brought a reign of terror, with mass expulsion in 1915 and many succumbing to typhoid and cholera epidemics. With the development of the town as a resort center in the 1920s economic conditions improved but the community was again hit hard by the economic crisis of the 1930s. Agudat Israel and the Zionists were the major political forces in the community. The Soviets put an end to all J. public life when they annexed Z. in Sept. 1939. Business enterprises were nationalized and artisans were forced to join cooperatives, though certain J. Communists occupied central administrative and economic positions. The Germans occupied the town on 8 July 1941 and on 14 Nov. assembled around 1,000 males between the ages of 15 and 50, sending 200 to the forced labor camp at Kamionka and executing the rest. The remaining Jews passed the winter under conditions of starvation and disease. On 20 Sept. 1942 they were dispersed to nearby ghettoes, most to the one at Tluste, ultimately to meet their end in the Belzec death camp.

ZALOZCE Tarnopol dist., Poland, today Ukraine. Jews were found in Z. from the early 17th cent. and the community grew in importance in the 18th and 19th cents. with many well-known rabbis and preachers residing there. The Zionists became active from the early 20th cent. The town was destroyed by fire in WWI and the J. pop. declined from 2,412 (total 6,928) in 1890 to 524 (less than 10%) in 1921. Soviet rule in 1939–41 curtailed J. economic and public life. The German occupation of 9 July 1941 brought with it forced labor and summary executions. Most of the Jews were expelled to the Zborow ghetto in Oct. 1942. Others were hunted down and murdered in 1943.

ZALTBOMMEL Gelderland dist., Holland. Jews lived in Z. in the 15th and 16th cents. but were expelled in 1546. Settlement was renewed in the late 17th cent. and the community grew rapidly in the second quarter of the 19th cent. The J. pop. in 1860 was 200 but began to dwindle from the 1860s. A number of J. organizations operated, including a branch of the Alliance Israelite. J. education was organized from 1845. The J. pop. in 1941 was 59 (total 4,219). Sixty-two Jews were deported and perished in Poland from Nov. 1942 to April 1943, with 15 others surviving.

ZALUKIEW Stanislawow dist., Poland, today Ukraine. The J. pop. in 1921 was 120. The Jews were sent to the Rodolf Mill camp in Stanislawow for liquidation in Sept.–Oct. 1942.

ZALUZ (Hung. Kisalmas; Yid. Zalysha) Carpatho-Russia, Czechoslovakia, today Ukraine. Jews probably settled in the early 19th cent., numbering 88 in 1880, 100 in 1921 under the Czechoslovakians, and 118 in 1941 under the Hungarians. In the Holocaust, most of the Jews perished in Auschwitz like the others in the region.

ZAMBERK Bohemia, Czechoslovakia. A J. community probably existed in the early 17th cent. Fires devastated the ghetto in 1810 and 1833. Many Jews left in the late 19th cent., leaving 74 in 1921 and 31 (1% of the total) in 1930. The Jews were deported to the Theresienstadt ghetto in 1942 and from there to the death camps. A concentration camp for J. women operated at nearby Bila Voda and 29 J. women who died on a death march from Auschwitz were buried in the area in Jan. 1945.

ZAMBROW Bialystok dist., Poland. The community was established in 1829 and grew substantially after the Russian army set up a base in Z. in 1863, requiring supplies and providing construction work for scores of craftsmen. The Jews provided kosher food and hospitality to the 400 J. soldiers at the base. After the abortive Polish rebellion (1863), antisemites killed several Jews and accused the Jews of betraying the Polish homeland in favor of Russian rule. By 1897 there were 2,400 Jews in Z. (63% of the total). Two major fires, one in 1895 and a second in 1910, gutted several hundred J. homes. J. emigration, which began after the first major fire, increased after the abortive revolution of 1905 and the second fire. In 1921 there were 3,216 Jews in Z. (about half the pop.). As antisemitism increased and the economic situation worsened between the World Wars, Zionist activity gained momentum and permits to Palestine were obtained for Hehalutz pioneers. Antisemitic violence and economic boycotts were routine in 1936–37. At the outset of WWII half the town was destroyed in air raids. The invading Nazis plundered J. property and businesses. The Ribbentrop-Molotov agreement temporarily permitted the Soviets to take over the town and many young Jews joined the Red Army. When Germany reoccupied Z. in June 1941, J. property was confiscated and the Jews were sent to forced labor. After the first, ineffective *Judenrat* was dispersed, a second *Judenrat* was appointed. The first *Aktion* took place a week later, in which 800 Jews were rounded up and shot in the forest outside the town. A second *Aktion* took place in Sept. 1941. In Dec. 1941, Z.'s remaining 2,000 Jews were removed to a ghetto and sent to forced labor. In Nov. 1942, the ghetto was transferred to the former Russian base, where about 14,000-17,000 Jews from the area were incarcerated. Some Jews fled in transit but later gave themselves up, unable to survive in the forests. The Nazis crushed an attempt at rebellion. To-

wards the end, many Jews died in a typhus epidemic and others, who tried to escape to the forests, were shot. In Jan. 1943 the remaining Jews were sent to Auschwitz.

ZAMEK MODLIBORZYCKI Lublin dist., Poland. The J. pop. stood at 150 (total 1,877) in 1921. During WWII, the Germans may have expelled the Jews to Tarnogrod prior to deportation with the local Jews to the Belzec death camp in the second half of 1942

ZAMIEKHOV Kamenets-Podolski dist., Ukraine. In 1734, 30 Jews were murdered in a Haidamak raid. The J. pop. included 505 poll tax payers in 1765 and numbered 891 (total 2,217) in 1897. After the Feb. 1917 Revolution, the Bund and Tze'irei Tziyyon became active. In 1919, the Petlyura gangs damaged J. property. In 1926, the J. pop. was about 1,000. The Germans arrived on 11 July 1941. On 20 Aug. 1942, the Jews were expelled to Novaya Ushitsa, where they were murdered together with Jews from neighboring settlements.

ZAMOSC Lublin dist., Poland. The first Jews were Sephardim from Turkey and Venice, apparently arriving in 1587 and granted equal rights with local residents by the town's proprietor. Around 1595 they consecrated a synagogue and cemetery. Unable to collect debts from the nobility, most left in the 1620s, their places taken by Ashkenazi Jews from the region. Thousands of J. refugees found refuge in Z. during the Chmielnicki massacres of 1648–49. Jews dealt in cattle, lumber, and grain and in 1726 were licensed to produce and sell alcoholic beverages. By 1846 they were operating three brickyards, three flour mills, a soap factory, and a number of sawmills. The J. pop. rose from 2,874 in 1827 to 7,034 (total 11,389) in 1897. In the first half of the 19th cent., large groups of Belz and Gur Hasidim resided in the city. Haskala made its first inroads in the period of Austrian rule (1772–1809), when German-J. schools were opened. In 1886, *maskilim* opened a J. boys' school. Among the leading Haskala figures in the early 19th cent. were Yosef Zederbaum and Yaakov Eichenbaum. The physician-poet Shelomo Ettinger (1803–56) lived in Z., urging Jews to take up productive occupations, and the author Y. L. Peretz (1852–1915) was born and raised there and commemorated the city in his writings. Z. was also the birthplace of the revolutionary Rosa Luxemburg (1870–1919). Under Haskala influence, Jews became active politically and took part in the Polish rebellions of 1830 and 1863. The Zionists and the Bund became active in the early 20th cent. During WWI, 11 Jews were executed by the Russians as alleged collaborators. Under the Austrian occupation of 1915–18, public life revived. Mizrachi formed a group in 1917 and opened a Yavne school that operated until 1923. In the aftermath of the war, Polish and Ukrainian soldiers murdered Jews and pillaged their property. The ensuing economic crises, the heavy tax burden, and anti-J. boycotts as antisemitism intensified in the 1930s reduced many to penury. Many of the young emigrated but community life continued to flourish with the Zionist movement the leading force. Kadima and CYSHO schools were opened and the Yiddish newspaper *Zamoshtsher Shtime* appeared in 1928–39 and from 1930 *Zamoshtsher Vort*. The community maintained a hospital, old age home, and orphanage and, through the TOZ organization, operated a shelter for needy children and sent many to summer camps. In 1931 the J. pop. was 10,265 (total 24,241). In 1928, half the city council was composed of Jews. In early Sept. 1939, heavy German bombardments claimed 500 J. lives as J. refugees flooded the city. Polish mobs attacked Jews prior to the permanent German occupation of the city on 7 Oct. Large numbers of Jews fled with the Red Army, leaving some 5,000 behind. In Dec., a *Judenrat* was set up under a regime of forced labor and "contributions." In mid-Dec. 1939, 500 more Jews arrived from Wloclawek and Kolo. The *Judenrat* opened a soup kitchen and school and a hospital to cope with typhus. During 1940, hundreds of Jews were sent to labor camps. In 1941, 1,500–2,000 from Z. and environs were sent to the Izbica labor camp. In April 1941, the remaining Jews were confined to a ghetto whose pop. reached 7,000 as thousands of Jews arrived from Czechoslovakia and Germany. Deportations commenced on 11 April 1942. About 3,000 Jews were transported to the Belzec death camp and nearly 250 left behind dead, mainly the old, the sick, and those trying to hide. A second *Aktion* commencing on 17 May sent the aged to Belzec on 26 or 27 May. Deportations were renewed in Aug.: 500 were sent to Belzec on 11 Aug. and 400 in early Sept., with Jews randomly seized off the streets. The final liquidation of the ghetto took place on 16 Oct. 1942 with the remaining Jews force-marched to Izbica 13 miles (21 km) away. Those who fell by the wayside were shot.

From Izbica, they were deported, beginning on 19 Oct., to Belzec, where about 4,000 are estimated to have died. Those still remaining in the city were killed on March 1943. The 1,000 Jews in the local labor camps, mostly from Z., were deported to the Majdanek concentration camp in May 1943. After the liberation by the Red Army in late 1944, about 300 Jews gathered in the city, most returning from the safety of the Soviet Union. When two were murdered by the Poles, most left, with only five remaining in 1947.

ZAMOSTEA Bukovina, Rumania, today Ukraine. A J. community existed in the late 19th cent. The J. pop. in 1930 was 129. In June 1941, the J. pop. was transferred to Storojineti and in Oct. 1941 the Jews were deported to Transnistria. Only 20 returned after the war.

ZAMOSTY Polesie dist., Poland, today Belarus. Z. was originally a J. farm settlement attached to Kamieniec. With the land sold off and economic decline, the J. pop. fell from 796 in 1897 to 305 (total 594) in 1921. They shared the fate of the Jews of Kamieniec in the Holocaust.

ZANDVOORT Noord-Holland dist., Holland. The J. community, organized in 1923, opened a hospital for needy J. children. In summer 1938 there were 20 German-J. refugees in Z. The J. pop. in 1941 was 553 (total 9,488). Persecution began in May 1940. In March 1942 the Jews were sent to Amsterdam, from where they were later deported; 17 returned after WWII.

ZANZUR Tripolitania dist., Libya. According to tradition, there was a large 16th cent. J. community in Z. The early 20th cent. saw 60 Jews in Z. During the Italian conquest of Z. in 1912 rioting Moslem extremists damaged both private and communal J. property. There were 117 Jews in Z. in 1936 and 100 in 1943. Z.'s Jews were always poor and the entire community lived in ten houses, interspersed among the Arab houses. Rather than depending solely on Tripoli, the Jews of Z. under Italian rule obtained their own rabbi, R. Yosef Khalon, who served from WWI to 1945 as *mohel* (ritual slaughterer) and teacher. WWII left Z. unscathed, but in 1945 Arab anti-J. riots, during the British occupation, resulted in the death of 34 of Z.'s 100 Jews. Others were injured and all homes and stores were destroyed. The Jews were transferred to Tripoli and never returned to Z. They left for Israel in 1948.

ZAPADNAYA DVINA Kalinin dist., Russia. Jews probably settled in the late 19th cent. In the Soviet period, their pop. was 439 in 1926 and 445 in 1939. Few Jews were present when the Germans arrived on 6 Oct. 1941. All were murdered during an occupation that lasted until Jan. 1942.

ZAPOROZHE (until 1921, Aleksandrovsk) Zaporozhe dist., Ukraine. Seven Jews were living in Z. in 1816. In 1897, their pop. was 5,290 (total 18,849). A pogrom was staged against the Jews on 1 May 1881. In subsequent attacks, on 6–7 Sept. 1904 and 22–23 Oct. 1905, dozens of Jews were killed and injured. In the early 20th cent., J. children attended a *talmud torah*, three boys' schools, and a coeducational school. Two vocational schools (one for girls) were opened by 1917. After the Feb. Revolution, the first secondary school for girls was established. In the Soviet period, hundreds of Jews were employed in the steel plant and at other factories established in the late 1920s.

Dozens of J. families were also employed in the nearby J. kolkhozes. By 1939, the J. pop. was 22,631 (total 289,280). The Germans captured the city on 3 Oct. 1941. On 24 March 1942, 3,700 Jews were murdered at the Stalin kolkhoz on the road to Melitopol. Shortly afterwards, the Germans murdered another few hundred Jews, mostly children from mixed marriages.

ZAPYSKIS (Yid. Sapizishok) Kaunas dist., Lithuania. Jews first settled at the beginning of the 19th cent., earning their livelihood in petty trade and crafts. The Zionist movement won widespread support. A Hebrew school was established in 1910. The J. pop. in 1923 was 293 (50% of the total). The Israeli artist Yehezkel Streichman was born in Z. in 1906. After the German occupation of June 1941, the Jews were confined to a ghetto. In mid-Aug., 40 J. men were killed and the rest on 4 Sept.

ZARASAI (Yid. Ezsherene) Zarasai dist., Lithuania. Jews from Troki requested permission from Czar Alexander I to settle in Z. in 1838. By 1866 the J. pop. was 3,562 (54% of the total). Jews served on the city council in 1924–1934 and in 1939 the J. pop.

High school students from Zarasai, Lithuania, celebrating spring

was 1,500. When the Soviets took control in 1940, Zionist and most communal institutions were dissolved and businesses nationalized. When the Germans entered Z., scores of Jews tried to flee to Russia, but armed Lithuanians blocked the roads and killed many. On 26 Aug. 1941 most Jews were put on carts to be taken to "work." Armed Lithuanians escorted them to previously prepared mass graves in the Deguciai forest and ordered them to strip naked. When the Jews resisted, the Lithuanians opened fire, killing all of them.

ZAREMBY KOSCIELNE (Yid. Zaromb) Bialystok dist., Poland. An organized community existed in the second half of the 17th cent. In the late 18th cent. Jews marketed estate produce under leaseholding agreements and engaged in crafts. In WWI Russian soldiers burned the J. settlement to the ground. In 1921 the J. pop. was 1,254 (total 1,630). Most J. tradesmen owned small stores and others worked only seasonally. In 1938, 150 of the community's 250 families required aid for the Passover season and 69 were left homeless after a fire. During the 1930s, J. livelihoods were further undermined by anti-J. boycotts and violence. The Zionists were particularly active among the young. A J. elementary school enrolled 200 children and a Beth Jacob school sponsored by Agudat Israel was attended by 80 girls. After a two-year Soviet occupation, the Germans entered the town on 22 June 1941. On 2 Sept., 1,500 Jews including refugees were taken to Szulborze, where German and Polish police bludgeoned dozens of children to death before their parents' eyes. The rest were taken to Mianowek and executed beside a freshly dug pit. Another 200 were sent to the death camps from the ghettoes where they had sought refuge or were hunted down and murdered in the forests.

ZARENAI (Yid. Zharan) Telsiai dist., Lithuania. Until WWI the area was owned by a family of squires who built houses on the land and rented them to Jews. Between the World Wars many Jews emigrated to South Africa. The J. pop. in 1941 was 95. Most of the Jews were killed in the Holocaust by Lithuanians.

ZARKI Kielce dist., Poland. Jews apparently settled with the founding of the town in the Middle Ages, forming an organized community by the late 17th cent. The J. pop. grew from 787 in 1765 to 1,544 in

1857. In the late 19th cent., Jews were active in the town's industrialization, setting up hide-processing plants, sawmills, brickyards, and flour mills. Z. was the birthplace of Yaakov Epstein, founder of a well-known family of bankers and industrialists, the printer Avraham Yosef Stiebel, and the hasidic leader Yitzhak of Warka. The community maintained two synagogues, two *battei midrash*, and a number of *shtiblekh*. In the late 19th cent., the attraction of the young to Zionism and socialism was a source of conflict in the tradition-oriented community. In WWI, economic life came to a standstill and in its aftermath the Joint Distribution Committee came to the community's assistance as the J. pop. rose to 2,536 in 1921 (total 4,406). At the time, Jews ran 89 workshops and small factories, nearly half in the garment industry. Most of the J. political parties and youth movements were represented and Hehalutz operated a pioneer training farm. Anti-J. agitation intensified in the 1930s and young Jews organized a self-defense group. In the German bombardment of 2 Sept. 1939, about 100 Jews were killed and in the ensuing occupation the Jews were subjected to severe persecution under a regime of forced labor and "contributions." In winter 1940–41, 250 refugees from Plock arrived and many died in a typhoid epidemic. By summer 1942, the J. pop. had dropped from a prewar figure of 600 families to just 130 as a result of sickness and starvation. On 6 Oct. 1942, 800 Jews were assembled in the market square and marched to the railroad station under a rain of blows while mothers with their infants and other stragglers were shot down. All were deported to the Treblinka death camp.

ZARNOVICA Slovakia, Czechoslovakia, today Republic of Slovakia. Jews settled in the 1840s after a longstanding settlement ban, reaching a peak pop. of 142 (total 1,862) in 1900. After WWI, J. property was looted in riots and the Jews organized themselves for self-defense. The Zionists were active from the 1920s. In 1940, the J. pop. was 77. Under Slovakian rule, J. businesses were liquidated or "Aryanized. "In spring 1942, the Jews were deported, the young to the Majdanek concentration camp in March and families to the death camps in the Lublin dist. (Poland) in June.

ZARNOWIEC Kielce dist., Poland. A J. community of 386 residents with a synagogue and school is mentioned in 1791. Its pop. increased to 814 in 1857 and 1,412 (total 2,472) in 1897. After WWI, J. life continued to revolve around the synagogue, although there were small Zionist and non-Zionist groups that were politically active. There were 1,000 Jews in Z., including refugees from Cracow, following the German occupation of Sept. 1939. A *Judenrat* was soon appointed, setting up a soup kitchen and health services that helped contain hunger and disease. On 5 Sept. 1942 the Jews were taken to neighboring Wolbrom and after a selection for the labor camps deported to the Belzec death camp.

ZARSZYN Lwow dist., Poland. J. settlement commenced in the late 18th cent. with community life centering around the *beit midrash*. The J. pop. was 128 in 1880 (total 959) and 181 in 1921. Persecution and forced labor came with the German occupation. Most were expelled to Sanok in summer 1942 to await their end.

ZARZECZE Stanislawow dist., Poland, today Ukraine. The J. pop. in 1921 was 106. The Jews were possibly executed locally in Oct. 1941.

ZARZIS (also Gaigis) Southern Tunisia. Although Judaized Berber tribes may have lived in the area, an organized J. community in Z. only sprang up at the end of the 19th cent. In 1909, Z. had 350 Jews; in 1936, 260 (3% of the total). The J. pop. increased to 1,026 (11.2%) in 1946. The Djerba origin of Z.'s Jews is apparent in the community's customs, traditions, and family names. No J. quarter developed though Jews preferred to live near each other and near the synagogue. The Jews played an active role in Z.'s economic life as owners of most local stores. Jews traded in agricultural produce, primarily olive oil, dates, and figs, operated fishing boats in partnership with Arabs, and engaged in traditional occupations such as tailoring, carpentry, and shoemaking. Virtually untouched by modernization, only their religion distinguished them from their Arab neighbors. Even under the French, J. boys studied only in the *talmud torah* while girls received no schooling at all until after WWII. The community maintained a synagogue, built in 1905, and a cemetery; community affairs were managed by a committee. There were incidental, unorganized attacks by Arabs on Jews and J. property. The French military administration generally preferred

not to interfere. No Zionist group ever formed and to the extent that there was Zionist activity, it was held in the synagogue and kept well hidden. In WWII, the Germans did not enter Z. but stayed near the area's French military camp. Although there were no anti-J. decrees and no men were taken for forced labor, Jews who could do so left during Jan.–April 1943. The economic havoc wreaked by the war led most Jews to abandon Z. after the war. The Joint Distribution Committee and OSE provided food, schooling, and health services. After the establishment of Israel, the Arab attitude to the Jews prompted *aliya* but only in 1952 did half the community leave together for Israel. In the early 1970s, there were still 300 Jews in Z., but in 1983 the synagogue was burned down, ending the history of the Jews there.

ZASHKOV Kiev dist., Ukraine. A small number of Jews were present in the 18th cent. Their pop. grew to 2,445 (total 5,181) in 1897. Most of the town's 26 stores were in J. hands and the weekly market day was an important source of J. income. Ten Jews were murdered in anti-J. riots on 20 Oct. 1918. In 1939, under the Soviets, the J. pop. was 877. The Germans occupied Z. on 19 July 1941, murdering nearly all the Jews. An underground group with J. members succeeded in saving Jews by providing them with forged "Aryan" documents.

ZASKIEWICZE Vilna dist., Poland, today Belarus. Jews probably arrived in the late 19th cent., numbering 200 (total pop. 253) in 1925 after losing most of their homes and property in WWI. Between the World Wars their small auxiliary farms often saved them from starvation. The Germans arrived in late June 1941 and set up a *Judenrat* and ghetto under a regime of forced labor. In June 1942 the Jews were apparently brought to the Smorgonie ghetto (if not murdered before) and in Oct. 1942 to the Oszmiana ghetto, where they were executed.

ZASLAVL Minsk dist., Belorussia. Jews probably settled in the mid-18th cent., numbering 158 in 1766 and 280 in 1897. A Hebrew printing press was founded in 1807. In 1926, under the Soviets, the J. pop. was 368 (total 1,648), dropping to 248 in 1939. In the mid-1920s, 35 Jews worked at a J. kolkhoz and from 1925 a four-year J. school was active. The Germans occupied the town on 28 June 1941.

The remaining Jews were herded into a ghetto and murdered in late Sept.

ZASLIAI (Yid. Zhosle) Troki dist., Lithuania. The J. pop. in 1897 was 1,325 (67% of the total). Many Jews joined the Hovevei Zion movement. During WWI the community took in Jews expelled by the Russians from other towns. Between the World Wars many emigrated to the West and to Palestine. After Germany's invasion in June 1941, Lithuanian nationalists arrested suspected Communist sympathizers, most of whom were Jews, and sent them to neighboring Kaisiadorys, where they were killed. Jews were also seized for forced labor and abused. In Aug. 1941 all the J. men and some of the women were taken to Kaisiadorys and then to the Strushon forest where they were murdered on 27 Aug. The remaining Jews were executed near Semeliskes on 6 Oct. 1941.

ZASTAVNA Bukovina, Rumania, today Ukraine. The J. community received official recognition in 1891. At the outbreak of WWI, most of the Jews fled to Austria, returning at the end of the war. Zionist activity began in 1904. The J. pop. was 629 in 1930 (12% of the total). A Betar training farm was opened in 1932 with 60–70 pioneers annually. In June 1940, the Soviets exiled Zionist functionaries to Siberia. The Germans and Rumanians deported the J. pop. to Transnistria in June 1941 and dispersed them among various camps and ghettoes. Only a tenth survived.

ZASULIE Sumy dist., Ukraine. J. residence was permitted only from 1902. In 1939, the J. pop. was 90 (total 7,018). The Germans captured Z. on 10 Sept. 1941 and murdered the few Jews who had neither fled nor been evacuated.

ZATEC Bohemia (Sudetenland) Czechoslovakia. Jews are mentioned in 1350 and in the 15th cent. as moneylenders. In 1541 they were attacked in their ghetto in a violent pogrom. Expelled by Ferdinand I in 1543, they returned only after the 1848 revolution. A synagogue was consecrated in 1872 as the J. pop. grew from 800 in 1860 to 1,262 in 1890. After WWI, WIZO and B'nai B'rith were active and Jews were prominent in the beer hop trade. In 1930 their pop. was 760 (total 18,100). After the annexation of the Sudetenland to the German Reich, most Jews left Z. The rest were mostly deported to the death camps of the

east in late 1942, with a few surviving the war in the Theresienstadt ghetto.

ZATISHIE Stalino dist., Ukraine. Jews numbered 527 (total 708) in 1897 and 449 in 1926. Under the German occupation, which began on 12 Nov. 1941, 95 Jews were murdered.

ZATOR Cracow dist., Poland. The small community was one of the 61 existing in Poland at the end of the Middle Ages, its pop. never exceeding 500 (a quarter of the total). The grievous J. suffering in WWI was compounded when rioters looted J. homes and stores in Nov. 1918. Economic conditions worsened between the World Wars and a devastating flood in 1934 added to the community's distress. Throughout the period the Zionists made few inroads owing to the opposition of traditional circles. With the arrival of the Germans in

Ceremonial procession bringing Torah scroll to synagogue, Zator, Poland

WWII the Jews were evicted from their homes and herded into substandard housing facilities. After two years of forced labor, all were expelled on 2 July 1942, making their way to Wadowice.

ZAVEREZHYE Mogilev dist., Belorussia. Z. was founded as a J. colony in 1835 and had a pop. of 259 Jews in 1898. The community maintained a prayer house, a cemetery, and a library with Yiddish and some Hebrew books. In 1924-25, under Soviet rule, 49 J. families engaged in farming and in 1930 the settlement became a kolkhoz. A four-grade J. school operated there. In 1939, the J. pop. was 130. The Germans arrived in late July 1941 and shortly afterwards executed all the Jews in the forest near the village of Pashkovka.

ZAVIDOVICI Bosnia-Hercegovina, Yugoslavia, today Republic of Bosnia. Jews settled there in the 19th cent. In 1930 the J. pop. was 200. In WWII the Ustase took the Jews of Z. to Sabac and handed them over to the Germans. Most were killed in the Banjica camp.

ZAVODY Kharkov dist., Ukraine. The J. pop. in 1939 was 251. The Germans captured Z. in late June 1942 and murdered all the Jews who had neither fled nor been evacuated.

ZAWALE Volhynia dist., Poland, today Ukraine. The J. pop. in 1921 was 129 (total 743). Under the German occupation, the Jews in this Czech village were transferred to Dubno.

ZAWALOW Tarnopol dist., Poland, today Ukraine. Jews were among the mid-16th cent. founders of the town. The J. pop. stood at 396 in 1890 and 137 (total 987) in 1921. All were presumably expelled to neighboring Podhajce in the fall of 1942 to share the fate of that community.

ZAWIA (also Zaouia) Tripolitania dist., Libya. J. settlement probably commenced in the 17th cent. from the neighboring city of Sorman after its destruction. The Jews were taken under the protection of the Bedouins of the Uhrshpana tribe but relations deteriorated under the influence of the fanatical Sunnites in the early 18th cent. When the Jews tried to rebuild a synagogue that had collapsed in 1780, Moslem zealots prevented it. In 1798, they again rioted to prevent its reconstruction. A threat to leave the city with its commercial implications led to reconciliation. Anti-J. action was rekindled when the synagogue was severely vandalized in 1879. A second synagogue was completed in 1895 in the face of Arab protests. Moslem persecution continued into the 20th cent., including desecration of the J. cemetery. The J. pop. rose from 310 in 1886 to 600 in 1906. The community was in effect divided into two rival neighborhood camps – the *Mubahiriya* and the *Muqabiliya* (the Northerners and Southerners, respectively), with separate ritual slaughter and fierce competition for leadership. In 1906, the president of the community was murdered at the instigation of the local Turkish governor, who was consequently dismissed. With the Arab Revolt in 1915, coming on the heels of the Italian occupation of 1911, many Jews fled, seeking refuge in the desert with the Bedouin tribes. Sheikh Lubay Ubayda took 30 J. families under his protection. After the suppression of the revolt, Jews resumed their former occupations, achieving prominence in most areas of trade and establishing a reputation for their metalworking ability. R. Khamus Sofer of Zarzis, Tunisia, served as chief rabbi in 1922-49, providing the community with outstanding spiritual leadership and helping bridge the gap between the rival factions. With the bombardment of Tripoli in WWII, many Jews fled to Z., giving local Jews their first taste of western ways. But for the deportation of J. foreign nationals, anti-J. measures were relatively mild in Z. and very few were sent to forced labor. With the arrival of the British and the return home of the Jews from Tripoli, the economic situation declined sharply and 80% of the community of 675 required relief. Many left for Tripoli and Benghazi and the Joint Distribution Committee rendered assistance. In the 1945 riots that spread from Tripoli, ten Jews were killed, 18 were injured, and much property was destroyed in outbreaks of particular savagery in which pregnant women, children, and the old were attacked and some crippled for life. Disturbances continued regularly until final emigration to Israel in 1949-51, organized by the J. Agency emissary for Libya, Barukh Duvdavani. Most of the Jews settled in Moshav Alma in Upper Galilee.

ZAWICHOST Kielce dist., Poland. Jews arrived in the early 18th cent., settling in Prosperowo, a settlement specifically built for Jews at the encouragement of King Augustus II to stimulate development. An organized community was formed and the J. pop. rose to

1,582 (total 2,966) in 1857. Despite economic hardship between the World Wars, which led many of the richer Jews to leave for the U.S. and other countries, community life flourished, with the Zionists, the Bund, and Agudat Israel active. The Germans captured Z. on 9 Sept. 1939, finding about 1,500 Jews there. A *Judenrat* was established in early 1940 under a regime of forced labor and extortionate tributes. In summer 1942, a ghetto was established and the pop. swelled to 5,000 with the arrival of refugees. All were deported to the Belzec death camp in Oct. 1942 after the elderly and sick were murdered in the ghetto along with the children.

ZAWIERCIE Kielce dist., Poland. Jews were permitted to settle and work the land by royal privilege in the late 17th cent. A community developed in the 19th cent., building a synagogue in 1881. The J. pop. reached 1,134 (total 5,224) in 1887. Jews were active in local industry, the Ginzburg textile plant employing 3,000 workers in the 1870s. They also operated a printing press which contributed to J. cultural life. In the late 19th cent., proponents of assimilation became prominent, regarding themselves as Polish patriots "of the J. persuasion" and engaging in a spirited struggle against the Orthodox for control of community institutions. The J. pop. numbered 6,095 (total 29,507) in 1921. In both 1919 and 1921, violent pogroms were staged against the Jews by local residents and by General Haller's Polish troops. Zionist influence spread in the 1920s. Mizrachi set up a reformed *heder* and in 1928 a Tarbut Hebrew school was opened. In 1926, the head of the J. community became mayor of the city. Antisemitism intensified in the 1930s under the influence of the Endecja Party, with anti-J. boycotts and heavy taxes reducing most of the community to penury. The Germans entered Z. on 4 Sept. 1939, finding about 7,000 Jews there and immediately exacting

Cantorial choir, Zawiercie, Poland, 1925–26

an exorbitant tribute. In early 1940, they began transferring J. businesses to "loyal" *Volksdeutsche*. In April 1940, 600 J. refugees arrived from Silesia and in June a ghetto and *Judenrat* were established under a regime of forced labor and further extortion. In 1942 Hashomer Hatzair members established an underground that succeeded in smuggling several J. families across the border using counterfeit documents supplied by a local resident posing as a Nazi. In Aug. (or May) 1942, 2,000 Jews were deported to Auschwitz. A new German factory making air force uniforms employed 2,500 Jews in early 1943. In Aug. 1943, all but 500 were included in the deportation of the remaining 6,000–7,000 Jews to Auschwitz. The rest of the factory workers were deported there in Oct. 1943.

ZAWISTY DZIKIE Bialystok dist., Poland. The J. pop. in 1921 was 181 (total 282). The Jews were expelled east of the Bug River by the Germans in fall 1939, most perishing in the Holocaust.

ZAWOJ Stanislawow dist., Poland, today Ukraine. The J. pop. in 1921 was 126. The Jews were expelled to Kalusz for liquidation in Aug. 1942.

ZBARAZ Tarnopol dist., Poland, today Ukraine. J. settlement dates from the late 15th cent. The community grew in the first half of the 17th and built a synagogue. However, the community suffered grievously in the Chmielnicki massacres of 1648–49, the Turkish occupation of 1675, and the Haidamak raids of 1708. Known for its illustrious rabbis, the community was also one of the early Galician strongholds of Haskala. In 1890 the J. pop. of Z. stood at 3,631 (total 8,785), leveling off at just under 3,000 after WWI. Despite the straitened economic circumstances of the community between the World Wars, Zionist activity continued unabated and the Hebrew school, founded in 1907, flourished with over 500 pupils. Refugees swelled the J. pop. to 5,000 at the outbreak of WWII. The Soviet regime brought J. life to a standstill. The Germans entered Z. on 6 July 1941. On 6 Sept., 76 Jews, mainly intellectuals, were taken to the Lubyanki forest for execution after a selection in the municipal square. In June 1942, 600 elderly and sick Jews were led away toward Tarnopol to be murdered and in a mass *Aktion* on 31 Aug.–1 Sept. a few hundred more were deported to the Belzec death camp. After a ghetto had been set up further large-scale deportations to Belzec were car-

ried out in Oct. and Nov., with 1,000 victims each time. Over 1,000 more were murdered outside the town on 7 April 1943. The ghetto was liquidated on 8 June.

ZBOJNIA Bialystok dist., Poland. The J. pop. in 1921 was 109 (total 681). The Jews were apparently expelled by the Germans to the Lomzha ghetto in July 1941 and subsequently deported to Auschwitz.

ZBONSZYN (Dzbanszyn; Ger. Bentschen) Poznan dist., Poland. A community of 89 Jews was present in 1765, with most engaged in crafts. J. trade expanded in the 19th cent., mainly in the export of grain and cloth to Prussia. The J. pop. reached a peak of 307 (total 1,670) in 1840, dropping to a few dozen after WWI as a result of emigration. About 10,000 Jews of Polish nationality expelled from Germany arrived in the city in Oct. 1938. They were supported by the Joint Distribution Committee and the local community until all who remained were expelled by the Germans to forced labor camps in Sept. 1939 and later to extermination camps.

ZBOROV (Hung. Zboro) Slovakia, Czechoslovakia, today Republic of Slovakia. Jews were present in the late 17th cent. Their pop. grew following the arrival of Galician Jews in the latter half of the 18th cent. A small wooden synagogue was built in the 1780s. R. Moshe Yosef Teitelbaum (d. 1897) maintained ties with the hasidic courts of Galicia and ran a *talmud torah*. A *beit midrash* was also built in this period. The J. pop. climbed from 198 in 1828 to 337 in 1850 and 645 (total 2,246) in 1900. A new synagogue was erected in the early 20th cent. The synagogue was destroyed in WWI but a large *beit midrash* was built in its place. After WWI, Mizrachi and Agudat Israel were influential and Jews owned most of the town's businesses. In 1940, 479 Jews remained. A J. elementary school was opened. In 1941, the authorities closed down J. businesses. About 40 J. girls were deported to Auschwitz on 25 March 1942. Young men were sent to the Majdanek concentration camp a few days later and on 14 May, 370 Jews were deported to the Pulawy ghetto in the Lublin dist. (Poland). Another 100 were sent to Opole on 16 May and most perished.

ZBOROW Tarnopol dist., Poland, today Ukraine. Jews were first recorded in Z. in the 1680s, enjoying wide-ranging privileges. The town accommodated

First grade of the Tarbut elementary school in Zborow, Poland

both Hasidim and *Mitnaggedim* and the Hovevei Zion were active in the 1890s, when the J. pop. was about 2,000 (45% of the total). Many fled to the interior of the Austrian Empire in WWI never to return, the pop. dropping to 1,086 (total 3,730) in 1921. In the chaos of the early postwar period Jews organized in self-defense groups. Between the World Wars many Jews joined the professional class and the poor received support from former townsmen residing in the U.S. The Soviet annexation of Sept. 1939 forestalled a pogrom at the hands of Ukrainian villagers and instituted a Communist regime. The Germans arrived on 4 July 1941 and immediately executed over 1,000 J. men. Dozens of J. Communist activists were executed in Aug. 1941. The Jews suffered from disease and hunger through the winter and on 29 August 1942, 1,300 were deported to the Belzec death camp. In the fall Jews from the surrounding villages were brought to Z. and a ghetto was fenced off along two streets where people were crowded 10–15 to a room. On 9 April 1943, 2,300 Jews were rounded up, forced to dig their own graves

behind the local sports arena, and executed. In the final *Aktion* of 5 June 1943, the Germans met with armed resistance from the J. underground in the ghetto and only prevailed after burning down the buildings where the Jews were making their stand. The two forced labor camps that remained were liquidated later in the month. Some 600 Jews were burned alive.

ZBRIZH Kamenets-Podolski dist., Ukraine. The J. pop. was 376 in 1787 with 138 houses under J. ownership. A J. printing press was founded in 1812. In 1897 the J. pop. was 281, dropping to 31 in the Soviet period in 1926. The Germans occupied Z. in July 1941 and murdered the few Jews still there.

ZBUCZYN Lublin dist., Poland. Jews were probably present in the 15th cent., earning a livelihood by operating distilleries. The J. pop. was 156 (of a total 2,562) in 1897 and 102 in 1921. The few Jews there on the approach of the Germans in Sept. 1939 presumably fled to Soviet-held territory and to Siedlce.

Market in Zdunska Wola, Poland

ZDANA (Hung. Hernadzsadany) Slovakia, Czechoslovakia, today Republic of Slovakia. Jews probably settled in the 18th cent., reaching a peak pop. of 130 (total 762) in 1828. A synagogue was erected in the 1860s and the community's first rabbi, Yitzhak Kahana (d. 1899), headed a *talmud torah* and yeshiva. The J. pop. dropped to 96 in 1880 and 49 in 1941, with Jews owning a few stores and workshops. After the annexation to Hungary, the Jews were pushed out of their businesses and jobs and seized for forced labor. In mid-May 1944, they were deported to Auschwitz.

ZDOLBUNOW Volhynia dist., Poland. The J. pop. expanded rapidly after Z. became an important railroad junction in 1903, reaching 1,262 (total 7,279) in 1921. A Hebrew school was in operation. The Germans arrived on 30 June 1941 and on 7 Aug. murdered 380 J. men. The representative of the German company responsible for railroad buildings in the area, Hermann Graebe, did much to protect his 3,000 J. workers from his headquarters in Z., forging documents that

helped some escape. Through his efforts the liquidation of Z.'s ghetto was delayed until Oct. 1942.

ZDUNSKA WOLA Lodz dist., Poland. Jews first settled here in 1788 and were active in the development of the textile industry. The community was established officially in 1828 and a synagogue built in 1858. The J. pop. in 1897 was 7,252. The first political movement was Hovevei Zion, founded at the beginning of the 20th cent. Jews were also members of the Polish Socialist Party (P.P.S.) and the Bund began its activities in 1905. The J. pop. in 1931 was 8,814 (39% of the total). Jews owned 70 textile factories employing over 1,000 workers, half of whom were Jews. Of the 2,063 employees in industry and trades, 1,559 were Jews. Agudat Israel, founded in 1919, had the strongest political influence in the community. In 1929 a Hehalutz branch was established and it organized a training farm for Zionist youth pioneers. Z. was occupied by the Germans on 6–7 Sept. 1939. They destroyed the main synagogue and burned the Torah scrolls. In

1940 a ghetto was set up housing 8,000–9,000 Jews. About 1,000 fled to the Soviet Union, but were replaced by Jews expelled from surrounding towns. In 1941, through the intervention of the *Judenrat*, workshops were organized and a large farm that supplied fruit, vegetables, and milk was set up in the ghetto. In June–July 1941, about 1,000 J. males over the age of 14 were sent to forced labor camps in the Poznan region. Twice in 1942, on Purim and Shavuot (14 March and 6 May) ten men were hanged publicly, charged with smuggling food. On 24 Aug. 1942 the Jews were rounded up and about 1,000–1,200 were sent to the Lodz ghetto and 6,000–8,000 deported to the Chelmno death camp.

ZDZIECIOL   (Yid. Zhetl; Rus. Diatlovo) Nowogrodek dist., Poland, today Belarus. Jews settled here around 1580 and established a community by 1670, when the first synagogue was built. Hayyim ha-Kohen Rapoport, who served as rabbi (1720–29), eventually moved to Lwow, where he took part in a major disputation with the Frankists (1759). Those born in Z. included R. Yaakov Kranz (1740–1804), the celebrated "*Maggid* of Dubno," and R. Yisrael Meir ha-Kohen ("Hafetz Hayyim"; 1838–1933), the great talmudic authority and ethical writer. Plagued by fires and other disasters from 1743, the community numbered 3,033 (76% of the total) in 1897. With help from relief organizations, Z. revived after WWI and the J. pop. rose to around 3,450 (75%) in 1926. Of the 621 J. families in the town, 303 earned their livelihoods as artisans (especially in tailoring and shoemaking) and 210 from trade (170 shopkeepers and 40 merchants). Conditions woresened, however, as a result of heavy taxes and competition from government-backed local tradesmen. The community ran a hospital and old age home. The Zionists and other J. political groups were active. Over the years several hundred pupils attended the CYSHO Yiddish school established in 1921 and the Tarbut Hebrew school set up in 1929. Following the Soviet occupation (1939–41), the Germans entered Z. on 30 June 1941. Subsequently 120 prominent Jews were rounded up and murdered near Nowogrodek on 25 July and another 400 Jews were sent to the Dworzec labor camp on 15 Dec. The rest were confined to a ghetto on 22 Feb. 1942, where about 1,400 refugees swelled their number to 4,000. On 30 April, 1,000–1,200 inhabitants of the ghetto were executed in the Kurpiesze forest and on 6 Aug. 1942, the last 1,500–

2,000 Jews were murdered at the J. cemetery. About 800 Jews escaped to the woods, however, many joining the partisans or the Red Army. Over 100 died fighting the Nazis.

ZECKENDORF   Upper Franconia, Germany. The community was founded in 1654 and was the first seat of the Bamberg regional chief rabbinate. R. Shemuel of Mezrich (Poland) was the first chief rabbi (1658–65). In 1742 the synagogue burned down and a new one was built the following year. The J. pop. numbered 166 in 1837 (total 285), declining to 22 in 1933. On *Kristallnacht* (9–10 Nov. 1938), the synagogue was vandalized. All but one of the 18 Jews remaining in 1942 were deported to Izbica in the Lublin dist. (Poland) via Bamberg on 25 April.

ZEHDENICK   Brandenburg, Germany. The first evidence of a J. presence in Z. dates from 1680. The J. pop. was five families in 1801 and about 115 individuals in the mid-19th cent. A cemetery was established in 1766–67 and a synagogue at the beginning of the 19th cent. Although still numbering 82 members in 1880, the community, unable to form a *minyan* in 1888, was compelled to close the synagogue and affiliate itself to the Templin community. In June 1933, about four months after the Nazis assumed power, there were 27 Jews in Z. By May 1939, there were five. No further information about their fate is available. Of those who moved away from the town seeking refuge elsewhere, at least nine perished in concentration camps.

ZEILITZHEIM   Lower Franconia, Germany. Jews are mentioned in 1607 and a synagogue is known from 1672. A new synagogue was built in 1836 when the J. pop. was 70 (total 655), subsequently declining to 23 in 1933. On *Kristallnacht* (9–10 Nov. 1938), J. homes were vandalized and soon afterwards Jews were forced to sell their houses and fields. Eleven left for other German cities in 1935–39; seven were deported to Izbica in the Lublin dist. (Poland) via Wuerzburg on 25 April 1942 and two to the Theresienstadt ghetto on 23 Sept. 1942.

ZEIMELIS   (Yid. Zheiml) Siauliai dist., Lithuania. Dating from the 18th cent., the J. community was one of the oldest in Lithuania. In the 1880s, a violent dispute broke out over the choice of a rabbi, only set-

Zeimelis community receiving an important guest, Lithuania

tled in 1887 with the election of Avraham Yitzhak ha-Kohen Kook, later chief rabbi of Palestine. In 1897 the J. pop. was 679 (54% of the total). After WWI many Jews emigrated to the U.S., South Africa, and Palestine. There was considerable Zionist activity. The J. pop. in 1940 was 205. After the German invasion in June 1941, Lithuanian nationalists murdered all the Jews in a forest outside the town (on 8 Aug. 1941).

ZEITLOFS   Lower Franconia, Germany. Jews are known from the 16th cent. A new synagogue was dedicated in 1885 after the old one burned down. The J. pop. was 74 in 1890 (total 688) and 33 in 1933. All left by July 1938, 23 to other German cities, and the synagogue was sold.

ZELECHOW   Lublin dist., Poland. J. settlement commenced in the first half of the 17th cent. and an organized community was formed in the early 18th cent. Among its prominent rabbis was Levi Yitzhak of Berdichev, who was forced to leave by the *Mitnaggedim* in the 1780s. In the 19th cent., R. Yitzhak She-

lomo Goldberg founded a hasidic dynasty that lasted until the Holocaust. J. political activity commenced in the 1860s against the background of Polish nationalism. The Zionists and the Bund became active in the early 20th cent. The J. pop. rose to 2,184 in 1857 (total 3,412) and continued to expand as economic horizons broadened in 1863 with the construction of Russian army barracks, with J. merchants supplying the soldiers with goods. In the late 19th cent., Jews opened a number of factories, producing sugar, soda water, and alcoholic beverages. In WWI, economic conditions worsened and serious food and fuel shortages were felt. The Joint Distribution Committee along with numerous local mutual aid and welfare societies came to the assistance of the Jews after the war. The Zionists became the dominant social force in the community. Antisemitism intensified in the 1930s, accompanied by economic boycotts and occasional violence. The Germans entered the city on 12 Sept. 1939, burning down the synagogue the next day. When they retreated for several days, the Poles rioted against the Jews. The Germans returned and in Nov. a *Judenrat* was established, charged with fur-

Senatorska St., Zelechow, Poland

nishing forced labor and "contributions." In Oct. 1940, large numbers of J. refugees began to arrive. By late 1941, the ghetto pop. reached 13,000. About 500 Jews were sent to labor camps in Vilna and the Minsk area. On 30 Sept., most of the others were deported to the Treblinka death camp after around 300 of the sick and elderly together with children were murdered on the spot. Another 800 in hiding were rounded up later and executed. A small group of artisans who remained were murdered on 28 Feb. 1943. A partisan group in the area, commanded by Shemuel Olshak, engaged in effective operations against the Germans, including the liberation of a prisoner-of-war camp near Demblin-Irena.

ZELENOPOLE Zaporozhe dist., Ukraine. Jews from the Vitebsk and Vilna regions founded Z. as a J. colony in 1853. It reached a pop. of 557, mostly Jews, in the same year. In 1897 the J. pop. was 658 and in 1926 it was 476. A J. council (soviet) and J. school were active in the mid-1920s and a J. kolkhoz was founded nearby in the late 1920s, reaching a pop. of 400 (122 households) in the early 1930s. The

Germans captured Z. in Oct. 1941 and in late Dec. murdered 74 Jews.

ZELIEZOVCE (Hung. Zseliz) Slovakia, Czechoslovakia, today Republic of Slovakia. Jews were banned from settlement until the mid-19th cent. and apparently organized a community in the early 20th cent. The J. pop. was 49 in 1910 and about 140 (5% of the total) between the World Wars, with the Zionists and Agudat Israel active and most businesses in J. hands. In 1941, 23 Jews were sent to concentration camps after torture by the Hungarians. On 8 May 1944, the Germans transferred 127 Jews to the Levice ghetto, from where they were deported to Auschwitz on 12 June.

ZELL (Mosel) Rhineland, Germany. The J. pop. was 23 in 1808 and 55 (total 2,503) in 1885. A synagogue was erected in the mid-19th cent., also serving affiliated communities, while local Jews used the J. cemetery in Bullay. The J. pop. remained stable at 40–45 until WWI and then dropped to 33 in 1925. Most left in the Nazi era. At least one died in Auschwitz. The

Members of Po'alei Zion, Zelow, Poland

synagogue was vandalized on *Kristallnacht* (9–10 Nov. 1938).

ZELOW Lodz dist., Poland. Jews who settled here in the mid-19th cent. supplied yarn to the textile industry developed by Czech immigrants. The J. pop. in 1897 was 922 (31% of the total). All Zionist organizations, the Bund, and Agudat Israel had their affiliates there. Z. was occupied on 6 Sept. 1939. The number of Jews increased from 4,500 in Dec. 1940 (including 2,300 refugees) to 6,000–7,000 in March 1941. They were prominent in smuggling goods, mainly textiles, between the Warthegau and General Gouvernement areas. Those who were caught were sent to forced labor or to extermination camps. From June 1942, groups of able-bodied Jews were sent to the Lodz ghetto, from where they were eventually transported to Chelmno. In Sept. 1942 the remaining J. inhabitants of Z. were murdered locally or deported to extermination camps. After the war a small group of survivors returned to the town.

ZELTINGEN-RACHTIG Rhineland, Germany. In 1808, 33 Jews lived in Z. and 17 in R. In 1895, the combined pop. was 78. The community in Z., which had a synagogue by 1821, constituted the center for the two. In 1853, however, the R. community formed its own congregation, building a synagogue c. 1910. A common cemetery was opened in 1876. In 1933, the combined pop. was 45, dwindling to 18 by 1938. In 1937, the community attached itself to the Neumagen congregation. The synagogue in Z. was sold before *Kristallnacht* (9–10 Nov. 1938), while the one in R. was desecrated during the pogrom. By Aug. 1939, the last Jews left the town. However, 23 met their deaths after being trapped by the Nazis in their places of refuge.

ZELTS Odessa dist., Ukraine. Z. was the center of a regional council (soviet) with a single, successful J. kolkhoz founded in 1924 in a predominantly German area. Called Geretenysh, the kolkhoz included 40 J. households (150–160 people) in 1934. After the German occupation of 1941, the Jews of Z. shared the fate of the rest of the Jews of the area. Most were murdered, probably with the assistance of the local German pop.

ZELVA (Yid. Podzelve, Zelve) Ukmerge dist., Lithuania. The J. community in Z. was one of the oldest in Lithuania. The J. pop. in 1897 stood at 643 (70% of the total). During WWI Z.'s Jews were expelled, though most returned later. In municipal elections two of the 17 elected representatives were Jews. In the 1930s, a boycott of J. merchants by Lithuanians led many to emigrate. Those who remained received financial aid from relatives in the U.S. and South Africa. The Zionist movement won widespread support. The J. pop. in 1923 was 364 (58%). After the German conquest of 1941, all the Jews were murdered in the Pivonija forest on 5 Sept. 1941.

ZELWA Bialystok dist., Poland, today Belarus. J. merchants apparently settled in the 17th cent. The organized community dates from the 18th cent., numbering 522 in 1766 including the neighboring villages. Jews traded mainly in grain, cattle, and lumber. With the coming of the railroad in 1847, they built large warehouses near the railroad station as trade expanded at the yearly fair, also giving rise to J.-owned inns, restaurants, and tea houses. In 1885 a group of railroad maintenance workers staged a drunken pogrom, destroying property and beating Jews until fought off. In 1895 a third of the town was destroyed in a fire. In 1897 the J. pop. reached 1,844 (total 2,803). Haskala made inroads in the late 19th cent. and Hovevei Zion was active A Bund group formed in the early 20th cent. Many left for the U.S. and Canada as economic conditions deteriorated and an anti-J. atmosphere began to prevail. After WWI, when the J. pop. dropped to 1,319, a J. cooperative bank helped Jews get back on their feet but heavy taxes and competition from a government-supported grain cooperative made J. recovery difficult. Continued economic crisis, compounded by antisemitism in the 1930s, led many to emigrate to Canada, Australia, Argentina, and Chile. Hebrew and Yiddish schools were opened and the Zionist youth movements were active. Under Soviet rule in 1939–41, stores were nationalized and artisans organized into cooperatives. With the arrival of the Germans in early July 1941, 50 Jews of the educated class were taken to the forest and executed. Jews were subjected to forced labor and prevented from obtaining the essentials of life. Seven butchers were publicly hanged for trading in meat. A ghetto was established and on 2 Nov. 1942 most were transported to the Wolkowysk transit camp and three weeks later to the Treblinka death camp. Dozens of the young were able to escape to the forest before the *Aktion*.

ZEMAICIU-NAUMIESTIS (Yid. Naishtot-Tavrig, Naishtot-Sugint) Taurage dist., Lithuania. Jews first settled here in the 17th cent. In the 1880s Zionism took root, though it had many opponents. Many emigrated to South Africa, England, and the U.S. The J. pop. in 1897 was 1,438 (59% of the total). In the 1930s there were antisemitic incidents and a boycott against J. businesses, leading to further emigration. The J. pop. in 1940 was about 120 families. After the German invasion in June 1941, all the Jews were put in a ghetto. The elderly and sick were murdered in the Siaudviciai valley. J. males were sent to the Silute labor camp for more than two years, some being killed. The women were murdered in Sept. 1941 in the Siaudviciai valley. In July 1943 the remaining men were sent to Auschwitz. Most of the others perished in Warsaw, where they had been sent to remove the ghetto debris, and in the Dachau concentration camp.

ZEMBIN Minsk dist., Belorussia. Jews probably settled in the late 18th cent., numbering 103 in 1811 and 1,037 (total 1,186) in 1897. In 1926, under the Soviets, the J. pop. dropped to 838. Many Jews earned their livelihoods at kolkhozes set up around the town, each accommodating dozens of families. A J. school and J. rural council (soviet) were also active. The Germans arrived in early July 1941 and on 18 Aug. murdered 927 Jews from Z. and the surrounding area.

ZEMIANSKA OLCA (Hung. Nemesolcsa) Slovakia, Czechoslovakia, today Republic of Slovakia. A community of over 100 with a synagogue and cemetery existed in the early 20th cent., dropping to 82 in 1930. Most Jews were deported to Auschwitz in June 1944.

ZEMPLENAGARD Zemplen dist., Hungary. Jews probably settled in the early 19th cent. and numbered 137 in 1930. They were deported to Auschwitz via Satoraljaujhely on 16–25 May 1944.

ZEMUN Croatia, Yugoslavia, today Republic of Croatia. Jews first settled in the first half of the 18th cent. and in the second half, Sephardi and Ashkenazi communities were established. During the 18th and

19th cents. Z. absorbed J. refugees from Zagreb. The Jews were sometimes discriminated against and restricted in their dealings, and in 1833 an attempt was made to force children to convert to Christianity. In 1862 unlimited J. settlement was permitted and in 1868 equal rights were granted. Between 1863 and 1900 the J. pop. grew from 211 to 955 (total 15,608). Notable members of the community were the Zionist precursor R. Yehuda ben Shelomo Hai Alkalai and the grandparents of Theodor Herzl. The former was the spiritual leader of Z.'s Sephardi community from 1823 until the 1870s, when he settled in Jerusalem. In the 20th cent., Zionism dominated the community. In the Holocaust the Jews were persecuted by the Ustase, and in summer 1942 they were taken to death camps. Some youths joined the partisans. Of the 585 Jews in Z. in 1940, 500 perished.

ZENICA   Bosnia-Hercegovina, Yugoslavia, today Republic of Bosnia. Jews first settled here in the 18th cent.; a community was established in 1880. All the 270 Jews there in 1931 (total 7,632) perished in the Holocaust.

ZEPCE   Bosnia-Hercegovina, Yugoslavia, today Republic of Bosnia. The first Jews settled in the 1820s. The J. pop. in 1931 was 218 (total 7,192). Most died in the Jasenovac death camp.

ZERBST   Anhalt, Germany. There is evidence of a J. presence in Z. from the first half of the 14th cent. and occasional references from the 15th cent. It was not until the 17th cent. that resettlement took place. A cemetery was established in the second half of the 18th cent. and a synagogue in 1794. In 1833 the community reached a peak pop. of 122. By 1933, there were 90–100 Jews living in Z. On *Kristallnacht* (9–10 Nov. 1938), the synagogue was looted and set on fire, homes and businesses were wrecked, and several J. residents were abused. By May 1939, 36 Jews were still living in the town. In April 1942, 34 were deported to Auschwitz and the Theresienstadt ghetto, while two, married to non-Jews, survived in Z.

ZERIND   (Hung. Nagyzerend) S. Transylvania dist., Rumania. A J. community was organized in 1842 and served as the spiritual center of the Arad and Bihor areas. R. Yeshayahu Jungreisz served the community from the beginning of the 20th cent. The J. pop. in 1930 stood at 89 (4% of the total). On 25 June 1941, the J. pop. was transferred to Arad, never to return to Z.

ZEVEN   Hanover, Germany. Numbering 22 in 1844, the Jews of Z. maintained their own prayer house and burial ground after amalgamating with the Bremervoerde community in 1858. Their pop. grew to 41 in 1928 and a new regional synagogue was dedicated in 1937. The Nazis vandalized its interior, burning the Torah scrolls on *Kristallnacht* (9–10 Nov. 1938). About ten Jews emigrated and 19 were deported to the Minsk ghetto. By 1941 the community had ceased to exist.

ZEVENAAR   Gelderland dist., Holland. The J. presence in Z. dates back to 1634; a community was organized in the early 19th cent. A synagogue was built in 1833 and the community numbered 94 in 1854. The J. pop. was 53 in 1941 (total 7,520). During the Holocaust 32 Jews were deported to camps; 14 survived in hiding.

ZGIEZH   Lodz dist., Poland. Jews first appeared in the mid-18th cent., but a community was organized only around 1827. In 1826 Jews were ordered to move to a special quarter of the city and the congestion and appalling sanitary conditions led to an outbreak of cholera in 1848. Jews were attracted to the industrial city and opened textile factories. Jews were also employed in transporting people and goods. The J. pop. in 1897 was 3,543 (18.5% of the total). In 1860 a large stone synagogue was erected and R. Shalom Tzvi Hirsch ha-Kohen opened a yeshiva that attracted hundreds of students. In the early 20th cent. Jews were active in the Polish Social Democratic Party and participated in the 1905 revolution. A government school for J. boys and girls was founded in 1885 and by 1918 five J. schools were operating. The first reformed *heder* was opened by the writer Yaakov Binyamin Katzenelson, whose son, the poet Itzhak, was born here. Antisemitic acts were widespread between the World Wars. Jews were attacked in the streets and their businesses boycotted. In 1937, Polish workers initiated a strike in three factories protesting the employment of Jews. About 4,800 Jews were living in Z. in 1939. When German troops occupied the city on 7 Sept. 1939 they arrested several hundred Jews and kept them in the church compound for two days without food and water, demanding large sums of ransom

Members of Zgiezh community council, Poland

money. Soldiers pillaged J. possessions and religious objects from their homes, ransacked their factories, and demanded payments of hundreds of thousands of zloty. Many Jews fled. In Nov. 1939 the Germans burned down the synagogue and the *beit midrash*. The cemetery was desecrated. On 26 Dec. 1939, almost all the remaining 2,500 Jews were rounded up and transported to Glowno, and from there to the Warsaw ghetto and to the Treblinka death camp.

ZGURITA   Bessarabia, Rumania, today Republic of Moldova. This J. settlement was founded in 1853. In 1930 the J. pop. was 2,541. On 3 July 1941 the Jews were deported to Transnistria and then moved from place to place, almost all dying or being killed on the way.

ZHABNO   Cracow dist., Poland. Jews first settled in the late 16th cent. and enjoyed wide-ranging privileges, constituting a majority of the pop. in the mid-18th cent. The burden of heavy taxation under Austrian rule from 1772 eroded the community's prosperity and a major fire in 1888 left many homeless and without a livelihood. A Baron Hirsch school was in operation from

1898 and the Zionists became active at the turn of the cent. In 1890 the J. pop. stood at 696 (total 1,420), but it dropped to 361 after WWI. Half the town's houses and much property were destroyed in the fighting and anti-J. riots in 1918 were accompanied by pillaging. After the German captured the town in Sept. 1939 a regime of forced labor was instituted, mostly on the neighboring Polish estates. A ghetto was set up in May 1942, swelled by refugees. All but 40 of the 700 Jews there were deported to the Belzec death camp in Sept.

ZHABOKRICH   Vinnitsa dist., Ukraine. Jews numbered 41 in 1765 and 1,307 (total 6,252) in 1897. Many Jews were beaten and robbed in a pogrom in late Oct. 1917. In 1926, the J. pop. was 924. Among the breadwinners, 41% were unemployed and the rest were tradesmen, white-collar workers, and farmers. A J. school was open throughout most of the 1920s and 1930s. The Germans occupied the town on 22 July 1941 and on 27–29 July about 435 Jews were executed in the city beside freshly dug pits. After the town was annexed to Transnistria in the fall, the Rumanians expelled hundreds of Jews from Bukovina and Bessarabia

Students of talmud torah, *Zhitomir, Ukraine (The Central Archive for the History of the Jewish People, Jerusalem/photo courtesy of Yad Vashem, The Holocaust Martyrs' and Heroes' Remembrance Authority, Jerusalem)*

there. About 40% of them died of starvation, disease, and the cold. On 1 Sept. 1943, 245 were still alive.

ZHARNOW Lodz dist., Poland. Jews were not permitted to live here until the 1790s. By 1897 the 1,171 Jews constituted 57% of the pop. In 1921 the J. pop. was 911. In May 1942, the Germans executed the community's leaders because a Communist was found hiding in the town. In Oct. 1942, 2,500 refugees were brought to Z. and together with the local Jews transported to Opoczno and then to the Treblinka death camp.

ZHELEZNOVODSK Stavropol territory, Russia. The Germans murdered the Jews of Z. on 10 Sept. 1942 at Mineralnyie Vody, together with Jews from the neighboring settlements (Yessentuki, Kislovodsk, Piatigorsk) and J. refugees who had arrived after the outbreak of war between the Soviet Union and Nazi Germany.

ZHGOW Lodz dist., Poland. In 1921 the 93 Jews constituted 51% of the inhabitants. In WWII they were

presumably deported to General Gouvernement territory.

ZHITKOVICHI Polesie dist., Belorussia. Despite a residence ban introduced in 1882, the J. pop. reached 293 (total 1,220) in 1897. J. residence was officially permitted in 1903. In 1918 the Balakhovich brigade staged a pogrom against the Jews, pillaging 400 J. homes and murdering four. Most Jews earned their livelihoods in trade and crafts. A J. kolkhoz founded in 1925 supported 40 families. A J. elementary school (four grades) operated until the late 1930s. In 1939, the J. pop. was 898. The Germans occupied the town on 20 July 1941. Some Jews managed to flee. About 150 were murdered in two *Aktions*, in Dec. 1941 and Jan. 1942.

ZHITOMIR Zhitomir dist., Ukraine. Jews settled in the early 18th cent. and numbered 346 in 1751 and 1,261 in 1791. In fall 1753, 33 Jews, including the rabbi from Pavoloch and a number of wealthy Jews from the area, were tried in a blood libel; 13 were executed after severe suffering and the rest forced to con-

Music club in the Jewish school of Zhitomir, Ukraine, 1938 (State Central Photo and Film Archive, Kiev/photo courtesy of Yad Vashem, The Holocaust Martyrs' and Heroes' Remembrance Authority, Jerusalem)

vert. In 1804, Z. was made the capital of the Volhynia dist. The Slavuta printing press moved to the city in 1837 and after the general shutdown of Hebrew printing presses in 1845, it remained one of the two still operating in Russia (the other being in Vilna). A state rabbinical seminary was opened in 1848, becoming a teachers' college in 1873. The writers Hayyim Zelig Slonimski and A. Zweifel and the poet Avraham Gottlober served on the faculty. A vocational school, the first in Russia, was opened in 1862 but was closed down by the authorities in 1885 together with the teachers' college. In 1897, the J. pop. was 30,738 (total 65,422). Of J. breadwinners, 45% were artisans, 30% in trade, and the rest in services. Mendele Mokher Seforim lived in the city in 1864-1882, producing his two greatest novels there: *Susati* (*Di Kliatshe* or "The

Nag") and *Masot Binyamin ha-Shelishi* ("Travels of Benjamin the Third"). The playwright and father of the J. theater Avraham Goldfaden also lived there and Hayyim Nahman Bialik spent his childhood in the city. The community had 54 *hadarim*, a *talmud torah*, and five private schools for girls. In the early 1920s, it also maintained a hospital, old age home, loan fund, and library. In a pogrom staged on 24–25 April 1905, 20 Jews were killed and over 100 seriously injured despite the intervention of J. self-defense groups. Additional pogroms occurred during the civil war (1918–21), with 317 Jews murdered and many injured by the Petlyura gangs on 22–26 March 1919. Polish soldiers murdered several dozen more Jews in early summer 1920. In the early 1920s, under the Soviets, Zionist youth groups such as Hashomer Hatzair,

Deror, and Tze'irei Tziyyon were active clandestinely, until many of their members were apprehended and either exiled or deported. In addition to the Yiddish elementary and secondary schools in operation, ORT opened three vocational schools in 1921, where shoemaking and carpentry were taught to the boys and sewing to girls. Weaving, tailoring, printing, and metalworking courses were also available. A three-year J. teachers' college was opened in 1925. By 1938, there were 512 graduates and enrollment stood at 340. There were also five J. schools at this time. The Shalom Aleichem J. National Theater of Z. operated from 1934, touring the towns of the dist. and the J. kolkhozes of the J. autonomous region in the southern Ukraine. The poet David Hofstein and the writer Asher Shvartzman were associated with the city and the Soviet army commander Yan Gamarnik, Bialik's brother-in-law, grew up there. In 1926-29, one of the local law courts transacted its deliberations in Yiddish. A J. kolkhoz was located on the outskirts of the city on the site of a J. colony from the time of Czar Nicholas. In 1939, the J. pop. of Z. was 29,503. The Germans captured the city on 9 July 1941. Some Jews managed to flee. The rest were confined in a ghetto and ordered to wear the yellow star on their sleeves. In July–Aug. 1941, about 4,000 were transported to the Dovzhik area and executed. Of the remaining Jews, 3,145 were murdered on 19 Sept. and 1,600 on 11 Oct., including 65 from the municipal home for the disabled and 80 from a children's home. The executions were carried out in the Vidumka area and at the Bogunia prisoner-of-war camp.

ZHIZDRA   Oriol dist., Russia. J. settlement dates from the mid-19th cent. The J. pop. was 554 in 1926 and 207 (total 8,109) in 1939. The Germans occupied the town in Oct. 1941 and murdered the few remaining Jews in late fall or early winter 1941.

ZHLOBIN   Gomel dist., Belorussia. The J. pop. rose from 268 in 1766 to 1,597 in 1847 and 1,760 in 1897. A devastating fire in 1882 destroyed all but ten houses in the town. All the communities in the area helped Z. recover. In 1923, under the Soviets, J. artisans formed an association. In 1926, 40 members of Hehalutz were active. A J. elementary school also operated. Thirty-five J. families worked at two nearby kolkhozes. In 1939 the J. pop. was 3,709. The Germans occupied Z. in Aug. 1941. Many Jews were evacuated before-

hand. In Sept., a ghetto was established under a regime of forced labor and abuse. On 12 April 1942, the 1,200 Jews there were executed in a field between Z. and the village of Lebedievka. Children were thrown into the burial pits alive. On 14 April, 282 Jews from the Streshin ghetto and 198 Jews from the settlements of the Streshin region were murdered at Z.

ZHMERINKA   Vinnitsa dist., Ukraine. The J. pop. was 2,396 (total 15,711) in 1897. On 27 April 1881, many J. homes and stores were looted and destroyed in a pogrom. Another pogrom was staged on 20–21 Oct. 1905 and on 3 July 1919, the Petlyura gangs attacked the Jews. Between the World Wars, under the Soviets, most Jews worked in artisan cooperatives or on kolkhozes. A J. elementary school was active. In 1939, the J. pop. was 4,630. The Germans occupied Z. on 17 July 1941. After the city was annexed to Transnistria in early Sept., the Rumanians concentrated the Jews in a ghetto, whose pop. reached 2,000–3,000. Jews also arrived after fleeing German-administered areas like the town of Brailow, as well as from Bukovina and Bessarabia after being expelled from there. The *Judenrat* that was established, along with a J. police force and various relief organizations, could not prevent the execution of 286 Jews from Brailow. Many local Jews survived. Almost 1,000 still resided in the ghetto in June 1944. The Jews of Z. later became known for a letter they sent to *Pravda* requesting that the Soviet authorities allow them to emigrate to Israel.

ZHMIEV   Kharkov dist., Ukraine. Jews numbered 21 in 1897 and 91 (total 6,956) in 1939. All were murdered after the German occupation of 22 Oct. 1941.

ZHMIGROD NOWY   Cracow dist., Poland. Jews were present in 1410 and within a cent. formed one of the largest communities in the region. Despite a major fire in 1577 and the Cossack and Swedish wars in the mid-17th cent. the community enjoyed a golden age up to the mid-18th cent. when the pop. reached 1,926 (including the surrounding villages). A yeshiva was in operation and the rabbinical seat carried much esteem. Under the Austrians a decline set in. Emigration resulting from straitened economic circumstances and the experiences of WWI further reduced the pop. from 1,330 (half the total) in 1880 to 940 in 1921. From the second half of the 19th cent., Zanz Hasidism came to the fore and maintained a local court. The decline continued between the World Wars. The German occupation brought forced labor and an influx of refugees. Two thousand Jews were crowded into a ghetto in the first half of 1942. On 7 July, after a selection, 1,250 of those defined as "unfit for work" – women, children, the sick, and the elderly – were executed. The able-bodied were consigned to the Zaslawie and Plaszow concentration camps and the remainder to the Belzec death camp.

ZHNIN Poznan dist., Poland. J. settlement was prohibited by the Church until annexation to Prussia in 1772. As merchants, the Jews contributed significantly to the economic development of the town, reaching a pop. of 428 (total 2,037) in 1871 before declining through emigration. The ten who remained in Sept. 1939 were expelled by the Germans to General Gouvernement territory.

ZHOLKIEWKA Lublin dist., Poland. Jews are mentioned in the 17th cent. but only developed a community in the 18th cent. The J. pop. rose to 1,476 (total 2,110) in 1897. Jews opened hide-processing shops and a flour mill and traded in farm produce and local factory wares. In the early 20th cent., their livelihoods were undermined by the creation of a Polish cooperative. The Zionists, the Bund, and Agudat Israel were all active between the World Wars as economic conditions continued to deteriorate. The J. pop. in 1921 was 1,308. In 1938, a fire destroyed the whole town. As the Germans and Russians contended for control of Z. in Sept.–Oct. 1939, local antisemites staged a pogrom leaving 20 Jews dead. In early 1940, the Germans set up a *Judenrat*. Hundreds of young Jews were sent to labor camps while refugees brought the J. pop. up to 2,300 by May 1942. On 15 May, 1,000 were deported to the Sobibor death camp; the rest were sent to the Belzec death camp via Izbica in the Lublin dist. (Poland) in Oct. 1942. The head of the Z. *Judenrat*, Leon Pelhandler, was among the leaders of an uprising at Sobibor.

ZHOLYNIA (Yid. Zhelin) Lwow dist., Poland. Founded in the 18th cent. the community achieved its maximum size of somewhat over 1,000 (more than half the total) with the arrival of R. Avraham Yosef Igra and his hasidic court in the 1880s. Subsequently, antisemitism, straitened economic circumstances, and the rigors of WWI reduced the J. pop. by 50%,

though social and cultirial life flourished under increasing Zionist influence. With the coming of the Germans, most of the community fled to Soviet-occupied territory; the remainder were apparently expelled later and ended their days in the Belzec death camp.

ZHOVTEN (until 1928, Petroverovka) Odessa dist., Ukraine. Jews settled in the late 19th cent. and numbered 819 in 1897 and 1,557 (total 1,608) in 1926. In the Soviet period, a J. rural council (soviet) was established as well as a J. elementary school (with six operating in council territory by 1932). Several artisan cooperatives with mostly J. members were founded under the Soviets and from the mid-1920s a number of J. colonies were established in the vicinity (Friling, Frayland, Ratenfeld). Frayland had 38 J. families in the late 1920s and Ratenfeld had 60 in the early 1930s along with a J. school (apparently two grades). A farm collective for 59 J. families (258 people) was set up in the J. colony of Rayzenfeld in the area. In 1939 the J. pop. of Z. was 470. The Germans captured the town on 7 Aug. 1941. In the same month, 28 Jews were murdered at the J. Nit Gedayget kolkhoz in the Ratenfeld colony. Another 22 were murdered in Aug. on the road to Tsebrikovka along with a few elderly Jews at the local J. cemetery. In early Sept., 25 more Jews were executed at Z. In all, over 200 people from the area were murdered during the Nazi occupation, most of them probably Jews.

ZHUKOVA Oriol dist., Russia. Jews probably settled in the late 19th cent. and numbered 674 in 1926 and 551 (total 10,097) in 1939. A J. school was in operation in the mid-1920s. Many of the 1,000 people the Germans murdered in Z. in the course of the war were Jews.

ZHURAVICHI Gomel dist., Belorussia. The J. pop. was 1,060 in 1847 and 1,606 in 1897. Most Jews engaged in petty trade; a few were cattle or grain merchants. In 1905, the Jews were attacked in a pogrom but without loss of life. In 1923, under the Soviets, the J. pop. was 938, dropping to 616 in 1939 (total 2,397). In 1929, 50% of J. breadwinners were artisans. Fifty-three J. families worked at nearby kolkhozes. A J. elementary school (four grades) was active. The Germans captured Z. on 14 Aug. 1941. In late Aug., they confined the Jews to two camps on the outskirts of the town and put them to forced labor repairing roads. In early Dec., they murdered 72 Jews aged 16–60. In a second *Aktion* on 1 Jan. 1942, the Nazis and the local police executed the remaining 171 Jews at Starina. Young children were thrown into the burial pits alive.

ZHVANIEC Kamenets-Podolski dist., Ukraine. The J. pop. included 1,134 poll tax payers in 1765 and reached 3,353 in 1897, most engaging in petty trade and crafts. A self-defense group was formed to counter antisemitic outbursts. Most Jews were Hasidim (Sadagora, Boyan, Husyatin). In the early 20th cent., Po'alei Zion and the Bund became active. The J. pop. was 1,383 in 1926. Local Jews founded a kolkhoz and artisan cooperatives where most worked. The Germans captured Z. on 5 July 1941. On 1 Sept., the Nazis murdered 1,224 Jews from Z. and its environs. The rest were sent to the Kamenets-Podolski labor camp. The last Jews of Z. were murdered in Nov. 1942.

ZHYRARDOW Warsaw dist., Poland. The first Jews settled in the early 1850s, buying up flax from the peasants and selling it to textile factories, whose goods they marketed. Jews also engaged in crafts and traded in forest products. A synagogue was erected in 1909. By 1921 the J. pop. stood at 2,547 (about 10% of the total), with Jews entering light industry (textiles, garments, hide processing, soft drinks) and providing services to vacationers arriving at the city's resort area. Between the World Wars the Zionists expanded their activity, preparing young laborers and artisans for *aliya*. A number of J. schools (Yavne, Beth Jacob, a WIZO kindergarten) served hundreds of children while hundreds more attended public schools. The Germans captured the city on 12 Sept. 1939. In Oct. about 3,000 Jews were confined to a ghetto and a *Judenrat* was appointed. On 14 April 1940 (Passover eve) the Jews were attacked and pillaged by hundreds of *Volksdeutsche*. By Jan. 1941 refugees had swelled the J. pop. to 5,000. All were expelled to the Warsaw ghetto on 1–2 Feb. 1941.

ZHYWIEC (Yid. Zeiwush) Cracow dist., Poland. Z. was the only Galician and republican Polish town where the 1603 ban on J. settlement was strictly enforced almost until WWII, thus confining Jews to the town's Zablowce suburb, where 624 resided alongside 3,000 Poles and Germans in 1921 (with another 5,320

non-Jews in the town proper). Jews there were regarded as "enlightened," though between the World Wars the traditional and hasidic pop. increased. The community was one of the wealthiest and best organized in W. Galicia, with some of the largest industrial plants in the country (for chemicals, lumber, hides, cigarette paper). Zionist activity was widespread with Bnei Akiva, founded in 1926, the leading youth movement and the Zionists controlling the community council. The pride of the community was its Baron Hirsch school accommodating most of the community's children in seven grades. Anti-J. agitation orchestrated by the Endecja Party (National Democrats) characterized the period, with economic consequences. The Germans took the town early in Sept. 1939 and shortly thereafter expelled the Jews to General Gouvernement territory, where they reached Cracow and other nearby settlements. From 1943 to Jan. 1945, Z. was the site of a labor camp.

ZICHNA (Nea-zihna, Ziliahovo) Macedonia, Greece. The earliest records of a J. presence date from the 14th cent. In WWII, the village was under Bulgarian rule and its 18 Jews were deported to death camps. None survived.

ZIDIKAI (Yid. Zhidik) Mazeikiai dist., Lithuania. Jews first settled here in the 17th cent. and its wooden synagogue built in 1780 was one of the first of its kind in Lithuania. Isolation made the community resistant to new ideas. In 1897 the J. pop. was 914 (73% of the total). Agudat Israel was active before WWI. The general poverty induced emigration to the U. S. and South Africa and, after WWI, to the larger cities in Lithuania. During WWI the Jews were expelled, only some of whom returned. The J. pop. in 1941 was 150. After Germany's invasion of the Soviet Union in June 1941 all the Jews were detained in the *beit midrash* for a week without food or water. In Aug. they were murdered by the Lithuanians.

ZIEGENHAIN Hesse–Nassau, Germany. After the Black Death persecutions of 1348–49 no Jews lived there until the 17th cent. The Jews opened a synagogue in 1840 and an elementary school in 1870. The J. pop. was 103 (6% of the total) in 1880. The community was affiliated with the rabbinate of Marburg. Anti-J. incitement and violence grew from 1904. The community declined to 53 in 1933 and disposed of its synagogue, most Jews leaving before *Kristallnacht* (9–10 Nov. 1938). Some 2,000 J. Displaced Persons housed nearby after WWII emigrated to Palestine.

ZIELENZIG   (Pol. Sulecin) Brandenburg, Germany, today Poland. The J. community grew from 24 individuals in 1801 to 147 in 1880. It maintained a synagogue and a cemetery. When the Nazis came to power in 1933, there were 82 Jews in the town. No further information about their fate under Nazi rule is available.

ZIELONA   Stanislawow dist., Poland, today Ukraine. The J. pop. in 1921 was 112. The Jews were expelled to Nadworna for liquidation in May 1942

ZIELUN   Warsaw dist., Poland. A small community existed in the 19th cent. and numbered 366 (total 839) in 1921. The 130 Jews remaining after post-WWI emigration were expelled by the Germans to the Mlawa ghetto in late 1941.

ZIERENBERG   Hesse–Nassau, Germany. Established in 1600, the J. community maintained an elementary school from 1837 to 1922 and numbered 132 (7% of the total) in 1861. It was affiliated with the rabbinate of Kassel and opened a new synagogue in 1899. Only 53 Jews remained in 1933. The Nazis destroyed the synagogue on *Kristallnacht* (9–10 Nov. 1938) and by 1939 all the Jews had left.

ZIERIKZEE   Zeeland dist., Holland. Jews lived here in the early 19th cent. and the community reached a peak pop. of 91 in 1860. The J. pop. in 1941 was 27 (total 6,902). Most were transferred to Amsterdam during WWII.

ZIEZMARIAI   (Yid. Zhezhmer) Troki dist., Lithuania. Jews first settled in Z. in the 16th cent. Zionism here predated the modern Zionist movement. In 1897 the J. pop. was 1,628 (58% of the total). Between the World Wars the J. community was helped finan-

Jewish orphanage in Ziezmariai, Lithuania

Young Maccabi members with Maccabi Seniors, Zilina, Slovakia, 1935

cially by former residents in the U.S. The community maintained a Hebrew school and library and sponsored Zionist youth groups. Many emigrated to the U.S., Uruguay, and Palestine. The J. pop. in 1940 was about 200 families. After the German invasion in June 1941, heads of J. families were taken to Kaisiadorys and executed. Men and women were sent to forced labor. On 27 Aug. 1941 all the men were taken to the Strosiunai forest and shot. The next day the women and children were killed there. The Germans established a labor camp here in 1943 for Jews from small ghettoes in the border areas of Lithuania and Belorussia. In May, 700 Jews were transferred to the Kovno ghetto.

ZILINA   (Hung. Zsolna) Slovakia, Czechoslovakia, today Republic of Slovakia. Jews from Varin began

to settle in the 1820s and an independent community was formed in 1852. The coming of the railroad brought economic prosperity and an influx of Jews, increasing the J. pop. to 619 in 1880 and 1,024 in 1900. A J. elementary school was opened in 1860 and a synagogue was consecrated in 1865. The congregation became Neologist after the split in 1869. A new 400-seat synagogue was built in 1881 and the J. school reached an attendance of 345, including 75 non-Jews. In 1912, a separate Orthodox congregation was formed, officially recognized in 1923. The Orthodox built their own synagogue and maintained separate community services for the congregation's 90-family membership but shared the school. The J. pop. rose to 2,006 (total 11,996) in 1919 and 2,919 in 1940. Jews served on the municipal council and as public officials. They owned 250 business establishments (the large majority) and 77 workshops in 1922. They owned wood-processing factories and were well represented in the professional class (12 of the city's 17 doctors; 22 of its 31 lawyers; 13 engineers; six pharmacists). Among the Zionists, WIZO was the most prominent organization with hundreds of members. The Maccabi sports club also attracted hundreds and Z. hosted the national Maccabiah Games in 1937. Most youngsters joined Zionist youth movements. After the establishment of the Slovakian state in March 1939, Jews were forced out of public positions and their 448 businesses. Dozens were seized for forced labor. On 27–28 March 1942, 100 J. girls were deported to Auschwitz and 120 young men to the Majdanek concentration camp. In the spring and summer, families were transferred to the local concentration camp and deported to Auschwitz and the death camps in the Lublin dist. (Poland). In all, 85% of local Jews were deported in 1942 and from late March to 20 Oct. nearly 59,000 Jews passed through the Z. concentration camp en route to the death camps. In fall 1944, the Germans seized those who remained and sent them to Auschwitz. A few dozen Jews joined the partisans and the Czech army. The postwar community numbered 531 in 1948. Nearly half emigrated to Israel or other places in 1949 and a few dozen remained through the 1990s.

ZILUPE (Yid. Rozinovsk) Latgale dist., Latvia. The J. community began c. 1900 with the founding of the town and grew to around 500 between the World Wars. The J. pop. dropped from 70–75% to 20% of the total when surrounding villages became part of the municipality in the mid-1930s. Economic conditions improved in the mid-1920s. Jews owned 59 of the town's 69 stores and a few merchants were engaged in the grain, flax, and lumber trade. A J. public school was opened in 1923. The Zionists with their youth movements were the dominant force in the community, sending a few dozen pioneers to Palestine. Under the nationalistic Ulmanis regime (from 1934), antisemitism began to manifest itself publicly and J. businesses were undermined by government support of the peasant cooperatives. Russian rule (1940–41) brought nationalization of J. enterprises. The Germans arrived around the end of June 1941. A number of J. families managed to flee to the Soviet Union. The rest were killed with Latvian participation.

ZIMMERSRODE (now part of Neuental) Hesse-

Nassau, Germany. Established around 1646, this regional community had an ancient J. cemetery and numbered 67 (11% of the total) in 1895. It was affiliated with the rabbinate of Kassel. The J. pop. declined to 39 in 1933 and by 1941 no Jews remained; at least 12 perished in the Holocaust.

ZINKOV (I) Kamenets-Podolski dist., Ukraine. Jews are first mentioned in 1526. In 1648 and 1651, Chmielnicki's Cossacks attacked them and injured many. The Haidamaks staged a pogrom against the Jews in 1702. The J. pop. was 522 in 1765 and 3,719 (53% of the total) in 1897. From the early 19th cent., Z. was one of the leading centers of Hasidism in Podolia. In the 1920s and 1930s, under the Soviets, a J. council and kolkhoz were active. In 1939, the J. pop. was 2,248. The Germans occupied Z. in July 1941. A ghetto and *Judenrat* were established and on 9 May 1942, 600 Jews were murdered. Another 1,882 were executed on 9–10 July and 9 Aug. 1942. Two hundred skilled J. workers were left in a labor camp. Within a short while, 150 of them were murdered. The rest were brought to Dunayevtsy and executed.

ZINKOV (II) Poltava dist., Ukraine. Jews settled in the early 19th cent. and numbered 1,263 (total 10,443) in 1897. Their pop. dropped to 142 in 1939. The Germans first occupied the town on 9 Oct. 1941 and then for a second time later in the month. Presumably they murdered the Jews early in the occupation.

ZINTEN (Rus. Kornevo) East Prussia, Germany, today Russia. The first Jew was allowed to settle in Z. in 1810. By 1817, the J. pop. was 70 individuals; in 1880, 80; and in 1925, 43. A synagogue was consecrated in 1869; a cemetery existed from the early days of the community. When the Nazis came to power in 1933, there were 32 Jews in Z. By April 1937, only four families were left. In Sept. 1937, the synagogue was sold. No information about the fate of the community is available.

ZIRNDORF Middle Franconia, Germany. An organized community existed in the late 16th cent., concentrated in a J. quarter. The synagogue was rebuilt in 1834 and the J. pop. stood at 100 in 1837 (total 1,690). Most of the Jews engaged in trade (cattle, textiles) and maintained a satisfactory economic and social position

*Great Synagogue of Zinkov, Ukraine, 19th cent. (Beth Hatefutsoth Photo Archive, Tel Aviv/photo courtesy of Yad Vashem, The Holocaust Martyrs'
and Heroes' Remembrance Authority, Jerusalem)*

until the spread of Bavarian antisemitism after WWI. In
1933 the J. pop. numbered 64 (total 7,069). Up to Nov.
1938, 24 emigrated, including 17 to the U.S., and 12
left for other German cities. After *Kristallnacht* (9–10
Nov. 1938), the rest dispersed, mainly to Nuremberg
and Fuerth.

ZITTAU   Saxony, Germany. From 1400 up to 1434
there is evidence of a small community maintaining a
prayer room. Resettlement commenced only in the
1860s or 1870s. A cemetery was established in 1887
and a synagogue was consecrated in 1906. Large numbers of Jews from Eastern Europe on their way to the
West stopped over in Z. and in around 1900 the community set up special relief organizations to assist
them. Probably also because of emigrants who decided
to stay in Z., the J. pop. rose to 200 in the 1920s. When
the Nazis came to power in 1933, the J. pop. was 159.
In Oct. 1938, there were only 70 Jews in Z.; 22 of non-
German citizenship were deported to Poland. On *Kris-*

tallnacht (9–10 Nov. 1938), the synagogue and the
mortuary at the cemetery were blown up, businesses
were wrecked, and the preacher and other Jews were
arrested and taken to the Buchenwald concentration
camp. By April 1941, 24 Jews and 29 persons of partial J. origin (*Mischlinge*) remained in Z. It is assumed
that most Jews were deported to the east. By Oct. 1942,
only six Jews were left in the town, probably protected
by marriage to non-Jews.

ZLATE MORAVCE   Slovakia, Czechoslovakia,
today Republic of Slovakia. Jews from the nearby village of Knazice and the Nitra dist. apparently settled in
the mid-1850s. A school was opened c. 1860 (closed in
1896) and a Neologist congregation was founded after
the 1869 split. An Orthodox congregation which ultimately became the larger of the two was formed in
1905. The J. pop. grew from 246 in 1880 to 370
(total 2,786) in 1900. A Zionist society was organized
in 1910 and after WWI most members of the commun-

ity became members, with WIZO, Hashomer Hatzair, and Bnei Akiva all active. Agudat Israel was also active and the J. National Party won six seats in the local council in 1923. Most of the town's businesses were in J. hands, including 30 of its 39 stores, 12 workshops, and the biggest *matza* (unleavened bread) factory in Slovakia. Jews also owned brickyards and a sawmill. When the Slovakian state was formed in March 1939, the J. pop. stood at about 500. In 1941, Jews were forced out of their businesses and in spring 1942 deportations commenced. Young women were sent to Auschwitz via Patronka on 28 March and young men to the Majdanek concentration camp via Novaky on 31 March. The deportation of families began on 11 April. The largest transport, including about 335 Jews from Z. and its environs, left from Novaky on 11 June for the Lublin dist. (Poland). Upon suppressing the Slovak uprising in Sept. 1944, the Germans trapped many of the remaining 119 Jews, who were also deported.

ZLATOPOL   Kirovograd dist., Ukraine. Jews probably settled in the early 19th cent. and numbered 6,373 (total 8,122) in 1897. The Brodski family was active here, endowing an old age home, hospital, and secondary school in the 19th cent. and two private girls' schools in the early 20th cent. A pogrom was staged on 2 May 1919. In the Soviet period, the J. pop. dropped to 3,863 in 1926 and 1,047 in 1939. A J. elementary school, a kindergarten, a children's home, a J. section in the local workers club, an artisans club, and a night school were still in operation in the late 1920s. The Germans captured Z. on 1 Aug. 1941. In Nov., 174 Jews were locked into the cellar of a local building and blown up with it. In Dec., the Jews were expelled to a ghetto-camp and soon afterwards many were executed near the village of Vinogradovka. The remaining 240 were murdered in Sept. 1942. In all, about 1,200 Jews from Z. and its environs were murdered by the Germans.

ZLIN   Moravia, Czechoslovakia. Jews settled after 1830, their pop. growing from 14 in 1848 to 49 in 1900 and 103 (total 21,582) in 1930. Most Jews were deported to the Theresienstadt ghetto in 1942 and from there to the death camps. Some survived as workers in the big Bata shoe factory.

ZLITEN   Tripolitania dist., Libya. A J. settlement ap-

parently existed in the Roman period, in the second cent. C.E. The modern settlement probably dates from the 16th cent., coming in the wake of the Spanish conquest of 1510, when many Jews fled the big cities. In the period of Qaramanli rule under the Ottomans (1711–1835), Jews traded mainly in oil and dates. In the 19th cent., they also began to trade in the popular *alafa* plant used to manufacture paper and cloth and exported to England. The J. pop. was 450 in 1902. In the early 20th cent., most Jews earned their living as jewelers, weavers, shoemakers, and peddlers. The economic prosperity of the Jews resulted in strained relations with their Arab neighbors. There was also religious rivalry since a Moslem holy site was located near the beautifully decorated ancient Tzallat Bu-Shaif synagogue, endowed by a pious J. women and a place of pilgrimage for Tripolitanian Jews. In 1867 it was burned by local Moslems and ordered rebuilt at their expense by the Ottoman authorities. In 1897 it was vandalized and looted and in 1915 again burned. It was rebuilt in 1918 with the assistance of the Italians and from then on became the site of yearly Lag ba-Omer festivities. A second synagogue was founded in 1892. During the Arab Revolt, until the Italians reestablished control of Z. in 1918, the Jews fled to Tripoli. Italian rule brought security and economic prosperity as well as ties with other communities and the beginnings of modernization in the city. Between the World Wars, when the J. pop. was 700–750 (about 2% of the total), Jews continued to be active in the flourishing date industry, marketing the popular *lagbi* date beverage. J. peddlers traded in seeds and beans; others owned small groceries and clothing stores. Many engaged in moneylending. The community owned two 150-room buildings which were used to house the Lag ba-Omer celebrants. The Ben-Yehuda Association opened its doors in Z. only in 1934. In the late 1930s, over 100 children studied Hebrew in Association classes. In 1937 Mussolini visited the city's J. quarter and the Bu-Shaif synagogue. It was only in 1940 that Italy's racial laws were felt and then in the Italian elementary school. Following Allied bombings, the Jews fled Z. to neighboring villages. Under the British occupation from early 1943, Jews were able to join the local police force and the Ben-Yehuda Association started operating again along with a scout group organized by J. soldiers. During the riots of 1945, J. property was damaged but no Jews were killed thanks to police intervention. Most Jews left for Tripoli in 1949 in anticipation of organized emigration to Israel, where the majority settled in the Galilean settlement of Zeitan.

ZLOCHEW   Lodz dist., Poland. At the end of the 17th cent. the first Jews settled here. The J. pop. in 1897 was 1,501 (65% of the total). During WWI and between the World Wars antisemitism was widespread. The Jews suffered from pogroms in the town and in the villages where they peddled their wares. In Nov. 1939 the majority of the 1,879 Jews there were expelled to General Gouvernement territory. The remaining 280 were deported to Chelmno in May–June 1942.

ZLOCZOW   Tarnopol dist., Poland, today Ukraine. J. settlement dates from the early 17th cent. with a synagogue erected around 1613 and the Jews receiving extensive residence and trade rights. When the synagogue burned down in 1727, the town's proprietor helped rebuild it. The Jews traded mainly in agricultural produce but with the coming of the railroad in the 1870s, economic horizons were broadened and Jews began to earn their living as contractors and carters. They also joined the professions and a large J.-owned printing house founded in 1870 produced about 1,000 Polish books up to WWI. Under Austrian rule (1772–1918) the Jews led an active political life, with two mayors serving the town and representatives in the Austrian parliament. Hasidism was the dominant force in the community throughout the 19th cent. A fire devastated Z. in 1903 but it was rebuilt in brick with aid from J. charitable organizations in Europe and J. emigrees in the U.S. The J. pop. reached 4,046 in 1890 and continued to grow despite the disruptions and anti-J. depredations of WWI and its aftermath. The J. pop. was 5,744 (total 11,130) in 1921. The Zionists were now the leading political force. Most children attended Polish schools. Antisemitism rose significantly in the 1930s. Under Soviet occupation (fall 1939–summer 1941), J. public, cultural, and economic life was shut down. The Germans arrived on 2 July 1941 and with the pop. swelled by refugees, the Ukrainians staged a massive pogrom claiming 4,000 J. lives. A *Judenrat* was immediately set up and required to supply forced labor and valuables. With the help of an anti-Nazi German administrator, many Jews were able to find employment in the town's vital food plants. When the *Judenrat* delayed supplying a list of the nonworking pop., about 2,700 Jews were rounded up and deported to the Belzec death camp in an *Aktion* commencing on

28 Aug. 1942. Another 2,500, mostly women, children, and the elderly, were deported on 2–3 Nov. A ghetto containing 7,500–9,000 Jews, including remnants from the surrounding area, was established on 1 Dec. 1942. A typhus epidemic took its toll in the winter. The ghetto was liquidated on 2 April 1943, when its 6,000 remaining Jews were brought outside the town and executed beside mass graves, many being buried alive. Members of the *Judenrat* were also murdered when they refused to sign an "authorization" for the liquidation of the ghetto for reasons of public health. Those who escaped were hunted down and shot, including partisan groups organizing in the forests.

ZLOTNIKI   Tarnopol dist., Poland, today Ukraine. Jews inhabited the village sporadically from the 16th cent. and numbered 225 in 1890 (total pop. 2,134). The J. pop. dropped by 50% after WWI. The Jews were murdered in a Ukrainian pogrom after the Soviet withdrawal in June 1941, or eliminated by the Germans.

ZLYNKA   Oriol dist., Russia. Jews probably settled in the mid-19th cent. and numbered 812 (total 5,408) in 1897. Much J. property was damaged in a pogrom staged on 21 Oct. 1921. The J. pop. declined in the Soviet period to 586 in 1926 and 432 in 1939. The Germans arrived on 25 Aug. 1941 and immediately concentrated the Jews of Z. and its environs on the grounds of the local tractor station. In Feb. 1942, they murdered 214.

ZNACOVO   (Hung. Ignecz or Iglinc) Carpatho-Russia, Czechoslovakia, today Ukraine. Jews probably settled in the late 18th cent. Their pop. was 13 in 1830 and 69 (total 1,315) in 1880. Twelve were tradesmen, four were artisans, and a few were farmers. In 1921, the J. pop. was 101 and in 1941 it was 110. The Hungarians occupied the town in March 1939. In mid-May 1944, the Jews were deported to Auschwitz.

ZNAMENKA   Kirovograd, Ukraine. Jews settled in the late 19th or early 20th cent., after the completion of the Odessa–Kharkov railway line in 1869 and the development of an urban settlement around the train station. The Jews were attacked in a pogrom on 3 May 1919. In the mid-1920s, under the Soviets, a *beit midrash* and a *heder* with 30 children were still active. The J. pop. in 1939 was 653 (total 13,604). The

Germans captured Z. on 6 Aug. 1941. The few Jews who had neither fled nor been evacuated were murdered in the nearby forest in Oct.–Nov. 1941.

ZNOJMO Moravia (Sudetenland), Czechoslovakia. Jews may have been present in the mid-11th cent. and a community existed from the first half of the 13th cent. at the latest. Many were massacred in the wake of the Pulkau blood libel of 1338 and during the Black Death persecutions of 1348–49. In the first half of the 15th cent., the community was one of the largest in Moravia but in 1454 King Ladislaus Posthumus expelled the Jews, who returned only 400 years later. With the arrival of Jews from the surrounding villages in the late 19th cent., the J. pop. rose from 36 in 1857 to 357 in 1869 and 674 in 1890. A synagogue was consecrated in 1888. The J. pop. reached a peak of 786 in 1928. The Zionists were active and the Jews became prominent in the preservative industry. Most Jews left during the Sudetenland crisis. The synagogue was burned on *Kristallnacht* (9–10 Nov. 1938) and the remaining Jews were deported to the Theresienstadt ghetto or the death camps of Poland in late 1942. Most of those in Theresienstadt survived the war.

ZOFJOWKA (Trochimbrod) Volhynia dist., Poland, today Ukraine. Z. was founded in 1835 as a J. farm settlement on 1,750 acres of land purchased from the local aristocracy by Belorussian and Volhynian Jews. Two glass factories boosted the economy as the pop. remained almost entirely J. (1,580 in 1897, 1,531 in 1921). In WWI the community suffered murder, rape, and robbery at the hands of the Cossacks and Ukrainians as well as hunger and disease. Economic recovery was rapid after the war though the economic crisis and the Polish cooperatives took their toll. The active Zionist movement sent 45 families to Palestine and the town hosted the first course for Irgun commanders in Poland in 1938. Under the German occupation from July 1941 J. farms were confiscated. The community was liquidated in *Aktions* on 25–27 Aug. and 21 Sept. 1942. Many escaped and a group of 15 engaging in effective partisan action joined the Kovpak partisan division.

ZOLKIEW Lwow dist., Poland. Jews, mostly from Lwow, received residence rights in 1600 and various other privileges throughout the 17th cent. Despite a destructive fire in 1645 and the Chmielnicki massacres of

Synagogue in Zolkiew, Poland (Bildarchiv der Oester. Nationalbibliothek, Wien/photo courtesy of Yad Vashem, The Holocaust Martyrs' and Heroes' Remembrance Authority, Jerusalem)

The Jewish quarter of Zolkiew, Poland, 1917 (Beth Hatefutsoth Photo Archive, Tel Aviv/courtesy of Polska Akademia Nauk, Warsaw)

German soldier buying from Jewish peddler, Zolkiew, Poland, 1917 (Beth Hatefutsoth Photo Archive, Tel Aviv/courtesy of Polska Akademia Nauk, Warsaw)

1648–49 the community grew to 270 households by 1680. In the 18th cent. Jews were engaged in international trade and the town became an important center of J. printing and was served by illustrious rabbis. The "Catholic reaction" in the Polish kingdom of the mid-18th cent. led to the imposition of certain disabilities on the Jews, exacting a heavy financial toll in addition to increasing taxation in order to circumvent the restrictions. The period of Austrian rule (1772–1918) brought economic stagnation with a particularly heavy tax burden. Most of the J. houses were destroyed in a fire in 1833. Neither the revolutionary spirit of 1848 nor the achievement of equal rights for the Jews of Galicia in 1867–68 could revive the community, whose pop. showed no growth from a late-19th cent. level of around 4,000 (approaching 50% of the total) right up to the eve of WWII. In the first half of the 19th cent., the community was a stronghold of the *Mitnaggedim*, but in the second half, Belz Hasidism came to the fore. The town was also a leading center of Haskala. Nahman Krochmal, one of the founders

of the Galician movement, resided in the town from 1798 to 1836. Together with the Hasidim its proponents put up effective resistance to the budding Zionist movement. Most of the Jews fled from the town with the approach of the Russians in Aug. 1914, returning only with the Austrian reconquest in May 1915. The postwar period, which saw an increase in Zionist influence, brought little alleviation of the economic plight of the Jews, 70% of whom were receiving aid from the Joint Distribution Committee. Under the Soviet rule of 1939–41, extensive aid was extended by the community to J. refugees escaping German-held territory. The Soviets, however, exiled many to Russia. With the German occupation of 28 June 1941, a regime of restrictions and forced labor was instituted. The winter brought hunger and disease but a semblance of normal life was maintained with children regularly attending clandestine classes. On 15 March 1942 a selection was made among 700 disabled Jews for deportation to the Belzec death camp. Hundreds of men were employed at forced labor. Throughout the summer transports bearing East Galician Jews to Belzec came through the town and those escaping from the trains, oftened injured, were hidden and cared for by the community. In a mass *Aktion* on 22 Nov. 1942, 2,000 Jews were rounded up; about 300 were murdered in the town and the rest deported to Belzec. Some local residents went so far as to carry tools for breaking out of the trains in just such an eventuality. On 1 Dec. 1942, a ghetto was established with Jews from neighboring settlements brought there and all crowded together ten to a room. A typhoid epidemic claimed 20 lives a day. Some managed to escape from the ghetto, a few finding shelter with Christian families, one of which concealed a group of 18 Jews. Another 600 Jews were taken to the Janowska Camp in Lwow on 15 March 1943. The liquidation of the ghetto commenced on 25 March with all but 230 workers executed in the forest outside the town. The last 40 Jews in the local forced labor camp were murdered on 10 July. The Germans continued hunting down Jews in hiding until the Soviets liberated the town on 23 July 1944.

ZOLOTONOSHA Poltava dist., Ukraine. Jews settled in the late 18th cent and numbered 2,749 (total 8,739) in 1897. Z. was the birthplace of Ber Borochov (1881–1917), the Zionist Socialist leader and ideologue, and the engineer Alexander Zarchin (1897–1988), who developed a desalination process used extensively in Israel. Much J. property was destroyed in a pogrom on 21 Oct. 1905. A *talmud torah* and private girls' school were operating in 1909. Another pogrom was staged on 12 May 1919. In the mid-1930s, about a quarter of the city's Jews were laborers; a third were white-collar workers; a third artisans; and the rest farmers and pensioners. About 80% of the artisans were organized in cooperatives. In 1939 the J. pop. was 2,087. The Germans entered Z. on 19 Sept. 1941. On 22 Sept., they murdered 300 Jews, most of them from the surrounding area or refugees. On 22 Nov., they executed another 3,500 Jews in a valley 2 miles (3 km) outside the city.

ZOLTANCE Stanislawow dist., Poland, today Ukraine. The J. pop. in 1921 was 293. The Jews were expelled to Kamionka Strumilowa for liquidation in June 1942.

ZOLUDEK Nowogrodek dist., Poland, today Ukraine. Jews are first mentioned in the mid-16th cent.

In the 1890s the community had a synagogue and *beit midrash* and a number of *shtiblekh* serving the Hasidim. The J. pop. grew to 1,372 (total 1,860) in 1897, dropping to 1,053 in 1921 after the depredations of WWI. A devastating fire in 1922 compounded the wartime suffering. Loan facilities sponsored by the YEKOPO relief organization helped the community recover. The Zionists with their youth movements were active between the World Wars and Hebrew and Yiddish schools together enrolled 200 children in the late 1930s. After two years of Soviet rule in 1939–41 the Germans entered Z. on 27 June 1941. A ghetto was established on 1 Nov. 1941 with the Jews subjected to forced labor and periodic killing. On 9 May 1942, 1,000–1,400 of the 1,500 Jews in the ghetto were murdered at the J. cemetery. The remaining skilled workers were sent to the Szczuczyn and Lida ghettoes, sharing the fate of local Jews.

ZOLUDZK Volhynia dist., Poland, today Ukraine. Z. was founded as a J. farm settlement in 1847. As farm income dropped, many engaged in peddling, the building trades, and light industry. The J. pop. stood at 418 (total 446) in 1921. Ten families emigrated to Palestine in 1934. Following the Soviet withdrawal in 1941, the Ukrainians staged a pogrom. The Germans expelled the community to the Rafalowka ghetto on 1 May 1942; all but ten who fled were murdered on 29 Aug.

ZOMBKOWICE Kielce dist., Poland. Twenty families from Bendzin settled in 1894 and set up glass and electrochemical plants employing hundreds of workers. Most were Hasidim. The Zionists were active between the World Wars. When the Germans entered Z. on 6 Sept. 1939, there were 400 Jews, their numbers increasing in Nov. with the arrival of 100 refugees from Austria and Germany. In May 1941, all were transferred to Dombrowa Gornicza and most were included in the first transport to Auschwitz in May 1942. There were 12 survivors after the war and the community was reconstituted but most left in the 1950s.

ZORNISCHE Vinnitsa dist., Ukraine. Jews numbered 174 in 1765 and 1,040 (total 3,518) in 1897. In the late 19th cent., the community had a stone-built synagogue and a prayer house. On 14 Nov. 1917, Jews were attacked in a pogrom. In 1926, under the Soviets, the J. pop. was 996. Religious life was still flourishing in the late 1920s. The Germans occupied the town in the latter part of July 1941. A few hundred Jews were executed in an *Aktion* in late May 1942.

ZOZHEV Vinnitsa dist., Ukraine. Nine Jews were present in 1765, growing to 414 (total 3,732) in 1897. The community had a stone synagogue and probably a *beit midrash* as well. In 1926, under the Soviets, the J. pop. dropped to 225. The few Jews who had not been able to escape prior to the German occupation were probably murdered in spring 1942 along with the rest of the Jews of the area.

ZRENJANIN Vojvodina dist., Yugoslavia. Jews first settled at the end of the 17th cent. and a community was organized in the second half of the 18th cent. A branch of the Alliance Israelite was very active from 1866. The Jews were well established economically and in the Yugoslavian era the community was one of the most active in the region. In 1931 there were 1,127 Jews in Z. (total 32,831). During WWII, Z. was taken by the Germans and by Sept. 1941 the Jews had been deported to Belgrade and killed. Less than 10% of the J. pop. survived the Holocaust.

ZSAKA Bihar dist., Hungary. Jews settled in the first half of the 19th cent., numbering 184 in 1880 and 50 in 1930. They were deported to Auschwitz via Nagyvarad at the beginning of June 1944.

ZSAMBEK Pest-Pilis-Solt-Kiskun dist., Hungary. Jews arrived in the first half of the 18th cent. and from 1812 enjoyed imperial protection. A synagogue was opened in 1810 and a school in 1878. The J. pop. reached a peak of 494 in 1840, dwindling to 222 in 1910 as Jews moved to the larger cities. Many fled during the White Terror attacks (1919–21) following WWI. All males were seized for forced labor in 1938. The few dozen remaining women and children were deported to Auschwitz on 30 June 1944.

ZUARA (also Zouara) Tripolitania dist., Libya. The modern community dates from the late 19th cent. and numbered 40 families in 1906, earning their livelihoods supplying the local army garrison and trading in the daily market. Between the World Wars, the J. pop. was 600–800 (less than 2% of the total). Children

attended the Italian elementary school in the morning and a *talmud torah* in the afternoons. A splendid synagogue seated 500. Relations with the Arab pop., based on mutual interests, were good. Arabs and Jews lived in mixed neighborhoods, with children visiting freely in one another's houses. The community was virtually untouched by WWII, with even Italy's racial laws barely felt. The city became a place of refuge for Jews, with 500–1,000 from Tripoli staying there during the German occupation. In the bombardment from the sea that preceded the British invasion in Dec. 1942, one Jew was killed. Z. was also spared the Arab riots of 1945, though their anxiety led many Jews to arm themselves. Zionist activity only took hold with the arrival of J. soldiers with the British. They set up a Hebrew school using a curriculum prepared in Palestine. After the 1945 riots, Z. became a transit point for Jews clandestinely leaving Libya for Tunisia en route to Palestine. Organized emigration from Z., as for all of Libya, took place in 1949–51. Some Jews settled in Moshav Alma in Upper Galilee and some in the various towns of Israel.

ZUELLICHAU (Pol. Sulechow) Brandenburg, Germany, today Poland. A J. community existed in the 19th cent., numbering 82 in 1849 and 169 in 1871. By 1900 it had already shrunk to 74 members. The community maintained a synagogue and a cemetery. When the Nazis came to power in 1933, there were 38 Jews in Z. By Oct. 1942, only one Jew, probably protected by marriage to a non-Jew, was still living in Z. No further information is available about the fate of the other Jews, but it is assumed that those who did not manage to emigrate were deported to the east.

ZUELPICH Rhineland, Germany. Most likely Jews were living in Z. from the 13th cent. on. They suffered during the Black Death persecutions of 1348–49. The community established a new synagogue in 1848 and a new cemetery in 1858. In 1885, the J. pop. was 113. When the Nazis came to power in 1933, there were 95 Jews living in Z. On *Kristallnacht* (9–10 Nov. 1938), the synagogue was burned down, J. stores and homes were wrecked, and J. men were arrested. By May 1939, about a third of the J. residents had managed to emigrate. The remaining Jews (with the exception of those married to non-J. partners) were deported from July 1942 on. In all, at least 27 Jews from Z. perished under Nazi rule.

ZUELZ (Pol. Biala) Upper Silesia, Germany, today Poland. Jews were present continuously from at least the 15th cent., when they were concentrated on their own street. The Jews of Z. and Glogau were the only ones allowed to remain following the general expulsion from Silesia and Bohemia in 1582. Consequently the community grew significantly and the town became known as "Z. of the Jews" (*Judenzuelz*) and in Hebrew as "*Makom Tzaddik.*" The J. pop. comprised 26 families in 1600. It again grew under conditions of economic prosperity in the late 17th cent. Until 1761, the Jews of Breslau were also buried in the local cemetery. A synagogue was erected in 1774. The J. pop. was 1,156 in 1787 but beginning in the 19th cent. Jews began leaving for places that offered greater economic opportunity. As a result, the J. pop. dropped to 755 in 1840 and continued to dwindle to such an extent that in 1914 the heretofore independent community was attached to the Neustadt congregation. Only twelve Jews remained in 1925–35. Their fate under the Nazis is unknown.

ZUENDORF-PORZ Rhineland, Germany. Jews settled in Z. in the 17th cent., and in 1713 a prayer room was set up in a private house. In 1882, a new synagogue was consecrated, and in 1920 a cemetery was established. Jews from Porz, who also belonged to the community, began to play an increasingly important role in the town's industrial life (wood processing) before WWI. The community was affiliated to the community of Muelheim-Rhein. In June 1933, some four months after the Nazi takeover, there were 64 Jews living in Z. Thirty-one Jews moved elsewhere in Germany and two emigrated abroad. By May 1939 there were only 26 Jews in Z. On 15 June 1942, 12 Jews were deported. Altogether, at least 30 Jews from Z. perished in the Holocaust.

ZUESCHEN (now part of Fritzlar) Hesse–Nassau, Germany. The J. community, numbering 50 in 1759, grew to 91 in 1847. It was affiliated with the rabbinate of Kassel. By 1933 it had dwindled to 13; the last three Jews were deported to the Lodz ghetto and perished.

ZUGRES Stalino dist., Ukraine. The J. pop. in 1939 was 188 (total 11,352). The Germans occupied Z. on 24 March 1941 and in late Dec. murdered the 15 Jews who had neither fled nor been evacuated

ZUIA Crimea, Russia, today Ukraine. Jews probably settled in the 1920s at the time of J. agricultural settlement in the area. In 1939, 33 were living in the town and 97 in its environs. The Germans occupied Z. in early Nov. 1941 and murdered 18 Jews at the village of Eni-Krymczak on 5 Feb. and in April 1942.

ZUIDLAND Zuid-Holland dist., Holland. An independent J. community was established in the second half of the 19th cent. and numbered about 60 in 1890. In Oct.–Nov. 1942 the nine Jews living there were deported. All perished.

ZURAWNO Stanislawow dist., Poland, today Ukraine. An organized community existed from the 18th cent., the Jews living as lessees and distillers as well as from petty trade and crafts. The community declined after WWI, dropping from 2,197 J. residents in 1880 (two-thirds of the pop.) to 865 (45%) in 1921 and supported by various forms of relief. The German occupation of 3 July 1941 introduced forced labor, mostly in the quarries. Over 150 Jews died of starvation and disease in the winter of 1941–42. In a large-scale *Aktion* on 4–5 Sept. 1942 a few hundred Jews were deported to the Belzec death camp and in the middle of the month a ghetto was sealed off. Some of the Jews were subsequently sent to the Stryj ghetto while the others were sporadically killed off, the last group on 5 June 1943.

ZUROMIN Warsaw dist., Poland. Jews are mentioned in the early 19th cent. and formed an organized community by the 1860s. They exported grain and horses to Danzig and operated a tannery and flour mill, reaching a pop. of 1,902 (total 3,962) in 1921. The Zionists, the Bund, and Agudat Israel were active after WWI. The Germans occupied the town in early Sept. 1939 and when the region was annexed to the Reich, the Jews were expelled.

ZUROW Stanislawow dist., Poland, today Ukraine. The J. pop. in 1921 was 104. The Jews were expelled to Rohatyn for liquidation in Oct. 1942.

ZUTPHEN (Zutfen) Gelderland dist., Holland. The J. presence in Z. dates back to the 14th cent. but settlement was prohibited from 1569 until 1796. In the 19th cent. the community grew rapidly. A synagogue was inaugurated in 1815 and was in use until a new synagogue was inaugurated in 1879. The J. pop. in 1901 was 670. Poverty kept many children from attending the J. school. A number of associations assisted the poor and others organized education. Prior to the Holocaust there was Zionist activity in Z. The J. pop. in 1941 was 579, with another 56 in nearby Gorssel and 59 in Voorst. In Oct. 1941 a number of Jews were arrested by the Nazis. Between Nov. 1942 and April 1943, 450–500 were deported; 109 spent the duration of the occupation in hiding. The community was reestablished after the war.

ZVENIGORODKA Kiev dist., Ukraine. A single J. lessee was present in 1765. In 1897, the J. pop. was 6,389. Jews set up a candle factory and a tobacco plant. Many worked on the estates during the grain harvest. Z. was the birthplace of Baron Horace Guenzburg and the Hebrew writer Natan Agmon Bistritski. In 1924, under the Soviets, 360 J. artisans were organized in unions. A few dozen J. families founded a kolkhoz nearby. Two Yiddish-language elementary schools and a vocational school were opened in the town. An educational institute for needy children (aged 4–8) was founded in 1927. In the same year, a J. law court began operating and in 1931 a Yiddish-language agricultural school was established. The J. pop. in 1939 was 1,957. The Germans occupied Z. on 29 July 1941, setting up a ghetto where the Jews of Katerynopol were also confined. On 14 June 1942, at least 1,500 Jews were executed in the Oforny forest.

ZVOLEN (Hung. Zolyom) Slovakia, Czechoslovakia, today Republic of Slovakia. Jews settled in the mid-19th cent. after residence restrictions were lifted, forming a Neologist congregation after the split of 1869. A synagogue was erected in 1895 and the J. pop. reached a peak of 611 (total 8,799) in 1910. During the 20th cent., Jews became increasingly active in public and economic life, owning 60 business establishments and 23 workshops and factories in 1921, including a big cheese factory and a sawmill. The young belonged to the Zionist youth movements (Hashomer Hatzair, Betar). In 1940, the J. pop. was 554. After the outbreak of war, the Jews were subjected to a regime of persecution and forced labor in the Slovakian state, soon being denied the means to earn a living. Refugees from Bratislava brought the J. pop. up to 679 in early 1942. In March, young men were deported to Novaky and the women to Patronka, with the latter

sent on to Auschwitz on 1 April. On 8 June, 606 Jews were deported to the Lublin dist. (Poland) with able-bodied men going to the Majdanek concentration camp and the women to the Sobibor death camp. Jews initially spared were murdered by the Germans in fall and winter 1944–45 at the J. cementery.

ZVORNIK Bosnia-Hercegovina, Yugoslavia, today Republic of Bosnia. Jews lived there from the 19th cent. The community numbered 75 Jews in 1931 (total 3,487). In May 1942 the Ustase took the Jews of Z. to Sabac and handed them over to the Germans. Most died in the Banjica camp.

ZWARTSLUIS Overijssel dist., Holland. In the 18th cent. a J. community was organized. The J. pop. in 1890 was 61 (total 4,029). After the Nazi invasion in 1941, 14 Jews remained; two went into hiding and 12 were deported, one of whom survived.

ZWEIBRUECKEN Palatinate, Germany. Individual Jews lived in the city during the Middle Ages. In the 19th cent., the J. pop grew from 24 in 1804 to 174 in 1827 and 238 (total 8,393) in 1871. Cattle dealing was a major source of livelihood. A synagogue is mentioned in 1815. A new Reform synagogue with an organ and a choir, built in the Eastern style, was consecrated in 1879. In 1878, Z. became the seat of the dist. rabbinate. The synagogue windows were smashed in 1927 during local New Year's celebrations. In 1933, the J. pop. was 149. In the Nazi period, 28 Jews belonged to a Zionist group. Fifteen children were removed from public schools in 1936. On *Kristallnacht* (9–10 Nov. 1938), the synagogue was burned, two J. stores were destroyed, and 20 J. men were arrested. A total of 30 Jews left the city, 16 for the U.S. Sixteen were deported to the Gurs concentration camp on 22 Oct. 1940. Nineteen perished in the Holocaust.

ZWESTEN Hesse–Nassau, Germany. The community dedicated a synagogue in 1741 (rebuilt in 1914) and maintained an elementary school. The J. pop. numbered 89 (11% of the total) in 1895. The community also drew members from neighboring villages. Affiliated with the Kassel rabbinate, it produced many Orthodox teachers and learned laymen. By 1933 the community had declined to 46. Its synagogue was vandalized on *Kristallnacht* (9–10 Nov. 1938), and most Jews emigrated before WWII.

ZWICKAU Saxony, Germany. Jews were living in Z. from the beginning of the 14th cent. There were several expulsions, the final one occurring in 1543. J. settlement was only renewed in the second half of the 19th cent. In 1907, the J. pop. was 120. In 1905, a synagogue and a cemetery were established. The immigration of East European Jews increased the J. pop. to 496 in 1925. Community associations included a number of charitable organizations, branches of the Central Union (C.V.) and the German Zionist Organization (from about 1912), and youth associations. The Orthodox members of the community maintained a prayer room. The publisher and philanthropist Salman Schocken (1877–1959) lived in Z. He and his brother Simon set up a department store which developed into the Schocken chain of department stores. Salman Schocken, a longtime Zionist supporter, within the community and throughout Saxony, helped Jews preparing for emigration by arranging for vocational training and financial aid. The Schocken department store chain was "Aryanized" in Aug. 1938. When the Nazis came to power in 1933, there were 473 Jews in Z. Of the 300 Jews in Z. in Oct. 1938, 68 did not have German citizenship and were deported to Poland. On *Kristallnacht* (9–10 Nov. 1938), the community's facilities and J. stores were wrecked. About 100 Jews were arrested and taken to the Buchenwald concentration camp. By 1939, there were only 64 Jews in Z. Those who did not manage to escape abroad were deported in 1941 with the exception of 15 Jews who were still living in the town in Oct. 1942, probably protected by marriage to non-Jews.

ZWINGENBERG Hesse, Germany. Banished in 1567, Jews returned 200 years later. Their independent community (1858), affiliated with the Orthodox rabbinate of Darmstadt, numbered 77 (5% of the total) in 1880. An imposing new synagogue was dedicated in 1903. Sigmund Nauheim (1879–1935) bequeathed his ritual art collection to the Frankfurt J. Museum. On *Kristallnacht* (9–10 Nov. 1938), the synagogue was not destroyed. By 1939 all the Jews had left Z., 18 emigrating (seven to Palestine); seven others perished in the Holocaust.

ZWOLEN Kielce dist., Poland. Jews are first mentioned in 1564. In 1579 they received a longstanding privilege from King Stephen Bathory granting them residence and trade rights. By 1765, there were 400

Jews in Z. A major fire and the Swedish invasion of the 1660s devastated the community, which only recovered fully in the mid-18th cent. In the 19th cent., R. Shemuel Eliyahu Taub (d. 1888) established a hasidic dynasty there. The J. pop. rose to 1,760 in 1864 and 3,787 (total 7,392) in 1921. Traditional circles continued to dominate the community until 1936, when the Zionists won the elections to the community council. The Germans arrived on 6 Sept. 1939, appointing a *Judenrat* and instituting a regime of forced labor and extortion. In early 1940, a ghetto was set up, its pop. doubling to 8,000 with the arrival of refugees in summer 1942. Almost all were deported to the Treblinka death camp in Sept. 1942. A small group of 200 was sent to a nearby work farm and then to a labor camp.

ZWOLLE Overijssel dist., Holland. Jews lived in Z. in the 14th cent. but their presence was not well received until the 16th cent. Their numbers began to increase from 1720, when a trading company largely owned by Jews in Amsterdam drew Jews to Z. Community activity also began in the 1720s. A synagogue was inaugurated in 1758. Most Jews were well-to-do and enjoyed equal civil rights by 1795. From 1814, Z. was the seat of the Overijssel chief rabbinate. A new synagogue was built in 1899 to serve the growing community, which reached its peak pop. by the end of the cent. (723 in 1901). A number of J. social and educational associations were active by that time. Chief Rabbi Shimon Hirsch (1872–1941) led the community in the 20th cent., while heading Holland's Agudat Israel organization. By 1938 there were 31 German-J. refugees in Z. and in 1941 there were 105 refugees from the coastal regions. The J. pop. in 1941 was 754 (total 43,301). In Oct. 1941 Jews were hunted down and taken to the Mauthausen concentration camp, where they perished. In Aug. 1942, 32 were taken to forced labor. Deportations began in Nov. 1942 and ended in April 1943. In all, 525 Jews were deported; 135 survived the Holocaust. A community was reestablished after the war.

ZYDACZOW Stanislawow dist., Poland, today Ukraine. Jews are recorded in the mid-15th cent. and an organized, independent community in the 18th. The dominant spiritual force was the hasidic Zhidachov dynasty founded by Tzevi Hirsh Eichenstein (1785–1831), which held sway for over 120 years. Zionist activity was extensive from the beginning of the 20th cent. and a J. mayor was elected in 1906. In 1921 the J. pop. stood at 823 (total 3,823). The Soviet annexation of 1939–41 brought a Communist regime. The Germans entered Z. on 3 July 1941. Hundreds of Jews were deported to the Belzec death camp on 4–5 Sept. 1942 and the rest transferred to the Stryj ghetto on 30 Sept. Those who escaped were hunted down in the forests and murdered by the Ukrainian peasants.

ZYKHLIN Lodz dist., Poland. Jews first settled in the mid-18th cent. and by 1897 they owned all but seven of the 184 stores in the town. The J. pop. at the end of the 19th cent was 2,268 (47% of the total). At this time members of the Gur hasidic sect settled, dominating the community up to the outbreak of WWI. About 1840 R. Shemuel Abba established the Z. dynasty and court. Members of J. youth movements organized self-defense units during the 1905 revolution and again during the pogroms in 1918. All Zionist parties were active and after the war they gained control of community affairs. In 1932 Po'alei Zion opened a pioneer training farm. Z. was occupied by the Germans on 17 Sept. 1939. In the fall of 1940 a ghetto was set up, divided into the "small" ghetto containing about 1,000 Jews and the "large" ghetto with about 1,800 Jews. Non-Jews were free to enter and purchase clothes, shoes, and other goods. Several hundred of the younger men were sent to forced labor camps and few returned. By 1942 there were 3,200 Jews in the ghetto, including local residents and refugees. On 3 March they were rounded up and transported to Chelmno.

ZYVOTOV Vinnitsa dist., Ukraine. Jews were murdered in 1648 during the Chmielnicki massacres. In 1765, they numbered 156. Many were murdered and robbed when the Haidamaks captured the town in 1768. In 1897, the J. pop. was 1,935 (total 3,733). A pogrom was staged against the Jews in Nov. 1917. In 1926, under the Soviets, their pop. was 405. The Germans arrived in late 1941 and murdered the Jews in Oct. together with the rest of the Jews in the area.

IN MEMORIAM

A Pictorial Supplement

SA men guarding entrance to a Jewish store on Boycott Day, 1 April 1933. The sign reads: "Germans, beware! Do not buy from Jews"

Burning of banned books on Berlin's Opera Square, 10 May 1933. As the German-Jewish poet Heinrich Heine wrote over a hundred years earlier: "Where books are burned, people will be burned too"

Viennese Jews being forced to scrub the streets of the city, March 1938

Burning of Boerneplatz Synagogue in Frankfurt, Germany, on 10 Nov. 1938

SS men "amusing" themselves by cutting off the beard of a Jew in Plock, Poland

Opposite page: Brutalization of Jews in Poland (location unknown)

Jews from Lodz, Poland, on their way to the ghetto

Warsaw Jews being taken to forced labor

Warsaw ghetto: children in rags

Warsaw ghetto: children in rags

Warsaw ghetto: Jewish child dying on the sidewalk (Steidel Verlag, Goettingen/photo courtesy of Yad Vashem, The Holocaust Martyrs' and Heroes' Remembrance Authority, Jerusalem)

The last journey: death and burial in the Warsaw ghetto

Jewish girl abused by Ukrainian mob

*Lwow, Poland, shortly after its occupation by German troops,
July 1941: Ukrainians dragging Jews through the streets*

Kaunas (Kovno): Lithuanians massacring Jews under the gaze of German soldiers, summer 1941

Kaunas (Kovno): Lithuanian collaborators escorting Jews to execution sites

Kaunas (Kovno): Lithuanian collaborators escorting Jews to execution sites

A bridge over an "Aryan" street connecting two sections of the Lodz ghetto

Lodz ghetto, Poland: deportation of Jews. Jewish policemen were forced to supervise the deportations

Lodz ghetto, Poland: deportation of Jewish children

Warsaw ghetto: deportation of Jewish children

Deportees bidding farewell to those left behind in the Lodz ghetto

Wloclawek, Poland: deportation of Jews to the Chelmno death camp

Budapest: roundup of Jewish women

Execution carried out by Einsatzgruppe *in the occupied Soviet Union during 1941–42 (exact location unknown)*

Kaunas (Kovno), the Seventh Fort: mass execution of Jews

Ponary, Lithuania: mass execution of Jews from Vilna

Jews digging their own graves before being shot by the Germans

Liepaja, Latvia: Jewish women before their execution

Auschwitz-Birkenau, Poland: the last journey

Opposite page: Vinnitsa, Ukraine: the last Jew alive being shot

Women in cattle cars en route to the death camps

Slovakia: Jews boarding trains bound for the death camps of the Lublin area of Poland and Auschwitz, March–Oct. 1942

Auschwitz-Birkenau, Poland: women and children before selection

Auschwitz-Birkenau, Poland: men and women being separated in selection

Auschwitz-Birkenau, Poland: the selection comtinues

Mauthausen concentration camp, Austria: prisoners' orchestra playing while an inmate caught trying to escape is led to execution

Overleaf: Men, women and children waiting in a grove before being taken to the gas chambers

Top and bottom: a crematorium in Majdanek, Poland

Zyklon B—the poison gas used in the gas chambers

A prisoner commits suicide by running into the electrified barbed-wire fence (Henning Langenheim, Berlin/photo courtesy of Yad Vashem, The Holocaust Martyrs' and Heroes' Remembrance Authority, Jerusalem)

Buchenwald, Germany: torture of prisoners

One of seven photographs taken clandestinely in Birkenau by a Sonderkommando worker (only three could be developed). The photos were smuggled out of Birkenau by the camp underground in order to alert the world to what was happening in the camps. Seen here are corpses being burned in the aftermath of gassing (Henning Langenheim, Berlin/photo courtesy of Yad Vashem, The Holocaust Martyrs' and Heroes' Remembrance Authority, Jerusalem)

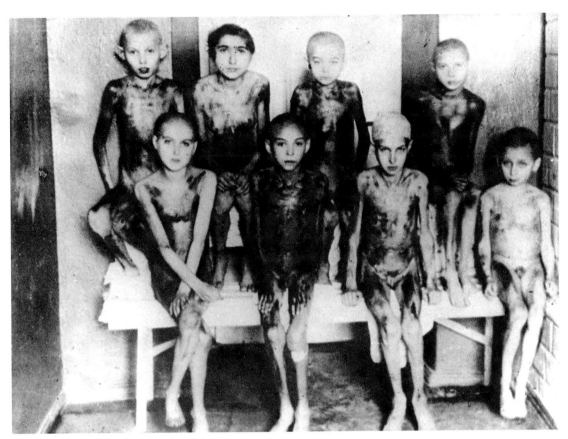

Auschwitz: medical experiments on children

Dachau, Germany: medical experiments by Nazi physicians

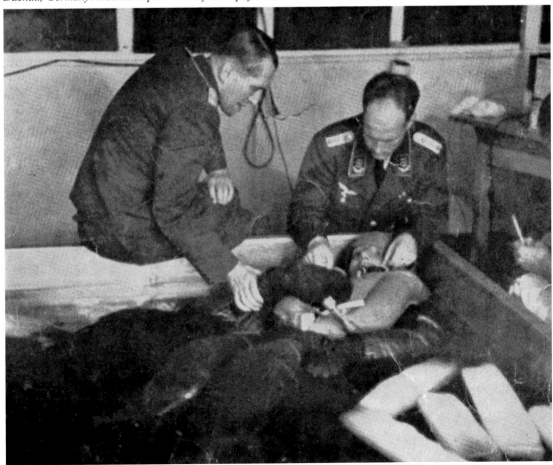

Top: man jumping from window of burning house in the Warsaw ghetto
Bottom: Warsaw ghetto going up in flames

Opposite page: Mordekhai Anielewicz, commander of the Warsaw ghetto
uprising against the background of the Warsaw ghetto in flames

Warsaw ghetto: group of Jews captured in the ghetto during the uprising

Opposite page: Warsaw ghetto: inhabitants captured during the uprising

Group of Jewish partisans from Vilna after the liberation of the city, July 1944. Standing in center: Abba Kovner, commander of the Jewish underground in the Vilna ghetto; on far right: Vitka Kempner; third from right: Reizl (Ruszka) Korczak; on far left: Elhanan Maggid

Hanging of two Jewish partisans in Minsk, Oct. 1941. On the left: 17-year-old Masha Bruskina

*Opposite page (bottom): left — Shalom Zorin, commander of a
Jewish partisan unit and the family camp from the Minsk ghetto;
right — Tuvia Bielski, commander of a Jewish partisan unit and the
family camp in the Nalibok forest (Belorussia)*

Child survivors of Auschwitz on the day of liberation in Jan. 1945, photographed by Soviet soldiers who liberated the camp

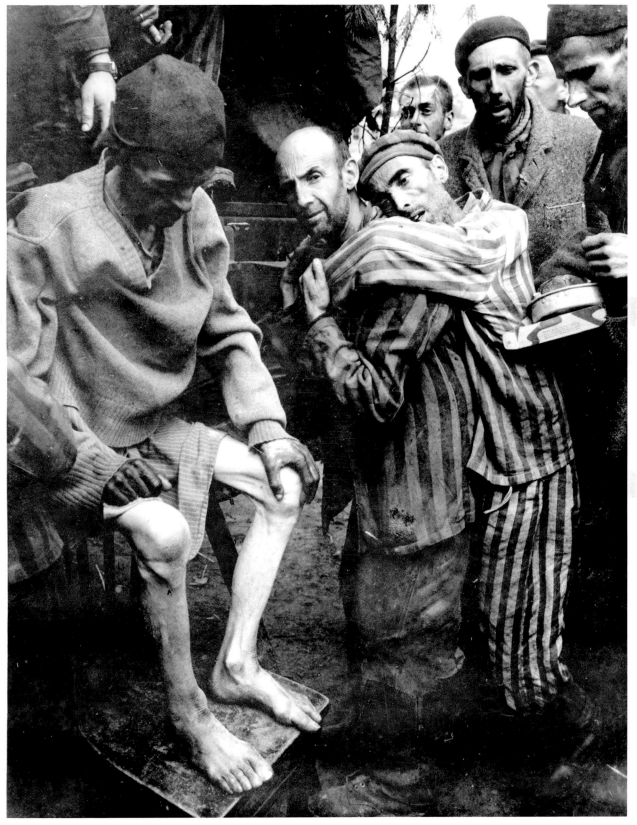

Wobbelin concentration camp, Germany, after liberation by American troops

Buchenwald, after the liberation: survivors in their barracks. Elie Wiesel, Nobel Peace Prize winner, 1986, is on the far right in the second tier from the bottom

Bergen-Belsen: female SS guards forced to bury the bodies of prisoners after liberation of the camp by the British

The joy of liberation

The "illegal" ship Theodor Herzl *captured by the British navy on 14 April 1947. The sign reads: "The Germans destroyed our families and homes. Don't you destroy our hope."*

Maps

LEGEND:

◙ CAPITAL
• SETTLEMENT
△ CAMP
✡ MASS MURDER SITE
–·– INTERNATIONAL BOUNDARIES
······· INTERNAL BOUNDARIES
–··– LINE OF FARTHEST GERMAN ADVANCE

MAIN TERRITORIAL CHANGES:
I WARTEGAU
II GENERAL GOUVERNEMENT OF POLAND
III TRANSNISTRIA
IV CARPATHO-RUSSIA (TO HUNGARY)
V PROTECTORATE OF BOHEMIA-MORAVIA
VI PROTECTORATE OF SLOVAKIA

NORWAY

Trondheim

SWEDEN

FINLAND

BALTIC SEA

Helsinki

Leningrad

Novgorod

Yaroslavl

Oslo

Stockholm

Tallinn

ESTONIA

"REICHSKOMMISSARIAT"

Kalinin

Moscow

DENMARK

Copenhagen

Pskov

LATVIA

OF OSTLAND

Riga

(Rumbula)

Daugavpils

(Dvinsk)

Polotsk

Vitebsk

UNION OF SOVIET

Hamburg

Bremen

Bergen-Belsen

Muenster

Stettin

Sachsenhausen-
Oranienburg

Klaipeda
(Memel)

Koenigsberg

Gdansk
(Danzig)

LITHUANIA

Kaunas

(Fort 9)

EAST
PRUSSIA

Vilna

(Ponary)

Minsk

(Maly Trostinec)

Grodno

Smolensk

Roslavl

SOCIALIST

Tula

Oriol

Berlin

Poznan

Kalisz

Bialystok

Brest Litovsk

Pinsk

Gomel

Mozyr

Chernigov

Kursk

REPUBLICS

Voronezh

Dortmund

Leipzig

Buchenwald

Chemnitz

Dresden

Breslau
(Wroclaw)

I

Lodz

Chelmno

Warsaw

POLAND

Lublin

Sobibor

Majdanek

Rowne

Kiev

(Babi Yar)

Sumy

Kharkov

Stalingrad

GERMANY

Frankfurt
am Main

Theresienstadt

Prague

Czenstochowa

Oswiencim
(Auschwitz)

II

Belzec

Cracow

Lwow

Proskurov

"REICHSKOMMISSARIAT"

OF UKRAINE

Berdichev

Poltava

Dnepropetrovsk

Voroshilovgrad
(Lugansk)

Rostov-on-Don

Nuremberg

Dachau

Munich

V

BOHEMIA

MORAVIA

SLOVAKIA

Stanislawow

Vinnitsa

Uman

Stalindorf

Zaporozhe

Voroshilovsk
(Stavropol)

Linz

Salzburg

Hohenems

Mauthausen

VI

Vienna

Bratislava

IV

YUGOSLAVIA

Sadagura
Cernauti
(Chernovtsy)
Iasi

Bogdanovka

III

Kalinindorf

Nikolaev

Mariupol

Krasnodar

Novorossiysk

Nalchik

Milan

Venice

Trieste

AUSTRIA

HUNGARY

Miskolc

Budapest

Sighet

Oradea Mare

Szeged

Chisinau
(Kishinev)

Odessa

Fraydorf

Sewastopol

Dzankoy

Larindorf

Kerch

ITALY

Ferrara

Bologna

Florence

Jasenovac

Zagreb

To
Hungary

CROATIA

Belgrade

RUMANIA

Timisoara

Ploesti

Galati

BLACK SEA

Ancona

Sarajevo

SERBIA

Ger Occup.

Craiova

Bucharest

Rome

Dubrovnik

BULGARIA

Sofia

Bari

To
Bulgaria

MACEDONIA

Istanbul

Naples

Tirana

ALBANIA

Salonika

TURKEY

Ankara

GREECE

Palermo

SICILY (It.)

Athens

SYRIA
(Fr.)

IRAQ

CYPRUS

RHODES

MALTA (Br.)

MEDITERRANEAN SEA

Chania

CRETE
(Gr.)

Djerba

Tripoli

Tripolitania

Benghazi

Cyrenaica

Tubruq

LIBYA

Alexandria

El Alamein

EGYPT

Haifa

PALESTINE
(Br. Mandate)

TRANS-
JORDAN
(Br.)

SAUDI ARABIA

Sfax

2. SOVIET UNION (BELORUSSIA, UKRAINE AND RUSSIA): MAIN JEWISH COMMUNITIES AND MASS MURDER SITES, 1940-1944

3. BALTIC STATES: MAIN JEWISH COMMUNITIES AND MASS MURDER SITES, 1941-1944

SWEDEN

FINLAND

LEGEND:
- ◉ CAPITAL
- ● SETTLEMENT
- ✡ MASS MURDER SITE
- —··— INTERNATIONAL BOUNDARIES

◉ STOCKHOLM

◉ HELSINKI

● LENINGRAD

DAGO

TALLINN ◉

NARVA ●

ESTONIA

OSEL

TARTU ●

● PERNU

GOTLAND
(SWEDEN)

B
A
L
T
I
C

S
E
A

VENTSPILS ●

VALGA ●

● PSKOV

TALSI ●

KULDIGA

● AIZPUTE

◉ RIGA
✡ (RUMBULA)

LATVIA

RUSSIAN SOVIET
FEDERATED SOCIALIST REPUBLIC

● LIEPAJA

● JELGAVA

SKUODAS ●

● VARAKLANI

PLUNGE ●
TELSIAI
(TELZ) ●
ZAGARE ●

● BAUSKA

REZEKNE ●

PALANGA ● ● KRETINGA

SIAULIAI
(SHAVL) ●

LUDZA ●

MEMEL (KLAIPEDA) ●

KELME ●

PANEVEZYS
(PONEVEZH) ●

● ROKISKIS

DAGDA ●

SEDUVA ●

DAUGAVPILS
(DVINSK) ●

RASEINIAI ●

UTENA ●

● KRASLAVA

● NEVEL

TILSIT
(SOVETSK) ●

JURBARKAS ●

● KEDAINIAI
(KEIDAN)

● UKMERGE
(VILKOMIR)

KOENIGSBERG
(KALININGRAD)

JONAVA ●

BRASLAW ●

SAKIAI ●

LITHUANIA

KAUNAS ◉
(KOVNO) ✡ (FORT 9)

GERMANY
(EAST PRUSSIA)

VILKAVISKIS ●
● MARIJAMPOLE

● ✡ (PONARY)
VILNA

VITEBSK ●

● KALVARIJA

● LYUBAVICHI

SUWALKI ●

WILEJKA ●

● SMOLENSK

BELORUSSIA

ALLENSTEIN
(OLSZTYN)
●

◉ MINSK

NOWOGRODEK ●

● MOGILEV

● MLAWA

POLAND

● SLUTSK

● BOBRUISK

4. POLAND: MAIN JEWISH COMMUNITIES, DEATH CAMPS AND MASS MURDER SITES, 1939-1945

5. RUMANIA: MAIN JEWISH COMMUNITIES, 1939-1945

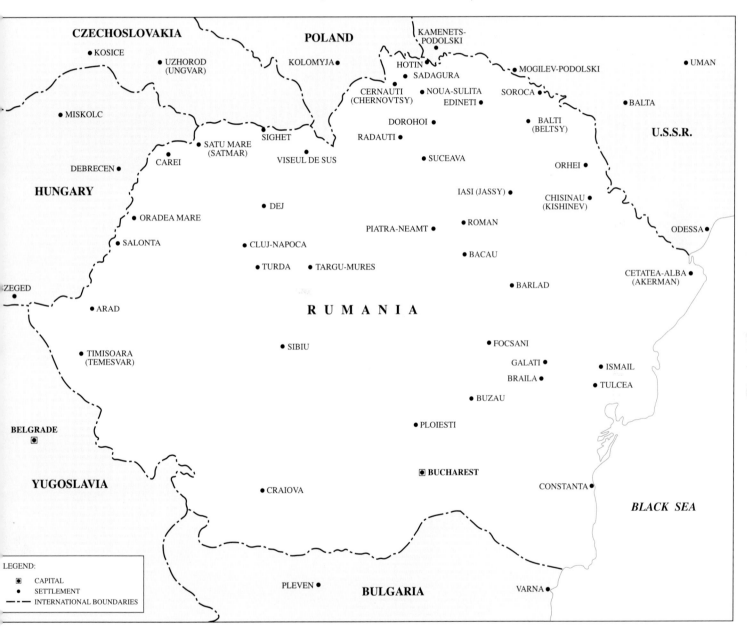

CZECHOSLOVAKIA

POLAND

KAMENETS-
PODOLSKI

• UMAN

• KOSICE

• UZHOROD
(UNGVAR)

KOLOMYJA •

HOTIN •

• MOGILEV-PODOLSKI

• SADAGURA

SOROCA

• MISKOLC

CERNAUTI
(CHERNOVTSY)

• NOUA-SULITA
EDINETI •

• BALTA

U.S.S.R.

• BALTI
(BELTSY)

SIGHET

DOROHOI •

• SATU MARE
(SATMAR)

RADAUTI •

• SUCEAVA

ORHEI •

DEBRECEN •

• CAREI

VISEUL DE SUS

HUNGARY

• DEJ

IASI (JASSY) •

CHISINAU
(KISHINEV) •

ODESSA •

• ORADEA MARE

PIATRA-NEAMT •

• ROMAN

• SALONTA

• CLUJ-NAPOCA

• TURDA • TARGU-MURES

• BACAU

ZEGED

CETATEA-ALBA
(AKERMAN) •

• BARLAD

R U M A N I A

• ARAD

• SIBIU

• FOCSANI

• TIMISOARA
(TEMESVAR)

GALATI •

• ISMAIL

BRAILA •

• TULCEA

• BUZAU

• PLOIESTI

BELGRADE
◉

◉ BUCHAREST

YUGOSLAVIA

CONSTANTA •

• CRAIOVA

BLACK SEA

LEGEND:

◉ CAPITAL

• SETTLEMENT

–··– INTERNATIONAL BOUNDARIES

PLEVEN •

BULGARIA

VARNA •

LEGEND:
- ◉ CAPITAL
- ● SETTLEMENT
- △ CAMP
- —·—·— INTERNATIONAL BOUNDARIES

7. HUNGARY: MAIN JEWISH COMMUNITIES AND DEPORTATION POINTS, 1939-1944

CZECHOSLOVAKIA

● KOSICE

● UZHOROD
(UNGVAR)

⊡ VIENNA

● BRATISLAVA

SATORALJAUJHELY ●

AUSTRIA

KISWARDA ●

MISKOLC ●

SALGOTARJAN

● NYIREGYHAZA

● EGER

● HAJDUNANAS
UJFEHERTO ●

SOPRON

● GYOR

● VAC

GYONGYOS ●

HAJDUHADHAZ ●
DEBRECEN ●

UJPEST ●

⊡ BUDAPEST

● PAPA

● SZOMBATHELY

SZEKESFEHERVAR ●

H U N G A R Y

BERETTYOUJFALU ●

● GRAZ

● SZOLNOK

● ORADEA MARE

● ZALAEGERSZEG

● KECSKEMET

BEKESCSABA ●

RUMANIA

NAGYKANIZSA

HODMEZOVASARHELY

CAKOVEC ●

● KAPOSVAR

● BONYHAD

SZEGED ● MAKO ●

● BAJA

● ARAD

● PECS

● ZAGREB

● TIMISOARA
(TEMESVAR)

● SOMBOR

YUGOSLAVIA

LEGEND:

⊡ CAPITAL
● SETTLEMENT
—·— INTERNATIONAL BOUNDARIES

8. CZECHOSLOVAKIA: MAIN JEWISH COMMUNITIES AND CONCENTRATION CAMPS, 1938-1944

9. AUSTRIA: MAIN JEWISH COMMUNITIES AND CONCENTRATION CAMPS, 1938-1945

10. YUGOSLAVIA: MAIN JEWISH COMMUNITIES AND CONCENTRATION CAMPS, 1941-1945

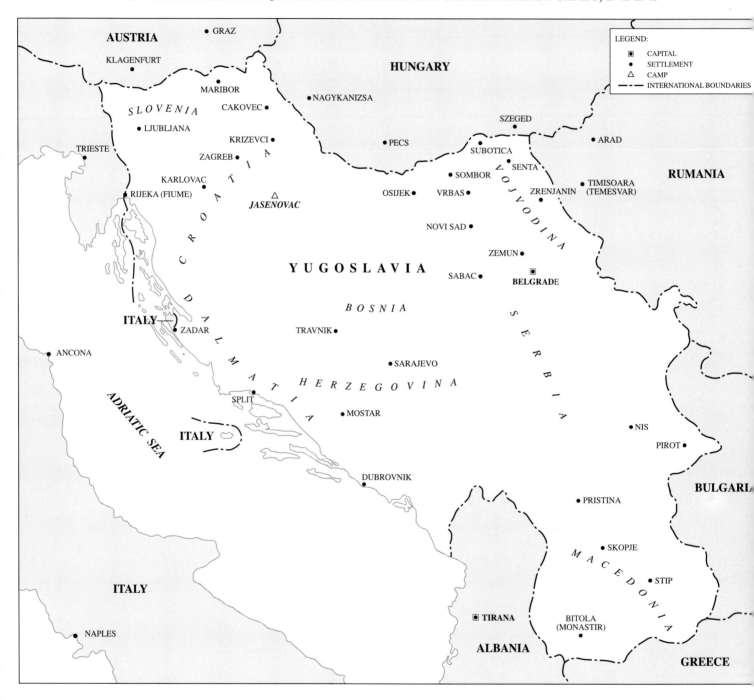

11. HOLLAND: MAIN JEWISH COMMUNITIES AND CONCENTRATION CAMPS, 1940-1944

LEGEND:

- ◉ CAPITAL
- • SETTLEMENT
- △ CAMP
- —·—·— INTERNATIONAL BOUNDARIES

NORTH SEA

EMDEN

• LEEUWARDEN   • GRONINGEN

• STEENWIJK

ALKMAAR •

• KAMPEN   △
ZWOLLE •   *WESTERBORK*

H O L L A N D

HAARLEM •   • DEVENTER

AMSTERDAM •

HILVERSUM •   • APELDOORN   • ENSCHEDE

• LEIDEN   • AMERSFOORT   • ZUTPHEN

◉ HAGUE

UTRECHT •   MUENSTER •

ARNHEM •

• ROTTERDAM

DORDRECHT •   NIJMEGEN •

• DEN BOSCH

GERMANY

MIDDELBURG •   • TILBURG

• EINDHOVEN

VENLO •

• OSTEND   △   • DUESSELDORF
BREENDONCK

ANTWERP   • SITTARD

BELGIUM

◉ BRUSSELS   • MAASTRICHT

BONN
FRANCE   LILLE •   •

12. BELGIUM: MAIN JEWISH COMMUNITIES AND CONCENTRATION CAMPS, 1940-1944

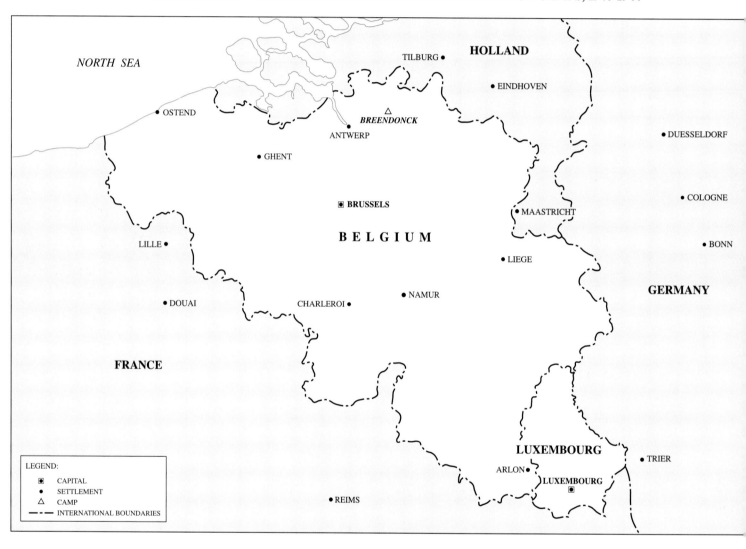

NORTH SEA

HOLLAND

TILBURG

• EINDHOVEN

• OSTEND

△
BREENDONCK

ANTWERP

• DUESSELDORF

• GHENT

• COLOGNE

▣ BRUSSELS

• MAASTRICHT

BELGIUM

• BONN

LILLE •

• LIEGE

GERMANY

• DOUAI

CHARLEROI •

• NAMUR

FRANCE

LUXEMBOURG

• TRIER

ARLON •

LUXEMBOURG
▣

• REIMS

LEGEND:
▣ CAPITAL
• SETTLEMENT
△ CAMP
—·— INTERNATIONAL BOUNDARIES

13. FRANCE: MAIN JEWISH COMMUNITIES AND CONCENTRATION CAMPS, 1940-1944

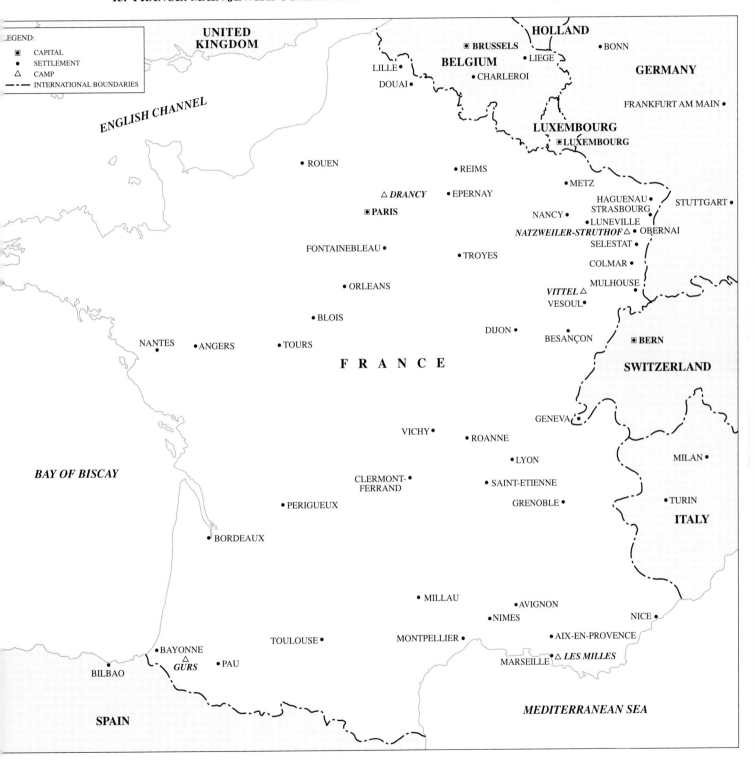

14. ITALY: MAIN JEWISH COMMUNITIES AND TRANSIT POINTS TO PALESTINE, 1939-1945

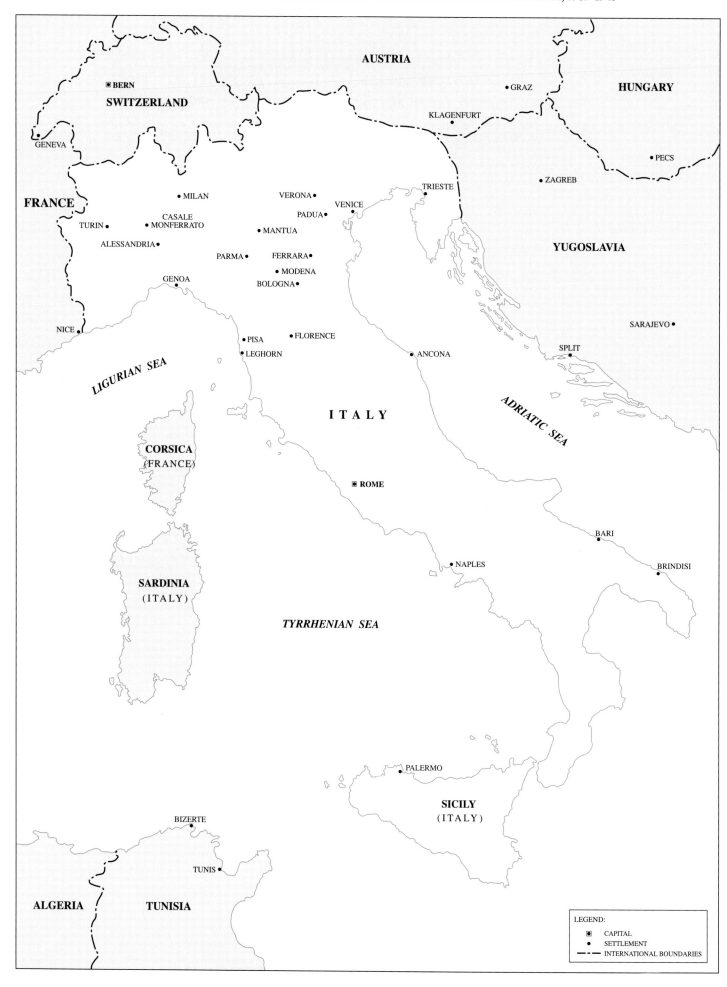

AUSTRIA

HUNGARY

• GRAZ

◙ BERN

SWITZERLAND

KLAGENFURT

• PECS

GENEVA •

• ZAGREB

TRIESTE •

FRANCE

• MILAN

VERONA •

VENICE •

YUGOSLAVIA

CASALE
MONFERRATO •

PADUA •

TURIN •

MANTUA •

ALESSANDRIA •

PARMA •

FERRARA •

GENOA •

• MODENA

BOLOGNA •

NICE •

PISA •

• FLORENCE

SARAJEVO •

LEGHORN •

• ANCONA

SPLIT •

LIGURIAN SEA

ADRIATIC SEA

CORSICA
(FRANCE)

I T A L Y

◙ ROME

SARDINIA
(ITALY)

BARI •

• NAPLES

BRINDISI •

TYRRHENIAN SEA

BIZERTE •

PALERMO •

SICILY
(ITALY)

TUNIS •

ALGERIA   TUNISIA

LEGEND:

◙   CAPITAL

•   SETTLEMENT

–·–·–   INTERNATIONAL BOUNDARIES

15. GREECE: MAIN JEWISH COMMUNITIES, 1939-1945

BLACK
SEA

YUGOSLAVIA

BULGARIA

⊡ TIRANA

DIDIMOTICHO

ISTANBUL

DRAMA •   • KSANTHI
SERES •   • KOMOTINI

ALBANIA

KAVALA •
ALEXANDROPOULIS

• FLORINA

• VERIA   • SALONIKA
• KASTORIA

G R E E C E

TURKEY

CORFU

• JANINA   LARISSA •
• TRIKALA
VOLOS •

AEGEAN SEA

• ARTA

PREVEZA •

ADRIATIC
SEA

AGRINION •

CHALKIS •

CHIOS •

PATRAS •

ATHENS
⊡

ZAKINTHOS

RHODES •
RHODES

MEDITERRANEAN SEA

CHANIA •

CRETE

LEGEND:

⊡   CAPITAL
•   SETTLEMENT
—·—·— INTERNATIONAL BOUNDARIES

16. NORTH AFRICA (TUNISIA AND LIBYA): MAIN JEWISH COMMUNITIES AND LABOR CAMPS, 1940s

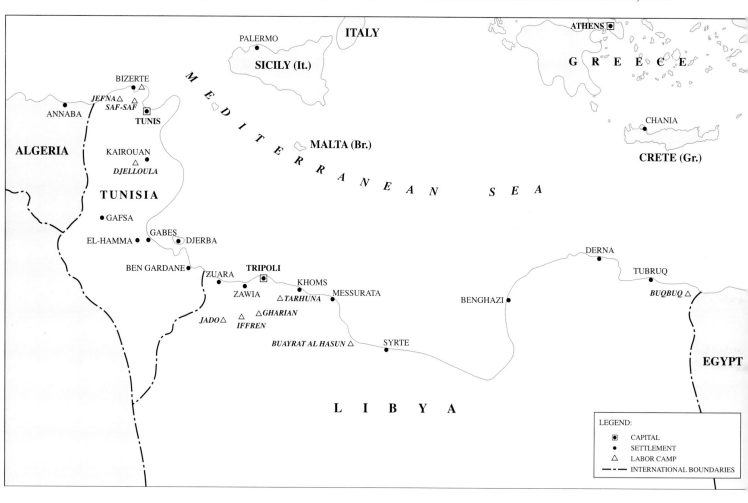

Glossary

Adass Jeshurun (also **Adass Jisroel**) Breakaway congregations in Germany with a Neo-Orthodox orientation. The first of these congregations came into being in the late 19th cent. Similar congregations also arose in other Jewish communities throughout the world during the 20th cent.

Agudat Israel Organization of Orthodox Jews founded in Kattowitz, Poland, in 1912 in reaction to the growth of political Zionism. Agudat Israel opposed the secular Zionist leadership's attempts to establish a Jewish state before WWII but eventually took part in the Zionist enterprise and has had representatives in the Israeli Knesset (Parliament) since the creation of the State of Israel.

Aktion German term for violent mass roundups of Jews by the Nazis and their collaborators during the Holocaust, for forced labor, for mass execution, and for deportation to the death camps.

Aliya (Heb. "ascent") Term for the immigration of Jews to Eretz Israel.

Alliance Israelite Universelle Jewish organization established in Paris in 1860. It actively promoted Jewish and secular education in the French language and sought to promote and defend Jewish civil and religious rights.

American Jewish Joint Distribution Committee (also **Joint** or **JDC**) American Jewish institution established soon after the outbreak of WWI in 1914 to provide aid to Jews in Europe and Palestine. The Joint was very active during the Holocaust era and its aftermath and continues to operate today.

Amora (pl. **amoraim**) Rabbis active in Babylonia and Eretz Israel between the third and sixth cents. and whose commentaries on the text of the Mishna, constituting what is referred to as the Gemara, represent the heart of the Talmud.

Amulets Dispute A controversy that broke out in 17th cent. Germany over the use of amulets said to contain the name of the false messiah Shabbetai Zvi. Rabbi Yaakov Emden accused Rabbi Yonatan Eybeschuetz of creating and distributing such amulets.

Anschluss (Ger. "annexation") Term used for the Nazi takeover of Austria in March 1938.

Anusim (Heb. "forced [converts]") Term for Jews in Spain who ostensibly converted to Christianity from the 14th cent. on but secretly continued to engage in Jewish religious practices or were suspected of doing so by the authorities. They are also known as Crypto-Jews, Marranos (Spanish for "pigs"), and Conversos.

Arbeitsgemeinschaft Nazi organization created to promote cooperation between labor and business in accordance with Nazi ideology.

Arenda (Pol.) Term for the leasing of property or certain economic prerogatives from the ruling class, such as mining, tax-collection, and liquor concessions. Certain Jews were granted these rights in Eastern Europe between the 15th and 18th cents.

Armia Krajowa (also **AK**; Pol. "Home Army") Main Polish armed resistance organization active in Nazi-occupied Poland. The AK was established in Feb. 1942 and was closely linked to the London-based Polish Government-in-Exile.

Armia Ludowa (also **Gwardia Ludowa**; Pol. "People's Army" or "People's Guard") Polish armed resistance organization active in Nazi-occupied Poland. The Armia Ludowa, established in spring 1942, was affiliated with the Polish Workers Party (Polska Partia Robotnicza or PPR), the Communist Party of Poland.

Armleder massacres Series of massacres of Jews carried out in Germany in 1336–39. The name derives from the leather armbands (*armleder*) worn by the marauding bands responsible for the killings.

Arrow Cross (Hung. Nyilaskeresztes or Nyilas) Hungarian pro-Nazi party established in 1937 by Ferenc Szalasi. The Arrow Cross came to power on 15 Oct. 1944 with Szalasi serving as prime minister. During the period of Arrow Cross rule, deportations of Jews to the Nazi camps resumed and tens of thousands of Jews were murdered by members of the Party in Budapest.

Aryanization (Ger. *Arisierung*) Nazi term for the transfer of Jewish businesses and property to non-Jews (in Nazi racial terminology, "Aryans"). In the 1933–1938 period of Nazi rule, the policy was carried out with less overt pressure, though by late 1937 the transfer of property was becoming more and more coercive. Following the *Kristallnacht* pogrom of Nov. 1938, forced Aryanization became legal. In various countries occupied by the Nazis and among the countries allied to the Nazis, Jewish property was also stolen by the authorities.

Ashkenazi (pl. **Ashkenazim**) Jews of European origin and their descendants as distinguished from Sephardi Jews.

Assembly of Notables Convocation of prominent Jews called together by Napoleon Bonaparte in 1806 to discuss questions put to them about possible conflicts between Judaism and French civic duties. The answers of the assembly were then confirmed by the French Sanhedrin.

Association of Jewish War Veterans (Ger. Reichsbund Juedischer Frontsoldaten, or RJF) Organization set up in Feb. 1919 by Jews who had fought for Germany in WWI. Its membership included some 30,000 men and it passionately championed German patriotism.

Auschwitz (Pol. Oswiencim) Nazi concentration and death camp complex. Auschwitz included the Auschwitz I concentration camp, the Auschwitz II (Birkenau) death camp, the Auschwitz III (Buna-Monowitz) labor camp, and 45 auxiliary camps for forced labor, all located near the Polish city of Oswiencim. Over one million Jews were murdered in Auschwitz-Birkenau as well as several hundred thousand Poles, gypsies, and others before it was liberated on 27 Jan. 1945.

Austrittsgemeinde Orthodox Jewish congregations in late 19th cent. Germany which separated themselves from official Jewish communities dominated by Reform Jews.

Ba'al Shem Tov (Yisrael ben Eliezer, also known as the "Besht"; 1700–1760). The founder and guiding light of Hasidism.

Bahad (Heb. acronym for Brit Halutzim Datiim). Religious Zionist youth movement affiliated with Mizrachi, the religious Zionist movement. Bahad was active in Germany, Czechoslovakia, and Hungary beginning in the 1930s.

Balakhovich Brigade Russian renegades who fought against the Bolsheviks during the Russian civil war (1918-21). They were infamous for the pogroms they staged against the Jews.

Bar Kochba Organization of Jewish students founded in Prague, Czechoslovakia. It is named after the leader of the second cent. revolt against the Romans, Shimon bar Kokhba. Soon after its creation in 1893 it adopted a pro-Zionist stance.

Bar Kokhba Jewish gymnastics clubs operating in Eastern and Central Europe from the late 19th cent. Forerunners of the Maccabi clubs.

Bar mitzvah Ceremony receiving a Jewish boy into the adult Jewish community at the age of 13, when he is considered to be responsible for his actions and for fulfilling the commandments of religious law.

Baron Hirsch schools Schools endowed in Eastern Europe by the Baron Maurice de Hirsch Foundation for the improvement of Jewish education. The Baron also contributed to Jewish education in Moslem countries in collaboration with the Alliance Israelite Universelle and set up an agricultural school in New Jersey and a trade school in New York City at the end of the 19th century.

Beilis trial Trial of Menahem Mendel Beilis, who was accused of ritual murder in Kiev in 1911. The trial was held in 1913 and Beilis was acquitted.

Beit din Rabbinical law court where questions of Jewish law are decided and suits arbitrated.

Beit midrash (pl. **battei midrash**) Place of study where religious texts are studied both formally and informally. Often a *beit midrash* adjoins or is part of a synagogue building.

Belzec One of the six death camps established by the Nazis in Poland. Belzec was set up in the southern Lublin district. Murder operations began on 17 March 1942 and ceased in Dec. 1942. About 600,000 Jews were executed there.

Bergen-Belsen Nazi camp located in northern Germany near the city of Celle. Set up in 1943, the camp at first served as an internment site for Jews destined to be exchanged for German nationals who had been stranded in Allied territory. In March 1944 Bergen-Belsen became a regular concentration camp and in the last few months of the war tens of thousands of Jews who had been evacuated from camps farther east were assembled there at the end of grueling death marches. Owing to the terrible conditions tens of thousands died before and after the liberation of the camp on 15 April 1945.

Berlin Rabbinical Seminary (Rabbinerseminar fuer das Orthodoxe Judentum) Seminary founded in the spirit of Neo-Orthodox Judaism in 1873 by Rabbi Azriel Hildesheimer. It continued to function until it was closed down by the Nazi regime in 1938.

Betar Youth movement of the Zionist Revisionist Organization or New Zionists, founded in Latvia in 1923.

Beth Jacob schools Network of schools for Orthodox Jewish girls. Founded in Cracow in 1917, the schools are associated with Agudat Israel and numbered 230 in Poland with about 27,000 pupils in 1938.

Betteljuden (Ger.) Term for Jewish beggars, especially in the 17th cent., when many Jews were reduced to wandering and begging because of the very strict regulations applying to Jewish residence in Germany.

Bizerta crisis Crisis occurring in 1961, when the Tunisians rebelled against the French occupation in the port of Bizerta. Threatened by their neighbors, the last Jews were shipped to safety in France just before the French evacuated the city.

Black Death persecutions Wave of atrocities committed against Jews in 1348–49 following the mass deaths caused by the bubonic plague that swept through Europe. Not knowing the true cause of the plague, people throughout Europe blamed the Jews, claiming they had poisoned the wells.

Black Hundreds (also known as Union of Russian People) Reactionary and violently antisemitic group. Active at the turn of the 20th cent., members of the Black Hundreds staged numerous pogroms against the Jews of Russia.

Blau-Weiss The first of the Zionist youth organizations. Founded in Germany in 1912, it was disbanded in 1926.

Blood libel Baseless but persisting allegation that Jews used the blood of Christian children for ritual purposes as well for medicines and sorcery. Also known as ritual murder, the accusation was most common at the time of Easter and Passover, when it was said that Jews required Christian blood to bake *matzot* (unleavened bread). Blood libels led to massacres and trials against Jews from the Middle Ages until the mid-20th cent.

Bnei Akiva Religious Zionist youth movement associated with the Mizrachi movement. Founded in Palestine in 1922 and active in Europe, the movement advocated the values of Torah, work, and kibbutz life.

B'nai B'rith Jewish fraternal organization. Patterned on other service organizations, it was established in 1843.

Body Tax (Ger. *Leibzoll*; Rus. *Gelietzoll*) Tax payed by Jews to gain exemptions from various restrictions (residence, travel, etc.). The tax was abolished in the German territories in the late 18th cent. and in the Russian Empire in 1862.

Boycott Day One-day boycott of Jewish businesses instituted by the Nazis throughout Germany on 1 April 1933. In some places it was accompanied by outbursts of violence against the Jews. Despite the declaration that the boycott would last only one day, it continued intermittently in some places for a protracted period.

Buchenwald Nazi concentration camp located near the German city of Weimar. Established in 1937, the camp was liberated on 11 April 1945. Nearly 240,000 prisoners representing over 30 nationalities, among them tens of thousands of Jews, were interned in Buchenwald during the camp's existence. About 43,000 perished there.

Bund (Yid.Yidisher Arbeter-Bund in Russland, Lite un Poiln [League of Jewish Workers in Russia, Lithuania and Poland]) Jewish socialist political organization. The Bund was established in Vilna, Lithuania (then Russia), in 1897. It aspired to achieve Jewish civil and cultural rights in a socialist economic milieu. The Bund advocated Yiddish as the Jewish national language and opposed Zionism and Hebrew culture.

Cantonists Term used for Jewish youth between the ages of 12 and 18 drafted into the army of Czarist Russia. Between 1827 and 1856, Jewish youth subject to the draft were forced to serve for 25 years. Since it was impossible for them to follow Jewish rituals and laws in the army, many parents took extreme measures to protect their sons from being drafted, while at the same time Jewish leaders were often forced by the authorities to provide the army with the conscripts.

Caisse de Secours et de Bienfaisance Israelite de Tunis (Tunisian Jewish Relief Fund) Following a series of decrees in the late 19th and early 20th cents., the Fund was established in the city of Tunis. Its primary role was to maintain synagogues and support rabbis. A committee, whose size varied, administered the Fund. Similar bodies were set up by other Jewish communities in Tunisia.

CENTOS (Federation of Associations for the Care of Orphans in Poland) Jewish organization set up in Poland in 1924 for the care of orphans.

Central Union of German Citizens of Jewish Faith (Ger. Centralverein Deutscher Staatsbuerger Juedischen Glaubens, or C.V.) Established in 1893, the Central Union was one of the foremost representative bodies of German Jewry. In 1938, following the *Kristallnacht* pogrom, the authorities closed it down.

Chelmno The first Nazi death camp. The camp was located near the village of Chelmno (Ger. Kulmhof) in the Pomerania dist. of Poland. The first Jewish victims arrived in the camp on 7 Dec. 1941. Until the final evacuation on 17 Jan. 1945, about 320,000 people, almost exclusively Jews, were murdered there.

Chmielnicki massacres Massacres of hundreds of thousands of Jews in the Ukraine during the uprising of 1648–49 led by the Cossak leader Bogdan Chmielnicki.

Commissariat Generale aux Questions Juives The Office of Jewish Affairs established by the collaborationist government of Vichy France in March 1941. Although the level of its cooperation with the German occupiers varied, the Office played a central role in the persecution of the Jews in France.

Comtat-Venaissin Area in southeastern France ruled by the Pope between 1274 and 1791. When Jews were expelled from the rest of France in the 14th cent. many of them found refuge there.

Congress Poland Semi-independent kingdom established in the traditional Polish heartland by the participants of the Congress of Vienna in 1815. The Russian Czar served as the king of Poland and the Polish gentry was granted a certain degree of autonomy to rule the country. The Polish uprising against Russia in 1863 brought the existence of the kingdom to an end.

Consistory (Fr. Consistoire) Jewish community organization set up by Napoleon Bonaparte. The Consistory remains in place today and is responsible for the religious life of French Jewry.

Council of the Four Lands (Heb. Va'ad Arba ha-Artzot) Body for autonomous Jewish self-government established in the Kingdom of Poland. Founded in the middle of the 16th cent. and in existence until 1764, the Council of the Four Lands represented Jewish interests before the crown and coordinated Jewish community activities.

Court Jew Jews who received special privileges from rulers in the 16th–18th cents. Court Jews, as the name implies, were able to attend the monarch's court and often acted as financial agents or advisors to the crown. Many Court Jews acquired great wealth and influence, and they frequently represented the Jewish community before the ruler and interceded on its behalf.

CYSHO (Central Yiddish School Organization) Network of Yiddish-language schools founded in Poland in 1921 and supported by the Bund. In 1929 it embraced 216 institutions and about 24,000 children.

Dachau The first concentration camp established by the Nazis in March 1933. Under its first commander, Theodor Eicke, Dachau became the model for the early concentration camps. Some 36 other camps were added to the Dachau complex and at the time of liberation on 29 April 1945 the camp held about 60,000 prisoners, of whom nearly a third were Jews.

Denikin, General Anton Leader of the anti-Bolshevik, counterrevolutionary White Russian forces during the period following the Russian Revolution of 1917.

De non tolerandis judaeis A papal bull or decree which gave a city or town the right to exclude Jews from its borders.

Der Stuermer Nazi antisemitic newspaper published weekly in Nuremberg by Julius Streicher between 1923 and 1945. It contained crude antisemitic diatribes and vulgar illustrations. At its height the newspaper's circulation was over 500,000.

Deutsche Volkspartei (also **DVP**; German People's Party) The DVP held right-wing democratic views and was the leading partner in the coalition that ruled Germany during the mid-1920s, until its support ebbed. In July 1933, several months after Hitler became chancellor, it disbanded.

Desecration of the Host Baseless allegation that Jews desecrated the holy wafer or bread used as part of the Eucharist ceremony, in which the wafer is said to become the body of Christ and the wine his blood through transubstantiation. The libel often led to violent attacks against Jews in the Middle Ages and in pre-modern Europe.

Dhimmi Laws Laws in Moslem lands that defined the relationship of the Jews to the Moslem majority. Jews were to be protected by the regimes under which they lived. In exchange they were not to engage in activities that would harm or dishonor Islam or the government and had to pay special taxes and undertake not to proselytize Moslems.

Displaced Persons (also known as **DPs**) Term used at the end of WWII for people who did not, could not, or would not return to their homes. Among them were many Jewish survivors of the Holocaust. DP camps were set up on the site of former Nazi camps in the American and British occupation zones of Germany, as well as in Italy. There were some 250,000 Jewish DPs 18 months after the end of the war. Most eventually emigrated. A few established residences near the camps. The last Jewish DP camp in Germany closed down in 1953.

District rabbi (Ger. Landesrabbiner, Landrabbiner; Heb. Av Bet Din) Position of responsibility and leadership held by Jews in Central Europe from the 14th through the 19th cents. The district rabbi was responsible for a country, state, or district, depending on the time and place, and had to distribute the tax burden fairly among his constituent Jews and act as the head of the religious court.

Einsatzgruppen (full name: Einsatzgruppen der Sicherheitsdienstes und der Sicherheitspolizei [Secret Service and Security Police Task Forces]). Special units of the SS set up by the Nazis in 1938. On the eve of the invasion of the Soviet Union in 1941, the *Einsatzgruppen* were reorganized into four main divisions (A, B, C, and D), each with a number of subunits known as *Einsatzkommandos* or *Sonderkommandos*. Their principal task was to carry out mass murder. It is estimated that they and their collaborators murdered over 1.25 million Jews and hundreds of thousands of others, among them Soviet prisoners of war, gypsies, and Communist officials.

Endecja Popular name for the right-wing Narodowa Demokracja Party in Poland founded at the end of the 19th cent. and particularly active from the end of WWI to the end of WWII. It advocated virulently antisemitic policies within the framework of an extreme nationalistic ideology.

Eretz Israel (Heb. "Land of Israel") Term for the geographic area of biblical Israel. Often used to avoid the complication of using the country's different names during different eras: Canaan, Palestine, and Israel.

Eruv (Heb. "mixing") The concept of the *eruv* is used in various ways in Jewish law to expand the space in which activities otherwise forbidden on the Sabbath and holidays may be performed. An *eruv tehumim* allows observant Jews to carry items in a wide and clearly defined area where otherwise such an act would be forbidden on the Sabbath and holidays. An *eruv tavshilim* allows food to be cooked for the Sabbath on a holiday that occurs on Friday.

Euthanasia Normally a term denoting mercy killing, it was used cynically by the Nazis for the murder of physically and mentally handicapped and chronically ill people.

Ezra Youth movement for Orthodox Jews founded in Germany in 1919. Although originally not oriented toward Zionism, by the 1930s it became more pro-Zionist.

Familiants Laws (Ger. *Familiantengesetz*) Laws restricting Jewish marriages in Bohemia, Moravia, and Silesia during much of the 18th and 19th cents.

Family camp During the period of the Holocaust, East European Jews fleeing to the forests and not able to fight as partisans because of age, sex, or other limitations were protected by Jewish partisans and lived in what were known as family camps. They often provided services to the partisans, such as cooking and sewing.

Fourth Aliya. The period from 1924 through 1931 when some 80,000 Jews, many of them from the middle class, immigrated to Palestine. Many of these immigrants were from Eastern Europe, especially Poland, which they left because of the anti-Jewish economic policies of Wladislaw Grabski.

Frankists Eighteenth century followers of Jakob Frank, who considered himself the successor to the popular 17th cent. pseudo-messiah Shabbetai Zvi. Especially active in Poland, the Frankists were excommunicated, renounced the Talmud, and some converted to Christianity.

French Sanhedrin Body convened by Napoleon Bonaparte in 1807, patterned on the ancient Sanhedrin that had acted as the highest Jewish court and legislature from the Second Temple period through the fourth cent. Napoleon wished to see the French Sanhedrin endorse the view that being Jewish was not incompatible with being a citizen of France. The Sanhedrin passed nine regulations satisfying Napoleon without violating Jewish religious law.

Gedud ha-Avoda (Heb. "Labor Battalion") Group established by immigrants to Palestine and active in the 1920s. The Labor Battalions engaged in various large-scale construction projects, founded settlements, and lived under a communal regime. They aspired to incorporate all the laborers of Palestine into a large commune.

General Gouvernement Following the German and Soviet invasions of Poland in autumn 1939, Poland was divided into three sections. The western section was incorporated into the German Reich, the eastern section was taken over by the Soviet Union, and the remaining part became known as the General Gouvernement, a semi-autonomous administrative region under the direction of the veteran Nazi Hans Frank. Ultimately it became the dumping ground for most of the Jews of Nazi-dominated Europe, with the six death camps of Poland either within its territory or directly adjacent to it.

Genizah Place where Jewish ritual objects no longer usable, such as books, Torah scrolls, and other parchments, are stored. Often it is adjacent to a synagogue.

Gestapo The German Secret State Police. During the Nazi regime, the Gestapo was the main instrument of state terror. It was deeply involved in the persecution and murder of the Jews.

Gordonia Zionist youth movement founded in Galicia in 1923 and following the teachings of A.D. Gordon, an ideologue of modern Zionism. Over time it merged with other Zionist youth movements.

Green Shirts Popular name for the Rumanian Fascist Iron Guard.

Grigoryev gangs Antisemitic gangs led by Ataman Grigoryev which attacked and killed Jews throughout the Ukraine during the Russian civil war (1918–21).

Gurs Nazi concentration camp in the south of France.

Habad Popular name for the Lubavich hasidic sect. The name is an acrostic for the Hebrew words for knowledge: *hohma*, *bina*, and *da'at*. Each has a different connotation: respectively, finding out the facts, logically thinking them through, and finally understanding them in their context. This process lies at the heart of the Lubavich world-view. Habad sponsors many activities throughout the world that seek to draw non-observant Jews closer to religion.

Habonim A Zionist youth movement associated with Labor Zionism. It is active in Europe, the Americas, South Africa, and Australia. Until the late 1930s, when it began merging with similar organizations, Habonim was an autonomous movement. Today it is part of Habonim–Deror.

Haidamaks Ukrainian Cossacks who staged numerous pograms against the Jews in the 18th cent.

Hakham (Heb. "sage"; pl. **hakhamim**) Title given to the third-ranking member of the Sanhedrin. It was also a title given to sages and Torah scholars in Oriental Jewish communities.

Hakhshara (Heb. "training" or "preparation") Facilities set up by the Zionist movement to teach skills for living in Palestine. Most commonly they were intended for young people.

Hakkafot Ritual circular procession. *Hakkafot* are part of the celebration of the Sukkot and Simhat Torah holidays. In some Jewish communities the bride also walks around the bridegroom during the marriage ceremony.

Haller's army Polish army under the command of General Jozef Haller, established by the Polish National Committee in Aug. 1917, before the creation of the Polish state at the end of WWI. Haller's forces were composed largely of Polish volunteers from the United States. The army fought in France toward the end of WWI and against Soviet forces until 1921. In Poland

and areas of the Soviet Union, Haller's soldiers killed many Jews and staged numerous pogroms.

Halukkah (Heb. "partition") Designation of a series of plans and proposals that surfaced throughout the 1930s and 1940s for the division of Palestine between Jewish and Arab residents. Ultimately, in 1948, the idea was rejected by the Arabs, leading to Israel's War of Independence.

Halutzim (Heb. "pioneers") Jews who settled in Palestine before the creation of the State of Israel, living a life of self-sacrifice in accordance with the Zionist ideal and often starting up new settlements.

Hame'assef The first secular Hebrew-language journal, published monthly in Germany from 1783 to 1829.

Ha-Meuhad Movement of collective kibbutz settlements founded in 1927. The movement has undergone many political changes and its successor organization belongs to the only remaining kibbutz movement in Israel.

Ha-No'ar ha-Tziyyoni Zionist youth movement founded in Poland in 1931. It united several Zionist youth organizations from Eastern, Central, and Western Europe under one banner. Ha-No'ar ha-Tziyyoni sought to encourage Jewish youth to adopt the ideal of kibbutz life and its graduates established a number of kibbutzim and educational centers.

Ha-Po'el ha-Mizrachi Orthodox Jewish Zionist organization, also known as Mizrachi. It was founded in Vilna in 1902 by rabbis and observant Jews who had adopted the Zionist idea of creating a Jewish national homeland in Palestine but sought to do so in a manner consistent with an Orthodox religious outlook. Mizrachi is a prominent political and ideological element in the mosaic of modern Zionism and the State of Israel.

Hasag Privately owned German armaments company using concentration camp inmates as forced laborers.

Hasidei Ashkenaz A Jewish religious movement that evolved in the Rhineland area of Germany in the 12th cent. following the atrocities committed against the Jews by the Crusaders. Hasidei Ashkenaz preached mysticism, martyrdom, and asceticism. Some of their liturgical verses are still used in the synagogue service today.

Hashomer Hatzair Zionist youth movement founded in Galicia in 1916. It combined socialism with Zionism, holding up life on the kibbutz as its ideal. One of the largest Zionist youth movements, its graduates founded many kibbutzim. Hashomer Hatzair has branches throughout the world.

Hasidism A spiritual branch of Judaism founded by the Ba'al Shem Tov in Eastern Europe in the 18th century. The followers of Hasidism are called Hasidim. In hasidic thought, prayer, joyousness, and mysticism are central elements. According to Hasidism, the Rabbi or Rebbe is a charismatic source of leadership and religious authority, fulfilling the role of intermediary between his disciples and God. Eventually, in a number of East European localities, diverse hasidic dynasties came into being, each centered on a different charismatic rabbi. Adherents of these dynasties now live in many parts of the world and their particular movements are named for the home town of the dynasties' founders (Gur [Gora Kalwaria], Lubavich [Lyubavichi], etc).

Haskala (Heb. "Enlightenment") Term generally used in the context of the turning of Jewish intellectual, cultural, and literary endeavor to secular fields and the surrounding Christian world. This activity accompanied the process of Jewish political emancipation from the second half of the 18th cent. through the end of the 19th cent.

Hazzan (pl. **hazzanim**; Heb. "cantor"). In many Jewish synagogues, in addition to the congregational rabbi, there is a cantor who regularly leads the prayer services, especially on the Sabbath and festivals, and is known as the *shali'ah tzibbur* ("representative of the congregation"). In other congregations this position is not formally held and various members of the prayer group may lead the service. The *hazzan* is not only well versed in the fine points of leading prayer, he usually has a fine voice as well.

Heder (pl. **hadarim**; Heb. "room") Elementary school for traditional Jewish religious instruction. In most Jewish communities before the advent of secular education, all young Jewish boys attended the *heder*, usually beginning at the age of five.

Hehalutz (Heb. "The Pioneer") Zionist movement for young single adults. Rooted in the reaction to the pogroms that swept Russia in 1881, it was set up officially in 1905. At its height in the 1930s it had tens of thousands of members. Hehalutz was associated with many Zionist youth movements and throughout the world prepared the graduates of these movements for immigration to Eretz Israel. Soon after the creation of the State of Israel, the movement ceased its activities.

Hep! Hep! riots Anti-Jewish riots that broke out in Germany in 1819. The riots were related to the nascent German nationalism and anti-Jewish feeling that accompanied the early stages of Jewish emancipation. The cry Hep! Hep! as a taunt apparently derived from the Latin Crusader slogan *Hierosolyma est perdita* ("Jerusalem is lost").

Hevra kaddisha Jewish burial society. In almost every traditional Jewish community there is a voluntary society to facilitate burial according to Jewish custom and to comfort the bereaved.

HIAS (Hebrew Immigrant Aid Society) Organization founded in 1902 to help Jewish newcomers in the United States. After WWI it set up offices in Europe as well to help Jewish immigrants.

Hilfsverein ("Relief Organization [of German Jews]") Founded in 1901, the Hilfsverein traditionally provided assistance to Jews in need in Eastern Europe, helping them move to other countries by way of Germany. After the Nazi rise to power in 1933 and until emigration from Germany was ended in autumn 1941, the Hilfsverein helped German Jews leave Germany for destinations other than Palestine.

Hitahdut Zionist party uniting Tze'irei Tziyyon and Ha-Po'el ha-Tza'ir (Palestine Workers Party) and active in Eastern Europe between the World Wars. It supported Hehaluz and the Tarbut school system.

Hitler Youth (Ger. Hitlerjugend) Nazi youth organization for boys. Founded in 1922 as part of the SA, it assumed its name in 1926. In 1928 a girls' youth organization, Bund Deutcher Maedel ("League of German Girls"), took its place alongside it. The Hitler Youth focused on the physical and ideological development of its members, with the aim of turning them into dedicated Nazis.

Hochdeutsch Ashkenazim (also known as **Hochdeutsch Juden**) Literally meaning "High German Jews" or "High German Jews from Ashkenaz," the term was coined to differentiate between Jews of Portuguese origin living in Hamburg and its environs and the Jews who had preceded them.

Horev schools A network of schools in Eastern Europe maintained by Agudat Israel and including *hadarim*, *talmudei torah*, and *yeshivot* and sometimes teaching general as well as Jewish subjects. In Poland the network embraced about 350 schools and over 47,000 children in the mid-1930s.

House of Catechumens House established in 16th cent. Rome by order of the government for Jews to be taught Christian precepts and to be given the opportunity to convert. If a Jew did not convert after residing there for a given period of time, he could return to the ghetto. Similar houses were also established in other parts of Italy.

Hovevei Zion (Heb. "Lovers of Zion") Members of the Hibbat Zion movement, which began in the 1860s and expressed the yearning of Jews to return to the Land of Israel. The Hovevei Zion generated much of the support that led to the creation of political Zionism by Theodore Herzl at the end of the 19th cent.

ICA (Jewish Colonization Association; also known as **JCA**) Founded by Baron Maurice de Hirsch in 1891, the Association facilitated the establishment of Jewish agricultural settlements in the Americas. It soon became involved in Jewish agricultural settlement in Palestine as well, shifting the focus of its activities to Israel after statehood.

Infamous Decree (Fr. *Decret Infame*) In 1808 Napoleon Bonaparte decreed that all debts owed to Jews by soldiers or women were canceled. In addition, Jews were no longer permitted to trade freely but were required to obtain special permits. The decree also banned Jews from residing in the Lower and Upper Rhine regions.

Inquisition A tribunal for rooting out suspected heresies, established by the Catholic Church in the 13th cent. In Spain, toward the end of the 15th cent., the Inquisition focused on Jews who had converted to Christianity and were accused of maintaining Jewish practices in secret. In the mid-16th cent., the Inquisition spread to Portugal and to Spanish and Portuguese holdings overseas. Many innocent Jews were burned at the stake during the Inquisition or expelled from their countries of residence.

Institut d'Etude des Questions Juives ("Institute for the Study of the Jewish Problem") Antisemitic institute established in Vichy France in 1941 and active until the summer of 1943. Primarily, the institute created and disseminated antisemitic propaganda.

Irgun Tzeva'i Le'ummi (also known by the Heb. acronym **Etzel**) Underground Jewish military organization founded in Palestine in 1931 and active until the creation of the State of Israel in 1948. The Irgun was associated with the Zionist Revisionists. Between 1939 and 1948, it brought many Jews to Palestine in defiance of the British in what was known as "Aliya Bet" or "Illegal Immigration."

Iron Guard Created in Rumania as the Legion of the Archangel Michael in 1927, its members were also known as Legionnaires or as Green Shirts after their uniforms. In 1940 the Iron Guard was included in the Rumanian government and in the following year attempted to take over completely. Their failed coup was accompanied by much violence against the Jews.

Jewish Brigade Unit in the British army composed of Jewish volunteers from Palestine. It was founded in 1944 and saw action near the end of WWII, fighting in Italy. Members of the Brigade were active after the war in helping Jewish Displaced Persons reach Palestine.

Jewish Fighting Organization (Pol. Zydowska Organizacja Bojowa, or ZOB; Yid. Yidishe Kamf Organizatsye) Main Jewish underground organization in the Warsaw Ghetto in 1942 and 1943. The ZOB spearheaded the Warsaw Ghetto Uprisings of Jan. and April 1943.

Jewish National Party (Ger. Juedische Volkspartei)

Zionist political party founded in Germany in 1919 to challenge assimilationist and conservative control of Jewish community councils.

Joint Distribution Committee   see **American Jewish Joint Distribution Committee**

Judendorf   (Ger.) Village in which the majority of residents were Jewish.

Judenfrei   (or **Judenrein**; Ger. "free of Jews") Self-congratulatory Nazi term designating the status of a locality where all the Jews had either been deported or executed.

Judengasse   (Ger.) Street where Jews resided and had their synagogue and other communal buildings.

Judenhaeuser   (Ger. "Jewish houses") Houses designated for Jews during the Nazi period. Jews were confined to such houses in the German Reich, where the Nazis did not establish ghettoes for the Jews after the outbreak of WWII, and also in Budapest in 1944.

Judenlager   (Ger. "Jewish camps") As part of the vast system of camps set up by the Nazis, some were designated specifically as Jewish camps.

Judenordnung   (Ger. "Jewish statute") Legal document defining the status of the Jews in a given locality. It outlined both their rights and obligations, including the payment of special taxes.

Judenrat   (Ger. "Jewish council") Soon after they invaded Poland in 1939 the Nazis began creating Jewish councils. These were to be composed of community leaders and charged with carrying out Nazi orders with reference to the Jews. The councils also represented the Jewish communities before the Nazi authorities. Though not every Jewish administrative body under the Nazis was called a Jewish council nor were they all constituted in the same way, *Judenrat* is nonetheless often used as a generic term for all such bodies.

Judenrein   see **Judenfrei**

Judenstern   (Ger. "Jewish star") The six-pointed Shield of David. In April 1933, during the boycott of Jewish businesses in Germany, the Jewish star was painted on Jewish storefronts by Nazi hooligans. Later on, during WWII, the symbol was usually used for the special badge the Jews were made to wear, and most commonly colored yellow.

Juedische Wissenschaft   (also known as **Wissenschaft des Judentums**; Ger. "Science of Judaism") Method of research developed in Germany in the 19th cent. in which Jewish scholars took a scientific approach to the study of Jewish religion, culture, history, literature, and thought.

Jugendstil   Artistic style that came into vogue in Germany at the end of the 19th cent. and persisted into the first decade of the 20th cent. It combined Art Nouveau and the style of Japanese prints. Later it assumed a more abstract form.

Kabbalah   The Jewish mystical tradition, first applied to mystical Jewish learning in medieval Spain and said to draw upon early rabbinical mystical traditions. It took on more importance in the 16th cent. with the teachings of Yitzhak Luria and Moshe Cordovera. The basic texts of the Kabbalah, such as the Zohar, continue to be studied today.

Kapp Putsch   An abortive attempt by German right-wing extremists to take over the government in March 1920. Named for its leader, Wolfgang Kapp, the coup was an early expression of the deep-seated and long-simmering resentment many Germans felt toward the Versailles Treaty and the republic it had imposed on them at the end of WWI. Unsupported by both the army and the civil service, Kapp was forced to back down several days after he seized power.

Karaites   Members of a Jewish sect that came into being in Persia during the eighth century. Karaites follow the word of the Bible, which they interpret literally. They do not accept the oral tradition of interpretation ultimately set down in writing in the Talmud and other rabbinical texts. Although they flourished for several centuries, by the modern period they had become a very small and marginal group.

Kasztner Group   The Relief and Rescue Committee in Budapest under the leadership of Israel (Rezso) Kasztner and Otto Komoly. In fall 1942 it first began helping Jewish refugees who reached Hungary, mostly from Slovakia. In early 1943 it was recognized by the Jewish Agency as an associated organization. Zionist in orientation, the Committee emerged as the unofficial Jewish leadership body during the period of the German occupation of Hungary in 1944 and early 1945. Kazstner and his group engaged in various rescue activities, including negotiations with the SS, some of which are still considered controversial.

Kattowitz Conference   The first large-scale meeting of members of the Hibbat Zion movement in Kattowitz (Katowice) in 1882. During the conference Jews were urged to move to Palestine and work the land there.

Keren Hayesod   (Palestine Foundation Fund) Company registered in 1921 as the financial arm of the Zionist Organization with the task of raising money to finance Zionist activity.

Khazars   A people whose kingdom in medieval Russia stretched from the Volga River to Kiev in present-day Ukraine. In the eighth cent. the king and his nobles converted to Judaism. Rabbi Yehuda Halevi, who lived in Spain from the mid-11th to the mid-12th cent., wrote a theological essay known as the *Kuzari* inspired by the conversion.

Kibbutz   (pl. **kibbutzim**) Collective farm settlement in Eretz Israel. A mainstay of the Zionist enterprise, the first, Deganya, called at the time a *kevutza*, was founded in 1909. The term was also used for pioneer training groups abroad.

Kindertransport   (Ger. "children's transport") Name given to the groups of Jewish refugee children and youth who reached the United Kingdom in the wake of the *Kristallnacht* pogrom. Between Dec. 1938 and Sept. 1939, when WWII broke out, nearly 10,000 Jewish children and youth from Germany, Austria, and former Czechoslovakia found refuge in the United Kingdom.

Kinot   (Heb. "lamentations") *Kinot* are texts expressing mourning recited in the synagogue on the 9th of Av, the day on which the First and Second Temples are said to have been destroyed.

Kishinev pogrom   Riot against the Jews in April 1903 in the Bessarabian city of Kishinev. During the pogrom some 41 Jews were killed and scores were injured. In its wake Jewish emigration from Russia increased greatly.

Klaus   (also **kloyz**) a prayer house or *beit midrash* common among Hasidim.

Komsomol   (Rus. Communist Youth League) Between its establishment in 1918 and its collapse in 1991, the Komsomol was the official organization of the Communist Party of the Soviet Union for people between the ages of 14 and 28. Its purpose was to prepare youth to become full-fledged members of the Communist Party.

KRBN   (Heb. acronym for the towns of Kolin, Roudnice, Bumsla (Mlada Boleslav), and Nachod. These were the most important Jewish communities in Bohemia during the 15th cent..

Krimchaks   Jews who lived in the Crimea for over 2,000 years. They continued to maintain traditional Jewish practices while at the same time adopting many elements of the Tartar culture around them, including modes of dress and language. About 70% of the Krimchaks were murdered in the Holocaust.

Kristallnacht   (Ger. "crystal night" or "Night of the Broken Glass") Name given by the Nazis to the pogrom against Jews on the night of 9–10 Nov. 1938. During the riots, about 40% of the synagogues in Germany and Austria were destroyed. Many Jewish stores were vandalized and their plate glass show windows smashed; hence the name. At the time of the violent spree, scores of Jews were killed and many more beaten. For the first time under the Nazi regime, Jewish men were arrested and placed in concentration camps simply for being Jews.

Kulturbund Deutscher Juden   (Jewish Cultural Association) Soon after the Nazi rise to power in 1933 and until it was disbanded in 1941, the Kulturbund fostered cultural and artistic activity among the Jews of Germany after they were excluded from Germany's artistic and cultural life. In particular, the Kulturbund provided an outlet for Jewish musicians, actors and, artists.

Kultur-Liga   (Culture League) First established in

Kiev in 1917, the aim of the Kultur-Liga was to foster Yiddish theater, literature, art, and scholarship. Local branches soon took root throughout Europe and the Americas. In 1921 the center of the League moved to Warsaw.

Kultusgemeinde   Designation of the Jewish community structure in Bohemia and Moravia created by the Austrian authorities and through which Jewish community life was organized and supervised between 1880 and the end of WWI.

Kultusverein   (Ger. "Religious Union") Framework through which Jewish community life was organized in the Austro-Hungarian Empire between 1848 and 1890. Each officially recognized Jewish community was constituted as a *Kultusverein.*

Lag ba-Omer   The 33rd day of the Omer, falling on the 18th day of the Hebrew month of Iyyar and considered a minor festival. Between the holidays of Passover and Shavuot, a seven-week period called the Omer is observed, characterized by some of the customs of mourning. On Lag ba-Omer, according to tradition, a plague that struck down the students of Rabbi Akiva came to an end. Lag ba-Omer is also said to be the anniversary of the death of Rabbi Shimon bar Yohai.

Landjudenschaft   Association of Jewish communities in Bohemia outside the city of Prague. Established in 1659 the association's main task was to collect taxes for the authorities. It was dissolved in 1884.

Land(es)rabbiner   see **District rabbi**

Landsmannschaft   Organization of former emigree residents of a given community. Such organizations were set up by Jewish immigrants to the United States, Israel, and other places, their organizations named for their home town or region.

Landtag   German term for the local parliament or diet of each of the German states (*Laender*).

Lehrhaus   A school for Jewish adults where Judaism and related subjects were taught. Such schools were active during the Nazi period, particularly in Frankfurt and Berlin.

Liberal Judaism   A movement in Judaism, also known as Reform Judaism or Progressive Judaism. Liberal Judaism emerged as a response of German Jews to their evolving emancipation in the middle of the 19th cent. It is characterized by a belief that traditional Jewish law is not binding in our time but rather a guide for Jewish practice, and by the extensive use of the local vernacular language in place of Hebrew in the synagogue service. Liberal Judaism has many adherents throughout the world, with large centers in the United States and Great Britain. Its main institutions include the Union of American Hebrew Congregations, Hebrew Union College–Jewish Institute of Religion, Leo Baeck College, and Central Conference of American Rabbis.

Lithuanian Council   Autonomous governing body for Jewish affairs in Lithuania during the 17th and 18th cents. It represented Jewish interests before the authorities and coordinated Jewish community affairs.

Maccabi World Union   Union of Jewish sports organizations established in 1895 in various European cities. It sponsors the Maccabiah Games, known as the Jewish Olympics.

Maggid   (Heb. "preacher") Usually a popular preacher who urged the Jews to behave morally and uphold Jewish religious law. Such preachers were especially common among the Hasidim of Eastern Europe.

Mahzikei ha-Dat   Ultra-Orthodox group formed in Lwow in 1879 to fight Reformist tendencies among the Jewish population. It was active in Galicia and Bukovina.

Mahzor   Prayer book used for the Jewish high holidays (Rosh Hashanah and Yom Kippur) and the festivals of Sukkot, Passover, and Shavuot.

Majdanek   Nazi death and concentration camp near Lublin in Poland. It opened as a concentration camp in Sept. 1941 and several months later assumed the function of a death camp as well. Until it was liberated in July 1944, some 360,000 inmates died there. About 40% of the victims were murdered in the gas chambers and the rest perished under the inhuman living conditions in the camp.

Ma'pilim   Hebrew term for Jews who circumvented

immigration laws in order to reach Palestine. They are also known as "illegal immigrants." Most arrived clandestinely to get around the strict immigration quotas imposed by the British from the late 1930s until the creation of the State of Israel in 1948. Their immigration is also known as Aliya Bet.

Marranos   see **Anusim**

Maskilim   (sing. **maskil**) Jews identified with the Haskala movement and turning to the secular world and its new knowledge at the time of the Enlightenment and Jewish Emancipation, from the mid-18th cent. to the end of the 19th cent.

Matrikel Laws   German laws limiting the number of Jewish marriages or households. The laws remained in effect until the emancipation of the Jews in the 19th cent.

May Laws   A series of laws passed in Czarist Russia in 1882 limiting Jewish residence to the Pale of Settlement. The May Laws also entailed various economic restrictions. They were abolished in 1917.

Melamed   (Heb. "teacher") The *melamed* was usually a junior teacher in the *heder* or a private tutor for young children.

Memorbuch   (Ger. "Memorial Book") Book usually published to commemorate a tragic event in the life of a Jewish community. After the Holocaust some 1,200 such books were published by the remnants of the shattered and obliterated Jewish communities of Europe. The books generally contain information about the history and social life of the community before the Holocaust, testimony and historical writings pertaining to the destruction of the community, and lists of the murdered Jews. Many books contain photographs of the community and even of some of the victims of the Holocaust. They are also known by the Hebrew term *Sifrei Yizkor* and as Yizkor Books.

Mikve   A Jewish ritual bath.

Mint Jews   Jews present in the courts of German rulers, especially during the 16th and 17th cents., with the responsibility of coining and distributing money.

Mintmaster   Person licensed by a local ruler to mint coins on his behalf. In Medieval Europe and into the 19th cent., many mintmasters were Jews.

Minyan   (pl. **minyanim**) A prayer quorum. For Orthodox Jews to engage in a public prayer service, a quorum of ten adult males is required.

Mischling   (pl. **Mischlinge**) Nazi term for people of mixed Jewish and "Aryan" descent. According to the Nuremberg Laws of Sept. 1935 and its many amendments, a full Jew was defined as having three or four Jewish grandparents and being part of the Jewish community. A person with two Jewish grandparents was considered a *Mischling* of the first degree and a person with one Jewish grandparent a *Mischling* of the second degree. At different times during the period of the Holocaust, certain anti-Jewish measures were applied to the *Mischlinge* in full, others in part, and some not at all.

Mitnaggedim   (Heb. "opponents") The term is used primarily to denote Orthodox Jews opposed to Hasidism. The first to clearly voice this opposition was the Vilna Gaon (Eliyahu ben Shelomo Zalman) at the end of the 18th cent.

Mizrachi   see **Ha-Po'el ha-Mizrachi**

Mohel   Jewish specialist performing ritual circumcision.

Monti di Pieta   Forerunners of modern banks established in Italy during the 15th and 16th cents. The Monti di Pieta loaned money at low interest, especially to Italian artisans and small businessmen, thereby providing an alternative to Jewish moneylenders.

More Judaico oath   Special oath taken by Jews at the start of legal proceedings between a Jew and a Gentile. In use from the medieval period through the 18th cent. in much of Europe, the *more judaica* oath assumed many forms and was often accompanied by an elaborate ceremony.

Moshav   (pl. **moshavim**) A cooperative smallholders' farm settlement in Eretz Israel. The first moshav, Nahalal, was founded in 1921. Farmers work their own land (10–25 acres) and utilize cooperative marketing and purchasing facilities.

Moshav shitufi A form of farm settlement in Eretz Israel combining elements of the moshav and kibbutz and featuring collective production and private consumption.

Mountain Jews (also known as Tats) A Jewish tribe living in Dagestan and the Eastern Caucasus. The Jews in this region were said to have arrived after the destruction of the First Temple. Historical evidence of their presence dates back to the third cent. The Mountain Jews took on many local customs and developed their own version of the local language, Tat, which they wrote in a cursive Hebrew script.

Munich Agreement Agreement signed between the British, French, Italians, and Germans in Sept. 1938 and allowing Hitler to take over the so-called Sudetenland from Czechoslovakia. The agreement was the first stage in the dismemberment of Czechoslovakia, which was completed in March 1939 with the establishment of the client state of Slovakia and the protectorate of Bohemia and Moravia under Nazi Germany. The Munich Agreement is usually seen as the symbol of the British policy of appeasement.

Musar movement Movement founded in the 19th cent. by Rabbi Yisrael Salanter in Lithuania. It stressed ethical instruction as part of traditional Jewish Torah education.

Nagid The head of the Jewish community in most of the Islamic world. The title was used from the eighth cent. through the 19th cent. In some times and places the title of Exilarch was used instead.

Neo-Dustur An Arab nationalist party active primarily in Tunisia. It was founded in 1934 as a revitalized version of the Dustur (Constitution) Party.

Neologism, Neologists The Hungarian branch of Reform Judaism. Many aligned themselves with the movement in the second half of the 19th cent., when Hungarian Jewish communities had to declare their religious orientation.

Neo-Orthodoxy Movement in Judaism founded in the second half of the 19th cent. by Rabbi Shimshon Rafael Hirsch in Germany. Neo-Orthodoxy sought to reconcile traditional Jewish practices and law with full integration into Western society.

Neturei Karta (Aram. "guardians of the city") An extreme ultra-Orthodox group that broke away from the Agudat Israel movement in 1935. It is fanatically anti-Zionist, even though one of its two large centers is in Israel, the other being in New York City.

Night of the Long Knives A bloody purge of leaders of the SA staged on 30 June 1934. In the wake of certain expressions of dissatisfaction with the course of the Nazi revolution by SA chief Ernst Roehm and some of his associates, Hitler ordered the SS under Heinrich Himmler to murder the malcontents. The official reason for the assassinations was that Roehm and his followers were engaged in homosexual debauchery.

NKVD (Rus. People's Commissariat of Internal Affairs) Forerunner of the KGB, the political and security police of the Soviet Union. The NKVD was formed in 1934 and retained its name until 1941, when it began to be known as NKGB, the People's Commissariat for State Security.

Nuremberg Laws A series of racial laws first promulgated in Nazi Germany on 15 Sept. 1935. The laws and their various amendments sought to define and fix the status of Jews on a racial basis. Those with three or four Jewish grandparents were deemed full-blooded Jews, those with one or two *Mischlinge* (half or quarter Jews). According to the laws, only "Aryans" could be full citizens of Germany, which meant that full and partial Jews could not. The laws also prohibited sexual relations between Jews and "Aryans." Lastly, they prohibited Jews to fly the German flag.

Oleh (pl. **olim**; Heb. "one who ascends") Term for an immigrant to Eretz Israel.

Operation Hindenburg WWI operation transferring Jews from the German-occupied areas of Eastern Europe to the Ruhr region to work.

ORT (Rus. "Society for the Encouragement of Handicrafts"). Established by Jews in Russia at the end of the 19th cent., ORT set up vocational schools for Jews throughout the world. It is still active today.

OSE   see **OZE**

Ostjuden   German term for East European Jews. The term was used especially for those who had immigrated to Western countries. Western Jews often used the word disdainfully and took pains to differentiate themselves from the *Ostjuden*.

OZE   (Rus. "Jewish Health Society"; Fr. OSE [Oeuvre de Secour aux Enfants]). Founded by Jews in Russia in 1912, OZE headquarters moved to France in 1919. The organization promoted child care, health, and hygiene.

Pale of Settlement   Area in Czarist Russia where Jews were permitted to live, often referred to as the Pale. The Pale was established by Catherine the Great in 1791 and abolished officially in 1917. It included 25 provinces in Belorussia, Bessarabia, the Crimea, Lithuania, Poland, and the Ukraine. In 1882, further restrictions, known as the May Laws, restricted Jewish residence to the cities, towns, and villages of the Pale.

Paris Sanhedrin   see **French Sanhedrin**

Parnas   (pl. **parnasim**; Heb. "provider") Term used for an elected leader of the Jewish community. Today the term is sometimes used for the president of a synagogue.

Partitions of Poland   The division of Poland by Russia, Austria, and Prussia in the 18th cent. In 1772, 1793, and 1795, territory was taken from Poland and allotted to its neighbors in an attempt to maintain a balance of power among them. The Second Partition produced an uprising led by Tadeusz Kosciuszko. The failure of the rebellion led to the Third Partition. The creation of Congress Poland by the Congress of Vienna in 1815 gave the Poles a modicum of autonomy, but it was only after WWI that Poland was reconstituted as an independent state.

Pastoureaux persecutions   Persecution of Jews during the second Pastoureaux (Shepherds') Rebellion that began in France in 1320. Clamoring for French participation in a Crusade against the Moslem rulers of the Holy Land, French peasants took up arms against their ruler Philip V. For awhile they held him hostage in Paris, while ransacking the city. Attacks against Jews occurred as the rebels made their way to the Garonne Valley. The uprising was put down in 1322.

Paytan   (pl. **paytanim**) Author of liturgical poems, known in Hebrew as *piyyutim*, many of which have been included in Jewish prayer services. Among the best known of these *paytanim* are Saadyah Gaon, Shelomo ibn Gabirol, and Yehuda Halevi.

Petlyura gangs   Ukrainian nationalist bands who murdered large numbers of Jews as they retreated before the Red Army in 1919. At the time of the pogroms Simon Petlyura was commander of the Ukrainian army and chairman of the provisional government but he did little to stop the violence.

Po'alei Agudat Israel   Orthodox Jewish labor party founded in Poland in 1922 and until 1960 formally associated with Agudat Israel. It reunited with Agudat Israel at the end of the 1980s.

Po'alei Zion   Movement founded in Russia in 1899 to promote the idea of Labor Zionism—the integration of political Zionism with socialist ideals. It spread throughout Europe and the rest of the Jewish world, and eventually evolved into a number of political parties.

Qa'id   (Arab. "leader") Title of heads of Jewish communities in Moslem lands under Turkish rule.

Rabbanites   Adherents of rabbinical Judaism, as opposed to Karaites.

Radanites   Group of Jewish traders who traveled between France and the Far East in the ninth cent. The origin of the name is unclear.

Rassenschande   (Ger. "racial defilement") Term used by racial antisemites, among them the Nazis, to describe the so-called crime of miscegnation.

Reformed heder   A religious Jewish elementary school operating along the lines of the traditional *heder* but considerably modernized.

Reform Judaism   see **Liberal Judaism**

Reichstag   The lower house of the German parliament in the period of the Second Reich (1871–1919) and the subsequent Weimar Republic.

Reichsvereinigung der Juden in Deutschland (Union of Jews of Germany) Organization created in 1939 as the successor of the Reichsvertretung der Deutschen Juden established in 1933. Both were the central bodies of Jewish leadership in Germany as set up by the Nazis. In 1943, the Reichsvereinigung was replaced by the Rest-Reichsvereinigung, which represented the remnant of German Jewry before the Nazi authorities.

Reichsvertretung   see **Reichsvereinigung**

Religionsgesellschaft   (also **Religionsgemeinde**) An officially recognized Jewish community.

Resh Kalla   Title of the second person in authority in the *yeshivot* of Babylonia in the first centuries after the destruction of the Second Temple.

Responsa   Written opinions ("responses") issued by rabbinical authorities with reference to questions of Jewish law, or published collections of such opinions.

Rindfleisch massacres   Attacks on Jews in Germany in 1298. After a series of blood libels in Mainz, Munich, and Oberwesel and a Host deseccration libel in Paris, a local mob led by a knight named Rindfleisch massacred 21 Jews in Roettingen. The pogroms quickly spread throughout southern and central Germany with thousands of Jews murdered.

Romaniots   Original Jewish settlers in the Byzantine Empire as opposed to Jews who reached the area after the expulsion from Spain. The name Romaniot apparently derives from notion that the Byzantine Empire was the successor of the Roman Empire. Most Romaniot Jews had Greek names.

Rouelle   Special circular badge that Jews were required to wear in Medieval France. It was usally red or yellow in color.

SA   (Ger. Sturmabteilung, or "stormtroopers") Nazi paramilitary organization. The SA, also known as the Brown Shirts for the color of its uniforms, was founded in 1922 to guard Nazi Party meetings. In

time it grew into the foremost grassroots organization of the Nazi Party. Its frequent public demonstrations and brawls with Nazi opponents thrust the SA into public prominence. In June 1934, Hitler had its leadership purged in the Night of the Long Knives, fearing it might challenge his power. Subsequently the SA continued to exist but with its standing significantly diminished.

Sanussi Brotherhood   Moslem religious organization established in North Africa in the 19th cent. It advocated a return to the Koran and Moslem unity and sought to throw off the yoke of European colonialism. In WWI and WWII members of the Brotherhood in Libya fought against the Italian occupation.

Sachsenhausen   Nazi concentration camp near Berlin, also known by its previous name of Oranienburg for the town in which it was located. Established in July 1936, it included 61 satellite forced labor camps by the time it was liberated in April 1945. About 200,000 prisoners passed through the Sachsenhausen camp complex and about 30,000 died there.

Shammash   (Heb. "beadle") The *shammash* served as the caretaker of the synagogue.

Schutzbrief   (Ger. "letter of protection") Charters granted to Jewish individuals and communities in Germany setting forth various rights against the payment of fees and taxes. Also issued by various foreign diplomats to Jews during the Holocaust. In particular in Hungary in 1944, the use of such documents (also known as a *Schutzpass*) was an important factor in the mass rescue campaign in which such diplomats as Friedrich Born, Charles Lutz, Angelo Rotta, Raoul Wallenberg, and others tried to help Jews. The Jewish underground also issued false papers in the tens of thousands as part of this rescue operation.

Schutzgeld   (Ger. "protection money") Special tax payed by Jews (*Schutzjuden*) under the protection of a local ruler.

Schutzhaft   (Ger. "protective custody") The legal fiction employed by the Nazis to imprison innocent people considered opponents of the regime.

Schutzjude   (pl. **Schutzjuden**; Ger. "protected Jew")

In pre-modern Germany, protected Jews were accorded special privileges, such as the right to live outside ghetto areas.

SD (Ger. Sicherheitsdienst des Reichsfuehrers-SS) The Security Service of the SS. The SD was set up in 1931 to provide intelligence to the SS. It was commanded by Reinhard Heydrich. During various reorganizations of the SS, the SD essentially incorporated the Gestapo. The lines that separated their activities remained blurred. Many SD men were deeply involved in the murder of the Jews.

Second Aliya Period of immigration of Jews to Eretz Israel beginning in 1905 and ending with the outbreak of WWI in 1914. During the Second Aliya the World Zionist Organization became an active partner in fostering immigration and building the Jewish community in the country and it was in this period that the foundations of Jewish society were laid there. Between 30,000 and 40,000 Jews arrived in Eretz Israel during these years.

Sejm The Polish parliament. First established in the 15th cent., the modern Sejm was convened during the period of Congress Poland (1815-1831) and again intermittently until the establishment of the Second Polish Republic in 1919. From then on, it has existed even while the government of Poland underwent changes of form.

Sephardi (pl. **Sephardim**) Jews of Spanish and Portuguese origin and their descendants as distinguished from Ashkenazi Jews

Seven Communities (Heb. *Sheva Kehillot*) The seven communities of Burgenland, Austria, were known for their learning, *yeshivot*, and rabbis. They included Eisenstadt, Mattersburg, Deutschkreutz, Frauenkirchen, Kittsee, Kovensdorf, and Lackenbach. They were also known as particularly strong separatist Orthodox communities from the end of the 19th cent. through the end of WWI.

Shabbateanism see **Shabbateans**

Shabbateans Followers of the Jewish false messiah Shabbetai Zvi, who died in 1676. The Shabbateans believed that Shabbetai Zvi would come back to life and usher in the Messianic Age. Their beliefs were known as Shabbateanism.

Shavuot Jewish Festival of Pentecost or Feast of Weeks. It is celebrated on the 6th day of the Hebrew month of Sivan. On Shavuot the receiving of the Torah – the Five Books of Moses or Pentateuch – is celebrated along with the first fruits of the new agricultural year. It is one of the three holidays named as festivals in the Torah.

Shehitah (Heb. "ritual slaughter") According to Jewish religious law, animals considered kosher must be slaughtered according to a particular procedure. Only a qualified ritual slaughterer, a *shohet*, may slaughter the animal.

Shofar The ram's horn sounded throughout the month preceding the New Year, on the New Year itself (Rosh Hashanah), and on the Day of Atonement (Yom Kippur).

Shohet (Heb. "ritual slaughterer") Jew authorized to slaughter kosher animals according to Jewish ritual. He must learn the laws of ritual slaughter (*shehita*) and train for his profession.

Shomer Israel Assimilationist movement founded in Galicia in 1869 with a German cultural orientation.

Shtadlan (pl. **shtadlanim**) A prominent Jew permitted to attend the court of a ruler and intercede on behalf of the Jewish community in the pre-modern period in Europe.

Shtetl Smalltown Jewish community in Eastern Europe. Famous in lore and literature for the unique warmth and flavor of its life.

Shtibl (pl. **shhtiblekh**) Yiddish term for a hasidic house of prayer.

Shum Hebrew acronym for the German cities of Speyer, Worms, and Mainz. The three cities were important centers of Jewish learning during the Middle Ages.

Sicarii A group of Jews who rebelled against the Roman authorities during the period of the Second

Temple. They were known for the dagger (*sica*) they carried.

Sobibor Death camp established by the Nazis near Lublin, Poland, in March 1942. About 250,000 Jews were murdered in the camp. On 14 Oct. 1943 prisoners staged an uprising in which several hundred escaped. Following the uprising, the SS ordered the camp closed and the area on which it stood was plowed under.

Sonderkommando (Ger. "special forces") In the Nazi period two uses of the term are most prominent. Some of the subunits of the *Einsatzgruppen* — the task forces that murdered Jews througout the occupied Soviet Union and eastern Poland — were called *Sonderkommandos*. In addition, the special prisoner unit at Auschwitz-Birkenau working in the area of the gas chambers and cremetoria was also called a *Sonderkommando*.

SS (Ger. Schutzstaffel, or "protection squad") Elite Nazi armed organization. Founded in 1923, the SS originally functioned as Adolf Hitler's personal bodyguard. Eventually it evolved into the elite police and military organization of the Nazi Party. The SS went through a series of organizational changes as it grew from a small band to an empire under Heinrich Himmler's command. It assumed responsibility for implementing the most brutal aspects of Nazi racial policies, especially the murder of the Jews. Almost all of the Nazi camps came under its control.

Status Quo Hungarian congregations adhering neither to Neologism nor Orthodoxy after the split of Jewish communities in 1869 but remaining unattached as previously (hence Status Quo Ante as their full nomenclature).

Stuermer boxes Glass display cases for the antisemitic Nazi newspaper *Der Stuermer*. Throughout Germany during the Nazi period such outdoor display cases were set up so that crowds could read the newspaper and absorb its virulent antisemitic message.

Subbotniki Sabbaterians or Seventh Day Adventists in Russia. The group came into being in the 18th cent. and adopted a number of Jewish practices while at the same time accepting the New Testament. They were often persecuted by the authorities.

Sukkot The Jewish Festival of Tabernacles. One of the three Jewish holidays defined as a festival in the Torah, Sukkot begins on the 15th day of the Hebrew month of Tishri and lasts for seven days. During Sukkot it is customary to live in a temporary structure called a *sukkah* (booth). During the morning prayer service a *lulav* (palm frond) and branches of myrtle and willow as well as an *etrog* (citron) are blessed and carried in a procession.

Sumptuary laws Laws regulating consumption and private spending adopted by Jewish communities from the Talmudic period through the Middle Ages and beyond. Many Jewish communities had regulations that attempted to limit ostentation and encourage modest behavior in dress and in private celebrations such as weddings and engagement parties. Such laws were also imposed occasionally by the authorities.

Svaz Cechu-zidu. (League of Czech Jews) Association established in 1919 to represent Czech Jews who believed in assimilation into Czech life. It opposed Zionism but supported the colonization of Palestine.

Szabasowki schools Polish state schools for Jewish children where classes were held on Sunday instead of on the Jewish Sabbath.

Takkana (pl. **takkanot**) A community regulation published by a rabbinical authority and based on religious law.

Talmud A compendium of Jewish religious law (*halakha*) and miscellaneous lore (*aggada*) based on the tradition of oral interpretation of the Torah. The Talmud is composed of two main parts: the Mishna, which contains the written record of discussions of points of law by the rabbinical *tannaim*, and the Gemara, which is a commentary on the Mishna evolving afterwards in the period of the *amoraim*. There are two versions of the Talmud, the Jerusalem Talmud, finalized in the fifth cent., and the Babylonian Talmud, edited in the sixth cent.

Talmud torah (pl. **talmudei torah**) Jewish religious school. After studying in the *heder* (elementary school), the next stage of religious study is in the *talmud torah*, followed by the yeshiva for advanced religious studies.

Tarbut Organization dedicated to Hebrew culture and education. Tarbut was founded in Russia in the beginning of the 20th cent. and was active throughout Eastern Europe. Students in the network of schools set up by Tarbut learned Hebrew and were encouraged to support Zionism. In 1935, 270 Tarbut schools were in operation with about 38,000 students in attendance.

Tartars (also **Tatars**) Members of one of the Turkic-speaking tribes living in the area of the former Russian Empire near the Volga River. Tartar is also used as a name for the Mongolians who conquered much of Europe in the 13th cent., since many of the Tartar tribes joined the forces of the Mongolian leader Genghis Khan.

Tats see **Mountain Jews**

Teutonic Order (Teutonic Knights of St. Mary's Hospital at Jerusalem) Together with Templars and Hospitallers, one of the the great religious and military orders born in the Crusades. Founded in Acre in 1189, it became a conquering force on the eastern frontiers of Germany and was active in Poland.

Theresienstadt (also known as Terezin) Supposed model ghetto set up by the Nazis. Established in Nov. 1941, the first inmates were from the Protectorate of Bohemia and Moravia. Soon Jews from Germany and Austria joined them, and later Jews from other countries as well. All told, about 140,000 Jews were imprisoned there. About 88,000 were subsequently sent to Nazi death camps and about 33,000 died in the ghetto itself.

Thirty Years War A series of wars from 1618 to 1648 that engulfed much of Europe. The wars were fought along religious lines—Roman Catholics vs. Lutherans vs. Calvinists—and by various rulers in an attempt to expand their territories. At the end of the period, with the signing of the Treaty of Westphalia, Europe assumed its modern form as an agglomerate of autonomous states.

Tiszaeszlar blood libel An accusation of ritual murder leveled against Jews in the Hungarian town of Tiszaeszlar in 1882. Before the accused Jews were acquitted, anti-Jewish attacks occurred in much of Hungary.

Todt Organization Large construction concern in Nazi Germany named for its founder, Dr. Fritz Todt. It used millions of forced laborers, many from concentration and prisoner-of-war camps, to build roads and fortifications.

Toleranzpatent (Ger. "Edict of Toleration") In 1782 the Austrian emperor Joseph II decreed that all statutes that restricted Jews were to be abolished.

Torah va-Avodah Confederation of pioneer and youth groups founded in Vienna in 1925 by Mizrachi and religious Hehalutz groups.

Tosafist Religious scholar compiling critical annotations to the Talmud. The tosafists flourished in France and Germany between the 12th and 14th cents.

Tosafot Yom Tov Seventeenth cent. commentary on the Mishna written by Yom Tov Lippman Heller in Poland.

Touansa Term for Jews living in Tunisia for generations.

TOZ (Pol. "Society for Safeguarding the Health of the Jewish Population") Founded in 1917, TOZ was affiliated with OZE. It emphasized preventive medicine, but also sponsored over 400 hospitals and clinics. In 1942 the German occupation authorities closed it down.

Transnistria Area in the Ukraine occupied by German and Rumanian forces in WWII and becoming a killing ground for local and deported Jews, particularly from Rumania. In all, over 250,000 Jews perished there.

Tzaddik (Heb. "righteous man") In hasidic thought the *tzaddik* is also a spiritual leader acting as a kind of intermediary between man and God.

Tze'irei Tziyyon Zionist youth movement founded in Russia and Galicia in 1905. It was aligned with the World Zionist Organization and came to include scores of youth groups. In the wake of the Russian Revolution its activities were curtailed in the Soviet Union, and within a few years the remaining groups outside the Soviet Union had merged with other Zionist youth movements.

Union Generale des Israelites de France (Fr. "Union of French Jews," or UGIF) Established in Nov. 1941 by the French Vichy government on the urging of the SS, the UGIF was designated as the official leadership body of the Jews of France during the Nazi period. All of the Jewish organizations in France were meant to be integrated into the UGIF, but some refused to cooperate with it. Although the UGIF was established by the authorities to serve their needs, it protested against anti-Jewish measures.

Union Universelle Jeunesse Juive (Fr. "World Union of Jewish Youth," or UUJJ) Organization for Jewish youth active in France and North Africa.

Ustase Nationalistic and Fascist movement founded in Croatia in 1930. Following the German invasion of Yugoslavia in 1941, the Ustase came to power in Croatia under Nazi patronage. It murdered 30,000 Croatian Jews, tens of thousands of gypsies, and half a million Serbs. It also expelled nearly a quarter of a million Serbs from the borders of Croatia and forced a similar number to convert to Catholicism.

Volksdeutsche Nazi term for ethnic Germans living outside Germany and Austria before the outbreak of WWII. Lists were compiled of *Volksdeutsche* in the territories conquered by the Nazis and they were given a status equal to that of Germans born in Germany itself. Many of them became involved in Nazi crimes on various levels.

Wehrmacht The official name of the German armed forces from 1935 until 1945.

Weimar Republic The republic established in Germany in 1919 after its defeat in WWI. Named for the place where it was founded, the city of Weimar. Never fully accepted by many of the German people, the democratic Weimar Republic began to dissolve at the start of the 1930s. When the Nazis came to power in 1933, they effectively abolished it, soon establishing in its place a dictatorial regime that came to be known as the Third Reich.

White Terror Acts of vengeance committed in Hungary by the anti-Communists. In 1919 a Communist regime under Bela Kun came to power for a short period. The opposition, known as the Whites (in contrast to the Communist color red), was led by Admiral Miklos Horthy. While fighting against the Communists – and eventually defeating them – the Whites committed numerous brutal acts against those they suspected of supporting the Communists, including many innocent Jews.

Wiener Gesera persecutions Measures directed against the Jews of Vienna and its environs in 1420 and 1421. Against the background of the allegation that a prominent Jew had desecrated the Host, all the approximately 1,500 Jews of Vienna and the surrounding communities were either murdered or expelled from the area.

WIZO (Women's International Zionist Organization) Established in 1920 in London and focusing on community and family welfare, WIZO was extensively active in Europe between the World Wars and continues to operate all over the world.

Yavne schools Network of religious Jewish schools with a Zionist orientation sponsored by Mizrachi in Lithuania and Poland. In 1938, its 235 schools were attended by over 23,000 children.

YEKOPO (Rus. "Jewish Relief Committee for War Victims") YEKOPO was founded in Russia in 1915 to aid Jews who had been expelled from the Baltic region of the Russian Empire during WWI.

Yeshiva (pl. **yeshivot**) Jewish institute of higher education for the study of the Talmud and rabbinical texts.

Yevsektsiya The Jewish section of the Russian Communist Party. The Yevsektsiya was founded in 1920 and operated until 1930. It lent a hand to the dismantling of traditional Jewish community institutions.

Yishuv Hebrew term for the Jewish community in Palestine before the creation of the State of Israel in 1948.

Youth Aliya (also known as Aliyat ha-No'ar and Jugend Alijah) Organization founded in Germany by Recha Freier in 1932. Youth Aliya sought to bring Jewish youth to Palestine and later to the State of Israel. It created educational frameworks abroad and in Israel to help prepare young people for life in Israel and to take them in upon their arrival.

Zeleny gangs.   Units under the command of the warlord Danylo Zeleny (Tepylo) that fought in the Ukraine during the Russian civil war (1918-1921). The Zeleny gangs fought against both the Communists and their opponents, the Whites.

ZOB   see **Jewish Fighting Organization**

Chronological Table

Date	Event
4th century B.C.E.	The Jewish community of Cyrene, the oldest in the Maghreb, is founded.
3rd century B.C.E.	First archeological evidence for Jewish presence in Greece.
c.140 B.C.E.	First evidence for Jewish settlement in Salonika.
161 B.C.E.	First documentation of Jews in Rome, where the oldest continuous Jewish community in the Diaspora is founded.
70 C.E.	Jerusalem falls to the Roman general Titus, who destroys the Temple. The start of the great Diaspora, the exile of Jews from the Land of Israel.
115–17	Revolt of the Jews in the Diaspora against Roman rule, started by the Jews of Cyrenaica and Alexandria, bringing destruction to many communities.
212	In the Antonine Constitution, promulgated by emperor Caracalla, the Jews are among those granted Roman citizenship.
312	Roman emperor Constantine converts to Christianity. The way is paved for the christianization of the Roman Empire, which will soon be accompanied by anti-Jewish legislation.
321	First evidence for Jewish presence in Cologne, the oldest Jewish settlement in Germany.
330	Constantinople is founded and made the capital of the Byzantine Empire.
465	Significant Jewish settlement in France begins.
600	Pope Gregory I sets guidelines for the treatment of Jews.
610	Muhammad, the founder of Islam, first comes on the scene.
814–40	Emperor Louis the Pious promotes Jewish trade, grants Jews certain juridical autonomy, and welcomes Jews at his court, disregarding the anti-Jewish demands of Agobard, archbishop of Lyon.
10th–11th centuries	Large-scale Jewish immigration to the Rhineland and the Danube regions in Germany.
1070	Rashi, Shelomo ben Yitzhak, completes his commentaries on the Pentateuch.
1096	The First Crusade is accompanied by murderous attacks on German Jews. The communities of Mainz, Speyer, Worms, and Cologne are destroyed by the sword. The Jews of Regensburg are forced to convert.
1147–1269	The fanatic Islamic Almohad dynasty in North Africa. The Jews of Tunisia and Libya are murdered or forced to convert to Islam. The family of Moses ben Maimon, the Rambam or Maimonides (1135–1204), leaves Cordoba/Spain and later Fez/Morocco because of the persecutions.
1156	A rabbinic synod in Troyes recognizes the rabbis of Speyer, Worms, and Mainz as supreme Beit Din for all German Jews.
1171	First blood libel in France; 30 Jews are burned at the stake in Blois.
1177	Jews are first allowed to mint coins in Poland; this will continue until 1296.
13th century	During the first half of the century, first Jews settle in Holland.
	Reestablishment of Jewish settlement in Tunisia under the Hafsid Dynasty.
1215	Fourth Lateran Council decrees that Jews must wear distinctive clothing.
1236	Emperor Frederick II adopts the concept of the Jews as "serfs of our chamber" in the Holy Roman Empire and thus extends the imperial protection to them.
1244	Duke Frederick II grants charter of privileges to the Jews of Austria.
1264	Duke Boleslaw V grants privileges to Jews in Poland in the Statute of Kalisz.

1288-93	The Jews in the south Italian Kingdom of Naples are expelled; many convert.
1290	Jews expelled from England settle in Germany, the Netherlands and France.
1289-98	Following several blood libels and Host desecration accusations, the Rindfleisch massacres are instigated in Germany. Some 146 communities, most of them in southern Germany, are destroyed.
1306	Jews are expelled from France with the exception of Provence.
1334	Polish King Casimir III upholds privileges granted to Jews in the Statute of Kalisz.
1348–49	Black Death Persecutions – Jews are accused of starting the Black Death (bubonic plague), which reached Europe in 1347 and led to the decimation of the European population. Massacres of Jews follow in several countries.
1360	A general expulsion order is issued against the Jews of Hungary but rescinded four years later.
1367	Expulsion of Jews from Hungary.
1370	In Brussels, Jews accused of desecrating the Host are burned at the stake.
1388	Vytautas (or Witold) the Great grants a charter of rights to the Jews in Brest-Litovsk, later extended to other communities in Lithuania.
1391	The era of forced conversions begins in the Iberian Peninsula; it will continue with the persecution by the Spanish Inquisition from 1479 on of converts (Marranos) suspected of maintaining Jewish practices.
1399–1586	Italian-Jewish synods established to guarantee centralized leadership of the communities.
1421	Expulsion of Jews from Austria.
1453	Constantinople falls to the Ottoman Turks, signaling the end of the Byzantine Empire.
1485–91	Following the anti-Jewish preaching of Franciscan and Dominican monks, Jews are expelled from several towns in northern Italy.
1492/3	The Jews of Spain, Sicily, and Sardinia are expelled. Together with the Jews of Portugal expelled in 1496/7 they settle mostly in Italy, North Africa, and Ottoman Turkey. There they form the nucleus of the Sephardi Greek communities.
1495	Expulsion of Jews from Lithuania. The Kingdom of Naples comes under Spanish control. Anti-Jewish legislation is followed by expulsions in 1510 and 1541.
1500	Jews are expelled from Provence.
1503	Jews are allowed to return to Lithuania.
1516	The first ghetto, or closed Jewish quarter, is established in Venice.
1519	Jews are expelled from Regensburg.
1536	Jews are expelled from Saxony.
1543	Luther publishes his pamphlet "On the Jews and Their Lies."
1544	Charles V in Germany grants Jews protection from expulsion.
1551	Ottoman conquest of Libya, followed by the reestablishment of Jewish settlement.
1553	The Talmud is burned throughout Italy on the order of Pope Julius III.
1569	Jews are expelled from the Papal States with the exception of Rome and Ancona.
1569	The Duchy of Lithuania and Poland are unified.
1571	Jews are expelled from most of Tuscany.
1579	The seven northern provinces of the Netherlands cast off Spanish rule and found the United Provinces. A little later, Marranos from Antwerp settle in Amsterdam, finally returning to Judaism and establishing c. 1600 the town's Sephardic community.
1581	The Council of the Four Lands is set up, signifying the beginning of Jewish autonomy in Poland.
1589	Venice grants Jews rights of residence on a ten-year renewable basis.
1593	The Medici invite Jews to settle in Leghorn/Tuscany, the only large Italian city where they are not forced to live in a ghetto. The Jews of Bucharest are massacred.
c.1600	Marranos from Spain and Portugal settle in the northern ports of Europe, such as Hamburg and Altona in Germany and Glueckstadt which is then under Danish rule.
1612–15	The rulers of Moldova invite Jewish merchants to trade in their principality.

1618–48	The Thirty Years War.
1626–76	Shabbetai Zvi, leader of the Messianic movement.
1623	The Council of Lithuanian Jews breaks away from the Council of the Four Lands.
1639	Ashkenazi Jews establish the Ashkenazi community of Amsterdam.
1648–49	Under Bogdan Chmielnicki there is an uprising in the Ukraine in which tens of thousands of Jews are massacred.
1657	Jews are permitted to settle in Denmark.
1670	Jews expelled from Vienna are invited to live in Brandenburg by the Elector.
1683	In the wake of the Messianic movement of Shabbetai Zvi some 300 Jewish families in Salonika convert to Islam, forming the sect of the Domne.
1700–60	Ba'al Shem Tov (Yisrael ben Eliezer), founder of the hasidic movement.
1720–97	Eliyahu ben Shelomo Zalman (Vilna Gaon), leader of the Mitnaggedim, the anti-hasidic opposition.
1723	The Marranos in Bordeaux/France are recognized as Jews.
1729–86	Moses Mendelssohn, leader of the Haskala movement.
1734–36	The Haidamak pogroms erupt in the Ukraine.
1735	Jews readmitted to the Kingdom of Naples.
1759	The followers of Jakob Frank, the successor of Shabbetai Zvi, convert to Christianity.
1764	The Council of the Four Lands is abolished by the Polish Sejm.
1768	The Haidamak pogroms recur.
1772	The First Partition of Poland between Austria, Prussia, and Russia.
1781	Joseph II issues his Edict of Tolerance in the Hapsburg Empire.
1783	Russia annexes the Crimea. Jews are allowed to serve on municipal councils in Russia.
1784	Louis XV rescinds the body tax which had been collected from Jews in Alsace.
1791	The Polish constitution grants the Jews emancipation.
1791	French Jews are granted emancipation.
1791	Catherine II establishes the Pale of Settlement for Jews in the Russian Empire.
1792–1815	In October 1792 Mainz is overrun by the French revolutionary army. In the ensuing years revolutionary and Napoleonic France will occupy many parts of Germany, including Berlin in 1806. The Jews in the French-occupied territories enjoy equal rights.
1793	The Second Partition of Poland.
1794	The Polish uprising breaks out. It is led by Thaddeus Kosciuszko and Jews participate in it.
1795	The Third Partition of Poland.
1797–99	French occupation of Italy brings in its wake temporary emancipation to the Jews in Italy.
1804	The First Jewish Statute in Russia allows Jews to study at any institute of learning.
1807/8	Napoleon Bonaparte convenes a Great Sanhedrin of the French Jews and creates a hierarchical organization of the Jewish communities under a central consistory.
1808	The "Infamous Decree" of Napoleon Bonaparte reimposes many of the former anti-Jewish disabilities.
1812	Prussian emancipation law.
1812	Russia annexes Bessarabia, where many Jews live.
1815–16	End of the Napoleonic era. The reactionary Congress of Vienna authorizes the German states to reinstate the status of the Jews obtaining before the French occupation.
1819	The Hep! Hep! riots against Jews begin in Germany and also spread to Denmark. The Verein fuer Cultur [sic] und Wissenschaft der Juden (Association for Culture and the Scientific Study of the Jews) is established in Berlin.
1821–29	The Greek War of Liberation. In the Peleponnesus many Jews are murdered. In the newly founded Greek state Jews are granted equal rights.
1824	Expulsion of Jews from villages in Russia.

1827	Czar Nicholas I decrees military conscription for Jews at age 18. Under the Cantonist Decrees Jewish boys at age 12 can be taken out of their homes for preparatory service.
1831	The constitution of the newly founded Belgian state grants equality to all citizens.
1837	Jews in Denmark may be elected to municipal posts.
1839–56	The Jews of Libya are granted equal rights but under the pressure of the peasant revolt of 1864 the law of emancipation is rescinded.
1848–49	During the revolutionary wave that sweeps across Europe, Jews in many places attain equal rights. However, the emancipation is revoked in several countries after the suppression of the revolt. It remains in force in Denmark, Holland, and several German and Italian states.
1856	Abrogation of the Cantonist Decrees in Russia.
1859–65	Gradual relaxation of the Pale of Settlement restrictions for rich Jewish merchants, university graduates, and artisans in the Russian Empire.
1860	The Alliance Israelite Universelle, the first international Jewish organization, is established in Paris.
1867	The Austro-Hungarian monarchy is established. Jews are granted equal rights. In Rumania, Jews are expelled from the villages.
1868	Split in Hungarian Jewry between Orthodox, Neologist (Reform), and Status Quo communities.
1869	Reichstag of the North German Confederation makes rights and obligations independent of religious affiliation.
1870	The ghetto in Rome is abolished and the emancipation of Italian Jews is completed.
1871	The Second German Empire is established. Emancipation is extended to all German Jews.
1876	The Ottoman Empire grants Jews equal rights.
1878	The beginning of political antisemitism in Germany. Rumania declares its independence from Turkish rule.
1881	France takes over Tunisia. Jews become citizens with equal rights.
1881–84	Pogroms break out in the Ukraine after the assasination of Czar Alexander II. A big wave of Jewish emigration begins, with many going to Central and Western European countries and the United States.
1881–1903	The First Aliya to Palestine.
1882	The Jewish communities of Greece are accorded legal status.
1884	The first conference of the Hovevei Zion movement convenes in Katowice, Poland.
1887	Admission of Jews to universities in the Russian Empire is subjected to quota restrictions.
1889	Serbia emancipates its Jews.
1891	Jews are expelled from Moscow. Jews in Norway are granted equal rights.
1893	In elections to the German Reichstag the antisemitic parties win 16 seats. The Central Union of German Citizens of the Jewish Faith is founded in Berlin to defend Jews against antisemitism.
1894	Alfred Dreyfus, a Jewish staff officer in France, is arrested and falsely accused of treason. His arrest and conviction spark off a public debate that will engage French society for many years.
1895	Founding of the Antisemitic League in Rumania.
1897	The antisemite Karl Lueger becomes mayor of Vienna.
	The First Zionist Congress meets in Basle, Switzerland.
	The Bund, the Jewish socialist movement, is founded in Vilna.
1899	Anti-Jewish riots begin in Prague and spread to the rest of Bohemia and Moravia.
1903–06	A bloody pogrom occurs in Chisinau (Kishinev); more pogroms will ensue until 1906, leading to a further wave of Jewish emigration.
1909–1910	Boycott against the Jews of Poland.
1910	Expulsion of Jews from Kiev.
1911	Italy takes over Libya.
1912	The First Balkan War breaks out, ending in the following year.

1914–18	WWI.
1915	Jews are expelled from hundreds of places in Lithuania and Poland to the Russian interior. This amounts to a de facto abrogation of the restrictions of the Pale of Settlement, which will be officially removed in 1917.
1917	The Bolshevik Revolution breaks out in Russia, followed by three years of civil war.
	The Balfour Declaration proclaims British support for the establishment of a Jewish National Home in Palestine.
1918	Russian participation in the war ends with the signing of the peace agreement at Brest-Litovsk.
	The Yevsektsiya (Jewish Section of the Communist Party) is established in Soviet Russia.
	The Polish State is established. Pogroms are carried out against Polish Jews during the course of this year and the next.
	Yugoslavia is established, with some 70,000 Jews living there.
	Rumania annexes Bessarabia, Bukovina, and Transnistria.
	The Weimar Republic, the first nationwide German democracy, is established under the shadow of defeat in war.
1919	The Versailles peace treaty ends WWI. Under its territorial arrangements, Germany loses Alsace-Lorraine to France in the west and the Saar comes under League of Nations administration. In the east, Germany loses Poznan and parts of West Prussia and eastern Upper Silesia.
1919–1923	The Third Aliya to Palestine.
1920	The Hungarian government imposes a quota restriction on the number of Jewish students in the universities.
	In Germany, the program of the newly founded Nazi Party advocates the exclusion of Jews from German society.
	Vilna passes to Poland.
1921	Jews are granted equal rights under the Polish constitution.
1923	Lithuania seizes the Memel from Germany.
	Anti-Jewish riots in Berlin.
1924–29	Fourth Aliya to Palestine.
1925	YIVO (Jewish Scientific Institute) is founded in Vilna.
1925	The Zionist Revisionist Organization is founded by Vladimir Jabotinsky.
1926	A conference of rabbis convenes in the Ukraine.
1927–35	In the Soviet Union five autonomous Jewish agricultural regions are established: Kalinindorf (Kalininskoye) in 1927, Nay Zlatopol in 1929, Stalindorf (Stalinskoye) in 1930 in the Ukraine, Fraydorf in 1931, and Larindorf in 1935 in the Crimea.
1928	Birobidzan, the so-called "Jewish Autonomous Region," is set up in the Soviet Union.
1929	The Stock Market crashes in New York, ushering in the period of the Great Depression.
1930	The Yevsektsiya (Jewish Section of the Communist Party) is abolished.
1932	Riots in Salonika.
1933–39	Period of the Fifth Aliya to Palestine.
30 Jan. 1933	Hitler becomes chancellor of Germany.
1 April 1933	A one-day countrywide anti-Jewish boycott is enforced in Germany; unofficial boycotts continue afterward.
March 1935	Germany retakes the Saar.
15 Sept. 1935	The Nuremberg Laws are issued at a Nazi Party rally.
March 1936	Pogroms in Poland.
1937	In Rumania the Cuza-Goga government passes antisemitic laws.
July 1937	The special status of Upper Silesia under the League of Nations is terminated; the Jewish residents are subjected to the racial discrimination in force throughout the Reich.

March 1938	Nazi Germany annexes Austria in what is known as the *Anschluss*. Forced emigration of Jews begins.
	Jewish communities in Germany lose their legal status as public corporate bodies.
July 1938	Representatives from 32 countries meet in Evian, France, to discuss the refugee problem, but do almost nothing.
	The Great Synagogue in Munich is razed on Nazi orders.
29 Sept. 1938	The Munich Agreement is signed.
Oct. 1938	Germany annexes the Sudetenland, the Czechoslovakian Republic is established, and Slovakia is given autonomy.
	Between 15,000 and 17,000 Jews are expelled from Germany and sent to Poland; most are detained in the border town of Zbonszyn.
9/10 Nov. 1938	The Kristallnacht pogrom signals the end of German Jewry.
Dec. 1938	Hungary annexes parts of Slovakia and the Transcarpathian Ukraine.
March 1939	Slovakia is declared an independent state.
	German forces enter Prague. The Protectorate of Bohemia-Moravia is established.
	Germany annexes Memel, Lithuania.
April 1939	Italy invades Albania.
May 1939	A law defining who is a Jew and restricting Jewish involvement in the economy is issued in Hungary.
	In the White Paper of 1939 the British government restricts Jewish immigration to Palestine.
23 Aug. 1939	Germany and the Soviet Union sign the Nazi-Soviet Pact.
1 Sept. 1939	The German army invades Poland.
28 Sept. 1939	Germany and the Soviet Union divide up Poland. In western Poland, the Germans set up the General Gouvernement. The Soviet Union takes over the eastern part of the country, including western Belorussia and western Ukraine. Vilna is handed over to Lithuania.
8 Oct. 1939	The first Nazi-established ghetto is set up in Piotrkow Trybunalski, Poland.
Oct. 1939	4,800 Jews from Ostrava, Katowice, and Vienna are deported to the Lublin area.
Nov. 1939	The Nazis begin to deport Jews from Lodz to other parts of Poland.
Nov. 1939	Hans Frank, governor-general of the General Gouvernement, orders the wearing of the Jewish badge.
Nov. 1939	The establishment of Judenraete in the General Gouvernement is decreed.
April 1940	German occupation of Denmark.
May 1940	German occupation of Holland and Belgium.
June 1940	German occupation of Norway.
	France is divided into a German-occupied northern zone and a "free" southern zone (Vichy France).
	The Soviet Union occupies the Baltic states (Lithuania, Latvia, and Estonia).
	Rumania is forced to hand over Bessarabia and northern Bukovina to the Soviet Union.
Oct. 1940	The first Statute des Juifs, a code of anti-Jewish laws, is promulgated by the French government.
22–25 Oct. 1940	The Jews of Baden, the Palatinate, and Wuerttemberg are deported to Gurs in southern France.
Jan. 1941	In Rumania, the Iron Guard unsuccessfully attempts to overthrow the government; riots against the Jews are rampant.
Feb. 1941	A total of 389 young Jewish men from Amsterdam are deported to Buchenwald.
25 Feb. 1941	A general anti-Nazi strike is observed in Amsterdam.
March 1941	The Cracow ghetto is ordered to be set up and is closed off on 20 March.
April 1941	German forces invade Greece and Yugoslavia.
April 1941	The Lublin ghetto is closed off.
June 1941	British forces retreat from Crete.

June 1941	In Rumania, Jews are expelled from the villages and towns of southern Bukovina.
22 June 1941	Operation Barbarossa: German forces invade the Soviet Union. They capture Kishinev, Kaunas, and other places.
	The Einsatzgruppen begin the mass systematic murder of Jews in Soviet territory.
27 June 1941	Hungary enters the war as a German ally.
29 June 1941	Black Sunday: In Iasi, thousands of Jews are shot in the courtyard of police headquarters.
July 1941	The Minsk ghetto is established.
	Rumanian forces occupy Bessarabia.
	The Kishinev ghetto is established; by this time some 10,000 Kishinev Jews have been killed.
	During the three Petlyura Days local Ukrainians carry out a pogrom against the Jews in Lwow.
31 July 1941	Hermann Goering instructs Heydrich to prepare a "final solution" to the Jewish question in Europe.
1 Aug. 1941	The Bialystok ghetto is established.
5 Aug. 1941	During the next three days over 10,500 Jews are murdered in Pinsk.
21 Aug. 1941	The first of some 70,000 Jews pass through the Drancy transit camp near Paris.
27 Aug. 1941	In Kamenets-Podolski, during two days, 23,600 Jews are murdered by German forces under Friedrich Jeckeln; at least 14,000 of the victims are from Hungary.
31 Aug. 1941	The murder of 8,000 Jews from Vilna begins in Ponary.
9 Sept. 1941	The Jewish Code is issued in Slovakia; this defines who is a Jew.
15 Sept. 1941	In the Netherlands, Jews are legally banned from many public places.
	The first batch of some 150,000 Jews from Bessarabia and Bukovina are deported to Transnistria; about 90,000 eventually die there.
19 Sept. 1941	In the Reich, Jews are required to wear the Jewish badge in public.
29 Sept. 1941	During two days some 33,000 Jews are murdered in Babi Yar.
Oct.–Dec. 1941	In Vilna, 33,500 Jews are murdered.
6 Oct. 1941	Beginning of the deportations from Prague.
13 Oct. 1941	In Dnepropetrovsk, 20,000 Jews are murdered.
15 Oct. 1941	Jews are deported from Germany and Austria and the Protectorate to Kaunas, Lodz, Minsk, and Riga.
18 Oct. 1941	Beginning of the deportations from Berlin.
19 Oct. 1941	Jews are murdered in Belgrade.
	Luxembourg Jews are deported to Lodz in eight transports.
23 Oct. 1941	Jews are forbidden to emigrate from Germany.
28 Oct. 1941	Some 9,000 Jews are murdered at the Ninth Fort outside Kaunas; 17,412 Jews remain in the Kaunas ghetto.
Nov. 1941	Sevastopol falls to the Germans after a seven-month battle.
Nov. 1941	20,000 Minsk Jews are killed at Tuchinka.
Nov. 1941	Jeckeln Aktion: 30,000 Jews are killed in the Rumbuli Forest outside Riga.
Dec. 1941	The first transport of Jews arrives at the Chelmno extermination camp; transports continue to arrive until March 1943, when the camp is temporarily closed. It will reopen to accommodate Lodz Jews whom the Nazis wish to murder in 1944.
Dec. 1941	Germany and Italy declare war on the United States and vice versa.
Dec. 1941	Some 54,000 Jews are murdered in the course of ten days in the Bogdanovka camp in Transnistria; 200 are left alive.
Dec. 1941	Mass killing of the Kharkov Jews begins. It will continue until Jan. 1942.
Jan. 1942	Dutch Jews begin to be assembled in Amsterdam.
1942	Deportations from Lodz to Chelmno begin; they continue until September 1942.
Jan. 1942	The Wannsee Conference: top Nazi officials attend a conference in a Berlin suburb in order to coordinate the Final Solution.

Jan. 1942	German forces launch a counteroffensive in North Africa.
Feb. 1942	Jews in Vilna create the United Partisan Organization.
Feb. 1942	The *Struma*, a ship loaded with 769 Jewish refugees, sinks off the coast of Turkey; only one person survives.
March 1942	Jews are deported from Lublin and Lwow to Belzec during the next six weeks.
March–Oct. 1942	Deportation of Jews from Slovakia.
March 1942	First transport of French Jews is sent to Auschwitz.
April 1942	In the Netherlands, Jews are ordered to wear the Jewish badge.
May 1942	In Belgium, Jews are ordered to wear the Jewish badge; the decree goes into effect on 3 June.
June 1942	In occupied France, Jews are required to wear the Jewish badge.
June 1942	Eichmann's office issues an order for the deportation of Jews from the Netherlands, Belgium, and France.
June 1942	German forces capture Tobruk from the British.
June 1942	The first transport from the Drancy transit camp leaves for Auschwitz.
June 1942	In the Netherlands, regular deportations begin to Westerbork and from Westerbork to Auschwitz.
July 1942	9,000 Jewish men from Salonika between the ages of 18 and 45 are made to do forced labor in Greece.
July 1942	In Paris, Jews are rounded up and sent to Drancy. From there they are deported to Auschwitz.
July–Sept. 1942	Mass deportation from Warsaw to Treblinka until the middle of September.
July 1942	In Warsaw, the Jewish Fighting Organization (ZOB) is founded.
July 1942	30,000 Jews from Germany who have been deported to Minsk are murdered at Maly Trostinec in a four-day period.
Aug. 1942	50,000 Jews are deported from Lwow to Belzec over the course of two weeks.
Aug. 1942	Most of the remaining Jews of Croatia are deported to Auschwitz.
Aug. 1942	Deportation of Belgian Jews to Auschwitz.
Sept. 1942	In Macedonia, the Jews are required to wear the Jewish badge.
Sept. 1942	The Battle of Stalingrad begins.
Oct. 1942	Nearly all the Jews of Pinsk are murdered by 1 November.
Nov. 1942	The deportation of Jews from the Bialystok district to Treblinka begins.
Nov. 1942	British forces capture El Alamein from the Germans.
Nov. 1942	American and British forces invade North Africa, launching Operation Torch.
Nov. 1942	German and Italian forces occupy Tunisia.
Nov. 1942	The Germans and Italians occupy southern France.
Nov. 1942	Deportation of Jews from Norway to Auschwitz.
Dec. 1942	In Tunisia, the German authorities order Jewish leaders to assemble 2,000 Jews for forced labor. Eventually, 5,000 Jews are sent to labor camps.
Jan. 1943	In Libya, British forces liberate Tripoli.
Feb. 1943	At Stalingrad, 91,000 German soldiers under Field Marshal Friedrich von Paulus surrender to the Soviet army.
Feb. 1943	In Bialystok, 2,000 Jews are murdered and 10,000 are deported to Treblinka. Jews actively resist the Germans.
March 1943	Almost all of the 4,000 Jews from Bulgarian Thrace are arrested and deported to Treblinka by 9 March.
March 1943	A total of 7,341 Macedonian Jews are assembled in Skopje; most are soon deported to Treblinka.
March 1943	The first transports from Salonika arrive at Auschwitz.
19 April–16 May 1943	The Warsaw Ghetto Uprising takes place and Himmler orders the razing of the Warsaw Ghetto.
May 1943	Tunisia is liberated by the Allies.
July 1943	Allied forces invade Sicily.
July 1943	Himmler orders the liquidation of the ghettoes in the Reichskommissariat Ostland.

July 1943	Mussolini is overthrown; Pietro Badoglio sets up a new government in Italy.
Aug. 1943	Nazi forces led by Odilo Globocnik surround the Bialystok Ghetto. The ghetto's remaining 30,000 Jews are ordered to report for evacuation. An uprising breaks out.
Sept. 1943	The last transport of Jews leaves Belgium.
Sept. 1943	The Allies invade southern Italy.
Sept. 1943	German forces occupy Athens; Italian forces surrender to the Germans in Rhodes.
11 Sept. 1943	The Minsk ghetto is liquidated and nearly all of its Jews are murdered during the next five days.
Sept. 1943	The Nazis liquidate the Vilna ghetto; 3,700 Jews are sent to labor camps in Estonia and 4,000 are deported to Sobibor.
Oct. 1943	In Denmark, German police begins rounding up Jews for deportation; the Danish population initiates the rescue of 7,200 Jews.
Oct. 1943	In Rome, mass arrests of Jews are launched and two days later, 1,035 Jews are deported to Auschwitz.
Nov. 1943	Operation Erntefest (Harvest Festival) begins. The Nazis murder the Jews of Poniatowa, Trawniki, and Majdanek. Other Jews are brought to Majdanek to be killed.
Nov. 1943	The Nazis order all Italian Jews concentrated in camps.
19 March 1944	German forces enter Hungary.
15 May 1944	The deportation of some 435,000 Hungarian Jews to Auschwitz begins; half are gassed soon after their arrival.
June 1944	The American Fifth Army liberates Rome.
6 June 1944	D-Day: Allied forces land in Normandy, France, with the largest force in history to arrive by sea.
June 1944	Transports from Lodz once again begin reaching Chelmno.
July 1944	The deportations from Hungary are halted temporarily.
July 1944	The Nazis liquidate the Kaunas ghetto.
July 1944	Soviet forces liberate Vilna.
July 1944	In France, American forces break through German lines. France is liberated by the end of August.
mid-1944	The death marches, the forced evacuation of concentration camp inmates into Germany, begins.
Aug.-Sept. 1944	The Polish Warsaw uprising.
1 Aug. 1944	Soviet forces liberate Kaunas.
7 Aug. 1944	For the next three weeks deportations from Lodz to Auschwitz take place.
23 Aug. 1944	The government of Ion Antonescu is overthrown; Rumania joins the Allies.
28 Aug. 1944	The Slovak National Uprising begins and is put down by the SS within a month.
3 Sept. 1944	The last transport of Jews leaves Westerbork.
4 Sept. 1944	Antwerp is liberated.
Oct. 1944	Soviet forces capture Riga.
Oct. 1944	In Hungary, Ferenc Szalasi and his Arrow Cross Party take over the government.
Nov. 1944	Deportations from Budapest are resumed under the Arrow Cross government.
Dec. 1944	Budapest falls to the Soviets.
Jan. 1945	The German evacuation of Auschwitz begins. About 60,000 prisoners are marched toward the German interior.
Jan. 1945	Soviet forces liberate Warsaw.
Jan. 1945	Soviet forces liberate Lodz.
Jan. 1945	Soviet forces enter Auschwitz; they find 7,650 prisoners.
March 1945	American forces cross the Rhine River.
April 1945	The United Nations meets in San Francisco.
2 May 1945	Soviet forces capture Berlin.
	German forces in Italy surrender to the Allies.
8 May 1945	V-E Day: the war in Europe is officially over.

1946	Survivors of the Holocaust are murdered in a bloody pogrom in Kielce, Poland.
15 May 1948	The State of Israel is established. Hundreds of thousands of Jews immigrate to Israel.
1949-62	Immigration of North African Jews to Israel and France.
1973	First mass wave of immigrants from the Soviet Union.
1989	Beginning of the main wave of mass immigration of Jews from the Soviet Union to Israel.

Selected Bibliography

I. GENERAL REFERENCE WORKS AND HISTORIES

Alfasi, Y.: *Encyclopedia of Hasidism* (Heb.). Jerusalem, 1980–1986.

——: *Sefer ha-Admorim* (Heb.). Tel Aviv, 1961.

Arad, Y., Gutman, Y., Margaliot, A. (eds.): *Documents on the Holocaust. Selected Sources on the Destruction of the Jews of Germany and Austria, Poland, and the Soviet Union.* Jerusalem-Oxford-New York, 1987.

Black Book of Localities whose Jewish Population was Exterminated by the Nazis. Jerusalem, 1965.

Dubnow, S.: *The History of the Hasidic Movement* (Heb.), 3 vols. Tel Aviv, 1944.

Encyclopaedia Judaica. Das Judentum in Geschichte und Gegenwart, 10 vols. (A–L). Berlin, 1928–1934.

Encyclopaedia Judaica. Jerusalem, 1971–1972.

Friedman, N.Z.: *Otzar ha-Rabanim* (Heb.). Benei Berak, 1975.

Gribetz, J., Greenstein, E.L., Stein, R.S.: *The Timetables of Jewish History. A Chronology of the Most Important People and Events in Jewish History.* New York, 1993.

Grosman, H. et al.: *The Book of Jewish Partisans* (Heb.). Merhavya, 1958.

Gottlieb, S.N.: *Sefer Oholei Shem* (Heb.). Pinsk, 1912.

Gutman, Y. (ed.): *Encyclopedia of the Holocaust*, 4 vols. New York, 1990.

Halahmi, D.: *Hakhamei Israel. Encyclopedia of Distinguished Jews during the Last Generations* (Heb.). Tel Aviv, 1958.

Hilberg, R.: *The Destruction of European Jews.* New York, 1985.

Jüdisches Lexikon, 5 vol. Berlin, 1927–1930.

Leshtchinsky, J.: *The Jewish Nation in Numbers* (Yid.). Berlin, 1922.

Mahler, R.: *History of the Jewish People in Modern Times. From the Late 18th Century until Our Day* (Heb.). Merhavya, 1955–1970.

Piekarz, M.: *Holocaust and Heroism as Reflected in the Hebrew Press. A Bibliography* (Heb.), 4 vols. Jerusalem, 1967.

——: *The Holocaust and its Aftermath as Reflected in the Hebrew Press. A Bibliography* (Heb.). Jerusalem, 1979.

——: *The Holocaust and its Aftermath in the Hebrew Books Published in the Years 1933–1972. A Bibliography* (Heb.), 2 vols. Jerusalem, 1974.

Rozett, R., Spector, S. (eds.): *Encyclopedia of the Holocaust.* New York, 2000.

Zarski, S.Z.: *Sefer Anshei Shem. World Lexicon of Rabbis* (Heb.), 2 vols. Jerusalem-Tel Aviv, 1940–1941.

II. INDIVIDUAL COUNTRIES

AUSTRIA

Altmann, A.: *Geschichte der Juden in Stadt und Land Salzburg von den frühesten Zeiten bis auf die Gegenwart.* Salzburg, new revised edition, 1990.

Dreier, W. (ed.): *Antisemitismus in Vorarlberg. Regionalstudie zur Geschichte einer Weltanschauung.* Bregenz, 1988.

Fellner, G.: *Antisemitismus in Salzburg 1918–1938.* Vienna, 1979.

Fraenkel, J. (ed.): *The Jews of Austria. Essays on Their Life, History and Destruction*. London, 1967.

Gold, H.: *Geschichte der Juden in Österreich. Ein Gedenkbuch*. Tel Aviv, 1971.

Karner, S.: *Die Steiermark im Dritten Reich 1938–1945. Aspekte ihrer politischen, wirtschaftlich-sozialen und kulturellen Entwicklung*. Graz-Vienna, 2nd edition, 1986.

Moser, J.: *Demographie der jüdischen Bevölkerung Österreichs 1938–1945*. Vienna, 1999.

Neuhauser-Pfeiffer, W., Ramsmaier, K.: *Vergessene Spuren. Die Geschichte der Juden in Steyr*. Linz, 1993.

Rabinovici, D.: *Instanzen der Ohnmacht. Wien 1938–1945: Der Weg zum Judenrat*. Frankfurt, 2000.

Rosenkranz, H.: *Verfolgung und Selbstbehauptung. Die Juden in Österreich 1938–1945*. Munich, 1978.

Schneider, G.: *Exile and Destruction. The Fate of Austrian Jews 1938– 1945*. Westport, 1995.

Schwarz, P.: *Tulln ist judenrein! Die Geschichte der Tullner Juden und ihr Schicksal von 1938 bis 1945. Verfolgung, Vertreibung, Vernichtung*. Vienna, 1997.

Sella, G. H.: *Die Juden Tirols. Ihr Leben und Schicksal*. Tel Aviv, 1979.

Slapnicka, H.: *Oberösterreich als es Oberdonau hiess (1938–1945)*. Linz, 1978.

Spitzer, S. (ed.): *Beiträge zur Geschichte der Juden im Burgenland*. Jerusalem, 1994.

Steines, P.: *Mahnmale. Jüdische Friedhöfe in Wien, Niederösterreich und Burgenland*. Vienna, 1992.

Streibel, R.: *Plötzlich waren sie alle weg. Die Juden der "Gauhauptstadt Krems" und ihre Mitbürger*. Vienna, 1991.

Taubes, L., Bloch, C.: *Jüdisches Jahrbuch für Österreich*. Vienna, 1932–1933.

Walzl, A.: *Die Juden in Kärnten und das Dritte Reich*. Klagenfurt, 1987.

Weinzierl, E., Kulka, O.D. (eds.): *Vertreibung und Neubeginn. Israelische Bürger Österreichischer Herkunft*. Vienna, 1992.

Widerstand und Verfolgung im Burgenland 1934–1945. Eine Dokumentation. Vienna, 2nd edition, 1983.

Widerstand und Verfolgung in Niederösterreich 1934–1945. Eine Dokumentation. Vienna, 1987.

Widerstand und Verfolgung in Oberösterreich 1934–1945. Eine Dokumentation. Vienna, 1982.

Widerstand und Verfolgung in Tirol 1934–1945. Eine Dokumentation. Vienna, 1984.

Widerstand und Verfolgung in Wien 1934–1945. Eine Dokumentation. Vienna, 2nd edition, 1984.

Wistrich, R.: *The Jews of Vienna in the Age of Franz Joseph*. Oxford, 1990.

BELGIUM

Doorslaer, R. v. et al. (eds.): *Les juifs de Belgique. De l'immigration au génocide, 1925–1945*. Brussels, 1994.

Dratwa, D.: *Répertoire des périodiques juifs parus en Belgique de 1841 à 1986*. Brussels, 1987.

Garfinkels, B.: *Les Belges face à la persécution raciale 1940–1944*. Brussels, 1965.

Hachez, F.: *Essai sur La Résidence à Mons. Des juifs et des Lombards*. Mons, 1853.

Klarsfeld, S., Steinberg, M.: *Die Endlösung der Judenfrage in Belgien. Dokumente*. New York, 1980.

——: *Mémorial de la déportation des juifs de Belgique*. Brussels, 1982.

La Grande Synagogue de Bruxelles 1878–1978. Brussels, 1995.

Michman, D. (ed.): *Belgium and the Holocaust. Jews, Belgians, Germans*. Jerusalem, 1998.

Ministère de la Justice, Commission des Crimes de Guerre: *Les crimes de guerre commis sous l'occupation de la Belgique 1940–1945*. Liège, 1947, 1948.

Ouverleaux, E.: *Notes et documents sur les juifs de Belgique sous l'Ancien Régime*. Paris, 1885.

Schmidt, E.: *L'histoire des juifs à Anvers*. Antwerpen, 1969.

Schreiber, J.P.: *Politique et religion. Le Consistoire Central Israélite de Belgique au XIXe siècle*. Brussels, 1995.

——: *L'Immigration juive en Belgique du moyen âge à la Première Guerre Mondiale*. Brussels, 1996.

Steinberg, L.: *Le Comité de défense des juifs en Belgique 1942–1944*. Brussels, 1973.

Steinberg, M.: *Dossier Bruxelles-Auschwitz. La police SS et l'extermination des juifs de Belgique*. Brussels, 1980.

——: *L'étoile et le fusil*, 3 vols. Brussels, 1983–1987.

——: *Un pays occupé et ses juifs. Belgique entre France et Pays-Bas*. Cerpinnes, 1998.

Stengers, J.: *Les Juifs dans les Pays-Bas au Moyen-Âge*. Brussels, 1949.

BELORUSSIA, UKRAINE, RUSSIA

"Akty o zaselenii iugo-zapadnoi Rossii," *Arkhiv iugo-zapadnoi Rossii*, part 7, vol. 2. Kiev, 1890.

Alexandrov, H.: "The Jewish Population of Belorussia at the Time of the Partitions of Poland. A Historical-Statistical Study," *Zeitschrift* (Yid.), 4 (1930).

Arad, Y., Krakowski, S., Spector, S. (eds.): *The Einsatzgruppen Reports*. New York, 1989.

Bershadskii, S.: *Russko-evreiskii arkhiv. Dokumenty i materialy dlia istorii evreev v Rossii*, 3 vols. St. Petersburg, 1882–1903.

Cherikover, I.: *Antisemitizm i evrei na Ukraine 1917–1918. K istorii ukrainsko-evreiskikh otnoshenii*. Berlin, 1923.

——: *The Pogroms in the Ukraine in 1919* (Yid.). New York, 1965.

Chernoglazova, R. (ed.): *Tragediia evreev Belorussii. Sbornik materialov i dokumentov*. Minsk, 1997.

Evrei v Krymu. Ocherki istorii. Simferopol-Jerusalem, 1997.

Evreiskaia entsiklopediia, 16 vols. St. Petersburg, 1906–1913.

Evreiskoe naselenie Rossii po dannym perepisi 1897 g. i po noveishim istochnikam. St. Petersburg, 1917.

Evreiskoe naselenie SSSR. Dvizhenie za vremia s 1897 po 1923 g. i raspredelenie po respublikam i poseleniiam. Moscow, 1927.

Greenbaum, A.: *Rabbis in the USSR between the World Wars 1917–1939* (Heb.). Jerusalem, 1994.

Grossman, V., Erenburg, I.: *Chernaia kniga*. Jerusalem, 1980.

Istoriia evreiskogo naroda, vols. 11–12. Moscow, 1914, 1921.

Istoriia mist i sil Ukrains'koi RSR. Kiev, 1967–1972.

Jews in the Belorussian SSR. Statistical Materials (Yid.). Minsk, 1929.

Kantor, I.: *Natsional'noe stroitel'stvo sredi evreev v SSSR*. Moscow, 1934.

Kiper, M.: *The Jewish "Shtetl" in the Ukraine* (Yid.). Kharkov, 1929.

Krasnyi-Admoni, G.: *Materialy dlia istorii antievreiskikh pogromov, vol. 2: Vos'midesiatye gody*. St. Petersburg-Moscow, 1923.

Kratkaia evreiskaia entsiklopediia, 9 vols. Jerusalem, 1976–1999.

Kruglov, A.: *Unichtozhenie evreiskogo naseleniia Ukrainy v 1941–1944 gg. Khronika sobytii*. Mogilev-Podolskii, 1997.

Levin, D.: *The Lesser of Two Evils. Eastern European Jewry under Soviet Rule*. Philadelphia, 1995.

Levin, V., Melzer, D.: *Chernaia kniga s krasnymi stranitsami*. Baltimore, 1996.

Levin, Y.: *History of Habad in the USSR, 1917–1950* (Heb.). New York, 1989.

Lukin, V., Khaimovich, B., Sokolova, A.: *100 evreiskikh mestechek Ukrainy. Podoliia*. Jerusalem-St. Petersburg, 2000.

Materialy ob antievreiskikh pogromakh. Pogromy v Belorussii. Moscow, 1922.

Neizvestnaia chernaia kniga. Svidetel'stva ochevidtsev o katastrofe sovetskikh evreev (1941–1944). Jerusalem-Moscow, 1993.

Nikitin, V.: *Evrei zemledel'tsy, 1807–1887*. St. Petersburg, 1887.

"Perepisi evreiskogo naseleniia v iugo-zapadnom krae v 1765–1791 gg.," *Arkhiv iugo-zapadnoi Rossi*, part V, vol. II, issue II. Kiev, 1890.

Regesty i nadpisi. Svod materialov dlia istorii evreev v Rossii, 3 vols. St. Petersburg, 1899–1913.

Rossiiskaia evreiskaia entsiklopediia, 4 vols. Moscow, 1994–2000.

Sbornik materialov ob ekonomicheskom polozhenii evreev v Rossii, 2 vols. St. Petersburg, 1904.

Slownik geograficzny Królestwa Polskiego i innych krajów slowiańskich, 16 vols. Warsaw, 1880–1902.

Spector, S.: *The Holocaust of Volhynian Jews, 1941–1944*. Jerusalem, 1990.

Stampfer, S.: "The 1764 Census of Polish Jewry," *Annual of Bar-Ilan University. Studies in Judaica and the Humanities: Studies in the History and Culture of East European Jews*, vol. 24–25 (1989), pp. 41–147.

Sud'by natsional'nykh men'shinstv na Smolenshchine, 1918–1938. Dokumenty i materialy. Smolensk, 1994.

Szmeruk, C.: *The Jewish Community and Jewish Agricultural Settlement in Soviet Belorussia (1918–1932)* (Heb.). Jerusalem, 1921.

Ves' iugo-zapadnyi krai. Spravochnaia i adresnaia kniga po Kievskoi, Podol'skoi i Volynskoi guberniiam. Kiev, 1914.

Veizblitt, I.: *The Dynamics of the Jewish Population in the Ukraine in the Years 1897–1926* (Yid.). Kharkov, 1930.

West, B. (ed.): *The Struggles of a Generation. The History of the Jews and the Zionist Movement in Soviet Russia* (Heb.). Israel, 1955.

Zinger, L.: *Evreiskoe naselenie SSSR*. Moscow, 1927.

CZECHOSLOVAKIA

Barkány, E., Dojč L.: *Židovské náboženské obce na Slovensku*. Bratislava, 1991.

Berger, N. (ed.): *Where Cultures Meet. The Story of the Jews of Czechoslovakia* (Heb.). Tel Aviv, 1990.

Bezdek, B. (ed.): *Menoslov obci na Slovensku*. Bratislava, 1920.

Bondy, G., Dworsky, F. (eds.): *Zur Geschichte der Juden in Böhmen, Mähren und Schlesien von 906 bis 1620*. Prague, 1906.

Bretholz, B.: *Geschichte der Juden in Mähren im Mittelalter*. Brünn, 1934.

—— (ed.): *Quellen zur Geschichte der Juden in Mähren*. Prague, 1935.

Bujnák, P. (ed.): *Slovenský náučný slovnik*, vols. I–III. Prague-Bratislava, 1932.

Československý statistický věstník. Prague, 1920–1930.

Chytil, A. (ed.): *Adresár Slovenska*, vol. I. Prague, 1921.

Dagan, A. et al. (ed.): *The Jews of Czechoslovakia*, vols. I–III. Philadelphia-New York, 1968–1984.

Erez, I.: *The Encyclopedia of Diasporas, vol. 7: Carpatho-Russia* (Heb.). Jerusalem-Tel Aviv, 1959.

Fiedler, J.: *Židovské památky v Čechach a na Morave*. Prague, 1992.

Filová, B. (ed.): *Etnografický atlas Slovenska*. Bratislava, 1990.

Freud, E., Questler, D.: *Immigrants from Czechoslovakia. Their Contribution to the Development of Israel* (Heb.). Jerusalem, 1998.

Friedmann, F.: *Einige Zahlen über die Juden in der Tschechoslowakei*. Prague, 1936.

Friss, A. et al. (eds.): *Monumenta Hungariae Judaica*, vols. I–XVII. Budapest, 1903–1974.

Gemeindelexikon von Böhmen. Vienna, 1905.

Gold, H.: *Die Juden und die Judengemeinde Bratislava in Vergangenheit und Gegenwart*. Brünn, 1932.

—— (ed.): *Die Juden und Judengemeinden Böhmens in Vergangenheit und Gegenwart*. Prague-Brünn, 1934.

—— (ed.): *Die Juden und die Judengemeinden Mährens in Vergangenheit und Gegenwart*. Brünn, 1929.

Goldelman, S.: "Die sozial-ökonomische Struktur der Juden Karpathorusslands," *Jüdischer Almanach 5694*. Prague, 1934.

Gross, D. (ed.): *Židovská ročenka pre Slovensko 5700/1940*. Bratislava, 1940.

Halperin, I.: *Takanot Medinat Mehrin 1650–1748* (Heb.). Jerusalem, 1952.

Herman, J.: *Židovské hrbitovy v Čechách a na Morave*. Prague, 1980.

Hermann, H. (ed.): *Jüdischer Kalender für die Tschechoslowakische Republik auf das Jahr 5683*. Brünn, 1923.

Hlošek, J.: *Židé na Morave*. Brno, 1925.

Horvát, P. (ed.): *Lexikon obcí v Slovenskej Republike*. Bratislava, 1942.

Iltis, R.: *Die jüdischen Gemeinden in der Tschechoslowakei nach dem Zweiten Weltkrieg*. Prague, 1957.

Kaiserlich Königliche Statistische Central-Commission, *Special Orts-Repertorium von Böhmen*. Vienna, 1893.

Kann, R.A.: *Geschichte des Habsburgreiches 1526-1917*. Vienna, 1977.

Kapras, J., Malypetr, J. (eds.): *Die Tschechoslowakische Republik*. Prague, 1937.

Karný, M. et al. (eds.): *Theresienstadt in der "Endlösung der Judenfrage"*. Prag, 1992.

Kerner, R.J.: *Czechoslovakia 20 Years of Indepedence*. Berkley, 1940.

Kestenberg-Gladstein, R.: *Neuere Geschichte der Juden in den böhmischen Ländern*, vol. I. Tübingen, 1969.

Kieval, H.J.: *The Making of Czech Jewry*. New York-Oxford, 1988.

Kolitz, Z. (ed.): "Czechoslovakian Jewry" (Heb.), *Gesher*, 2–3 (59–60), 1969.

Kropilák, M. (ed.): *Vlastivedný slovník obcí na Slovensku*, vols. I–III. Bratislava, 1987.

Mamatey, V.S., Luža, R.: *A History of the Czechoslovak Republic 1918-1948*. Princeton, 1973.

Prečan, V. (ed.): *Slovenské národné povstanie. Dokumenty*. Bratislava, 1965.

Rothkirchen, L.: *The Destruction of Slovakian Jewry* (Heb.). Jerusalem, 1968.

Rozman, S.: *Sefer Shefer Harerei Kedem. The Diaspora of Carpatho-Russia–Marmarosh in its Glory and in its Destruction* (Heb.). Brooklyn, 1991.

Sole, A.: *Light in Mountains. Hebrew-Zionist Education in Carpatho-Russia 1920–1944* (Heb.). Tel Aviv, 1986.

Statistical Survey of the Czechoslovak Republic. Prague, 1930.

Statistický lexikon obcí v Republike Československé. Prague, 1935.

Steinherz, S.: "Die Einwanderung der Juden in Böhmen," *Die Juden in Prag*, edited by S. Steinherz. Prague, 1927.

Tomek, V.V.: *Dějepis mesta Prahy*, vols. I–XII. Prague, 1855-1901.

Trestik, D.: *České a Československé dějiny. Dokumenty a materialy*. Prague, 1992.

Ujvári P. Magyar Zsidó Lexikon. Budapest, 1929.

Wandruszka, A., Urbanitsch, P. (eds.): *Die Habsburgermonarchie 1840–1918, vol. 3: Die Völker des Reiches*. Vienna, 1980.

Weiner, L. (ed.): *Review of the Society for the History of Czechoslovak Jews*, vols. I–V. New York, 1987–1992.

Zatloukal, J. (ed.): *Podkarpatská Rus*. Bratislava, 1936.

DENMARK

Altschul, S.: *The History of the Jews in Denmark* (Yid.). Copenhagen, 1921.

Arnold, E.: *A Night of Watching*. New York, 1967.

Balslev, B.: *De danske Jøders historie*. Copenhagen, 1932.

Barfod, J.H.: *The Escape from Nazi Terror*. Copenhagen, 1969.

Derry, T.K.: *A History of Scandinavia. Norway, Sweden, Denmark, Finland and Iceland*. Minneapolis, 1979.

Haestrup, J.: *From Occupied to Ally. Denmark's Fight for Freedom, 1940–1945*. Copenhagen, 1963.

Hevra Kaddischa 1858–1958. Copenhagen, 1958.

Kings and Citizens. The History of the Jews in Denmark, 1622–1983. New York, 1983.

Levine, E.: *Darkness over Denmark. The Danish Resistance and the Rescue of the Jews*. New York, 1999.

Margolinsky, J.: *Jødiske dødsfald i Danmark 1693–1976*. Copenhagen, 1978.

Nytrup, P.: *An Outline of the German Occupation of Denmark 1940–45*. Copenhagen, 1966.

Petrow, R.: *The Bitter Years. The Invasion and Occupation of Denmark and Norway April 1940–May 1945*. New York, 1974.

Pundik, H.: *In Denmark It Could Not Happen. The Flight of the Jews to Sweden in 1943*. Jerusalem, 1998.

    Yahil, L.: *The Rescue of Danish Jewry*. Philadelphia, 1969.

——: "Methods of Persecution. A Comparison of the Final Solution in Holland and Denmark," *Scripta Hierosoly-mita*, 23 (1972).

ESTONIA – *see* **LATVIA, ESTONIA**

FRANCE

Adler, J.: *The Jews of Paris and the Final Solution*. New York, 1987.

Albert, P.C.: *The Modernization of French Jewry. Consistory and Community in the Nineteenth Century*. Hanover (New England), 1977.

Anchel, R.: *Napoléon et les juifs*. Paris, 1928.

——: *Les juifs de France*. Paris, 1946.

Benbassa, E.: *The Jews of France. A History from Antiquity to the Present*. New Jersey, 1999.

Birnbaum, P.: *Antisemitism in France. A Political History from Léon Blum to the Present*. Cambridge, 1992.

——: *The Jews of the Republic. A Political History of State Jews in France from Gambetta to Vichy*. Stanford, 1996.

Blumenkranz, B. (ed.): *Histoire des juifs en France*. Paris, 1972.

——: *Bibliographie des juifs en France*. Toulouse, 1974.

Caron, V.: *Uneasy Asylum. France and the Jewish Refugee Crisis, 1933–1942*. Stanford, 1999.

Carpi, D.: *Between Mussolini and Hitler. The Jews and the Italian Authorities in France and Tunisia*. Hanover (New England), 1994.

Cohen, A.: *History of the Holocaust. France* (Heb.). Jerusalem, 1996.

Duclos, J.C., Loiseau, J. (eds.): *Être juif en Isère entre 1939 et 1945*. Isère, 1997.

Guide Religieux de la France. Paris, 1967.

Iancu, C. (ed.): *Juifs à Montpellier et dans le Languedoc à travers l'histoire du Moyen Âge à nos jours*. Montpellier, 1988.

Iancu, C., Iancu, D.: *Les juifs du Midi. Une histoire millénaire*. Avignon, 1995.

Iancu, D.: *Les juifs en Provence (1475–1501). De l'insertion à l'expulsion*. Marseilles, 1981.

Job, F.: *Les juifs de Nancy. Du XIIe au XXe siècle*. Nancy, 1991.

Kott, A., Kott, J.: *Roanne. Enquête sur les origines d'une communauté juive atypique*. Paris, 1998.

Klarsfeld, S.: *Mémorial de la déportation des juifs de France*. Paris, 1978.

——: *Le calendrier de la persécution des juifs en France, 1940–1944*. Paris, 1993.

Laloum, J.: *Les juifs dans la banlieue parisienne des années 20 aux années 50. Montreuil, Bagnolet et Vincennes*. Paris, 1998.

Lambert, A., Tocze, C.: *Être Juif à Nantes sous Vichy*. Nantes, 1994.

Lazare, L.: *La Résistance juive en France*. Paris, 1987.

Lewi, M.: *Histoire d'une communauté juive: Roanne*. Roanne, 1976.

Lunel, A.: *Juifs du Languedoc, de la Provence et des États français du Pape*. Paris, 1975.

Malino, F.: *The Sephardic Jews of Bordeaux. Assimilation and Emancipation in Revolutionary and Napoleonic France*. Tuscaloosa, 1978.

Marrus, M.: *The Politics of Assimilation. A Study of the French Jewish Community at the Time of the Dreyfus Affair*. Oxford, 1971.

Marrus, M., Paxton, R.: *Vichy France and the Jews*. New York, 1981.

Paxton, R.: *Vichy France. Old Guard and New Order, 1940–1944*. New York, 1982.

Poliakov, L.: *L'étoile jaune*. Paris, 1949.

——: *La condition des juifs en France sous l'occupation italienne*. Paris, 1955.

Poznanski, R.: *Être juif en France pendant la Seconde Guerre Mondiale*. Paris, 1994.

Raphael, F., Weyl, R.: *Juifs en Alsace. Société, culture, histoire*. Strasbourg, 1977.

Reinach, T.: *Histoire des Israélites depuis l'époque de leur dispersion jusqu'à nos jours*. Paris, 1885.

Roblin, M.: *Les juifs de Paris. Démographie, économie, culture*. Paris, 1952.

Ryan, D.F.: *The Holocaust and the Jews of Marseilles. The Enforcement of Anti-Semitic Policies in Vichy France*. Urbana, 1996.

Schnurmann, E.: *La population juive en Alsace*. Paris, 1936.

Schwarzfuchs, S.: *Du Juif à l'Israélite. Histoire d'une mutation 1770–1870*. Paris, 1989.

——: *Aux prises avec Vichy. Histoire politique des Juifs de France 1940–1944*. Paris, 1998.

Simon, L.: *Les juifs à Nîmes et dans le Gard durant la Deuxième Guerre Mondiale de 1939 à 1944*. Nîmes, 1985.

Szajkowski, Z.: *Analytical Franco-Jewish Gazetteer 1939–1945*. New York, 1966.

Vidal-Naquet, P.: *Les juifs, la mémoire et le présent*, 3 vols. Paris, 1981–1995.

Weinberg, D.: *Les Juifs à Paris de 1933 à 1939*. Paris, 1974.

Weisberg, R.H.: *Vichy Law and the Holocaust in France*. New York, 1996.

Wellers, G.: *L'étoile jaune à l'heure de Vichy*. Paris, 1973.

Wellers, G., Kaspi, A., Klarsfeld, S. (eds.): *La France et la Question Juive 1940–1944*. Paris, 1981.

Zuccotti, S.: *The Holocaust, the French and the Jews*. New York, 1993.

GERMANY

Adam, U.D.: *Judenpolitik im Dritten Reich*. Düsseldorf, 1972.

Andernacht, D., Sterling, E. (eds.): *Dokumente zur Geschichte der Frankfurter Juden 1933–1945*. Frankfurt, 1963.

Brann, M.: *Geschichte der Juden in Schlesien*. Breslau, 1896.

Brocke, M., Schwarz, M. (eds.): *Feuer an Dein Heiligtum gelegt. Zerstörte Synagogen 1938. Nordrhein-Westfalen*. Bochum, 1999.

Brocke, M., Heitmann, M., Lordick, H. (eds.): *Zur Geschichte und Kultur der Juden in Ost- und Westpreussen* ditto NETIVA. Wege deutsch-jüdischer Geschichte und Kultur. Studien des Salomon Ludwig Steinheim-Instituts, vol. II. Hildesheim-Zürich-New York, 2000.

Dick, J., Sassenberg, M. (ed.): *Wegweiser durch das jüdische Sachsen-Anhalt* ditto Beiträge zur Geschichte und Kultur der Juden in Brandenburg, Mecklenburg-Vorpommern, Sachsen-Anhalt, Sachsen und Thüringen, vol. III. Potsdam, 1998.

Diekmann, I. (ed.): *Wegweiser durch das jüdische Mecklenburg-Vorpommern* ditto Beiträge zur Geschichte und Kultur der Juden in Brandenburg, Mecklenburg-Vorpommern, Sachsen-Anhalt, Sachsen und Thüringen, vol. II. Potsdam, 1998.

Diekmann, I., Schoeps, J.H. (eds.): *Wegweiser durch das jüdische Brandenburg* ditto Beiträge zur Geschichte und Kultur der Juden in Brandenburg, Mecklenburg-Vorpommern, Sachsen-Anhalt, Sachsen und Thüringen, vol. I. Berlin, 1995.

Friedländer, S.: *Nazi Germany and the Jews, vol. I: The Years of Persecution 1933–1939*. New York, 1997.

Germania Judaica, vols. I–III/2. Tübingen, 1968–1995.

Hahn, J.: *Erinnerungen und Zeugnisse jüdischer Geschichte in Baden-Württemberg*. Stuttgart, 1988.

Heid, L., Schoeps, J.H.: *Wegweiser durch das jüdische Rheinland*. Berlin, 1992.

Jersch-Wenzel, S., Rürup, R. (eds.): *Quellen zur Geschichte der Juden in den Archiven der neuen Bundesländer*, vols. I–IV. Munich, 1996–1999.

Keyser, E., Stoob, H. (eds.): *Deutsches Städtebuch. Handbuch städtischer Geschichte*, 10 vols. Stuttgart, 1952–2000.

Marx, A.: *Die Geschichte der Juden im Saarland. Vom Ancien Régime bis zum Zweiten Weltkrieg.* Saarbrücken, 1992.

——: *Die Geschichte der Juden in Niedersachsen.* Hanover, 1995.

Meyer, M.A. (ed.): *German-Jewish History in Modern Times*, vols. I–IV. New York, 1996–1998.

Paul, G., Gillis-Carlebach, M.: *Menora und Hakenkreuz. Zur Geschichte der Juden in und aus Schleswig-Holstein, Lübeck und Altona 1918–1998.* Neumünster, 1998.

Post, B. (ed.): *Jüdische Geschichte in Hessen erforschen. Ein Wegweiser zu Archiven, Forschungsstätten und Hilfsmitteln.* Wiesbaden, 1994.

Pracht, E.: *Jüdisches Kulturerbe in Nordrhein-Westfalen*, 5 vols. Cologne, 1997–.

Reicher, B.: *Jüdische Geschichte und Kultur in NRW. Ein Handbuch.* Essen, 1993.

Richarz, M. (ed.): *Jewish Life in Germany. Memoirs from Three Centuries.* Bloomington, 1991.

Rürup, R. (ed.): *Jüdische Geschichte in Berlin. Essays und Studien.* Berlin, 1995.

State Archives of Rhineland-Palatinate, State Archive Saarbrücken (eds.): *Dokumente zur Geschichte der jüdischen Bevölkerung in Rheinland-Pfalz und im Saarland von 1800 bis 1945*, 9 vols. Koblenz, 1972–1982.

Stern, S.: *Der preussische Staat und die Juden.* Tübingen, 1962–1971.

Treml, M., Weigand, S. (eds.): *Geschichte und Kultur der Juden in Bayern. Aufsätze.* Munich, 1988.

——: *Geschichte und Kultur der Juden in Bayern. Lebensläufe.* Munich, 1988.

Walk, J. (ed.): *Das Sonderrecht für die Juden im NS-Staat.* Heidelberg, 2nd edition, 1996.

GREECE

Attal, R.: *Les Juifs de Grèce de l'expulsion d'Espagne à nos jours. Bibliographie.* Jerusalem, 1984.

——: *Bibliographie additive à la première édition.* Jerusalem, 1996.

Biblio Mnimis. Athens, 1979.

Bowman, S.B.: *The Jews of Byzantium 1204–1453.* Alabama, 1985.

Carpi, D. (ed.): *Italian Diplomatic Documents of the History of the Holocaust in Greece (1941–1943).* Tel Aviv, 1999.

Chary, F.B.: *The Bulgarian Jews and the Final Solution 1940–1944.* Pittsburgh, 1972.

Constantopoulou, P., Veremis, T. (eds.): *Documents on the History of the Greek Jews.* Athens, 1998.

Dalven, R.: *The Jews of Ioannina.* Philadelphia, 1990.

Enepekides, P.K.: *I diogmi ton Evreon en Elladi 1941–1944 epi ti vasi ton mistikon archion ton Es-Es.* Athens, 1969.

Fintz Menascé, E.: *Gli ebrei a Rodi. Storia di un antica communita annientata dai nazisti.* Milan, 1991.

Frey, J.B.: *Corpus of Jewish Inscriptions and Prolegomenon.* New York, 1975.

Galante, A.: *Histoire des Juifs de Rhodes, Chio, Cos, etc..* Istanbul, 1935.

——: *Appendice à l'histoire des Juifs de Rhodes.* Istanbul, 1948.

Hondros, J.L.: *Occupation & Resistance. The Greek Agony 1941–1944.* New York, 1983.

Mazower, M.: *Inside Hitler's Greece. The Experience of Occupation 1941–44.* New Haven-London, 1993.

Messinas, E.V.: *The Synagogues of Salonika and Veroia.* Athens, 1997.

Molho, M.: *In Memoriam. Hommage aux victimes juives des Nazis en Grèce.* Salonika, 2nd edition, 1973.

Novitch, M.: *The Passage of the Barbarians. Contribution to the History of the Deportation and the Resistance of Greek Jews.* Hull, 1989.

Picciotto Fargion, L.: *Il Libro della Memoria. Gli Ebrei deportati dall'Italia (1943–1945).* Milan, 1991.

Pierron, B.: *Juifs et Chrétiens de la Grèce moderne. Histoire des relations intercommunautaires de 1821 à 1945.* Paris, 1996.

Plaut, J.: *Greek Jewry in the Twentieth Century 1913–1983. Patterns of Jewish Survival in the Greek Provinces before and after the Holocaust.* Madison, 1996.

Rafael, S. (ed.): *Be-Netivei Sheol. The Jews of Greece in the Holocaust. Testimony* (Heb.). Tel Aviv, 1988.

Reccanati, D.A., (ed.): *Remembering Salonika. The Greatness and Destruction of the Jerusalem of the Balkans* (Heb.), 2 vols. Tel Aviv, 1972, 1986.

Salonika. Town and Mother in Israel (Heb.). Jerusalem-Tel Aviv, 1967.

Shmuelevitz, A.: *The Jews of the Ottoman Empire in the Late Fifteenth and Sixteenth Centuries.* Leiden, 1984.

Starr, J.: *The Jews in the Byzantine Empire 641–1204.* Athens, 1939.

——: *Romania. The Jewries of the Levant after the Fourth Crusade.* Paris, 1949.

Stavroulakis, N.P., De Vinney, T.J.: *Jewish Sites and Synagogues of Greece.* Athens, 1992.

HOLLAND

Aalders, R.: *De Ontvreemding van Joods bezit Tijdens de Tweede Wereldoorlog.* The Hague, 1999.

Agt, J.F. van, Voolen, E. van: *Synagogen in Nederland.* Hilversum, 1988.

Beem, H.: *Jerosche. Jiddische Spreekwoorden en Zegswijzen uit het Nederlandse Taalgebied.* Amsterdam, 1998.

——: *Sje-erith. Resten van een Taal.* Assen, 1967.

Belinfante, J.: "The Ideal of Jewish Nation Versus the Reality of the Jewish Poor. The Dilemma of the Ashkenazi Jewish Nation," *Studia Rosenthaliana,* 30 (1996), pp. 213–224.

Berg, J. van den, Wall, E.G.E. van der (eds.): *Jewish-Christian Relations in the Seventeenth Century: Studies and Documents.* Dordrecht, 1988.

Bloemgarten, S., Velzen, J. van: *Joods Amsterdam in een Bewogen Tij, 1890–1940.* Zwolle, 1997.

Blom, J.C.H.: "De Vervolging van de Joden in Nederland in Internationaal Vergelijkend Perspectief," *De Gids,* (1987) 6–7, pp. 494–507.

Blom, J.C.H., Fuks-Mansfeld, R.G., Schöffer, I. (eds.): *Geschiedenis van de Joden in Nederland.* Amsterdam, 1995.

Boekman, E.: *Demografie van de Joden in Nederland.* Amsterdam, 1936.

Braber, B.: *Passage naar Vrijheid. Joods Verzet in Nederland 1940–1945.* Amsterdam, 1987.

Brasz, C.: *Removing the Yellow Badge. The Struggle for a Jewish Community in the Postwar Netherlands, 1944–1945.* Jerusalem, 1995.

Brasz, C., Kaplan, Y. (eds.): *Dutch Jews as Perceived by Themselves and by Others.* Leiden-Boston-Cologne, 2001.

Cleeff-Hiegentlich, F. van: "De Transformatie van het Nederlandse Jodendom in de Eerste Helft van de Negentiende Eeuw," *De Gids,* 148 (1985) 3–4, pp. 232–242.

Flim, B.: *Omdat hun Hart Sprak. Geschiedenis van de Georganiseerde Hulp aan Joodse Kinderen in Nederland 1942–1945.* Kampen, 1996.

Fuks, L., Fuks-Mansfeld, R.G.: *Hebrew Typography in the Northern Netherlands 1585–1818,* 2 vols. Leiden, 1984–1987.

Fuks-Mansfeld, R. G.: "Yiddish Historiography in the Time of the Dutch Republic," *Studia Rosenthaliana,* 15 (1981), pp. 9–19.

Galen Last, D. van, Wolfwinkel, R.: *Anne Frank and After. Dutch Holocaust Literature in a Historical Perspective.* Amsterdam, 1996.

Gans, M.H.: *Memorbook.* Baarn, 1977.

Giebels, L.: *De Zionistische Beweging in Nederland 1899–1914*. Assen, 1975.

Haan, I. de: *Na de Ondergang. De Herinnering aan de Jodenvervolging in Nederland 1945–1995*. The Hague, 1997.

Hiegentlich, E.P.: "Reflections on the Relationship between the Dutch Haskala and the German Haskalah," *Dutch Jewish History*, 1 (1984), pp. 207–219.

Hofmeester, K.: *Van Talmoed tot Statuut. Joodse en Arbeidersbewegingen in Amsterdam, Londen en Parijs 1880–1914*. Amsterdam, 1999.

Houwink ten Cate, J.: "Heydrich's Security Police and the Amsterdam Jewish Council (February 1941–October 1942)," *Dutch Jewish History*, 3 (1993), pp. 381–393.

Huussen, A.H., Wedman, H.J.: "Politieke en Sociaal-Culturele Aspecten van de Emancipatie der Joden in de Republiek der Verenigde Nederlanden," *Documentatieblad Werkgroep Achttiende Eeuw*, 51–52 (1981), pp. 207–224.

Israel, J.: *Empires and Entrepots. The Dutch, the Spanish Monarchy and the Jews, 1585–1713*. London, 1990.

——: *European Jewry in the Age of Mercantilism 1550–1750*. London, 1998.

Jong, L. de: *Het Koninkrijk der Nederlanden in de Tweede Wereldoorlog*, vols. 1–14. The Hague, 1969–1991.

Kaplan, Y.: "Amsterdam and Ashkenazic Migration in the Seventeenth Century," *Studia Rosenthaliana*, 23 (1989) 2, pp. 22–45.

——: "Eighteenth-Century Rulings by the Rabbinical Court of Amsterdam's Community and Their Socio-Historical Significance" (Heb.), *Studies on the History of Dutch Jewry*, 5 (1988), pp. 1–55.

——: "The Portuguese Jews in Amsterdam. From Forced Conversion to a Return to Judaism," *Studia Rosenthaliana*, 15 (1981), pp. 37–51.

Leydesdorff, S.: *Wij Hebben als Mens Geleefd. Het Joodse Proletariaat van Amsterdamse 1900–1940*. Amsterdam, 1987.

Michman, D.: *Het Liberale Jodendom in Nederland 1929–1943*. Amsterdam, 1988.

——: "Joods Onderwijs in Nederland (1616–1905)," *JBO. Stichting Joodse Scholengemeenschap*. Amsterdam, 1973, pp. 13–29.

——: "La 'période Batave' et la 'période Française' dans l'histoire des juifs de Hollande (1795–1813) et son évaluation dans l'historiographie," *Tsafon. Revue d'études juives*, 5 (1991), pp. 3–49.

——: "Migration versus 'Species Hollandia Judaica.' The Role of Migration in the Nineteenth and Twentienth Centuries in Preserving Ties between Dutch and World Jewry," *Studia Rosenthaliana*, 23 (1989) 2, pp. 54–77.

——: "The Uniqueness of the Joodse Raad in the Western European Context," *Dutch Jewish History*, 3 (1993), pp. 371–380.

Michman, J.: "A Decade of Historiography of Dutch Jewry," *Dutch Jewish History*, 3 (1993), pp. 9–18.

——: *Dutch Jewry during the Emancipation Period, 1787–1813. Gothic Turrets on a Corinthian Building*. Amsterdam, 1995.

——: "Historiography of the Jews in the Netherlands," *Dutch Jewish History*, 1 (1984), pp. 7–29.

——: "The Conflicts between Orthodox and Enlightened Jews and the Governmental Decision of 26th February 1814," *Studia Rosenthaliana*, 15 (1981) 1, pp. 20–36.

——: "The Jewish Essence of Dutch Jewry," *Dutch Jewish History*, 2 (1989), pp. 1–23.

—— (ed.): *Studies on the History of Dutch Jewry* (Heb.), vols. 1–5. Jerusalem, 1975–1988.

Michman, J., Levie, T. (eds.): *Dutch Jewish History*, vols. I–III. Jerusalem, 1980–1993.

Moore, B.: *Refugees from Nazi Germany in the Netherlands 1933–1940*. Dordecht, 1986.

——: *Victims and Survivors*. London, 1997.

Pieterse, W.Chr.: "The Sephardi Jews of Amsterdam," *The Western Sephardim. The Sephardi Heritage*, vol. II., edited by R. Barnett, W. Schwab. Grendon, 1989, pp. 75–100.

Praag, Ph. van: "Between Speculation and Reality," *Studia Rosenthaliana*, 23 (1989) 2, pp. 175–180.

——: *Demography of the Jews in the Netherlands*. Jerusalem, 1976.

Presser, J.: *Ashes in the Wind*. London, 1968.

Reijnders, C.: *Van "Joodsche Natien" tot Joodse Nederlanders*. Amsterdam, 1969.

Rosenberg, A.: "The Adoption of the Dutch Language by Dutch Jewry," *Studia Rosenthaliana*, 30 (1996) 1, pp. 151–163.

Stengers, J.: *Les Juifs dans les Pays-Bas au Moyen-Âge*. Brussels, 1949.

Verheij, E.: *Om het Joodse Kind*. Amsterdam, 1991.

Vlessing, O.: "New Light on the Earliest History of the Amsterdam Portuguese Jews," *Dutch Jewish History*, 3 (1993), pp. 43–75.

——: "The Jewish Community in Transition. From Acceptance to Emancipation," *Studia Rosenthaliana*, 30 (1996) 1, pp. 195–212.

Vries, B.W. de: *From Pedlars to Textile Barons. The Economic Development of a Jewish Minority Group in the Netherlands*. Amsterdam, 1989.

Yogev, G.: *Diamonds and Corals. Anglo Dutch Jews and 18th Century Trade*. Leicester, 1978.

HUNGARY

Ben-Tov, A.: *The Red Cross Came Too Late* (Heb.). Jerusalem, 1994.

Beri-Lichtner, J.: *Együtt-élés. A zsidóság szerepe Magyarország legūjabbkori történetében 1790–1918*. Budapest, 1995.

Braham, R. L.: *The Hungarian Labor Service System, 1935–1945*. Boulder, 1977.

——: *The Politics of Genocide*. Detroit, 1981.

—— (ed.): *The Hungarian Jewish Catastrophe. A Selected and Annotated Bibliography*. New York, 1984.

Fischer, R.: *Entwicklungsstufen des Antisemitismus in Ungarn 1867–1939. Die Zerstörung der magyarisch-jüdischen Symbiose*. Munich, 1988.

Friss, A. et al. (eds.): *Monumenta Hungariae Judaica*, vols. I–XVII. Budapest, 1903–1974.

Karády, V.: *Zsidóság az 1945 utáni Magyarországon*. Paris, 1984.

Katzburg, N.: *Hungary and the Jews. Policy and Legislation 1920–1943*. Ramat Gan, 1981.

Kohn, S.: *A zsidók története Magyarországon*. Budapest, 1884.

——: *Héber kútforrások és adatok a Magyarország történetéhez*. Budapest, 1881.

Komoróczy, G. (ed.): *Jewish Budapest. Monuments, Rites, History*. Budapest, 1999.

Lelkes, G.: *Magyar helységnév-azonos'itó szótár*. Budapest, 1992.

Levai, J.: *Fekete könyv a Magyar zsidóság szenvedéseiröl*. Budapest, 1946.

——: *Zsidósors Magyarországon*. Budapest, 1948.

Magyar Királyi Központi Statisztikai Hivatal: *Magyar Statisztikai Évkönyv*. Budapest, 1943.

Moskovits, C.: *Jesivák Magyarországon. Adalékok a zsidó hitközségek 1944. Áprilisi össze'rásának történeti értékléséhez*. Budapest, 1999.

Munkácsi, E.: *Hogyan történt? Adatok és okmányok a magyar zsidóság tragédiájához*. Budapest, 1947.

Ránki, G.: *The Politics of Inclusion and Exclusion. Jews and Nationalism in Hungary*. New York, 1999.

Reuveni, S.: "Antisemitism in Hungary 1945–1946," *Holocaust and Genocide Studies*, vol. 4 (1989), 1, pp. 41–61.

——: "Circumstances that Furthered and Impeded Rescue amongst the Jews of Hungary" (Heb.), *Dapim le-Heker Tekufat ha-Shoah*, 31 (1997), pp. 313–325.

——: "Special Deportations in Late Trains from Hungary to Auschwitz," *Yalkut Moreshet*, May 1985, pp. 123–134.

Ronen, A.: *Harc az életért. Cionista (Somer) ellenállás Budapesten 1944*. Budapest, 1998.

Rozett, R.: *From Poland to Hungary. Rescue Attempts* (Heb.). Jerusalem, 1995.

——: *The Protected Children's House Rescue. Budapest 1944–45*. Jerusalem, 1981.

——: *The Wartime System of Labor Service in Hungary (ABOUT)*. New York, 1998.

Ságvári, Á. (ed).: *Archival Documents on Data Concerning [the] Jewish Holocaust in Hungary*. Budapest, 1996.

Schläger, U.: *Und wann wir? Die Vernichtung der ungarischen Juden und der Budapester Judenrat 1944*. Cologne, 1996.

Sebok, L.: *Magyar neve?* Budapest, 1990.

Shvarts, Y. (ed.): *The Jews of Hungary during the Holocaust, Including the "Kasztner Trial"* (Heb.). Hadera, 1990.

Spitzer, S.: *Die Rabbiner Ungarns, 1944 (Die orthodoxen Gemeinden)*. Budapest, 1999.

Stark, T.: *Hungarian Jews during the Holocaust and after the Second World War, 1939–1949. A Statistical Review*. Boulder, 2000.

Sūgár, P.F. (ed.): *A History of Hungary*. Bloomington, 1994.

Szita, S.: *Verschleppt, verhungert, vernichtet. Die Deportation von ungarischen Juden auf das Gebiet des annektierten Österreich 1944–1945*. Vienna, 1999.

Teleki, É.: *Nyilas uralom Magyarországon: 1944. Október 16–1945. Április 4*. Budapest, 1974.

Újvári, P.: *Zsidó Lexikon*. Budapest, 1922.

Underground Rescue. Bnei Akiva in Hungary during the Holocaust (Heb.). Ramat Gan, 1993.

Valley, E.: *The Great Jewish Cities of Central and Eastern Europe. A Travel Guide and Resource Book to Prague, Warsaw, Crakow, and Budapest*. Northvale, 1999.

Venetianer, L.: *A magyar zsidóság története a világháború kitöréséig*. Budapest, 1922.

ITALY

Bemporad, D.L., Tedeschi Falco, A.: *Toscana Itinerari ebraici. I luoghi, la storia, l'arte*. Venice, 1994.

Benigni, M. L.M.: *Marche Itinerari ebraici. I luoghi, la storia, l'arte*. Venice, 1996.

Bonfil, R.: *Rabbis and Jewish Community in Renaissance Italy*. Oxford, 1990.

Brandes, F.: *Veneto Itinerari ebraici. I luoghi, la storia, l'arte*. Venice, 1995.

Calimani, R.: *The Ghetto of Venice*. New York, 1987.

Campus, G.: *Il treno di Piazza Giulia. La deportazione degli ebrei di Roma*. Cuneo, 1995.

Caracciolo, N.: *Gli Ebrei e l'Italia durante la guerra 1940–1945*. Rome, 1986.

Caravita, G.: *Ebrei in Romagna (1938–45). Dalle leggi razziali allo sterminio*. Ravenna, 1991.

Carpi, D. (ed.): *Bibliotheca Italo-Ebraica. Bibliografia per la storia degli Ebrei in Italia 1964–1973*. Rome, 1982.

De Felice, R.: *Storia degli ebrei italiani sotto il fascismo*. Turin, 1988.

Del Bianco Cotrozzi, M.: *La comunita ebraica di Gradisca d'Isonzo*. Udine, 1983.

Enciclopedia Italiana di Scienze, Lettere ed Arte. Milan, 1929.

Fortis, U.: *Il ghetto sulla laguna. Guida storico-artistica al Ghetto di Venezia (1516–1797)*. Venice, 1987.

Italia-Judaica. Saggio d'una bibliografia storica e archeologica degli Ebrei d'Italia. Rome, 1924.

Levi, F.: *L'ebreo in oggetto. L'applicazione della normativa antiebraica a Torino 1938–1943*. Turin, 1991.

Migliau, B., Procaccia, M.: *Lazio Jewish Itineraries. Places, Histories and Art*. Venice, 1997.

Milano, A.: *Storia degli ebrei in Italia*. Turin, 1992.

Onorfi, N.S.: *Ebrei e fascismo a Bologna*. Bologna, 1989.

Picciotto Fargion, L.: *Gli ebrei in provincia di Milano 1943–1945. Persecuzione e deportazione*. Milan, 1992.

——: *Il Libro della Memoria. Gli Ebrei deportati dall'Italia (1943–1945)*. Milan, 1991.

——: *L'occupazione Tedesca e gli ebrei di Roma.* Milan, 1979.

——: *Per ignota destinazione. Gli ebrei sotto il nazismo.* Milan, 1994.

Sacerdoti, A., Tedeschi Falco, A.: *Emilia Romagna Itinerari ebraici. I luoghi, la storia, l'arte.* Venice, 1992.

——: *Lombardia Itinerari ebraici. I luoghi, la storia, l'arte.* Venice, 1993.

——: *Piemonte Itinerari ebraici. I luoghi, la storia, l'arte.* Venice, 1994.

Salvadori, R.G.: *Breve storia degli ebrei toscani, IX–XX secolo.* Florence, 1995.

Sarfatti, M.: *Mussolini contro gli ebrei. Cronaca dell'elaborazione delle leggi del 1938.* Turin, 1994.

—— (ed.): *1938. Le leggi contro gli ebrei.* Rome, 1988.

Segre, R. (ed.): *Gli ebrei a Venezia 1938–1945. Una comunita tra persecuzione e rinascita.* Venice, 1995.

Simonsohn, S.: *The Jews in the Duchy of Milan. A Documentary History of the Jews in Italy.* Jerusalem, 1986.

—— (ed.): *Biblioteca Italo-Ebraica. Bibliografia per la storia degli Ebrei in Italia 1986–1995.* Rome, 1997.

Toaff, R.: *La nazione ebrea a Livorno e a Pisa (1591–1700).* Florence, 1990.

——: *The Jews in Umbria. A Documentary History of the Jews in Italy,* 3 vols. Leiden-New York-Cologne, 1993–1994.

Urbani, R., Zazzu, G.N.: *The Jews in Genoa.* Leiden-Boston-Cologne, 1999.

Wistrich, R., Della Pergola, S. (eds.): *Fascist Antisemitism and the Italian Jews.* Jerusalem, 1995.

LATVIA, ESTONIA

Arbusow, L.: *Grundriss der Geschichte Liv-, Est- und Kurlands.* Riga, 1908.

Bobe, M.: Chapters in the History of Latvian Jewry, 1651–1918 (Heb.). Tel Aviv, 1965.

Bobe, M. et al. (eds.): *The Jews in Latvia.* Tel Aviv, 1971.

Buchholtz, A.: *Geschichte der Juden in Riga bis zur Begründung der rigischen Hebräergemeinde im J. 1842.* Riga, 1899.

Gerz, M.: *25 Years of the Jewish Press in Latvia* (Yid.). Riga, 1933.

Itai, A.: *The History of a Movement. Netzah in Latvia* (Heb.). Tel Aviv, 1972.

Joffe, J. (ed.): *Regesten und Urkunden zur Geschichte der Juden in Riga und Kurland,* 3 vols. Riga, 1910–1912.

Kaufmann, M.: *Die Vernichtung der Juden Lettlands. Churbn Lettland.* Munich, 1947.

Krausnick, H., Wilhelm, H.H.: *Die Truppe des Weltanschauungskrieges. Die Einsatzgruppen der Sicherheitspolizei und des SD 1938–1942.* Stuttgart, 1981.

Latvju Enciklopedija. Stockholm, 1953–1955.

Lejins, J.: *Latvian Jewish Relations.* Canada, 1975.

Levin, D.: *With Their Backs to the Wall. The Struggle of the Jews of Latvia against the Nazis 1941–1945* (Heb.). Jerusalem, 1978.

Lithuania Latvia Estonia. Statistical Abstract. Vilna, 1991.

Maor, Y.: "On Latvian and Estonian Jewry" (Heb.), *Hapoel Hatzair,* 42 (1950), 11.

Mark, M.: *The Jewish Secular School in Latvia* (Yid.). Tel Aviv, 1973.

Mikhelson, F.: *I survived Rumbuli.* New York, 1974.

Obchinski, L., Ben Duber, Y.: *History of the Settlement of the Jews in Courland (1561–1901)* (Heb.). Vilna, 1912.

Porat, E.: "The Jewish Press in Latvia," *Jewish Press of the Past,* edited by Y. Gothelf. Tel Aviv, 1973.

Press, B.: *Judenmord in Lettland. 1941–1945.* Berlin, 1992.

Rutkis, J. (ed.): *Latvia. Country and People.* Stockholm, 1967.

Schatz-Anin, M.: *The Jews in Latvia* (Yid.). Riga, 1924.

Schneider, G.: *Journey into Terror. Story of the Riga Ghetto.* New York, 1979.

Vesterman, M.: *Fragments of the Jewish History of Riga. A Brief Guide-Book with a Map for a Walking Tour.* Riga, 1991.

Wunderbar, R.J.: *Geschichte der Juden in den Provinzen Liv- und Kurland. Seit ihrer frühesten Niederlassung daselbst bis auf die gegenwärtige Zeit.* Mitau, 1853.

LIBYA, TUNISIA

Abitbol, M.: *Les juifs d'Afrique du Nord sous Vichy.* Paris, 1983.

——: *The North African Jews during World War II* (Heb.). Jerusalem, 1986.

Attal, R.: "The Jewish Population in Libya," *Jewish Folktales from Libya,* edited by D. Noy. Jerusalem, 1967, pp. 234–236.

——: "Tunisian Jewry during the Last Twenty Years," *Jewish Journal of Sociology,* II (1969), pp. 4–15.

Attal, R., Sitbon, C.: *Regards sur les Juifs de Tunisie.* Paris, 1979.

Avrahami, Y.: "Ideological and Public Struggles among the Jews of Tunis at the Beginning of French Rule, 1881–1914" (Heb.), *Kav Lakav. Mehkarim al Yahadut ha-Magrib.* Jerusalem, 1983.

——: "Libyan Jewry's Response to World War II" (Heb.), *Proceedings of the 11th World Congress on Jewish Studies,* II/2. Jerusalem, 1994.

——: "The Grana in Tunis as Reflected in Its Records. The Struggle for Autonomy" (Heb.), *North African Jewry in the 19th and 20th Centuries,* edited by M. Abitbol. Jerusalem, 1980.

——: "The Jewish Communities in Tunisia at the Time of the German Occupation. Financial Aspects" (Heb.), *Pe'amim,* 28 (1986), pp. 107–125.

——: "The Jews of Tunisia under Vichy and the German Occupation. October 1940–May 1943. The Attitude of the Government and the Population" (Heb.), *Shorashim Bamizrah,* 2 (1986), pp. 403–440.

Borgel, R.: *Étoile jaune et croix gammée. Récit d'une servitude.* Tunis, 1944.

Carpi, D.: *Between Mussolini and Hitler. The Jews and the Italian Authorities in France and Tunisia.* Hanover (New England), 1994.

Cohen, B.R.: *Sefer Malkhei Tarshish* (Heb.). Jerusalem, 1986.

De Felice, R.: *Jews in an Arab Land.* Austin, 1985.

Goldberg, H.: "Ecologic & Demographic Aspects of Rural Tripolitanian Jewry. 1853–1949," *VIJMES,* (1971), pp. 245–265.

——: "Rites & Riots. The Tripolitanian Pogrom of 1945," *Plural Societies,* 1 (1977), pp. 35–56.

Ghez, P.: *Six mois sous la botte.* Tunis, 1944.

Hacohen, M.: *The Book of Mordechai,* edited by H. Goldberg. Philadelphia, 1980.

Hirschberg, H.Z.: *A History of the Jews in North Africa,* 2 vols. Leiden, 1974, 1981.

Khalfon, H.: *For Us and for Our Sons* (Heb.). Tel Aviv, 1986.

Lasker, M.: *The Jews of the Maghreb under the Shadow of Vichy and the Swastika* (Heb.). Tel Aviv, 1992.

Sabille, J.: *Les Juifs de Tunisie sous Vichy et l'Occupation.* Paris, 1954.

Sebag, P.: *Les Juifs de Tunisie. Images et textes.* Paris, 1989.

——: *Histoire des Juifs de Tunisie.* Paris, 1991.

Simon, R.: "The Hebrew Movement in Libya" (Heb.), *Shorashim Bamizrah,* 2 (1989), pp. 173–210.

——: "The Jews of Libya on the Brink of the Holocaust" (Heb.), *Pe'amim,* 28 (1986), pp. 44–79.

——: "The Socio-Economic Role of the Tripolitanian Jews in the Late Ottoman Period," *Communautés juives des marges sahariennes du Maghreb,* edited by Michel Abitbol. Jerusalem, 1982, pp. 321–328.

Slouschz, N.: *The Jews of North Africa. Travels.* Philadelphia, 1927.

Tsur, Y.: *France and the Jews of Tunisia. The French Policy towards the Jews of the State and the Activities of the*

Jewish Elites at the Transition Point from Independent Muslim Rule to Colonial Rule, 1873–1888 (Heb.). Jerusalem, 1988.

——: "The Jews of Tunis at the Time of the Nazi Occupation. A Divided Community in Days of Crisis" (Heb.), *Yahadut Zemanenu*, 2 (1985), pp. 153–175.

Udovitch, A., Valensi, L.: *The Last Arab Jews*. New York, 1984.

Zuarez, F. (ed.): *Libyan Jewry* (Heb.). Tel Aviv, 1960.

LITHUANIA

Bershadski, S.A.: *Litovskie Yevrei, 1388–1569. Regesti I Nadpisi*, vol. I. St. Petersburg, 1883.

Cepenas, P.: *Naujujutu laiku Lietuvos istorija*. Vilna, 1992.

Chase, T.G.: *The Story of Lithuania*. New York, 1964.

Cohen, B.: *Jewish Towns, Shtetls and Villages in Lithuania until 1918* (Yid.). New York, 1991.

Dubnow, S. (ed.): *Pinkas ha-Medina shel Va'ad ha-Kehillot ha-rashiot be-Medinat Lita. A Collection of Statutes and Halakhic Decisions from 1623 until 1761* (Heb.). Berlin, 1925.

Elimor (Volkovski), G.: "The Jewish Press in Independent Lithuania," *Jewish Press of the Past*, edited by Y. Gothelf. Tel Aviv, 1973.

Goldberg, J. (ed.): *Jewish Privileges in the Polish Commonwealth. Nature of Rights Granted to Jewish Communities in Poland-Lithuania in the Sixteenth to Eighteenth Centuries* (Heb.). Jerusalem, 1985.

Goren, N. et al. (eds.): *The Jews of Lithuania from the 15th Century until 1918* (Heb.). Tel Aviv, 1960.

Halpern, Y.: *Supplements and Additions to "Pinkas Medinat Lita"* (Heb.). Jerusalem, 1935.

Joffe, M. (ed.): *Hitlerine okupacija Lietuvoje, Straipsniu rinkinys*. Vilna, 1961.

Katz, B.: *History of the Jews in Russia, Poland and Lithuania in the 16th and 17th Centuries* (Heb.). Tel Aviv, 1970.

Khasman et al. (eds.): *The Jews of Lithuania*, vols. 1–4. Tel Aviv, 1960–1984.

Kloizner, Y.: *Lithuanian Hasidism from its Beginning to the Present Day* (Heb.). Jerusalem, 1961.

Lazar-Litai, H.: "The Zahar and Betar in Lithuania" (Heb.), *Publications of the Partisans and Fighters Museum*, vol. 4, no. 10 (50).

Levin, D.: *Baltic Jews under the Soviets, 1940–1946*. Jerusalem, 1994.

——: *Fighting Back. Lithuanian Jewry's Armed Resistance to the Nazis, 1941–45*. New York, 1984.

Lietuviu Enciklopedija, vols I–XXXII. Boston, 1953–1965.

Lietuvos Statistikos Metrastis 1929–1930m. Annuaire statistique de la Lithuanie. Années 1929–1930. Kaunas, 1931.

Lietuvos Statistikos Metrastis 1939m. Annuaire statistique de la Lithuanie. Année 1939. Vilna, 1940.

Lithuania (Yid.), vols. 1–2. New York, 1951.

Lithuania, Latvia, Estonia. Statistical Abstract. Vilna, 1991.

Shatzky, J.: *A Cultural History of the Haskala in Lithuania. From the Earliest Times to Hibbat Zion* (Yid.). Buenos Aires, 1956.

Shohat, A.: "The Beginnings of Anti-Semitism in Independent Lithuania," *Yad Vashem Studies*, 11 (1958), pp. 7–48.

Smoliakovas, H.: "Zydu svietimas Lietuvos Respublikoje 1918–1940," *Tevynes sviesa*, 22-27-29 rugsejo (September) 1989.

The Jews of Lithuania. Pictures and Landmarks, photographed by Y.D. Kemson. Jerusalem, 1959.

The Jewish Craftsmen in Lithuania in Figures (Yid.). Kaunas, 1938.

Ziegelman, S.A.: *The Jews of Poland and Lithuania until 1648* (Heb.). Jerusalem, 1999.

LUXEMBOURG

Bech, J. (ed.): *Luxembourg and the German Invasion. Before and After.* London, 1942.

Cerf, P.: *L'étoile juive au Luxembourg.* Luxembourg, 1986.

——: *Longtemps j'aurai mémoire. Documents et témoignages sur les juifs du Grand-Duché de Luxembourg durant la seconde guerre mondiale.* Luxembourg, 1974.

Friedrich, E.: *Als Luxemburg entvölkert werden sollte.* Luxembourg, 1969.

Hoffmann, S. (ed.): *Le Grand-Duché de Luxembourg pendant la deuxième guerre mondiale.* n.p., 1991.

Lehrmann, C., Lehrmann, G.: *La communauté juive du Luxembourg dans le passé et dans le présent. Histoire illustrée.* Esch-sur-Alzette, 1953.

Weber, P.: *Geschichte Luxemburgs im Zweiten Weltkrieg.* Luxembourg, 1958.

NORWAY

Abrahamsen, S.: *Norway's Response to the Holocaust.* New York, 1991.

Andenaes, J., Riste, O., Skodvin, M.: *Norway and the Second World War.* Oslo, 1966.

Derry, T.K.: *A History of Modern Norway, 1814–1972.* Oxford, 1973.

——: *A History of Scandinavia. Norway, Sweden, Denmark, Finland and Iceland.* Minneapolis, 1979.

Eckstein, H.: *Division and Cohesion in a Democracy. A Study of Norway.* Princeton, 1966.

Friedmann, T. (ed.): *Dokumentensammlung über "Die Deportierung der Juden aus Norwegen nach Auschwitz."* Ramat Gan, 1963.

Hambro, C.: *I Saw It Happen in Norway.* New York-London, 1940.

Høye, B., Ager, T.M.: *The Fight of the Norwegian Church Against Nazism.* New York, 1943.

Johansen, P.O.: *Oss selv nærmest. Norge og jødene, 1914–1943.* Oslo, 1984.

Koritzinsky, H.M.: *Jødernes historie i Norge. Henrik Wergelands kamp for jødesaken.* Kirchhain (N.-L.), 1922.

Mendelsohn, O.: *Jødenes historie i Norge gjennom 300 år.* Oslo, 1969.

Paneth, P.: *Haakon VII. Norway's Fighting King.* London, 1944.

Petrow, R.: *The Bitter Years. The Invasion and Occupation of Denmark and Norway.* New York, 1974.

Riste, O. *Norway 1940–45.* Oslo, 1978.

POLAND

Almanach Gmin Żydowskich w Polsce, vol. 1. Warsaw, 1939.

An-Ski, S.: *The Destruction of the Jews in Poland, Galicia and Bukovina* (Heb.). Tel Aviv, 1936.

Azulai, H.: *Sifrei Shem ha-Gedolim* (Heb.). Jerusalem, 1990.

Balaban, M.: *Historia i Literatura Żydowska*, vols. II–III. Lwow-Warsaw-Cracow, 1925.

——: *The History of the Frankist Movement*, 2 vols. Tel Aviv, 1934–1935.

Balinski, B., Lipinski, T.: *Starożytna Polska pod względem historycznym, geograficznym I statystycznym.* Warsaw, 1885.

Bersohn, M. (ed.): *Dyplomataryusz dotyczący Żydów w dawnej Polsce. Na zródlach archiwalnych osnuty (1388–1782).* Warsaw, 1910.

Bielawski, W.: *Zbrodnie na Polakach dokonane przez hitlerowców za pomoc udzieloną Żydom.* Warsaw, 1981.

Blatman, D.: *For Our Freedom and Yours. The Bund in Poland, 1939–1949* (Heb.). Jerusalem, 1996.

Bornstein, I.: *Budżety gmin żydowskich w Polsce.* Warsaw, 1929.

Bronsztejn, S.: *Ludność żydowska w Polsce w okresie międzywojennym.* Wroclaw (Breslau)-Warsaw-Cracow, 1963.

Bystrzycki, T. (ed.): *Skorowidz miejscowości Rzeczypospolitej Polskiej z oznaczeniem terytorialne im własciwych władz I urzędów oraz urządzen komunikacyjnych.* Przemysl, 1937.

Czerniakiewicz, J.: *Repatriacja Ludności polskiej z ZSRR 1944–1948*. Warsaw, 1987.

Datner, S.: *55 dni Wehrmachtu w Polsce*. Warsaw, 1967.

Davidovitch, D.: *Synagogues in Poland and Their Destruction* (Heb.). Jerusalem, 1960.

Eisenbach, A.: *Hitlerowska polityka eksterminacji Żydów w latach 1939–1945 jako jeden z przejawów imperializmu niemieckiego*. Warsaw, 1953.

——: *Kwestia równouprawnienia Żydów w królestwie Polskim*. Warsaw, 1972.

Ele Ezkera. Collection of the History of the Martyrs, 1940–1945 (Heb.). New York, 1956–1972.

Encyklopedia Powszechna. Warsaw, 1859–1868.

Goldberg, J. (ed.): *Jewish Privileges in the Polish Commonwealth. Nature of Rights Granted to Jewish Communities in Poland-Lithuania in the Sixteenth to Eighteenth Centuries* (Heb.). Jerusalem, 1985.

Gutman, Y.: *The Jews in Poland after World War II* (Heb.). Jerusalem, 1985.

——: *The Jews of Warsaw, 1939–1943. Ghetto, Underground, Revolt*. Bloomington, 1982.

Gutman, Y. et al. (eds.): *The Jews of Poland between Two World Wars*. Hanover (New England)-London, 1989.

Halpern, Y. (ed.): *Pinkas Va'ad Arba ha-Artzot. Acta Congressus generalis Judaeorum regni Polaniae (1580–1764)* (Heb.). Jerusalem, 1945.

Hirszhorn, S.: *Historia Żydów w Polsce*. Warsaw, 1921.

Katz, B.: *History of the Jews in Russia, Poland and Lithuania in the 16th and 17th Centuries* (Heb.). Tel Aviv, 1970.

Kazdan, T.: *The History of the Jewish School System in Independent Poland* (Yid.). Mexico City, 1947.

Krakowski, S.: *The War of the Doomed. Jewish Armed Resistance in Poland, 1942–1944*. New York, 1984.

Leshtchinsky, J.: *The Jews in Contemporary Poland*. Paris, 1937.

——: "The Jews in the Cities of the Republic of Poland," *YIVO Annual of Jewish Social Science*, vol. I. New York, 1946.

Leszczynski, A.: *Żydzi ziemi Bielskiej od polowy XVII e. do 1795 r. Studium osadnicze, prawne I ekonomiczne*. Wroclaw (Breslau), 1980.

Mahler, R.: *History of the Jews in Poland* (Heb.). Tel Aviv, 1946.

——: *Jews in Poland between the Two World Wars. A Socio-Economic History on a Statistical Basis* (Heb.). Tel Aviv, 1968.

Mendelsohn, E.: *Zionism in Poland. The Formative Years*. New Haven, 1981.

Miasta polskie w Tysiącleciu. Wroclaw (Breslau)-Warsaw-Cracow, 1967.

Oppenheim, Y.: *The Hehalutz Movement in Poland 1917–1939* (Heb.). Jerusalem, 1982.

Piechotkowie, M., Piechotkowie, K.: *Bóżnice drewniane*. Warsaw, 1957.

Ringelblum, I.: *Last Writings. Polish-Jewish Relations, January 1943–April 1944* (Heb.), edited by Y. Gutman et al. Jerusalem, 1994.

Schepansky, Y.: *The Holocaust Calendar of Polish Jewry* (Heb.). New York, 1974.

Schiper, I.: *Cultural History of the Jews in Poland in the Middle Ages* (Yid.). Warsaw, 1926.

——: *Dzieje handlu żydowskiego na ziemiach polskich*. Warsaw, 1937.

——: *Economic History of the Jews in Poland in the Middle Ages* (Yid.). Warsaw, 1926.

Schiper, I., Tartakowrer, A., Haftka, A. (eds.): *Dzieje Żydów w Polsce Odrodzonej*. Warsaw, 1933–1934.

Shamir, Y. (ed.): *Hashomer Hatzair in Poland 1913–1950* (Heb.). Givat Haviva, 1991.

Sulimierski, F. (ed.): *Slownik geograficzny Królestwa Polskiego i innych krajów slowiańskich*. Warsaw, 1880–1902.

Trunk, I.: *Judenrat. The Jewish Councils in Eastern Europe under Nazi Occupation*. New York, 1972.

Wasiutynski, B.: *Ludność żydowska w Polsce w wiekach XIX I XX*. Warsaw, 1930.

Weichert, M.: *Jewish Self-Help 1939–1945* (Yid.). Tel Aviv, 1962.

Weinryb, B.D.: *The Jews of Poland. Social and Economic History of the Jewish Community in Poland from 1100 to 1800.* Philadelphia, 1973.

Wielka Encyklopedia Powszechna (PWN). Warsaw, 1968–1970.

Wischnitzer, M.: *A History of Jewish Crafts and Guilds.* New York, 1965.

Ziegelman, S.A.: *The Jews of Poland and Lithuania until 1648* (Heb.). Jerusalem, 1999.

Żydzi w Polsce Odrodzonej, 2 vols. Warsaw, 1936.

RUMANIA

Academia Română, Institutul de Geografie (ed.): *România. Atlas istorico-geografic.* Bucharest, 1996.

Ancel, J.: *Transnistria.* Bucharest, 1998.

—— (ed.): *Documents Concerning the Fate of Romanian Jewry during the Holocaust.* New York, 1986.

Benjamin, L. (ed.): *Evreii din România între anii 1940–1944.* Bucharest, 1993–1998.

Braham, R.: *Romanian Nationalists and the Holocaust. The Political Exploitation of Unfounded Rescue Accounts.* New York, 1998.

—— (ed.): *The Tragedy of Romanian Jewry.* New York, 1994.

Butnaru, I.C.: *The Silent Holocaust. Romania and Its Jews.* New York, 1992.

——: *Waiting for Jerusalem. Surviving the Holocaust in Romania.* Westport, 1993.

Carmelly Steigman, F.: *Shattered! 50 Years of Silence. History and Voices of the Tragedy in Romania and Transnistria.* Scarborough, 1997.

Carp, M.: *Holocaust in Rumania. Facts and Documents on the Annihilation of Rumania's Jews 1940–44.* Budapest, 1994.

Federaţia Comunitâţilor Evreieşti din Republica Socialistâ România Sectia de documentare (ed.): *Remember. 40 de ani de la masacrarea evreilor din Ardealul de Nord sub ocupaţia horthystâ.* Bucharest, 1985.

Evreii din România in războiul de reintregire a ţării (1916–18). Bucharest, 1996.

Finkelstein, A.: *Être ou ne pas naître. Chronique de l'Holocauste en Roumanie.* Paris, 1997.

Geller, Y.: *The Sephardi Jews in Rumania. The Flowering and Decline of the Sephardi Community in Bucharest* (Heb.). Tel Aviv, 1983.

"Genocide and Ethnocide of the Jews and Hungarians in Rumania," *Toward the Understanding and Prevention of Genocide. Proceedings of the International Conference on the Holocaust and Genocide,* edited by I.W. Charny. Tel Aviv, 1984.

Gursan-Salzmann, A.: *The Last Jews of Radauti.* Garden City, 1983.

Iancu, C.: *Emanciparea evreilor din România (1913–1919).* Bucharest, 1998.

——: *Jews in Romania 1866–1919. From Exclusion to Emancipation.* Boulder, 1996.

Ioanid, R.: *Evreii sub regimul Antonescu.* Bucharest, 1998.

——: *The Holocaust in Romania. The Destruction of Jews and Gypsies under the Antonescu Regime, 1940–1944.* Chicago, 2000.

——: *The Sword of the Archangel. Fascist Ideology in Romania.* Boulder, 1990.

Kara, I. [pseud.]: *Contribuţii la istoria obştii evreilor din Iaşi.* Bucharest, 1997.

Krausz, A.Ch.I.: *A Regi Erdely Arad,* vol. I. Tel Aviv, 1993.

Kuller, H.: *Presa evreiasca bucuresteana, 1857–1994.* Bucharest, 1996.

Levanon, Y.: *Remnants of the Sword. Chapters in the History of Religious Zionism in Rumania* (Heb.). Jerusalem, 1998.

Lowy, D.: *A téglagyártól a tehervonatig. Kolozsvár zsidó lakosságának története.* Kolozsvar, 1998.

Mircu, M.: *Oameni de omenie în vremuri de neomenie.* Bucharest, 1996.

Mozes, T.: *Evreii din Oradea.* Bucharest, revised edition, 1997.

Nathanson, E.: *The Position of the Rumanian Authorities regarding the Jews in the Period between the Two World Wars, 1919-1939* (Heb.). Haifa, 1985.

Ofir, E.: *Zionists in the Lions' Den. The Zionist Movement in Rumania during the Second World War, 1938-1944* (Heb.). Tel Aviv, 1992.

Pascu, S. (ed.): *Atlas pentru istoria României.* Bucharest, 1983.

Pavel, A.: *Pictori evrei din România, 1848-1948.* Bucharest, 1996.

Peri, Y.: *Chapters in the History of the Jews in Transylvania in Modern Times* (Heb.). Tel Aviv, 1977.

Petreu, M.: *Un passé coupable ou La transfiguration de la Roumanie.* Cluj, 2000.

Rozen, M.: *Involuţia demografică a evreilor din România în perioada 1940-2000.* Bucharest, 1998.

Safran, A.: *Resisting the Storm. Romania, 1940-1947.* Jerusalem, 1987.

Sanie, S. (ed.): *Studia et acta historiae iudaeorum romaniae.* Bucharest, 1996-1998.

Serbanescu, I. (ed.): *Parlamentari evrei in forul legislativ al României 1919-1940. Documente (extrase).* Bucharest, 1998.

Shelomoh, D. (ed.): *Generations of Judaism and Zionism. Dorohoi, Saveni, Mikhaileni, Darabani, Herta, Radauti-Prut* (Heb.). Kiryat Bialik, 1992.

Siperco, A. (ed.): *Ecouri dintr-o epocă tulbure. Documente elveţiene 1940-1944.* Bucharest, 1998.

Stern, N. (ed.): *Remember Satmar. Memorial Book of the Jews of Satmar* (Heb.). Benei Berak, 1984.

Stoenescu, A.M.: *Armata, mareşalul şi evreii. Cazurile D Doroho. Bucureşti, Iaşi, Odessa.* Bucharest, 1998.

Streja, A.: *Sinagogi din România.* Bucharest, 1996.

Treptow, K.W.: *Historical Dictionary of Romania.* Lanham, 1996.

Vago, R.: *Anti-Semitism in Romania 1989-1992.* Tel Aviv, 1995.

Volovici, L.: *Nationalist Ideology and Antisemitism. The Case of Romanian Intellectuals in the 1930s.* Oxford, 1991.

RUSSIA — *see* **BELORUSSIA, UKRAINE, RUSSIA**

TUNISIA — *see* **LIBYA, TUNISIA**

UKRAINE — *see* **BELORUSSIA, UKRAINE, RUSSIA**

YUGOSLAVIA

Browning, C.R.: "The Final Solution in Serbia. The Semlin Judenlager. A Case Study," *Yad Vashem Studies,* XV (1984), pp. 55–90.

Deak, A.: *Razzia in Novi Sad.* Zurich, 1967.

Keckemet, D.: *Zidovi U Povijesti Splita.* Split, 1971.

Krizman, B.: *Pavelic Izmedju Hitlera I Musolinija.* Zagreb, 1979.

——: *Utase I Treci Rajh.* Zagreb, 1981.

Levi, M.: *Die Sephardim in Bosnien.* Sarajevo, 1911.

Levntal, Z. (ed.): *The Crime of the Fascist Occupants [sic!] and Their Collaborators against Jews in Yugoslavia.* Belgrade, 1957.

Matkovsky, A.: *A History of the Jews in Macedonia.* Skopje, 1982.

Military Historical Institute of the Yugoslav People's Army: *The National Liberation War. Revolution in Yugoslavia (1941–1945). Selected Documents*. Belgrade, 1982.

Pass-Freidenreich, H.: *The Jews of Yugoslavia. A Quest for Community*. Philadelphia, 1979.

Romano, S.J.: *Jevreji Jugoslavije 1941–1945. Zrtve Genocida I Ucesnici Narodnooslobodilackog Rata*. Belgrade, 1980.

Schwarz, G.: *Povijest Zagrebacke Zidovske Opcine Od Osnuta Do 50-tih Godina 19 Vijeka*. Zagreb, 1939.

Shelach, M.: *A Blood Account. The Rescue of the Croatian Jews by the Italians, 1941–1943* (Heb.). Tel Aviv, 1986.

—— (ed.): *History of the Holocaust. Yugoslavia* (Heb.). Jerusalem, 1990.

Slang, I.: *Jevreji U Beogradu*. Belgrade, 1926.

Tadic, J.: *Jevreji U Dubrovniku Do Polovine XVII Stoljeca*. Sarajevo, 1937.

Index of Communities

A

AACH 17

AACHEN 17

Aahof see LEJASCIEMS

AALTEN 18

Aarbergen see KETTENBACH

Aarlen see ARLON

ABA 19

ABADSZALOK 19

ABAUJSZANTO 19

Abbazra see OPATIJA

Abolnik see VABALNINKAS

ABONY 19

ABRAMOWO 19

ABRENE 19

ABTERODE 19

ACAS 19

Achelous see KEFALONIA

ACHIM 19

Acholshausen see GAUKOENIGSHOFEN

Acqui see ALESSANDRIA

ACS 19

ADA 19

ADAMOW 20

Adamus see TARNAVENI

ADELEBSEN 20

ADELSBERG 20

ADELSDORF 20

ADELSHEIM 20

ADJUD 20

ADONY 20

ADORF 20

Adrianople see KSANTHI

AFFALTRACH 21

Agenhof see IGENE

Aghiresu see CLUJ DISTRICT

Agram see ZAGREB

Agriboz see CHALKIS

Agrinio see AGRINION

AGRINION 21

AHAUS 21

AHLEN 22

AHRENSBURG 22

AHRWEILER 23

Ahsen see RECKLINGHAUSEN

AIDHAUSEN 23

AIUD 23

Aix see AIX-EN-PROVENCE

AIX-EN-PROVENCE 24

AIZPUTE 24

Ajaccio see BASTIA

AJAK 24

AJDABIYA 24

Akerman see CETATEA-ALBA

AKHTYRKA 25

AKMENE 25

Akmian see AKMENE

Aknasugatag see OCNA SUGATAG

AKNISTE 25

Akos see ACAS

Alaksandrabal see ALEKSANDROBOLIS

al-Ariana see L'ARIANA

Alave see ALOVE

ALBA-IULIA 25

ALBANIA 26

Albano Laziale see ROME

ALBERSWEILER 27

ALBERTFALVA 27

ALBERT-IRSA 27

Albrekhtovo see ROSSONY

Albsheim see GRUENSTADT

Alchevsk see VOROSHILOVSK (II)

Aldingen see LUDWIGSBURG

Aldorf see PRUNDUL BARGAULUI

Aleksander see ALEKSANDROW

ALEKSANDRIA 27

ALEKSANDROBOLIS 27

Aleksandrovsk see ZAPOROZHE

ALEKSANDROW 27

ALEKSANSROW-KUJAWSKI 28

ALEKSIN 28

Alersha see ALLERSHEIM

Aleshki see TSURIUPINSK

ALESSANDRIA 28

H

Pecsujfalu see PECOVSKA NOVA VES
PECSVARAD   978
PECZENIZYN   978
PEINE   978
PEISKRETSCHAM   979
PEKELA, OUDE EN NIEWE   979
Pelczyce see BERNSTEIN
PELHRIMOV   979
Pels see PSZCZYNA
Pelsoc see PLESIVEC
PENESZLAK   979
PERBENIK   979
Pereche see DEMIDOV
PERED   979
PEREHINSKO   979
PEREKOP   979
PERETZ FELD   979
PERIGUEUX   979
Perleberg see WITTENBERGE
Perlitz see PARLITA
PERNU   980
Pershetravneve see ERSHTMAYSK
PERUGIA   980
PERVOMAYSK (I)   980
PERVOMAYSK (II)   980
PERVOMAYSK (III)   980
Pervomayskoye see DZHURCHI
Pesaro see ANCONA
PESCHANAYA   981
Peschanka see PESCHANAYA
PESCHANNAYA   981
Pesochnaya see KIROV
PESTSZENTERZSEBET   981
PESTSZENTLORINC   981
PESTUJHELY   981
Petcheneydorf see PECOVSKA NOVA VES
Petchuz see PETSERI
PETERGOF   981
PETERSHAGEN   981
PETERVASARA   982
PETNEHAZA   982
PETRAUTI   982
Petrautz see PETRAUTI
PETRIKOV   982
PETRILA   982
Petrilla see PETRILA
Petrodvorets see PETERGOF
Petrograd see LENINGRAD

Petrokrepost see SHLISSELBURG
Petro-Marievka see PERVOMAYSK (II)
PETROSANI V
PETROVA   982
Petroverovka see ZHOVTEN
PETROVICHI   982
Petrozseny see PETROSANI
PETRZALKA   983
PETSERI   983
Peyrehorade see BAYONNE, BIARRITZ
PEZINOK   983
PFAFFEN-BEERFURTH   983
PFAFFENHOFFEN   983
PFEDDERSHEIM   983
PFLAUMLOCH   983
PFORZHEIM   983
PFUNGSTADT   984
Pharsala see FARSALA
PHILIPPSBURG   984
PHILLIPE THOMAS   984
Piacenza see PARMA
PIASECZNO (I)   984
PIASECZNO (II)   984
PIASKI   985
PIASKI LUTERSKIE   985
PIASKOVKA   985
PIATEK   985
PIATIGORSK   985
PIATIGORY   985
PIATKA   985
PIATKOWA   986
PIATNICA   986
PIATRA-NEAMT   986
PIATYKHATKA   987
PIEDRUJA   987
PIENIONZKI   987
PIEREJASLAV   987
PIERZCHNICA   987
PIESOCHIN   987
PIESTANY   987
Pietrasanta see PISA
PIKELIAI   988
Pikeln see PIKELIAI
PIKOV   988
Pila see SCHNEIDEMUEHL
PILAWA   988
PILDA   988
PILICA   988

W

Index of Persons

A

Abba (*amora*) see CARTHAGE

Abba, Shemuel see ZYKHLIN

Aboab, Shemuel see VENICE

Abrabanel, Shemuel see FERRARA

Abraham of Leipzig see LEIPZIG

Abraham, Max see LEIPZIG

Abramowitsch, Shalom Yaakov see Mendele Mokher Seforim

Abramsky, Yehiel see SLUTSK

Abravanel, Yitzhak see CORFU

Adadi, Shaul see TRIPOLI

Adadi, Tziyyon see TRIPOLI

Adler, Abraham see LEIPZIG

Adler, Felix see ALZEY

Adler, Immanuel see KITZINGEN

Adler, Jankel see LODZ

Adler, Karl see SPEYER, STUTTGART

Adler, Lazarus Levi see BAD KISSINGEN, KASSEL

Adler, Natan ha-Kohen see FRANKFURT AM MAIN

Adler, Nathan Marcus see HANOVER, OLDENBURG, WUERZBURG

Adler, Samuel see ALZEY

Adler, Yoav see HUNUSOVCE

Adorno, Theodor see FRANKFURT AM MAIN

Agnon (Chachkes), Shemuel Yosef see BERLIN, BUCZACZ

Ahad Ha-Am (Asher Ginsberg) see ODESSA, SKVIRA

Aharon, Yehuda see CHELM

Aharon of Zhitomir see CAREI

Aharon the Great (of Karlin) see Karlin, Aharon ben Yaakov

Alatini, Azriel see FERRARA

Alatini, Moshe see FERRARA

Alatri, Samuel see ROME

Alcalay, Yitzhak see BELGRADE

Alexander, Kurt see KREFELD

Alexandrov, Shemuel see BOBRUISK, BORISOV

Algazi, Leon see PARIS

Alkalai, David see BELGRADE

Alkalai, Dora see BELGRADE

Alkalai, Yehuda ben Shelomo Hai see ZEMUN

Allouche, Felix see SFAX, TUNIS

Almanzi, Giuseppe see PADUA

Almogi, Yosef see HRUBIESZOW

Almosnino, Moshe see SALONIKA

Alten, Mark see LUBLIN (II)

Alter, Avraham Mordekhai see GORA KALWARIA, WARSAW

Alter, Victor see MLAWA

Alter, Yehuda Aryeh Leib see GORA KALWARIA

Alter (Rothenberg), Yitzhak Meir see GORA KALWARIA

Altkonstatt, Yaakov Koppel see VRBOVE

Altmann, Adolf see SALZBURG

Alush, Humani see MEDENINE

Amiel, Moshe Avigdor see ANTWERP, GRAJEWO

Amirov, Hizkiyahu see NALCHIK

Amnon of Mainz see MAINZ

Ancona, Alessandro d' see PISA

Angel, Shemuel see KOSICE

Anielewicz, Mordekhai see BENDZIN, SOSNOWIEC, WARSAW, WYSZKOW

Ansbacher, Jonas see WIESBADEN

An-Ski, S. see VITEBSK

Antokolski, Mark see BAD HOMBURG, VILNA

Appel, Meir see KARLSRUHE

Archi, Yisrael see BIZERTE

Archivolti, Shemuel de see BOLOGNA, PADUA

Arendt, Hannah see HANOVER

Arikha (Dolgin), Yosef see OLEVSK

Arlosoroff, Hayyim see ROMNY

Armando, Sorani see FERRARA

Arnstein, Fanny von see VIENNA

Artom, Benjamin see NAPLES

Artom, Elia S. see FLORENCE, TRIPOLI

Artom, Eugenio S. see FLORENCE

Asad, Yehuda see DENUJSKA STREDA

Asch, Avraham see CELLE

Asch, Bruno see HOECHST AM MAIN

Asch, Nahum see CZENSTOCHOWA

Asch, Sholem see KUTNO, WARSAW

Ascoli, Graziadio Isaia see GORIZIA

Asher ben Yehiel (ha-Rosh) see COLOGNE, KOBLENZ

Ashkenazi, Gershon see HANAU

Ashkenazi, Shelomo Natan see CRACOW, UDINE

Ashkenazi, Tzevi Hirsch ben Yaakov ("Hakham Tzevi") see ALTONA, EMDEN, LWOW, SARAJEVO

Ashkenazi, Yaakov see JANOW (III)

Ashman, Aharon see KAMENETS-PODOLSKI

Asimov, Isaac see PETROVICHI

Asscher, Abraham see AMSTERDAM

C

D

I

J

Acknowledgments

The Publishers wish to express their appreciation to the following individuals and institutions for their help:

to Yisrael Gutman — the initiator of the idea;

to Avner Shalev and Ishai Amrami — who supported and encouraged the project all the way;

to Miriam Aviezer, Tamar Avraham, Nadia Cohen, Bracha Freundlich, Shaul Greenstein, Ilana Guri, Bella Gutterman, Rodica Jacob, Tova Katz, Yitzhak Len, Effi Neuman, Daniel Uziel, Ahron Weiss — for assistance and advise;

to Ami Green, Veronika Mostoslavsky, Zvi Ohev-Zion, Tal Zeidani — for their professional work.

Unless otherwise stated, all photographs were provided by the Yad Vashem Archives in Jerusalem. "Warsaw Ghetto Uprising" (p.1525) was sculpted by Nathan Rapaport.

The Publishers have attempted to observe the legal requirements with respect to copyright. However, in view of the large number of illustrations included in this volume, the Publishers wish to apologize in advance for any involuntary omission or error and invite persons or bodies concerned to write to the Publishers.

Prepress: Keterpress, Jerusalem